TEACHER'S ANNOTATED EDITION

SPANISH for MASTERY 2

Entre nosotros

Jean-Paul Valette

Rebecca M. Valette

Editor-Consultant
Teresa Carrera-Hanley

Contributing Writer
Frederick Suárez Richard

D.C. HEATH AND COMPANY
Lexington, Massachusetts / Toronto, Ontario

EXECUTIVE EDITOR, MODERN LANGUAGES
Roger D. Coulombe

PROJECT EDITORS
Jayne Cotton
Valentia Dermer

NATIONAL MODERN LANGUAGE PRODUCT SPECIALIST
Teresa Carrera-Hanley

MODERN LANGUAGE PRODUCT MANAGER
Natalie St. John

D.C. HEATH CONSULTANTS
Alison King
Karen Ralston
Ramón Morales-Sánchez

DESIGN AND PRODUCTION
Will Tenney, Executive Designer
Donna Lee Porter, Senior Production Coordinator
Marianna Frew Palmer, Editorial Services
Susan Gerould/Perspectives, Cover Designer

SPANISH for MASTERY
1989 Video Edition

Welcome to the video edition of SPANISH for MASTERY. As its name indicates, this new edition has been enriched by the addition of a video component entitled ¡ADELANTE! In developing this video program, we wanted to respond to the significant trends in teaching foreign languages that have emerged over the past few years. These trends stress communicative proficiency and cultural understanding as major instructional goals. Consequently our aim is to assist you, the teacher, in developing the corresponding skills in your students, especially . . .

- cultural awareness of the Spanish-speaking world with an emphasis on young people
- listening comprehension skills
- communication skills, especially in proficiency-type situations
- vocabulary acquisition in context

By bringing Hispanic culture into the classroom, our video program will also motivate students to continue their study of Spanish.

¡ADELANTE! is a flexible and versatile pedagogical tool. Although it is correlated to SPANISH for MASTERY, Level One, it can be used effectively at Level Two as a basis for communication activities and for cultural enrichment.

Buena suerte a todos y, ¡adelante con el español!

Jean-Paul Valette   Rebecca M. Valette

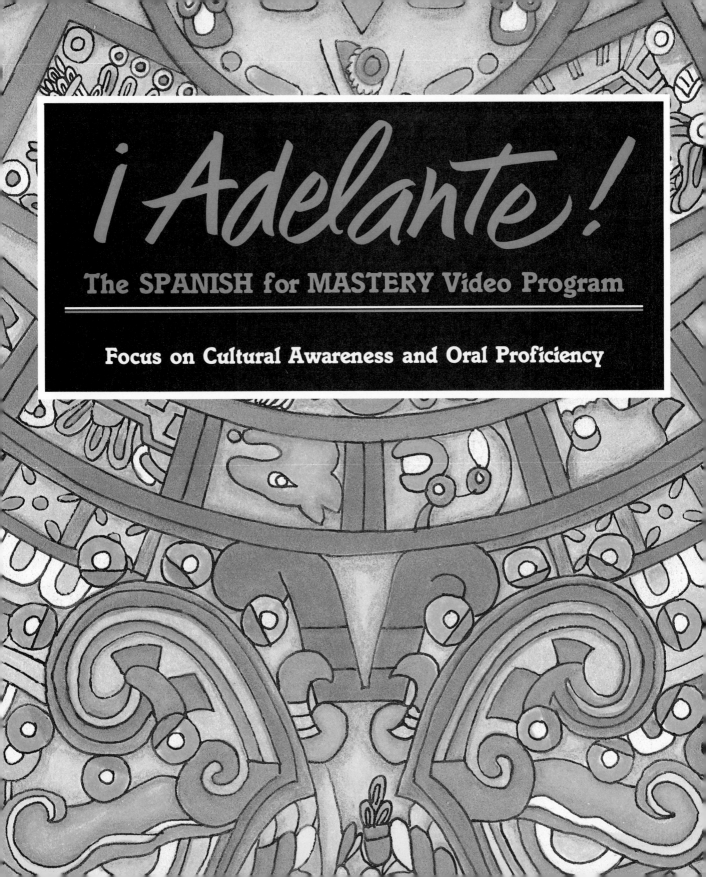

¡Adelante!

The SPANISH for MASTERY Video Program

Focus on Cultural Awareness and Oral Proficiency

STRUCTURE AND ORGANIZATION

Contents of the Video Program

¡ADELANTE! consists of 20 modules contained in two video packs. Each pack includes two video cassettes, two audio cassettes, and a Reference guide.

Scope and Sequence

The purpose of ¡ADELANTE! is to present a realistic and diversified image of the Spanish-speaking world to students in the United States. Each module is built around a specific cultural theme and focuses on an important aspect of daily life in a part of the Spanish-speaking world. The chart on the following pages give the titles of the twenty modules and indicates the corresponding cultural topics and proficiency activities.

VIDEO PACK I

CASSETTE 1

MODULE	CULTURAL TOPIC	PROFICIENCY ACTIVITY
1 ¡Hola, amigos!	Introduction to the Hispanic world; Greetings	Introducing oneself
2 ¿Cuánto es?	Shopping; The café: a meeting place	Shopping; Ordering and paying in a café
3 ¿Qué hora es?	A day in the life of a Spanish city	Telling time
4 ¿Qué tiempo hace?	Geographical variety in the Hispanic world	Talking about the weather
5 Nosotros, los hispanoamericanos	A fiesta in San Antonio	Talking about leisure activities
6 En Miami	Hispanic life in Miami	Talking about studies and career plans

CASSETTE 2

MODULE	CULTURAL TOPIC	PROFICIENCY ACTIVITY
7 ¿Quién es?	A secondary school in Spain	Describing people
8 En el club hispano	Leisure activities	Relating to other people; Talking about possessions
9 Y ahora, México	A provincial Mexican city	Talking about future plans
10 En la capital	Visiting Mexico City	Getting around the city
11 La familia de Maritza	Puerto Rican family	Talking about home and family life
12 En mi casa	Mexican home	Talking about oneself and others

MODULE	CULTURAL TOPIC	PROFICIENCY ACTIVITY	
13 El mundo de los deportes	Sports	Talking about sports activities	CASSETTE 3
14 Los espectáculos	Movies, theater, and other weekend activities	Talking about leisure activities	CASSETTE 3
15 Comprando ropa	Clothes and clothing shops	Shopping for clothes	CASSETTE 3
16 El pobre Sr. Peña	The morning routine	Describing one's daily routine	CASSETTE 3
17 La vida escolar	A school day in Mexico	Talking about past activities	CASSETTE 4
18 A comer	Spanish cafés and restaurants	Ordering foods and beverages	CASSETTE 4
19 El mundo profesional	Professional life	Describing one's professional activities	CASSETTE 4
20 La paella	A food market; Spanish cuisine	Shopping for food; Cooking	CASSETTE 4

VIDEO PACK II

Organization of a Module

The typical module of ¡ADELANTE! consists of three parts:

- the cultural opener
- the dialogs
- the expansion or "ampliación" section

The first two parts are integrated into a unified segment.

The *cultural opener* is accompanied by a brief narration. Its purpose is to present visually the theme of the module and to introduce the dialogs.

The *dialogs,* short exchanges in conversational Spanish, serve to develop listening comprehension.

The last part, entitled "ampliación," is a separate segment that focuses on specific vocabulary and/or grammar points. The speaking activities in this section range from simple listening and repetition to answering personal questions.

Each module is presented in both a captioned and uncaptioned version.

HOW TO USE ¡ADELANTE!
SPANISH for MASTERY, LEVEL TWO

¡ADELANTE! is a flexible teaching instrument that can be used in many different ways and at various points in the learning process. In particular, this video program can be used to meet the following objectives:

- to review previously learned material
- to stimulate cultural awareness
- to develop oral proficiency
- to expand the vocabulary base
- to develop writing skills

Reviewing Previously Learned Material

Although the main teaching objective at Level Two is to expand students' vocabulary and strengthen their grammar base, it is important that students handle the material presented in Level One with confidence. To this end SPANISH for MASTERY, Level Two, contains several chapters devoted primarily to reviewing Level One structures and vocabulary.

The review process can be enhanced by using the appropriate modules of ¡ADELANTE! Modules 1-4, which present basic conversational topics (greetings, numbers, time, dates, and weather) may be used to renew interest in the language. The other modules may then be used as a basis for review of stuctures and vocabulary. Some teachers may wish to base the review of the linguistic material presented in Level 1 exclusively on the video program. This would be especially appropriate for higher-track classes.

The video program may also be used as a diagnostic instrument. For example, the teacher may review a particular grammar point by first showing the corresponding video module. If students have no difficulty, the teacher may then proceed with the presentation of another grammar point, again using the corresponding module. If students do experience difficulty, the teacher can use the student text for the needed remedial work.

The following chart presents the review lessons of SPANISH for MASTERY, Level Two, and lists the video modules of ¡ADELANTE! that contain the corresponding structures and/or vocabulary.

SPANISH for MASTERY   Level Two

Unit	Lesson	Structure/Vocabulary	Corresponding Modules in ¡Adelante!
1	1	-*ar* verbs	Modules 5, 6
		daily and weekend activities	
	2	*ser*	Modules 7, 8
		noun group	
		people	Modules 7, 8, 11
		family	
		nationalities	
	3	*tener*	Module 8
		ir, ir a	Module 9
		everyday objects	Module 8
		names of places	Modules 9, 10
	4	*estar*	Module 9
		ser vs. *estar*	Module 10
		-*er* and -*ir* verbs	Module 11
		estar + present participle	

Unit	Lesson	Structure/Vocabulary	Corresponding Modules in ¡Adelante!
2	1	*conocer*	Module 14
		possessive adjectives	Module 11
		direct object pronouns	Modules 10, 12
		jobs and workplaces	Module 19
	2	indirect object pronouns	Module 12
		decir	
	3	indirect and direct object pronouns	Module 12
		personal belongings	Module 8
	4	*me gusta*	Module 13
		movies and theater	Module 14
3	1	stem-changing verbs	Module 14
	2	reflexive verbs	Module 16
		personal care	
		daily activities	
	4	verbs that are irregular in the first person	Module 14
4	2, 3, 4	preterite	Modules 17, 18, 19
7	1	comparative	Module 15
8	1	informal commands	Module 20

Stimulating Cultural Awareness

¡ADELANTE! is not only visually attractive but also culturally rich. While each module focuses on a specific aspect of life in a part of the Spanish-speaking world, it also contains many other cultural subthemes, which can be expanded in class. The primary object of Module 1 (**¡Hola, amigos!**), for instance, is to give an overall impression of the Spanish-speaking world. The images contained in the module can also serve to introduce secondary themes, such as the landmarks of Madrid (Plaza de Cibeles, Palacio Real, Puerta del Sol, Plaza Mayor) or the modern contrasted with the traditional (high-rise buildings in Mexico City and San Juan vs. Aztec pyramids or old San Juan).

A module can be played many times for different purposes. During the first presentation, students' attention may be drawn to the main cultural theme of the unit. Students may then be asked to formulate a general impression by noting broad similarities and differences between customs of the United States and those of various parts of the Spanish-speaking world. Then, as the module is shown again, attention may be drawn to more specific points (for example, personal appearance: clothing, hair styles, bearing, and body language; style of houses; types of shops). Such observations may become points of departure for class discussion, elaboration by the teacher, or student reports. It is clear that the more often students view the modules of ¡ADELANTE! the more cultural details they will observe.

The chart on the following page indicates the broad cultural topics that are illustrated in the modules of ¡ADELANTE!

City life	
City life in general	Modules 1, 3, 9, 10
Madrid	Module 1
Mexico City	Module 10
Family life	Modules 11, 12, 16
Friends	Modules 1, 5, 7, 8, 9, 18
School	Modules 6, 7, 17
Shopping	
Shopping for school supplies	Module 2
Shopping for clothes	Module 15
Shopping for food	Module 20
Leisure-time activities	
At a party	Modules 5, 8
At the movies	Module 14
Other cultural activities	Modules 10, 14
Sports	Module 13 .
Weekend activities	Module 14
Eating and drinking	
At the café	Modules 1, 2, 18, 19
At the restaurant	Module 20
At work	Module 19
Diversity of the Spanish-speaking world	Modules 1, 4, 5, 6, 9, 11
CULTURAL THEMES	CORRESPONDING MODULES IN ¡ADELANTE!

Developing Oral Proficiency

As students' linguistic knowledge expands, their oral proficiency skills can be strengthened using the video as a basis for communicative activities. These activities may take a variety of forms.

Answering questions

After viewing a module, students may be asked different kinds of questions.

- Factual questions

  Students are asked to describe with precision what they have observed in the video module: **¿Dónde y cuándo ocurre esta escena? ¿En qúe tienda entra X? ¿Qué ropa lleva Y? ¿Qué compra la Sra. A? ¿Qué contesta el Sr. B?**

- Interpretation questions

  Students are asked to give an analysis or interpretation of the situation presented in the module: **¿Qué piensas de X? ¿Por qué? ¿Qué piensas de Y? ¿Qué piensas de la actitud de Z? En tu opinión, ¿qué va a hacer el Sr. A? En tu opinión, ¿por qué compra la Sra. B esas cosas?**

- Personal questions

  Students are asked to describe their own preferences, experiences, and activities in relation to the topic presented in the module. For instance, after viewing Module 13 on sports, students may be asked questions such as: **¿Cuáles son tus deportes favoritos? ¿Juegas al tenis? ¿Cuándo? ¿Dónde? ¿Qué deportes practicas en verano? ¿En invierno?**

- Cross-cultural questions

  After viewing a given module, students are asked to compare daily life in a Spanish-speaking country and in the United States. For example, after viewing Module 20, students may be asked questions such as: **¿Hay mercados al aire libre en los Estados Unidos? ¿Cuáles son los productos que se venden allí? ¿Cuáles son las ventajas de un mercado al aire libre? ¿Cuáles son las desventajas?**

To develop oral proficiency, questions may be constructed so as to practice and review specific grammar points, especially verb tenses. For example:

(present)	**¿Adónde va X ¿Qué hace Y?**
(preterite)	**¿Adónde fue X? ¿Qué hizo Y?**
(future)	**¿Adónde ira X después . . . ? ¿Qué hara Y?**
(conditional)	**Si estuvieras en México, ¿adónde irías para . . . ? ¿Qué harías?**
(subjunctive)	**¿Qué debe hacer X para . . . ? (Es necesario que vaya a . . .)**

Dialogs and skits

Students may be asked to create their own scripts based on the modules they have seen. Such activities may take various forms:

- interviews
- skits (ordering in a café, food shopping, and so on)
- dialogs (talking about weekend activities, and so on)

Oral presentations

Students may be asked to make brief oral presentations based on a given module. These reports may take various forms:

- description of the action of the module
- description of a subtheme (such as a specific sport)
- description of cross-cultural differences

Expanding the Vocabulary Base

¡ADELANTE! utilizes the vocabulary base of SPANISH for MASTERY, Level One. This vocabulary base can be expanded for Level Two students by introducing new lexical terms. For example, the teacher might view a given module and prepare a list of five or ten unfamiliar Spanish words that are illustrated in the video. Then, as the module is presented in class, the teacher can introduce the new words within the cultural context of the film. For instance, Module 20 (**La paella**) can be used to introduce students to the names of additional foods such as **pimiento, cebolla, aceituna.**

Developing writing skills

Students may be assigned written compositions based on a video module. These compositions could be formulated so as to include the new supplementary vocabulary related to the module. Compositions can range from simple descriptions of the video to narratives using specific tenses. For more creative assignments, students could be asked to write the imagined diary of one of the characters or a phone conversaton between two of the characters.

INTRODUCTION

The Teacher's Edition of SPANISH for MASTERY is an enlarged version of the Student Text. The manual at the front of the book consists of four parts: (1) a description of the characteristics and organization of the SPANISH for MASTERY program including a Scope and Sequence chart; (2) suggestions on how to use the various components of the program; (3) hints on how to supplement the basic materials; (4) a Reference Guide containing useful classroom expressions and a detailed listing of the contents of the program.

In the textbook itself, an overprint of small, blue type provides the teacher with several kinds of information.

- Unit summaries of the main communicative, grammatical, and cultural objectives
- Comprehension questions on the *Presentation texts* and **Notas culturales**
- Supplementary grammatical information
- Supplementary cultural information
- Suggested realia to enliven the presentation of culture
- Supplementary vocabulary
- Suggestions for expanding and modifying exercises
- Suggested optional activities
- Responses to **Observaciones** questions
- Material designated as optional
- Correlation of the text to the components

It is important to note here that the term "optional" does not mean that the material so designated should be left out. It simply signals material that can be adapted or omitted according to specific objectives of the class, and/or material that can be assigned as supplementary work for better students or for students with a particular interest in the topic.

Contents

PART 1: Description of SPANISH for MASTERY

1 | GENERAL CHARACTERISTICS OF THE PROGRAM

SPANISH for MASTERY is a complete three-level program for junior/senior high school students. SPANISH for MASTERY 1, *¿Qué tal?*, and SPANISH for MASTERY 2, *Entre nosotros*, are accompanied by the following components:

- Teacher's Annotated Edition
- Video Program ¡ADELANTE!
- Workbook
- Teacher's Annotated Edition of the Workbook
- Cassette Program
- Tapescript

- Testing Program
- Activity Masters
- Overhead Transparencies
- Song Binder
- Computer Software
- Teacher's Resource Binder
- Answer Key/Student Text

The core program is contained in the Student Text and the Teacher's Edition. The other components are optional.

SPANISH for MASTERY 3, *Situaciones,* is a program for third-level students.

1.1 Objectives and Philosophy

The basic objectives of SPANISH for MASTERY are the following:

- to help each student attain proficiency in the four skills of listening, speaking, reading, and writing within a minimum period of time and in a way that makes language learning a meaningful activity;
- to present the language within the context of the contemporary Spanish-speaking world and the various cultures it includes.

In pursuing these goals, the authors have adopted a pragmatic approach and purposely have avoided relying on any one theory of language learning. To elicit a high level of student participation in the learning process, they have evaluated a variety of pedagogical techniques and have selected those that would produce the best results. This integration of techniques is at the heart of SPANISH for MASTERY. Furthermore, teachers can adapt the program to their own teaching styles and to the needs of their students.

1.2 Key Features

1.2.1 Close articulation between levels.   The success of a secondary program depends to a large extent on the careful articulation among levels. SPANISH for MASTERY 2, *Entre nosotros,* is designed not only for students who finished SPANISH for MASTERY 1, *¿Qué tal?,* and who may have lost contact with Spanish over the summer, but also for students who did not finish the Level One text or who used a different program for the first level of instruction.

Unit 1 helps students and teachers to get acquainted—or reacquainted—while reviewing the basic structures introduced in Units 2–4 of Level One: the present tense of **-ar, -er,** and **-ir** verbs: **ser, estar, tener,** and **ir;** and the forms and uses of articles, nouns, and adjectives. Unit 2 reviews possessive adjectives, demonstrative adjectives, and object pronouns (corresponding to Units 5, 6, and 7 of Level One), as well as other common irregular verbs. Unit 3 focuses on stem-changing and reflexive verbs (introduced in Units 6 and 7 of Level One). Unit 4 reviews the preterite tense (presented in Unit 8 of Level One), and begins the introduction of new structures.

The rate at which these first units are covered will depend on the level of the students and on their background. The time given to strengthening this common foundation, however, is well spent, for the students will be able to continue their acquisition of new structures and vocabulary on a strong footing.

1.2.2 Broad cultural focus.

In SPANISH for MASTERY, cultural material is integrated into the learning process so that students gain an awareness of the culture of the Spanish-speaking world as they study each lesson. In addition, specific segments of the program have been especially designed to emphasize culture:

- the *Nota cultural* of each lesson
- the five full-color, illustrated *Vista* sections
- the *Rincón cultural* sections of the Workbook
- the photographs and realia presented throughout the text

From the start of the program, students are made aware of the geographic and cultural variety of the Spanish-speaking world, from South America to the Caribbean, from Mexico and Central America to Europe. A second but no less important goal is to make students aware that Hispanic culture in their own country is a reality that directly affects their lives. For many students this awareness will broaden their horizons and stimulate their interest in learning Spanish.

1.2.3 Accent on youth.

An effective way of involving students in language learning is to make communication in the new language relevant to their own lives. The majority of the activities in this program have youth-related themes: hobbies, travel, schoolwork, dating, choice of career, relationships with parents, and attitudes toward love, friendship, money, success, and failure.

1.2.4 Adaptability of the program.

SPANISH for MASTERY can be used in a variety of teaching situations:

- large or small classes
- slow or fast tracks
- language programs stressing oral proficiency or more traditional classes

The program is also adaptable to small-group teaching and lends itself to self-paced instruction. Part Two of this manual suggests various ways in which the teacher can organize the lessons.

1.2.5 Several approaches to grammar.

Because there is no one way of teaching a foreign language, SPANISH for MASTERY incorporates several classroom-proven approaches into the presentation of Spanish structures:

- **Guided discovery approach.** The new structures in each lesson are presented in key sentences in the *Presentation text* that begins each lesson. The *Conversación/Observación* section that follows presents a limited number of short questions that pertain to the new structures. The questions are phrased to allow students to make their own generalizations about the new material.
- **Descriptive approach.** In the *Estructuras* sections, the new material is explained in English and, where appropriate, presented graphically with examples and related exercises. These sections also serve as a grammar reference manual.

- **Modified contrastive approach.** Where appropriate, new structures are compared to and contrasted with previously learned structures or English equivalents. Areas of potential interference between Spanish and English are mentioned explicitly: see, for example, Lesson 4.1, the English present perfect versus the Spanish present with **hace.**
- **Analytic-synthetic approach.** More complex points of grammar are introduced across two or more lessons in minimal learning steps. Finally, the entire pattern is summarized in a table (for example, the summary of the main uses of the subjunctive, Lesson 10.2).

1.2.6 Variety in the learning material.   Variety in presentation as well as in content is an essential element in fostering and maintaining student interest. Throughout SPANISH for MASTERY, this feature has been given particular attention. For instance, instead of relying exclusively on dialogs, the lessons are also built around narratives, interviews, questionnaires, cartoon series, or advertisements. Similarly, the exercises encompass a wide variety of formats: role-playing activities, *Preguntas personales,* open-ended sentences requiring a personal completion, and so on.

1.2.7 Focus on communication.   To elicit active participation in the learning process, all exercises of SPANISH for MASTERY, including those of the Cassette Program and the Workbook, are set in situational contexts. The situations are sometimes practical (planning a sightseeing trip) and sometimes thought-provoking (deciding on future goals). The purpose of these contextual exercises is to have students use Spanish as a means of communication and self-expression rather than as a rote response in artificial drills. This approach gives students extensive practice with the **yo** and **tú** forms, as they communicate with one another.

1.2.8 Flexibility in developing language skills.   The language is presented and practiced across all four language skills. However, if the teacher wishes to focus on only one or two skills, the parts of the program emphasizing these skills can be stressed. For instance, if speaking is a priority, the teacher can stress the program's communicative activities: *Preguntas personales,* role-playing activities, and *Conversación* activities as well as the *Speaking* activities of the Cassette Program. The teacher could also use the *Rincón cultural* sections of the Workbook.

Each skill is developed in its several aspects. For instance, in building reading skills, the teacher may use many types of materials: *Presentation texts, Notas culturales, Variedades,* and *Vistas.* Similar breadth of development characterizes the listening activities of the Cassette Program, which include active listening to recorded material from the Student Text, selective listening for grammatical signals such as verb tenses or forms of pronouns, and general listening comprehension of unfamiliar passages.

1.2.9 Logical organization.   In learning Spanish students are carefully guided through a concise, measured grammatical progression. The presentation of the simpler and more frequently used structures precedes that of the more complex and less common ones. Each lesson in SPANISH for MASTERY concentrates on two to four aspects of grammar, and the amount of new vocabulary is carefully controlled. The introductory *Presentation text* of the lesson incorporates the new material into the context of previously mastered patterns and structures. Any unknown words are glossed in the margin or presented in the *Vocabulario* section immediately following the *Presentation text.*

1.2.10 Systematic reentry of grammar and vocabulary.   Level 2 of SPANISH for MASTERY opens with a systematic review, in new contexts, of all the important material presented in Level 1. Therefore, second-year students who have not completed Level 1 or who have used materials other than SPANISH for MASTERY can confidently begin the second year with the material in Level 2.

All vocabulary in the *Vocabulario* and *Vocabulario práctico* sections is active, as is the vocabulary in the *Estructuras;* that is, they should be mastered by the students. Lists of these words and expressions by unit appear in the Activity Masters. Passive vocabulary, for recognition only, is glossed when it appears.

As the program progresses, structures and vocabulary items are reentered in the exercises and reading materials. Suggestions for reviewing structures and vocabulary are given in the overprint if the mastery of these elements is a requisite for learning the new material of the lesson.

All basic aspects of grammar and active vocabulary are incorporated into the ***Test/Repaso*** which concludes each unit of the Workbook. The teacher may use these tests informally for review if desired.

1.2.11 Emphasis on Spanish.   SPANISH for MASTERY has been written so that Spanish can be used almost exclusively in class. Note that all exercise instructions and ***Notas culturales*** are written in Spanish. Spanish classroom expressions (see section 7.1 of this manual) should be used from the beginning of the year. However, the ***Observación*** questions and the grammatical explanations in the ***Estructuras*** sections are in English throughout to prevent possible misunderstandings and to ensure that all students may use them for out-of-class reference and study.

1.2.12 Careful vocabulary choice.   A concern for simplicity and authenticity governed the choice of vocabulary. In instances in which Spanish speakers from different areas have different words for an object or concept, SPANISH for MASTERY has chosen the word that consultants felt would be most appropriate for secondary school students in the United States.

2 ORGANIZATION OF SPANISH FOR MASTERY

The following pages describe SPANISH for MASTERY 2, *Entre nosotros*.

2.1 The Student Text

The Student Text contains ten basic units and five illustrated culture sections. The book concludes with appendices, a complete Spanish-English vocabulary, and an active English-Spanish vocabulary.

Unit 1

Vista 1: Los Estados Unidos

Units 2 and 3

Vista 2: El Caribe

Units 4 and 5

Vista 3: México y Centroamérica

Units 6 and 7

Vista 4: La América del Sur

Units 8 and 9

Vista 5: España

Unit 10

Appendices

Spanish-English Vocabulary

English-Spanish Vocabulary

2.1.1 Organization of a unit. Each unit is built around a particular theme (such as the world of today, attitudes toward the future) and has a main grammatical focus (such as object pronouns, the imperfect, the subjunctive). It is divided into four basic lessons, which present the new structures and vocabulary of the unit, and ends with the reading section **Variedades.**

Unit organization	
Lesson 1	
Lesson 2	Presentation of new material
Lesson 3	(structure and vocabulary)
Lesson 4	
Variedades	Reading practice

2.1.2 Organization of a basic lesson. Each basic lesson consists of three parts: the presentation material, the instructional material, and the recombination material. The diagram below shows the construction of a typical lesson.

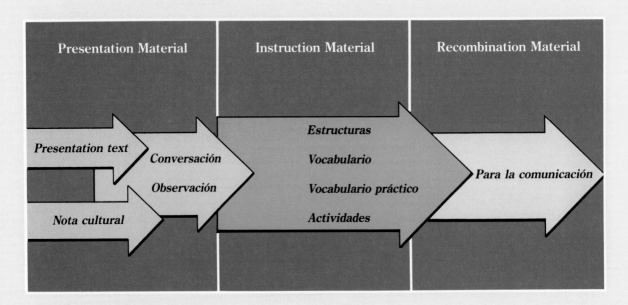

- **The Presentation Material.** The function of the *Presentation text* is to introduce, in context, samples of the basic structures and vocabulary taught in the lesson. The context used may assume a variety of formats:

—A dialog (**Dos chicas**—Lesson 6.3)

—A personality or psychological questionnaire (**Un psicotest: ¿sociable o no?**—Lesson 2.1)

—A series of humorous cartoons (¡**Así es la vida!**—Lesson 2.2)

—A game (**Un accidente en Cartegena**—Lesson 5.4)

The *Presentation text* is built on previously learned material and contains samples of the new structures and vocabulary of the lesson. Unfamiliar words are glossed and are usually part of the ***Vocabulario*** and ***Vocabulario práctico*** sections.

The ***Nota cultural*** explains and develops cultural references made in the *Presentation text*. For example, in Lesson 4.3, after a reading about a car accident, the ***Nota cultural*** explains the role of the automobile in Hispanic culture.

Beginning in Unit 5, Lesson 2, the ***Conversación/Observación*** section provides the link between the presentation material and the instruction material. Through the ***Observación*** questions, students are able to generalize about the new grammatical material of the lesson.

- **The Instruction Material.** The grammatical structures in the ***Estructuras*** are functionally related to the theme of the unit. For example, the grammar of Unit 3, which focuses on careers and plans for the future, presents the future tense.
- New grammar in the ***Estructuras*** section is explained in a simple, clear and schematic manner. Immediately after the grammar explanations, the rules are applied in situational exercises *(Actividades)*.

The ***Actividades*** assume a variety of formats:

—Situational activities, which are simple transformational drills

—***Diálogos,*** which are activities that two or more students act out, often requiring a personal yes/no answer

—***Preguntas personales,*** which are yes/no and open-ended questions about the student's life, incorporating the new grammatical structures of the lesson while reviewing previously learned structures

—***Expressión personal,*** similar to the ***Preguntas personales*** but containing more complex constructions

—¡Un poco de lógical, a recombination drill/game in which students are asked to derive as many logical sentences as they can from a given set of elements containing the new grammatical structures

The ***Vocabulario*** lists active vocabulary items from the *Presentation text* and the ***Notas culturales.***

In the ***Vocabulario práctico,*** active vocabulary items are grouped thematically (family, entertainment, emotions, and so on). Whenever possible the vocabulary is presented pictorially or in sentences.

- **The Recombination material.** The ***Para la comunicación*** sections reinforce the new material of the lessons and help students further develop communication skills. Students can prepare these exercises orally or in writing.

Answers to the activities are provided in the Answer Key to the Student Edition, a separate booklet available to the teacher.

2.1.3 *Variedades*. Each unit concludes with a ***Variedades*** section consisting of a reading passage in the form of a narrative, poem, a guessing game, or a project. The ***Variedades*** provide a great variety of material in order to motivate students.

2.1.4 *Vista*.   The purpose of the illustrated ***Vista*** sections is to show the breadth of the Spanish-speaking world—Spain, Latin America, and the United States.

CONTENTS	
Vista 1	***Los Estados Unidos***
Vista 2	***El Caribe***
Vista 3	***México y Centroamérica***
Vista 4	***La América del Sur***
Vista 5	***España***

The ***Vistas*** focus on the Spanish-speaking world—its customs, its contributions, its heroes and heroines. Students assimilate culture from illustrations, photographs, and varied readings in an exciting magazine format.

Since the ***Vistas*** are entirely in Spanish, they provide extensive practice in developing reading skills. The illustrations, photographs, and realia may provide points of departure for conversation. The cultural projects at the end of each ***Vista*** suggest further areas of exploration. In addition, the Activity Masters contain comprehension and reading exercises based on the ***Vistas***.

2.1.5 End matter.   The end matter contains the following elements:

- **Appendices:**
  Appendix 1—Cardinal and ordinal numbers
  Appendix 2—Selected vocabulary
  Appendix 3—Verb charts
- **Spanish-English Vocabulary**
  This vocabulary lists the words in the text, except for specialized vocabulary glossed in the ***Vista*** and ***Notas culturales.*** Each word and expression that is considered "active" is followed by a reference number giving the unit and lesson where the word or expression first appears actively in the text.
- **English-Spanish Vocabulary**
  This vocabulary lists only the active words and expressions: those found in the ***Vocabulario, Vocabulario práctico,*** and ***Estructuras*** sections. Each entry has a unit and lesson number referring the student to the first active usage in the text.

2.2 The Workbook

The Workbook supplements the Student Text. In addition to providing written exercises to accompany the instructional material of the text, each unit of the Workbook contains an illustrated cultural section, ***El rincón cultural,*** and a ***Test/Repaso.*** The Teacher's Annotated Edition of the Workbook provides answers to all the activities, in position, to facilitate correction of students' work.

2.2.1 Written exercises.   For each basic lesson of the Student Text, the Workbook contains two to four pages of written exercises. Each lesson begins on a right-hand page so that students can tear out specific pages to hand in if the teacher so requests.

To stimulate students' interest, all basic exercises are set in situational or game contexts. Most exercises require thoughtful rather than mechanical answers. Where appropriate, the activites are based on visual cues.

2.2.2 *El rincón cultural.* Each Workbook unit ends with a section called *El rincón cultural.* This section contains realia, games, and exercises. The realia reinforce the cultural themes developed in the unit.

2.2.3 *Test/Repaso.* Each unit closes with a *Test/Repaso* consisting of a series of situational review exercises. Students take these tests individually and check their responses against the Answer Key at the back of the Workbook. The Answer Key contains a diagnostic section to help students interpret their results. It also refers them back to specific sections of the unit for additional study and review.

2.3 The Cassette Program

The Cassette Program for SPANISH for MASTERY is designed to supplement the Student Text by providing additional practice in the development of listening and speaking skills.

2.3.1 General description. The Cassette Program for each lesson of SPANISH for MASTERY runs approximately 25 minutes. All the activities in the Cassette Program, together with the correct oral and written responses, are printed in the Tapescript, a separate booklet available to the teacher.

2.3.2 Types of activities on cassette. The cassette for each lesson contains a variety of activities. These are introduced in English so that all students may work independently with the Cassette Program. The activities include the following categories:

- **Listening.** Students listen to an unpaused, dramatized reading of the *Presentation text* and **Nota cultural.**
- **Listening and Repeating.** The speaker models words from the vocabulary and verb charts. When the vocabulary or verb chart contains both a word and a sentence in which the word is used, students will repeat both.
- **Listening for Signals.** Students hear a series of sentences and are asked to discriminate among sounds that signal grammatical information such as singular or plural, preterite or imperfect, indicative or subjunctive. Students may mark their responses either on the grid provided in the Activity Masters or on a separate sheet of paper. At the end of the activity, the speaker gives the correct answers.
- **Listening Comprehension with Visual Cues.** Students see a diagram or illustration and hear several statements pertaining to it. They indicate whether these statements are true or false, or match statements, or locate specific items. For example, students hear six witnesses being interviewed about a burglary that occurred the previous evening. By looking at a map of the burglary site and by listening to the interviews, students determine which witnesses give the most accurate accounts.
- **Speaking.** Directed activities: Students participate in situation drills similar to the exercises in the Student Text. These drills require only a simple transformation (for example, from masculine to feminine) and provide variety in oral practice while helping to develop listening comprehension skills. In these activities, the cues are followed by a pause for the student response. A confirmation of the appropriate response is then given by the speaker on the tape.

- **Conversación.** The Cassette Program contains free-response activities similar to those in the **Conversación** section of the Student Text. Students answer the questions using answer sheets provided in the Activity Masters. Because students supply original answers, no response is given on the tape.
- **Pronunciación.** The cassette for each lesson of Units 1-5 ends with a brief review of one aspect of Spanish pronunciation and sound-spelling correspondence. The sample words, phrases, or sentences to be repeated appear in the Tapescript.
- **Spanish songs.** Each unit features a different traditional Spanish song. The melody serves as a recurrent theme that is heard at the beginning of the tape and at brief intervals between selected activities. At the end of the unit, the entire song is sung by a Spanish speaker. Music and lyrics are printed in the Activity Masters for student participation.

A cassette with all the unit songs from Levels 1 and 2, with the music and lyrics, is available separately in a special Song Binder.

2.4 The Activity Masters

The SPANISH for MASTERY Activity Masters are a set of copymasters that include the following teaching aids:

- **Cassette Program Material**
  —Activity Sheets containing answer grids and visual cues, write-on lines for the **Conversación** activities, and the music and lyrics of the unit songs
- **Other Material**
  —Reading Activities to accompany the **Vistas**
  —Active Vocabulary Sheets by unit for reference and review
  —Useful Expressions, including Classroom Expressions and Expressions for the **Actividades** (reprinted from the Teacher's Edition)

2.5 Testing Program

The SPANISH for MASTERY Testing Program offers three types of testing materials: *Lesson Quizzes, Unit Tests,* and *Achievement Tests.* The tests are printed on copymasters and the listening portions are recorded on cassettes. The Answer Key to the Testing Program is found in the accompanying Test Guide.

2.5.1 Lesson Quizzes.   *The Lesson Quiz,* designed to be administered in about 20 minutes, permits quick and frequent evaluation of students' mastery of the structures and vocabulary of a lesson. The test items are based on aural, visual, or printed word cues to accommodated learning styles. A Student Progress Chart (on a copymaster) allows the teacher to track each student's progress.

2.5.2 Unit Tests.   The *Unit Test,* designed to be administered in about 45 minutes, focuses on the content of the unit and also evaluates communication skills. In addition to responding to items similar to those in the *Lesson Quiz,* students may be asked to use Spanish in practical situations, such as listening for specific information; in creative situations, such as deciding which of two expressions most logically completes a thought or sentence; and in cultural contexts.

2.5.3 Achievement Tests. The Testing Program provides two *Achievement Tests* (to follow Units 5 and 10), each designed to be administered over two 45-minute class periods. Broader in scope than the *Unit Tests*, the *Achievement Tests* are cumulative and recombine elements of language in expanded contexts.

2.6 The Overhead Transparencies

The SPANISH for MASTERY 2, *Entre nosotros*, program includes a set of 50 Overhead Transparencies available in a convenient binder. The transparencies correspond to specific visual items in the Student Text to which it is keyed with identifying titles and page numbers.

The Overhead Transparencies have been provided to teach and reinforce vocabulary, to practice essential verb forms, to present the geography of the Spanish-speaking world, to serve as a basis for conversation and composition, and to help teachers minimize the use of English in the classroom.

2.7 The Teacher's Resource Binder

The Teacher's Resource Binder is a three-ring binder that contains the following items.

- **Question Cards—additional communicative activities**
- **Student Text Answer Key**
- **Workbook: Teacher's Annotated Edition**
- **Activity Masters, as copymasters**
- **Testing Program, as copymasters**
- **Tapescript**
- **Test Guide**
- **"Teaching with SPANISH FOR MASTERY"—a booklet of teaching strategies**
- **Newsletters**
- **Unit Correlation Charts**

2.8 The SPANISH for MASTERY Newsletter

The SPANISH for MASTERY Newsletter is an invaluable supplement to the SPANISH for MASTERY program. Published three times a year, it is available to all SPANISH for MASTERY users free of charge. Each issue contains up-to-date information of interest to teachers and students alike. The **Accent on . . .** column gives suggestions for using the program and highlights current trends in teaching. The ***Vistazo*** column (in Spanish) focuses on the culture and language of the Spanish-speaking world. **Para su calendario** lists upcoming conferences and meetings. Each issue also includes a listing of schools that have recently adopted SPANISH for MASTERY. Teachers can file the newsletters in the Teacher's Resource Binder for reference.

SCOPE AND SEQUENCE

Students' lesson-to-lesson progression through SPANISH for MASTERY 2, *Entre nosotros,* is represented on the following Scope and Sequence chart. This chart correlates each lesson's communication functions and objectives (comprehension and self-expresson) and linguistic objectives (Vocabulary consolidation and expansion and Grammatical accuracy).

SPANISH for MASTERY 2
Entre Nosotros: SCOPE AND SEQUENCE

Building for Communicative Proficiency

UNIT 1 ¡Nosotros, los jóvenes!

COMMUNICATION FUNCTIONS AND OBJECTIVES Comprehension and self-expression	LINGUISTIC OBJECTIVES Vocabulary consolidation and expansion	LINGUISTIC OBJECTIVES Grammatical accuracy
1.1 Describing one's activities at home and at school Discussing what one does on vacation Expressing preferences	1.1 Daily activities and vacation activities	1.1 The present tense of *-ar* verbs (Review) Infinitive constructions (Review) Forming questions (Review)
1.2 Describing and talking about oneself and others: Appearance, personality, and nationality	1.2 Family members and others Physical description, personality traits, and nationality	1.2 The verb *ser* (Review) The noun group: gender and number of nouns and articles (Review) Using descriptive adjectives: forms and position (Review)
1.3 Talking about one's belongings and those of others Talking about going somewhere Discussing future plans	1.3 Everyday objects Activities involving other people Places and buildings	1.3 The verb *tener* (Review) The use of the definite article with days of the week (Review) The contractions *al* and *del* (Review) The personal *a* (Review) The verb *ir* (Review) The construction *ir a* + infinitive (Review)
1.4 Expressing feelings and physical state Indicating location Describing others: Origin, profession, and basic characteristics Talking about daily activities and ongoing actions	1.4 Adjectives of feeling Time expressions Common activities	1.4 The verb *estar* (Review) *Ser* vs. *estar* (Review) The present tense of *-er* and *-ir* verbs (Review)

COMMUNICATION FUNCTIONS AND OBJECTIVES

Comprehension and self-expression

2.1 Talking about acquaintances
Identifying one's belongings and those of others
Discussing relationships with others

2.2 Talking about what and whom one knows
Pointing out specific people or objects
Discussing relationships with others

2.3 Asking for information
Engaging in conversation with others
Asking others for specific things
Asking the help of other people

2.4 Talking about leisure activities
Asking and talking about one's likes, dislikes, and concerns
Being specific about people or objects

LINGUISTIC OBJECTIVES

Vocabulary consolidation and expansion

2.1 Service occupations

2.2 Beach activities
Activities involving other people

2.3 Everyday objects

2.4 Leisure activities
Sports; hobbies; movies, theater, television, music
Verbs that express preference, interest, need, and concern

LINGUISTIC OBJECTIVES

Grammatical accuracy

2.1 The verb *conocer* (Review)
The use of *de* **to indicate ownership or relationship**
Possessive adjectives (Review)
Using direct object pronouns: *lo, la, los, las* (Review)

2.2 Distinguishing between *saber* **and** *conocer* (Review)
Using demonstrative adjectives and pronouns
Using indirect object pronouns: *le, les* (Review)

2.3 Using object pronouns: *me, te, nos* (Review)
Double object pronouns (Review)
the pronoun *se* (Review)
the pronoun *lo*

2.4 The use of the definite article in a general sense (Review)
gustar (Review)
The constructions
el + adjective
el + *de*
el + *que*

FUTBOL EN EL MUNDO

COMMUNICATION FUNCTIONS AND OBJECTIVES	LINGUISTIC OBJECTIVES	LINGUISTIC OBJECTIVES
Comprehension and self-expression	**Vocabulary consolidation and expansion**	**Grammatical accuracy**
3.1 Expression feelings about something Expressing what one wants to do or can do Talking about one's daily activities	3.1 Everyday activities	3.1 **The present of stem-changing verbs** (Review)
3.2 Talking about personal care and grooming Describing daily activities	3.2 **Personal care** **The daily routine**	3.2 **Reflexive verbs: forms and uses**
3.3 Expressing feelings and emotions	3.3 **Feelings and emotions**	3.3 **The use of reflexive verbs to express emotions and describe behavior**
3.4 Talking about daily activities Expressing reciprocity	3.4 **Everyday activities** **Love** Friendship, affection, love, and marriage	3.4 **Irregular verbs with irregular *yo* forms in the present** **The use of reflexive verbs to express reciprocal action** **Reflexive verbs in the infinitive and the present progressive**

UNIT 4   El coche del Sr. Molina

COMMUNICATION FUNCTIONS AND OBJECTIVES	LINGUISTIC OBJECTIVES	LINGUISTIC OBJECTIVES
Comprehension and self-expression	**Vocabulary consolidation and expansion**	**Grammatical accuracy**
4.1 Saying how long an action has been going on Talking about events that happened recently Ranking persons or objects Expressing how much and how many	4.1 Vacations	4.1 The use of the present tense with *hace* (Review) The construction *acabar de + infinitive* (Review) Ordinal numbers (Review) Indefinite adjectives (Review)
4.2 Talking about one's belongings and those of others Reporting past events	4.2 The car	4.2 Possessive pronouns and stressed possessive adjectives The preterite of *-ar* verbs (Review) The diminutive *-ito*
4.3 Reporting past events Indicating that two actions are occurring almost simultaneously Expressing surprise or horror	4.3 Verbs of motion Accidents	4.3 Forms of the preterite: ■ verbs in *-er* and *-ir* (Review) ■ stem-changing verbs in *-ir* (Review) ■ *ir* and *ser* (Review) The construction *al + infinitive*
4.4 Reporting past events Saying how long ago something took place Describing the manner in which something is done	4.4 Common descriptive adjectives	4.4 Forms of the preterite: ■ verbs like *conducir* (Review) ■ other irregular verbs (Review) The use of the preterite with *hace* Adverbs with *-mente*

Avianca del Sur

Avianca

Primera línea aérea de las Américas

COMMUNICATION FUNCTIONS AND OBJECTIVES	LINGUISTIC OBJECTIVES	LINGUISTIC OBJECTIVES
Comprehension and self-expression	**Vocabulary consolidation and expansion**	**Grammatical accuracy**
5.1 Expressing negative concepts	5.1 **Personality types** **Affirmative and negative expressions** **Descriptive adjectives**	5.1 **Affirmative and negative expressions** **The constructions** *lo* **+ adjective and** *lo que* (Review)
5.2 Describing habitual past actions	5.2 **Good and bad manners**	5.2 **The imperfect tense:** regular forms **The use of the imperfect to describe habitual or repeated events**
5.3 Describing what was going on when another action occurred	5.3 **Mishaps**	5.3 **The imperfect tense:** irregular forms **The use of the imperfect to describe ongoing actions**
5.4 Describing the circumstances of a specific event Describing past events Describing how one feels	5.4 **Physical and psychological states**	5.4 **The use of the imperfect tense:** imperfect vs. preterite (summary)

COMMUNICATION FUNCTIONS AND OBJECTIVES

Comprehension and self-expression

6.1 Describing actions

6.2 Describing physical and emotional states
Describing the location of people and objects

6.3 Describing what one has done recently
Showing indifference

6.4 Describing what had already happened by the time something else occurred

LINGUISTIC OBJECTIVES

Vocabulary consolidation and expansion

6.1 Shops, merchandise, and services

6.2 Physical states and conditions
Prepositions of place

6.3 Expressions of time

6.4 The natural environment
Expressions of time

LINGUISTIC OBJECTIVES

Grammatical accuracy

6.1 The use of the reflexive pronoun *se* in impersonal constructions

6.2 The use of past participles as adjectives
Prepositions of place

6.3 The present perfect tense: forms and use
irregular past participles

6.4 The pluperfect tense: forms and use

UNIT 7 Mañana será otro día

COMMUNICATION FUNCTIONS AND OBJECTIVES	LINGUISTIC OBJECTIVES	LINGUISTIC OBJECTIVES
Comprehension and self-expression	**Vocabulary consolidation and expansion**	**Grammatical accuracy**
7.1 Describing plans for the future Making predictions about the future Expressing a goal or destination Making comparisons	**7.1 Progress and technology**	**7.1 The future tense:** forms and use **Using *para*** **Using the comparative of adjectives** (Review)
7.2 Talking about the future Making a guess about a present situation Expressing duration, manner, movement, and cause		**7.2 Irregular future forms** **Using the future tense to express probability** **Using *por***
7.3 Describing how one would act in a certain situation Making polite requests Explaining the purpose of an action	**7.3 Adventures**	**7.3 The conditional:** forms and uses **The construction preposition + infinitive** (Review)
7.4 Expressing that an action will have happened by a certain time in the future Expressing the cause of an action	**7.4 Parts of the home**	**7.4 Using the future perfect tense** **The construction *por* + infinitive**

UNIT 8   Perspectivas de hoy

COMMUNICATION FUNCTIONS AND OBJECTIVES

Comprehension and self-expression

8.1 Telling a friend what to do
Giving directions
Describing the timing of an action

8.2 Telling others what to do and what not to do
Persuading others

8.3 Making suggestions

8.4 Expressing wishes
Giving advice
Making requests

LINGUISTIC OBJECTIVES

Vocabulary consolidation and expansion

8.1 City traffic and highway travel

8.2 Verbs used with infinitives

8.3 Camping equipment

8.4 Verbs indicating wishes and preferences

LINGUISTIC OBJECTIVES

Grammatical accuracy

8.1 Giving an order or advice:
affirmative *tú* commands (Review)
The construction preposition of time + infinitive (Review)

8.2 Giving an order or advice:
negative *tú* commands:
regular and irregular forms
Ud., Uds. commands:
regular and irregular forms
The construction verb + preposition + infinitive

8.3 Giving an order or advice:
nosotros commands
position of object pronouns
using two object pronouns

8.4 Using the subjunctive to make a request or express a wish
Indicative mood vs. subjunctive mood

CONSULTE LAS PÁGINAS AMARILLAS

OXIGENO PARA FUTBOLISTAS

Páginas Amarillas

La consulta que resulta!

COMMUNICATION FUNCTIONS AND OBJECTIVES

Comprehension and self-expression

9.1 Expressing feelings and emotions about people or events

9.2 Expressing opinions about people or events

9.3 Expressing doubt or uncertainty about people or things
Expressing feelings or doubt about past events

9.4 Expressing what is and what may be
Stating preferences

LINGUISTIC OBJECTIVES

Vocabulary consolidation and expansion

9.1 Verbs and expressions indicating feelings and emotions

9.2 Impersonal expressions followed by the subjunctive

9.3 Verbs and expressions expressing doubt and uncertainty

LINGUISTIC OBJECTIVES

Grammatical accuracy

9.1 Irregular subjunctive forms
Using the subjunctive to express emotion

9.2 Using the subjunctive after impersonal expressions
The subjunctive of stem-changing verbs in -ar, -er, -ir

9.3 Using the subjunctive to express doubt and uncertainty
Using the present perfect subjunctive

9.4 Relative pronouns
Using the subjunctive or the indicative after a relative pronoun

Mujer, lee Mujeres es tu revista

UNIT 10 Cambios

COMMUNICATION FUNCTIONS AND OBJECTIVES	LINGUISTIC OBJECTIVES	LINGUISTIC OBJECTIVES
Comprehension and self-expression	**Vocabulary consolidation and expansion**	**Grammatical accuracy**
10.1 Expressing objectives Describing actions that are subject to certain conditions	**10.1** Conjunctions expressing conditions or limitations	**10.1** Using the subjunctive after *para que* and other conjunctions
10.2 Describing future events that depend on specific conditions		**10.2** The future tense (Review) Using the indicative or the subjunctive after *cuando* Uses of the subjunctive (summary)
10.3 Expressing attitudes, wishes, and feelings about events in the past		**10.3** Using the imperfect subjunctive
10.4 Formulating hypotheses Describing what would happen if certain events were to occur		**10.4** The conditional (Review) Using the imperfect subjunctive in *si* clauses

PART 2: Using SPANISH for MASTERY

4 | SUGGESTED TECHNIQUES

A basic characteristic of the SPANISH for MASTERY program is its flexibility. The classroom teacher can easily adapt the textbook and its related components to the students' needs and learning styles. Each unit of SPANISH for MASTERY contains more activities than can be completed by the average class. The teacher should therefore select those that are most appropriate for specific classes and individuals. The purpose of this section is to help the teacher make these choices by showing how each component may be used. The suggestions are not exhaustive, but they form a base upon which the teacher may wish to build.

4.1 Teaching Unit 1

In the first week(s) of instruction, the teacher will get to know students and determine to what extent they have retained or forgotten the material they learned in their Level 1 class. On the basis of this assessment, Unit 1, which reviews some of the most basic vocabulary items and structures of Level 1, may be skipped entirely or it may be used for light or heavy review. Here are several ways in which the first four lessons of Unit 1 may be presented.

4.1.1 The Presentation texts and the *Notas culturales*.   In the *Presentation texts* of these lessons teenagers from Chile, Mexico, Panama, and Spain introduce themselves. The teacher may want to play each person's short monolog (recorded on the Cassette Program) several times while students keep their books closed. Each time they hear the text, students should be able to understand a little more. When students have understood as much as they can from the cassette, they should open their books and read along as the cassette is played once more. Brief comprehension questions are included in the overprint of the Teacher's Edition.

Reading skills are practiced in the *Notas culturales,* which focus on specific parts of the Spanish-speaking world. The Teacher may want to play the recorded *Notas* as students read along.

4.1.2 *Conversación*.   In the *Conversación* section of the lesson, students are encouraged to talk about themselves by answering short questions that reintroduce basic structures. The teacher may first want to ask questions of individual students as a full-class activity. Once students can handle accurately the material being practiced, they can continue by working in pairs, interviewing each other. As a culminating activity, students may be asked to tell the class what they have learned about their partners.

4.1.3 *Vocabulario práctico* and *Estructuras* sections.   These sections review basic vocabulary and structures from the first half of Level 1 of SPANISH for MASTERY. Students practice this material through a variety of related activities. If appropriate, the activities may be done orally since written practice is provided in the Workbook. For classes not using the Workbook, selected activities may be assigned for written homework.

4.2 Teaching the Basic Lesson

4.2.1 Using the Presentation text.   The *Presentation text* (not intended for memorization) serves as initial exposure to the basic structures of the lesson and as a point of departure for other activities. The *Presentation text* can be used in the following ways:

- Students listen to an unpaused version either as provided in the Cassette Program or as read by the teacher.
  —*With books closed.* The teacher first plays or reads the entire *Presentation text* once or twice without pauses so that students can try to get the gist of the text. Then the teacher pauses the cassette or stops reading at various intervals to ask questions.
  —*With books open.* Students see if they can understand the spoken word well enough to follow in their books. Students also hear the correct pronunciation as they are seeing the words.
- The teacher presents the **Vocabulario** before students hear the *Presentation text*. With faster groups, the teacher may ask students to guess the new words from their contexts.
- The students perform various activities based on the *Presentation texts*.
  —Students dramatize the text as the cassette is being played.
  —Students guess from illustrations what is going to happen and explain their ideas in Spanish.
  —Students use the illustrations to make up stories.
  —Students bring in visuals (posters, maps, original drawings) and explain how they are related to the *Presentation text*.
  —At the end of the lesson, students reread, summarize, or enact the *Presentation text*.

4.2.2 Using the *Nota cultural.*   The purpose of the **Nota cultural** is twofold: to familiarize students with the culture of the Spanish-speaking world and to develop reading skills. The culture notes provide general cultural information such as geography and history as well as insights into customs or patterns of behavior of interest to young people.

   The cultural notes can serve as a point of departure for more extended classroom activities. The teacher may wish to bring in photos, slides, or realia relating to the topic of the note. The teacher could also create a cultural bulletin board or involve students in cultural projects.

4.2.3 Using the *Conversación/Observación.*   In the **Conversación** section of the lesson, students are encouraged to talk about themselves—their preferences, their activities, and people they know. In the first four units the questions of the **Conversación** allow students to practice the structures and vocabulary being reviewed in these early units. Beginning with Unit 5 the **Conversación** allows students to use some of the new structures of the lesson; it also serves as a springboard to the **Observación** segment, which in turn leads to the **Estructuras** sections.

   In going over the **Observación** sections with students, the teacher may ask them to open their textbooks to the appropriate page. In many lessons it is also possible, and sometimes preferable, to show the **Conversación** sentences on the chalkboard, on a chart, or on an overhead transparency. In this way, the teacher can more readily focus on specific features of the sentences, drawing attention to those points under discussion. If the sentences are reproduced on larger visuals, color or boxing may replace the boldface used in the text.

4.2.4 Teaching structure.   In the **Estructuras** sections, each grammar point is presented with succinct explanations in English, with examples in Spanish, and, where appropriate, with illustrations. These descriptions, however, are intended to serve as reference sections, because in most classes the teacher will first introduce the grammar of the lesson orally. This oral introduction to the grammar may be done in one of the following ways:

- The teacher may introduce the structure in the context of the *Presentation text*.
- The teacher may prefer to begin with the questions that appear in the overprint.

- The teacher may begin by explaining why students need to know the new structure. For example, in Unit 3 the teacher may explain that to talk about many common activities it is useful to know how to use reflexive verbs.
- For some lessons it may be possible to present certain structures with props. For example, in order to review direct object pronouns (Unit 2, Lesson 1), teachers may ask questions about items the students have on their desks or in their pockets. For example: **Miren este bolígrafo. Ana, ¿lo quieres?**
- When students learn a new structure, the teacher should have them practice with the *Listening for Signals* activities in the Cassette Program until they can hear the targeted differences—gender and number, for example. Some students may need to listen to these cassette activities several times before they can recognize the new forms.

4.2.5 Using the *Actividades*.

After the teacher presents the structure orally, students must internalize it. At this point, differences in learning rate and learning style become most apparent. In order to accommodate these differences, SPANISH for MASTERY provides many kinds of learning activities—more than any one teacher would be likely to use in a year. These cover a wide range, from simple to more challenging. They also encompass a variety of formats so that students who need extra practice in a structure will not be repeating the same kinds of activities. These learning activities are found in the Student Text (with variations suggested in the overprint of the Teacher's Edition), in the Workbook, and in the Cassette Program.

Students internalize new structures by practicing them in role-playing or situational exercises and by using the language for personal expression. In SPANISH for MASTERY students are never given a series of unrelated sentences to manipulate; they always practice new structures in a situational context.

Answers to the activities are printed in the Answer Key to the Student Edition, a separate booklet available to the teacher.

Types of Activities

Simple situational activities. The first activity after the presentation of a new structure is usually a situational activity requiring a transformation. Students of all abilities should do this first activity.

- The teacher gives the situation and cues while students give responses with their books closed. It is better if the teacher gives the cue before mentioning a student's name so that everyone will pay attention.
- Students could work in pairs or small groups and cue each other for responses.

Role-play and directed responses. In activities of this type, students respond according to specific instructions.

- The teacher can request full-class responses or have both halves of the class play roles.
- The teacher can call on individual students to give responses.
- Students can do the activities in pairs or groups.
- Faster learners can practice an activity with books closed and then write out responses to one or two cues.

Guided self-expression. These activities may be **Preguntas personales** (yes/no questions, information questions) or **Expresión personal** (open-ended sentences) that require students to use Spanish for personal expression.

- The teacher can foster communication by encouraging students to listen to each other. For example, the teacher asks: **Juan, ¿a qué hora cenas?** After Juan answers, the teacher calls on another student: **Ana, ¿a qué hora cena Juan?** If Ana cannot answer, the teacher tells her to ask Juan. In this type of activity, students learn to listen to each other as they practice the language.

- The *Preguntas personales* also lend themselves to working in pairs. One student with the book open asks another student a question. The second student answers without looking in the book.
- The teacher may prefer to assign these personal activities as written homework since the responses will differ from student to student. The teacher then corrects the papers and asks students to rewrite the sentences that have errors.
- For an in-class writing activity, one student can give a response, which the other class members write down.
- Additional communicative activities can be developed using the Question Cards that are found in the Teacher's Resource Binder.

¡Un poco de lógica! This activity requires knowledge of the structures and basic vocabulary of the lesson. It is also challenging and fun, as students must use the words given in the three or four columns of the activity to create sentences that are logical and grammatically correct.

- As an oral activity, each student can be called upon to create a sentence which other students could judge for logic and correctness.
- As a special challenge, students may compete to see who can write the greatest number of logical, correct sentences within a given time, such a five or ten minutes.

4.2.6 Teaching Vocabulary.

Words are essential to communication. If students can identify and understand the key words in a conversation or a written text, they can grasp the gist of the message. When they have acquired a basic vocabulary, they can begin to express their own ideas.

In SPANISH FOR MASTERY, vocabulary is introduced in small "doses," with one or two thematic lists per lesson. This approach allows students to master new words in manageable amounts and meaningful contexts. The new vocabulary is reinforced in the activities and readings in the textbook, as well as in the activities in the Workbook and Cassette Program. All the new lexical items of a given unit are grouped together for review on a one-page "Active Vocabulary Sheet," available for duplication and distribution in the Activity Masters component.

Most of the vocabulary in SPANISH FOR MASTERY consists of concrete, everyday words that students can easily relate to. Probably the most important thing to keep in mind is that students need a great amount of comprehension practice with new vocabulary items before they are able to use these words actively themselves. Here are a few suggestions:

- Pre-teaching new vocabulary, for listening comprehension only, via classroom warm-up activities. For example, the teacher may spend a couple of minutes at the beginning of the hour talking about current events of interest to the students (whether it is the success of the local school basketball team or an international confrontation), writing key words on the board and using gestures, pictures, maps, and drawings to convey meaning. The teacher may also retell familiar stories or fairy tales in Spanish.
- Teaching new vocabulary using the Overhead Transparencies. For example the teacher gives a series of sentences using the various verbs shown on Transparency 27 (Los verbos reflexivos: **El arreglo personal**). Volunteers may come forward and with a pointer indicate the corresponding picture. Once it is clear that all students understand all the verbs used in context, the teacher can begin modeling the verbs for repetition and writing the forms on the transparency with washable markers.
- Teach new vocabulary using magazine cutouts. For instance, when teaching house vocabulary (Unit 7.4) the teacher can easily find magazine pictures of rooms and furniture. Get a supply of red and blue construction paper, and mount masculine nouns on blue and feminine nouns on red. This way all pictures will be of the same size, and the color coding will help students remember gender. If desired, the teacher can use a felt market to write the corresponding noun on the back of the

picture card. When students can respond quickly to questions and commands containing the new vocabulary words, collect the cards, put them along the chalkboard, and have students pronounce the new vocabulary.

■ Reviewing Level One vocabulary using the video program ¡ADELANTE! Many Level One vocabuary items are visually illustrated in the video program. These items may therefore be reviewed using the video. The chart on pages 12T–13T indicates in which module of the video specific vocabulary topics and themes are presented.

■ Reviewing Level One vocabulary using the SPANISH for MASTERY Software program. Here, students have the advantage of working at their own pace and with immediate feedback.

4.2.7 Improving pronunciation.

The best way for students to acquire good Spanish pronunciation is to have them listen to as much Spanish as possible and to have them imitate authentic models.

The first four units of the Cassette Program contain special **Pronunciación** sections that review the Spanish sound system as it was presented in SPANISH for MASTERY 1, *¿Qué tal?*

Unit 1: Review of Spanish vowels. Pronunciation of cognates.
Unit 2: Stress and accent. Diphthongs. Linking. The "jota."
Unit 3: Review of Spanish consonant sounds **r; rr; b, v; d, g.**
Unit 4: Review of Spanish consonants **c, s, z; l, ll; ñ, ch;** initial p, t, c, /k/.

Since all the activities in the Cassette Program help students develop better Spanish pronunciation, the teacher should play the tapes as frequently as possible in class and let students work with the Activity Masters in the language laboratory. Have students learn the songs that accompany each unit: the rhythm of the music sometimes makes pronunciation easier.

The SPANISH for MASTERY video program also provides an opportunity for students to develop good Spanish pronunciation. In the modules students hear Spanish-speaking people communicating in an authentic context. Ask students to imitate the dialogs or perform them.

Finally, depending on the region in which you are teaching, encourage students to listen to Spanish radio and TV programs and urge them to take advantage of every opportunity to listen to Spanish being spoken.

4.2.8 Using *Para la comunicación.*

The *Para la comunicación* section, found at the end of each lesson, reenters the main structures and vocabulary. The teacher may use these sections as they occur or wait until the end of the unit and use them as part of a review.

■ If the teacher uses these sections at the end of the unit, the class can be divided into four groups, each group being given a *Para la comunicación* activity to develop. The groups could then share their results with the rest of the class.

■ The *Para la comunicación* sections may be used as practice for the faster learners while the teacher reviews with other students.

4.3 Using the *Variedades*

The *Variedades* sections, which occur at the end of the units, contain varied reading materials: narratives, poems, a how-to project, and games; they have a cultural focus, are youth-oriented, and can be used in a variety of ways.

■ **For in-class activities.** The *Variedades* sections can serve as the basis for cultural discussions, comparing and contrasting customs of the United States and of the Hispanic world. They also promote conversation, as when students try to solve a crime or learn to express wishes and desires. Where there are game-oriented activities, the teacher can hold team, group, or individual competitions, to see who can correctly answer all the questions first. An activity such as this encourages quick reading for comprehension and can be of great help in improving reading skills.

- **For individual activities.** When the teacher is conducting a review for a class test, those who do not need the review can read the *Variedades* section. They could summarize it in Spanish to practice their writing skills.
- **For out-of-class activities.** The *Variedades* can be assigned as homework or extra-credit work. Students could be encouraged to find and label pictures in magazines or newspapers to illustrate the topics of the *Variedades.* Some students might want to draw their own pictures. These illustrations can become bulletin-board or class decorations and will serve as a good review of vocabulary and structure.

The *Variedades* sections do not have to be done at the end of the units they accompany. Although they should probably not be used before their accompanying unit has been studied, they can be used any time afterwards, to reinforce grammar or to provide a change of pace before or after a vacation.

4.4 Using the *Vistas*

The purpose of the *Vistas* is, first and foremost, to engage students and to encourage them to explore Hispanic culture and civilization. These sections also furnish additional reading practice and provide the basis for discussions and mini-talks in Spanish. They should be considered optional and supplementary.

- The *Vistas* can be used to reinforce oral communication skills. Students can prepare simple questions about the reading or the illustrations, or they can give short talks on related topics.
- For homework the teacher may assign a selection from a *Vista* for which students prepare four true/false statements about the reading. For example, **Guadalajara es la capital de México** (based on **México y los países de Centroamérica** in *Vista 3*). In class, students form small groups and select ten of their best questions. At a given signal, each group passes its questions to another group, which answers them. The group that correctly answers all the questions first wins.
- Some teachers prefer to select parts of the *Vista* to supplement classroom instruction and choose a segment a week for a lesson in culture and reading practice. The teacher should take care not to chose a *Vista* before the vocabulary and structure in it has been taught.
- The teachers may assign special cultural projects or have students think up projects of their own. Students may also enjoy expanding the material of particular articles. For example, for **La cocina del suroeste** in *Vista 1,* students can bring in other recipes or foods from the region.
- The teacher and students can bring in posters, photographs, or other materials related to the *Vistas.* In addition to materials such as photographs of Spanish-speaking areas, students can bring in realia as well. For example, after reading **Pequeñas biografías de grandes hispanos** in *Vista 1,* students can expand the topic by bringing in newspaper and magazine articles about notable Hispanics in the news.
- The teacher can have students complete the corresponding exercises in the Activity Masters. These written activities encourage close reading and focus on comprehension.
- Students will find that the photographs, realia, and art inspire discussion. They can discuss what is in a given piece, tell a story about it, or create a conversation among the people pictured. Students may also enjoy providing captions for various pictures. The more students work with the visual material, the more they will internalize the cultural content.
- The teacher can use the magazine sections as points of departure for short compositions. For example, students can write about their favorite singers in the style of **Ojos que no ven, corazón que siente** (*Vista 2*), or prepare a slide show on Spain and write their own script (*Vista 5*).

4.5 Using the Workbook

The Workbook has been carefully designed to develop the writing skill. The activities are sequenced in order of increasing difficulty so that students first write out cued responses before using the new structures to express their own feelings and ideas. The activities are related to situations or illustrations so that students concentrate on the meaning of what they are writing as well as on accuracy of forms. Most lessons end with suggestions for brief original sentences.

4.5.1 Using the written exercises.
The Workbook contains numerous situational activities based on the structures and vocabulary of the lesson. Each Workbook activity is keyed to the text so that the teacher will know at what point he or she can assign a particular activity. Each Workbook lesson begins on a right-hand page so that students can tear out specific lessons to hand in. The Teacher's Annotated Edition of the Workbook provides answers to all activities.

- The teacher can assign these activities as written homework for all students, for students who need extra drill on specific items, or for students seeking extra credit.
- Part of the class can do the Workbook activities individually while the teacher provides help to other members of the class.
- The teacher can assign selected activities upon completion of a unit as a review.

4.5.2 Using *El rincón cultural.*
An original feature of the SPANISH for MASTERY Workbook is the *El rincón cultural* section at the end of each unit. This section provides a change of pace between units. The activities, which are built around realia, introduce the students to authentic samples of the Spanish language and provide a point for departure for oral communication. The activities may be assigned as homework or may be done in class in pairs or small groups.

4.5.3 Using the *Test/Repaso.*
The *Test/Repaso,* found at the end of each unit of the Workbook, provides a written review of the basic structures and vocabulary of each unit. The *Test/Repaso* should be assigned as preparation for the Unit Test.

- The teacher may use these tests for review in class.
- Students may take these tests on their own and check their answers in the Answer Key at the back of the Workbook. It contains *Interpretation* segments that refer students to the structure, vocabulary section, or cultural note of their texts corresponding to the various parts of the *Test/Repaso.*

4.6 Using the Cassette Program

The Cassette Program introduces students to spoken Spanish through the voices of Spanish speakers, thus supplementing the model provided by the teacher. Because the activities are recorded at natural conversational speed, students should be warned that they may not understand everything the first time they hear the cassette. In some cases the teacher may wish to present a passage or exercise before playing the cassette. At other times the teacher may stop the cassette to have students repeat a sentence or phrase that they have just heard. The more students listen to the cassette, the better able they will be to understand spoken Spanish.

- **Listening to the Presentation text.** The teacher may wish to play the *Presentation text* as an introduction to the lesson. Students can listen with their books closed or follow along with their books open. Later, the teacher may play the *Presentation text* again (repeating if necessary) as students listen carefully. Students can then do the comprehension activity that follows.
- **Listening for Signals.** These exercises test students' ability to distinguish among sounds that signal grammatical information.

- **Listening Comprehension.** The listening comprehension activities focus on the vocabulary of the lesson. The visuals (in the Activity Masters), which accompany many of these activities, provide a lively format for student practice.
- **Speaking/Conversation.** (1) Like the activities in the textbook, the speaking activities are situational. Since students cannot rely on any printed cues, the listening skill is all important. (2) In the conversation sections, students write answers to personalized, free-response questions. They express themselves using the vocabulary and structures of the lesson.
- **Pronunciation.** In the pronunciation review activities, students should be encouraged to listen carefully and to approximate the sounds of Spanish.
- **Spanish Songs.** The songs (one at the end of each unit) feature lyrics appropriate for students at the intermediate level. Students may sing along with the cassette, reading from the music and lyrics in the Activity Masters. For extra credit, students may learn and perform the songs for the class; whole-class performances can become part of a larger school festivals.
- A cassette with all the unit songs from Levels 1 and 2, along with the music and lyrics, is available separately in a special Song Binder.

4.7 Using the Testing Program

The SPANISH for MASTERY Testing Program includes four *Lesson Quizzes* and a *Unit Test* for each unit, and two *Achievement Tests*. In addition, the Test Guide includes ideas for developing speaking tests and written composition tests.

4.7.1 Using the *Lesson Quizzes*. The four *Lesson Quizzes* that accompany each unit are designed to be administered upon completion of each lesson. The *Quiz* items include a variety of formats, such as fill-ins, short answers, multiple choice, statement completion, and full answers. Students should be able to complete each *Lesson Quiz* in about 20 minutes.

4.7.2 Using the *Unit Tests*. The *Unit Tests* are designed to be administered upon completion of each unit. Students should be able to complete each *Test* in about 45 minutes. All the material of the unit is evaluated in discrete-point exercises.

For slower learners, the teacher may wish to administer each *Unit Test* over two days. The listening portion could be given on the first day and the written portion on the second day.

4.7.3 Using the *Achievement Tests*. The *Achievement Tests* are designed to be administered upon completion of the corresponding units (*Achievement Test 1:* Units 1–5; *Achievement Test 2:* Units 6–10). Students should be able to complete each *Test* in two 45-minute class periods. The teacher may choose to administer the listening portion of the first day, and the written portion on the second day.

For slower learners, the teacher may wish to include only selected items from each part of the *Test,* adjusting the scoring as necessary.

4.8 Using the Overhead Transparencies

4.8.1 When to use them. The SPANISH for MASTERY Overhead Transparencies have been selected with particular attention to flexibility and multiple use. The transparencies may be used for (1) review (structures and vocabulary); (2) testing (especially vocabulary; (3) reentry and variety (previously learned vocabulary, and familiar transparencies in new contexts): (4) guided self-expression (conversation and composition); (5) cultural awareness (maps).

4.8.2 How to use them.
The following are basic techniques for using the Overhead Transparencies:

- **Transparencies plus pointer.** The teacher projects the transparency and uses a pencil, a ruler, or a pointer to point to various images.
- **Transparency plus marker.** The teacher may write on the transparency with a water-soluble transparency marker that can be easily wiped off with a damp cloth or paper towel. Colored markers may be used to distinguish and reinforce various linguistic features.
- **Transparency plus overlay.** An overlay is a second transparency used to add visual material to another transparency. Besides the overlays provided in the box of visuals, teachers may use blank sheets of acetate to develop their own.
- **Transparency plus mask.** If the teacher wishes to project only a portion of the visual, a sheet of paper may be laid on the transparency as a mask.
- **Transparency plus moving elements.** It is possible to project both a still image (the original transparency) and a moving image. Adding movable hands to a clock face is perhaps the most common example.

5 SCHEDULING AND LESSON PLANS

5.1 Scheduling

SPANISH for MASTERY 2, *Entre nosotros,* may be completed in one school year; however, it is the individual teacher who decides how many units will ultimately be covered.

When planning the teaching of SPANISH for MASTERY, the teacher should be aware of the following facts:

(1) In order to complete SPANISH for MASTERY 2 within the school year, each unit should take about 15 class days.

(2) It will probably not be possible for a class to do all the suggested activities. Some will have to be shortened and others omitted entirely. For the teacher's convenience, certain sections, exercises, and grammatical presentations are labeled "optional" in the overprint of the Teacher's Edition.

The following chart shows how a unit may be presented in 15 school days with and without scheduled language laboratory sessions.

SAMPLE LESSON SCHEDULE FOR A UNIT	
Day 1	Lesson 1
Day 2	Lesson 1
Day 3	(Lab: Lesson 1) Lesson 1
Day 4	Quiz 1 Lesson 2
Day 5	Lesson 2
Day 6	(Lab: Lesson 2) Lesson 2
Day 7	Quiz 2 Lesson 3
Day 8	Lesson 3
Day 9	(Lab: Lesson 3) Lesson 3
Day 10	Quiz 3 Lesson 4
Day 11	Lesson 4
Day 12	(Lab: Lesson 4) Lesson 4
Day 13	Quiz 4 Unit Review *(Test/Repaso)*
Day 14	Unit Test
Day 15	Test Results *Variedades* or *Vistas*

Notes:

(1) The video program ¡ADELANTE! can be used at various points in the lesson plan and in different ways. Pages 5T–17T of this teacher's manual describe how to use the Video Program with SPANISH for MASTERY 2.

(2) The Cassette Program may be used effectively both in the classroom and in the language laboratory.

(3) The *Unit Test* may take less than a full period.

(4) In the average school year, there will be ample time to work with the selections in the **Vistas.**

5.2 Preparing Lesson Plans

Drawing up lesson plans helps the teacher to visualize how a unit is going to be presented. By emphasizing certain aspects of the program and playing down others, the teacher can change the focus of a unit to meet students' needs.

The following lesson plan shows how Lesson 5.1 may be taught using some of the techniques presented in Section 3 of this manual. Suggestions are given for several types of classes.

5.2.1 Basic lesson plan Lesson 5.1

Day 1

1. Warm up with a review of adjectives of personality: **tonto(a), egoísta, paciente, impaciente, simpático(a), generoso(a), amable, nervioso(a).** Ask questions: **¿Eres paciente? ¿Tienes amigos interesantes? ¿Es nervioso(a) tu mejor amigo(a)?** (5 minutes)

2. Play the tape of the *Presentation text* and test student comprehension with the activity in the overprint. (5 minutes)

3. Ask the questions in the **Conversación** section. Have students elaborate on their answers by asking **¿Dónde?** or **¿Qué paso?** (10 minutes)

4. Present **Estructura A.** Ask questions to elicit affirmative and negative responses. Briefly go over **Vocabulario práctico.** Do **Actividades 1, 2, 3.** (20 minutes)

5. Assignment: Have students write a short paragraph of 3–4 sentences describing a friend or acquaintance that fits one of the personality types from pp. 186–187. (5 minutes)

Day 2

1. Go over homework by having some students read their paragraphs aloud. (5 minutes)

2. Read **Nota cultural.** Ask different students to give adjectives that describe Don Quijote. (5 minutes)

3. Present **Estructura B** by asking about Don Quijote: **¿Quiere hacer lo imposible? ¿Prefiere lo común o lo raro?** (10 minutes)

4. Ask students personalized questions using the **lo** +adjective construction and **Vocabulario práctico: ¿Prefieres lo moderno o lo antiguo?** (5 minutes)

5. Do **Actividades 4, 5, 6.** (15 minutes)

6. Assignment: Suggest that students do some research on Don Quijote or Miguel de Cervantes. Write **Actividad 7.** (Or: have students do corresponding Workbook exercises.) (5 minutes)

Day 3	1. Go over written homework, asking individual students to read the sentences they wrote for *Actividad 7.* (5 minutes)
	2. Briefly review **lo** + adjective. Present *Estructura C.* Ask personalized questions such as: **¿Comprendes lo que digo?** Do *Actividades* **8, 9, 10** orally. (20 minutes)
	3. In the language lab or in the classroom, do the corresponding Cassette Program activities with the Activity Masters. (15 minutes)
	4. Assignment: Prepare for Lesson Quiz. (Give some sample quiz questions.) Write out *Para la comunicación.* (5 minutes)
Day 4	1. Go over *Para la comunicación.* Ask individual students for their sentences. (5 minutes)
	2. Give Lesson Quiz. (15 minutes)
	3. Begin Lesson 5.2.

5.2.2 Variations on the basic lesson plan. The basic lesson plan may easily be modified to meet the needs of individual classes. Since SPANISH for MASTERY offers a wealth of teaching materials and activities, it is expected that teachers will differ in the way they teach the lesson. Here are a few sample variations.

(1) Regular class without the Cassette Program

If a school does not have a language laboratory, nor the facilities to use the Cassette Program in the classroom, the teacher can serve as a model by reading the *Presentation texts* and directing the oral activities. If the teacher wants to use the activities in the Cassette Program together with the Activity Masters, he or she can work with the Tapescript, which is available separately. The teacher can, for example, read the *Listening for Signals* activities while students record their answers on the corresponding activity sheet.

(2) Regular class with emphasis on oral communication skills

In order to emphasize oral skills, the teacher should have access to a high-quality cassette recorder in the classroom. On Day 1 the teacher can play the recording of the *Presentation text* while students keep their books closed. The teacher asks students if they understand any words or phrases. The teacher plays the cassette again and asks students to write down fragments that they understand. The teacher plays the cassette a third time, stopping after each exchange and asking students to try to reconstitute what is said. Finally, the teacher plays the cassette a fourth time and has students follow with their books open.

On Days 2 and 3 the teacher plays the *Nota cultural* as a warm-up activity while students read softly along with the speaker. The teacher uses the cassette activities, playing them two or three times if needed. When possible, the teacher conducts the textbook *Actividades* orally with students' books closed.

On Day 4 the teacher might give a taped listening quiz consisting entirely of aural cues: *Listening for Signals* exercises, written responses to situational cues, and perhaps a brief dictation.

Throughout the school year, the communicative proficiency skills of Level 2 students can be strengthened by using the SPANISH for MASTERY Video Program as a point of departure for communication activities. For example, after viewing a module the teacher could ask students factual, interpretive, personal, or cross-cultural questions. Students could also be asked to create interviews, skits, and dialogs, or to make brief oral presentations based on the module.

(3) Regular class with emphasis on written skills

In order to develop reading and writing skills, students need regular practice. It is often effective to have one or two students write responses at the board or on an overhead transparency while the rest of the class writes at their seats. It is also helpful to use the Workbook.

On Day 1 the teacher can ask students to answer the *Presentation text* comprehension questions in writing. Once negation and negative expressions have been presented, students can turn to a selection in the **Vistas** and pick out negative words and expressions.

On Day 2 the teacher can ask personalized questions to which students write negative responses. Selected responses to the **Actividades** can also be done in writing as well as orally.

On Day 3 students can write out answers to warm-up review questions on the *Presentation text*. Or they can write selected sentences from the *Presentation text* as dictation exercises.

On Day 4 a quiz may consist of written cues and responses.

The self-instructional nature of the Software program makes it an ideal tool for review of vocabulary and structures which will result in improved writing skills. The program may be used at various points throughout the year.

More extensive writing activities derive from the use of the video modules. Students may be assigned written compositions the topic of which can range from simple descriptions of the video to narratives using specific tenses. For more creative assignments, students could be asked to write the imagined diary of one of the characters in the video dialog or a phone conversation between two of the characters.

(4) Slower class

With slower learners it is important to stress comprehension, both oral and written, and to pay less attention to such details as spelling.

On Day 1 the teacher should play the *Presentation text* several times in order for students to begin to understand what is said. Encourage students to speak quietly along with the cassette and to read along in their books. The teacher may want to give the English equivalent of a sentence from the *Presentation text* and have students find the corresponding Spanish sentence. (Example: "He repeats everything his friends tell him." Students respond, **"Repite todo lo que le dicen sus amigos."**) To check comprehension, it may be better to use true/false statements about the text rather than the activity.

On Days 2 and 3 more time will be spent on the **Actividades.** Students should first practice with full-class and half-class responses before responding individually. An exercise done chorally can then be repeated by having students work in pairs. *Listening for Signals* activities should be repeated twice. **Estructura B** can be either omitted or presented only for recognition. As a change of pace, ask students for homework to find a comic strip with a character like one of the people described in the *Presentation text.*

On Day 4 the Quiz can consist mainly of short-answer and fill-in items.

Both the Software and Video Programs are ideal teaching tools for the slower class. Slower students benefit from computer work because each individual can work at his or her own pace and receive immediate feedback. The Video Program with its blend of media—moving image and sound— makes for optimal language learning. The captioned version allows students to see the relationship between the spoken language and the printed word.

PART 3: How to Supplement SPANISH for MASTERY

6 | SUPPLEMENTARY MATERIAL AND ACTIVITIES

Foreign language methodologists stress the importance of using realia and supplementary cultural activities for a number of reasons:

- They enliven the atmosphere of the class.
- They provide a sometimes much-needed change of pace.
- They allow for a more natural exchange between student and teacher.
- They permit students who are not linguistically oriented to express themselves in other areas such as music, art, or cooking.
- They present students with a practical application of the skills learned in the classroom.
- They provide an interdisciplinary link to students' other studies.

6.1 How to Find and Use Realía

Spanish teachers, in contrast to teachers of other languages, have easy access to materials in the language they are teaching. From the Northeast to the Southwest, the United States has a rich source of Hispanic culture: newspapers, magazines, information about food, music, dances, and customs are accessible to everyone for the price of a postage stamp.

This section lists some good sources of materials and suggests how and when to use them. The listing is not exhaustive, but seeks to provide variety.

6.1.1 The written language

Spanish-language magazines and newspapers distributed in the United States

NAME	COUNTRY	APPROX. COST	TYPE	USEFUL CONTENTS	(U.S.) DISTRIBUTOR	FREQUENCY
ABC	Spain	$3.00 $4.00 (Sunday)	newspaper	ads money tables (values) stock market weather reports	Roig 29 West 19th St. New York, NY 10011	daily
as color	Spain	$2.50	sports	pictures cartoons	Roig	daily
Buenhogor	Panama	$2.50	family	ads articles with checklists recipes cartoons personality questionnaires correspondence	Roig	bi-weekly

				El Diario-La Prensa 143 Varick St. New York, NY 10013	
El Diario-La Prensa	U.S.	.35, $1.00 (Sunday)	newspaper	entertainment section comics Sunday colored section ads	daily except Sat.
Estrellas	Puerto Rico	$1.75	personality	ads	Roig — bi-weekly
GeoMundo	U.S.	$3.00	geography	pictures ads	Roig — monthly
¡Hola!	Spain	$4.50	personality	cartoons ads pictures	Roig — weekly
Lecturas	Spain	$4.00	personality	ads cartoons TV section	Roig — weekly
Réplica	U.S.	$2.00	personality	ads comics	Roig — monthly
Semana	Spain	$4.25	general	ads with forms cartoons TV section	Roig — weekly
Siete días	Argentina	$3.50	news	ads cartoons chess section	E. Castellón 207 Piaget Ave. Clifton, NJ 07011 — weekly
Vanidades	Panama	$2.50	modern living	ads forms to fill out recipes (wordless) comics	Roig — monthly
Vistazo	Ecuador	$4.00	news current events sports	ads with forms charts	E. Castellón — weekly

U.S. magazine printed in Spanish: *Selecciones del Reader's Digest*

6.1.2 The spoken language. In many states and in most large urban centers of the country, there are a variety of Spanish language radio broadcasts. If your state does not have a station that broadcasts programs in Spanish, you still might be able to receive broadcasts from a station in a nearby state. Check your local newspapers for listings.

Local Spanish Radio Programs		
City	**State**	**Radio station call letters**
Boston	MA	WUNR
Chicago	IL	WCRW; WEDC
Houston	TX	KEYH; KLAT; KXYZ
Los Angeles	CA	KLVE/FM
Miami	FL	WCMQ; WOCN; WHTT
New York	NY	WADO; WBNX; WJIT
Philadelphia	PA	WTEL
San Antonio	TX	KCOR; KEDA; KFHM
San Francisco	CA	KBRG/FM

Local Spanish Television Programs		
City	**State**	**TV station call letters**
Chicago	IL	WCIU/TV; WSNS/TV
Houston	TX	KRIV/TV
Los Angeles	CA	KMEX/TV; KSCI/TV; KVEA/TV
Miami	FL	WLRN/TV; WLTV
New York	NY	WNJU/TV; WXTV/TV
Phoenix	AZ	KTVW/TV
San Francisco	CA	KDTV/TV; KTZO/TV
Tijuana	MEX	XETV

Again, if your state does not have Spanish-language television stations, you may be within the reception area of another state that does. There are now two national networks, Univisión and Telemundo, which supply local television stations with programs in Spanish. Check your local newspapers for listings.

6.1.3 Other sources. In the local community, there may be the following:

—Hispanic clubs and organizations sponsoring festivals that feature food, song, and dance.

—stores and shops catering to Spanish-speaking clientele.

—restaurants offering Spanish or Latin American cuisine.

—travel agencies offering brochures and posters.

—consulates, embassies, and other cultural missions.

—food product companies (Kellogg's, Del Monte, Campbell) that sell their products abroad and in Spanish-speaking domestic outlets.

A pen pal exchange program can also be arranged with a class studying English in a Hispanic country. Classes can exchange letters, realia, and other cultural material difficult to locate in the United States.

6.1.4 How to use the material. The teacher may want to use realia to enrich classroom activities and to develop greater student awareness of the Spanish-speaking world.

- **Preparing realia for students.** Teachers should be selective in the realia they bring to class. The realia should have visuals that reinforce familiar vocabulary and structures. The teacher might edit realia by underlining words or structures that students already know and by preparing a brief glossary of items that they don't know. Students should not translate but try to understand the message from the context.
- **Useful materials.** In newspapers and magazines, TV guides, movies schedules, weather reports, and ads for restaurants, food, or clothes provide useful teaching tools that are easy to understand. They can be used for the following purposes:

—identification of vocabulary and structures already learned

—vocabulary building (new words, especially concrete nouns)

—culture expansion

—points of departure for conversation

The following are examples of realia to teach specific points:

—listings of concerts, movies, TV programs to illustrate kinds of entertainment

—ads from various stores to illustrate store and merchandise vocabulary

—instructions on food labels to illustrate use of the imperative

Many Hispanic periodicals contain ads for U.S. products and carry publicity (and even articles) patterned after U.S. models. This may give the impression that the Spanish-speaking world tends to copy the American model. While "Americanization" is a very real phenomenon, the teacher should make sure that students understand that Spanish speakers have their own traditions and values. (Observant students will notice that some U.S. products are marketed with different types of ads in Spanish, reflecting the Hispanic value system rather than that of the United States.)

6.2 How to Prepare and Use Games

Games are useful learning tools, accessible to every teacher, that provide variety. At the beginning of the class, games capture students' attention. In the middle of the period, games may serve as a transition from one activity to the next. At the end of the class, they fill in the few minutes between the final activity and the bell. The teacher can play games with the entire class or use them for pair and small-group activity. The main purpose of games is to enliven the linguistic aim of the lesson; they should not become the exclusive focus of the class.

The following section provides sample games that the teacher can use or adapt.

6.2.1 Commercial games.   Many board games are now available in Spanish editions. Games in this category include classics like Monopoly (good practice in using numbers with dice and money). Scrabble (for vocabulary practice, can be played in teams and simplified), and Lotto (excellent vocabulary practice). There are many other Spanish games with English-language counterparts that are also useful in reviewing Spanish structures and vocabulary. These are all available through companies that sell foreign language realia.

6.2.2 Teacher-created games.   Teacher-created games have a distinct advantage over commercial games: they can be "custom made" to fit the needs of a particular class or a lesson. Following are sample games that the teacher can use in the classroom.

A. Oral games

The teacher may suggest this game as a way to review vocabulary prior to the unit test. One student thinks of a word from a *Vocabulario práctico* section of one of the lessons in the unit. This student writes on the chalkboard a series of blanks corresponding to the number of letters in the word and draws a noose. When someone from the class guesses a letter that appears in the word, the student at the board enters that letter in all the spaces where it occurs. When someone guesses a letter that is not in the word, the student leading the game adds a part of the body to the person in the noose. The object, of course, is to guess the word before being hanged. As the final activity, no matter who wins, a student should spell the complete word and supply the gender or identify the part of speech of the word.

¡ADIÓS!

This game is similar to "Ghost" in English. Playing in groups of five or six, each student has a turn to say a letter that contributes to the spelling of the Spanish word. If in so doing the student completes a word, he or she gets an **A,** the next time a **D,** and so on. Any student who completes the word **Adiós** is out. The last person remaining in the game is the winner. If a student says a letter that the next person does not believe contributes toward the building of a word, the student who said may be challenged. If the challenged student cannot come up with a word, he or she receives a letter toward being eliminated from the game. However, if the challenged student does know a Spanish word with that sequence of letters, the student who challenged receives one of the letters of **Adiós.**

WORD GEOGRAPHY

This game is an adaptation of the English language game "Geography." One student starts by saying a word. The next student must say a word that begins with the last letter of the previous word. Anyone who fails to do so is eliminated, and the game continues until one person remains.

Example: Student 1: bueno
Student 2: ojos
Student 3: sol
Student 4: la
Student 5: aquí
and so on

TWENTY QUESTIONS

One student thinks of an object (**¿Qué es?**), and the others, in turn, try to guess what it is by asking yes/no questions. The student who guesses correctly is "it," but if no one guesses after twenty questions, the student who was "it" thinks of another object and the game begins again.

(Other possible questions: **¿Quién soy?**, **¿Dónde estoy?**, **¿Cuál es mi profesión?**)

CHALLENGE

The teacher divides the class into several teams and assigns each team a section of the chalkboard. One person from each team goes to the board and the teacher announces the category. The students at the board write as many words as they can think of in that category in ten seconds. After they return to their seats, a second student from each team goes to the board. The teacher announces a new category and the members of this group write as many words as they can think of in ten seconds. When every member of the team has been to the board, the class checks all the teams entries and counts them. The team with the most correct words is the winner. If desired, the class can subtract the number of wrong words from the correct ones in calculating the team score. The teacher may use the themes of the *Vocabulario práctico* as categories.

TIC-TAC-TOE

The class is divided into two teams. A tic-tac-toe board with one subject pronoun written on each of the squares is set up and then covered. One member of the team chooses a square. The teacher (or another student) uncovers the pronoun and gives the team member a verb to conjugate in a particular tense, corresponding to the subject pronoun. If the student does it correctly, his or her team wins the square. If not, the turn is forfeited and the other team selects a square. A team wins the game when it has won three squares in a row.

¡CARAMBA!

After distributing sheets of paper divided into sixteen squares, the teacher gives a category, such as food, clothing, or school life. Students then fill in the spaces with Spanish words belonging to the category. One at a time, the teacher then calls out words that belong in the category; if students have the words, they cross them off their sheets. The first student to get four words in a row horizontally, vertically, or diagonally calls out **¡Caramba!** and wins the game.

BÚSCALO

This is an adaptation of the card game "Go Fish," and is best played in groups of four or five. Five cards are given to each player, and any pairs are placed face up on the desk. The object of the game is to get the most pairs. To begin one student asks another group member if he or she has the card that would give the student a pair. The student can continue asking whomever he or she wishes for cards until someone does not have the card asked for. The player is then told **"¡Búscalo!"** He or she picks up the top card from the remaining deck, and the person to his or her right asks for cards. (ace = **as;** king = **rey;** queen = **reina;** jack = **sota**)

B. Written games

BUSCAPALABRAS

This can best be described as a "block of letters" in which various Spanish words are hidden. These words may be written forward, backward, diagonally, or upside down, as long as there is consecutive placement of the letters of the word. Students are given the list of words they are to find (in Spanish or in English) and a set amount of time in which to find them. The game may also be set up as a contest, and the first student to find all words is declared the winner.

P	R	O	S	O	M	I	L	I	A	B
R	A	T	R	A	B	A	J	A	R	M
E	T	A	R	L	R	A	T	R	O	C
P	R	E	E	A	E	C	H	O	C	O
A	A	V	C	H	V	E	A	M	T	S
R	B	S	I	A	I	R	B	U	S	C
A	U	T	V	B	V	E	L	P	A	P
B	T	S	O	M	E	M	O	C	R	A

BUSCAR
COMEMOS
CORTAR
HABLO
PREPARA
TRABAJAR
VIVE

CROSSWORD PUZZLES

These are simple to prepare and can be imaginative and creative. The following is an example of a puzzle that reviews clothing:

HORIZONTALMENTE

4. Clothing

7.

6.

VERTICALMENTE

1.

2.

3.

5.

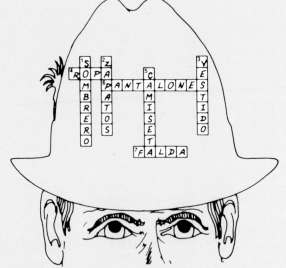

64T

CATEGORIES

Students are given a chart with categories on the horizontal axis and letters on the vertical axis. Students must write one word for each category beginning with each of the letters.

	alimentos	lugares	colores
M	manzana	México	morado
A	azúcar	Argentina	azul
C	café	Colombia	café

FOLLOW THE DOTS

This is an adaptation of the juvenile game, but with the numbers written out. Students connect the dots in numbered order to discover a hidden figure or message.

UNSCRAMBLE

Students rearrange scrambled letters to form a Spanish word. Each group of scrambled words should pertain to a common theme, for example, parts of the body.

EAIRNP = P I E R N A

CAAR = C A R A

PLEASAD = E S P A L D A

In addition to the above suggestions, teachers can adapt any popular television game show (for example, "Password," "Jeopardy," "The $25,000 Pyramid," "Wheel of Fortune") to Spanish. Students can also submit ideas for games and receive extra credit for making up a game and writing the rules.

6.3 Cultural Activities

Since Hispanic communities in the United States are so numerous, it is not difficult to bring cultural activities into the classroom.

6.3.1 Dancing.   By learning Hispanic dances, students will also be learning about Hispanic music. If information is available, the teacher should explain the origins of the dance.

6.3.2 Cooking.   Cooking usually ranks as one of students' favorite activities; even those who are not keen on preparing food will not turn down the opportunity to eat. Recipes for Hispanic dishes abound, and many are very simple to prepare.

6.3.3 Other classroom cultural activities.   Some teachers regularly prepare "foreign festivals" that include regional food specialties, dances, and performances by students. Although time consuming to prepare, these fiestas can be enjoyable and valuable parts of a foreign language week.

6.3.4 Outside the classroom.   Field trips are also a good way to provide an introduction to Hispanic culture. Some possible excursions might be:

- going to a Hispanic restaurant
- going to a Hispanic shop
- going to a Hispanic museum
- visiting a Hispanic community

In order for these activities to be successful and to make students see and experience the relevance of Spanish, they need to be carefully planned. Students could be given special assignments or research, and could report to the class before the trip. Or, the assignment could be given to everyone for homework.

PART 4: Reference Guide for SPANISH for MASTERY

This part of the teacher's manual contains reference materials for easy accessibility.

7 | USEFUL EXPRESSIONS

The teacher who wishes to conduct the class entirely in Spanish may use the following vocabulary supplements.

7.1 Classroom Expressions

These classroom expressions may be copied and distributed to students.

7.1.1 Palabras

un bolígrafo   un lápiz   la tiza   un cuaderno   una hoja de papel

un borrador   una regla   un libro   un bolso   un objeto *object*
    una cosa *thing*

una silla   un mapa   un pupitre   un sacapuntas

una pantalla   un proyector   una tocacintas   una cassette   un televisor

un tablón de anuncios   la pizarra   una cassette (del video)   una videograbadora

7.1.2 Expresiones

Both the plural (Escuchen) and the singular (Escucha) command forms are given here.

Escuchen (Escucha).	*Listen.*
Escuchen (Escucha) la cinta (cassette).	*Listen to the cassette.*
Miren (Mira) el video.	*Watch the videotape.*
Repitan (Repite).	*Repeat.*
No repitan (No repitas).	*Don't repeat.*
Hablen (Habla) más alto.	*Speak up. Speak louder.*
Escuchen (Escucha) la pregunta.	*Listen to the question.*
Contesten (Contesta).	*Answer.*
No contesten (No contestes).	*Don't answer.*
Vengan (Ven) aquí (enfrente de la clase).	*Come here (in front of the class).*
Hagan (Haz) el papel de . . .	*Play the part of . . .*
Empiecen (Empieza).	*Begin.*
Gracias.	*Thank you.*
Siéntense (Siéntate).	*Sit down.*
Saquen (Saca) los libros (cuadernos).	*Take out your books (workbooks).*
Abran (Abre) los libros a la página . . .	*Open your books to page . . .*
Cierren (Cierra) los libros.	*Close your books.*
Saquen (Saca) un bolígrafo (un lápiz).	*Take out a pen (pencil).*
Saquen (Saca) papel.	*Take out some paper.*
Lean (Lee) en voz alta.	*Read aloud.*
Continúen (Continúa)	*Continue.*
Escriban (Escribe).	*Write.*
No escriban (No escribas).	*Don't write.*
Levántense (Levántate).	*Get up.*
Vayan (Ve) a la pizarra.	*Go to the board.*
Miren (Mira) la pizarra.	*Look at the board.*
Mírenme (Mírame).	*Look at me.*
Pongan (Pon) atención.	*Pay attention.*
Silencio.	*Silence.*
No hablen (No hables).	*Don't talk.*
Cuidado con la pronunciación (la ortografía).	*Careful with the pronunciation (spelling).*
Digan (Di) . . .	*Say . . .*
Díganle (Dile) . . .	*Tell him/her . . .*
Todos juntos.	*All together.*
Todo el mundo.	*Everyone.*
Otra vez.	*Again. Once more.*
Muy bien.	*Very good.*
Excelente.	*Excellent.*
No, no es eso.	*That's not it.*
Otra vez.	*Once again.*
Para mañana . . .	*For tomorrow . . .*
Para la próxima vez . . .	*For the next time . . .*
Preparen (Prepara) . . .	*Prepare . . .*
Hagan (Haz) el ejercicio (los ejercicios) . . .	*Do the exercise (the exercises) . . .*

En español.	In Spanish.
En inglés.	In English.
¿Qué quiere decir . . . ?	What does . . . mean?
¿Cómo se dice . . . ?	How do you say . . . ?
¿Hay preguntas?	Are there any questions?
Levanten (Levanta) la mano.	Raise your hand.
¿Comprenden? (¿Comprendes?)	Do you understand?
No comprendo.	I don't understand?
No sé.	I don't know.

7.2 Expressions for the *Actividades*

Cambia.	Change. Conjugate.
Compara.	Compare.
Contesta.	Answer.
Cuenta.	Tell, relate.
Da.	Give.
Describe.	Describe.
Di.	Say, tell.
Empieza.	Start, begin.
Escoge.	Choose.
Escribe (un párrafo; una oración).	Write (a paragraph; a sentence).
Explica.	Explain.
Expresa.	Express.
Haz el papel (los papeles) de . . .	Play the part (parts) of . . .
Hazle una pregunta (según el modelo).	Ask him/her a question (according to the model).
Imagina.	Imagine.
Lee.	Read.
Manda.	Send.
Pide.	Ask for.
Piensa.	Think.
Pon.	Put.
Pregunta.	Ask.
Prepara.	Prepare.
Usa.	Use.
la columna	column
la frase (oración)	sentence
la palabra	word
la respuesta (contestación)	answer
un elemento	an element
siguiente	following

8 DETAILED LISTING OF THE CONTENTS

This section lists the contents of SPANISH FOR MASTERY 2, *Entre nosotros,* in chart form. The teacher will find these charts useful in preparing course objectives, lesson plans, study guides, and tests. As the course progresses, the teacher may use the charts to recall where specific sounds, words, structures, or cultural topics were introduced. Lists have been established under the following headings: Structure, Vocabulary, and Culture.

8.1 Structure

These charts list the grammar sections of the Student Text and cross-reference the related exercises.

ESTRUCTURAS	TEXT EXERCISES	WORKBOOK EXERCISES	TAPESCRIPT ACTIVITIES
Unit 1 ¡Nosotros, los jóvenes!			
Lesson 1.1 A. Repaso: los verbos que terminan en -*ar*	1	A1	5
B. Repaso: la negación	2,3,4	B1	4
C. Repaso: el uso del infinitivo	5,6,7	C1	
D. Repaso: preguntas	8,9	D1,D2	8
Lesson 1.2 A. Repaso: *ser*	1	A1	
B. Repaso: el género: sustantivos, artículos y adjetivos	2	B1	4,5
C. Repaso: el plural: sustantivos, artículos y adjetivos	3,4	C1	
D. Repaso: la posición de los adjetivos	5,6	D1,D2	6,7
Lesson 1.3 A. Repaso: *tener*	3,4		3
B. Repaso: el artículo definido con los días de la semana	5,6		
C. Repaso: *al, del*	7	C1	4
D. Repaso: la *a* personal	8,9,10	D1	
E. Repaso: *ir, ir a*	11,12,13	E1,E2	3,5
Lesson 1.4 A. Repaso: *estar*	2,4		4
B. Repaso: *ser y estar*	3,5	B1,B2	
C. Repaso: los verbos que terminan en -*er* y en -*ir*	6,7,8	C1,C2,C3	
D. Repaso: *estar* + el participio presente	9,10	D1,D2	5

ESTRUCTURAS	TEXT EXERCISES	WORKBOOK EXERCISES	TAPESCRIPT ACTIVITIES
Unit 2 Nuestro mundo personal			
Lesson 2.1 A. Repaso: *conocer*	1	A1	
B. Repaso: el uso de *de* para indicar la posesión	3,4	B1	
C. Repaso: los adjetivos posesivos	5,6	C1,C2	4,5
D. Repaso: complementos directos: pronombres	7,8,9	D1,D2	6,7
Lesson 2.2 A. Repaso: *saber*	2	A1,A2	
B. Adjetivos y pronombres demostrativos	3,4	B1	4
C. Repaso: el complemento indirecto: *le, les*	5,6,7	C1,C2,C3	5,6
D. Repaso: *decir*	8	D1	
Lesson 2.3 A. Repaso: los pronombres *me, te, nos*	3,4	A1,A2	5
B. Repaso: pronombre indirecto + pronombre directo	5,6,7	B1	6
C. Repaso: el pronombre *se*	8.9	C1	
D. Repaso: el pronombre neutro *lo*	10		
Lesson 2.4 A. Repaso: el uso del articulo en el sentido general	2,3	A1,A2	5
B. Repaso: la construción *me gusta(n)*	4,5,6,7	B1,B2	6
C. La construcción *el (la, los, las)* + adjetivo	8	C1	8
D. La construcción *el (la, los, las)* + *que*	9		8
Unit 3 Día tras día			
Lesson 3.1 A. Repaso: los verbos con cambio en el radical (*e → ie*)	1,2		4
B. Repaso: los verbos con cambio en el radical (*o, u → ue*)	3,4,5	B1,B2,B3	6
C. Repaso: los verbos con cambio en el radical (*e → i*)	6,7,8	C1,C2,C3, C4	8
Lesson 3.2 A. Repaso: la construcción reflexiva	1,2,3	A1,A2	4,5
B. Repaso: los verbos reflexivos: el arreglo personal	4,5	B1	7
C. Repaso: los verbos reflexivos: las actividades diarias	6,7,8	C1,C2,C3	8
Lesson 3.3 A. Los verbos reflexivos: las emociones	1,2,3	A1	4,5,6
B. Los verbos casi siempre reflexivos	4,5	B1,B2,B3	
Lesson 3.4 A. Repaso: verbos irregulares en la primera persona	1,2,3	A1,A2	4
B. El uso de los verbos reflexivos para indicar la reciprocidad	5,6	B1	5,6,7
C. Los verbos reflexivos en el infinitivo y con *estar* + el participio presente	8,9,10	C1,C2	

ESTRUCTURAS	TEXT EXERCISES	WORKBOOK EXERCISES	TAPESCRIPT ACTIVITIES
Unit 4 El coche del Sr. Molina			
Lesson 4.1 A. Repaso: la duración: *hace* + el presente	1,2	A1,A2,A3	5
B. Repaso: *acabar de* + infinitivo	3,4	B1,B2	3,4
C. Repaso: los numerales ordinales	5,6	C1	
D. Repaso: algunos adjetivos indefinidos	7,8		
Lesson 4.2 A. Los adjetivos y los pronombres posesivos	1,2,3,4	A1	3,4
B. Repaso: el pretérito de los verbos que terminan en *-ar*	5,6,7	B1,B2,B3	6,7,8
C. El diminutivo *-ito*	10		
Lesson 4.3 A. Repaso: el pretérito de los verbos que terminan en *-er* y en *-ir*	1,2,3,4,5	A1,A2,A3	
B. Repaso: el pretérito de los verbos con cambios que terminan en *-ir*	6	B1	3
C. Repaso: el pretérito de *ir* y *ser*	7	C1	5
D. *Al* + infinitivo	8,9,10	D1	
Lesson 4.4 A. El pretérito del verbo *conducir*	1	A1	
B. Repaso: otros pretéritos irregulares	2,3,4,5,6	B1,B2	5
C. El pretérito + *hace*	7,8	C1,C2	7
D. Los adverbios que terminan en *-mente*	9,10	D1	6,8
Unit 5 ¡Cómo transcurre el tiempo!			
Lesson 5.1 A. La construcción negativa	1,2,3	A1,A2	4,6
B. La construcción *lo* + adjetivo	4,5,6,7	B1	
C. Repaso: *lo que*	8,9,10	C1	7
Lesson 5.2 A. El imperfecto de los verbos que terminan en *-ar*	1,2	A1	4
B. El imperfecto de los verbos que terminan en *-er* y en *-ir*	3,4,5,6	B1,B2	
C. El uso del imperfecto para describir sucesos repetidos	7,8,9,10	C1,C2,C3	7
Lesson 5.3 A. El imperfecto de *ir, ser* y *ver*	1,2	A1	
B. El uso del imperfecto para describir acciones continuas	3,4,5,6	B1,B2,B3	
Lesson 5.4 A. El imperfecto y el pretérito: circunstancias y acciones	1,2,3,4,5	A1,A2,A3	
B. Resumen: el uso del pretérito y del imperfecto	7,8	B1,B2	
Unit 6 Hoy y ayer			
Lesson 6.1 A. El uso impersonal del pronombre reflexivo *se*	1,2,3	A1	4,5,6
B. Otro uso impersonal del pronombre reflexivo *se*	4,5,6,7, 8,9	B1,B2	7

ESTRUCTURAS	TEXT EXERCISES	WORKBOOK EXERCISES	TAPESCRIPT ACTIVITIES
Lesson 6.2 A. Los participios pasados regulares	1,2,3,4, 5,6	A1,A2,A3	4,5
B. Preposiciones de lugar	7,8	B1	
Lesson 6.3 A. La formación del pretérito perfecto	1,2,3,4,5	A1,A2	4,5
B. El uso del pretérito perfecto	6,7	B1	6,7
C. Los participios pasados irregulares	8,9	C1	9
Lesson 6.4 A. El pluscuamperfecto	2,3,4,5	A1,A2,A3	4,5
Unit 7 Mañana será otro día			
Lesson 7.1 A. El futuro	1,2,3	A1,A2,A3	4,5,6
B. *Para* + sustantivo	4	B1	7
C. Repaso: el comparativo de los adjetivos	5	C1	9
Lesson 7.2 A. Futuros irregulares	1,2,3,4	A1,A2	5,6
B. El uso del futuro para indicar probabilidad	5,6,7	B1,B2	
C. *Por* + sustantivo	8,9,10	C1,C2	
Lesson 7.3 A. El condicional	1,2,3,4,5	A1,A2,A3	5,6,7,8
B. Repaso: preposición + infinitivo	6,7,8	B1,B2	
Lesson 7.4 A. El futuro perfecto	2,3,4	A1,A2,A3	4
B. *Por* + infinitivo	5,6	B1,B2,B3	6
Unit 8 Perspectivas de hoy			
Lesson 8.1 A. Repaso: mandatos afirmativos: la forma familiar (*tú*)	1,2	A1,A2	3,4
B. Repaso: mandatos afirmativos: la forma familiar (*tú*) irregular	3,4	B1,B2	6
C. Repaso: preposición de tiempo + infinitivo	5,6,7	C1,C2	
Lesson 8.2 A. Mandatos: las formas negativas regulares de *tú* y de *Ud., Uds.*	1,2,3,4	A1,A2, A3,A4	3,4
B. Mandatos: las formas negativas irregulares de *tú* y de *Ud., Uds.*	5,6	B1	
C. Repaso: verbo + preposición + infinitivo	7,8,9	C1	7,8
Lesson 8.3 A. Mandatos: la primera persona del plural (*nosotros*)	1,2	A1,A2	
B. La posición de los pronombres con los mandatos	3,4,5	B1,B2	5,7
C. Los mandatos con dos pronombres	6,7	C1	6
Lesson 8.4 A. El subjuntivo: la formación regular	1,2,3,4		4,5
B. El uso del subjuntivo: mandatos indirectos	5,6,7,8,9	B1,B2,B3	7,8
C. El concepto del subjuntivo	10,11	C1,C2,C3	9,10

ESTRUCTURAS	TEXT EXERCISES	WORKBOOK EXERCISES	TAPESCRIPT ACTIVITIES
Unit 9 ¡Así es la vida!			
Lesson 9.1 A. Los subjuntivos irregulares	1,2	A1	
B. El uso del subjuntivo después de las expresiones que muestran emociones	3,4,5,6,7 8,9	B1,B2,B3	5,6,8
Lesson 9.2 A. El uso del subjuntivo después de expresiones impersonales	1,2,3,4,5 6,7	A1,A2, A3,A4	4
B. El subjuntivo de los verbos en -*ar* y en -*er* con cambios en el radical	8	B1,B2	
C. El subjuntivo de los verbos en -*ir* con cambios en el radical	9,10		6
Lesson 9.3 A. El uso del subjuntivo después de expresiones de duda	1,2,3,4	A1,A2,A3	3,4,5
B. El presente perfecto del subjuntivo	5,6,7	B1,B2	7
Lesson 9.4 A. Los pronombres relativos	1,2,3	A1	7
B. El uso del subjuntivo después de los pronombres relativos	4,5,6,7,8, 9,10	B1,B2,B3, B4	5,6,7
Unit 10 Cambios			
Lesson 10.1 A. El subjuntivo después de *para que*	1,2,3	A1,A2,A3	5
B. El subjuntivo después de ciertas conjunciones	4,5,6	B1,B2,B3	
Lesson 10.2 A. Repaso: el futuro	1,2	A1,A2	
B. El subjuntivo o el indicativo después de algunas conjunciones de tiempo	3,4,5,6,7 8	B1,B2,B3, B4	6
C. Resumen: el uso del subjuntivo	9		
Lesson 10.3 A. El imperfecto del subjuntivo: formas regulares	1,2,3	A1,A2,A3	4,5
B. El imperfecto del subjuntivo: usos	4,5,6,7	B1,B2	6
Lesson 10.4 A. El imperfecto del subjuntivo: formas irregulares	1,2,3	A1,A2	4
B. Repaso: el condicional	4,5	B1,B2	
C. El uso del imperfecto del subjuntivo: después de *si*	6,7,8,9	C1,C2	6,7

8.2 **Vocabulary**

The following tables summarize the contents of the *Vocabulario práctico* sections.

8.3 Culture

The following list contains the cultural topics of each **Nota cultural** section and the **Vistas.** A specific cultural reading may be listed more than once if its topic fits several catgories.

TOPIC	VISTAS	NOTAS CULTURALES
Países y ciudades hispanos		
Chile, un país de contrastes		3
México, el país más grande de habla hispana	227–239	13
Panamá: el cruce del mundo		21
España, un país de tradiciones	409–421	30
El Caribe	133–145	
Los países hispanos de la América del Sur	315–327	
¿Por qué se llama «Ecuador»?		288
Buenos Aires, la capital de la Argentina		107
Cartagena		216
La República Dominicana		259
Las líneas misteriosas de Nazca		392
Una ciudad peridida y encontrada (Machu Picchu)	322	
Los hispanos en los Estados Unidos		
Los Estados Unidos	41–51	
Población hispana en algunas ciudades norteamericanas	45	
El mundo hispánico		
Los inmigrantes		3
El rodeo y otras cosas de origen español	48	
Los caballos tienen nombres españols	50	
El respeto		55
Las estaciones en la América del Sur		66
La autoridad paternal		83
El dinero		97
El matrimonio		123
Lo antillano en nuestra lengua	140	
La plaza mayor		157
El coche		165
El honor familiar		174
Un tipo de la literatura española: don Quijote		188
La idea de ser bien educado		197
La supersticiones		207
«El Libertador»		216
El mensaje de las piedras	234–235	
Las manos creadoras	236	
La creación del hombre	237	
El tabaco, un producto de origen indio		244
Las posadas	239	
El teléfono		252
El tuteo		259
El valor del tiempo		268

The following are used in the overprint to cue the use of the various ancillaries of SPANISH for MASTERY 1.

(cassette icon)	material recorded on the Cassette Program
WB	additional exercises in the Workbook
SCRIPT (cassette icon)	additional activities in the Cassette Program with text in the Tapescript
MASTERS	answer sheets for written Cassette Program activities and additional activities found in the Activity Masters
(cube/transparency icon)	visual material on the Overhead Transparencies
QUIZ	indicates a *Lesson Quiz* in the Testing Program
TEST	indicates a *Unit Test* in the Testing Program
ACHIEVEMENT TEST	indicates an *Achievement Test* in the Testing Program
(pencil icon)	is used to signal **Actividades** suitable for writing
(disk icon)	additional practice on disks of the Computer Software
(TV icon)	additional material in the Video Program
(card icon) TRB	additional activities on Question Cards in the Teacher's Resource Binder

SPANISH for MASTERY 2

Entre nosotros

Jean-Paul Valette
Rebecca M. Valette

Editor-Consultant
Teresa Carrera-Hanley

Contributing Writer
Frederick Suárez Richard

 D.C. HEATH AND COMPANY
Lexington, Massachusetts / Toronto, Ontario

TEACHER CONSULTANTS
Susan Crichton, Lynnfield H.S., Massachusetts
Karen Davis, McLean Middle School, Texas
Elena Marsh, Columbine H.S., Colorado
Judith Morrow, Bloomington H.S. South, Indiana
Delores Rodríguez, San Jose Unified School Dist., California

LINGUISTIC CONSULTANT
Kenneth Chastain, University of Virginia

EXECUTIVE EDITOR, MODERN LANGUAGES
Roger D. Coulombe

PROJECT EDITORS
Jayne Cotton
Valentia Dermer

NATIONAL MODERN LANGUAGE PRODUCT SPECIALIST
Teresa Carrera-Hanley

MODERN LANGUAGE PRODUCT MANAGER
Natalie St. John

D.C. HEATH CONSULTANTS
Alison King
Karen Ralston
Ramón Morales-Sánchez

DESIGN AND PRODUCTION
Will Tenney, Executive Designer
Donna Lee Porter, Senior Production Coordinator
Marianna Frew Palmer, Editorial Services
Susan Gerould/Perspectives, Cover Designer
M. L. Dietmeier, Illustrator

Contents

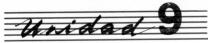

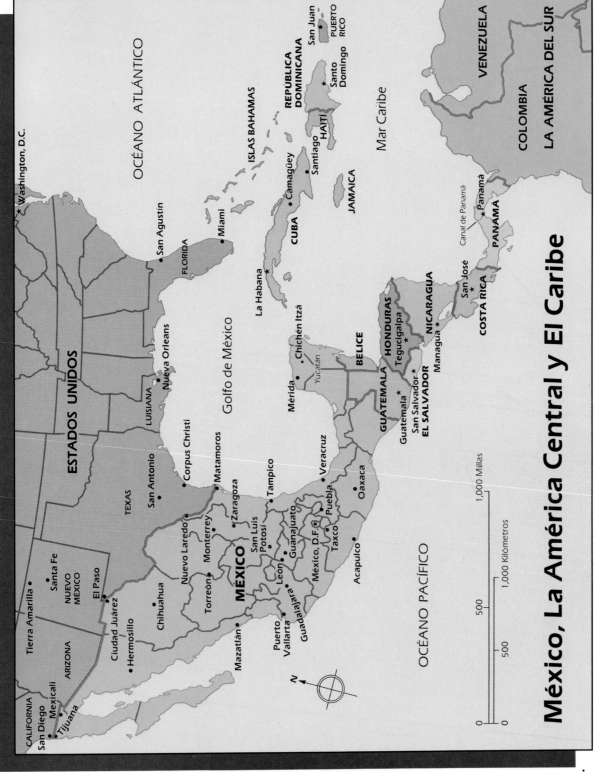

México, La América Central y El Caribe

CALIFORNIA
San Diego
Mexicali
Tijuana

Tierra Amarilla
Santa Fe
NUEVO MÉXICO
ARIZONA
El Paso
Ciudad Juárez
Hermosillo

Chihuahua

ESTADOS UNIDOS

Washington, D.C.

OCÉANO ATLÁNTICO

San Agustín
FLORIDA
Miami

ISLAS BAHAMAS

REPÚBLICA DOMINICANA
San Juan
PUERTO RICO
Santo Domingo
HAITÍ

VENEZUELA

COLOMBIA

LA AMÉRICA DEL SUR

Nueva Orleans
LUISIANA

Camagüey
Santiago
CUBA

Mar Caribe

JAMAICA

Panamá
Canal de Panamá
PANAMÁ

TEXAS
San Antonio
Corpus Christi
Matamoros

Golfo de México

La Habana

Chichén Itzá
Yucatán

BELICE

GUATEMALA
Guatemala
San Salvador
EL SALVADOR

HONDURAS
Tegucigalpa

NICARAGUA
Managua

San José
COSTA RICA

Nuevo Laredo
Monterrey
Torreón
Zaragoza
San Luis Potosí
Guanajuato
León
Guadalajara
Tampico
Veracruz
Puebla
México, D.F.
Taxco
Oaxaca
Acapulco

Mérida

MÉXICO

Mazatlán
Puerto Vallarta

OCÉANO PACÍFICO

N

0   500   1,000 Millas
0   500   1,000 Kilómetros

ix

3–4

Mar Caribe

Canal de Panamá

COSTA RICA
Cartagena · Maracaibo   Caracas ★
PANAMÁ
VENEZUELA
Medellín ·
Bogotá ★
Cali ·
COLOMBIA
GUYANA
SURINAM
GUAYANA FRANCESA

Quito ★
ECUADOR
Guayaquil ·
Iquitos ·
Manaus ·
Belém ·
Fortaleza ·

Trujillo ·
PERÚ
B R A S I L

El Callao ·
Lima ★
Machu Picchu ·
Cuzco ·
La Paz ★
BOLIVIA
Salvador ·
★ Brasilia
Arequipa ·
Sucre ·

Antofagasta ·
PARAGUAY
Rio de Janeiro ·
São Paulo ·

OCÉANO
PACÍFICO
Asunción ★
San Miguel
de Tucumán ·
Pôrto Alegre ·

CHILE
Córdoba ·

URUGUAY
Valparaíso ·
Santiago ★
LA PAMPA
Buenos
Aires ★
Montevideo ★
Punto del Este ·

Concepción ·
ARGENTINA
OCÉANO ATLÁNTICO

N

La América del Sur

ISLAS MALVINAS

Tierra del Fuego

0   400   800 Millas
0   400   800 Kilómetros

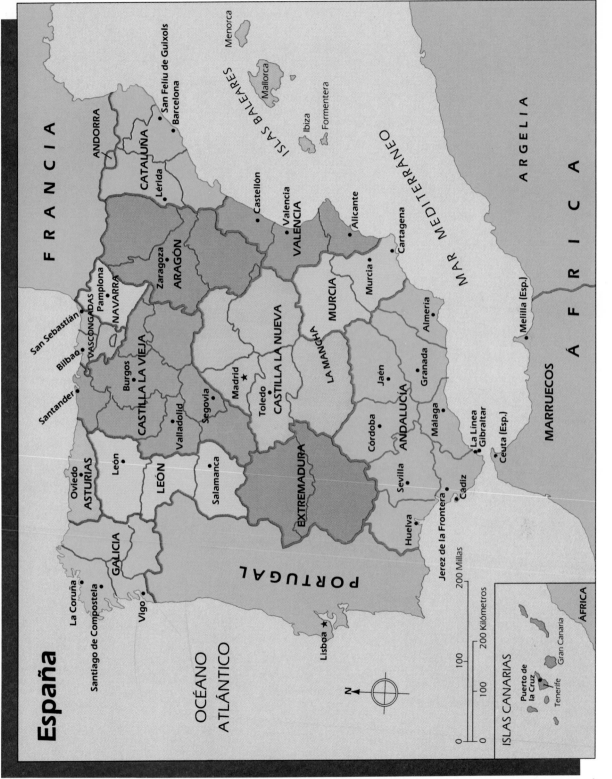

España

Unidad 1

¡Nosotros, los jóvenes!

1.1 **Chile: Enrique Pirelli**

1.2 **México: Ana María González**

1.3 **Panamá: Graciela Cortez**

1.4 **España: Carlos Espínel**

VARIEDADES Unos ruidos en español

OBJECTIVES

Communication

In this unit, students use Spanish:
- To talk about daily activities at home and at school
- To discuss what they do on vacations and in their free time
- To describe themselves and their friends
- To express their feelings and preferences

Language

The first four units of this book review and expand on the grammar and vocabulary presented in Level 1. This unit focuses on the following topics:
- Adjective-noun agreement
- Forms and uses of the definite and indefinite articles
- Present tense of regular verbs (in **-ar, -er, -ir**)
- **Ser, estar, ir, tener**
- **Ser** vs. **estar**
- The future with **ir a** + infinitive
- The present progressive

Culture

This unit stresses the breadth of the Hispanic world and focuses on Chile, Mexico, Panama, and Spain.

 Review   Modules 5, 6, 7, 8, 9, 10, 11

1

STRUCTURES TO REVIEW:
- Present tense of **-ar** verbs
- Negation
- **Me gusta** + infinitive
- Questions

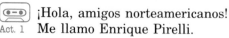

¡Hola, amigos norteamericanos!
Me llamo Enrique Pirelli.

Act. 1

See the last page of the Teacher's Manual for an explanation of the overprinted symbols.

Soy de Chile.
En el colegio, estudio matemáticas, biología e inglés.
De hecho, el inglés es mi clase favorita porque me gustan las canciones norteamericanas.
Canto todo el tiempo. ¡Soy un cantante maravilloso!
(¡No es verdad!)
También me gusta la fotografía.
Quiero ser fotógrafo y viajar a varios países.
Un día espero visitar los Estados Unidos.
¿Cuándo?
En uno, dos, cinco o diez años. ¡No sé!
Y Uds., ¿esperan visitar Chile?
¡Es un país muy lindo!

colegio: *high school*
De hecho: *In fact*

cantante: *singer*
maravilloso:
  marvelous
¡No es verdad!:
  That's not true!
Un día: *One day*

¿Cómo se llama el chico? ¿De dónde es? ¿Qué estudia? ¿Por qué el inglés es su clase favorita? ¿Qué quiere ser? ¿Qué país espera visitar? ¿Qué dice de su país?

NOTAS CULTURALES OPTIONAL

Los inmigrantes

¿Piensas que el nombre° Enrique Pirelli es más italiano que español? ¡Tienes razón!° Chile es un país hispánico, pero muchos de sus habitantes tienen antepasados° de otros países además de España: Italia, Alemania, Francia, Inglaterra y hasta° la China y el Japón. De hecho,° el héroe de la independencia de Chile se llama . . . ¡Bernardo O'Higgins!

Esta misma mezcla° de inmigrantes es típica en la Argentina, en el Uruguay y en muchos de los países latinoamericanos.

nombre *name* **Tienes razón** *You are right*
antepasados *ancestors* **hasta** *even* **De hecho** *In fact*
mezcla *mixture*   ¿De qué origen es el nombre Pirelli?
¿Son todos los habitantes de Chile de origen español?
¿De qué otros países vienen? ¿Cómo se llama el héroe
de la independencia de Chile?

Chile, un país de contrastes

Sí, ¡Chile es un país de muchos contrastes!

Este país sudamericano tiene una extensión de más de cuatro mil kilómetros o dos mil seiscientas millas de norte a sur, por las altas montañas de los Andes hasta° la Isla° de la Tierra del Fuego. Esto° explica la gran variedad de climas y paisajes.° Se puede° esquiar en los Andes y nadar en las playas del Pacífico. En el norte el clima es caliente° y en el sur es frío y húmedo.°

Y con sus territorios, Chile se extiende° también hasta la parte sur del Pacífico. La Isla de Pascua,° con sus famosas estatuas gigantes de piedra,° es una posesión chilena.

hasta *down to* **Isla** *Island* **Esto** *This* **paisajes** *landscapes*
Se puede *One can* **caliente** *hot* **húmedo** *humid* **se
extiende** *extends* **La Isla de Pascua** *Easter Island* **piedra**
stone

Soccer game at the foot of the Andes in Chile

¿Dónde está Chile? ¿Es un país grande o pequeño? ¿Hay montañas en Chile? ¿Cómo se llaman? ¿Dónde esquían los chilenos? ¿Dónde nadan? ¿Cómo es el clima en el sur? ¿Dónde está situada la Isla de Pascua?

— Vocabulario —

sustantivo	*la verdad	the truth
adjetivo	*maravilloso	marvelous
expresiones	*de hecho	in fact
	*¡Es verdad!	That's right. That's true.
	*¡No es verdad!	That's not true.
	*un día	one day, some day

An asterisk signals
new vocabulary in
Units 1–4.

Other facts about Chile:
• 450 miles to the west lies Juan Fernández Island where Alexander Selkirk (the real-life Robinson Crusoe) was shipwrecked.
• The Christ of the Andes, a gigantic statue made of melted-down cannons, marks the border between Chile and Argentina. It symbolizes eternal peace between the two countries.

Vamos a hablar de las actividades de la escuela.

¿Cómo te llamas?

¿Estudias español?

¿Estudias mucho? ¿Sacas buenas notas?

¿Hablas español bien?

¿Siempre hablas español en la clase?

¿Qué más estudias? ¿inglés? ¿matemáticas? ¿biología? ¿historia?

¿Cómo se llama tu profesor(a) de español? ¿de inglés? ¿de matemáticas?

7

VOCABULARIO PRÁCTICO   Algunos verbos que terminan en *-ar*

actividades de todos los días

*cocinar	to cook
escuchar (música)	to listen to (music)
estudiar (matemáticas, francés)	to study (math, French)
ganar (dinero)	to earn (money)
hablar (español, inglés)	to speak (Spanish, English)
llevar (libros, discos)	to take (books, records)
mirar (la televisión)	to watch (television)
sacar (una buena o mala nota)	to get (a good or bad grade)
tomar (el autobús, el tren)	to take (the bus, the train)
tomar (café, té, agua)	to have or drink (coffee, tea, water)
trabajar (en una oficina)	to work (in an office)

Most of these words were presented in Level 1.

Ahora vamos a hablar de tus actividades del fin de semana.

¿Trabajas? ¿Dónde trabajas?

¿Miras la televisión?

¿Qué programas te gustan? ¿los programas de deportes? ¿las comedias?

¿Escuchas música?

¿Qué tipo de música escuchas? ¿música clásica? ¿música popular?

¿Te gusta nadar? ¿esquiar?

¿Te gusta jugar al volibol? ¿al tenis: ¿al ping pong? ¿al fútbol?

¿Te gusta bailar? ¿cantar? ¿Cómo cantas? ¿bien o mal?

actividades de vacaciones

bailar	to dance
cantar (una canción)	to sing (a song)
* **descansar**	to rest
* **esquiar** (en las montañas)	to ski (in the mountains)
nadar (en el mar)	to swim (in the sea)
sacar (fotos)	to take (pictures)
tocar (la guitarra, el piano)	to play (the guitar, the piano)
* **tomar el sol**	to sunbathe
viajar (a los Estados Unidos)	to travel (to the United States)
visitar (un museo)	to visit (a museum)

NOTA: Note the difference between **tomar** *(to take, to drink)* and **llevar** *(to take along, to carry).*

Elena **toma** un taxi.   *Elena **is taking** (riding in) a taxi.*

Felipe **toma** leche.   *Felipe **is drinking** milk.*

Clara **lleva** discos a la fiesta.   *Clara **is taking** records **(along)** to the party.*

Carlos **lleva** a Ana a la fiesta.   *Carlos **is taking** Ana **(along)** to the party.*

Lección uno

5

Estructuras

A. Repaso: los verbos que terminan en -ar

In Spanish, the *present tense* is a *simple tense*. It is composed of one word which is formed as follows:

$$\text{stem} + \text{ending}$$

Review the present tense of **estudiar** *(to study)* in the affirmative and negative sentences below. The stem for each form is **estudi-** (the infinitive minus **-ar**). Pay attention to the endings which correspond to each subject pronoun.

INFINITIVE	**estudiar**			
PRESENT				
(yo)	Estudio	español.	**No** estudio	italiano.
(tú)	Estudias	inglés.	**No** estudias	física.
(él, ella, Ud.)	Estudia	matemáticas.	**No** estudia	geografía.
(nosotros)	Estudi**amos**	historia.	**No** estudi**amos**	latín.
(vosotros)	Estudi**áis**	biología.	**No** estudi**áis**	francés.
(ellos, ellas, Uds.)	Estudi**an**	música.	**No** estudi**an**	ciencias.

⟫ Most verbs ending in **–ar** follow the above pattern. They are called *regular –ar verbs*.

⟫ The Spanish present tense has several English equivalents:

Estudio español.
$\begin{cases} I \textbf{ study } Spanish. \\ I \textbf{ am studying } Spanish. \\ I \textbf{ do study } Spanish. \end{cases}$

⟫ Since the verb endings usually indicate the subject, Spanish subject pronouns, except for **Ud.** and **Uds.**, are often omitted. Subject pronouns are used for emphasis or clarification.

Yo voto
Tú votas
El vota
Todos
debemos
votar
El 4 de Julio

ACTIVIDAD 1 En Santiago de Chile

Imagina que estás en Santiago de Chile con tus amigos. Prepara diez frases describiendo algunas actividades. Usa los elementos de las columnas A, B y C.

A	B	C
yo	visitar	Santiago
tú	mirar	la alameda Bernardo O'Higgins
Mónica	admirar	el Cerro Santa Lucía
nosotros	sacar fotos de	el Museo de Arte Popular
Luis y José		los monumentos
		el Jardín Zoológico
		la catedral
		la Virgen de San Cristóbal

The "Alameda" is the main thoroughfare of Santiago. Santa Lucía Hill is where Don Pedro de Valdivia founded the city in 1541. The Museo de Arte Popular is on Cerro Santa Lucía in the former dungeons of the old fortress Castillo Hidalgo. The Jardín Zoológico is on Cerro San Cristóbal, on the top of which hill is a large statue of the Virgin Mary. This statue was a gift from France to Chile. The cathedral dates back to 1558.

WB
A1

SCRIPT
Act. 5

⟷ (Nosotros) visitamos Santiago.   Sacamos fotos de los monumentos . . .

You may remind the students of the contraction: **de** + **el** → **del**.

SUGGESTED REALIA: tour book of Chile, travel brochures, map of Santiago. Also see **Vista** 4, pp. 315–327.

B. Repaso: la negación

Review the negative sentences in the verb chart for **estudiar**. Then read the sentences below.

Elena **no** habla inglés.   *Elena does **not** speak English.*
Carlos y Enrique **no** trabajan.   *Carlos and Enrique do **not** work.*

To make a sentence negative, Spanish speakers use the construction:

$$\boxed{\textbf{no} \quad + \quad \text{verb}}$$

⟷ In sentences where **nunca** *(never)* is used, the constructions can be either:

$$\boxed{\textbf{no} + \text{verb} + \textbf{nunca}} \quad \text{or} \quad \boxed{\textbf{nunca} + \text{verb}}$$

Andrés **no** trabaja **nunca**.   Andrés **nunca** trabaja.

VOCABULARIO PRÁCTICO   Algunos adverbios

bien	≠	**mal**	well	≠ badly
mucho	≠	**poco**	much, a lot	≠ a little
más	≠	**menos**	more	≠ less
siempre	≠	**nunca**	always	≠ never
también			also	
muy			very	
bastante			rather, enough	
demasiado			too, too much	

ACTIVIDAD 2 Nunca los domingos *(Never on Sundays)*

Durante la semana, Miguel y sus amigos hacen las siguientes cosas, pero no las hacen los sábados, y nunca las hacen los domingos. Expresa eso según el modelo.

∽ Miguel estudia.   Los sábados no estudia.
                      Los domingos no estudia nunca.

1. Carmen trabaja.
2. Felipe mira la televisión.
3. Esteban y Carlos sacan fotos.
4. Luisa toma el tren.

5. Uds. viajan.
6. Nosotros trabajamos mucho.
7. Yo hablo inglés.
8. Tú ganas dinero.

ACTIVIDAD 3 ¿Qué haces bien?

Di si haces las siguientes cosas. Entonces da una explicación según el modelo.

∽ nadar   Nado. Nado muy bien (mal, un poco, bastante bien).
           (No nado.)

1. cantar
2. esquiar
3. bailar
4. hablar español

5. hablar francés
6. tocar la guitarra
7. cocinar
8. tocar el piano

VARIATION: Ask about student responses. **¿Canta Betty? ¿Canta bien o mal?**

ACTIVIDAD 4 Diálogo: Actividades

Pregúntales a tus compañeros si hacen las siguientes cosas.

∽ tocar el trombón   Estudiante 1: ¿Tocas el trombón?
                      Estudiante 2: Sí (No, no) toco el trombón.

WB
B1

SCRIPT
Act. 4

MASTERS
p. 1

1. hablar ruso
2. hablar japonés
3. estudiar filosofía
4. trabajar en un zoológico
5. trabajar como mecánico
6. bailar el rock
7. cantar ópera

8. ganar mucho dinero
9. llevar discos a la clase
10. descansar en la clase de español
11. descansar en la clase de matemáticas
12. tomar café en la cafetería
13. viajar mucho
14. tomar el sol en la cafetería

VARIATION: Use the plural, asking two or more class-
mates the questions.
   —¿Tocan Uds. el trombón?
   —Sí (No, no) tocamos...

C. Repaso: el uso del infinitivo

In Spanish, the infinitive is used after certain verbs and expressions.

desear	to wish	**Deseo hablar** español bien.
esperar	to hope	**Espero visitar** Chile.
* **odiar**	to hate	**Odio escuchar** canciones tontas.
* **me / te encanta**	I / you very much like	**Me encanta viajar.**
me / te gusta	I / you like	**Me gusta estudiar** inglés.
* **me / te gusta más**	I / you prefer	**Me gusta más estudiar** español.
* **me / te gustaría**	I / you would like	**¿Te gustaría visitar** Puerto Rico?

ACTIVIDAD 5   Diálogo

Pregúntales a tus compañeros si les gusta hacer las siguientes cosas.

escuchar música clásica   Estudiante 1: ¿Te gusta escuchar música clásica?
                        Estudiante 2: Sí (No, no) me gusta escuchar música clásica.
                                      (Odio escuchar música clásica.)

1. viajar
2. nadar en el mar
3. hablar español
4. estudiar
5. trabajar en una oficina
6. bailar
7. ganar dinero
8. tomar el sol
9. mirar la televisión

10. tomar el tren
11. cantar canciones españolas
12. llevar libros a la clase
13. cocinar
14. visitar museos
15. tomar medicina
16. esquiar en las montañas
17. sacar fotos
18. sacar malas notas

ACTIVIDAD 6 Según las circunstancias (According to circumstances) OPTIONAL

¿Qué te gusta hacer y qué no te gusta hacer en las siguientes situaciones?

>> En una fiesta ...

En una fiesta me gusta (me encanta, no me gusta, odio) bailar
(escuchar música, hablar con mis amigos ...).

1. En la cafetería ...
2. En casa ...
3. Con mis amigos ...
4. Con mis amigas ...
5. Cuando estudio ...
6. Cuando viajo ...
7. En el verano ...
8. En el invierno ...

ACTIVIDAD 7 Esperanzas (Hopes) OPTIONAL

Di lo que esperas hacer en las siguientes circunstancias.

>> Después de la clase de español ...

Después de la clase de español, espero hablar con mis amigos
(tomar una Coca-Cola ...).

1. Esta noche ...
2. Mañana ...
3. El fin de semana ...
4. Durante las vacaciones ...
5. Después de la escuela secundaria ...
6. En la vida (life) ...

D. Repaso: preguntas

Note the position of the subject in the following questions.

¿Habla español **María?**	*Does **María** speak Spanish?*
¿Trabaja mucho **Luis?**	*Does **Luis** work a lot?*
¿Escucha la radio **Carlos?**	*Is **Carlos** listening to the radio?*
¿Dónde trabajas **(tú)?**	*Where do **you** work?*
¿Qué estudian **Uds.?**	*What are **you** studying?*

To ask a question, Spanish speakers usually use the following construction:

¿question word(s) + verb + rest of sentence + subject?
  (if any)   (if any)   (when expressed)

>> The subject may also come immediately *after* the verb.

ACTIVIDAD 8 Los estudiantes chilenos

Imagina que un grupo de estudiantes chilenos va a visitar tu escuela.
Quieres saber algo de ellos. Haz las preguntas necesarias según el modelo.

>> Carlos: hablar inglés   ¿Habla inglés Carlos?

1. Adela e Inés: hablar inglés
2. Tomás: cocinar bien
3. Silvia: bailar bien
4. Enrique: tocar la guitarra
5. Paco y Felipe: sacar fotos
6. Emilia y Rosita: cantar bien

You may remind the students that:
• Question words have an accent.
• The plural of **quién** is **quiénes**.

VOCABULARIO PRÁCTICO   **Palabras interrogativas**

Act. 7

¿cuánto?	how much?	¿**Cuánto** ganas?
¿cómo?	how?	¿**Cómo** tocas el piano? ¿bien o mal?
¿cuándo?	when?	¿**Cuándo** descansa Felipe?
¿dónde?	where?	¿**Dónde** esquías?
¿por qué?	why?	¿**Por qué** estudias español?
¿qué?	what?	¿**Qué** escuchas?
¿quién?	who?	¿**Quién** habla francés aquí?

ACTIVIDAD 9   Preguntas personales

You may review:
• adónde   ¿Adónde viajas?
• de dónde   ¿De dónde eres?

1. ¿Cómo hablas español? ¿bien o muy bien?
2. ¿Cómo nadas? ¿bien o mal?
3. ¿Cómo cantas? ¿bastante bien?
4. ¿Dónde estudias? ¿en una escuela pública o en una escuela privada?
5. ¿Dónde hablas español? ¿en casa o en clase?
6. ¿Cuándo miras la televisión? ¿por la noche o por la mañana?
7. ¿Qué estudias? ¿italiano o español?
8. ¿Qué te gusta escuchar? ¿música clásica o música popular?

Ask about student responses.
¿Cómo habla español Charles?
¿Quién nada? ¿Quiénes nadan bien?

WB
D1, D2
Trad.

SCRIPT

Act. 6, 8, 9

MASTERS
p. 1

TRB

QUIZ
pp. 1–2

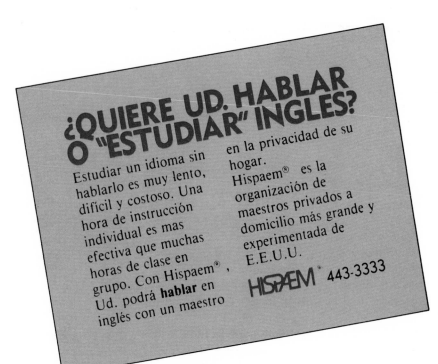

Act. 1

Me llamo Ana María González.
Soy mexicana, de Puebla.
¿Cómo soy?
Soy alta, morena y tengo el pelo corto.
Tal vez no soy la mexicana típica pero soy ciento por ciento
    mexicana.
¿Qué tipo de persona soy? A ver . . .
Según mis amigos soy idealista y muy independiente.
Y aunque soy independiente también soy buena compañera.
En clase soy un poco tímida, pero generalmente soy buena alumna.
Después del colegio espero ir a la universidad y estudiar química o
    geología.
Me gustaría mucho ser ingeniera y trabajar para la industria
    petrolera nacional.
Y a ti, ¿qué te gustaría hacer en la vida?

STRUCTURES TO REVIEW:
• **Ser**
• Noun-adjective agreement
• Definite and indefinite articles
• Position of adjectives

Tal vez: *Maybe*
ciento por ciento:
    100%

A ver: *Let's see*

Según: *According to*
aunque: *although*
compañera:
    companion
química: *chemistry*

ingeniera: *engineer*
industria petrolera:
    oil industry

¿Cómo se llama la chica? ¿De dónde es? ¿Es alta o baja? ¿Es rubia o morena? ¿Qué espera hacer después
del colegio? ¿Por qué?

Vamos a hablar de tu escuela.

¿Son estrictos los profesores? ¿Son pacientes? ¿justos?
¿Son dinámicos los profesores? ¿Son divertidos? ¿simpáticos? ¿interesantes?
¿Son simpáticos tus compañeros? ¿Son interesantes? ¿perezosos? ¿ . . . un
poco locos (crazy)?

Vamos a hablar de tu familia.

¿Son estrictos tus padres? ¿Son justos? ¿pacientes? ¿generosos?
¿Tienes un hermano? ¿Es guapo? ¿alto? ¿moreno? ¿simpático? ¿divertido?
¿aburrido? ¿loco? ¿listo (smart)?
¿Tienes una hermana? ¿Es bonita? ¿simpática? ¿divertida? ¿perezosa?
¿lista?
¿Tienes primos? ¿Son simpáticos? ¿aburridos? ¿tontos? ¿flacos?
¿gordos?

Tener is reviewed in the next lesson, p. 24. Have students answer **tener** questions with **sí** or **no**.

La personalidad
  el aspecto físico

moreno	≠ **rubio**	dark	≠ blond
guapo ⎫	≠ **feo**	handsome, beautiful ⎫	≠ ugly
bonito ⎭		pretty ⎭	
bajo	≠ **alto**	short	≠ tall
* **flaco** ⎫	≠ **gordo**	skinny ⎫	≠ fat
delgado ⎭		thin ⎭	
joven	≠ **viejo**	young	≠ old

  el aspecto moral y social

bueno	≠ **malo**	good	≠ bad
* **activo**	* ≠ **perezoso**	active	≠ lazy
* **deportista**		athletic, sports-loving	
divertido ⎫	≠ **aburrido**	amusing, fun ⎫	≠ boring
interesante ⎭		interesting ⎭	
* **inteligente**	* ≠ **estúpido**	intelligent	≠ stupid
* **listo**	≠ **tonto**	clever, smart	≠ foolish, silly
serio	* ≠ **loco**	serious	≠ crazy
rico	≠ **pobre**	rich	≠ poor
simpático	≠ **antipático**	nice	≠ unpleasant, disagreeable

La nacionalidad

* **canadiense**	Canadian	**inglés (inglesa)**	English
español	Spanish	* **mexicano**	Mexican
francés (francesa)	French	**norteamericano**	American (from US)

• In Spanish, adjectives of nationality are not capitalized.
• For other adjectives of nationality, see Appendix 2.

Estructuras

A. Repaso: *ser*

Review the forms and uses of **ser** *(to be)* in the following sentences.

Act. 3

(yo)	**Soy** simpático.	(nosotros)	**Somos** mexicanos.
(tú)	**Eres** estudiante.	(vosotros)	**¿Sois** de aquí?
(él, ella, Ud.)	**Es** de México.	(ellos, ellas, Uds.)	**Son** muy inteligentes.

ACTIVIDAD 1 La conferencia internacional

Los siguientes estudiantes asisten a una conferencia internacional. Cada uno(a) habla el idioma de su país. ¿Puedes decir de qué ciudad es cada estudiante? **Buenos Aires, París, Chicago, Roma, Moscú**

⟩⟩ Linda habla inglés.   Es de Chicago.

1. Juan habla español.
2. Nosotros hablamos italiano.
3. Uds. hablan inglés.
4. Yo hablo francés.

5. Tú hablas ruso.
6. Mario y Teresa hablan italiano.
7. Nancy e Irene hablan inglés.
8. Ud. habla francés.

WB
A1

B. Repaso: el género: sustantivos, artículos y adjetivos

Look at the forms of the articles and adjectives in the following sentences.

Roberto es **el** amigo de Luis.   Es **un** chico **inteligente, simpático** e **intelectual.**
Amalia es **la** amiga de Roberto.   Es **una** chica **inteligente, simpática** e **intelectual.**

All nouns, whether they designate people, animals or things, have a *gender:* they are either masculine or feminine.

Most nouns ending in **–o** are masculine.
Most nouns ending in **–a** are feminine.

Exception: **la mano**
There are many exceptions: **el día, el telegrama** (and nouns ending in **-ama, -ema**), **el pianista** (and male persons).

⟩⟩ Masculine nouns are introduced by masculine articles (**el, un**) and are modified by masculine adjectives.

⟩⟩ Feminine nouns are introduced by feminine articles (**la, una**) and are modified by feminine adjectives.

Adjectives which end in **–o** in the masculine end in **–a** in the feminine.
Many adjectives which do not end in **–o** in the masculine remain the same in the feminine.   Exception: **trabajador → trabajadora**

⟩⟩ Adjectives of nationality which end in a consonant in the masculine add an **–a** in the feminine.

Juan es **español.**   Juana es **española.** Also: **francés, francesa; inglés, inglesa;** etc.

ACTIVIDAD 2   Retratos   OPTIONAL

Usa por lo menos *(at least)* tres adjetivos del **Vocabulario práctico**
para describir a las siguientes personas.

⟩⟩   Robert Redford   Es norteamericano. Es rubio. ¡Es muy guapo!

1. el amigo ideal
2. la amiga ideal
3. el hijo ideal
4. la hija ideal
5. el profesor ideal
6. Michael J. Fox
7. Raquel Welch
8. Bill Cosby

9. Tom Cruise
10. Dan Rather
11. Whitney Houston
12. Blancanieves *(Snow White)*
13. Carlitos *(Charlie Brown)*
14. Drácula
15. King Kong

WB
B1

SCRIPT

Act. 4, 5

MASTERS
p. 2

C. Repaso: el plural: sustantivos, artículos y adjetivos

Note the forms of the articles and adjectives in the following sentences.

>Luis tiene **(unos) amigos** en México.
>**Los amigos mexicanos** de Luis son **simpáticos, interesantes** e **intelectuales.**
>Olga tiene **(unas) amigas** en México.
>**Las amigas mexicanas** de Olga son **simpáticas, interesantes** e **intelectuales.**

Plural nouns are introduced by plural articles and are modified by plural adjectives.

The plural of nouns and adjectives is formed by adding:

-s   if the singular form ends in a vowel;
-es   if the singular form ends in a consonant.

Exceptions:

⟩⟩   Nouns and adjectives ending in **-z** in the singular end in **-ces** in the plural.
Raquel Welch es **actriz.**   Jane Fonda y Barbara Streisand son **actrices.**

⟩⟩   Nouns and adjectives which have an accent mark on the last syllable
in the singular drop this accent mark in the plural.
Pierre es **francés.**   Jean y Jacques son **franceses.**

⟩⟩   The articles **unos** and **unas** *(some)* are usually omitted.

Resumen:

	DEFINITE ARTICLE		INDEFINITE ARTICLE		ADJECTIVES	
MASCULINE	**el**	**los**	**un**	**unos**	**simpático(s)**	**inteligente(s)**
FEMININE	**la**	**las**	**una**	**unas**	**simpática(s)**	**inteligente(s)**

Manos Unidas
CAMPAÑA CONTRA EL HAMBRE

ACTIVIDAD 3   Las personas que figuran en mi vida

Describe a las personas que figuran en tu vida, completando las siguientes frases con adjetivos apropiados. ¡Usa tu imaginación!

1. Mis profesores son . . .
2. Mis padres son . . .
3. Mis amigos son . . .
4. Mis amigas son . . .
5. Mis hermanos son . . .
6. Mis hermanas son . . .
7. Mis compañeros son . . .
8. Mis compañeras son . . .
9. Mis abuelos son . . .
10. Mis primos son . . .

ACTIVIDAD 4   Estereotipos   OPTIONAL

Los estereotipos son exageraciones de la realidad. En tu opinión, ¿cuáles son los estereotipos más comunes de las siguientes personas? Usa los adjetivos de la lección en frases afirmativas o negativas.

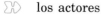 los actores   Los actores son guapos y ricos. No son siempre muy inteligentes.

1. las actrices
2. los atletas
3. los políticos
4. los artistas
5. los estudiantes
6. las personas flacas
7. las chicas francesas
8. los abuelos
9. las mujeres norteamericanas
10. los hombres latinoamericanos

WB
C1

D. Repaso: la posición de los adjetivos

Note the position of the adjectives in the following sentences.

Luis es un chico **simpático**.   *Luis is a **pleasant** boy.*
Amalia es una muchacha **mexicana**.   *Amalia is a **Mexican** girl.*

In Spanish, descriptive adjectives usually come *after* the nouns they modify. A few such adjectives may come before or after the noun:

bueno *(good)*   La Srta. Montez es una **buena** profesora.
malo *(bad)*   Luis y Felipe son estudiantes **malos**.

When used before a noun, the masculine singular adjectives **bueno** and **malo** become **buen** and **mal**.

Enrique es un **buen** compañero pero un **mal** estudiante.

ACTIVIDAD 5 Los amigos

Algunas personas tienden a seleccionar amigos que tienen características similares. Expresa esto según el modelo.

Laura es intelectual.   Tiene amigos intelectuales.

1. Luis es perezoso.
2. Marta es inteligente.
3. Felipe es divertido.
4. Carmen es seria.
5. Alberto es deportista.
6. Inés es lista.

7. Juan es tonto.
8. Tere es guapa.
9. Mónica es aburrida.
10. Dolores es simpática.
11. Manuel es interesante.
12. Concepción es delgada.

ACTIVIDAD 6 ¡Un poco de lógica! OPTIONAL

May be assigned as a special challenge activity.

Describe la personalidad de las personas en la columna A. En cinco minutos, ¿cuántas frases lógicas puedes crear? Usa los elementos de las columnas A, B, C y D en frases afirmativas o negativas.

A	B	C	D
yo	estudiar	chico(a)	pobre
Roberto	trabajar mucho	estudiante	rico
el Sr. Montez	nadar bien	muchacho(a)	serio
la Sra. de Ochoa	ganar mucho dinero	hombre	activo
nosotros	sacar buenas / malas notas	mujer	perezoso
Mari-Carmen y Adela		joven	deportista
mis amigos			listo

Isabel   Isabel (no) saca buenas notas. (No) Es una chica (muchacha, estudiante) seria (lista, perezosa).

WB
D1, D2
Trad.

SCRIPT

Act. 6, 7,
8

MASTERS
p. 2

TRB

QUIZ
pp. 3–4

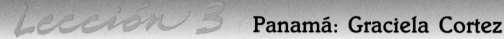

Panamá: Graciela Cortez

STRUCTURES TO REVIEW: • **Tener, ir, ir a** + infinitive
• Definite articles with days of the week
• **Al** and **del**
• Personal **a**

Act. 1

Me llamo Graciela Cortez y tengo diez y nueve años.

Uds. son estudiantes, ¿verdad?

¡Yo no!

Trabajo para Panavisión, en el canal 5.

Tengo un trabajo muy interesante.

Soy asistente de producción.

Ayudo a las personas que presentan las noticias.

Trabajo mucho, pero no todo el tiempo.

Generalmente, los sábados voy al cine con mi novio, y los domingos
voy a la playa con mis compañeras.

Pero, el sábado próximo no vamos al cine.

Vamos a una gran fiesta en casa de mi primo Andrés.

Es su cumpleaños y va a invitar a mucha gente.

¿Qué regalo le voy a comprar? ¿un libro? ¿un disco compact? ¿una
camisa? ¿y por qué no una corbata bonita?

¡Caramba esto sí que es un problema!

¡Qué complicada es la vida!

canal: *channel*

todo el tiempo: *all
the time*

¡Caramba!: *Wow!*
la vida: *life*

¿Cómo se llama la chica? ¿Cuántos años tiene? ¿Es estudiante? ¿Qué trabajo tiene? ¿Adónde va los
domingos? ¿Adónde va el sábado próximo? ¿Cómo se llama su primo?

NOTA CULTURAL

OPTIONAL

SUGGESTED REALIA: travel brochures, map of Central America. See also **Vista** 3.

Panamá: el cruce° del mundo

Tú sabes que hay un Canal de Panamá. Pero, ¿sabes que en 1524 (mil quinientos veinte y cuatro) el rey° de España Carlos V ya° se interesaba° en construir° el canal? Y, ¿sabes que sus ingenieros hicieron las primeras investigaciones? En 1880 (mil ochocientos ochenta), el ingeniero francés Ferdinand de Lesseps empezó la construcción del canal actual,° pero su proyecto° fracasó.° Finalmente, los Estados Unidos empezaron a trabajar en el canal en 1904 (mil novecientos cuatro), y lo inauguraron en 1914 (mil novecientos catorce). El canal conecta el At-

lántico y el Pacífico. Es la conexión entre° Europa y Asia y Australia, entre el viejo y el nuevo mundo.

Los habitantes de Panamá representan una mezcla° de muchas culturas. Son de origen indio, negro, europeo y asiático. Hablan español, pero también hay gente que habla inglés, portugués, chino, japonés, árabe . . .

Hoy día, Panamá es sin duda el cruce del mundo.

cruce *crossroads* **rey** *king* **ya** *already* **se interesaba** *was interested* **en construir** *in building* **actual** *present* **proyecto** *plan* **fracasó** *failed* **entre** *between* **mezcla** *mixture*

¿Quién es Carlos Quinto? ¿Quién es Ferdinand de Lesseps? ¿Qué océanos conecta el canal de Panamá? ¿Qué continentes conecta? ¿De qué orígenes son los panameños? ¿Qué lenguas hablan?

—— Vocabulario ——

sustantivos	*el mundo	the world	**la vida**	life
expresiones	¡Caramba!	Wow!		
	*todo el tiempo	all the time		

"Panamá la Vieja," the old Panama City, was an important settlement during the Spanish conquest of America. It was founded in 1519. It is from there a few years later that Pizarro planned his expedition to Peru. The city was destroyed in the 17th century by English pirates. Panama, which once belonged to Colombia, is today an independent country.

Vamos a hablar de ti.

¿Cuántos años tienes?

¿Tienes muchos amigos? ¿muchas amigas?

¿Cuántos años tiene tu mejor amigo? ¿tu mejor amiga?

¿Tienes hermanos? ¿Cuántos? ¿Cuántos años tienen?

¿Tienes hermanas? ¿Cuántas? ¿Cuántos años tienen?

¿Tienes abuelos? ¿abuelas? ¿tíos? ¿tías?

¿Tienes una guitarra? ¿un piano? ¿otro instrumento musical?

¿Tienes un radio? ¿un tocadiscos? ¿una grabadora? ¿discos? ¿cintas?

¿Tienen tus padres un coche? ¿De qué marca *(make)*?

VOCABULARIO PRÁCTICO   **Algunos objetos de la vida diaria**

algunos objetos

un objeto	object, thing	**una cosa**	thing
un coche	car	**una bicicleta**	bicycle
un disco	record	***una calculadora**	calculator
un libro	book	**una cámara**	camera
un periódico	newspaper	**una cinta**	tape, cassette
un radio	radio	**una grabadora**	tape recorder
un regalo	present, gift	**una moto**	motorcycle
un reloj	watch, clock	***una pelota**	ball
un televisor	TV set	***una raqueta**	racket
un tocadiscos	record player	**una revista**	magazine

algunos verbos

comprar	to buy	**tener**	to have
necesitar	to need		

algunos adjetivos

nuevo	new	**viejo**	old
grande	big, large; great	**pequeño**	small, little
¿cuántos?	how many?	**muchos**	many
otro	other, another		

Mucho(a, os, as), ¿cuánto(a, os, as)?, otro(a, os, as) agree with the nouns they introduce. The indefinite
article (un, una) is never used with **otro: otro chico** (another boy); **otra vez** (another time).

Ahora vamos a hablar de tu vida diaria *(daily).*

¿Estudias mucho? ¿Tienes que estudiar mucho para la clase de español?
   ¿para la clase de inglés? ¿para la clase de matemáticas?
¿Tienes que hablar español en la clase de español?
¿Ayudas mucho en casa? ¿Tienes que ayudar a tu papá? ¿a tu mamá?
¿Tienes trabajo? ¿Tienes que trabajar mucho?

Ahora vamos a hablar de tus diversiones.

¿Vas a menudo al cine? ¿al teatro? ¿a los conciertos? ¿a las fiestas?
El fin de semana próximo, ¿vas a estudiar? ¿a mirar la televisión? ¿a visitar
   a tus amigos? ¿a comprar discos?
Durante las vacaciones de Navidad, ¿vas a trabajar? ¿a viajar? ¿a esquiar?
Durante las vacaciones, ¿vas a menudo a la playa? ¿a la piscina? ¿al campo?

otras palabras y expresiones

para	for	¿Tienen Uds. un regalo **para** Amanda?
pero	but	No me gusta cantar, **pero** bailo muy bien.
y (e)	and	Luis **y** Ana tienen un libro nuevo **e** interesante.
o (u)	or	¿Desea Ud. un periódico **o** una revista **u** otra cosa?
a menudo	often	Compro revistas **a menudo**.
a veces	sometimes	**A veces** compro discos nuevos.

NOTAS: 1. **Nuevo** and **grande** may be used before the noun.
When used before a singular noun, **grande** becomes **gran**.
Note the two meanings:

   Nueva York es una ciudad **grande**.   *New York is a **big** city.*
   ¡Nueva York es una **gran** ciudad!   *New York is a **great** city!*

When used before a noun, **nuevo** means *another* or *different*.
When used after a noun, **nuevo** means *brand new.*
Note the two meanings:

   Tengo un coche **nuevo**.   *I have a **new** car (**a brand new car**).*
   Tengo un **nuevo** coche.   *I have a **new** car (**another car**).*

   2. Note the following variants of **y** and **o**.

   y becomes **e** before **i** or **hi**
   o becomes **u** before **o** or **ho**

ACTIVIDAD 1 El regalo ideal

¿Cuáles son los regalos ideales para las siguientes personas?

Para un chico intelectual . . .

Para un chico intelectual, el regalo ideal es un libro.

1. Para un chico de 12 años . . .
2. Para una chica de 14 años . . .
3. Para un chico de 16 años . . .
4. Para un chico de 18 años . . .

5. Para una chica de 20 años . . .
6. Para una persona que no es puntual . . .
7. Para una chica a quien le gusta la fotografía . . .

ACTIVIDAD 2 ¿Cuánto?

Review the numbers in Appendix 1.

Di cuántos dólares necesitas para comprar las siguientes cosas. No necesitas el precio exacto.

un disco   Para comprar un disco, necesito cinco dólares.

1. una bicicleta nueva
2. un televisor de color
3. un reloj viejo
4. una calculadora pequeña
5. una cámara grande

6. una pelota de béisbol
7. una buena raqueta de tenis
8. un libro interesante
9. un radio pequeño
10. un periódico

11. diez cintas
12. una grabadora nueva
13. una moto vieja
14. un coche nuevo
15. un coche viejo

Estructuras

A. Repaso: *tener*

Review the forms of **tener** *(to have)* in the following sentences.

(yo)	**Tengo** un radio	(nosotros)	No **tenemos** raqueta de tenis.
(tú)	**Tienes** una revista.	(vosotros)	No **tenéis** grabadora.
(él, ella, Ud.)	**Tiene** un reloj.	(ellos, ellas, Uds.)	No **tienen** bicicleta.

After **tener**, the indefinite article (**un, una**) is sometimes omitted, especially in negative sentences.

Tener is used in many idiomatic expressions.

tener . . . años	to be . . . (years old)	¿Cuántos **años tienes**, Marta? **Tengo** diez y seis **años**.
tener suerte	to be lucky	Pedro tiene una moto. ¡**Tiene suerte!**
tener que + infinitive	to have to	**Tenemos que** hablar español en la clase de español.
tener ganas de + infinitive	to wish to, to feel very much like	¿**Tienes ganas de** visitar Puerto Rico?

ACTIVIDAD 3   ¿Suerte?

¿Tienen suerte las siguientes personas? Expresa tu opinión según los modelos.

⚉ Carlos (un coche)   Carlos tiene un coche. ¡Tiene suerte!
⚉ Esteban (muchas tareas)   Esteban tiene muchas tareas. ¡Tiene mala suerte!

1. Juan (una moto)
2. Silvia y Luisa (un tocadiscos nuevo)
3. Anita (amigos simpáticos)
4. tú (un hermano aburrido)
5. yo (un profesor estricto)
6. nosotros (una profesora muy seria)

7. mis primos (padres muy estrictos)
8. mis amigos (un televisor de color)
9. mis padres (un[a] hijo[a] muy inteligente)
10. mi prima (hermanos tontos)

ACTIVIDAD 4   El baile *(The dance)*

Esta noche hay un gran baile. Las siguientes personas quieren ir pero desgraciadamente tienen que hacer otras cosas. Di esto según el modelo.

⚉ Carmen (estudiar)   Carmen tiene ganas de bailar.
                         Pero tiene que estudiar.

1. Luis (trabajar)
2. nosotros (estudiar para el examen)
3. tú (estudiar)

4. yo (reparar mi bicicleta)
5. José y Felipe (estudiar)
6. Antonio y Rita (trabajar)

SCRIPT
⌸
Act. 3

MASTERS
p. 3

B. Repaso: el artículo definido con los días de la semana

Review the days of the week: **lunes, martes, miércoles, jueves, viernes, sábado, domingo.**

Note how the days of the week are used in the following sentences:

Hoy es **lunes**.   *Today is **Monday**.*
Tengo una cita **el viernes**.   *I have a date **(on) Friday**.*
Los sábados no trabajamos nunca.   ***(On) Saturdays** we never work.*

Except after the verb **ser,** the definite article is always used with days of the week.

el lunes, **el** martes . . .   *(on) Monday, (on) Tuesday . . .*
los miércoles, **los** jueves . . .   *(on) Wednesdays, (on) Thursdays . . .*

Sábado and **domingo** are the only days of the week that have different forms in the singular and plural.

ACTIVIDAD 5   Citas

Las siguientes personas tienen citas. Expresa eso según el modelo.

⚉ Héctor: lunes   Héctor tiene una cita el lunes.

VARIATION using the negative:
Héctor no tiene cita el lunes.

1. yo: sábado
2. nosotros: miércoles
3. Juana: viernes

4. Enrique: martes
5. mis parientes: domingo
6. tú: jueves

ACTIVIDAD 6   Obligaciones

Di que las siguientes personas siempre tienen que hacer las mismas cosas
los mismos días de la semana.

⟩⟩ El profesor descansa el domingo.   Siempre tiene que descansar los domingos.

1. Las muchachas cocinan el sábado.
2. Llevo los libros a casa el lunes.
3. Trabajamos el miércoles.

4. Margarita viaja el martes.
5. Sacas fotos el viernes.
6. Ud. visita el museo el jueves.

C. Repaso: *al, del*

The prepositions **a** and **de** contract with **el** to form **al** and **del**.

	a + el → al	**de + el → del**
el chico	Luisa habla **al** chico.	Cora habla **del** chico.
el profesor	¿Por qué hablas **al** profesor?	¿Tienes el libro **del** profesor?
el teatro	¡Vamos **al** teatro!	Paco saca una foto **del** teatro.

There is no contraction with **la, los** and **las.**

ACTIVIDAD 7   Entrevistas *(Interviews)*

Mientras *(while)* Luisa habla a ciertas personas, Felipe habla de ellas.
Expresa esto según el modelo.

⟩⟩   el chico mexicano   Luisa habla al chico mexicano.
                          Felipe habla del chico mexicano.

WB
C1

SCRIPT

Act. 4

1. la chica argentina
2. el muchacho canadiense
3. los muchachos españoles
4. el profesor de francés

5. la profesora de inglés
6. las amigas de Luis
7. el abuelo de Carmen
8. el primo de Roberto

D. Repaso: la *a* personal

In the sentences on the left, the direct objects are things. In the sentences
on the right, the direct objects are people. Compare each pair of sentences.

Enrique visita **Puerto Rico**.   Manuel visita **a Teresa**.
Paco busca **los libros de Miguel**.   Ana busca **a los hermanos de Miguel**.
Luisa espera **el autobús**.   Roberto espera **al estudiante mexicano**.

When the direct object is a person, Spanish speakers use the construction:

verb   +   **a**   +   person(s)

⟩⟩   Also note the construction:

    ¿**A quién (quiénes)** invitas al baile?   *Whom do you invite to the dance?*

⟩⟩   The personal **a** is not used after **tener**: Tengo hermanos.

VOCABULARIO PRÁCTICO

Algunos verbos que usan complementos directos

*admirar	to admire	¿A qué tipo de personas **admiras?**
ayudar	to help	**¿Ayudas a** tu papá?
buscar	to look for	**¿Buscan** Uds. **a** Ramón?
*criticar	to criticize	El profesor no **critica a** los estudiantes.
esperar	to wait for	Susana **espera a** Josefina.
invitar	to invite	**Invito a** mis primos al café.
llamar	to call	La mujer **llama a** los niños.
llamar por teléfono	to phone, call up	**Llamo a** mi tía **por teléfono**.
*respetar	to respect	Los niños **respetan a** los abuelos.

ACTIVIDAD 8   Invitaciones

Imagina que estás organizando una fiesta para estudiantes españoles. Di si
vas a invitar a las siguientes personas o no.

⚭   el profesor de francés   Sí (No, no) invito al profesor de francés.

VARIATIONS: with **admirar,
ayudar, criticar, respetar.**

1. el (la) profesor(a) de español
2. el (la) director(a) de la escuela
3. los chicos de la clase de español
4. las chicas de la clase de español
5. mi mejor amigo
6. mi mejor amiga
7. mis padres
8. el (la) presidente del club de español

ACTIVIDAD 9   Tomás el distraído *(Scatterbrained Thomas)*

Tomás no sabe nunca dónde están sus amigos y sus posesiones. Siempre
está buscándolos. Expresa esto según el modelo.

⚭   el libro de español   Tomás busca el libro de español.

1. el profesor de español
2. María
3. Pedro
4. los libros
5. los discos
6. el chico mexicano
7. la chica española
8. la grabadora
9. el tocadiscos
10. sus amigos
11. la calculadora
12. los niños
13. la cámara
14. la pelota de tenis
15. la raqueta de tenis

ACTIVIDAD 10 Preguntas personales

1. ¿Ayudas a tu mejor amigo? ¿a tu mejor amiga? ¿a los otros alumnos?

2. ¿Criticas a los profesores? ¿a tus amigos?

3. ¿Llamas por teléfono a tus amigos? ¿a los amigos de tus amigos?

4. ¿Respetas a tus padres? ¿a tus profesores?

5. ¿Admiras a los actores? ¿al presidente? ¿a Mohamed Alí? ¿a Martin Luther King? ¿a Jorge Washington? ¿a tus profesores? ¿a tus padres?

6. ¿Esperas a veces a tus amigos? ¿a tus hermanos? ¿a tus padres?

Use the appropriate forms of **mi** / **mis** if necessary. Possessive adjectives are formally reviewed on p. 60.

E. Repaso: *ir, ir a*

Review the forms and uses of **ir** *(to go)* in the following sentences.

(yo)	**Voy** a la playa.	**Voy a** nadar.
(tú)	**Vas** al concierto.	**Vas a** escuchar música latina.
(él, ella, Ud.)	**Va** a la escuela.	**Va a** estudiar.
(nosotros)	**Vamos** a casa.	**Vamos a** mirar la televisión.
(vosotros)	**Vais** a la fiesta.	**Vais a** bailar.
(ellos, ellas, Uds.)	**Van** al centro.	**Van a** comprar discos.

To express an action which is going to happen, Spanish speakers use the construction:

$$\textbf{ir a}\ +\ \text{infinitive}$$

María **va a comprar** una raqueta.   *María is going to buy a racket.*

You may review the use of the question word **¿adónde?** with **ir**. **¿Adónde vas?**

ACTIVIDAD 11 Un año en el extranjero *(A year abroad)*

Los siguientes estudiantes van a pasar el año en el extranjero. Di adónde va cada uno y qué idioma va a estudiar.

⤳ Vicente (Nueva York: inglés)   Vicente va a Nueva York.
Va a estudiar inglés.

1. nosotros (París: francés)
2. yo (Roma: italiano)
3. Linda (Madrid: español)
4. tú (Lisboa: portugués)
5. Enrique y Paco (Tokio: japonés)
6. Uds. (Moscú: ruso)
7. Ud. (Chicago: inglés)
8. Luisa y Carmen (Quebec: francés)

VOCABULARIO PRÁCTICO   Algunos lugares

*el almacén	(department) store	*la biblioteca	library
el campo	country	la casa	house, home
el centro	downtown	la ciudad	city
el cine	movie theater	la escuela	school
*el concierto	concert	*la fiesta	fiesta, party
*el mercado	market	la piscina	swimming pool
el restaurante	restaurant	la playa	beach
el teatro	theater	la tienda	store

NOTA: Review the expressions with **casa**:

Voy **a casa**.   *I am going **home**.*
Voy **a la casa de Roberto**.   *I am going **to Roberto's (house)**.*

You may also review: **Estoy en casa. Estoy en la casa de Pedro.**

ACTIVIDAD 12   ¡Un poco de lógica!

En cinco minutos, ¿cuántas frases lógicas puedes crear? Usa **ir a** y los elementos de las columnas A, B y C.

A	B	C
yo	el centro	escuchar música
tú	la biblioteca	bailar
el profesor	la playa	nadar
nosotros	el café	tomar el sol
mis amigos	el almacén	tomar té
	la discoteca	comprar cintas
	el supermercado	mirar revistas
	el cine	trabajar
	el campo	sacar fotos
	el concierto	escuchar una comedia musical
	la fiesta	visitar los monumentos
	la tienda	comprar discos

Voy a la fiesta. Voy a bailar.

ACTIVIDAD 13   Preferencias

Di adónde te gustaría ir los siguientes días.

domingo   El domingo me gustaría ir a la piscina.

1. lunes   3. sábado   5. martes
2. jueves   4. miércoles   6. viernes

TEATROS DEL

IMSS

'87 AÑO DEL TEATRO MEXICANO

EL PORTON

EL PORTON RESTAURANTE

Act. 1

Me llamo Carlos Espinel y tengo diez y seis años.
Soy de Madrid, España.
Soy bastante atlético y juego muchos deportes.
Mis favoritos son el fútbol y el tenis, un deporte muy a la moda
    ahora.
¿Qué tipo de persona soy?
Generalmente soy muy tranquilo, pero en ese momento estoy un
    poco nervioso.
¿Por qué estoy nervioso?
Porque mañana tengo un partido de fútbol muy importante.
Ahora, mientras que mis amigos están en el café escuchando música,
    yo estoy practicando con el equipo.
Ellos me preguntan: Carlos, ¿por qué no pasas
    tiempo con nosotros?
    ¡No es justo! ¡Qué barbaridad!
Tal vez no es justo, pero entre las diversiones,
    hay que escoger.
    Y yo prefiero los deportes.

¿Cómo se llama el chico? ¿Cuántos años tiene? ¿De dónde es?
¿Cómo es? ¿Por qué está nervioso? ¿Dónde están sus amigos?
¿Qué está haciendo él?

STRUCTURES TO REVIEW:
• Estar
• Ser vs. estar
• Verbs in -er and -ir
• The present progressive

a la moda: *in style*

¡Qué barbaridad!:
    What nonsense!

escoger: *choose*

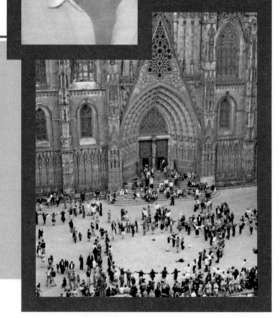

Act. 2

NOTA CULTURAL   OPTIONAL

España fue el país más próspero y poderoso°
del mundo durante los siglos° XVI (dieciséis) y XVII
(diecisiete). Durante estos siglos los españoles ex-
ploraron, conquistaron y colonizaron el Nuevo
Mundo.

Hoy día,° gracias a° la industria y un turismo°
muy desarrollado,° España es todavía un país próspero. Es moderno y dinámico y al mismo tiempo°
mantiene° su larga tradición de cultura.

poderoso *powerful* **siglos** *centuries* **Hoy día** *Today*
gracias a *thanks to* **turismo** *tourism* **desarrollado**
developed **al mismo tiempo** *at the same time* **mantiene**
maintains

• For more information on Spain, see **Vista** 5, pp. 409–421.
• SUGGESTED REALIA: map of Spain, travel brochures,
  posters.

Vocabulario

sustantivo	*la moda	fashion
adjetivos	*justo	fair
	*único	unique, only
expresión	*¡Qué barbaridad!	What nonsense!

CONVERSACIÓN OPTIONAL

Vamos a hablar de tu personalidad.

¿Eres generoso(a)?
¿Eres paciente con todos?
¿Eres una persona optimista?
¿Eres buen(a) compañero(a)?

Ahora vamos a hablar de cómo te sientes actualmente (at present).

¿Estás tranquilo(a) o nervioso(a)?
¿Estás cansado(a)?
¿Estás alegre o triste?

Ahora vamos a hablar de lo que (what) **haces en este momento**

¿Estás en casa o en las escuela?
¿Estás en clase o en la biblioteca?
¿Estás hablando con tus amigos?
¿Estás hablando español?
¿Estás escuchando al profesor?
¿Estás mirando a los otros alumnos?

VOCABULARIO PRÁCTICO   Algunos sentimientos

¿Cómo estás?

alegre

* preocupado

contento

* enamorado

* de buen humor

triste

* irritable

* furioso

* de mal humor

cansado

enfermo

* nervioso

* aburrido

* tranquilo

VOCABULARIO PRÁCTICO

Algunas expresiones de tiempo

ahora	now	* **(por) la mañana**	(in) the morning
hoy	today	* **(por) la tarde**	(in) the afternoon
mañana	tomorrow	* **(por) la noche**	(in) the evening, (at) night
antes (de)	before	**el fin de semana**	(on) the weekend
después (de)	after	**(el sábado) próximo**	next (Saturday)
durante	during	**(el viernes) pasado**	last (Friday)

ACTIVIDAD 1 Preguntas personales

1. ¿Miras la televisión por la noche?
2. ¿Cuándo estudias en casa, por la tarde o por la noche?
3. ¿Vas a jugar después de la clase de español?
4. ¿Vas a nadar el próximo fin de semana?
5. ¿Vas a ir al colegio mañana por la mañana?
6. ¿Vas a ayudar a tu mamá antes de la comida? ¿después de la comida?
7. ¿Quién estudia contigo?   You may want to review the forms **conmigo** / **contigo**.
8. ¿Quién va al cine contigo? ¿al teatro? ¿a la heladería *(ice cream parlor)*?

Ask about student responses. **¿Quién mira la televisión por la noche? ¿Cuándo estudia Karen?**

Estructuras

A. Repaso: *estar*

11

Act. 3

Review the forms of **estar** in the following sentences.

(yo)	**Estoy** en la clase.
(tú)	**Estás** aquí.
(él, ella, Ud.)	**Está** allá.
(nosotros)	**Estamos** en los Estados Unidos.
(vosotros)	**Estáis** en casa.
(ellos, ellas, Uds.)	**Están** con sus amigos.

ACTIVIDAD 2 El sábado

VARIATION: On Monday they are all in class and are not in the places mentioned. **Carmen no está en la playa. Está en la clase.**

Es sábado y las siguientes personas no están en casa. Expresa esto y di dónde están.

SCRIPT
Act. 4

MASTERS p. 4

⟴ Carmen (en la playa)   Carmen no está en casa. Está en la playa.

1. Felipe (en la piscina)
2. Silvia y Mónica (con sus amigos)
3. Luis y Ramón (con sus amigas)
4. nosotros (en el campo)
5. yo (en el centro)
6. tú (en el museo)
7. Ud. (en el cine)
8. Uds. (en el restaurante)
9. Dolores (en el mercado)

B. Repaso: *ser* y *estar*

Compare the uses of the verbs in each pair of sentences.

11

Carlos **es** de México.	Ahora, no **está** en México. **Está** en España.
El Sr. Gómez **es** médico.	Ahora **está** en el hospital.
Elena **es** inteligente.	Ahora **está** muy nerviosa.

Although **ser** and **estar** both mean *to be*, they have very specific uses. **Ser** and **estar** cannot be substituted for one another in most cases.

Ser is used to describe basic traits and permanent characteristics. **Ser** tells *who* the subject is.

Ser is used to indicate:

nationality or origin	Paco **es** mexicano. **Es** de Puebla.
profession	**Somos** estudiantes. El Sr. Montero **es** profesor.
physical traits	Carmen **es** morena. Enrique **es** bajo.
basic personality traits	María **es** inteligente. Pedro **es** generoso.

Estar is used to describe temporary conditions, that is, conditions which may change. **Estar** tells *where* the subject is and *how* the subject feels.

Estar is used to indicate:

location	**Estamos** en la clase. Alberto **está** en Puerto Rico.
physical condition	¿Cómo **estás**? **Estoy** cansado.
feelings	Luisa **está** enamorada. Felipe **está** preocupado.

- After **ser**, nouns designating professions are usually used without **un** or **una**, unless they are modified by an adjective.

  El Sr. Gómez es dentista. Es **un** buen dentista.

- Sometimes the meaning of an adjective changes, depending on whether it is used with **ser** or **estar**.

	ser: permanent trait	**estar:** temporary condition
malo	Lucía **es mala.** *(a bad person)*	Elisa **está mala.** *(sick)*
aburrido	El profesor **es aburrido.** *(boring)*	Los alumnos **están aburridos.** *(bored)*
listo	Emilio **es listo.** *(smart, clever)*	Jaime **está listo.** *(ready, prepared)*

Also:
bonito: Sara **es bonita** (is pretty);   Adela **está bonita** (looks pretty).
verde: : La hierba **es verde** (green is its natural color);   Las bananas **están verdes** (green: unripe).

ACTIVIDAD 3   Lugares de trabajo

A menudo es posible saber dónde trabajan las personas si uno sabe qué
trabajo tienen. Expresa esto según el modelo.

⟴   la Sra. de Montez (profesora: la escuela)   La Sra. de Montez es profesora.
                                                    Está en la escuela.

1. nosotros (alumnos: el colegio)
2. la Srta. Ochoa (secretaria: la oficina)
3. la Sra. de Muñoz (doctora: el hospital)
4. Luisa (estudiante: la universidad)
5. Carmen (ingeniera: el laboratorio)
6. mi padre (farmacéutico: la farmacia)
7. tú (actor: el teatro)
8. yo (presidente: la Casa Blanca)

ACTIVIDAD 4   Sentimientos   OPTIONAL

¿Cómo te sientes en las siguientes situaciones? Expresa tus sentimientos en
frases afirmativas o negativas, usando una de las expresiones del vocabulario.

⟴   Cuando estoy con mis amigos . . .
            Cuando estoy con mis amigos, estoy alegre (de buen humor . . .).

1. Cuando estoy en la clase de
   español . . .
2. Cuando hablo en público . . .
3. Después de un partido de
   básquetbol . . .
4. Cuando estoy en una fiesta . . .
5. Antes de un examen . . .
6. Después de un examen . . .
7. Cuando saco una mala nota . . .
8. Cuando saco una buena nota . . .
9. Cuando tengo una cita con una
   persona simpática . . .
10. Cuando tengo una cita con una
    persona aburrida . . .
11. Cuando no tengo dinero . . .
12. Cuando mis padres me critican . . .
13. Cuando estoy de vacaciones . . .
14. Cuando estoy en un avión . . .

ACTIVIDAD 5 **Retratos** *(Portraits)*

Describe a las siguientes personas en un párrafo corto. Usa las expresiones entre paréntesis y la forma apropiada de **ser** o **estar**.

⚡️ Paco (español / de Sevilla / en Barcelona / estudiante / simpático / enamorado de Felicia / alegre)

> Paco es español. Es de Sevilla, pero ahora no está en Sevilla. Está en Barcelona. Es estudiante. Es muy simpático. Ahora está enamorado de Felicia. ¡Está alegre!

1. Luisa (fotógrafa / mexicana / morena / alta / de Guadalajara / en Los Ángeles / contenta)

2. Roberto (moreno / alto / puertorriqueño / de San Juan / en Nueva York / mecánico / ambicioso)

3. Felipe (en la clase / aburrido / irritable / un alumno malo)

4. Cora (deportista / en el estadio / con amigas / alegre / cansada)

5. mis abuelos (viejos / de Italia / en Boston / enfermos / de buen humor)

6. mis primos (nunca puntuales / nunca listos / preocupados / irritables / nerviosos / antipáticos)

WB
B1, B2

7. yo (triste / enfermo / malo / en casa / aburrido / de mal humor / furioso)

C. Repaso: los verbos que terminan en *-er* y en *-ir*

Review the forms of **aprender** *(to learn)* and **vivir** *(to live)* in the sentences below.

INFINITIVE	**aprender**	**vivir**	ENDINGS
PRESENT			
(yo)	Aprend**o** francés.	Viv**o** en París.	-o
(tú)	Aprend**es** italiano.	Viv**es** en Milán.	-es
(él, ella, Ud.)	Aprend**e** inglés.	Viv**e** en Nueva York.	-e
(nosotros)	Aprend**emos** español.	Viv**imos** en Lima.	-emos, -imos
(vosotros)	Aprend**éis** japonés.	Viv**ís** en Tokio.	-éis, -ís
(ellos, ellas, Uds.)	Aprend**en** portugués.	Viv**en** en Río.	-en

Many verbs ending in **-er** and **-ir** in the infinitive are conjugated like **aprender** and **vivir**. They are regular **-er** and **-ir** verbs.

VOCABULARIO PRÁCTICO   Verbos que terminan en –er y en –ir

aprender (algo)	to learn (something)
beber (leche)	to drink (milk)
comer (dulces)	to eat (candy)
comprender (la tarea)	to understand (the homework)
*__correr__ (rápidamente, despacio)	to run (fast, slowly)
creer (la verdad)	to believe (the truth)
*__deber__ (diez dólares)	to owe (ten dollars)
leer (un cuento)	to read (a story)
*__responder__ (a una carta)	to answer (a letter)
vender (helados)	to sell (ice cream)
ver (a alguien)	to see (someone)
*__abrir__ (la puerta)	to open (the door)
escribir (una carta)	to write (a letter)
recibir (una tarjeta)	to receive, get (a card)
vivir (con la familia)	to live (with the family)

NOTAS: 1. Note the construction: **aprender a** + infinitive

¿**Aprendes a tocar** la guitarra?   *Are you learning to play* the guitar?

2. The verb **ver** is irregular only in the **yo** form: **veo.** Note the expressions:

¡**Vamos a ver!** ⎫
¡**A ver!** ⎬ *Let's see!*

3. The construction   **deber** + infinitive   is used to express an obligation.

Debemos respetar a los profesores.   *We should (ought to)* respect the teachers.

ACTIVIDAD 6   Las bebidas nacionales *(National drinks)*

Las siguientes personas beben las bebidas nacionales de los países en donde viven. Expresa eso según el modelo.

Carlos (en el Brasil: café)   Carlos vive en el Brasil. Bebe café.

1. yo (en los Estados Unidos: Coca-Cola)
2. Felipe (en Inglaterra: té)
3. nosotros (en la Argentina: mate)
4. mis amigos (en Francia: vino)
5. Lucía (en Colombia: café)
6. tú (en Guatemala: chocolate)

• **Mate** is an herb tea commonly drunk in Argentina and Paraguay.
• ADDITIONAL CUES: **Ud.: (en Italia: vino);
Uds.: (en Puerto Rico: Coca-Cola).**

ACTIVIDAD 7 Preguntas personales

1. ¿Aprendes italiano? ¿francés?

2. ¿Aprendes a tocar la guitarra? ¿a tocar el piano? ¿a jugar al tenis? ¿a esquiar?

Ask about student responses. **¿Aprende italiano Roberto? ¿Quiénes aprenden francés?**

3. ¿Comprendes bien cuando el (la) profesor(a) habla español?

4. ¿En casa bebes leche? ¿Coca-Cola? ¿té? ¿agua?

5. ¿En casa comes muchas frutas? ¿vegetales? ¿tacos?

6. ¿Comes bien en la cafetería de la escuela?

7. ¿Te gusta correr? ¿Corres rápidamente o despacio? ¿Cuántos kilómetros corres?

8. ¿Recibes muchas cartas? ¿De quién?

9. ¿Respondes inmediatamente cuando recibes una carta?

10. ¿Escribes poemas? ¿cuentos? ¿artículos para el periódico de la escuela?

11. ¿Lees mucho? ¿Lees poesía? ¿novelas? ¿cuentos de ciencia-ficción? ¿historietas (comics)?

12. ¿Dónde vives? ¿Vives en una ciudad o en el campo?

13. ¿Ves a menudo a tus abuelos? ¿Dónde viven?

14. ¿Ves a menudo a tus primos? ¿Dónde viven?

15. ¿Crees en los fantasmas (ghosts)? ¿en el Papá Noel? ¿en la percepción extrasensorial? ¿en la amistad (friendship)? ¿en la vida extraterrestre? ¿en la vida en Marte (Mars)?

16. En tu opinión, ¿deben los hijos ayudar a sus padres? ¿Deben los estudiantes respetar a los profesores? ¿Debe un estudiante ayudar a un compañero en un examen?

OPTIONAL

May be assigned as a special challenge activity.

ACTIVIDAD 8 ¡Un poco de lógica!

En cinco minutos, ¿cuántas frases lógicas (afirmativas o negativas) puedes crear? Usa **estar** y los elementos de las columnas A, B, C y D. ¡Estudia el modelo!

A	B	C	D
yo	alegre	comer	cartas
Mari-Carmen	contento	beber	buenas / malas notas
el gato	de buen / mal humor	correr	buenas noticias (news)
el Sr. Camacho	cansado	leer	diez kilómetros
nosotros	triste	recibir	leche
mis amigos	preocupado		dulces
			helados
			una novela interesante / triste

WB
C1, C2,
C3

 (No) Estoy de buen humor cuando (no) recibo cartas.

D. Repaso: *estar* + el participio presente

Review the present progressive in the sentences below.

Cora **está escuchando** discos.	*Cora is listening to records.*
Pedro y Luis **están comiendo**.	*Pedro and Luis are eating.*
Estoy escribiendo una carta.	*I am writing a letter.*

To express an action which is currently in progress, use the construction:

$$\boxed{\textbf{estar} \quad + \quad \text{present participle}}$$

In such constructions, only **estar** changes with the subject. The present participle is formed as follows:

infinitive	−	-ar	+	**ando**	cantar	**cantando**
		-er		**iendo**	beber	**bebiendo**
		-ir		**iendo**	vivir	**viviendo**

The present participle of verbs ending in **–eer** is formed by replacing **-er** by **-yendo**.

$$\text{leer} \rightarrow \textbf{leyendo} \qquad \text{¿Qué estás \textbf{leyendo} ahora?}$$

The present progressive occurs much less frequently in Spanish than in English. It is used to emphasize that an action is occurring *now*. It is not used to refer to regular activities or to future actions.

Carlos **repara** coches.	*Carlos repairs cars.* (generally speaking)
Carlos **está reparando** un Mercedes.	*Carlos is repairing a Mercedes.* (now)

¿Por qué el SEAT 127 es el coche más vendido?

SEAT-127

1.000.000 de coches fabricados en España, 4.000.000 en el mundo.

ACTIVIDAD 9   En la biblioteca

VARIATION: The students have just heard there is an exam next period. **Carlos está estudiando. No está mirando una revista.**

Los siguientes estudiantes que están en la biblioteca no están estudiando.
Expresa esto y di lo que están haciendo.

 Carlos (mirar una revista)   Carlos no está estudiando.
                                                    Está mirando una revista.

1. Felipe (mirar a las chicas)
2. Isabel y Patricia (mirar a los chicos)
3. nosotros (hablar con nuestros amigos)
4. tú (hablar con el profesor)
5. yo (comer dulces)

6. Uds. (escuchar a un muchacho)
7. Pilar (escribir una tarjeta)
8. Ud. (leer un periódico)
9. Margarita (abrir una carta)
10. Esteban y Jorge (descansar)

ACTIVIDAD 10   ¡Un poco de lógica!   OPTIONAL

May be assigned as a special challenge activity.

¿Dónde están y qué están haciendo las siguientes personas? En cinco
minutos, ¿cuántas frases lógicas puedes escribir? Usa los elementos de
A, B y C.

A	B	C
yo	en casa	trabajar
el (la) profesor(a)	en clase	estudiar
mi papá	en la oficina	hablar por teléfono
mi mamá	en la Casa Blanca	tomar café
mis hermanos	en el restaurante	mirar la televisión
mis amigos	en el centro	comprar revistas
el presidente	en el café	comer helados
nosotros		beber Coca-Cola
		aprender español
		escribir cartas
		leer un cuento
		ayudar a los estudiantes

 Ahora mi mamá está en la oficina.   Está trabajando.

Estamos
haciendo futuro.

Telefónica

Variedades   Unos ruidos en español

¿Son diferentes los ruidos° para las personas que hablan español y las personas que hablan inglés? ¡Claro que no! Pero los hispanos expresan los ruidos en una manera diferente.

ruidos: *sounds*

Aquí tienes una lista de algunos ruidos de la vida diaria.°

la vida diaria: *everyday life*

VISTA

Los Estados Unidos

1

Un poco de historia

¿La historia de los Estados Unidos en un libro de español? ¡Sí, claro! Pero no vamos a hablar ni de Jorge Washington ni° del Cuatro de Julio. Vamos a recordar otros hechos° que también son memorables.

Juan Ponce de León

1513

El conquistador español Juan Ponce de León accidentalmente descubre la Florida. Lo que realmente quiere encontrar es la fuente° de la eterna juventud.° Según la leyenda,° la gente vuelve a ser° joven cuando se baña en esta fuente.

1528

Un tornado destruye una expedición española cerca de las costas de Texas. Álvar Núñez Cabeza de Vaca es uno de los pocos° hombres que sobreviven.° Durante ocho años tiene aventuras fantásticas, huyendo° de los indios de Texas o viviendo entre ellos como esclavo.°

1539

Cerca de Tampa, Florida, 570 hombres y 220 caballos° desembarcan. Dos años más tarde, esta expedición, bajo el mando de° Hernando de Soto, descubre el río° Misisipí.

1565

Pedro Menéndez de Avilés funda° la ciudad de San Agustín en la Florida. Es la primera ciudad permanente de origen europeo en los Estados Unidos.

Pedro Menéndez de Avilés

1610

Pedro de Peralta funda otra ciudad importante: la Villa Real de la Santa Fe de San Francisco. Hoy esta ciudad es la capital del estado de Nuevo México y se llama simplemente Santa Fe.

ni . . . ni *neither . . . nor* **hechos** *facts* **fuente** *fountain* **juventud** *youth* **leyenda** *legend* **vuelve a ser** *are again* **pocos** *few* **sobreviven** *survive* **huyendo** *fleeing* **esclavo** *slave* **caballos** *horses* **bajo el mando de** *under* **río** *River* **funda** *founds*

1718

El padre Antonio Olivares funda la Misión de San Antonio de Valero para cristianizar a los indios de Texas. Así empieza la ciudad de San Antonio. Hoy la misión del padre Olivares se llama El Álamo.

1769

Comienza° la colonización de California. Fray Junípero Serra, un sacerdote° franciscano, funda la primera misión, San Diego de Alcalá. En menos de 60 años los franciscanos fundan 20 misiones más. Todas estas misiones forman una cadena° por una ruta que todavía se llama El Camino Real.°

1819

La Florida deja de ser española. España cede° este territorio a los Estados Unidos por cinco millones de dólares.

1836

En San Antonio ocurre una batalla famosa. Bajo el mando de David Crockett, 183 texanos mueren° defendiendo el Álamo. El ejército° mexicano batalla con los separatistas texanos. Texas (entonces parte de México) declara su independencia.

1910

Comienza una fuerte emigración de mexicanos hacia los Estados Unidos. De 1910 a 1930, medio millón de mexicanos vienen a vivir en este país, especialmente en los estados fronterizos.

1917

El Congreso declara ciudadanos° de los Estados Unidos a los puertorriqueños. (España cedió° Puerto Rico a los Estados Unidos en 1898.) Miles° de puertorriqueños comienzan a emigrar a las ciudades industriales de este país.

1966

Comienzan los «vuelos° de la libertad». Bajo el auspicio del gobierno° de los Estados Unidos, de 3000 a 4000 refugiados cubanos comienzan a llegar a Miami cada mes. Son cubanos que no quieren vivir bajo el régimen de Fidel Castro.

1990

Unos diecinueve millones de las personas que viven en los Estados Unidos son de origen hispano.

El Álamo

Comienza *Begins* **sacerdote** *priest* **cadena** *chain* **El Camino Real** *The Royal Way*
cede *gives up* **mueren** *die* **ejército** *army* **ciudadanos** *citizens* **cedió** *ceded*
Miles *Thousands* **vuelos** *flights* **gobierno** *government*

43

MÉXICO-AMERICANO: UN CORRIDO

Rumel Fuentes es un méxico-americano del estado de Texas. A su padre le gustan°
mucho los corridos, canciones° típicas del pueblo mexicano que hablan de la vida
diaria.° Desde niño, Rumel los oye° cantar en casa. Más tarde él escribe sus
propios° corridos.

El corrido MÉXICO-AMERICANO muestra° el orgullo° de Rumel, que pertenece°
a dos países° y tiene dos culturas. Para comprender al méxico-americano, es
necesario comprender que viene° de dos mundos.

El Grito Vol. 6 No. 3 Spring 1973. Copyright © Rumel Fuentes.

Por mi madre yo soy mexicano,
Por destino soy americano,
Yo soy de la raza de oro,
Yo soy méxico-americano.

Yo te comprendo el inglés
También te hablo el castellano,
Yo soy de la raza noble,
Yo soy méxico-americano.

Zacatecas a Minnesota,
De Tijuana a Nueva York,
Dos países son mi tierra,°
Los defiendo con mi honor.

Dos idiomas° y dos países,
Dos culturas tengo yo,
Es mi suerte y tengo orgullo,
Porque así lo manda° Dios.

44

le gustan *likes*   **canciones** *songs*   **vida diaria** *daily life*   **oye** *hears*   **sus propios** *his own*
muestra *shows*   **orgullo** *pride*   **pertenece** *belongs*   **países** *countries*   **viene** *comes*
tierra *homeland*   **idiomas** *languages*   **manda** *commands*

Población hispana en algunas ciudades norteamericanas

CIUDAD	POBLACIÓN TOTAL	POBLACIÓN DE ORIGEN HISPANO (%)	
Miami	380.000	194.000	(51%)
San Antonio	843.000	422.000	(50%)
Los Ángeles	3.215.000	815.000	(25%)
Nueva York	7.165.000	1.406.000	(20%)
Chicago	2.992.000	423.000	(14%)

Pequeñas biografías

Aquí presentamos una galería de hispanos famosos. ¿Sabes quiénes son?

RITA MORENO

Rita Moreno es la puertorriqueña más famosa del mundo del espectáculo.° Actriz de cine, ella apareció° en películas clásicas como *Singing in the Rain, The King and I* y *West Side Story.*

Es la única actriz que tiene los cuatro premios° más importantes de su profesión: ha ganado° un «Oscar», un «Tony», un «Grammy» y dos «Emmies». Todos recuerdan° su participación en programas de televisión para niños como *Los Muppets* y *La Compañía Eléctrica.* Su interés en los niños incluye° las causas humanitarias. Es miembro° de la junta directiva° de la «Free Arts Clinic» en Los Ángeles, que presenta obras de teatro a los niños pobres. Orgullosa° de su herencia,° lucha por mejorar° la vida° de los hispanos.

PLÁCIDO DOMINGO

Plácido Domingo es uno de los mejores tenores del mundo de la ópera. Nació° en España pero creció° en México donde empezó su carrera° a los 18 años. Se conoce° por su magnífica voz° y su excepcional calidad° de actor. Ha cantado° en los teatros de ópera más importantes del mundo.

Plácido no sólo se conoce por ser gran músico, sino° también por ser gran amigo de la humanidad y de su patria adoptiva.° En 1985, cuando un terremoto° devastó una parte de la ciudad de México, Plácido tomó parte° en las operaciones de salvamento.° Ayudó a buscar a los perdidos° y, mediante° la televisión, pidió ayuda a los Estados Unidos. Poco tiempo después, viajó por el mundo° dando° una serie de conciertos a beneficio de° las familias de las víctimas. Todos los mexicanos le agradecen° mucho su sincera compasión y su generosa labor.

espectáculo *entertainment* **apareció** *appeared* **desempeñó** *she played* **premios** *awards* **ha ganado** *she has won* **recuerdan** *remember* **incluye** *includes* **miembro** *member* **junta directiva** *board of directors* **Orgullosa** *Proud* **herencia** *heritage* **lucha por mejorar** *she strives to improve* **vida** *life* **Nació** *He was born* **creció** *he grew up* **carrera** *career* **Se conoce** *He is known* **voz** *voice* **calidad** *quality* **Ha cantado** *He has sung* **sino** *but* **patria adoptiva** *adopted country* **terremoto** *earthquake* **tomó parte** *participated* **salvamento** *rescue* **los perdidos** *those who were lost* **mediante** *via* **viajó por el mundo** *travelled throughout the world* **dando** *giving* **a beneficio de** *to benefit* **agradecen** *are grateful for*

de grandes hispanos

JAVIER PÉREZ DE CUÉLLAR

Javier Pérez de Cuéllar, originario° del Perú, es Secretario General de la Organización de las Naciones Unidas (ONU) desde° 1982. Empezó su carrera diplomática en la embajada° peruana en Francia, Inglaterra, Bolivia y Brasil. También fue el embajador° del Perú en Suiza, la Unión Soviética, Polonia y Venezuela. Más tarde sirvió en la ONU como representante del Perú en la Asamblea General y en el Consejo de Seguridad.°

El secretario General de la ONU es uno de los más importantes puestos del mundo. En esta posición, Pérez de Cuéllar desempeña un papel crucial en mantener la paz° y la armonía° entre las naciones del mundo.

ROBERTO CLEMENTE

Roberto Clemente fue° uno de los grandes jugadores° hispanos de béisbol de todos los tiempos. Tuvo° una carrera impresionante con los Piratas de Pittsburgh. Clemente recibió su primer contrato profesional en Puerto Rico a la edad de 17 años. Desde entonces° recibió todos los premios que un jugador de béisbol puede recibir. Él es el primer jugador hispano elegido° miembro del Salón de la Fama.° Pero Clemente fue más que un buen jugador de béisbol; luchó° por las causas humanitarias. Murió° trágicamente en un accidente de avión° cuando iba° a Nicaragua a ayudar a las víctimas de un terremoto.

Puerto Rico todavía recuerda al atleta más famoso de la historia de la isla. Recientemente,° en San Juan, se presentó° *Clemente,* una obra musical basada° en la vida del gran jugador. También en su honor existe la "Ciudad Deportiva Roberto Clemente" en San Juan. Éste es un lugar° donde los jóvenes de todas las razas° y clases sociales vienen para competir juntos° en deportes.

originario *native* **desde** *since* **embajada** *embassy* **embajador** *ambassador* **Consejo de Seguridad** *Security Council* **paz** *peace* **armonía** *harmony* **fue** *was* **jugadores** *players* **Tuvo** *He had* **Desde entonces** *From then on* **elegido** *elected* **Salón de la Fama** *Hall of Fame* **luchó** *he fought* **Murió** *He died* **avión** *airplane* **iba** *he was going* **Recientemente** *Recently* **se presentó** *was performed* **basada** *based* **lugar** *place* **razas** *races* **juntos** *together*

47

EL RODEO Y OTRAS COSAS DE ORIGEN ESPAÑOL

¿Qué es un rodeo sin «broncos»?
¿Qué es una película del oeste sin vaqueros?°
¿Qué es la comida norteamericana sin rosbif o hamburguesas?

Y todo porque a lugares como Texas y Nuevo México, los españoles
trajeron caballos,° vacas,° toros° y otros animales.

Los toros y las vacas vinieron de Europa. Las primeras cabezas de
ganado° llegaron al Caribe en el segundo viaje de Colón. Del Caribe
pasaron a México y de México a los Estados Unidos.

Con los toros y las vacas, llegaron los vaqueros. Los primeros vaqueros
de los Estados Unidos fueron españoles y mexicanos. Los norteamericanos
aprendieron a ser vaqueros cuando ocuparon el lejano° oeste.° Y así muchas
palabras españolas se hicieron° inglesas.

Éstas, por ejemplo:

español	*inglés*	*español*	*inglés*
lazo	lasso	corral	corral
la reata	lariat	bonanza	bonanza
vaquero	buckaroo	rancho	ranch
rodeo	rodeo		

vaqueros *cowboys*   **caballos** *horses*   **vacas** *cows*   **toros** *bulls*   **ganado** *cattle*   **lejano** *far*
oeste *West*   **se hicieron** *became*

La cocina del suroeste

¿Te gusta el chile con carne? Éste, y otros platos° populares en el suroeste,° son adaptaciones norteamericanas de la cocina° mexicana.

En Texas, el chile con carne es un plato especial. Para muchos texanos es otro de los símbolos de Texas, como el escudo° y la bandera° del estado.

Cuando el chile con carne se prepara en casa, huele° muy bien y . . . ¡es exquisito! Para prepararlo necesitas:

1 libra° de carne molida°

1 cebolla° mediana° en rodajas°

2 dientes de ajo picados°

3 tazas de jugo de tomate

2 cucharadas° de chile en polvo°

1 cucharada de comino° molido

sal y pimienta al gusto°

Preparación:

1. Dora° la carne en una sartén,° con la cebolla y los ajos.
2. A la carne dorada° échale° el jugo de tomate y todos los condimentos: el chile, el comino, la sal y la pimienta.
3. Ahora, deja que la carne se cueza° despacio,° durante una hora. ¡Eso es todo! Fácil, ¿verdad?

NOTA: Los puristas dicen que el chile auténtico no lleva frijoles. Si lo que más te gusta del chile son los frijoles, olvídate de esta receta.°

platos *dishes*   **suroeste** *Southwest*   **cocina** *cooking*   **escudo** *coat of arms*   **bandera** *flag*   **huele** *it smells*
libra *pound*   **molida** *ground*   **cebolla** *onion*   **mediana** *medium-sized*   **rodajas** *slices*   **dientes de ajo**
picados *cloves of chopped garlic*   **cucharadas** *spoonfuls*   **en polvo** *powder*   **comino** *cumin*
al gusto *to taste*   **Dora** *Brown*   **sartén** *frying pan*   **dorada** *browned*   **échale** *add*   **se cueza** *cook*
despacio *slowly*   **receta** *recipe*

Los caballos°
tienen nombres españoles

El caballo no es un animal de origen americano. Los primeros caballos llegaron° al continente americano con los conquistadores españoles. Por eso varios° tipos de caballos tienen nombres° que vienen de° palabras españolas.

La palabra inglesa «mustang» viene de la palabra española «mesteño». Mesteño significa salvaje.° Este tipo de caballo vive en un estado de semi-libertad en las mesetas y desiertos del suroeste° de los Estados Unidos.

Otro tipo de caballo es el «jennet». La palabra «jennet» en inglés es una transformación de la palabra española «jinete».° Un «jennet» es un caballo de mezcla° árabe y española. Son pequeños y muy trabajadores.°

Los palominos son caballos hispanoamericanos que viven en el suroeste de los Estados Unidos. Se llaman palominos porque tienen el mismo color que las palomas.°

caballos *horses*   **llegaron** *arrived*   **varios** *several*
nombres *names*   **vienen de** *come from*   **salvaje** *wild*
suroeste *southwest*   **jinete** *rider, jockey*
mezcla *mixture*   **trabajadores** *hard-working*
palomas *doves*

Los artistas del barrio

San Francisco. Estamos en la esquina° de las calles Misión y Veintidós ... ¿O es la Veinticuatro? Bueno, no importa. Éste es el corazón° del barrio chicano de San Francisco.

Los niños juegan en el parque. Los jóvenes conversan en una esquina. La gente va y viene. Nadie se da cuenta° ... Sólo nosotros. Éste no es un barrio. ¡Es un museo! Estamos rodeados de° murales.

¡Qué artistas los chicanos!

Actividades culturales

1. *Escoge° uno de los españoles de las páginas 42–43 y prepara un informe° sobre° su vida y sus logros.°*

2. *En el periódico, busca un artículo sobre un(a) hispano(a). Prepara un resumen° del artículo en español para la clase.*

3. *Prepara una lista de 10–15 palabras inglesas de origen español.*

4. *Prepara una lista de 10–15 ciudades norteamericanas con nombre° de origen español.*

5. *Ve° al supermercado° y prepara una lista de los productos agrícolas típicamente hispánicos que allí se venden (por ejemplo: chile, frijoles, tacos). Si es posible, ilustra la lista con etiquetas.°*

Escoge *Choose*   **informe** *report*   **sobre** *about*   **logros** *accomplishments*   **resumen** *summary*
nombre *name*   **Ve** *Go*   **supermercado** *supermarket*   **etiquetas** *labels*

Unidad 2

Nuestro mundo personal

2.1 Un psicotest: ¿sociable o no?

2.2 ¡Así es la vida!

2.3 Intercambios

2.4 ¡No hay democracia!

VARIEDADES Dos poetas españoles: Machado y Bécquer

OBJECTIVES

Communication

In this unit, students use Spanish to talk about:
- Dating and social life
- Friendships and free-time activities
- Family relations and conflicts
- People in their community

Language

The process of review and expansion is continued in this unit, which focuses on the following structures:
- Possessive adjectives
- Demonstrative adjectives and pronouns
- Nominalization with **el** (**el** + **de**, **el** + adjective, **el que**)
- Direct and indirect object pronouns
- The construction **me gusta(n)**
- **Decir, saber, conocer**

Culture

The cultural themes of this unit relate mainly to leisure-time activities: music, the beach, the movies.

 Review   Modules 8, 11, 12, 13, 14, 19, 20

53

Un psicotest: ¿sociable o no?

Act. 1

Conoces a tu familia y tus amigos muy bien, ¿verdad? ¡Por supuesto! Pero hay otras personas fuera de tu familia y de tus amigos que figuran en tu vida . . . personas que ves a menudo, quizá todos los días . . . ¿Conoces bien a esas personas? ¡Vamos a ver!

fuera de: *outside of*
quizá: *maybe*

12

	A muy bien	**B** solamente un poco	**C** muy poco	
1. El cartero Lo conozco . . .	☐	☐	☐	cartero: *mailman*
2. La secretaria de la escuela La conozco . . .	☐	☐	☐	
3. El (la) director(a) de la escuela Lo (la) conozco . . .	☐	☐	☐	
4. Los padres de tus compañeros Los conozco . . .	☐	☐	☐	
5. Los amigos de tus amigos Los conozco . . .	☐	☐	☐	
6. Las amigas de tus amigas Las conozco . . .	☐	☐	☐	
7. Tus vecinos Los conozco . . .	☐	☐	☐	vecinos: *neighbors*
8. Los amigos de tus vecinos Los conozco . . .	☐	☐	☐	

INTERPRETACIÓN

Ahora, marca   dos puntos por cada respuesta «A»
                 un punto por cada respuesta «B»
                 cero por cada respuesta «C»

Suma tus puntos.

Si tienes catorce puntos (o más) . . .

Eres una persona muy sociable porque te gusta conocer a otros.
Pero, ¿los conoces bien o sólo superficialmente?

Si tienes entre ocho y trece puntos . . .

Eres sociable y amable con todos. Eres realista también porque sabes
que no es posible ser el amigo íntimo de todos.

entre: between
amable: kind

Si tienes entre cuatro y siete puntos . . .

Eres tímido(a) o indiferente al mundo que te rodea.

rodea: surrounds

Si tienes menos de tres puntos . . .

¿Por qué no te gusta la compañía de otros?

Act. 2

NOTA CULTURAL   OPTIONAL

El respeto

En los países hispanos, el respeto° a los demás°
es muy importante y se manifiesta° en muchas for-
mas. Algunas de las manifestaciones de respeto
son la cortesía, la amabilidad,° la consideración y
el cariño.°

Dentro de la familia no sólo se tiene respeto a
los padres, sino también a los abuelos que ocupan
un lugar muy importante, y a los hermanos mayores
que son considerados como modelos.°

Entre los amigos, el respeto se muestra° a través
de° la sinceridad y el cariño. Es común° ver chicas
y chicos besarse en la mejilla° o darse un abrazo.

A los servidores públicos° como el cartero, el

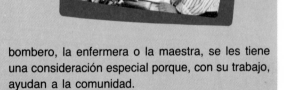

bombero, la enfermera o la maestra, se les tiene
una consideración especial porque, con su trabajo,
ayudan a la comunidad.

el respeto *respect* **a los demás** *for others* **se manifiesta** *it
is demonstrated* **la amabilidad** *kindness* **el cariño**
affection **modelos** *role models* **se muestra** *is
demonstrated* **a través de** *through* **común**
common **besarse en la mejilla** *kiss each other on the
cheek* **servidores públicos** *public servants*

¿Cuáles son algunas de las manifestaciones de respeto?
¿Por qué existe una consideración especial para los servidores públicos?

—— Vocabulario ——

sustantivos	**las noticias**	the news	* **una respuesta**	answer, response
	* **una sorpresa**	surprise		
adjetivos	* **amable**	kind	**mismo**	same
expresiones	* **quizá**	perhaps, maybe	* **fuera (de)**	outside (of)
	* **tan**	so	* **solamente**	only
	un poco	a little	**todos**	all, everyone

Vamos a hablar del futuro.

¿Deseas ser policía? ¿Te gustaría dirigir
(*direct*) el tráfico?

¿Deseas ser cartero? ¿Te gustaría
entregar (*deliver*) cartas y tarjetas?

¿Deseas ser mecánico(a)? ¿Te gustaría
reparar coches y motos?

¿Deseas ser gerente (*manager*) en un almacén
(*department store*)? ¿Te gustaría ser
el (la) jefe(a) (*boss*) de los dependientes
(*clerks*)?

¿Deseas ser empleado(a) de correos? ¿Te
gustaría vender sellos (*stamps*)?

¿Deseas ser médico(a)? ¿Te gustaría cuidar
a los pacientes?

¿Deseas ser enfermero(a)? ¿Te gustaría
cuidar a los enfermos?

¿Deseas ser dentista? ¿Te gustaría
arreglar (*fix*) los dientes?

Vamos a hablar del presente.

¿Trabajas como camarero(a)? ¿Dónde
trabajas? ¿en un café? ¿en un
restaurante? ¿en una heladería?

¿Trabajas como dependiente(a)? ¿Dónde
trabajas? ¿en una tienda? ¿en un
almacén?

¿Trabajas como mecánico(a)? ¿Dónde
trabajas? ¿en una estación de servicio?
¿en una agencia de coches?

Act. 3

WB
V1

13–19

VOCABULARIO PRÁCTICO   Las personas que vemos a menudo

en **la calle**	
*un(a) **vecino(a)** (*neighbor*)	**Los vecinos** son las personas que viven en la misma calle.
*un **policía**	**El policía** dirige (*directs*) el tráfico.
en **el café** o *la **heladería** (*ice cream parlor*)	
un(a) **camarero(a)** (*waiter, waitress*)	**El camarero** les sirve café o helado a los clientes.
en **el almacén** (*department store*)	
*el (la) **gerente** (*manager*)	**El gerente** es *el jefe (*boss*) de los dependientes.
*un(a) **dependiente(a)** (*clerk*)	**La dependienta** les vende varios artículos a los clientes.
en **la estación de servicio**	
*un **mecánico**	**El mecánico** repara los coches.
en *el **correo** (*post office*)	
un(a) **empleado(a)** (*employee*)	**El empleado** de correos vende los *sellos (*stamps*).
*un **cartero** (*mail carrier*)	**El cartero** entrega (*delivers*) las cartas.
en *el **hospital**	
*el (la) **médico(a)**	**Los médicos** ayudan a los *enfermos (*sick people*).
el (la) **enfermero(a)** (*nurse*)	**Las enfermeras** cuidan (*take care of*) a los pacientes.
el (la) **dentista**	**Los dentistas** arreglan (*fix*) los dientes.

56 EXTRA VOCAB.: **En la oficina: el (la) secretario(a), el (la) recepcionista. En la fábrica** (factory): **el (la) obrero(a)**
(worker); **el (la) ingeniero(a)** (engineer); **el (la) laboratorista** (lab technician). **En la casa municipal** (city hall): **el alcalde** (mayor);
el político, el juez (judge); **el (la) abogado(a)** (lawyer). **En el banco: el (la) banquero(a); el (la) cajero(a)** (teller, cashier). **Los
servicios: el electricista; el plomero** (plumber); **el bombero** (fireman).

Estructuras

A. Repaso: *conocer*

Review the forms and uses of **conocer** *(to know)*.

(yo)	**Conozco** a Pedro.
(tú)	**Conoces** a Mónica.
(él, ella, Ud.)	**Conoce** Madrid.
(nosotros)	**Conocemos** bien al profesor.
(vosotros)	**¿Conocéis** a los estudiantes?
(ellos, ellas, Uds.)	**Conocen** Nueva York muy bien.

> **Conocer** means *to know* in the sense of *to be acquainted with, to be familiar with*. It is always used with nouns and pronouns referring to people and places.

> **Conocer** and most verbs ending in **–cer** and **–cir** have an irregular **yo** form: **c → zc**.

ACTIVIDAD 1   Turismo

Un grupo de estudiantes norteamericanos está visitando Madrid. Ésta es su segunda visita. Di que ellos conocen los siguientes lugares.

> Eric: el Museo del Prado   Eric conoce el Museo del Prado.

1. yo: el Parque del Retiro
2. nosotros: la Plaza Mayor
3. Uds.: la Puerta del Sol
4. los chicos: el Escorial
5. Ud.: el Rastro *(the Flea Market)*
6. Linda: el Palacio Real

- The Prado Museum, opened in 1823, has a superb collection of Spanish, Flemish, and Italian masterpieces (especially works of Goya, Velázquez, and Bosch). The Retiro, behind the Prado, is Madrid's most popular park. The Plaza Mayor dates back to the 17th century. The Palacio Real was built in the 18th century. In Spain all distances are measured from the historic Puerta del Sol. The Rastro is most active on Sunday mornings. The Escorial, 31 miles from Madrid, is the burial place of Spain's kings and queens.
- SUGGESTED REALIA: reproductions of paintings in the Prado, map of Madrid, travel brochures.

VOCABULARIO PRÁCTICO

verbos que terminan en –cer

*merecer	to deserve	**Merezco** una buena nota.
obedecer	to obey	No **obedezco** siempre a mis padres.
ofrecer	to offer, to give	Te **ofrezco** consejos, pero dinero, ¡no!
*parecer	to seem, to look	Carlos **parece** triste.
*pertenecer	to belong (to), to be a member (of)	**Pertenezco** a un club de tenis.

verbos que terminan en –cir

conducir	to drive	Mi mamá **conduce** muy bien.
traducir	to translate	El profesor **traduce** un poema.

In many Latin American countries, the verb **manejar** (to drive) is used.

ACTIVIDAD 2   Preguntas personales

1. ¿Conduces el coche de tus padres?
2. ¿Conduce bien tu papá? ¿tu mamá? ¿Qué tipo de coche conducen?
3. En la clase de español, ¿traduces las palabras nuevas? ¿las lecturas?
4. ¿Mereces una «A» en la clase de español? ¿Qué nota mereces en la clase de inglés? ¿en la clase de matemáticas? ¿en la clase de ciencias?
5. ¿Obedeces las reglas (rules) de la escuela? ¿las reglas de la casa? ¿las reglas de la cortesía?
6. ¿Ahora parece el (la) profesor(a) contento(a)? ¿ de buen humor? ¿cansado(a)?
7. ¿Les ofreces chocolate a tus amigos? ¿consejos? ¿ayuda?

WB
A1

Ask about student responses. **¿Conduce Bob el coche de sus padres?**
Note: Possessives are reviewed in Section C.

B. Repaso: el uso de *de* para indicar la posesión

Note the use of **de** and the word order in the following sentences.

¿Dónde está el radio **de Elena?**	*Where is **Elena's** radio?*
No tengo los libros **del profesor.**	*I do not have **the teacher's** books.*
Paco es el hermano **del amigo de Luisa.**	*Paco is **Luisa's friend's** brother.*
	*Paco is the brother **of Luisa's friend**.*

To indicate possession or relationship, Spanish speakers often use the construction:

Remind the students of the contraction **de + el → del**.

$$\boxed{\text{noun } + \textbf{ de } + \text{ (article) } + \text{ noun}}$$

De is used in the following expressions:

ser de	*to belong to*	La guitarra **es de** Elena.
¿de quién(es) ...**?**	*whose?*	**¿De quién** son los discos?

Note also the construction: definite article + **de** + noun.   OPTIONAL

¿Tienes las revistas de Carmen?	*Do you have Carmen's magazines?*
No, pero tengo **las de Luisa.**	*No, but I have **Luisa's (those of Luisa, those belonging to Luisa)**.*
No conozco a la hermana de José, pero conozco a **la de Pilar.**	*I do not know José's sister, but I know **Pilar's (that of Pilar)**.*

In the above constructions, the definite article replaces a noun.   This is new material.

las de Luisa = las revistas de Luisa
la de Pilar = la hermana de Pilar

ACTIVIDAD 3   Curiosidad

Quieres saber cómo se llaman los amigos y parientes de las siguientes
personas. Haz las preguntas necesarias.

Carmen tiene un hermano.   ¿Cómo se llama el hermano de Carmen?

1. Pedro tiene una hermana.
2. Isabel tiene un novio.
3. El profesor tiene unos amigos.
4. El doctor Sánchez tiene una secretaria.
5. Federico tiene dos primos.
6. Los vecinos tienen dos hijos.

ACTIVIDAD 4   Las cosas de otros   OPTIONAL

A veces, no tenemos ciertas cosas que necesitamos. Tenemos que usar las
de otros. Expresa esto, según el modelo.

Cuando no tengo mi bicicleta ... (Enrique)
    Cuando no tengo mi bicicleta, uso la de Enrique.

1. Cuando no tengo mi radio ...
   (mi hermano)
2. Cuando no tengo mi libro de español ...
   (mi amigo)
3. Cuando no tengo mi pelota ...
   (Rosita)
4. Cuando no tengo mis discos nuevos ...
   (Alfredo)
5. Cuando no tengo mi calculadora ...
   (mi papá)
6. Cuando no tengo mi raqueta ...
   (mi prima)

WB
B1

C. Repaso: los adjetivos posesivos

Another way to indicate possession or relationship in Spanish is to use possessive adjectives. Review the forms of these adjectives:

POSSESSOR	SINGULAR		PLURAL		
yo	**mi** hermano	**mi** hermana	**mis** hermanos	**mis** hermanas	(my)
tú	**tu** primo	**tu** prima	**tus** primos	**tus** primas	(your)
él					(his, its)
ella	**su** amigo	**su** amiga	**sus** amigos	**sus** amigas	(her, its)
Ud.					(your)
nosotros	**nuestro** tío	**nuestra** tía	**nuestros** tíos	**nuestras** tías	(our)
vosotros	**vuestro** hijo	**vuestra** hija	**vuestros** hijos	**vuestras** hijas	(your)
ellos					(their)
ellas	**su** profesor	**su** profesora	**sus** profesores	**sus** profesoras	(their)
Uds.					(your)

- All possessive adjectives agree in number with the nouns which they introduce: they have singular and plural forms. Note that **nuestro** and **vuestro** also agree in gender.

- **Su** and **sus** have several English equivalents:

el coche de Paco	**su** coche	*his* car
el coche de Marta	**su** coche	*her* car
el coche de Ud.	**su** coche	*your* car
el coche de mis amigos	**su** coche	*their* car
el coche de Uds.	**su** coche	*your* car

When clarification is necessary, Spanish speakers use the expressions **de él** (**de ella, de Ud., de ellos, de ellas, de Uds.**) instead of **su/sus**.

—¿Conocen Uds. a los amigos de Miguel y Mercedes?
—Conocemos a **los amigos de él,** pero no conocemos a **los de ella.**

ACTIVIDAD 5   Para ir al trabajo

Di cómo van al trabajo las siguientes personas, según el modelo.

- El doctor Velázquez tiene un coche.
    Para ir al trabajo, el doctor Velázquez usa su coche.

1. La Srta. Vilar tiene una bicicleta.
2. Mi papá tiene un Fiat.
3. Alberto tiene una moto.
4. Mis primos tienen un Mercedes.
5. Tú tienes una bicicleta.
6. El cartero tiene un Toyota.
7. La secretaria de la escuela tiene un Volvo.
8. Tenemos dos pies.
9. Tengo patines de ruedas (*roller skates*).

ACTIVIDAD 6   Los pedigüeños *(Leeches)*

Un pedigüeño es una persona que siempre pide cosas a sus amigos para usarlas. Di que las siguientes personas son pedigüeñas, según el modelo.

⟩⟩   Carmen (los discos / la amiga)   Carmen no usa sus discos.
Usa los discos de su amiga.

WB
C1, C2

SCRIPT
Act. 4, 5

MASTERS
p. 5

1. el Sr. Montero (el coche / los empleados)
2. el doctor Valdez (la máquina de escribir / la secretaria)
3. nosotros (la grabadora / los vecinos)
4. yo (el reloj / la hermana)
5. tú (la pelota / los hermanos)
6. Ud. (la cámara / los primos)
7. Uds. (el teléfono / el vecino)
8. mis primos (la moto / los amigos)

D. Repaso: complementos directos: pronombres

Compare the direct objects and the corresponding object pronouns in the questions and answers below.

¿Invitas a **Pedro** a la fiesta?	Sí, **lo** invito.
¿Conoces a **Emilia?**	No, no **la** conozco.
¿Llevas **tus discos** a la fiesta?	Sí, **los** llevo.
¿Llamas a **tus amigas** por teléfono?	No, no **las** llamo.

⟩⟩   The direct object pronoun usually comes before the verb.

⟩⟩   In an infinitive or present progressive construction, the direct object pronoun may come either before the conjugated verb or after the infinitive or present participle, to which it is attached.

¿Vas a invitar a Luisa al cine?	Sí, voy a invitar**la**.
	Sí, **la** voy a invitar.
¿Estás llamando a Rafael?	No, no estoy llamándo**lo**.
	No, no **lo** estoy llamando.

When the pronoun is attached to the present participle, an accent mark is placed on the next-to-last syllable of the participle to preserve the original stress pattern.

⟩⟩   The direct object pronouns **lo (la)** and **los (las)** are used when speaking to people addressed as **Ud.** and **Uds.**

Voy a llamar**lo** por teléfono, Sr. Sánchez.
Voy a invitar**los** a mi fiesta de cumpleaños, Sr. y Sra. López.

Di si conoces a las siguientes personas personalmente. Di también si las ves a menudo.

∽ el cartero   (No) Conozco personalmente al cartero.
              (No) Lo veo a menudo.

1. la secretaria de la escuela
2. los vecinos
3. la empleada de correos
4. el mecánico que repara el coche de tu papá
5. los dependientes de la tienda donde compras tus discos
6. las camareras de la heladería donde vas con tus amigos

7. la empleada del banco donde van tus padres
8. los policías que dirigen el tráfico en tu barrio
9. el jefe de la policía
10. el presidente de los Estados Unidos

ACTIVIDAD 8   La maleta

Imagina que vas a México. Estás preparando tu maleta. Di si necesitas los siguientes objetos y si vas a llevarlos contigo.

∽ tu calculadora   (No) La necesito. (No) Voy a llevarla conmigo.

SCRIPT
Act. 6

MASTERS
p. 5

1. tus anteojos de sol   (sunglasses)
2. tu diccionario de español
3. tu raqueta de tenis
4. la dirección (address) de tus vecinos

5. tu bolígrafo   (ballpoint pen)
6. una máquina de escribir   (typewriter)
7. tus sandalias
8. el mapa de los Estados Unidos

ADDITIONAL CUES: una grabadora, tu cámara, tu reloj, tu libro de matemáticas.

ACTIVIDAD 9   Preguntas personales

Usa el pronombre del complemento directo en cada respuesta.

1. ¿Aceptas la injusticia? ¿las ideas revolucionarias? ¿las opiniones diferentes? ¿los defectos de tus amigos? ¿su negligencia? ¿su egoísmo (selfishness)?

2. ¿Admiras a tus profesores? ¿a tus padres? ¿a la policía? ¿a los artistas? ¿a los políticos? ¿a las personas famosas?

3. ¿Ayudas a menudo a tu papá? ¿a tu mamá? ¿a tus hermanos? ¿a tus abuelos? ¿a tus vecinos?

4. ¿Criticas un poco a tu mejor amigo? ¿a tu mejor amiga? ¿a tus parientes? ¿la sociedad moderna?

5. ¿Perdonas los insultos? ¿la ingratitud? ¿las culpas (mistakes) de tus amigos?

6. ¿Respetas siempre a los políticos? ¿al presidente de los Estados Unidos? ¿las reglas (rules) de la escuela?

7. ¿Toleras a las personas aburridas? ¿a las personas arrogantes? ¿a las personas mal educadas (impolite)? ¿a los presumidos (snobs)?

Unidad dos   Ask about student responses. ¿Acepta Bill la injusticia?

62

8. ¿Conoces el Perú? ¿el Ecuador? ¿la Argentina? ¿el Canadá? ¿los Estados Unidos? ¿la India?

9. ¿Conduces a veces el coche de tus padres?

10. ¿Mereces solamente buenas notas? ¿malas notas?

11. ¿Vas a invitar a tu mejor amigo a tu fiesta de cumpleaños? ¿a tu mejor amiga? ¿a tus primos? ¿a tus vecinos? ¿a tus compañeros de clase? ¿a todos?

12. ¿Deben los niños obedecer a sus abuelos? ¿a su papá? ¿a su mamá?

WB
D1, D2

SCRIPT

Act. 7

ACTIVIDAD 10   ¡Un poco de lógica!   OPTIONAL

Prepara diez frases lógicas (afirmativas o negativas) usando los elementos de las columnas A, B, C y D.

May be assigned as a special challenge activity.

A	B	C	D
yo	ayudar	el amigo	Verónica
María	conducir	la amiga	Luis
nosotros	conocer	los padres	el profesor
mis primos	criticar	el coche	la escuela
Ud.	merecer	las reglas (rules)	un periodista
	obedecer	la disciplina	español
	traducir	las felicitaciones	los vecinos
	cuidar	(congratulations)	
		los artículos	
		los niños	

María no conduce el coche de sus vecinos.

Para la comunicación   OPTIONAL

WB
Trad.

SCRIPT

Act. 8, 9, 10

MASTERS
p. 6

TRB

QUIZ
pp. 14–15

Escribe un pequeño párrafo sobre una persona que conoces bien. Puede ser una persona del vocabulario especializado u otra persona.

Puedes usar frases como:
Conozco a un (una) . . .
Lo (La) respeto porque . . .
Lo (La) admiro . . .
Es una persona . . .
(No) Deseo ser como él (ella) porque (no) me gusta . . .

- May be assigned as homework.
- VARIATION: Select a magazine picture of a well-known person and write a similar paragraph.

Lección 2 ¡Así es la vida!

STRUCTURES TO REVIEW: • **Saber**
• Indirect object pronouns
• **Decir**

Hoy es el diez de enero . . .
   un día de verano muy soleado . . .
   un día ideal para correr las olas.

Have students review months and dates
in Appendix 2.

soleado: *sunny*
correr las olas: *to surf*
tabla hawaiana:
   surfboard

Ramón, un chico de Lima, lleva su tabla hawaiana y va a la playa.
Allí, ve a una chica que está tomando el sol.
¿Quién es?
Ramón no sabe cómo se llama.
No sabe de dónde es.
No sabe nada de ella . . . sólo que es una chica muy bonita . . .
¡Le gustaría mucho conocerla!
Sí, pero, ¿cómo?
Vamos a ver.

20–21

Esa chica es muy guapa y parece muy simpática.
Me gustaría mucho hablarle . . . pero, ¿qué voy a decirle?

¿Le pregunto si pasa las vacaciones aquí?
. . . No, ¡es obvio!

¿Le digo que es muy guapa?
. . . No, ¡es ridículo!

¿Cuál es la fecha? ¿Qué tiempo hace? ¿De dónde es Ramón? ¿Qué lleva Ramón en la playa? ¿Qué hace la chica? ¿Qué sabe Ramón de la chica? ¿Por qué no le pregunta Ramón si pasa las vacaciones en Lima? ¿Por qué no le dice que es muy guapa? ¿Por qué no le pregunta si tiene muchos amigos en Lima? ¿Por qué no le pregunta si tiene ganas de ir al cine con él? ¿Qué le pregunta el otro chico? ¿Quién tiene suerte hoy?

NOTAS CULTURALES

OPTIONAL Note: On a world map show where the Equator cuts across South America.

Las estaciones en la América del Sur

Como la mayoría de la América del Sur está en el hemisferio sur, las estaciones del año son lo contrario de las de los Estados Unidos. Los meses del verano son enero, febrero y marzo. Los meses del invierno son julio, agosto y septiembre.

Act. 2

La playa

¿Qué haces un día de verano en que hace mucho sol? ¿Vas a la playa?

Como muchos de los países hispanos tienen veranos largos° y calurosos,° el ir a la playa° es uno de los pasatiempos favoritos de muchos jóvenes hispanohablantes.°

¿Y qué hacen allí? Depende un poco de donde viven. En todas las playas pueden nadar o tomar el sol o jugar al volibol. En el Caribe, pueden también bucear.° En el Pacífico, pueden navegar en un bote de vela.° En Puerto Rico, Colombia y el Perú pueden correr las olas. En Lima, el correr las olas es un deporte tan favorito como en California o Hawai y allí hay muchas competencias° internacionales.

Pero sobre todo,° el ir a la playa es para gozar de° la compañía de los amigos . . . y claro, para hacer nuevos amigos.

largos *long* **calurosos** *hot*
el ir a la playa *going to the beach*
hispanohablantes *Spanish-speaking* **bucear**
go scuba diving **navegar un bote de vela** *sail*
competencias *competitions* **sobre todo** *above all*
gozar de *enjoy*

¿Cuáles son los meses del invierno en los Estados Unidos? ¿Cuáles son los meses del invierno en el Perú? ¿Adónde van los jóvenes en el verano? ¿Qué hacen en la playa? ¿Qué pueden hacer en el Caribe? ¿Qué pueden hacer en el Pacífico? ¿Qué pueden hacer en Colombia y el Perú?

You may want to review other expressions of weather in Appendix 2.

—— Vocabulario ——

¿Qué tiempo hace?	How's the weather?
Hace calor (frío,*fresco).	It is hot (cold, cool).
Hace sol (viento).	It is sunny (windy).
El día **está*soleado (nublado).**	The day is sunny (cloudy).
El verano **es muy*caluroso.**	Summer is very hot.

CONVERSACIÓN OPTIONAL

¿Sabes nadar? Sí (No, no) sé nadar.

¿Sabes nadar a crol *(crawl)*?

¿Sabes nadar de espalda *(on your back)*?

¿Sabes esquiar?

¿Sabes esquiar en el agua *(to waterski)*?

¿Sabes navegar un bote de vela *(to sail)*?

¿Sabes correr las olas *(to surf)*?

VOCABULARIO PRÁCTICO

Cuando voy a la playa, llevo

unos anteojos de sol  **un traje de baño**

Also: **gafas de sol, espejuelos para el sol, lentes de sol.**

un sombrero * **una toalla**

En la playa, hay* **arena** *(sand)* y* **piedras** *(stones)*.

Hay muchas cosas que hacer en la playa:

* **caminar** *(to walk)*   En la playa, **caminamos** en la arena.
* **correr** *(to run)*   No me gusta **correr** en las piedras.
* **correr las olas** *(to surf)*   En el Perú, muchos chicos **corren las olas.**
* **esquiar en el agua** *(to waterski)*   Para **esquiar en el agua,** es necesario tener un * **bote** *(boat)* y esquís acuáticos.
* **navegar un bote de vela** *(to sail)*   Cuando hace viento, es fácil **navegar un bote de vela.**
  Un barco is another word for boat.
* **pescar** *(to fish)*   Para **pescar,** no es necesario tener bote.
  tomar el sol *(to sunbathe)*   Carlos está muy* **tostado** *(tanned)* porque **toma** mucho **sol.**

EXTRA VOCAB.: **el colchón de aire** (air mattress), **bucear** (to go scuba diving), **la mascarilla** (goggles), **las aletas** (fins), **bucear con mascarilla** (to go snorkeling).

ACTIVIDAD 1   Preguntas personales

Ask about student responses. **¿De qué color son los anteojos de Jane?**

1. ¿Tienes anteojos de sol? ¿De qué color?

2. ¿Tienes un traje de baño? ¿De qué color?

3. ¿Tienes un sombrero para el sol? ¿Es grande?

You may want to review the colors in Appendix 2.

4. ¿Tienes toallas? ¿De qué colores?

5. ¿Cómo vas a la escuela? ¿Caminas o tomas el autobús?

6. ¿A qué playa vas durante las vacaciones? ¿Es una playa con arena o con piedras?

7. ¿Te gusta correr en la arena? ¿Te gusta correr donde hay muchas piedras?

8. ¿Te gustaría correr las olas? ¿Dónde?

9. ¿Te gustaría esquiar en el agua? ¿Dónde?

10. ¿Te gustaría pescar en el mar Mediterráneo?

11. En tu opinión, ¿es fácil correr las olas? ¿esquiar en el agua? ¿navegar un bote de vela?

12. En tu opinión, ¿es peligroso *(dangerous)* esquiar en el agua? ¿navegar un bote de vela?

13. ¿Te gusta tomar el sol? ¿Dónde tomas el sol? ¿Usas una crema especial para el sol? ¿Ahora estás tostado(a)?

SCRIPT
Act. 7
MASTERS
p. 7

Estructuras

A. Repaso: *saber*

Review the forms and uses of **saber** *(to know)* in the sentences below.

(yo)	**Sé** cómo se llama la chica.
(tú)	**¿Sabes** dónde vive?
(él, ella, Ud.)	**Sabe** quién es.
(nosotros)	**Sabemos** su dirección *(address)*.
(vosotros)	**Sabéis** su número de teléfono.
(ellos, ellas, Uds.)	**Saben** nadar.

Although **saber** and **conocer** both correspond to the English verb *to know*, their uses are quite different. These two verbs cannot be substituted for each other. Remind students that **conocer** is used with people and places.

⚡ **Saber** means *to know information or facts*. It can be followed by:
— a noun or pronoun representing this information or fact.

¿Sabes **mi dirección?**   *Do you know **my address?***

— a clause.

¿Sabes . . . **dónde vivo?**   *Do you know . . . **where I live?***
　　　　　quién trabaja conmigo?   ***who works with me?***
　　　　　por qué estudio español?   ***why I am studying Spanish?***

⚡ **Saber** is never used with nouns representing persons or places.

Conozco a María . . . pero no **sé** dónde vive.
Miguel **conoce** una playa bonita . . . pero no **sabe** si hay olas hoy.

⚡ When **saber** is followed by an infinitive it means *to know how to do something*.

Raquel no **sabe nadar.**   *Raquel does not **know how to swim**.*

ACTIVIDAD 2   La misteriosa Cristina

Las siguientes personas conocen a Cristina pero no saben mucho de ella.
Expresa esto según el modelo.

⚡ Carlos (dónde vive)   Carlos conoce a Cristina . . . pero no sabe dónde vive.

1. Luis (si tiene muchos amigos)
2. mis amigos (cuál es su número de teléfono)
3. yo (por qué estudia francés)
4. nosotros (cuántos hermanos tiene)
5. sus vecinos (dónde trabaja)
6. Enrique (cómo se llama su novio)
7. Felipe (si nada bien)
8. mis hermanas (si tiene esquís acuáticos)

B. Adjetivos y pronombres demostrativos

The forms and uses of demonstrative adjectives are summarized in the following diagram.

(aquí)	*(ahí)	(allá)
este perro	**ese** perro	**aquel** perro
esta chica	**esa** chica	**aquella** chica
estos discos	**esos** discos	**aquellos** discos
estas casas	**esas** casas	**aquellas** casas

yo	**este** perro *(this dog)*	**ese** perro *(that dog)*	**aquel** perro *(that dog over there)*

Demonstrative adjectives *introduce* nouns.

    Mira **ese** libro.   *Look at that book.*

Demonstrative pronouns *replace* nouns.

    ¿Cuál es tu libro? *¡**Éste** o *aquél?   *Which is your book? This one or that one?*

In Spanish, demonstrative pronouns have the same forms as demonstrative adjectives, but with an accent on the stressed syllable.

*You may practice the distinction between **este, ese,** and **aquel** with a book that you place at various distances from the students.*

ACTIVIDAD 3   En la playa

Luisa y Felipe están en la playa. Luisa le pregunta a Felipe si conoce a las personas que están caminando. Haz los dos papeles.

*VARIATIONS: with **este** and **aquel.***

    el muchacho (no)   Luisa: ¿Conoces a ese muchacho?
                               Felipe: No, no lo conozco.

1. la mujer (sí)
2. el hombre (no)
3. la muchacha (sí)
4. el pescador (no)

5. los niños (sí)
6. las chicas (no)
7. los turistas (sí)
8. los jóvenes (sí)

ACTIVIDAD 4   En la tienda de la playa

Ahora Felipe y Luisa están en una tienda. Felipe le pregunta a Luisa
qué cosas prefiere. Luisa dice que prefiere otras cosas. Haz los dos
papeles.

⟯   una revista   Felipe: ¿Prefieres esa revista o ésta?
                    Luisa: Prefiero aquélla.

1. un traje de baño
2. unos anteojos de sol
3. un sombrero
4. un parasol

5. unas cañas de pescar (*fishing poles*)
6. una toalla
7. una tabla hawaiana (*surfboard*)
8. unos esquís acuáticos

C. Repaso: el complemento indirecto: *le, les*

Note the forms and position of the indirect object pronouns.

¿**Le** habla **al cartero**?   No, no **le** habla.
¿**Le** escribes **a Luisa**?   Sí, **le** escribo una carta.
¿Qué **les** mandas **a tus primos**? **Les** mando un regalo.
¿Vas a escribir**les a tus abuelos**? Sí, voy a escribir**les**.

The third person indirect object pronoun has only two forms:

> **le** (singular) and **les** (plural)

Indirect object pronouns also follow affirmative
commands. This will be actively reviewed on
p. 352. **¡Escríbele una tarjeta a Carlos! ¡Háblales
a las chicas!**

⟯   Like other object pronouns, it usually comes *before* the verb.
    In an infinitive or present progressive construction, the indirect object
    pronoun may come either before the conjugated verb or after and
    attached to the infinitive or present participle.

Le voy a hablar.   ⎫
Voy a hablar**le**.   ⎬ *I am going to talk* **to him**.

Le estoy hablando.   ⎫
Estoy hablándo**le**.   ⎬ *I am talking* **to him**.

⟯   Spanish speakers may use an indirect object pronoun in a sentence that
    also contains an indirect object noun.

    Le hablo **a Paco**.   *I am speaking* **to Paco**.

⟯   **Le** and **les** are the indirect object pronouns used with persons
    addressed as **Ud.** or **Uds.**

    Le digo la verdad, Sr. Montero.   *I am telling* **you** *the truth, Sr. Montero.*

You may clarify the distinction between direct and indirect objects with English examples.
Direct Object:
I invite *Carmen* to the party.   Who is *invited*?
Luis calls *Carmen*.   Who is *called*?
Since Carmen is directly affected by the action of the verb, she is the direct object of the sentence.
Indirect Object:
I am speaking *to Carmen*.   Who is *spoken to*?
I am writing *Carmen*.   Who is *written to*?
Carmen is indirectly affected by the action of the verb. She is the indirect object of the sentence.
Direct and Indirect Objects:

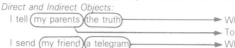

I tell (my parents) (the truth) → What is told?	(direct object)
→ To whom is it told?	(indirect object)
I send (my friend) (a telegram) → What is being sent?	(direct object)
→ To whom is it sent?	(indirect object)

ACTIVIDAD 5   Los conocidos (*Acquaintances*)

Para cada una de las siguientes personas, di si la ves todos los días y si le hablas todos los días también.

Ask about student responses. **¿Lo ven Sally y Jim...? ¿Le hablan...?**

▷ el médico   (No) Lo veo todos los días. (No) Le hablo todos los días.

1. el dentista
2. el cartero
3. la secretaria de la escuela
4. tus primos

5. tus abuelos
6. los vecinos
7. las amigas de tus amigos
8. los padres de tus amigos

Other verbs: **ofrecer, escribir, vender.**

VOCABULARIO PRÁCTICO   Verbos con complementos indirectos

comprar	to buy	Luis le **compra** un helado a Isabel.
dar	to give	Les **doy** consejos a mis amigos.
decir	to tell, say	Le **digo** la verdad al maestro.
enseñar	to show	No les **enseño** mis fotos a mis padres.
	to teach	El profesor les **enseña** francés a los alumnos.
mandar	to send	Le **mando** una carta a mi primo.
prestar	to lend	No les **presto** dinero a mis amigos.
*regalar	to give (as a present)	Voy a **regalarle** un disco a mi primo para su cumpleaños.

NOTAS: 1. In the above sentences, the verbs are used with indirect object pronouns and with direct objects.
2. Note the **yo** forms of **dar (doy)** and **decir (digo).**

ACTIVIDAD 6   Regalos de Navidad

Imagina que compras las cosas de la columna A para Navidad. Di a qué persona de la columna B vas a darle cada regalo.

VARIATIONS with: **regalar, comprar, ofrecer.**

A	B
una suscripción a *Mad*	mi mejor amigo
un cartel (*poster*)	mi mejor amiga
un sombrero	mi papá
unos discos	mi mamá
unos anteojos de sol	mis abuelos
unos esquís acuáticos	mi tía
una novela	mis primos
un mapa de los Estados Unidos	mis hermanas
una tabla hawaiana	un amigo deportista
un rompecabezas (*puzzle*)	una amiga que va a menudo a la playa
una suscripción a *Deportes ilustrados*	un amigo que no es puntual
un reloj	unas amigas que viven en España

SCRIPT
Act. 5

MASTERS
p. 7

▷ Les doy una suscripción a *Mad* a mis primos.

ACTIVIDAD 7   Preguntas personales

Usa un pronombre complemento indirecto en tus respuestas.

1. Durante las vacaciones, ¿le escribes a tu mejor amigo? ¿a tu mejor amiga? ¿a tu profesor de español? ¿Les escribes a tus abuelos? ¿a tus compañeros?

2. ¿Les das consejos a tus amigos? ¿a tus compañeros? ¿a tus primos?

3. ¿Le prestas tus anteojos de sol a tu mejor amigo? ¿a tu mejor amiga? ¿a tu novio(a)?

4. ¿Les enseñas tus fotos a tus profesores? ¿a tus compañeros? ¿a tus amigos?

5. ¿Qué vas a regalarle a tu papá para su cumpleaños? ¿a tu mamá? ¿a tu mejor amigo? ¿a tu mejor amiga?

6. ¿Les lees cuentos a tus hermanos? ¿a tus hermanas? ¿a tus primos?

WB
C1, C2, C3

SCRIPT

Act. 6

7. ¿Les prestas a tus compañeros tus revistas viejas? ¿tus notas de español?

8. Cuando estás de viaje, ¿les mandas tarjetas a tus compañeros? ¿a tus vecinos? ¿a tus tíos? ¿a tus abuelos?

D. Repaso: *decir*

Review the forms of **decir** (*to say, to tell*).

Other verbs conjugated like **decir** are **contradecir** (to contradict) and **predecir** (to predict).

(yo)	**Digo** que Ana es guapa.
(tú)	**Dices** que es lista.
(él, ella, Ud.)	**Dice** que está cansada.
(nosotros)	**Decimos** que Ramón es deportista.
(vosotros)	**Decís** que es tímido.
(ellos, ellas, Uds.)	**Dicen** que no tiene suerte.

ACTIVIDAD 8   El secreto

Mari-Carmen tiene un secreto que le dice a Carlos. Carlos le dice el secreto a Manuel, que le dice el secreto a . . . . Expresa esto usando la forma apropiada del verbo **decir**.

WB
D1

⟩⟩   Mari-Carmen: Carlos   Mari-Carmen le dice el secreto a Carlos.

1. Carlos: Manuel
2. yo: Enrique
3. mis primos: Isabel
4. tú: Felipe

5. Roberto y Andrés: Alberto
6. mis primos: mis primas
7. Uds.: el profesor

VARIATIONS:
• Each person contradicts the other. **Mari-Carmen contradice a Carlos.**
• Each person predicts a brilliant future for the other. **Mari-Carmen le predice a Carlos un futuro brillante.**

Para la comunicación   OPTIONAL

Imagina que estás en una playa cerca de Lima. Si tú eres un chico, ves a una chica. Si eres una chica, ves a un chico. Esta persona es guapa y parece interesante. Prepara seis frases o preguntas que puedes decirle. (Si quieres, usa «Así es la vida» como tu inspiración.)

May be assigned as homework.
VARIATION: Pairs of students can prepare skits inspired by "Así es la vida."

WB
Trad.

SCRIPT
Act. 8, 9

MASTERS
p. 7

TRB

QUIZ
pp. 16–17

STRUCTURES TO REVIEW: • Pronouns **me** and **te**
• Indirect/direct object pronoun sequence
• The indirect object pronoun **se**

Lección 3

Intercambios

Act. 1

¡Chantaje!

Manuel: ¡Oye, Luis!

Luis: ¿Qué hay?

Manuel: Tienes una bicicleta nueva, ¿verdad?

Luis: ¡Sí! ¿Por qué?

Manuel: ¿Me la prestas?

Luis: Claro... Te la presto... ¡si me prestas mil pesetas!

Manuel: Mil pesetas, ¡no!

Luis: ¡Si no hay dinero, no hay bicicleta!

Manuel: ¡Va por quinientas pesetas! ¡Pero esto es chantaje!

¿Qué hay?: What's new?

Va por: It's a deal for
esto: this
chantaje: blackmail

¿Un tocadiscos por una guitarra?

Pedro: ¡Dime, Carmen! ¿Adónde vas con tu guitarra?

Carmen: Voy a venderla.

Pedro: ¿A quién?

Carmen: ¡A Carlos!

Pedro (inquisitivo): ¿Por cuánto se la vendes a Carlos?

Carmen (un poco impaciente): Por treinta dólares.

Pedro (insistente): ¿Por treinta dólares... no quieres cambiármela?

Carmen (curiosa): Eso depende ... ¿Por qué me la cambias?

Pedro (misterioso): Por algo magnífico, maravilloso, estupendo ...

Carmen (un poco sospechosa): ¿Qué cosa?

Pedro (con un aire indiferente): ¡Mi tocadiscos!

Carmen (furiosa): ¿Quieres cambiar tu tocadiscos por mi guitarra, eh? ... ¿Crees que soy tonta? ... ¡Yo sé bien que tu tocadiscos está descompuesto!

Dime: Tell me

cambiármela: to trade it with me
Eso: That

sospechosa: suspicious

está descompuesto: doesn't work

• ¿Quién tiene una bicicleta nueva? ¿Quién desea usar esta bicicleta? ¿Va a prestársela Luis a Manuel? Si Manuel desea usar la bicicleta, ¿qué tiene que prestarle a Luis? ¿Cuánto dinero va a prestarle a Luis al fin? En tu opinión, ¿es chantaje? ¿Por qué?

• ¿Quién va a vender su guitarra? ¿A quién va a vendérsela? ¿Por cuánto se la vende? ¿Qué quiere Pedro? ¿Tiene un tocadiscos magnífico Pedro? En tu opinión, ¿es un ladrón Pedro? ¿Por qué?

NOTA CULTURAL   OPTIONAL

¡La guitarra!

La guitarra es uno de los instrumentos de cuerda más usado en la música popular española. La música y el baile flamenco, por ejemplo, se acompañan° con palmadas, ° zapateados,° y ¡con la guitarra!

En este siglo,° Andrés Segovia, famoso guitarrista español, fue el principal responsable del resurgimiento° del interés por la guitarra. Segovia mostró° que la guitarra era un instrumento de muchas posibilidades. Tocaba° música clásica.

La guitarra sigue siendo° el instrumento musical favorito de los jóvenes hispanos. Tocan la guitarra en las fiestas, en la playa, en los picnics, en los cafés, en las calles, en las plazas . . . y en todos los lugares donde se reúnen.° En algunos países hispanos, los jóvenes conservan° la tradición de dar una serenata° cerca de la ventana o del balcón de las chicas de que° están enamorados.°

de cuerda *string*   **se acompañan** *are accompanied*   **palmadas** *clapping*   **zapateados** *foot stamping*   **siglo** *century*   **resurgim iento** *resurgence*   **mostró** *demonstrated*   **Tocaba** *He played*   **sigue siendo** *continues to be*   **se reúnen** *they get together* **conservan** *keep*   **dar una serenata** *to serenade*   **de que** *with whom*   **están enamorados** *they are in love*

- Other words for picnic: **jira campestre, merienda campestre.**
- See reading on **La guitarra,** SFM Book 1, p. 303.

── Vocabulario ──

sustantivo	*el chantaje	blackmail
adjetivos	*inquisitivo	curious, inquisitive
	*misterioso	mysterious
	*sospechoso	suspicious
verbo	cambiar	to change, to exchange
preposiciones	con	with
	por	for, in exchange for
pronombres	*eso, esto	that, this (neuter)
exclamaciones	*¡Dime!	Say! Tell me!
	¡Oye!	Listen!
	*¿Qué cosa?	What is it? What thing?
	*¿Qué hay?	What's up? What is it?
	*¡Va por . . .!	It's a deal for . . .!

- You may review the forms: **conmigo / contigo.**
- **Por** and **para** are reviewed and contrasted in Unit 7.

NOTA: **Eso** and **esto** are neuter demonstrative pronouns. They are used to refer to a general idea rather than a specific object.

CONVERSACIÓN OPTIONAL

¿Tienes tocadiscos?
  ¿Se lo prestas a tus amigos?
¿Tienes discos?
  ¿Se los prestas a tus hermanos?
¿Recibes muchas cartas?
  ¿Se las lees a tus padres?
¿Tienes secretos?
  ¿Se los dices a tu mejor amigo? ¿a tu mejor amiga? ¿a tus padres?

Act. 3

23–24

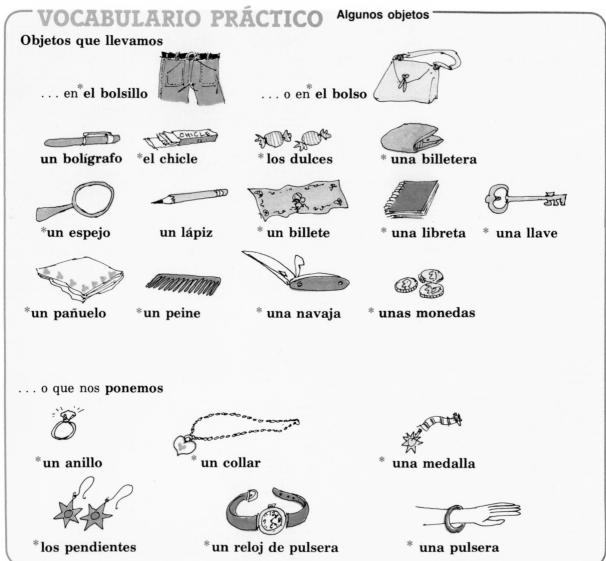

VOCABULARIO PRÁCTICO   Algunos objetos

Objetos que llevamos

. . . en* el bolsillo   . . . o en* el bolso

un bolígrafo   *el chicle   * los dulces   * una billetera

*un espejo   un lápiz   * un billete   * una libreta   * una llave

*un pañuelo   *un peine   * una navaja   * unas monedas

. . . o que nos **ponemos**

*un anillo   * un collar   * una medalla

*los pendientes   * un reloj de pulsera   * una pulsera

ACTIVITY: Have each student show one of these objects and give a descriptive sentence. **Tengo un peine pequeño.**

ACTIVIDAD 1 El costo de la vida *(The cost of living)*

If necessary, review numbers in Appendix 1.

¿Puedes decir cuánto cuestan las siguientes cosas? No es necesario saber el precio exacto.

⚡ un paquete de chicle   Un paquete de chicle cuesta veinte centavos.
⚡ un espejo   Un espejo cuesta un dólar.

1. un bolígrafo
2. un lápiz
3. una libreta
4. una billetera de plástico
5. una billetera de cuero *(leather)*
6. un pañuelo
7. un peine
8. una navaja
9. un anillo barato
10. un anillo de plata *(silver)*
11. un anillo de oro *(gold)*
12. una pulsera barata
13. una pulsera de plata
14. un reloj de pulsera
15. unos pendientes
16. un collar barato
17. un collar de perlas
18. una medalla de oro

ACTIVIDAD 2 Preguntas personales

1. ¿Tienes bolígrafo? ¿De qué marca?
2. ¿Compras chicle a menudo? ¿De qué marca?
3. ¿Comes muchos dulces?
4. ¿Tienes la llave de tu casa? ¿la llave del coche de tus padres? ¿la llave de la escuela?
5. ¿Usas pañuelos de tela *(cloth)* o pañuelos de papel *(paper)*?
6. ¿Tienes reloj de pulsera? ¿De qué marca? ¿Anda *(does it work)* bien?
7. ¿Escribes tus citas en una libreta?
8. ¿Tienes billetera? ¿De qué color es?
9. ¿Llevas anillos? ¿Cuántos?
10. ¿Llevas medallas? ¿Qué representan?
11. ¿Qué hay en tus bolsillos?

Ask about student responses.
¿Quién tiene un bolígrafo?

Estructuras

A. Repaso: los pronombres *me, te, nos*

Compare the subject and object pronouns in the chart below.

SUBJECT PRONOUNS	DIRECT AND INDIRECT OBJECT PRONOUNS		
yo	**me**	¿**Me** escuchas?	¿Vas a escuchar**me**?
tú	**te**	No **te** ayudo hoy.	Voy a ayudar**te** mañana.
nosotros(as)	**nos**	¿**Nos** ayudas, Pepe?	¿Vas a prestar**nos** tu guitarra?

> **Me, te** and **nos** can be used as both direct and indirect object pronouns.

> These pronouns have the same position as other object pronouns.

You may remind the students that the pronouns that correspond to **Ud.** and **Uds.** are: direct object: **lo / la** and **los / las** indirect object: **le** and **les**

ACTIVIDAD 3 ¿Tienes buenas relaciones con otros?

Describe tus relaciones con otros, según el modelo. Puedes usar expresiones como **a veces, nunca.**

> tu papá (ayudar)   Mi papá (no) me ayuda (nunca).

VARIATION: Talk about you and your brothers and sisters using the pronoun **nos**: Nuestro papá (no) nos ayuda.

1. tu papá (ayudar / comprender / dar consejos / prestar el coche)
2. tu mamá (comprender / dar dinero / comprar regalos / respetar)
3. tus abuelos (escribir / llamar por teléfono / mandar regalos)
4. tus profesores (dar consejos / dar buenas notas / criticar)
5. tus amigos (visitar / llamar por teléfono / admirar / criticar / tolerar)

ACTIVIDAD 4 Diálogo: La amistad *(Friendship)*

Pregúntales a tus compañeros si van a hacer las siguientes cosas para ti durante las vacaciones.

WB
A1, A2

SCRIPT
Act. 5

> escribir   Estudiante 1: ¿Vas a escribirme?
> Estudiante 2: Sí (No, no) voy a escribirte.

1. invitar al cine
2. visitar
3. invitar a la playa

4. ayudar
5. presentar a tus amigos
6. mandar tarjetas

B. Repaso: pronombre indirecto + pronombre directo

The answers below contain two object pronouns. Note the sequence of these pronouns.

¿Me prestas tu coche?	Sí, **te lo** presto.
¿Me vendes tu bicicleta?	No, no **te la** vendo.
¿Vas a mandarme los libros?	Sí, voy a mandár**telos**.

In sentences which contain two object pronouns, the sequence is:

indirect object + direct object

ACTIVIDAD 5   La envidia *(Envy)*

Clara quiere usar las cosas nuevas de su amiga Cecilia. Haz los dos papeles según el modelo.

unos pendientes (prestar)   Cecilia: ¡Mira mis pendientes nuevos!
                              Clara: ¿Me los prestas?

VARIATION with **poder:** Clara: **¿Puedes prestármelos?**

1. un anillo (dar)
2. una pulsera (regalar)
3. un peine (prestar)
4. una billetera (enseñar)
5. unas medallas (dar)
6. unos discos (ofrecer)

ACTIVIDAD 6   Peticiones

Raúl le pide a Carmen algunas cosas. Carmen le dice que sí a ciertas cosas y a otras, no.

el espejo (no)   Raúl: ¿Me prestas tu espejo?
                   Carmen: No, no te lo presto.

VARIATION with **ir:** Carmen: **No, no voy a prestártelo.**

1. el peine (sí)
2. la libreta (sí)
3. el bolígrafo (sí)
4. los pendientes (no)
5. las monedas (no)
6. la pulsera (no)
7. los anteojos de sol (no)
8. la toalla (sí)
9. el sombrero (no)
10. la guitarra (sí)
11. el pañuelo (no)
12. la navaja (sí)

ACTIVIDAD 7   Intercambios

Roberto le propone a Elena ciertos intercambios, pero sin éxito *(success)*. Haz los dos papeles.

el anillo / la medalla   Roberto: ¿Me das tu anillo?
                           Elena: Sí, te lo doy . . . por tu medalla.
                           Roberto: ¡Por mi medalla! ¡No! No quiero cambiártela.

1. la billetera / la libreta
2. los pendientes / las medallas
3. los dulces / el chicle
4. los billetes / las monedas
5. la pulsera / el anillo
6. el peine / el espejo
7. los esquís acuáticos / la tabla hawaiana
8. el sombrero / los anteojos de sol
9. el reloj de pulsera / la navaja
10. el lápiz / el bolígrafo

C. Repaso: el pronombre *se*

Review the use of the pronoun **se** in the sentences below.

¿**Le** prestas tu moto **a Carlos?**	Sí, **se** la presto.
¿**Le** vendes tus libros **a María?**	No, no **se** los vendo.
¿**Les** mandas el telegrama **a tus primos?**	Sí, voy a mandár**se**lo.

Se replaces **le** and **les** before the direct object pronouns **lo, la, los, las.**

ACTIVIDAD 8   Isabel

Isabel actúa positivamente con chicas y actúa negativamente con chicos. Di cómo va a actuar ella.   VARIATION with **ir: No, no va a dársela.**

> ¿Le da su dirección a Andrés?   No, no se la da.
>
> ¿Le da sus tareas a Rita?   Sí, se las da.

1. ¿Le enseña sus fotos a Roberto?
2. ¿Le enseña sus notas a Luisa?
3. ¿Les presta sus pulseras a sus amigas?
4. ¿Le presta su libreta a Ramón?
5. ¿Le manda el telegrama a su primo?
6. ¿Les manda la tarjeta a sus primas?
7. ¿Les da el chicle a León y Felipe?
8. ¿Le ofrece los dulces a Beatriz?

ACTIVIDAD 9   Regalos

Imagina que tienes dos amigos: Elena, a quien le gustan los deportes, y Ramón, a quien le gusta la música. Di a cuál de los dos vas a regalarle los siguientes objetos.

> una tabla hawaiana   Se la doy a Elena.

1. unos discos
2. unas pelotas de tenis
3. una guitarra
4. un tocadiscos
5. una raqueta
6. unos zapatos de tenis

D. Repaso: el pronombre neutro *lo*   OPTIONAL

This may be presented for recognition only.

Review the use of the neuter pronoun **lo** in the sentencas below.

¿**Sabes dónde vive María?**	No, no **lo** sé. *(I do not know it.)*
Juan dice **que tiene suerte.**	No **lo** creo. *(I don't believe it.)*

The neuter pronoun **lo** replaces a part of a sentence (rather than a specific noun). It is often the equivalent of the English *it* or *so*. Note also the expression:

Lo siento.   *I am sorry (about that).*

Lo may also be used with **ser** and **estar.**
Pablo es muy guapo, ¿no? Sí, lo es.
¿Son tus lápices? Sí, lo son.
¿Está contenta Alicia? No, no lo está.

ACTIVIDAD 10 Preguntas personales

1. ¿Sabes si vas a sacar una buena nota en español?
2. ¿Sabes dónde vive el (la) profesor(a)?
3. ¿Sabes dónde trabaja el papá de tu mejor amigo?
4. ¿Sabes dónde vas a pasar las vacaciones próximas?
5. ¿Sabes cuál es el signo del zodíaco de tu mejor amiga?
6. ¿Sabes si vas a ser millonario(a) un día?

Para la comunicación   OPTIONAL

Proponles ciertos intercambios a tus compañeros con dos cosas que
tienes en tu bolsillo o en tu bolso.
Por ejemplo: —Tengo un lápiz. Te lo cambio por tu bolígrafo.
　　　　　　—Pero no necesito un lápiz. Te cambio mi bolígrafo por tus
　　　　　　　llaves . . .

This activity may be as-
signed as homework.

VARIATION: Pairs of stu-
dents can give short skits.

Lección 4 ¡No hay democracia!

Hoy es domingo. Como todos los domingos, la familia Morales va al cine. Pero, ¿qué película va a ver? ¡Eso es un problema! Cuando hay cinco hijos en una familia, casi siempre hay cinco opiniones diferentes. Pero en una familia tan organizada como la familia Morales, siempre hay una solución para los problemas de esa clase. . . .

STRUCTURES TO REVIEW:
- The construction **me gusta(n)**
- The use of the definite article in the general sense

Sra. de Morales:	¿Chicos, quieren ir al cine?
Roberto:	¡Claro, mamá!
Silvia:	¡Qué idea tan buena!
Carmen:	¡Vamos a ver una película romántica!
Manuel:	¡Qué ideas tan estúpidas tienes, Carmen! ¡Las películas románticas son tan tontas! ¡A mí me gustan las películas de aventuras!
Enrique:	¡Y a mí no me gustan! ¡Solamente me agradan las películas cómicas!
Silvia:	¡Y a mí me gustan las películas de horror!
Roberto:	¡Y a mí me gustan las películas del oeste!
Sra. de Morales:	Un momento, jóvenes. . . . ¿Quién va a comprar las entradas?
Silvia:	¡Espero que papá!
Roberto:	¡Lo espero también!
Sra. de Morales:	¡Entonces, papá tiene que decidir. . . ! Julio, ¿qué clase de película te gustaría ver?
Sr. Morales:	Una comedia musical, ¡por supuesto!
Enrique:	¡No es justo!
Sra. de Morales:	¿Quieren ir con nosotros, o no?
Carmen:	Bueno . . . vamos a ver una comedia musical . . . pero . . .
Roberto:	En esta familia . . .
Silvia:	. . .¡NO HAY DEMOCRACIA!

me agradan: *I like*

entradas: *tickets*

¡Espero que papá! =
Espero que papá va
a comprar las
entradas.

justo: *fair*

¿Qué día es hoy? ¿Adónde va la familia Morales todos los domingos? ¿Cuántos hijos hay en la familia Morales? ¿Cómo se llaman? ¿Quién desea ver una película romántica? ¿A quién le gustan las películas de aventuras? ¿A quién le agradan las películas cómicas? ¿A quién le gustan las películas de horror? ¿A quién le gustan las películas del oeste? ¿Quién va a comprar las entradas? ¿Qué clase de película le gusta al Sr. Morales? ¿Qué clase de película va a ver la familia Morales? ¿Hay democracia en esta familia?

La autoridad paternal

¿Quién decide adónde vas de vacaciones, o qué clase de coche o de ropa vas a comprar? Tal vez tu mamá, tu papá o quizá ambos°. . . o a veces tú decides.

En las familias hispanas tradicionales, es el padre quien gana el dinero. Por lo tanto° él toma las decisiones grandes o pequeñas que conciernen a la familia. ¡Y sus decisiones son finales! Sin embargo, el papel° de la madre en asuntos° familiares° es importantísimo. Aunque ella no toma las decisiones finales, ella toma parte en ellas y hasta° puede influir en los resultados. Cuando un joven tiene miedo° de pedirle algo a su padre, su mejor estrategia es ir a hablar con su madre.

ambos *both* **Por lo tanto** *Therefore* **papel** *role* **asuntos** *matters* **familiares** *family* **hasta** *even* **tiene miedo** *is afraid*

¡Vamos al cine!

¿Te gusta ver películas? En los Estados Unidos, los jóvenes van a menudo al cine. También pueden ver buenas películas en la televisión por los sistemas de cable. Los jóvenes que tienen una videograbadora° en casa pueden alquilar° videos de sus películas favoritas y verlas sin salir de casa.

A los jóvenes hispánicos también les encanta ver películas. Sin embargo,° en los países hispanos generalmente en la televisión no se presentan pelí-

culas modernas. La mayoría de las familias no tiene videograbadora. Entonces, no hay más remedio. ¡Hay que° ir al cine!

A veces, cuando se estrena° una película es necesario hacer cola° para entrar en el cine. Las funciones° empiezan regularmente por la tarde, aunque hay cines que tienen funciones de matinée. Algunos cines presentan dos películas y durante el intermedio° se puede comprar rositas de maíz° y refrescos y además hablar con los amigos. Las películas más populares entre los jóvenes hispánicos son las películas cómicas, policíacas, de misterio, de horror, de comedias musicales, de vaqueros° y, por supuesto, las de ciencia ficción.

videograbadora *VCR* **alquilar** *rent* **Sin embargo** *However* **Hay que** *One has to* **se estrena** *premières* **hacer cola** *to stand in line* **funciones** *shows* **intermedio** *intermission* **rositas de maíz** *popcorn* **vaqueros** *cowboys*

¿Qué tipo de películas les gusta a los jóvenes hispánicos? ¿Son interesantes las películas que se presentan el la televisión? ¿Cuántas películas presentan los cines? ¿Qué puedes hacer durante el intermedio?

Vocabulario

sustantivos	*una clase	type, kind	*una entrada	ticket
expresiones	casi	almost	¿cuál? ¿cuáles?	which?
	entonces	then	*hay que	one must, it is
	*un momento	wait a minute		necessary to
	*no es justo	it's not fair	todos los	every
	*¡qué . . .!	what (a) . . .!	(todas las)	

NOTA: **¿Cuál?** is usually used instead of **¿qué?** in front of the verb **ser**.
It suggests a choice between several possibilities.

　　　　¿Cuál es la mejor película?　　*Which is the best picture?*

¿Te gusta el cine?
¿Te gustan las películas de horror?
¿Te gusta la violencia?
¿Te gustan los deportes violentos?
¿Te gusta la música?
¿Te gustan las comedias musicales?

Act. 3

25

VOCABULARIO PRÁCTICO **Las diversiones**

los deportes

Hay deportes individuales y deportes de **equipo** *(team)*.
Un **deporte** puede ser *sano (healthy),* **peligroso** *(dangerous)* o **violento.**

  bailar
  *****cazar** *(to hunt)* ✓
  *****escalar** *(to climb)* la montaña
  jugar al básquetbol, al fútbol,
      al ping pong, al tenis ✓
  *****montar a caballo** *(to ride)*
  nadar ✓
  *****patinar** *(to skate)* ✓
  *****el baile** moderno, clásico
  *****la caza** *(hunting)*
  *****el alpinismo** *(mountain climbing)* ✓
  el básquetbol, el fútbol, ✓
   *****el ping pong, el tenis**
  *****la equitación** *(horseback riding)* ✓
  la natación *(swimming)*
  *****el patinaje** *(skating)*

SCRIPT

Act. 4

The present tense of **jugar** is reviewed on p. 101.
EXTRA VOCAB.: **trotar** (to jog), **las telenovelas** (TV serials).

ACTIVIDAD 1   Diálogo: Las diversiones

Pregúntales a tus compañeros si les gustan las siguientes diversiones,
según el modelo.

ADDITIONAL CUES: **el ping pong, el golf,
el fútbol, la pintura.**

 el baile   Estudiante 1: ¿Te gusta el baile?
                    Estudiante 2: Sí, me gusta bailar.
                             (No, no me gusta bailar.)

1. el alpinismo	4. la cerámica	7. la fotografía
2. el tenis	5. la lectura	8. la caza
3. la equitación	6. el patinaje	9. la cocina

26

los pasatiempos

Hay pasatiempos artísticos. Otros son intelectuales.

cocinar	**la cocina** (*cooking*)
coleccionar	**la colección de sellos** (*stamps*)**, de monedas**
hacer cerámica	**la cerámica** (*pottery*)
leer	**la lectura** (*reading*)
pintar (*to paint*)	**la pintura**
sacar fotos	**la fotografía**

los espectáculos

A veces somos espectadores.

el cine: **una película** de aventuras, de horror, del oeste

el teatro: **una obra de teatro** (*play*),* **una tragedia,** * **una comedia**

la televisión o la radio: **las noticias** (*news*), **un programa** de variedades,
                          un partido (*game, match*) de fútbol o de tenis

la música:* **una ópera, un concierto**

Estructuras

A. Repaso: el uso del artículo en el sentido general

Note the use of the definite article in the following sentences.

¿Qué piensas de **la** música moderna?	*What do you think of modern music (in general)?*
¿Es **el** fútbol un deporte bueno?	*Is soccer (generally) a good sport?*
Las comedias musicales son aburridas.	*Musical comedies (in general) are boring.*
¿Estás en pro o en contra de **la** violencia en la televisión?	*Are you for or against violence on TV (in general)?*

Spanish speakers use the definite article before a noun used in a general or collective sense. In English the article is omitted.

ACTIVIDAD 2   Tus opiniones

Expresa lo que piensas de las siguientes diversiones, usando los elementos de A y B.

1. fútbol
2. volibol
3. natación
4. cine
5. teatro
6. fotografía
7. lectura
8. televisión
9. cerámica
10. películas románticas
11. películas de ciencia-ficción
12. películas del oeste
13. baile
14. alpinismo
15. cocina
16. pintura
17. patinaje
18. caza
19. equitación
20. atletismo

You may use this activity as the basis of a class survey, asking each student to name the three hobbies or sports that he/she likes the best (least).

A	B	
deporte	estupendo	difícil
espectáculo	interesante	peligroso
pasatiempo	aburrido	sano
	tonto	violento
	útil	artístico

☞ tenis   El tenis es un deporte interesante.

ACTIVIDAD 3   ¿En pro o en contra?

¿Estás en pro o en contra de las siguientes cosas? Explica tu opinión, usando los siguientes adjetivos en frases afirmativas o negativas: **útil, inútil, necesario, sano, peligroso, bueno, malo** (* indica que el sustantivo es femenino).

> violencia*   Estoy en contra (en pro) de la violencia.
> La violencia es mala (buena).

WB
A1, A2

SCRIPT
🎞
Act. 5

1. justicia*
2. progreso social
3. progreso técnico
4. democracia*
5. libertad* *(freedom)*

6. injusticia*
7. revolución*
8. anarquía*
9. contaminación* *(pollution)* del aire
10. exámenes

B. Repaso: la construcción *me gusta(n)*

Note the forms of the expression **me gusta** in the following sentences.

¿**Te gusta** el jazz?   No, **me gusta** solamente la música clásica.

¿**Te gustan** los deportes?   Sí, **me gustan** especialmente los deportes como el tenis y la natación.

> Literally, **gustar** means *to please* or *to be pleasing.*
> In expressions such as **me gusta la música, me gustan los deportes,** the verb **gustar** agrees with the subject (**la música, los deportes**) and not with **me,** which is the indirect object.

> **Me** can be replaced by the other indirect object pronouns: **te, le, nos, les**.

Nos gusta el español, ¿verdad?   *We like Spanish, don't we?*
*(Spanish **is pleasing to us** . . .)*

A Rita le gusta el tenis y   *Rita likes tennis and*
a Esteban **le gusta** la natación.   ***Esteban likes** swimming.*

¿**Le gustan** las películas   *Do you like American movies,*
norteamericanas, Sr. Morales?   *Mr. Morales?*

ACTIVIDAD 4   El turista mexicano

Imagina que un periodista norteamericano le hace una entrevista a un turista mexicano. Le pregunta a él si le gustan las siguientes cosas. Haz los dos papeles.

> Nueva York (sí)   El periodista: ¿Le gusta Nueva York?
> El turista: Sí, me gusta mucho.

1. el béisbol (sí)
2. el fútbol americano (no)
3. la hospitalidad (sí)
4. las películas (no)

5. los programas de televisión (no)
6. la cocina (no)
7. los restaurantes (no)
8. los hoteles (sí)

VOCABULARIO PRÁCTICO   Expresiones como *me gusta*

me gusta(n) más	I prefer (. . . please[s] me more)	Me gusta la televisión, pero **me gusta más** el cine.
me gustaría(n)	I would like (. . . would please me)	**Me gustaría** ir a México.
me agrada(n)	I enjoy (. . . please[s] me)	**Me agradan** las películas del oeste.
me disgusta(n)	I hate (. . . disgust[s] me)	**Me disgustan** las películas de violencia.
me encanta(n)	I like very much (. . . please[s] me very much)	**Me encanta** la música.
me interesa(n)	I am interested in (. . . interest[s] me)	**Nos interesa** la clase.
me importa(n)	. . . matter(s) to me	No **me importan** tus ideas.
me preocupa(n)	I am worried by (. . . worry[ies] me)	**Me preocupa** el futuro.
me falta(n)	I lack (. . . is[are] lacking to me) I do not have	**Nos falta** experiencia. **Me faltan** dos dólares para ir al cine.

Have students suggest other completions, either nouns or infinitives, e.g. **Me gustaría bailar ahora. Me encanta la fotografía.**

ACTIVIDAD 5   Expresión personal

Expresa tus reacciones personales a las siguientes cosas, usando las
expresiones del vocabulario en frases afirmativas o negativas.

  mis estudios   (No) Me interesan (preocupan, importan . . .) mis estudios.

1. la música clásica
2. el baile tradicional
3. los deportes violentos
4. las películas de violencia
5. los exámenes

6. las vacaciones
7. mis relaciones con mis amigos
8. mis relaciones con mis padres
9. mis notas
10. el futuro del mundo

ACTIVIDAD 6   Lo que nos falta *(What we don't have)*

Hay muchas cosas que no podemos hacer porque nos falta algo. Expresa
eso, completando las frases con una idea personal.

  Me falta dinero para . . .   Me falta dinero para comprar una moto.

1. Me falta experiencia para . . .
2. Me falta tiempo para . . .
3. Me falta paciencia para . . .

4. Me falta ambición para . . .
5. Me falta talento para . . .
6. Me falta inspiración para . . .

En cinco minutos, ¿cuántas frases lógicas puedes crear? Usa los elementos
de las columnas A, B, C y D, según el modelo.

May be assigned as a
special challenge activity.

A	B	C	D
Marina	loco	gustar	el tenis
el Sr. Chávez	deportista	encantar	la música clásica
la Srta. Velázquez	intelectual	disgustar	los conciertos de rock
nosotros	liberal	agradar	el comunismo
mis amigos	músico		la ópera
	conservador		la violencia
	artístico		las modas extravagantes
			la libertad *(freedom)*
			el peligro *(danger)*
			las ideas revolucionarias
			la escultura
			la pintura
			la equitación
			la caza

WB
B1, B2

SCRIPT
Act. 6

Marina es música. Le gusta la ópera.

C. La construcción *el (la, los, las)* + adjetivo   OPTIONAL

This may be presented for recognition only.

Note the use of the definite articles in the following questions and
answers.

¿Te gusta más el teatro moderno o el clásico?   **El** moderno. *(The modern **one**.)*
¿Te gusta más la música norteamericana o la hispana? **La** hispana. *(The Spanish **one**.)*
¿Prefieres los programas cómicos o los dramáticos?   **Los** cómicos. *(The funny **ones**.)*
¿Prefieres las chicas morenas o las rubias?   **Las** morenas. *(The brunette **ones**.)*

To avoid repeating a noun, Spanish speakers often use the construction:

The equivalent English construction is: the +
adjective + one(s).

> **el, la, los, las** + adjective

In the above sentences,   el clásico = el teatro clásico
                          la hispana = la música hispana

There is a similar construction with the indefinite article:

un(a) joven   a young man (woman)
un(a) viejo(a)   an old man (woman)
un(a) francés(esa)   a French man (woman)

Lección cuatro
89

ACTIVIDAD 8   El honor nacional

Un chico español está discutiendo *(arguing)* con una chica mexicana. El chico español dice que las cosas españolas son buenas. La chica mexicana dice que las cosas mexicanas son mejores. Haz los dos papeles.

Ɔ⟩   las películas   El chico español: Las películas españolas son muy buenas.
La chica mexicana: ¡Quizá! Pero las mexicanas son mejores.

1. el teatro
2. la literatura
3. el arte
4. el clima *(climate)*
5. los restaurantes
6. la cocina
7. los atletas
8. los artistas
9. los museos
10. las comedias

D. La construcción *el (la, los, las) + que*   OPTIONAL

This may be presented for recognition only.

We have seen several instances in which the definite article can be used to replace a noun which has already been expressed.

el (la, los, las) + de

¿Es la moto de Juan?
No, es **la de** Ramón.   *No, it is Ramón's **(the one of** Ramón).*
       (la moto de Ramón)

el (la, los, las) + adjetivo

¿Te gustan los programas cómicos?
Sí, pero me gustan **los dramáticos** también.   *Yes, but I also like the **dramatic ones**.*
       (los programas dramáticos)

Also note the construction   **el (la, los, las) + que**

Hay dos chicas aquí.
Alicia es **la que** estudia conmigo.   *Alicia is **the one who** studies with me.*
       (la chica que)
¿Cuál es el muchacho francés?
    Es **el que** habla con Luisa.   *It's **the one who** is talking with Luisa.*
       (el muchacho que)

Unidad 3

Día tras día

3.1 Ocho cosas que no me gustan

3.2 La rutina diaria

3.3 El chinchoso

3.4 ¡Viva el amor!

VARIEDADES Una chica como ninguna otra

OBJECTIVES
Communication
In this unit students use Spanish to talk about:
- Personal opinions (thinking, liking, wishing to do various things)
- Their daily routine (getting up, washing, getting dressed)
- Personal care and clothes
- Their feelings and emotions

Language
This unit continues review and expansion, treating the following topics:
- Stem-changing verbs
- Verbs with first-person irregularity (in **-go**)
- Forms and position of reflexive pronouns
- Uses of reflexive verbs to indicate reflexive and reciprocal actions

Culture
This unit treats Hispanic attitudes toward money and marriage and presents Buenos Aires.

 Review   Modules 14, 16

Lección 1 Ocho cosas que no me gustan

Act. 1

La vida no es siempre color de rosa . . . De vez en cuando, tenemos nuestros pequeños problemas . . . ¡Éstas son algunas cosas que no me gustan a mí, Patricia Álvarez!

color de rosa: *fun*

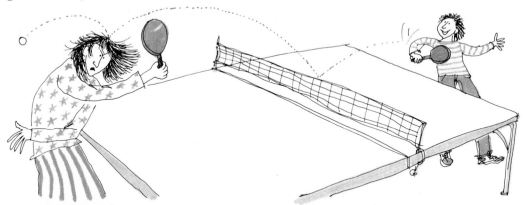

No me gusta . . .

... jugar al ping pong con mi hermano.
Juego bastante bien y él juega mal. No es divertido jugar
con él. ¡Qué va!

¡Qué va!: *Nonsense!*

... jugar al tenis con mis primas.
Juego bien pero ellas juegan mejor. Cuando jugamos
juntas, ellas ganan y yo pierdo. ¡Siempre! ¡Qué lástima!

juntas: *together*

... perder el tiempo.
¡Especialmente cuando lo pierdo con personas aburridas!
¡Qué lata!

¡Qué lata!: *What a bore!*
chistes: *jokes*

... contar chistes.
¡No los cuento bien! ¡Qué lío!

¡Qué lío!: *What a mess!*

... pedirle dinero a mi papá.
Mi papá es generoso conmigo solamente cuando recibo
buenas notas. ¡Ay! Por eso no le pido dinero a menudo.
. . . ¡Se lo pido a mi mamá!

Have the students compare the **yo** forms and the infinitives of the verbs in the reading: **jugar, perder, contar, pedir, almorzar, encontrar, dormir**. Be sure they remember the meanings of these verbs.

... almorzar en la cafetería de la escuela.
Almuerzo allí cinco días por semana y cuarenta semanas
por año . . . ¡Qué horror!

... encontrar a personas antipáticas.
¡Afortunadamente, no las encuentro a menudo! ¡Qué
bueno!

... dormir más de nueve horas por día.
Cuando duermo más, me duele la cabeza y me siento de
mal humor el resto del día. ¡Qué malo!

más de: *more than*
me duele la cabeza:
my head aches

¿Cómo se llama la chica que habla? ¿Con quién juega al ping pong? ¿Quién gana? ¿Con quiénes juega al tenis? ¿Quién pierde? ¿Por qué no le gusta contar chistes? ¿Cuándo le da dinero su papá? ¿A qué otra persona le pide dinero? ¿Dónde almuerza? ¿Por qué no le gusta dormir demasiado?

Act. 2

El dinero

Muchos padres hispanos no suelen° darles una mensualidad° a sus hijos. Generalmente si los jóvenes reciben dinero es en ocasiones especiales como el cumpleaños, la Navidad, el Año Nuevo, visitas de parientes generosos o cuando reciben buenas notas. Sin embargo, los jóvenes no tienen muchos gastos.° Los padres les pagan el colegio, los libros, los gastos de transporte y las menudencias.°

El dinero regalado° por los padres a sus hijos en esas ocasiones especiales tiene nombres diferentes en cada país. Por ejemplo, en México se le llama "el domingo" porque tradicionalmente los jóvenes recibían° este dinero los domingos. En otros países, como Colombia, se le llama "la cuelga" a la cantidad° de dinero que se da principalmente como regalo de cumpleaños.

suelen *usually* **mensualidad** *(monthly) allowance* **gastos** *expenses* **menudencias** *small things* **regalado** *given* **recibían** *received* **cantidad** *quantity, sum*

• ¿Siempre dan una mensualidad a sus hijos los padres hispanos? ¿En qué ocasiones especiales reciben dinero? ¿Quién les paga las menudencias? ¿En México, cómo se llama el dinero que reciben los hijos de sus padres en ocasiones especiales? ¿Por qué se llama así?
• SUGGESTED REALIA: Hispanic coins and bills.

Vocabulario

sustantivo	*un chiste	joke
adjetivo	*juntos(as)	together
expresiones	*así (es que)	therefore, so (it is that)
	de vez en cuando	from time to time, once in a while
	*me duele(n) . . .	my . . . hurt(s)
	mejor	better
	*por eso	because of that
exclamaciones	¡Qué lástima!	Too bad!
	*¡Qué lata!	What a bore!
	*¡Qué lío!	What a mixup! What a mess!
	¡Qué malo / bueno!	How awful / great!
	*¡Qué va!	Nonsense!

NOTAS: 1. The construction **me duele** is similar to **me gusta.**

Me duele la cabeza.   *I have a headache. (Literally, the head hurts me.)*

Me duelen los ojos.   *My eyes hurt.*

2. **¡Qué. . .!** To express your feelings about something, you may use the following exclamations:

¡Qué + noun!   What a . . .!   ¡Qué lástima!

¡Qué + adjective!   How . . .!   ¡Qué bueno!

Di si te gusta hacer las siguientes actividades. Di también si las haces
frecuentemente.

∑ᐈ   ¿Te gusta jugar al volibol?

Sí (No, no) me gusta jugar al volibol.   (No) Juego al volibol frecuentemente.

¿Te gusta jugar al tenis?
¿Te gusta jugar al básquetbol?
¿Te gusta jugar al ping pong?
¿Te gusta jugar al béisbol?
¿Te gusta contar chistes?

Estructuras

A. Repaso: los verbos con cambio en el radical *(e → ie)*

Review the changes which occur in the present tense stem of the verbs
pensar *(to think, to intend),* **querer** *(to like),* **preferir** *(to prefer).*

INFINITIVE	pensar	querer	preferir
PRESENT			
(yo)	pienso	quiero	prefiero
(tú)	piensas	quieres	prefieres
(él, ella, Ud.)	piensa	quiere	prefiere
(nosotros)	pensamos	queremos	preferimos
(vosotros)	pensáis	queréis	preferís
(ellos, ellas, Uds.)	piensan	quieren	prefieren
PRESENT PARTICIPLE	pensando	queriendo	prefiriendo

∑ᐈ   In many verbs that have an **e** in the stem, the **e** becomes **ie** in the
yo, tú, él, and **ellos** forms of the present tense.

∑ᐈ   For **-ir** verbs only, another stem change occurs in the present
participle: **e → i.**

∑ᐈ   The endings of all stem-changing verbs are regular.

ACTIVIDAD 1   A cada uno su gusto *(Everyone to his or her own taste)*

Todos no tenemos los mismos gustos. Las siguientes personas no quieren hacer ciertas cosas porque prefieren hacer otras. Expresa esto, según el modelo.

Paco: estudiar francés / inglés   Paco no quiere estudiar francés.
Prefiere estudiar inglés.

1. Rafael: leer novelas / historietas *(comics)*
2. mis hermanas: escuchar la radio / discos
3. tú: salir con Teresa / con Roberto
4. yo: ir a México / a España
5. nosotros: jugar al tenis / al béisbol
6. Enrique: comer dulces / helado
7. Ud.: correr las olas / en la playa
8. Uds.: caminar por el centro / por el campo

Act. 3

SCRIPT

Act. 4

VOCABULARIO PRÁCTICO   Verbos con cambio en el radical (e → ie)

verbos que terminan en -ar

*cerrar	to close, to shut	Lucía **cierra** la ventana.
*cerrar con llave	to lock	¿**Cierras** tu cuarto **con llave**?
comenzar	to begin, to start	Mateo **comienza** una novela.
comenzar a (+ infinitivo)	to begin, to start	**Comenzamos a** trabajar a las ocho.
empezar	to begin, to start	La película **empieza** a las nueve.
empezar a (+ infinitivo)	to begin, to start	Está **empezando** a llover.
pensar de	to think of, to have an opinion about	¿Qué **piensas de** Roberto?
pensar en	to think about	¿**Piensas** mucho **en** el futuro?
pensar (+ infinitivo)	to intend, to plan	¿**Piensas** hacer un viaje durante las vacaciones próximas?

verbos que terminan en -er

entender	to understand	No **entiendo** al profesor.
perder	to lose	¿Por qué **pierdes** la paciencia?
	to waste	No me gusta **perder** el tiempo con personas aburridas.
	to miss	No **pierdo** nunca el autobús.
querer	to want (something)	¿**Quieres** té o café?
querer a	to like, love (someone)	Pedro **quiere a** Anita.
querer (+ infinitivo)	to want	¿**Quiere** Ud. ir al cine conmigo?

verbos que terminan en -ir

*mentir	to lie	No me gustan las personas que **mienten.**
preferir	to prefer	¿**Prefieres** ir al cine o al teatro?
sentir	to feel	**Siento** admiración por Rosita.
	to regret, to be sorry about	Mis hermanos **sienten** mucho su accidente.

ACTIVIDAD 2 Preguntas personales

Ask questions rapidly to develop listening comprehension. Let students give **sí/no** answers.

1. ¿Cierras la puerta de tu cuarto cuando estudias? ¿cuando escuchas música? ¿cuando estás allí con tus amigos?

2. Cuando vas al colegio, ¿cierras con llave tu cuarto? ¿los cajones *(drawers)* de tu escritorio *(desk)*?

3. ¿Cierras los ojos cuando ves una película de horror? ¿un accidente?

4. ¿A qué hora empieza la clase de español? ¿la clase de inglés? ¿la clase de matemáticas?

5. ¿Piensas mucho en los estudios? ¿en las fiestas? ¿en el futuro? ¿en los problemas del mundo?

6. De vez en cuando, ¿pierdes la paciencia? ¿el tiempo? ¿el dominio de ti mismo *(self-control)*? ¿la cabeza? ¿tus facultades *(senses)*?

7. ¿Entiendes español? ¿francés? ¿inglés? ¿otro idioma *(language)*? ¿cuál?

8. ¿Entiendes bien cuando el (la) profesor(a) habla español?

9. ¿Quieres mucho a tus amigos? ¿a tus compañeros?

10. ¿Quieres ser ingeniero(a)? ¿fotógrafo(a)? ¿profesor(a)? ¿médico(a)? ¿artista?

11. ¿De vez en cuando, ¿les mientes a tus amigos? ¿a tus padres? ¿a tus profesores?

12. ¿Sientes mucha admiración por los atletas? ¿por los artistas? ¿por tus padres? ¿por tus profesores?

13. ¿Sientes pena *(grief)* cuando tus amigos están tristes?

B. Repaso: los verbos con cambio en el radical (o, u → ue)

Review the stem changes in the verbs **contar** (*to tell*), **volver** (*to return*), and **dormir** (*to sleep*).

INFINITIVE	contar	volver	dormir
PRESENT			
(yo)	cuento	vuelvo	duermo
(tú)	cuentas	vuelves	duermes
(él, ella, Ud.)	cuenta	vuelve	duerme
(nosotros)	contamos	volvemos	dormimos
(vosotros)	contáis	volvéis	dormís
(ellos, ellas, Uds.)	cuentan	vuelven	duermen
PRESENT PARTICIPLE	contando	volviendo	durmiendo

> In many verbs that have an **o** in the stem, the **o** becomes **ue** in the **yo, tú, él,** and **ellos** forms of the present tense.

> In addition, the **-ir** verbs have another stem change in the present participle: **o → u.**

> **Jugar** (*to play*) has the stem change **u → ue** in the **yo, tú, él,** and **ellos** forms of the present tense.
>
> **Ju**ego al tenis con Silvia.   **Ju**gamos a menudo.

ACTIVIDAD 3   El insomnio

Las siguientes personas no pueden dormir. Explica su insomnio según el modelo.

> Jaime / enfermo   Jaime duerme mal. No puede dormir porque está enfermo.

1. Elena / nerviosa
2. tú / de mal humor
3. mis primos y yo / constipados (*congested with a cold*)
4. nosotros / preocupados
5. yo / enfermo
6. Isabel y Chela / agitadas
7. Ud. / furioso
8. Uds. / de muy mal humor

VARIATION: They sleep well. **Jaime duerme bien. No está enfermo.**

When the cue to an exercise is a compound subject containing **yo** (e.g., **María y yo, tú y yo**), the students should use the **nosotros** form of the verb.

VOCABULARIO PRÁCTICO
Verbos con cambio en el radical (o, u → ue)

verbos que terminan en -ar

almorzar	to have lunch	**Almuerzo** en la cafetería.
contar	to count	Pedro **cuenta** su dinero.
	to tell	Elena **cuenta** un chiste.
costar	to cost	¿Cuánto **cuestan** tus libros?
encontrar	to find (like)	¿Cómo **encuentras** esta película?
	to meet	Espero **encontrar** a mis amigos en el café.
jugar (a + deporte)	to play	Esteban **juega** muy bien **al** tenis.
* **mostrar**	to show	Clara le **muestra** sus fotos a Pedro.
* **probar**	to try (out), to test	Inés **prueba** su bicicleta nueva.
	to taste	Roberto **prueba** el café.
* **recordar**	to remember	No **recuerdo** tu visita.
* **soñar (con)**	to dream (about)	**Sueñas con** cosas imposibles.
		Sueño con ser rico.

verbos que terminan en -er

* **devolver**	to give back, to return (an object)	Le **devuelvo** los discos a Pedro.
poder	can, to be able	¿**Puedes** prestarme cinco dólares?
volver	to return, to come back	¿A qué hora **vuelves**?

verbos que terminan en -ir

dormir	to sleep	No **duermo** bien.

ACTIVIDAD 4   ¿Cuántas veces? *(How often?)*

Di si haces las siguientes cosas. Usa expresiones como **siempre, de vez en cuando, nunca, casi siempre, a menudo, raras veces.**

⟩⟩ dormir bien   Casi siempre, duermo bien.

1. dormir en clase
2. soñar
3. soñar despierto(a) *(to daydream)*
4. soñar con cosas imposibles
5. soñar con ser rico(a)
6. almorzar en la cafetería de la escuela
7. almorzar en restaurantes elegantes
8. contar chistes
9. contar mentiras *(lies)*
10. contar tu dinero
11. recordar tus sueños *(dreams)*
12. devolver las cosas de tus amigos
13. probar las cosas que compras
14. mostrarles tus notas a tus padres
15. volver a casa muy tarde

SCRIPT / Act. 6

VARIATION using the plural:
¿Juegan Uds. al tenis? Sí, jugamos...

ACTIVIDAD 5   Diálogo: Las diversiones

Pregúntales a tus amigos si juegan a las siguientes cosas y con quién.

⟩⟩ al tenis   Estudiante 1: ¿Juegas al tenis?
　　　　　　　Estudiante 2: Sí, juego al tenis. (No, no juego al tenis.)
　　　　　　　Estudiante 1: ¿Con quién juegas?
　　　　　　　Estudiante 2: Juego con mi hermana (Manuel, Bárbara . . .).

1. al volibol
2. al básquetbol
3. al fútbol
4. al ajedrez *(chess)*
5. a las damas *(checkers)*
6. a los naipes *(cards)*
7. al bridge
8. al póker
9. al chaquete *(backgammon)*
10. al béisbol

WB
B1, B2, B3

The English word *backgammon* is also used by many Spanish speakers.

C. Repaso: los verbos con cambio en el radical (e → i)

Review the changes which occur in the stem of **pedir** *(to ask for)*.

Act. 7

INFINITIVE	pedir		
PRESENT			
(yo)	pido	(nosotros)	pedimos
(tú)	pides	(vosotros)	pedís
(él, ella, Ud.)	pide	(ellos, ellas, Uds.)	piden
PRESENT PARTICIPLE	pidiendo		

⟩⟩ In certain verbs in **-ir** that have an **e** in the stem, the **e** becomes **i** in the **yo, tú, él** and **ellos** forms of the present tense and in the present participle.

You may review the difference between **pedir** (to ask for, in the sense of to request) and **preguntar** (to ask a question).

Note that **reír** and **sonreír** are often used in the reflexive form **reírse** and **sonreírse**. The reflexive construction is presented on page 108.

VOCABULARIO PRÁCTICO — Verbos con cambio en el radical (e → i)

pedir	to ask for	Inés le **pide** su foto a Luisa.
*reír	to laugh	**Reímos** a menudo en la clase.
*repetir	to repeat	Roberto **repite** los verbos.
*seguir	to follow	**Sigo** los consejos de mi profesor.
*seguir (+ pres. part.)	to keep on	Carlos **sigue** trabajando.
servir	to serve	¿Qué **sirven** en la cafetería?
*sonreír	to smile	¿Por qué estás **sonriendo**?

NOTAS:

1. The accent on the **í** of **reír** and **sonreír** exists in all forms of the present: **río, ríes, ríe, reímos, reís, ríen.** Note that there is no written accent in the present participle: **riendo.**

   Río cuando mis amigos cuentan chistes.
   Mis padres no **ríen** cuando saco una mala nota.

2. The **gu** of **seguir** becomes **g** before **o**.

   No **sigo** tus instrucciones.

3. The construction **seguir** + present participle means *to keep on* or *to continue doing something.*

Marta sigue estudiando.	*Marta keeps on (continues) studying.*
Sigo escribiéndoles a mis amigos.	*I keep on writing to my friends.*

Number 3 under **NOTAS** above is optional. It may be presented for recognition.

ACTIVIDAD 6   Preguntas personales

1. ¿Le pides consejos a tu papá? ¿a tu mamá? ¿Les pides consejos a tus amigos? ¿a tus profesores?

2. ¿Sigues los consejos de tus amigos? ¿de tus profesores? ¿de tus padres?

3. ¿Sigues los buenos consejos? ¿los buenos ejemplos? ¿los malos ejemplos? ¿la moda?

4. ¿Sirven buenas comidas en la cafetería de tu colegio? ¿Sirven pizza? ¿hamburguesas? ¿tacos?

5. ¿Ríes mucho? ¿Ríes cuando un amigo te cuenta un chiste? ¿cuando el profesor te da una mala nota?

6. ¿Sonríes a los chicos (las chicas) cuando caminas por la calle? ¿cuando estás en la clase?

7. ¿Te gusta repetir los verbos? ¿Los repites a menudo?

ACTIVIDAD 7 Los fines de semana

OPTIONAL

Hay personas que siempre hacen una cierta cosa los fines de semana.
Pregunta a las personas entre paréntesis si siguen haciendo esta misma
actividad. Expresa esto según el modelo.

Silvia siempre juega al tenis los fines de semana. (tú) ¿Sigues jugando
al tenis los fines de semana?

1. Siempre nado los fines de semana. (tú)
2. Siempre monto en bicicleta los fines de semana. (Ud.)
3. Carmen siempre baila los fines de semana. (Uds.)
4. Mi hermana y yo siempre jugamos a las damas (checkers) los fines de semana. (Paco y su tío)
5. Mis hermanas siempre juegan al ajedrez (chess) los fines de semana. (Andrés y Marisol)
6. Clara siempre toca el piano los fines de semana. (Luís)

ACTIVIDAD 8 Causas y consecuencias OPTIONAL

Nuestras acciones producen ciertos resultados. Expresa esto según el
modelo.

María: estar muy cansada / jugar al tenis
María va a estar muy cansada si sigue jugando al tenis.

1. Carlos: engordar (get fat) / comer mucho
2. Ana y yo: adelgazar (get thin) / comer poco
3. nosotros: ganar dinero / trabajar los fines de semana
4. yo: aprender mucho / estudiar
5. tú: aburrir (bore) a tus amigos / hablar siempre
6. Uds.: correr el maratón / correr todos los días

WB
C1, C2,
C3, C4

Para la comunicación OPTIONAL May be assigned as homework.

WB
Trad.

SCRIPT

Act. 8, 9,
10

MASTERS
p. 10

TRB

QUIZ
pp. 26–27

Imagina cuatro actividades que te gusta hacer y cuatro que no te gusta
hacer. Di cuándo, dónde, por qué y con quién haces estas actividades.
Puedes usar «Ocho cosas que no me gustan» como modelo.

Me gusta bailar. Bailo los sábados por la noche . . .

VARIATION: Have students
illustrate their preferences with
magazine pictures.

Lección 2   La rutina diaria

Act. 1

Cada mañana, nos levantamos.

¿Y qué hacemos después? Probablemente, nos miramos en el espejo, y a veces nos admiramos. Nos lavamos, nos peinamos, nos vestimos, nos desayunamos, luego vamos a la escuela o al trabajo . . . Y cada noche, nos acostamos y nos dormimos.

¿Es decir que no hay originalidad en nuestra vida?

¡Claro que no! Hacemos las mismas cosas, pero las hacemos de una manera un poco diferente. Considera a los siguientes amigos porteños. La rutina diaria de cada uno empieza a una hora diferente.

Es decir: Is that to say

porteños: from Buenos Aires

diaria: daily

Jaime (diez y ocho años)

—Yo soy estudiante en la universidad de Buenos Aires. Generalmente, me levanto a las siete, pero los martes no tengo clases por la mañana y no me levanto antes de las diez . . . excepto cuando tengo una cita.

Isabel (veinte y un años)

—Soy enfermera en el Hospital General. Mi trabajo empieza a las ocho. Pero como vivo lejos, tengo que levantarme a las seis . . . ¡Qué lata!

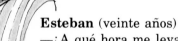

Esteban (veinte años)

—¿A qué hora me levanto? ¿Yo? Me levanto a las dos. No a las dos de la mañana . . . a las dos de la tarde. Soy guitarrista en un club de jazz. Toco toda la noche y me acuesto generalmente a las siete de la mañana.

Ramón (veinte y dos años)

—Soy portero de noche en el Hotel República. Yo también trabajo por la noche y duermo por el día . . . ¿Cuándo me levanto? Depende . . . A las tres o cuatro de la tarde . . .

portero: doorman

¿Quién es Jaime? ¿A qué hora se levanta? ¿A qué hora se levanta los martes?
¿Quién es Isabel? ¿Por qué se levanta a las seis?
¿Quién es Esteban? ¿A qué hora se levanta? ¿Por qué?
¿Dónde trabaja Ramón? ¿A qué hora se levanta?

ct. 2

Buenos Aires, la capital de la Argentina

¿Sabes quiénes son los porteños? Así se llama a los habitantes de Buenos Aires. La capital de la Argentina es una ciudad cosmopolita y enorme. Por su población, es la segunda ciudad de habla hispana° del mundo. Los porteños se sienten muy orgullosos° de su ciudad. Y, ¿por qué? ¡Porque hay muchas cosas interesantes que hacer y ver en Buenos Aires!

• Buenos Aires es la ciudad más europea de las Américas. Muchos la llaman el París de Latinoamérica, porque es una ciudad muy bonita donde hay mucha cultura.

• En el centro de la ciudad está la hermosísima° Plaza de la República con el famoso Obelisco.

• La Avenida 9 de Julio es la más ancha del mundo.

• El teatro Colón está considerado como uno de los mejores del mundo por su acústica.

• Allí está La Boca, parte de la ciudad muy pintoresca donde el tango se hizo° famoso.

Y hay muchísimas razones° más. Si vas a Buenos Aires un día, no olvides° ver esa casa elegante de color de rosa, donde está la oficina del presidente. ¡Ésa es la Casa Rosada!°

de habla hispana *Spanish-speaking*   **orgullosos** *proud* **hermosísima** *very beautiful*   **se hizo** *became*   **razones** *reasons*   **no olvides** *don't forget*   **Rosada** *Pink*

The Obelisk on the Avenida 9 de Julio

¿Cómo se llama la capital de la Argentina? ¿Cómo se llaman los habitantes de Buenos Aires? ¿Por qué se dice de Buenos Aires que es el París de Latinoamérica? ¿Cómo se llama la avenida más ancha del mundo? ¿Dónde vive el presidente de la Argentina?

Vocabulario

expresiones		
	cada	each
	*cada uno	each one
	*como	since
	*de una manera	in a way
	*diario	daily
	luego	then
	*por el día	during the day

NOTAS:
1. **Cada** *(each)* introduces masculine and feminine singular nouns. It has only one form.
   Cada noche.   **Cada** día.

2. **Cada uno** *(each one)* replaces nouns. It has two forms:
   Mira a los chicos.   **Cada uno** tiene una raqueta.
   Mira a las chicas.   **Cada una** tiene una bicicleta.

3. **Como** has different meanings:
   like, as   Te hablo **como** a un hermano.
                      Isabel trabaja **como** enfermera.
   since, because   **Como** vivo lejos del centro, tomo el autobús.

• The word **porteño** means *resident of the port*. Buenos Aires is the port of Argentina and contains one-third of the country's population. The residents of the rest of the country are called **provincianos**.

• The Avenida 9 de Julio, with its ten lanes of traffic, commemorates the day in 1816 when the country, under the leadership of José de San Martín (1778-1850), el Libertador, declared its independence from Spain.

• REALIA: travel brochures on Argentina. See also **Vista** 4.

Ahora vamos a hablar de la rutina diaria de tu familia.

¿A qué hora te levantas los lunes?
¿A qué hora te levantas los domingos?
¿A qué hora se levanta tu papá durante la semana?
¿A qué hora se levanta tu mamá?
¿A qué hora se levantan tus padres los domingos?
¿A qué hora te acuestas durante la semana?

Estructuras

A. Repaso: la construcción reflexiva

Note the form and position of the pronoun in the conjugation of the reflexive verb **lavarse** *(to wash oneself)*.

INFINITIVE	**lavar**se		
PRESENT			
(yo)	**me** lavo	(nosotros)	**nos** lavamos
(tú)	**te** lavas	(vosotros)	**os** laváis
(él, ella, Ud.)	**se** lava	(ellos, ellas, Uds.)	**se** lavan
PRESENT PARTICIPLE	lavánd**ose**		

For practice, you may model the conjugation of other reflexive verbs, such as **mirarse en el espejo** or **peinarse**.

Reflexive verbs are formed with reflexive pronouns.

Reflexive pronouns have the same position as other object pronouns. They usually come before the verb, except in affirmative commands:

¡Lávate!   Commands are presented in Unit 8, Lessons 1-3.

In an infinitive or present progressive construction, the reflexive pronouns come before the conjugated verb or after the infinitive or present participle.

Carlos va a lavar**se**.   **Se** va a lavar.
Isabel está peinándo**se**.   **Se** está peinando.

Compare the reflexive and nonreflexive constructions in the following sentences:

(nonreflexive)   (reflexive)

Clara **lava** el perro.
*Clara **washes** the dog.*

Después, **se lava.**
*Afterwards, **she washes herself.***

Spanish speakers may or may not use the personal **a** with animals depending on whether or not a close relationship exists between the owner and the animal. For simplicity, the personal **a** is not used in this text with animals.

Act. 3

(nonreflexive)   (reflexive)

Manuel **mira** a Isabel.   Isabel **se mira** en el espejo.
*Manuel **looks at** Isabel.*   *Isabel **looks at herself** in the mirror.*

Compro un helado para mi prima.   **Me compro** una Coca-Cola.
*I **buy** an ice cream cone for my cousin.*   *I **buy myself** a coke.*

María **prepara** un sándwich para Tomás.   María **se prepara** para la fiesta.
*María **prepares** a sandwich for Tomás.* *María **prepares herself** for the party.*

- In a reflexive construction, the subject performs the action for or on himself: the reflexive pronoun represents the same person as the subject.

- Reflexive verbs are used very frequently in Spanish. Sometimes the reflexive pronouns **me, te, se** . . . are the equivalent of the English pronouns *myself, yourself, himself* . . . Most of the time, however, the English pronouns are implied but not expressed.

Me lavo.   *I am washing (that is, I am washing myself).*
Ramón se compra un reloj.   *Ramón is buying a watch (that is, Ramón is buying a watch for himself).*

ACTIVIDAD 1   En la feria de San Isidro *(At Saint Isidro's fair)*

VARIATION with infinitive:
Isabel quiere comprarse un anillo.

Hay muchos vendedores ambulantes *(traveling)* y muchos compradores en la feria de San Isidro. Di lo que se compran las siguientes personas.

- Isabel (un anillo)   Isabel se compra un anillo.

1. Roberto (una navaja)   4. yo (un sombrero)   7. Uds. (un bolso)
2. Inés (una pulsera)   5. tú (un helado)   8. nosotros (un collar)
3. mis primas (pendientes)   6. Ud. (un reloj)   9. tú y yo (dulces)

ACTIVIDAD 2   El cumpleaños de Roberto

Hoy es la fiesta de cumpleaños de Roberto. Los amigos de Roberto preparan sus regalos. Después se preparan para la fiesta. Expresa esto según el modelo.

🎵 Chela   Chela prepara su regalo. Después, se prepara para la fiesta.

1. Uds.
2. Carmen y Felicia
3. la novia de Roberto
4. mis amigos
5. tú

6. yo
7. nosotros
8. Uds.
9. tú y yo
10. Luis y yo

ACTIVIDAD 3   Diferencias de opinión

Las siguientes personas tienen una opinión elevada de ellas mismas. Pero sus amigos (entre paréntesis) tienen otra opinión. Expresa esto según el modelo.

🎵 Juan: inteligente (Pedro: tonto)   Juan se cree inteligente, pero Pedro lo cree tonto.

1. Silvia: bonita (Rita: ordinaria)
2. Ramón: interesante (Olga: aburrido)
3. Mis primos: superiores a todos (sus compañeros: tontos)
4. yo: muy inteligente (el profesor: perezoso[a])

WB
A1, A2

SCRIPT
🔊
Act. 4, 5

MASTERS
p. 11

5. tú: extraordinario (tu hermano: vanidoso [*vain*])
6. nosotros: simpáticos (los otros alumnos: presumidos [*stuck up*])
7. Ud.: delgado (yo: un poco gordo)
8. Tomás y yo: muy deportistas (nuestras hermanas: perezosos)

B. Repaso: los verbos reflexivos: el arreglo personal

Note the use of reflexive verbs in the following sentences.

Te bañas.	*You take a bath.*
Me corto el pelo.	*I cut my hair.*
Pepita **se lava las** manos.	*Pepita washes her hands.*
Mis hermanos **se quitan los** zapatos.	*My brothers take off their shoes.*

You may have the students review the parts of the body and items of clothing (Appendix 2), for this vocabulary is used in some of the exercises that follow.

🎵 In Spanish, most of the verbs relating to personal care are used in the reflexive when the subject performs the action on or for the subject.

🎵 After such verbs, Spanish speakers often use the definite article before parts of the body and articles of clothing. (In English, the possessive adjective is used.)

VOCABULARIO PRÁCTICO

El arreglo personal (Personal care)

sustantivos

*un cepillo

*el champú

un espejo

*el jabón

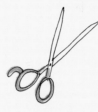

*el lápiz de labios

*una afeitadora

*unas tijeras

un peine

ACTIVITY: Use the sentences below for student practice by varying the subjects. **Mi tío se afeita... Tú te bañas...**

verbos

afeitarse	to shave (oneself)	Mi padre **se afeita** con una afeitadora.
bañarse	to take a bath	**Me baño** en el baño.
*cepillarse	to brush	**Nos cepillamos** los dientes y las*uñas *(nails)*.
cortarse	to cut (oneself)	Pedro **se corta** el pelo, la barba, el*bigote *(mustache)* y las uñas.
lavarse	to wash (oneself)	**Te lavas** la cara, las manos, los pies y el pelo.
peinarse	to comb (one's hair)	**Me peino** con un peine.
*pintarse	to put on makeup	Mi prima **se pinta** los ojos, la boca . . .
*prepararse	to get ready	**Nos preparamos** para la fiesta.
*quitarse	to take (something) off	Andrés **se quita** el suéter, los zapatos y los calcetines.
*secarse	to dry	**Me seco** el pelo con la*secadora *(dryer)*.
vestirse (e → i)	to dress, to get dressed	¡**Te vistes** con mucha elegancia, Carmen!

NOTA: Many of the above verbs can be used in reflexive and nonreflexive constructions with a slightly different meaning.

nonreflexive:	Ana **baña** el perro.	*Ana gives a bath to the dog.*
reflexive:	Ana **se baña**.	*Ana takes a bath (herself).*
nonreflexive:	Carmen **pinta** su cuarto.	*Carmen paints her room.*
reflexive:	Carmen **se pinta**.	*Carmen puts on makeup (that is, paints herself).*

Remind the students that in a reflexive construction the pronouns **me, te,**... correspond to the English pronouns myself, yourself,...which are implied but not expressed.

EXTRA VOCAB.: **los rulos** (curlers), **el desodorante** (deodorant), **el maquillaje** (makeup), **la pasta de dientes, el dentífrico** (toothpaste), **la crema de afeitar** (shaving cream), **el perfume** (perfume), **la colonia** (cologne), **ducharse, tomar una ducha** (to [take a] shower).

ACTIVIDAD 4   En el cuarto de baño *(In the bathroom)*

Las siguientes personas usan ciertos objetos. Puedes decir qué hace cada una.

> Manuel usa jabón.   (Se baña, se lava las manos . . .)

1. Inés usa tijeras.
2. Felipe usa una secadora.
3. El Sr. Montero usa una afeitadora.
4. La Sra. de Martínez usa champú.
5. Isabel usa un peine.
6. Pablo usa un cepillo.
7. María usa un lápiz de labios.
8. Elena usa el espejo.

ACTIVIDAD 5   El orden lógico

Tenemos que hacer ciertas cosas antes de hacer otras. Para cada una de las siguientes personas, crea un párrafo usando las expresiones entre paréntesis en el orden lógico.

> Pedro (bañarse / quitarse la camisa / quitarse la corbata)
>   Pedro se quita la corbata. Se quita la camisa. Se baña.

1. María (pintarse / bañarse / vestirse)
2. la Sra. de Ojeda (lavarse el pelo / peinarse / secarse el pelo)
3. Enrique (lavarse los pies / quitarse los calcetines / quitarse los zapatos)
4. tú (quitarse los pijamas / vestirse / lavarse)

C. Repaso: los verbos reflexivos: las actividades diarias

Review the use of reflexive verbs in the following sentences.

Me levanto a las siete.	*I get up at seven.*
¿A qué hora **te acuestas?**	*At what time do you go to bed?*
Mi padre **se va** al trabajo a las ocho.	*My father leaves for work at eight.*

> Many daily activities are expressed in Spanish by reflexive verbs, especially when these activities involve physical movement.

> Note that in the corresponding English expressions, the reflexive pronouns *(myself, yourself . . .)* are often implied but not expressed. For instance, the sentence **Pedro se acuesta** *(Pedro goes to bed)* literally means *Pedro puts himself to bed.*

VOCABULARIO PRÁCTICO

Nuestras actividades diarias

*despertarse (e → ie)	to wake up	Carlos **se despierta** a las siete,
levantarse	to get up	. . . pero no **se levanta** hasta
		las siete y media.
sentarse (e → ie)	to sit down	María **se sienta** en la silla.
acostarse (o → ue)	to go to bed	Elena **se acuesta** a las diez,
dormirse (o → ue)	to fall asleep	. . . pero no **se duerme**
		inmediatamente.
*callarse	to keep quiet, silent	**¿Se callan** los alumnos
		cuando el profesor habla?
*quedarse	to stay	Cuando estoy enfermo, **me**
		quedo en la cama.
*despedirse (e → i)	to take leave, say good-bye	Cuando **me despido,** les digo
		«Adiós» a mis amigos.
irse (a)	to leave (for), go (away)	¿A qué hora **te vas** a la escuela?
*marcharse	to leave	Si no me gusta la película, voy
		a **marcharme.**
*darse prisa	to hurry	No **me doy prisa** para ir al colegio.
*reunirse (con)	to meet	**Me reúno con** mis amigos en
		la heladería.

NOTA: Most of the above verbs can be used in nonreflexive constructions. Although there is a relationship between the reflexive and nonreflexive verbs, their meanings are different. Compare:

La Sra. de Morales **despierta** a Carlos.	*Mrs. Morales **wakes** Carlos **up.***
Carlos **se despierta.**	*Carlos **wakes up.***
Levanto la maleta.	*I **lift** the suitcase.*
Me levanto.	*I **get up** (that is, I **lift myself up**).*
Voy a la escuela.	*I **go** to school.*
Me voy a la escuela.	*I **leave** for school.*

Remember that **reunirse** has a written accent on the **u** in some forms.

• The expression **irse de** means *to leave* in the sense of not planning to return.

• The expression **salir de** is used to mean *to leave* with the intent of returning: **Salimos de la escuela a las tres.**

ACTIVIDAD 6 Quince horas después

Las siguientes personas se acuestan exactamente quince horas después de despertarse. Expresa eso según el modelo.

la Sra. de Martínez (6:30 / 9:30) La Sra. de Martínez se despierta a las seis y media. Se acuesta a las nueve y media.

1. el Sr. Ayala (6:00 / 9:00)
2. mi hermano (7:00 / 10:00)
3. yo (8:30 / 11:30)
4. Inés (8:15 / 11:15)
5. mis padres (7:30 / 10:30)
6. tú (7:45 / 10:45)
7. nosotros (10:00 / 1:00)
8. Uds. y yo (9:45 / 12:45)

ACTIVIDAD 7 Preguntas personales

Ask about student responses. **¿A qué hora se levanta Julie los lunes?**

1. ¿A qué hora te levantas los lunes? ¿los sábados? ¿los domingos?

2. ¿A qué hora te acuestas los lunes? ¿los viernes? ¿los sábados?

3. ¿Dónde se reúnen tú y tus amigos después de las clases? ¿los sábados? ¿cuando van a una película?

4. Cuando no te gusta una película, ¿te marchas del cine?

5. ¿Te das prisa cuando vas al colegio? ¿a una cita? ¿al cine?

6. ¿Dónde te sientas cuando miras la televisión? ¿en una silla? ¿en el sofá? ¿en el suelo *(on the floor)*?

7. ¿Te duermes cuando el programa es aburrido?

8. ¿Te marchas cuando asistes a una clase aburrida? ¿a una película estúpida? ¿a un concierto ridículo?

9. Cuando vas al cine, ¿te sientas en la primera fila *(row)*? ¿en la última fila?

10. En la clase de español, ¿quién se sienta a tu derecha *(on your right)*? ¿a tu izquierda *(on your left)*?

11. ¿Te callas en clase? ¿en la presencia de mayores *(adults)*? ¿cuando estás en la compañía de personas aburridas? ¿durante un concierto de música clásica? ¿durante un concierto de rock? ¿durante un partido de fútbol muy emocionante *(exciting)*? ¿durante una película de horror?

12. ¿Qué les dices a tus amigos cuando te despides? ¿a tus padres? ¿a tus abuelos?

13. ¿Te quedas en casa los sábados? ¿los domingos? ¿durante el verano?

14. ¿A qué hora te vas a la escuela los lunes? ¿los miércoles?

ACTIVIDAD 8   Las causas y las consecuencias   OPTIONAL

May be assigned as a special challenge activity.

Para expresar las consecuencias lógicas de ciertas situaciones, forma frases afirmativas y negativas usando elementos de A, B, C y D, según el modelo.

A	B	C	D
yo	estar enfermo(a)	levantarse	a las nueve
tú	estar cansado(a)	acostarse	en el sofá
Carlos	estar aburrido(a)	quedarse	en la cama
mis amigos	tener mucho que hacer	marcharse	en el sillón *(armchair)*
Jaime y yo	tener una cita	darse	en casa
	encontrar la película aburrida	dormirse	de casa
		sentarse	del cine
			prisa
			en la silla

WB
C1, C2,
C3

Cuando estoy enfermo, me quedo en casa.

WB
Trad.

SCRIPT

Act. 7, 8, 9

MASTERS
p. 12

TRB

QUIZ
pp. 28–29

Para la comunicación   OPTIONAL

May be assigned as homework.

1. Describe detalladamente *(in detail)* tus actividades de un día de la semana y de un sábado típico. Usa por lo menos *(at least)* diez verbos reflexivos.

2. Entrevista *(Interview)* a una persona que tiene un horario *(schedule)* especial y describe este horario. (O si no puedes hacer una entrevista, usa tu imaginación.) Puedes entrevistar a una de las siguientes personas: un(a) enfermero(a), un(a) conductor(a) de autobús, un guardia nocturno *(night guard)*, un(a) portero(a), un(a) empleado(a) de hotel, un(a) camarero(a), un(a) policía, un(a) aeromozo(a).

VARIATION: Pairs of students can prepare these **Entrevistas** as skits.

Lección 3   El chinchoso

¿Qué es un chinchoso o una chinchosa? Es lo contrario de la persona ideal . . . El chinchoso lo critica todo . . . El chinchoso molesta a sus amigos . . . El chinchoso crea problemas para todo el mundo.

Esto es lo que hace el chinchoso:

1. Se siente superior a todos.

2. Se toma por un gran genio.

3. Se enoja con todos.

4. Se irrita por los más pequeños detalles.

5. Se impacienta fácilmente.

6. Se enfada cuando alguien lo critica.

7. No se preocupa por los demás.

8. Se alegra de los problemas de sus compañeros.

9. Se siente de mal humor cuando los otros están alegres.

10. Se siente de buen humor cuando los otros están tristes.

¿Conoces a tal persona? ¿Eres tú chinchoso(a) de vez en cuando?

Se toma: *He takes himself*
Se enoja: *He gets annoyed*
detalles: *details*

Se enfada: *He gets angry*
los demás: *others*

tal: *such a*

NOTA CULTURAL

Las peculiaridades de los profesores

Aunque los profesores son las personas más importantes fuera de° la familia y de los amigos, son también personas como los demás° . . .

¿Cuáles son las palabras que usan los jóvenes hispánicos para describir a los profesores? Aquí tenemos algunos cumplidos° y críticas:°

¡estricto(a)! En su clase, no debes mascar° chicle, llegar tarde o charlar° con tus compañeros.

¡generoso(a)! Te da buenas notas y poco trabajo.

¡chismoso(a)!° Llama a tus padres cuando no haces tu trabajo.

Por supuesto, la crítica es solamente entre° los estudiantes y nunca debe llegar a oídos° de los padres ni° de los profesores. ¡Ay, pobre de ti,° si te oyen criticándolos!

fuera de *outside of*   **los demás** *the rest*   **cumplidos**
compliments   **críticas** *criticisms*   **mascar** *chew*   **charlar**
chat   **chismoso(a)** *tattle-tale*   **entre** *among*   **llegar a oídos**
reach the ears   **ni** *nor*   **pobre de ti** *poor you*

Vocabulario

sustantivos	*un(a) chinchoso(a)	a "pain"
	*un detalle	detail
	*un genio	genius
verbos	*crear	to create
	*molestar	to bother, to annoy
	*tomarse por	to take oneself for, to think one is
expresiones	*los demás	others, the other people, the rest
	*tal (persona)	such a (person)
	todo	everything
	*todo el mundo	everyone, everybody

CONVERSACIÓN

Ahora vamos a hablar de ti. ¿Qué tipo de persona eres?

¿Te sientes superior a todos?
¿Te enojas con todos?
¿Te impacientas fácilmente?

¿Te enfadas cuando alguien te critica?
¿Te preocupas por tus amigos?
¿Te preocupas por los demás?

Estructuras

A. Los verbos reflexivos: las emociones

Note the use of reflexive verbs in the following sentences.

Carlos **se preocupa** sin razón.	*Carlos **gets worried** without any reason.*
¿Por qué **te enojas?**	*Why **do you get angry?***

Spanish speakers often use reflexive verbs to indicate emotions.

Act. 3

VOCABULARIO PRÁCTICO   El mundo de las emociones

*aburrirse	to get bored
*alegrarse (de)	to get / be happy (because of)
*cansarse (de)	to get tired (of)
divertirse (e → ie)	to have fun
*enfadarse (con)	to get angry (at)
*enojarse (con)	to get angry (at)
*impacientarse (con)	to get impatient (because of)
*irritarse (con)	to get irritated (at, with)
*ocuparse (de)	to occupy oneself (in)
*preocuparse (por)	to get worried (because of)
sentirse (e → ie) (triste . . .)	to feel (sad . . .)

NOTAS: 1. The above verbs express emotional (or physical) states. Many of them correspond to English expressions beginning with *to get*.

2. The above verbs may be used in reflexive and nonreflexive constructions, with somewhat different meanings. Compare:

nonreflexive:	Juana **divierte** a sus amigos.	*Juana **amuses** her friends.*
reflexive:	Juana **se divierte.**	*Juana **is having fun** (that is, **is amusing herself**).*
nonreflexive:	Este problema **preocupa** a Carlos.	*This problem **worries** Carlos.*
reflexive:	Carlos **se preocupa.**	*Carlos **is getting worried** (that is, **he worries himself**).*

ACTIVIDAD 1 Las personas que figuran en tu vida

Las siguientes personas son muy importantes: tu mejor amigo, tu mejor
amiga, tus hermanos, tus padres, tu profesor(a) de español. Escoge (choose)
una de esas personas y di si hace las siguientes cosas.

⚑ preocuparse por tus estudios   Mi mejor amigo no se preocupa por mis estudios.
                                    (Mis padres se preocupan por mis estudios.)

1. preocuparse por tu salud (health)
2. preocuparse por tus problemas
   personales
3. divertirse contigo
4. alegrarse de tus éxitos (successes)

5. alegrarse de tu progreso en español
6. impacientarse contigo
7. enojarse mucho contigo
8. enojarse cuando llegas tarde

ACTIVIDAD 2 Tus sentimientos (Your feelings)

Describe tus sentimientos en las siguientes circunstancias.

⚑ Cuando saco una buena nota . . .   Cuando saco una buena nota, me alegro.

1. Cuando saco una mala nota . . .
2. Cuando un amigo está enfermo . . .
3. Cuando un amigo no viene a una
   cita . . .
4. Cuando el profesor no viene a
   clase . . .
5. Cuando mi mejor amigo no me dice la
   verdad . . .
6. Cuando mi mejor amigo se siente
   triste . . .
7. Cuando mi mejor amigo está de buen
   humor . . .

8. Cuando mi mejor amigo se enoja
   conmigo . . .
9. Cuando mi hermano rompe mis
   cosas . . .
10. Cuando alguien coquetea (flirts) con
    mi novio(a) . . .
11. Cuando estoy en una fiesta . . .
12. Cuando estoy en una fiesta donde no
    conozco a nadie . . .
13. Cuando el equipo de la escuela gana
    un partido importante . . .
14. Cuando el equipo pierde . . .

ACTIVIDAD 3 Nuestro humor   OPTIONAL

Nuestro humor cambia. A veces estamos alegres; a veces estamos tristes.
Di en qué ocasiones sientes los siguientes sentimientos.

⚑ Me aburro cuando . . .
      Me aburro cuando estoy enfermo(a) (cuando asisto a una película estúpida . . .).

1. Estoy de buen humor cuando . . .
2. Estoy de mal humor cuando . . .
3. Me impaciento cuando . . .
4. Me irrito cuando . . .
5. Me enojo cuando . . .

6. Me alegro cuando . . .
7. Me divierto mucho cuando . . .
8. Me preocupo cuando . . .
9. Me canso cuando . . .
10. Me siento feliz cuando . . .

VARIATION: Ask groups of students to respond. **Nos aburrimos...**

VB
1

CRIPT

ct. 4, 5,

ASTERS
13

B. Los verbos casi siempre reflexivos

As you have seen, most reflexive verbs can be used in nonreflexive constructions with a somewhat different meaning. Certain verbs, however, are almost always used in reflexive constructions.

Carlos **se porta** bien.	*Carlos **is behaving**.*
Sus hermanos no **se portan** bien.	*His brothers **are** not **behaving** properly.*

The verb **portarse** is always reflexive. Most of the verbs which are always reflexive are used to describe certain aspects of social behavior.

In some countries, the verb **portar** is used nonreflexively to mean *to carry*. This usage is not common.

VOCABULARIO PRÁCTICO   Algunos verbos siempre reflexivos

* **burlarse (de)**	to make fun of
* **darse cuenta (de)**	to realize
equivocarse (de, en)	to make a mistake, to be mistaken
* **portarse bien**	to behave
* **portarse mal**	to misbehave
* **quejarse (de)**	to complain about

ACTIVIDAD 4   Expresión personal

1. De vez en cuando, ¿te burlas de tus amigos? ¿de tus profesores?

2. De vez en cuando, ¿te quejas de tus estudios? ¿de los exámenes? ¿de la vida en general?

3. Generalmente, ¿te portas bien o mal en clase? ¿en casa? ¿con tus amigos? ¿cuando estás en una fiesta?

4. ¿Te das cuenta de tus errores? ¿de las cualidades de tus amigos? ¿de la suerte que tienes?

5. ¿Te equivocas en tus tareas de español? ¿en tus tareas de matemáticas?

Instituto Mexicano de la Radio — comunicación social radiofónica

XERIN@ 660 AM
TIEMPO DE TAREAS
Radio Infantil dedica 60 minutos para que resuelvas las dudas de tus labores escolares, con ayuda profesional

ACTIVIDAD 5   Según nuestro carácter

A veces nuestro carácter influye en nuestras acciones. Expresa esto usando los elementos de A, B, C y D para construir frases lógicas, según el modelo.

A	B	C	D
yo	divertido(a)	alegrarse	bien
María	simpático(a)	divertirse	mal
nosotros	antipático(a)	impacientarse	a menudo
mis amigos	bien educado(a)	enojarse	mucho
	(polite)	criticarse	siempre
	mal educado(a)	portarse	nunca
	(impolite)	equivocarse	de vez en cuando
	irritable	quejarse	
	feliz		

María es simpática. Se divierte siempre.

Para la comunicación

OPTIONAL   May be assigned as homework.

Reacciones

Describe lo que ocurre cuando . . .

- vuelves a casa a las tres de la mañana.
- rompes algo (un vaso o una lámpara, por ejemplo).
- el televisor no funciona.

Describe las reacciones de cada miembro de tu familia. Puedes usar los siguientes verbos en frases afirmativas o negativas:

alegrarse / divertirse / enfadarse / impacientarse / criticarse / preocuparse / sentirse / burlarse / quejarse

Lección 4 ¡Viva el amor!

Act. 1

Ramón es un estudiante universitario.
Lucía trabaja en un banco.
Ramón no conoce a Lucía y Lucía no conoce a Ramón.
No se conocen . . . pero ¡van a conocerse!

Un sábado, Ramón va a un baile.
Lucía va al mismo baile.
Ramón mira a Lucía.
Lucía mira a Ramón.
Se miran . . . y se hablan.
¡Ahora se conocen!

El lunes siguiente, Ramón llama a Lucía por teléfono y la invita al cine.
El miércoles, Ramón y Lucía se encuentran en un café.
El jueves, se reúnen en el cine.
El sábado, se ven de nuevo en el teatro.

de nuevo: *again*

Ahora, Ramón y Lucía se llaman por teléfono todos los días.
Se ven casi todos los días y cuando no se ven, se escriben . . .
Un día, se declaran su amor y se prometen quererse siempre . . .

se prometen: *promise each other*

¿Van a casarse Ramón y Lucía?
¡Tal vez! Pero primero Ramón va a terminar sus estudios y a graduarse.
Luego van a comprometerse, y después de unos meses, van a casarse.
¡Ay, qué romántico!

casarse: *to get married*

terminar: *to finish*
graduarse: *to graduate*
comprometerse: *to get engaged*

¿Cómo se llama el chico? ¿Cómo se llama la chica? ¿Dónde se encuentran por primera vez? ¿Qué hace Ramón el lunes siguiente? ¿Dónde se encuentran Ramón y Lucía el miércoles? ¿Qué hacen el jueves? ¿Qué hacen el sábado? ¿Qué quiere hacer Ramón antes de casarse?

Act. 2

OPTIONAL

El matrimonio

En los países hispánicos, el matrimonio es algo muy serio, algo que dura° toda la° vida. Los divorcios son raros y en algunos países el divorcio no existe. El matrimonio se considera° como una de las grandes y felices ocasiones de la vida.

Tradicionalmente, antes de la boda° hay otra ceremonia: la de compromiso° matrimonial. Allí se hace° la promesa de casamiento.° Esta ceremonia de compromiso es una gran ocasión social para los familiares.° Los padres del novio visitan la casa de los padres de la novia y les piden la mano de ella para su hijo. Los futuros esposos cambian los anillos matrimoniales y fijan° la fecha de la boda.

Unos pocos meses más tarde la boda se realiza.° Casi siempre hay dos bodas: la ceremonia civil y la religiosa. Generalmente ambas° tienen lugar° el mismo día.

dura *lasts*   **toda la** *the whole*   **se considera** *is considered*
boda *wedding*   **compromiso** *engagement*   **se hace** *is made*   **casamiento** *marriage*   **familiares** *family members*
fijan *fix*   **se realiza** *occurs*   **ambas** *both*   **tienen lugar** *take place*

¿Son frecuentes los divorcios en los países hispánicos? ¿Qué es el compromiso matrimonial? ¿Qué hacen los padres del novio? ¿Qué hacen los futuros esposos?

Vocabulario

sustantivos	* **un banco**	bank
	un país	country
verbos	* **durar**	to last
	* **prometer**	to promise
	* **terminar**	to finish, to end
expresiones	* **de nuevo**	again
	* **más o menos**	more or less
	primero	first

CONVERSACIÓN   OPTIONAL

¿Sales mucho?   Sí (No, no) salgo . . .
¿Sales todos los fines de semana?
¿Sales con tus amigos o solo(a)?
¿A qué hora sales de casa cuando vas al cine?

¿A qué hora sales cuando vas a un partido de fútbol?
¿A qué hora sales cuando vas a la heladería?

Estructuras

A. Repaso: verbos irregulares en la primera persona

Compare the **yo** and **tú** forms of the verb **salir** *(to go out)*:

> ¿Con quién **sales?**
> **Salgo** con Elena y Carmen.

In the present, a few verbs have an irregular **yo** form which ends in **-go.**

Act. 3

VOCABULARIO PRÁCTICO — Verbos irregulares en la primera persona

no reflexivos

caer	to fall	Mi cumpleaños **cae** el miércoles.
decir (e → i)	to say	**Digo** siempre la verdad.
hacer	to do	**Hago** la tarea.
	to make	**Hago** muchos planes.
oír	to hear	**Oigo** un *ruido *(noise).
poner	to put	**Pongo** un disco de música clásica.
salir	to leave	**Salgo** de casa a las siete.
	to go out	**Salgo** con Enrique.
traer	to bring	**Traigo** mi tocadiscos a la fiesta.

reflexivos

*****caerse**	to fall	Nunca **me caigo** de mi bicicleta.
*****hacerse** (+ sustantivo)	to become	Carlos quiere **hacerse** médico.
ponerse (+ ropa)	to put on (clothes)	Teresa **se pone** un suéter.
*****ponerse** (+ adjetivo)	to get, become	**Me pongo** (triste, alegre, furioso, nervioso).

NOTAS: 1. **Oír** *(to hear)* has the following forms: **oigo, oyes, oye, oímos, oís, oyen.**
2. **Caer** and **traer** have the ending **-igo** in the **yo** form: ca**igo**, tra**igo.**
3. Note the following expressions with **hacer:**

hacer la maleta	*to pack a suitcase*
*****hacer un papel**	*to play a part, to play a role*
hacer un viaje	*to take a trip*

Unidad tres Both **caer** and **caerse** mean *to fall.* **Caerse** is used when the subject is a person or an animal.

124

ACTIVIDAD 1 Diálogo

Pregúntales a tus compañeros si hacen las siguientes actividades.

⟩⟩ hacer la tarea todas las noches

Estudiante 1: ¿Haces la tarea todas las noches?
Estudiante 2: Sí (No, no) hago la tarea.

1. hacer tu cama todas las mañanas
2. hacer muchos viajes
3. hacer muchos planes
4. decir mentiras de vez en cuando
5. salir mucho
6. salir todos los sábados
7. poner discos populares todas las noches
8. traer muchos libros a la clase
9. oír ruidos por la noche
10. ponerse blue-jeans los domingos
11. caerse a veces de la bicicleta

ACTIVIDAD 2 ¿Por qué se ponen rojos? *(Why do they blush?)*

Las siguientes personas muestran sus emociones poniéndose rojas *(by blushing)*. Expresa eso según el modelo.

⟩⟩ Cuando una chica lo mira, Carlos . . .

Cuando una chica lo mira, Carlos se pone rojo.

1. Cuando un chico la mira, Anita . . .
2. Cuando me enojo, (yo) . . .
3. Cuando me equivoco, (yo) . . .
4. Cuando nos ponemos furiosos, (nosotros) . . .
5. Cuando mi hermano dice una mentira, (él) . . .
6. Cuando el profesor les pregunta algo, mis compañeros . . .
7. Cuando hablan con chicas, Carlos y Enrique . . .
8. Cuando un chico les da una ojeada *(glance),* mis primas . . .

ACTIVIDAD 3 Tus reacciones

Di cómo reaccionas en las siguientes circunstancias. Para eso, usa el verbo **ponerse** con uno de estos adjetivos: **alegre, triste, enfermo, rojo, furioso, nervioso, triste.**

Ask about student responses.
¿Qué hace Joe cuando un amigo se burla de él?

⟩⟩ Un amigo se burla de mí.   Me pongo furioso(a) (rojo[a], triste . . .).

1. Saco una buena nota.
2. Mi hermano pierde mi disco favorito.
3. Pierdo mis tareas.
4. No digo la verdad.
5. Mi mejor amigo no me dice la verdad.
6. Me caigo de mi bicicleta en frente de mis amigos.
7. El profesor me pregunta algo y no puedo contestarle.
8. Hace mucho frío y salgo sin chaqueta.
9. Mi mejor amigo no me invita a su fiesta de cumpleaños.
10. Estoy en un barco y el mar está revuelto *(rough).*
11. Mis compañeros se ríen de mí.
12. Un(a) chico(a) me sonríe.

ACTIVIDAD 4   Ropa para cada ocasión

VARIATION: Ask students what they wear in similar situations.

Carmenza tiene los siguientes artículos:

accesorios: una pulsera, un anillo, unos pendientes, un collar, unos anteojos de sol, un bolso

ropa: una blusa blanca, un suéter, una falda azul, un vestido amarillo, una camisa azul, una camiseta, unos pantalones negros, unos blue-jeans, unos pantalones cortos, un traje de baño

zapatos: unos zapatos negros, unas sandalias, unos zapatos de tenis

Di qué se pone Carmenza para las siguientes ocasiones.

Cuando va a una entrevista profesional . . .
> Cuando va a una entrevista profesional, Carmenza se pone un vestido amarillo . . .

1. Cuando va a la playa . . .
2. Cuando va a una discoteca . . .
3. Cuando va a un restaurante . . .
4. Cuando va al mercado . . .
5. Cuando hace un viaje . . .
6. Cuando va al colegio . . .
7. Cuando va a una cita con Ramón . . .
8. Cuando va a una cita con Isabel . . .
9. Cuando va a la iglesia . . .
10. Cuando juega al tenis . . .

WB
A1, A2

SCRIPT

Act. 4

B. El uso de los verbos reflexivos para indicar la reciprocidad

Note the use of reflexive verbs in the following sentences.

Carlos quiere a Elena.
Elena quiere a Carlos. } **Se quieren.**   *They **love each other.***

Ana le escribe a Luis.
Luis le escribe a Ana. } **Se escriben.**   *They **write to each other.***

Reflexive verbs are sometimes used to express reciprocal actions or interaction between two or more subjects.

> Since interaction involves at least two people, reflexive verbs indicating reciprocal actions are generally used in the *plural.*

Nos llamamos por teléfono.   *We phone each other.*

> In Spanish, reflexive pronouns cannot be omitted with verbs expressing reciprocal action. (In English, the expressions *each other* or *one another* are frequently left out.)

Se casan.   ***They are getting married (to each other).***

ACTIVIDAD 5   Reciprocidad

Ramón habla de las actividades de sus amigos. Julia quiere saber si ésas
son actividades recíprocas. Ramón dice que sí. Haz los dos papeles según el
modelo.

> Carlos invita a Rodrigo al café.   Ramón: Carlos invita a Rodrigo al café.
> Julia: ¿Y Rodrigo invita a Carlos al café?
> Ramón: ¡Sí! Se invitan.

1. Paco quiere a Carmen.
2. Elena quiere a Felipe.
3. José adora a Sofía.
4. Silvia llama a Tomás.
5. Eduardo mira a Ana.

6. Roberto insulta a Rafael.
7. Rubén ve a Sarita.
8. Jaime encuentra a Pilar.
9. Andrés admira a Beatriz.
10. Emilia visita a Elena.

ACTIVIDAD 6   Tú y tus amigos

¿Tienes buenas relaciones con tus amigos? Vamos a ver. Contesta según
el modelo.

> ¿Se conocen bien, tú y tus amigos?   Sí, (No, no) nos conocemos bien.

1. ¿Se llaman por teléfono, tú y tus amigos?
2. ¿Se invitan al cine, tú y tus amigos?
3. ¿Se visitan, tú y tus amigos?
4. ¿Se escriben durante las vacaciones, tú y tus amigos?
5. ¿Se hablan de sus problemas, tú y tus amigos?
6. ¿Se ayudan con la tarea, tú y tus amigos?
7. ¿Se cuentan chistes, tú y tus amigos?
8. ¿Se encuentran a menudo tú y tus amigos?
9. ¿Se muestran fotos, tú y tus amigos?
10. ¿Se piden consejos, tú y tus amigos?

VOCABULARIO PRÁCTICO   ¡Amor!

*el amor	love	*la amistad	friendship
*el cariño	affection		
el esposo	husband	la esposa	wife
*el matrimonio	marriage	*la boda	wedding (ceremony)

los estados de la vida social

*casarse	to get married	Jamie y yo **nos casamos** el cinco de julio.
*casarse con	to marry	Manuel va a **casarse con** Luisa.
*enamorarse (de)	to fall in love (with)	Luis **se enamora de** todas las chicas que encuentra.
*llevarse (con)	to get along (with)	Pablo **se lleva** bien **con** sus amigos.
*pelearse	to fight, to quarrel	***Aun** *(Even)* los buenos amigos **se pelean** de vez en cuando.

EXTRA VOCAB.: **el anillo de matrimonio** (wedding ring), **el caballero de honor** (best man), **la dama de honor** (maid or matron of honor), **el novio** (groom; fiancé), **la novia** (bride; fiancée).

ACTIVIDAD 7   Expresión personal

1. ¿Sientes mucho cariño por tus padres? ¿por tus parientes? ¿por tus hermanos?

2. ¿Sientes mucha amistad por tus amigos? ¿por tus compañeros de clase?

3. ¿Sientes simpatía *(liking)* por tus profesores? ¿por los políticos? ¿por tus vecinos?

4. Generalmente, ¿te llevas bien con tus profesores? ¿con tus compañeros? ¿con tus vecinos? ¿con las personas que no conoces bien?

5. De vez en cuando, ¿te peleas con tu mejor amigo? ¿con tu mejor amiga? ¿con tus hermanos? ¿con tus padres?

6. ¿Eres una persona muy sentimental? ¿Te enamoras a menudo? ¿fácilmente? ¿Qué piensas de las personas que se enamoran fácilmente?

7. ¿Quieres casarte o quedarte soltero(a) *(single)*? Si te casas, ¿quieres tener una familia grande?

WB
B1

SCRIPT

Act. 5

MASTERS
p. 14

C. Los verbos reflexivos en el infinitivo y con *estar* + el participio presente

Compare the position and the form of the reflexive pronouns in the sentences on the right and on the left.

Clara **se** casa.	Va a casar**se** con Ramón.
	(**Se** va a casar con Ramón.)
Me peleo con mi hermano.	No quiero pelear**me** con él.
	(No **me** quiero pelear con él.)
Nos lavamos.	Estamos lavándo**nos** la cara.
	(**Nos** estamos lavando la cara.)

The basic infinitive form of a reflexive verb is always given with the pronoun **se**: **casarse**.

When the reflexive verb is used in the infinitive form or in a present progressive construction, the reflexive pronoun changes to agree with the subject.

Voy a **casarme**.   *I am going to **get married**.*

ACTIVIDAD 8   El ejemplo de Francisca

Las amigas siguen el ejemplo de Francisca. Ellas también quieren casarse.
Di cuándo va a casarse cada una.

⋙ Elena (en julio)   Elena va a casarse en julio.

1. Carmen (en agosto)
2. Susana y Luisa (el 3 de abril)
3. nosotros (el año próximo)
4. yo (antes de la Navidad)
5. tú (en septiembre)
6. la hermana de Silvia (el 2 de octubre)
7. tú y yo (después de las vacaciones)
8. Uds. (el primero de junio)

ACTIVIDAD 9   Planes profesionales

Unos amigos están hablando del futuro. Di lo que cada uno quiere hacerse.

Roberto: periodista   Roberto quiere hacerse periodista.

1. Susana: médica
2. Luis y Guillermo: ingenieros
3. nosotros: pilotos
4. yo: trabajador social

5. tú: el mejor actor del mundo
6. Ud.: explorador
7. Uds.: policías
8. Enrique y yo: astronautas

ACTIVIDAD 10   Unas actividades peligrosas

Algunas de nuestras actividades son más peligrosas que otras. Di qué
parte del cuerpo (por ejemplo: **el brazo, la mano, el pie, la pierna, la
nariz, los dientes**) pueden romperse las siguientes personas en las
siguientes situaciones.

You may want to review the
parts of the body (Appendix 2).

Si esquías . . .   Si esquías, puedes romperte el brazo (la pierna).

1. Si jugamos al fútbol . . .
2. Si juegas al volibol . . .
3. Si me caigo del tercer piso . . .
4. Si boxeas contra *(against)* Mohamed
   Alí . . .
5. Si Carlos tiene un accidente de
   automóvil . . .

6. Si Enrique tropieza contra *(bumps
   against)* un árbol . . .
7. Si mis primos tienen un accidente de
   bicicleta . . .
8. Si Clara y Elena se lanzan en
   paracaídas *(parachute jump)* . . .
9. Si te caes de tu moto . . .

Para la comunicación

May be assigned as homework.

a) Las personas ideales

En un pequeño párrafo describe a las siguientes personas. Puedes usar
estos verbos en frases negativas o afirmativas: **visitar / hacer / decir / traer /
ponerse / pelearse / llevarse / reunirse / quererse.**

This may be assigned as a group composition to teams of 3-5 students. Set a
time limit of 10 or 15 minutes.

- los amigos ideales
- los esposos ideales
- los hermanos ideales
- los vecinos ideales

$\backsim$ los novios ideales

Hacen muchos planes. Se traen regalos y se dicen cosas amables...

b) ¡Qué romántico!

Éste es el principio *(beginning)* de la historia de un gran amor:

Linda es una estudiante norteamericana de veinte y un años. Es muy
inteligente y bastante independiente. Como estudia español, decide pasar
el tercer año de la universidad en España. En Madrid una amiga la
presenta a Vicente. Vicente es moreno, bastante guapo, romántico...
Trabaja como intérprete en una agencia de viajes...

Ahora, imagina la continuación de la historia. (Si quieres, puedes
encontrar inspiración en «¡Viva el amor!».)

WB
Trad.

SCRIPT

Act. 6, 8,
9

MASTERS
p. 14

TRB

QUIZ
pp. 32–33

WB   Test / Repaso   TEST   pp. 34–37

Variedades Una chica como ninguna otra

Se llama Maribel Atienza. Es pequeña, tiene ojos de color café y pelo castaño. Y a los diez y ocho años, ¡ya° era° una de las mujeres más famosas de España!

ya: *already*
era: *she was*

¿Es una actriz o una cantante? No. Maribel Atienza tiene una profesión totalmente diferente. Es torera.° Y aunque ella pesa° menos de cincuenta kilos, se enfrenta° regularmente a toros° de más de quinientos kilos.

torera: *bullfighter*
pesa: *weighs*
se enfrenta: *she faces*
toros: *bulls*

¿Por qué decidió ser torera? Porque un día un amigo le dijo que el peligro físico° no era para las mujeres. Desde° entonces, ella ha matado° a más de doscientos toros. Y ahora es una celebridad no solamente en España, sino° también en Venezuela y Colombia.

peligro físico: *physical danger*
Desde: *Since*
ha matado: *has killed*
sino: *but*

La profesión de torera no es solamente muy peligrosa. Requiere entrenamiento° físico. Maribel se levanta a las ocho, se desayuna y hace sus ejercicios° diarios° hasta las dos de la tarde. También juega al tenis, nada, monta a caballo . . . Después se dedica° a otras actividades más personales: sale con sus amigos y ayuda a su mamá en casa.

entrenamiento: *training*
ejercicios: *exercises*
diarios: *daily*
se dedica: *she devotes her time*

El día antes de la corrida° es muy diferente. Se despierta tarde y no se levanta antes de las diez. Se queda en la cama, leyendo los periódicos. Se lava el pelo y se desayuna. Y pasa el resto del día mirando la televisión o visitando a sus amigos. Finalmente, llega el día de la corrida. Se pone su traje de luces,° es decir, su traje de torera. Y nunca olvida° rezar° para ponerse bajo° la protección de Cristo, de la Virgen y de todos los santos.°

¿Se siente nerviosa Maribel antes de la corrida? ¡Claro que sí! Después de todo, el toro es un animal peligroso. Es feroz,° fuerte y está listo a matar. Pero cuando Maribel entra en el ruedo° y cuando el público grita° «olé», ella no se siente nerviosa. Se siente calmada, orgullosa° y lista.

corrida: *bullfight*

traje de luces: *"suit of lights"*
olvida: *she forgets*
rezar: *to pray*
bajo: *under*
santos: *saints*
feroz: *ferocious*
ruedo: *ring*
grita: *shouts*
orgullosa: *proud*

LA CORRIDA
Tres cosas importantes

estoque

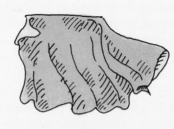

muleta

banderillas

Uno de los pases—el pase por alto

El pase por alto: *a high, right-handed pass*

VISTA
El Caribe

2

Un poco de historia

El Caribe es la puerta por donde Europa entró° en América. ¿Y cómo llegaron los europeos a América? En barco, ¡claro! El mar hizo un gran papel en la historia de la región. Vamos a ver.

1300

Los indios caribes comienzan a invadir las islas° donde viven los indios arawakos. Los caribes son agresivos y guerreros.° Así es que dominan fácilmente a los arawakos.

Cristóbal Colón

1492

A las costas del Caribe llega el primer europeo (Cristóbal Colón) y sus tres barcos (la Niña, la Pinta y la Santa María).

Bartolomé Colón

1496

En la costa de una isla, Bartolomé Colón (un hermano de Cristóbal) funda° Santo Domingo, hoy capital de la República Dominicana. Es la ciudad fundada° por los españoles más vieja del Nuevo Mundo.

1512

Los barcos españoles comienzan a llegar con esclavos° negros para trabajar en las plantaciones de caña de azúcar° en Cuba y otras islas.

entró *entered*   **islas** *islands*   **guerreros** *warlike*   **funda** *founds*   **fundada** *founded*
esclavos *slaves*   **caña de azúcar** *sugar cane*

1853

Los Estados Unidos quieren comprar Cuba. España no acepta la oferta: ¡130 millones de dólares por Cuba!

1868

En Cuba comienza la Guerra° de los Diez Años. Los patriotas cubanos demandan dos cosas: la independencia de la isla y la abolición de la esclavitud.° España anuncia la abolición de la esclavitud en la isla, pero no declara su independencia.

El barco Maine

1898

En el puerto° de La Habana una explosión de origen misterioso destruye el barco *Maine* de los Estados Unidos. Los Estados Unidos le declaran la guerra a España e intervienen en la segunda guerra de la independencia de Cuba. La guerra es corta y España pierde sus últimas colonias en América: Cuba y Puerto Rico.

1917

La nacionalidad estadounidense es concedida° a todos los puertorriqueños.

1952

Los Estados Unidos aprueban° una constitución para Puerto Rico creando así el Estado Libre Asociado.° Esta constitución establece una relación muy especial entre° los Estados Unidos y Puerto Rico. Puerto Rico no es un estado pero con esta relación especial se preservan la ciudadanía común,° el comercio libre° y la autonomía fiscal.°

1959

Después de años de lucha,° Fidel Castro asume el poder° en Cuba. Castro establece en Cuba el primer gobierno° comunista en América. Muchos cubanos, descontentos con el nuevo régimen, deciden emigrar a otros países, incluyendo los Estados Unidos.

1992

Los países hispanos del Caribe celebran el Quinto Centenario° del descubrimiento° de América.

Guerra *War* **esclavitud** *slavery* **puerto** *port* **es concedida** *is granted* **aprueban** *approve*
Estado Libre Asociado *Commonwealth* **entre** *between* **ciudadanía común** *common citizenship*
comercio libre *free trade* **autonomía fiscal** *fiscal autonomy* **lucha** *fighting* **poder** *power*
gobierno *government* **Quinto Centenario** *Five-hundredth Anniversary* **descubrimiento** *discovery*

Cuba

Población: 10.200.000
Ciudad capital: La Habana
Unidad monetaria: el peso
Productos principales:
   azúcar, níquel
Otros datos:°
   Cuba no se compone solamente de
   la isla donde están La Habana y
   otras provincias, sino° también de
   más de 1600 islotes — islas
   pequeñas y rocosas.

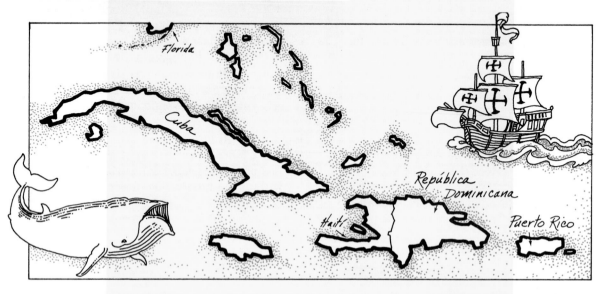

La República Dominicana

Población: 6.400.000
Ciudad capital: Santo Domingo
Unidad monetaria: el peso
Productos principales:
    caña de azúcar, bauxita
Otros datos:
    La universidad más vieja del Nuevo
    Mundo está en Santo Domingo.
    Fue fundada en 1538.

Puerto Rico

Población: 3.197.000
Ciudad capital: San Juan
Unidad monetaria: el dólar
Productos principales:
    azúcar, café, bananas
Animal típico:
    el coquí, una rana° encantadora°
Otros datos:
    El Yunque es la única selva
    tropical° de los Estados Unidos.
    Allí se encuentran 240 tipos de
    árboles diferentes.

rana *frog*   **encantadora** *delightful*
selva tropical *rain forest*

CRISTÓBAL COLÓN
el misterioso descubridor de América

Cristóbal Colón. Un hombre lleno° de gloria. Y lleno de misterio también. Descubrir la verdadera° vida de este hombre parece una misión imposible. Su vida es una sucesión de enigmas.

¿Dónde nació?°

Mucha gente dice que Colón fue un navegante italiano. Pero esto no es completamente seguro. Fue navegante, sí, pero, ¿nació realmente en Génova, Italia? Hay investigadores° convencidos de que Colón fue portugués. Otros dicen que nació en España, en Grecia,° en . . . Bueno, son muchos los países que pelean por la cuna° de Colón.

El descubrimiento°

Todo el mundo sabe que Colón llegó a América por primera vez el 12 de octubre. Es un día que se conmemora con «Columbus Day» en los Estados Unidos y con «Día de la Raza» en los países hispanos. Pero, ¿adónde llegó? ¿Fue a la isla de Guanahaní,° como dicen los historiadores? ¡No, según algunos! Dicen que la isla de Guanahaní y la

LOS CUATRO VIAJES DE CRISTÓBAL COLÓN

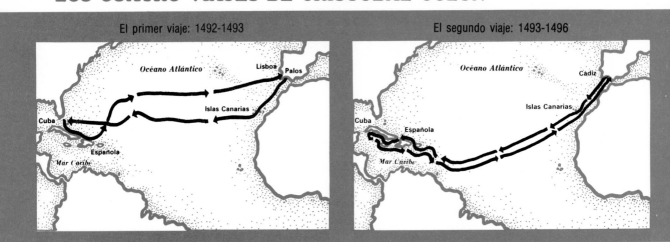

El primer viaje: 1492-1493

El segundo viaje: 1493-1496

138   lleno *full*   verdadera *true*   nació *was he born*   investigadores *researchers*   Grecia *Greece*
cuna *cradle, birthplace*   descubrimiento *discovery*   Guanahaní *island in the Bahamas*

descripción de esta isla en el diario de Colón son dos cosas muy diferentes. ¿Describió Colón una isla que no existe?

Sus otros viajes

Cuando volvió a España después de su primer viaje, Colón fue recibido como un héroe. Pero después, hizo tres viajes más y ¿qué pasó? Después del segundo viaje Colón fue a vivir a un monasterio. Durante el tercer viaje fue arrestado, y volvió a España encadenado.°

Sus últimos días

Colón murió° dos años después de su cuarto y último viaje. ¿El año? 1506. ¿La ciudad? Valladolid, España. Murió sin amigos, sin honores, sin dinero. Es difícil creer que murió así, pero es cierto. El lugar donde Colón está enterrado° es un misterio. Colón descubrió la República Dominicana en 1492. Los dominicanos dicen que Colón sigue° allí todavía.

Hay muchos monumentos en todo el mundo en honor a Colón. No todos son estatuas. Por ejemplo, el colón es el nombre de la moneda de El Salvador y la moneda de Costa Rica. Colombia es un país que se llama así en honor al gran navegante.° También hay ciudades (Colón en Panamá), universidades (Colombia, en Nueva York), calles, avenidas, plazas, parques . . .

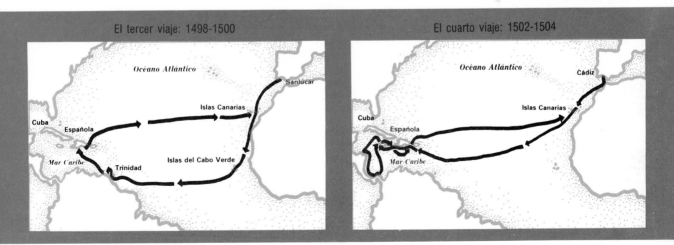

El tercer viaje: 1498-1500

Océano Atlántico

Sanlúcar

Islas Canarias

Cuba

Española

Mar Caribe

Trinidad

Islas del Cabo Verde

El cuarto viaje: 1502-1504

Océano Atlántico

Cádiz

Islas Canarias

Cuba

Española

Mar Caribe

---

encadenado *in chains* **murió** *died* **enterrado** *buried* **sigue** *is* **navegante** *navigator*

LO ANTILLANO° EN NUESTRA LENGUA

¿Sabes de dónde viene la palabra «huracán»? Viene de la palabra taína «Jurakan».

Los taínos fueron una tribu arawaka que pobló° Puerto Rico antes de la llegada° de los españoles. Y Jurakan se refiere a un espíritu malo y destructivo. Jurakan es el espíritu que causa tormentas° violentas y devastadoras.

Cuando los españoles llegan al Caribe, el nombre° Jurakan da origen a la palabra «huracán» en español. Pasa al inglés como «hurricane».

En inglés hay muchas palabras que vienen del español. En algunos casos son palabras que (como «hurricane») tienen su origen en las lenguas° indígenas° del Caribe.

Aquí hay algunas:

español	*inglés*	*español*	*inglés*
canoa	canoe	papaya	papaya
barbacoa	barbecue	sabana	savanna
hamaca	hammock	tabaco	tobacco
maíz	maize		

Antillano *Caribbean*   **pobló** *populated*   **llegada** *arrival*   **tormentas** *storms*   **nombre** *name*
lenguas *tongues*   **indígenas** *native*

corazón *heart*   **ciego** *blind*   **Nació** *He was born*
felicidad *happiness*   **edad** *age*   **descubierto** *discovered*
ha visto *has he seen*   **sueño** *dream*   **hecho** *made*

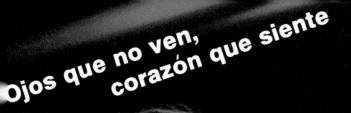

Ojos que no ven, corazón que siente

Todos conocemos el refrán que dice, «Ojos que no ven, corazón° que no siente». Pero en el caso de José Feliciano no es así. José Feliciano es ciego,° pero canta con la emoción de los grandes artistas. Es un cantante puertorriqueño muy famoso.

Nació° ciego, pero optimista. Su apellido, Feliciano, nos hace pensar en *feliz, felicidad.*° A la edad° de seis años aprendió a tocar su primer instrumento musical. Y como un niño ciego, la música fue siempre su mejor amiga. Pasaron los años ... Un día, fue descubierto° cantando en un café del Greenwich Village en Nueva York.

Cuando este gran artista canta, multitudes lo escuchan. Sus discos se venden por millones. José Feliciano es un cantante internacional, muy popular en todo el mundo. Nunca ha visto° el color de su guitarra. Nunca ha visto las caras del público que lo admira. Pero para este muchacho puertorriqueño, la vida es un sueño° hecho° realidad.

Los «galeones fantasmas»°

phantom galleons
(galleon = large
Spanish sailing
ship)

La mayoría de° la gente tiene una vida tranquila y normal. Trabaja en algo común y quizá repetitivo. Las personas que tienen una vida de aventura son muy pocas. Este cuento es sobre uno de esos pocos individuos con una vida diferente, una vida de incertidumbre,° de peligro, de esperanza y finalmente de éxito.° Mel Fisher es un hombre con un sueño:° encontrar uno de los tesoros° más valiosos° del mundo. Sus elementos son la historia, un equipo de buzos° y, lo más importante, la paciencia y la inteligencia.

Ésta es la historia que Mel Fisher conoce. Durante el período colonial español, el centro de transporte entre el Nuevo Mundo y España es las islas grandes del Caribe. Todo el oro° y la plata° de las minas de Latinoamérica pasan por la Española° y Cuba. Los peligros para los barcos° son muchos: la distancia, los piratas, las tormentas° tropicales. Por eso,° los barcos van en grupos grandes. El 4 de septiembre de 1622, un grupo de 28 galeones sale de La Habana, Cuba, con una carga importante. Llevan cobre,° índigo, tabaco y mucho oro y plata. Los navegantes tienen miedo,° no de los piratas, sino° de los huracanes del mes de septiembre. Pero el día 4 hace buen tiempo y la luna° nueva es una señal° favorable. ¡Con suerte van a llegar sin problemas!

Todo va bien y los galeones pasan por el Estrecho de Florida. El quinto día de viaje hace mucho viento, pero ya° es difícil volver a tierra.° Deciden continuar. De repente° vienen los vientos y la lluvia de un violento huracán. La atmósfera de los barcos cambia de tranquilidad a terror y los hombres luchan° por salvar sus vidas. Todo se moja.° Las velas° se rompen.° Los vientos llevan los galeones cerca de° los Cayos° de Florida. El día 9, después de cuatro días de lucha contra° la tormenta, todos los barcos se hunden° en olas que son más y más altas. Ninguno se salva. Quizá los últimos en hundirse son los más grandes, los barcos de guardia, la «Nuestra Señora de Atocha» y la «Santa Margarita». Con ellos se va al fondo° del mar una cantidad de oro y plata con un valor° equivalente a millones de dólares.

En España nadie quiere creer que la flota° está perdida. El tesoro es de un valor tan grande que pasan unos 40 años buscando los barcos. Los españoles mandan varias expediciones en busca de los barcos. Buscan en el golfo de México. Buscan en muchas partes inexploradas del Caribe. También buscan en el Atlántico y en los puertos° de África. Buscan por todas partes. Durante mucho tiempo esperan en España la llegada de los barcos misteriosamente perdidos. Pero esperan en vano. Finalmente los barcos cargados° de oro y plata se transforman en leyenda . . . en «galeones fantasmas» que aparecen° en cuentos y visiones.

Esto es todo lo que Mel Fisher sabe cuando comienza a soñar con el tesoro perdido. Viaja primero a Sevilla en España para visitar los archivos principales del período colonial. Allí encuentra mapas mostrando la ruta de los barcos desde°

Most

uncertainty;
success
dream; treasures;
valuable
divers

gold; silver
Hispaniola; ships

storms; Therefore

copper

are afraid; but

moon; sign

by now; land
Suddenly
fight
gets soaked; sails;
break
near; Keys; against
sink

bottom; value

fleet

ports

loaded

appear

from

el Caribe a España. Allí encuentra también libros viejos que describen los barcos. Los manuscritos son difíciles de leer. La lengua° española del siglo° XVII es muy diferente del español moderno. Mel Fisher tiene que llevar los documentos a expertos. ¡Ni° ellos están seguros del significado de ciertas frases! Cuando Mel Fisher reúne° toda la información no sabe exactamente dónde tiene que buscar. Sólo sabe que su expedición va a ser difícil pero tiene esperanza y determinación.

language; century

Not even

gathers

Con la información de los documentos y mapas Mel Fisher vuelve a Florida y comienza la búsqueda° en las aguas claras del Caribe. Su equipo consiste en un barco pequeño y cinco personas. Entre° ellas está su hijo, que comparte° el sueño del padre: vivir una vida de aventura bajo el agua y encontrar los «galeones fantasmas». El equipo pasa cuatro años al este° del Cayo de las Marquesas, pero no encuentra nada. Ya están pensando en abandonar todo cuando un amigo examina otra vez los mapas. El amigo descubre° que hay un problema con la letra° antigua de los mapas. El mapa dice «veste» (oeste)°, no «leste» (este). ¡Están buscando en el lado° equivocado° del Cayo de las Marquesas!

search

Among; shares

east

discovers

handwriting; west

side; wrong

Comienzan de nuevo en el otro lado de la isla . . . y esta vez encuentran un ancla.° Más tarde encuentran cadenas° de oro y luego unas monedas de plata. Éstas son pistas° importantes. ¡Los barcos tienen que estar cerca! Después de buscar durante tres años, encuentran más oro y más monedas, en total un tesoro con un valor de seis millones de dólares. ¿De qué barco viene? Se dan cuenta que es parte de la carga de «Nuestra Señora de Atocha». El barco tenía muchas barras de plata y oro, pero sólo encuentran el oro. Continúan buscando el resto de la carga.

anchor; chains

clues

El trabajo continúa hasta que° un día hay un accidente . . . un accidente fatal. El hijo de Mel Fisher se ahoga° buceando.° La muerte° del hijo causa una crisis terrible de duda° y culpa° en el padre. ¡Por culpa de° su sueño, su hijo ha muerto!° Durante mucho tiempo Mel Fisher deja de° buscar. Tiene además problemas con el gobierno.° Para él, el trabajo es imposible.

until

drowns; diving; death

doubt; guilt; because of

has died; stops

government

Pero Mel Fisher vuelve finalmente al mar, a su sueño, y descubre más oro y esta vez descubre también una parte de un barco. El oro y quizá esta parte del barco vienen de la Santa Margarita. ¡El sueño se está realizando! El

descubrimiento llena° al buscador de alegría,° no por el dinero sino porque está viviendo lo que tanto° había deseado: recuperar° un tesoro perdido en las olas y en el tiempo.

fills; joy

so much; to recover

El hallazgo° atrae° más gente interesada en el trabajo . . . más gente que quiere resolver el misterio de los «galeones fantasmas».

discovery; attracts

La voz poética de un líder revolucionario

José Martí (1853-1895): periodista, poeta y líder político. Dedicó su vida a la libertad° y, en particular, a la libertad política de Cuba. A los 16 años de edad° fue deportado de Cuba por sus actividades revolucionarias. Después, la segunda vez que volvió, murió° en una batalla, peleando contra° las fuerzas españolas por la independencia de Cuba. En La Habana hay un monumento grande dedicado a Martí.

Los poemas de Martí revelan su gran idealismo. ¿Los conoces? Algunos versos de Martí se usaron para hacer una canción que fue muy popular.

Yo soy un hombre sincero
de donde crece° la palma,
y antes de morirme° quiero
echar° mis versos del alma.°

Con los pobres de la tierra
quiero yo mi suerte echar:°
el arroyo° de la sierra
me complace° más que el mar.

Cultivo una rosa blanca,
En julio como en enero,
Para el amigo sincero
Que me da su mano franca.

Y para el cruel que me arranca°
El corazón con que vivo,
Cardo° ni oruga° cultivo;
Cultivo la rosa blanca.

libertad *liberty* **edad** *age* **murió** *he died* **contra** *against* **crece** *grows* **morirme** *dying* **echar** *to pour out* **alma** *soul* **echar** *cast* **arroyo** *stream* **complace** *pleases* **me arranca** *pulls from me* **Cardo** *Thistle* **oruga** *plant*

Plátanos fritos°

Necesitas: *2 plátanos, verdes o maduros*
(Si no encuentras plátanos, ¡usa bananas!)
aceite° para freír°
sal o azúcar

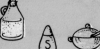

Preparación:

1. Corta° los plátanos diagonalmente, en rodajas° delgadas.

2. Calienta° aceite en una sartén.°

3. Fríe° los plátanos en aceite bien caliente.°

4. Ponlos° en una toalla de papel° para quitar el exceso de aceite.

5. Si usaste plátanos verdes: échales sal° y sírvelos con el plato principal.
   Si usaste plátanos maduros: échales azúcar y sírvelos como postre.°
   ¡Buen provecho!°

Actividades culturales

1. *Prepara un informe breve° sobre° la ciudad de Santo Domingo.*
2. *Prepara una exhibición° sobre uno de los países hispanos del Caribe. Puedes usar mapas, tarjetas postales, fotos y folletos° turísticos.*
3. *Prepara un informe sobre el primer viaje de Cristóbal Colón.*
4. *Busca un disco español, como uno de Julio Iglesias, y escucha una canción. ¿Cuenta una historia? Di° a la clase lo que expresa.*
5. *Lee unos poemas de José Martí.*

informe breve *brief report* **sobre** *on* **exhibición** *exhibit* **folletos** *brochures* **Di** *Tell*

fritos *fried* **aceite** *oil* **freir** *frying* **Corta** *Cut* **rodajas** *slices* **Calienta** *Heat* **sartén** *frying pan*
Fríe *Fry* **caliente** *hot* **Ponlos** *Put them* **toalla de papel** *paper towel* **échales sal** *salt them*
postre *dessert* **¡Buen provecho!** *Enjoy it!*

Unidad 4

El coche del Sr. Molina

4.1 ¡Sola en casa!

4.2 La decisión de Isabel

4.3 ¡Qué tragedia!

4.4 ¿Un coche nuevo?

VARIEDADES ¿Tienes sentido de orientación?

OBJECTIVES
Communication
In this unit students use Spanish to talk about past events.
Language
This unit focuses on a review of the preterite. It also presents:
- The construction **acabar de** + infinitive
- Hace + present
- Hace + preterite
- The construction **al** + infinitive
- The possessive adjectives and pronouns (long forms)
- The adverbs in **-mente**

Culture
This unit focuses on life in Spain.

The four presentation texts of this unit form a continuous mini-drama. The main characters are Isabel, her mother, her father, and Anita, a friend. You may want to select students to dramatize the story. Or students may mime the action while you play the tape recording.

 Review   Modules 17, 18, 19

147

Act. 1

28

Estamos en julio. Hace muchísimo calor. La familia Molina, una familia española, está de vacaciones. Todos los años pasa las vacaciones en San Felíu, una playa en la Costa Brava. Ahora Isabel, la hija menor (tiene diez y siete años), regresa de la calle.

STRUCTURES TO REVIEW:
• **Acabar de** + infinitive
• **Hace** + present

regresa: *returns*

Isabel:	¡Hola, mamá!
Sra. de Molina:	¡Hola, Isabel!
Isabel:	¿No está aquí Elena?
Sra. de Molina:	¡No! Tu hermana acaba de salir con una amiga.
Isabel:	¿Y Ricardo?
Sra. de Molina:	Acaba de llamar por teléfono. Hace unas dos horas que está en la playa con sus amigos. Dijo que después van a ir a una discoteca.
Isabel:	¿Papá está también en la calle?
Sra. de Molina:	¡Sí! Acaba de salir con el Sr. Martínez. Van a ver un partido de fútbol.
Isabel:	Y tú, mamá, ¿vas a salir?
Sra. de Molina:	Sí, hija. Tengo que ir de compras con la Sra. de Onís.
Isabel:	¿Me voy a quedar sola en este apartamento?
Sra. de Molina:	Sí, ¡pero no es una tragedia!
Isabel:	¡Claro que no! Voy a leer las revistas que acabo de comprar.

acaba de salir: *has just gone out*

¿está . . . en la calle?: *is he out?*

ir de compras: *go shopping*

• • • • • • • • • • • • • •

Hace unos diez minutos que Isabel está sola en casa . . .
¿Va a leer sus revistas?
¡No! Isabel tiene otra idea . . .
¡y esta idea es mucho más interesante!

¿En qué mes estamos? ¿Qué tiempo hace? ¿Dónde pasa las vacaciones la familia Molina? ¿Cuántos años tiene Isabel? ¿Quién es Elena? ¿Quién es Ricardo? ¿Dónde está Ricardo? ¿Dónde está el Sr. Molina? ¿Con quién está él? ¿Con quién va a salir la Sra. de Molina? ¿Qué acaba de comprar Isabel? ¿Lee las revistas Isabel cuando está sola en casa?

Act. 2

NOTA CULTURAL OPTIONAL

Las vacaciones de verano en España

Tradicionalmente, julio y agosto son los meses de vacaciones en España. Los estudiantes españoles tienen más o menos tres meses de vacaciones y sus padres tienen más o menos cuatro semanas. Como los veranos son muy calurosos, muchas familias van a veranear° a la playa.

Las playas españolas son unas de las más bonitas del mundo. También en el verano son unas de las más llenas.° Durante esta temporada,° millones de turistas (de Alemania, de Francia, de Inglaterra, de los Países Bajos° y de Suiza°) vienen a las playas de la Costa Brava y la Costa del Sol. Los españoles y los extranjeros° vienen a descansar y a gozar del° sol . . . ¡y a recibir quemaduras de sol° si no tienen cuidado!°

veranear to spend the summer   **llenas** crowded
temporada season   **Países Bajos** Belgium, Luxembourg, The Netherlands   **Suiza** Switzerland   **extranjeros** foreigners
gozar del enjoy the   **quemaduras de sol** sunburns   **no tienen cuidado** they are not careful

SUGGESTED REALIA: a map of Spain, tourist brochures.
¿Cuántos meses de vacaciones tienen los estudiantes en España? ¿Cuántas semanas de vacaciones tienen sus padres? ¿Qué tiempo hace en el verano? ¿De dónde son los turistas que visitan España?

Vocabulario

sustantivos	*las compras	shopping
	*las vacaciones	vacation(s)
verbos	*estar de vacaciones	to be on a vacation
	*estar en la calle	to be out
	*gozar de (las vacaciones)	to enjoy (the vacation)
	*ir de compras	to go shopping
	*ir de vacaciones	to go on a vacation
	pasar (las vacaciones)	to spend (one's vacation)
	*regresar	to return, to come back
adjetivos	menor	younger
	solo	alone
expresión	*hace muchísimo calor	it is *very* hot

NOTA: The endings **–ísimo(s)** and **–ísima(s)** added to an adjective are equivalent to the English words *very* or *extremely*.

When the adjective ends in a consonant, the ending is attached directly to it:

difícil → dificil**ísimo**   una tarea dificil**ísima**

When the adjective ends in a vowel, this vowel is dropped before attaching the ending:

guapo → guap**ísimo**   unos chicos guap**ísimos**
interesante → interesant**ísimo**   unas novelas interesant**ísimas**

The following final consonants change to retain the sound of the stem:

c → qu   rico → riquísimo
g → gu   largo → larguísimo
z → c   feliz → felicísimo

Lección uno
149

Vamos a hablar de lo que hiciste recientemente.

¿Acabas de levantarte?
¿Acabas de comer?
¿Acabas de leer una novela
   interesante?
¿Acabas de escuchar un buen chiste?
¿Acabas de hacer un viaje?
¿Acabas de recibir noticias de tus
   primas?

Estructuras

A. Repaso: la duración: *hace* + el presente

In Spanish, the present tense is used to describe actions or conditions
which began in the past and which are still going on now. Compare the
use of verb tenses in Spanish and English.

Hace una hora que **espero** a Carlos.	I **have been waiting** for Carlos **for** one hour.
Hace dos semanas que Isabel **está** de vacaciones.	Isabel **has been** on vacation **for** two weeks.
Hace dos años que **estudiamos** español.	We **have been studying** Spanish **for** two years.

To express the duration of such actions, Spanish speakers use the following
constructions:

> **hace** + period of time + **que** + present + rest of sentence

Note also the question constructions:

> ¿Hace cuánto tiempo que (+ present)?
> ¿Cuánto tiempo hace que (+ present)?

¿Hace cuánto tiempo que estás aquí?	*(For) How long* have you been here?
¿Cuánto tiempo hace que estudias español?	*(For) How long* have you been studying Spanish?

ACTIVIDAD 1 Una entrevista

Una periodista en Miami hace una entrevista a un músico español famoso.
Haz los dos papeles según el modelo.

📼 Ud. toca la guitarra. (10 años)

La periodista: ¿Hace cuánto tiempo que Ud. toca la guitarra?

El músico: Hace diez años que toco la guitarra.

1. Ud. canta. (12 años)
2. Ud. vive en Madrid. (20 años)
3. Ud. da conciertos. (8 años)
4. Ud. está casado. (1 año)

5. Ud. graba (record) discos. (6 años)
6. Ud. está de viaje. (3 semanas)
7. Ud. está en los Estados Unidos. (1 semana)
8. Ud. está en Miami. (2 días)

ACTIVIDAD 2 Diálogo: ¿Cuánto tiempo hace que ... ?

Pregúntales a tus amigos cuánto tiempo hace que hacen las siguientes cosas.

📼 estudiar español (¿cuántos años?)

Estudiante 1: ¿Cuántos años hace que estudias español?

Estudiante 2: Hace dos años que estudio español.

WB
A1, A2, A3

SCRIPT
🔊
Act. 5

1. vivir en esta ciudad (¿cuántos años?)
2. asistir a este colegio (¿cuántos años?)
3. conocer a tu mejor amigo (¿cuántos años?)
4. ser amigo(a) de él (¿cuántos años?)

5. conocer a tu mejor amiga (¿cuántos meses?)
6. ser amigo(a) de ella (¿cuántos meses?)
7. estar en la clase (¿cuántos minutos?)
8. hacer esta tarea (¿cuántos minutos?)

B. Repaso: *acabar de* + infinitivo

Note the use of the expression **acabar de** in the sentences below.

Acabo de llamar a Isabel.	*I just called Isabel.* / *I have just called Isabel.*
Ricardo **acaba de salir.**	*Ricardo just went out.* / *Ricardo has just gone out.*
Acabamos de llegar.	*We just arrived.* / *We have just arrived.*

Have students compare the recent past and the immediate future.
Voy a llamar a Elena.
Va a salir con Ana.
Vamos a tomar algo.

To express an event which has just happened, Spanish speakers use the construction:

> present tense of **acabar** + **de** + infinitive

📼 Object pronouns and reflexive pronouns are attached to the infinitive.

Acabo de levantar**me**.   *I just got up.*

—¿Sabes dónde está Isabel?
—Sí, acabo de ver**la**.   *Yes, I just saw her.*

Furiosos y contentos

...gos de Isabel están furiosos. Otros están contentos. Describe
...tos de cada persona (¿Está furiosa o contenta?) y explica por
... modelos.

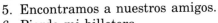 ...os saca una mala nota.   Carlos está furioso porque acaba de sacar una mala nota.
Luisa saca una buena nota.   Luisa está contenta porque acaba de sacar una buena nota.

1. Enrique pierde el partido de tenis.
2. Felicia gana el partido.
3. Francisco recibe una carta de su novia.
4. Silvia vende su bicicleta a buen precio (price).
5. Encontramos a nuestros amigos.
6. Pierdo mi billetera.
7. Tú recibes diez dólares de tu papá.
8. Elena se enoja con su novio.
9. Me peleo con mis amigos.
10. Enrique y Ana se llaman por teléfono.

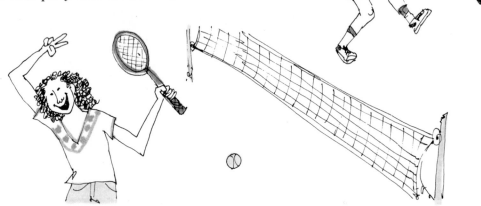

ACTIVIDAD 4 ¿Por qué?   OPTIONAL

¿Puedes explicar por qué las siguientes personas tienen varios
sentimientos? Tienes que usar la imaginación . . . y la construcción **acabar
de** + infinitivo, según el modelo.

   Isabel está contenta porque . . .
        Isabel está contenta porque acaba de llamar a su novio.
        (Isabel está contenta porque su amiga acaba de llamarla.)
        (Isabel está contenta porque su papá acaba de comprarle un coche.)

WB
B1, B2

SCRIPT
Act. 3, 4

MASTERS
p. 15

1. Rafael está triste porque . . .
2. Ramón y Luis están enojados porque . . .
3. Estoy muy contento porque . . .
4. Estamos de buen humor porque . . .
5. Tú estás de mal humor porque . . .
6. El profesor está de un humor horrible porque . . .

C. Repaso: los numerales ordinales

Ordinal numbers, such as first, second, third, are used to rank people and things.

1°	**primero**	6°	**sexto**
2°	**segundo**	7°	**séptimo**
3°	**tercero**	8°	**octavo**
4°	**cuarto**	9°	**noveno**
5°	**quinto**	10°	**décimo**

Note the superscript (°), which is used in Spanish to designate ordinal numbers. (The feminine forms are 1ª, 2ª, etc.) It corresponds to the English superscripts 1st, 2nd, 5th.

Ordinal numbers are adjectives. They agree in gender and number with the nouns they introduce.

Ordinal numbers may also be used as adverbs. Hoy voy a hacer muchas cosas. *Primero* voy a ir de compras. *Segundo* voy a llamar a...

Carmen es la **primera** chica a quien voy a invitar.

Primero and **tercero** become **primer** and **tercer** before a masculine singular noun.

Ordinal adjectives can be used alone when the noun has already been expressed. **La primera se llama Carmen.** *The first (one) is called Carmen.* **No conozco a la segunda.** *I don't know the second (one). (i.e., I don't know the second girl.)*

Enero es el **primer** mes del año.
¿Vas a ver el **tercer** acto?

Beyond **décimo**, you would use cardinal numbers instead of ordinal numbers.

Carlos vive en **el piso trece**.   *Carlos lives on **the thirteenth floor (floor thirteen)**.*
En **el siglo veinte** . . .   *In the twentieth century (century twenty). . .*

ACTIVIDAD 5   El torneo de tenis *(The tennis tournament)*

Hay un torneo de tenis en tu escuela. Les anuncias los resultados a los siguientes participantes.

Jaime: 10   Jaime, eres décimo.
Juana: 9   Juana, eres novena.

1. Julia: 2
2. Felipe: 4
3. Isabel y Luisa: 5

4. Ramón y Manuel: 7
5. Silvia: 6
6. Antonio: 8

7. Esteban: 3
8. . . . y yo: 1

ACTIVIDAD 6   El rascacielos *(The skyscraper)*

Este rascacielos tiene veinte pisos. Tú tienes muchos amigos que viven allí. Di en qué piso viven.

Ricardo: 4   Ricardo vive en el cuarto piso.

1. Raúl: 9
2. los Montoya: 12
3. Consuelo: 7
4. el Dr. Vega: 5
5. Enrique: 15

6. la Srta. Arroyo: 3
7. Alberto: 8
8. mi tío Ignacio: 6
9. el Dr. Ramos: 14
10. Anita: 1

Algunos adjetivos indefinidos

in heavy print below do not refer to a specific number of
. They are indefinite adjectives. Note the uses and forms of

algún, alguna	some	Algún día, voy a visitar España.
algunos, algunas	some, several	Tengo algunos amigos allá.
cada	each	Para la fiesta, cada chico va a invitar a una chica.
otro		
otro(a)	other, another	¿Cómo se llama la otra amiga de Inés?
		¿Tiene otro hermano, Isabel?
otros(as)	other	Mis otros amigos no pueden venir a la fiesta.
todo		
todo(a)	the whole, all	—¿Vas a leer toda la novela?
todos(as)	all, every	—No, pero voy a leer todas las revistas.

Ⅺ Alguno → algún before a masculine singular noun.

Ⅺ The indefinite article (un, una) is never used before the word otro.

Dame otra revista, por favor.   *Please give me another magazine.*

Ⅺ The above indefinite expressions can be used to replace a noun which
has already been expressed.

Conozco a aquella chica pero no
  conozco a la otra (= la otra chica).

*I know this girl, but I do not
  know the other one.*

No me gustan estas revistas.
  Dame otras (= otras revistas).

*I do not like these magazines.
  Give me other ones.*

Exception: Cada cannot be used alone. Cada uno(a) is used when
the noun is not expressed.

Tengo muchas amigas.

I have many friends.

Cada una me escribe por mi
  cumpleaños.

Each one writes me on my birthday.

ACTIVIDAD 7   Generalizaciones

Ricardo hace generalizaciones, pero Isabel no está de acuerdo *(in
agreement)* con él. Haz los dos papeles según el modelo.

Ⅺ Los muchachos son inteligentes. Ricardo: ¿Son inteligentes todos los muchachos?
                                                     Isabel: ¡No, claro que no! No todos son inteligentes.

1. Las muchachas son simpáticas.
2. Los norteamericanos son altos.
3. Las norteamericanas son rubias.
4. Los españoles son bajos.

5. Las españolas son morenas.
6. Las novelas son interesantes.
7. Los profesores son interesantes.
8. Las generalizaciones son tontas.

ACTIVIDAD 8   No, gracias

Elena le dice a Ricardo que acaba de terminar varias cosas. Ricardo le ofrece otras, pero Elena no acepta su oferta. Haz los dos papeles.

 Elena lee un libro.   Elena: Acabo de leer el libro.
                        Ricardo: ¿Quieres otro?
                          Elena: No, gracias.

1. Elena lee una revista.
2. Mira unas fotos.
3. Come unos dulces.

4. Lee unos periódicos.
5. Toma una aspirina.
6. Bebe una Coca-Cola.

Para la comunicación   OPTIONAL   May be assigned as homework.

1) La autobiografía

Imagina que acabas de recibir un premio *(prize)* importante. Un periodista habla contigo. Él quiere saber cuáles son tus actividades y cuánto tiempo hace que las haces. Contéstale en un párrafo de ocho frases. Puedes usar los siguientes verbos.

vivir / estudiar / asistir a / trabajar / jugar a / ir / hablar / tocar

 Vivo en Miami. Hace diez años que vivo aquí . . .

2) Las noticias del día

Elige *(Choose)* seis noticias recientes (políticas, artísticas, deportivas . . .) y descríbelas usando la construcción **acabar de** + infinitivo.

 El presidente acaba de hacer un viaje a Latinoamérica.
 Los Patriotas de Nueva Inglaterra acaban de vencer *(beat)* a los Delfines de Miami.
 El FBI acaba de arrestar a un criminal . . .

3) En la ventana

Asómate *(Look out)* a la ventana (de tu casa, de la sala de clase . . .) por unos diez minutos y describe en ocho frases qué ocurrió, usando la construcción **acabar de** + infinitivo. Si quieres, puedes usar los siguientes verbos:

salir / llegar / regresar / pasar / entrar / caerse / ver / hablar / charlar *(chat)*

 La vecina acaba de salir. Dos coches acaban de pasar . . .

WB
Trad.

SCRIPT

Act. 6, 7, 8

MASTERS
pp. 15–16

TRB
QUIZ
pp. 38–39

Lección 2

Segundo acto:
La decisión de Isabel

Act. 1

28

Hace varios días que Isabel piensa en esta idea: ¡probar el SEAT de su padre! ... En secreto, por supuesto, porque el Sr. Molina nunca presta su coche nuevo...
Pero hay una voz interior que no está de acuerdo con Isabel.

varios: *several*

voz: *voice*
  de acuerdo: *in agreement*

Esta voz le dice:
—¡Escúchame, Isabel!
  Hace solamente unos dos meses que tienes el permiso de conducir.
  No sabes todavía conducir bien ...
  Además, ¿de quién es el coche?
  ¿Es tuyo? ¡No! Es de tu papá ... Y si lo tomas, ¡sabes que él va a enojarse!

el permiso de conducir: *driver's license*

tuyo: *yours*

También hay otra voz, y ésta le dice:
—Por supuesto, el coche es de tu papá ...
  Pero si es suyo, es un poco tuyo también, ¿no? ¡Isabelita, estás sola! ¡Es tu oportunidad! (*Es una voz fuerte, muy fuerte...*) —¿Suyo, mío? ¿Qué importa? — piensa Isabel, sin poder resistir la tentación ...

suyo: *his*

mío: *mine*
  ¿Qué importa?: *What does it matter?*

• • • • • • • • • • •

Isabel decidió no perder más tiempo. Llamó por teléfono a Anita, su mejor amiga. Le explicó su idea. La invitó a dar una vuelta en el coche. Anita aceptó la invitación, con mucho gusto. Isabel tomó las llaves del coche de su padre. Entró en el garaje y arrancó el coche. ¡Lo sacó del garaje muy de prisa y con mucho ruido!
—¿No sabes conducir bien? Vamos a ver,—se dice Isabel, empujando el acelerador ... Se dirige hacia la plaza mayor, donde vive Anita.

Have students identify the **él** form of the preterite and give the infinitives of the -ar verbs in this paragraph.

arrancó: *started up*
de prisa: *quickly*
  ruido: *noise*
empujando: *stepping on*

Se dirige: *She heads*

Br-u-u-m

¿Hace cuánto tiempo que Isabel tiene el permiso de conducir? ¿Sabe conducir Isabel? ¿Qué va a hacer el Sr. Molina si Isabel toma el coche? ¿Cuál de las dos voces escucha Isabel — la primera o la segunda? ¿Cómo se llama la mejor amiga de Isabel? ¿Qué le explicó Isabel? ¿Qué tomó Isabel? ¿Dónde vive Anita?

ct. 2

La plaza mayor

Todas las ciudades de España y hasta° los pueblos pequeños tienen una plaza mayor.° Esta plaza tiene una arquitectura cuadrangular° y casi siempre está rodeada de° casas muy antiguas. La plaza mayor es el centro histórico de la ciudad. En el pasado° (¡y todavía ahora!) servía° para fiestas, corridas, competencias,° dramas y obras de teatro.

Hoy día la plaza mayor es el centro de mucha actividad. Hay apartamentos. También hay tiendas y cafés al aire libre.° Es agradable sentarse en uno de estos cafés y contemplar la belleza° y perfección de la arquitectura de la plaza. ¡Qué maravilla!

hasta *even*   **plaza mayor** *main square*   **cuadrangular** *square*   **rodeada de** *surrounded by*   **pasado** *past*
servía *it was used*   **competencias** *contests*   **al aire libre** *outdoor*   **belleza** *beauty*

¿Cómo se llama la plaza que se encuentra en muchas ciudades de España? ¿Son modernas las casas que están en esta plaza? ¿Qué tipo de eventos tienen lugar en la Plaza Mayor?

Vocabulario

sustantivos	* **un permiso**	permission, permit	**una voz**	voice
	* **el permiso**		(pl. **voces**)	
	de conducir	driver's license		
	un ruido	noise		
verbos	* **arrancar**	to start (a car), to pull out		
	* **dirigirse (a)**	to go (towards)		
	* **empujar**	to push		
	* **explicar**	to explain		
	probar (o → ue)	to try		
	sacar	to take out		
expresiones	* **dar una vuelta**	to go for a ride		
	* **de prisa**	fast, quickly		
	* **estar de acuerdo**	to agree		
	hacia	toward, in the direction of		
	todavía	still, yet		

NOTA: **Unos (unas)** is used in front of a number to indicate an approximation.

Hace **unos** ocho años   *I have been living in Madrid for **about***
que vivo en Madrid.   *(**approximately, more or less**) eight years.*

In Spanish-speaking countries there are several terms for "driver's license": **la licencia de manejar, la tarjeta de circulación, el carnet de conductor** (Argentina).

Lección dos
157

Vamos a hablar de lo que hizo tu papá (o tu mamá, si prefieres) ayer.

¿Se levantó temprano él (ella)?
¿Preparó el desayuno?
¿Tomó café?
¿Tomó el autobús para ir al trabajo?
¿Compró algo especial? ¿Qué?
¿Miró la televisión?
¿A qué hora se acostó?

Estructuras

A. Los adjetivos y los pronombres posesivos

There are two kinds of possessive adjectives in Spanish:

—the short or *unstressed adjectives* (**mi, tu, su, nuestro**);
—the long or *stressed adjectives*.

Note the masculine singular forms of the stressed adjectives in the chart below.

POSSESSOR		POSSESSOR	
(yo)	el coche **mío**	(nosotros)	el coche **nuestro**
(tú)	el coche **tuyo**	(vosotros)	el coche **vuestro**
(él, ella, Ud.)	el coche **suyo**	(ellos, ellas, Uds.)	el coche **suyo**

Stressed possessive adjectives agree in gender and number with the noun they modify (and *not* with the possessor).

Carmen es amiga **mía**.	*Carmen is a friend **of mine**.*
Vamos a invitar a unas amigas **nuestras** a la fiesta.	*We are going to invite a few friends **of ours** to the party.*

The stressed possessive adjectives correspond to the English forms *of mine, of yours,* etc. They always come *after* the noun. When the noun comes after **ser,** the indefinite article may be omitted.

Inés es **amiga tuya,** ¿verdad?	*Inés is **a friend of yours,** isn't she?*

Stressed possessives may also be used alone after **ser.**

Los periódicos son **míos,** pero las revistas son **tuyas**.	*The newspapers are **mine,** but the magazines are **yours**.*

Note also the following construction.

Carlos y yo tenemos bicicletas.

La mía (= mi bicicleta) es roja.	*Mine is red.*
La suya (= su bicicleta) es blanca.	*His is white.*

In the preceding sentences, the expressions in heavy print replace nouns already expressed: they are *possessive pronouns*. Possessive pronouns are formed as follows:

definite article + stressed possessive adjective

Note that both parts agree with the noun which is replaced.

mi coche = **el mío**   mis discos = **los míos**
mi casa = **la mía**   mis revistas = **las mías**

ACTIVIDAD 1   Los amigos de Raquel

Raquel quiere saber si Enrique conoce a varias personas. Enrique le pregunta si esas personas son amigas suyas. Raquel le contesta afirmativamente.

Isabel   Raquel: ¿Conoces a Isabel?
              Enrique: Es amiga tuya, ¿verdad?
              Raquel: Sí, es buena amiga mía.

1. Felipe   3. Ramón   5. Roberto y Paco
2. Carlos y su hermano   4. Elena y Felicia   6. Luisa y Silvia

ACTIVIDAD 2   Durante las vacaciones

Durante las vacaciones, las siguientes personas van a visitar a amigos o parientes. Expresa eso según el modelo.

Carlos (una amiga)   Carlos va a visitar a una amiga suya.

1. Elena (un amigo)   6. yo (un primo)
2. Roberto (un amigo)   7. tú (una prima)
3. Federico (una amiga)   8. mis hermanas (unos compañeros de colegio)
4. Ud. (un tío)   9. nosotros (un amigo)
5. Uds. (unos amigos)   10. Ana y yo (una prima)

ACTIVIDAD 3   ¿Qué vas a escoger *(choose)*?

En cada par *(pair)* de objetos, puedes escoger un objeto para ti y otro para un(a) compañero(a). Di qué escoges para ti y qué para él (ella).

VARIATION: Use plural forms. **El coche es nuestro. La moto es suya.**

un coche / una moto   El coche es mío. La moto es tuya.
                       (La moto es mía. El coche es tuyo.)

1. un reloj de pulsera / una calculadora
2. una revista de historietas *(comics)* / una novela policíaca *(detective)*
3. unos discos de jazz / unas revistas de modas

4. unos esquís acuáticos / una tabla hawaiana *(surfboard)*
5. un televisor / una bicicleta
6. unos anteojos de sol / un bolso

ACTIVIDAD 4   Diálogo: ¿Puedes usar . . .?

Pídeles a tus compañeros varios objetos suyos.

WB
A1

SCRIPT

Act. 3, 4

MASTERS
p. 17

la bicicleta   Estudiante 1: No tengo mi bicicleta. ¿Puedo usar la tuya?
                       Estudiante 2: ¡Claro! Puedes usar la mía.
                                  (No, no puedes usar la mía.)

1. el espejo
2. el peine
3. las revistas
4. el reloj
5. la calculadora
6. la guitarra
7. los discos
8. la navaja

B. Repaso: el pretérito de los verbos que terminan en -ar

The *preterite* is used to describe actions that took place in the *past*. All
regular -ar verbs have the same preterite endings. Note these endings in
the chart below.

Act. 5

INFINITIVE	**hablar**		
PRETERITE			
(yo)	habl**é**	(nosotros)	habl**amos**
(tú)	habl**aste**	(vosotros)	habl**asteis**
(él, ella, Ud.)	habl**ó**	(ellos, ellas, Uds.)	habl**aron**

Many **-ar** verbs that have a stem change in the present do *not*
have this stem change in the preterite.

pensar	¿Qué **pensaste** de esa película estúpida?
despertarse	Ayer, me **desperté** a las nueve.
encontrar	**Encontré** a María en la **cafetería**.
acostarse	Anoche, Carlos se **acostó** temprano.

Verbs that end in **-car, -gar,** and **-zar** have a spelling change in
the preterite. This change concerns only the **yo** form and is made to
preserve the sound of the stem.

-car (c → qu)	¿**Sacaste** fotos el fin de semana pasado?
	Sí, **saqué** muchas fotos.
-gar (g → gu)	¿Con quién **jugaste** al tenis?
	Jugué con Roberto.
-zar (z → c)	¿Dónde **almorzaste** ayer?
	Almorcé en un restaurante mexicano.

ACTIVIDAD 5   De compras

Isabel y sus amigos van de compras. Di qué compró cada uno y si, según
tú, gastó mucho dinero o no.

ADDITIONAL CUES: **Ud.:**
una grabadora; Uds.: un
SEAT; tú y yo: helados.

> Isabel: una revista   Isabel compró una revista.
> No gastó mucho dinero.

1. Tere: una camiseta
2. Enrique: una bicicleta
3. los hermanos de Tere: dulces
4. yo: chicle
5. tú: postales (postcards)
6. nosotros: una moto

ACTIVIDAD 6   Diálogo: El fin de semana pasado

Pregúntales a tus compañeros qué hicieron el fin de semana pasado.

Ask about student responses.
¿Con quién habló Sally?

> hablar (¿con quién?)

> Estudiante 1: ¿Con quién hablaste el fin de semana pasado?
> Estudiante 2: Hablé con un chico de Panamá.

1. llamar por teléfono (¿a quiénes?)
2. visitar (¿a quiénes?)
3. encontrar (¿a quiénes?)
4. levantarse (¿cuándo?)
5. acostarse (¿a qué hora?)
6. jugar (¿a qué?)
7. almorzar (¿dónde?)
8. bailar (¿dónde?)
9. comprar (¿qué?)

ACTIVIDAD 7   Nunca los domingos (Never on Sundays)

Éstas son las cosas que las siguientes personas hacen durante la semana.
Di que no hicieron esas cosas el domingo pasado.

WB
B1, B2, B3

SCRIPT

Act. 6, 7

MASTERS
p. 17

> Mi hermana se despierta temprano.   El domingo pasado, no se despertó temprano.

1. Me acuesto tarde.
2. Te acuestas a las diez.
3. Pedro encuentra al profesor en la calle.
4. Juego al tenis.
5. Juegas al volibol.
6. Jugamos al fútbol.
7. Almuerzo en la cafetería.
8. Almorzamos de prisa.
9. Ud. toca el piano.
10. Practico la guitarra.
11. Busco apartamento.

Make sure that students use the correct preterite forms of stem-changing verbs and verbs in **-car**, **-gar**, and **-zar**.

VOCABULARIO PRÁCTICO   El automóvil

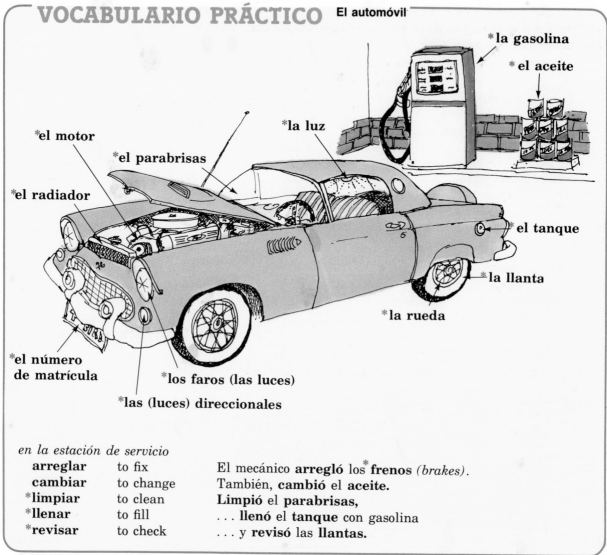

*la gasolina

*el aceite

*la luz

*el motor

*el parabrisas

*el radiador

*el tanque

*la llanta

*la rueda

*el número
de matrícula

*los faros (las luces)

*las (luces) direccionales

en la estación de servicio

arreglar	to fix	El mecánico **arregló** los *frenos (brakes)*.	
cambiar	to change	También, **cambió** el **aceite**.	
***limpiar**	to clean	**Limpió** el **parabrisas**,	
***llenar**	to fill	. . . **llenó** el **tanque** con gasolina	
***revisar**	to check	. . . y **revisó** las **llantas**.	

EXTRA VOCAB.: **el volante** (steering wheel), **el acelerador** (gas pedal), **el capó** (hood), **el claxon / la bocina** (horn), **el cambio de velocidades** (gear shift), **estacionar** (to park), **poner aire en las llantas** (put air in the tires), **revisar el nivel del aceite** (check the level of the oil).

ACTIVIDAD 8   Preguntas personales

1. ¿Tiene coche tu familia? ¿De qué marca *(make)*? ¿Es viejo o nuevo? ¿De qué color es? ¿Usa mucha gasolina? ¿mucho aceite?

2. ¿Lavas el coche de tu familia? Si no, ¿quién lo limpia?

3. ¿Sabes conducir? ¿Tienes el permiso de conducir? Si no, ¿cuándo esperas obtenerlo?

4. ¿Sueñas con tener un coche deportivo? ¿Qué clase de coche prefieres?

ACTIVIDAD 9 Un buen mecánico

Imagina que llevaste tu coche a una estación de servicio. Di qué hizo el mecánico, usando los verbos del vocabulario.

SCRIPT
Act. 8

MASTERS
p. 18

⤳ los frenos   Arregló (revisó) los frenos.

1. el tanque
2. el parabrisas
3. el radiador
4. las llantas
5. el motor
6. los faros
7. el aceite
8. las luces direccionales

C. El diminutivo –ito   OPTIONAL

This may be presented for recognition only.

Note the endings in heavy print.

Carlos tiene una herman**ita.**	*Carlos has a **little** sister.*
Vivimos en una cas**ita.**	*We live in a **small** house.*
¿Quién es ese hombre**cito?**	*Who is that **little** man?*
¿Dónde está Carmen**cita?**	*Where is **dear** Carmen?*

To convey affection or smallness, Spanish speakers often use the endings:

-ito(a)   with nouns ending in **-o, -a, -l**
-cito(a)   with other nouns

The diminutives are much more common in Spanish than in English. Since the endings also are used to show affection, they are used with adults as well as children.

ACTIVIDAD 10 Elena y Silvia   OPTIONAL

Elena le pregunta muchas cosas a Silvia. Haz el papel de Silvia, según el modelo.

⤳ ¿Tienes un hermano menor?   Silvia: Sí, tengo un hermanito.

1. ¿Tienes hermanas menores?
2. ¿Vives en una casa pequeña?
3. ¿Tienes un perro pequeño?
4. ¿Tienes un gato pequeño?
5. ¿Me esperas un momento?
6. ¿Conoces a Carmen?
7. ¿Conoces a Miguel?
8. ¿Conoces a ese hombre pequeño?

Para la comunicación   OPTIONAL

May be assigned as homework.

WB
Una
página

SCRIPT
Act. 9, 10

MASTERS
p. 18

TRB
QUIZ
pp. 40–41

El fin de semana pasado
En un pequeño párrafo describe lo que hizo cada miembro de tu familia. Puedes usar los siguientes verbos.

en casa: quedarse / limpiar / arreglar / escuchar / mirar / llamar
fuera de la casa: visitar / jugar / encontrar / regresar / mirar

- Mi hermano . . .
- Mi hermana . . .
- Mis padres . . .

VARIATION: Have students describe the imagined weekend events of someone in one of the drawings or photos of this book.

⤳ Yo: ¿Me quedé en casa? ¡Yo, no! Llamé a un amigo y salimos . . .

Lección dos
163

Lección 3

Tercer acto: ¡Qué tragedia!

Act. 1

28

Isabel estacionó el coche frente al edificio de apartamentos de Anita. Entró en el edificio y subió de prisa al apartamento de su amiga en el segundo piso.

estacionó: *parked*
edificio: *building*
subió: *went up*

Al entrar en el apartamento, Isabel oyó un ruido increíble, un ruido horrible, realmente.
—¡Dios mío! — exclamó Anita. —¡Es el coche de tu papá!
Las chicas corrieron a la ventana.
Desde allí vieron un espectáculo desastroso:
¡Un automovilista acaba de chocar con el coche nuevo del Sr. Molina!
¡Qué tragedia!

Desde allí: *From there*
chocar con: *run into*

Isabel abrió la ventana, vio al conductor culpable y exclamó:
—¡Un momentito, señor! ¡Ud. acaba de chocar con mi coche! ¡Voy a bajar!
    ¡Señor, señor . . . !

culpable: *guilty*

bajar: *come down*

Pero el conductor no oyó a Isabel y no la esperó. ¡Al contrario!
Al verla se fue muy de prisa.
—¡Válgame Dios!—exclamó Isabel.—¿Qué hago ahora?

Al verla: *On seeing her*

• • • • • • • • • • • • •

Los problemas de Isabel acaban de comenzar.
¿Qué puede hacer?
¿Cómo va a explicarle el accidente a su papá?
. . . ¿Y qué le va a decir?
Isabel está muy triste y muy nerviosa.

¿Dónde estacionó el coche Isabel? ¿Dónde está el apartamento de su amiga? ¿Qué oyó Isabel? ¿Adónde corrieron las chicas? ¿Qué vieron? ¿Qué le dijo Isabel al conductor culpable? ¿Qué hizo el conductor? ¿Cómo se siente Isabel? ¿Por qué se siente así?

Act. 2

—— Vocabulario ——

sustantivos	*un edificio de apartamentos	apartment building	**una ventana**	window
	*un espectáculo	sight, spectacle		
	un piso	floor	*In Spain, the word* **piso** *also means "apartment."*	
adjetivos	*culpable	guilty		
	*increíble	unbelievable		
	*propio	(one's) own		
verbo	*exclamar	to exclaim, to say		
expresiones	*al contrario	on the contrary		
	*desde allí	from there		
	¡Dios mío!	My goodness!		
	*frente a	facing, opposite		
	*¡Válgame Dios!	God help me!		

CONVERSACIÓN   OPTIONAL

Vamos a hablar de lo que hiciste el sábado pasado.

¿Fuiste al campo?
  Sí (No, no) fui al campo.
¿Fuiste al cine?
¿Fuiste a un restaurante?
¿Fuiste a casa de tus amigos?

¿Asististe a un concierto?
  Sí (No, no) asistí a un concierto.
¿Asististe a un partido de fútbol?
¿Asististe a un espectáculo extraordinario?
¿Asististe a la ópera?

Estructuras

A. Repaso: el pretérito de los verbos que terminan en -er y en -ir

In the preterite, most verbs which end in **-er** and **-ir** have the same endings. Note the preterite endings of **correr** *(to run)* and **subir** *(to climb)*.

Act. 3

INFINITIVE	correr	subir
PRETERITE		
(yo)	corrí	subí
(tú)	corriste	subiste
(él, ella, Ud.)	corrió	subió
(nosotros)	corrimos	subimos
(vosotros)	corristeis	subisteis
(ellos, ellas, Uds.)	corrieron	subieron

⚙ Verbs in **-er** (but not those in **-ir**) which have a stem change in the present tense have no stem change in the preterite.

entender Carlos no **entendió** al profesor.
volver Anoche **volví** a casa a las once.

⚙ In the preterite, **dar** *(to give)* and **ver** *(to see)* take the endings of **-er** and **-ir** verbs with one exception: there are no accents on the **yo** and **él** forms.

Vi a mi primo ayer. Me **dio** noticias de la familia.

⚙ Verbs in **-aer, -eer, -uir** and the verb **oír** have a spelling change in the preterite. In the **él** and **ellos** forms, the **i** of the ending becomes **y**.

caer(se) *(to fall)*	Carlos **se cayó** en la calle.
	Inés y Luisa **se cayeron** en el suelo *(ground)*.
leer *(to read)*	Isabel no **leyó** la novela.
	Mis amigos **leyeron** historietas.
oír *(to hear)*	Enrique **oyó** un ruido *(noise)* terrible.
	Mis hermanas no te **oyeron** bien.
✱**construir** *(to build)*	Roberto **construyó** un radio.
	Tus primos **construyeron** un garaje.

In addition, the **i** of these verbs (with the exception of verbs in **-uir**) has an accent in all other preterite forms.

¿Por qué **leíste** esa novela aburrida?

ACTIVIDAD 1   Diálogo: La semana pasada

Pregúntales a tus compañeros si hicieron las siguientes cosas durante la semana pasada.

⟩⟩   asistir a un concierto   Estudiante 1: ¿Asististe a un concierto?

Estudiante 2: Sí (No, no) asistí a un (ningún) concierto.

1. asistir a un partido de fútbol
2. comer en casa de un amigo
3. comer en un restaurante
4. ver a tus primas
5. recibir buenas notas
6. recibir una carta de tus abuelos

7. escribir a tus tíos
8. reunirte con tus parientes
9. salir con tus amigos
10. volver a casa después de las once
11. leer una novela policíaca
12. asistir a una película de horror

ACTIVIDAD 2   La casa encantada (The haunted house)

Hay una casa encantada en el pueblo donde vive Ramón. Un día, Ramón y sus amigos decidieron entrar en la casa. Di que oyeron ruidos raros (strange) pero que no vieron al fantasma (ghost).

⟩⟩   Ramón   Ramón oyó ruidos raros pero no vio al fantasma.

1. las hermanas de Ramón
2. yo
3. tú

4. tú y yo
5. nosotros
6. el perro de Ramón

7. Susana
8. Uds.
9. Susana y Raúl

VOCABULARIO PRÁCTICO   Algunos verbos de movimiento

*andar	to walk	**Andamos** de prisa.
	to work, to run	Mi moto **anda** bien.
*parar	to stop	Isabel **paró** el coche frente a la casa de Anita.
*pararse	to stop (oneself)	**Me paré** delante del cine.
darse prisa	to hurry	Carlos **se dio prisa** para tomar el autobús.
*subir (a)	to get (in, on), to go up	**Subí** al taxi.
	to climb	Elena **subió** la **escalera** (stairs) de prisa.
*bajar (de)	to get off, to descend	**Bajé del** autobús enfrente del colegio.
*dar un paseo	to go for a walk, ride	Ayer, **dimos un paseo** a pie (en coche, en bicicleta, a caballo).
dar una vuelta	to take a walk, ride	**Di una vuelta** en el parque.

• You may review other verbs of motion, such as **caminar** (to walk) and **correr** (to run).
• The preterite of **andar** is irregular. The forms are presented in Lesson 4.4.

ACTIVIDAD 3   ¡En vano! *(In vain)*

Las siguientes personas se dieron mucha prisa, ¡pero fue en vano! Explica
eso según el modelo.

   Carmen / perder el autobús   Carmen se dio mucha prisa, pero perdió el autobús.

1. mi papá / perder el avión
2. yo / perder el tren
3. tú / no encontrar a tus amigos
4. los ladrones *(thieves)* / no escapar
   de la policía

5. nosotros / llegar tarde al concierto
6. Ricardo y yo / no ver la película
7. Ud. / no asistir al partido de fútbol
8. Uds. / no llegar a tiempo

ACTIVIDAD 4   ¿Por qué?

Explica por qué las siguientes personas están sin aliento *(out of breath)*.

   Elena / correr dos millas   Elena corrió dos millas.

1. yo / nadar unas dos millas
2. nosotros / correr unas tres millas
3. mi prima / subir la escalera muy de
   prisa
4. los vecinos / subir cinco pisos

5. tú / darse mucha prisa
6. Isabel y yo / bajar la escalera de prisa
7. Uds. / correr dos kilómetros
8. Ud. / nadar mil metros

VOCABULARIO PRÁCTICO   Accidentes

caer	to fall	El vaso **cayó** al***suelo** *(floor)*.
caerse	to fall down	**Me caí** en la calle.
***chocar (con)**	to bump into	El coche **chocó con** un árbol.

romper	to break	Carlos **rompió** el espejo.
romperse (la pierna)	to break (one's leg)	**Me rompí** la pierna esquiando.
***tropezar (con)**	to stumble (against)	**Tropecé con** la mesa.

ACTIVIDAD 5   Unos accidentes

Unos amigos se cuentan unos accidentes que pasaron. Ahora, cuenta los elementos principales de cada accidente en un párrafo pequeño, usando los verbos en frases afirmativas o negativas.

> Carlos: tomar el coche de su papá / ver una luz roja / parar / chocar con un autobús / romperse la pierna

> Un día Carlos tomó el coche de su papá. Desafortunadamente no vio la luz roja. No paró. Chocó con un autobús y se rompió la pierna.

1. yo: entrar en la cocina de prisa / tropezar con la mesa / romper algunos vasos
2. tú: dar una vuelta por la noche / ver un árbol / chocar con él / caerte / romper tus anteojos
3. Enrique: visitar a Elena / subir la escalera de prisa / tropezar con el gato de Elena / caerse / bajar la escalera con ruido / romperse la pierna
4. nosotros: dar un paseo en auto / ver un perro en la calle / subir a la acera *(sidewalk)* / chocar con un poste telegráfico
5. los ladrones *(thieves)*: salir del banco / subir a su coche / salir de prisa / ver a los policías / chocar con una pared *(wall)*

B. Repaso: el pretérito de los verbos con cambios que terminan en *-ir*

Verbs in **-ir** which have a stem change in the present have a stem change in the preterite.
The following stem change occurs only in the **él** and **ellos** forms:

e → i	pedir	Carlos le **pidió** el coche a su papá.
		Mis amigos me **pidieron** cinco dólares.
o → u	dormir	Pedro no **durmió** bien ayer.
		Mis amigos **durmieron** en mi casa.

ACTIVIDAD 6   En la fiesta de Ana María

Ana María invitó a sus amigos a una fiesta. Algunos se sintieron contentos toda la fiesta y se divirtieron. Otros no. Expresa esto según el modelo.

> tú: enfermo   Te sentiste enfermo. No te divertiste.

1. Clara: contenta
2. Paco: mal
3. mis hermanas: muy contentas
4. tus amigos: enfermos
5. nosotros: bien
6. yo: bien también
7. Uds. y yo: cansados
8. Ud.: aburrido

C. Repaso: el pretérito de *ir* y *ser*

Ir *(to go)* and **ser** *(to be)* have the same irregular preterite.

(yo)	**fui**	(nosotros)	**fuimos**
(tú)	**fuiste**	(vosotros)	**fuisteis**
(él, ella, Ud.)	**fue**	(ellos, ellas, Uds.)	**fueron**

Usually the context helps clarify the meaning of the above preterite forms.

Mi hermano **fue** a la universidad. — *My brother **went** to the university.*
¡**Fue** un estudiante malo! — *He **was** a bad student!*

ACTIVIDAD 7 El sábado pasado

Unos amigos se cuentan lo que hicieron el sábado pasado. Di adónde fue cada uno y qué hizo. Usa por lo menos *(at least)* tres de los verbos en paréntesis . . . y tu imaginación.

WB
C1

SCRIPT
Act. 4, 5

MASTERS
p. 19

Manuel: el centro (ver, comprar, asistir, dar un paseo)
   Manuel fue al centro. Compró unos discos. Después dio un paseo en el parque donde vio a una amiga.

1. Rafael: una fiesta (escuchar, mirar, bailar, divertirse, contar)
2. nosotros: el campo (ver, dar una vuelta, almorzar, sacar fotos, volver a casa)
3. yo: el museo (mirar, admirar, romper, salir, darse prisa)
4. tú: una cita (buscar, esperar, enojarse, impacientarse, excusarse)
5. Elena y Cora: el estadio (correr, jugar, subir, caerse, irse)

VARIATION: Each cue may be assigned to a group of two or three students who have three minutes to prepare a short description. These may then be read aloud.

D. *Al* + infinitivo

Note the construction in heavy type in the following sentences:

Al entrar, Isabel oyó un ruido. — ***When she came in,** Isabel heard a noise.*
Al ver el accidente, Anita no se sintió bien. — ***On seeing** the accident (**when she saw** the accident), Anita did not feel well.*
Supimos la noticia **al hablar** con nuestros amigos. — *We learned the news **while talking** to our friends.*

The preterite of **saber** is reviewed in the next lesson.

To express the fact that two actions are going on at about the same time, you may use the construction:

al + infinitive

In this construction, **al** is the contraction of **a** + **el.** It means *at the (moment of)* and corresponds to the English expressions *on (doing something), upon (doing something), while, when.*

ACTIVIDAD 8   Preguntas personales

Ask questions in the plural. ¿**Se sienten Uds. nerviosos al ver un accidente?** Sí, (No, no) nos sentimos...

1. ¿Te pones nervioso(a) al ver un accidente?
2. ¿Te pones contento(a) al encontrar a tus amigos?
3. ¿Te pones nervioso(a) al hablar en público?
4. ¿Saludas *(do you greet)* a tus amigos al encontrarlos?
5. ¿Te acuestas al regresar a casa?
6. ¿Te duermes al mirar la televisión?
7. ¿Qué vas a hacer hoy al regresar a casa?
8. ¿Qué vas a hacer al graduarte?

ACTIVIDAD 9   Nuestras emociones

Describe las emociones de las siguientes personas, usando la construcción
al + infinitivo y el verbo **ponerse (nervioso, triste, contento, furioso, rojo . . .).**

Carmen encuentra a su novio.   Se pone contenta al encontrar a su novio.

1. Roberto encuentra a su novia.
2. Paco dice una mentira *(lie)*.
3. Felipe recibe un regalo de su tía.
4. Recibimos buenas noticias.
5. Mis amigos se informan de la muerte *(death)* de su abuelo.
6. Bailas por la primera vez *(time)*.

ACTIVIDAD 10   El accidente

Di cómo y cuándo las siguientes personas se informaron del accidente, usando la construcción **al** + infinitivo.

Leí el periódico.   Me informé del accidente al leer el periódico.

1. Esteban escuchó la radio.
2. Miraste la televisión.
3. Hablamos con nuestros amigos.
4. Carmen llegó al colegio.
5. Mis amigos fueron al centro.
6. El Sr. Vargas entró en su oficina.
7. Juan y Felipe entraron en el café.
8. Salimos del cine.

Para la comunicación

OPTIONAL
May be assigned as homework.

Lo que *(what)* hicimos

Escribe por lo menos siete frases lógicas, usando un elemento de A, B y C según el modelo.

(For more input sentences)

A	B	C
yo	ir al cine	el domingo
tú	visitar a los abuelos	a las dos
Elena	ver una película	la semana pasada
Tomás	leer un libro interesante	el verano pasado
Cristóbal	llamar a Miguel	esta mañana
	levantarse a las siete	el sábado pasado

Yo fui al cine el sábado pasado.

Lección 4   Cuarto acto: ¿Un coche nuevo?

Have students try to identify the irregular preterites in the reading.

Act. 1

28

El Sr. Molina volvió a su casa a las siete . . . ¿Y qué fue la primera cosa que vio? Su coche nuevo, por supuesto . . . ¡pero en qué estado! También vio a la policía, a los fotógrafos y a los periodistas.

policía: *police*

Entonces, vio a Isabel.

Sr. Molina:	¡Dime, hija! ¿Qué pasó? ¿Por qué está el coche así? Y esta gente, ¿qué quiere? ¿Por qué está en nuestra casa?
Isabel:	¡Yo soy la culpable, papá!
Sr. Molina:	¿Tú, la culpable? ¿Tomaste mi coche?
Isabel:	¡Sí, papá! ¡Quise probarlo!

Esta vez, el Sr. Molina se puso furioso.

Sr. Molina:	¿Cómo? ¡Quisiste probarlo! ¡Mira lo que hiciste . . .! ¡Dios mío! ¿No sabes cuánto dinero gasté en ese coche?
Isabel:	Papá, por favor . . . ¡no te enojes! ¡Te voy a comprar un coche nuevo!
Sr. Molina:	¿Qué dices? Que me vas a comprar qué . . . ¿Otro coche? ¿Y con qué dinero?
Isabel:	¡Con el mío, por supuesto! Ahora te voy a explicar cómo.

• • • • • • • • • •

Isabel le explicó a su papá el accidente y le explicó otras cosas también:

—Cuando el conductor se fue de prisa, naturalmente me sorprendí ... Pero me quedé tranquila y afortunadamente, pude ver su número de matrícula y lo escribí en un papel. Inmediatamente llamé a la policía, les di ese número y, ¿adivina qué pasó? ...

Veinte minutos después de mi llamada, la policía pudo arrestar al conductor culpable. ¿Y quién crees que es él? ¡Nada menos que el ladrón del Banco de Bilbao en Barcelona! ¡El ladrón que la semana pasada huyó con quinientos millones de pesetas! La policía encontró casi todo el dinero en el coche.

¡Qué suerte! ¿Verdad?

Pero eso no es todo ... Hace unos dos minutos, el director del banco me llamó por teléfono. Naturalmente me felicitó y me dijo también que gané la recompensa: ¡un millón de pesetas! ¡Es bastante para comprarte un coche nuevo, papá! Y por supuesto, no te voy a comprar un SEAT, sino un Jaguar.

• • • • • • • • • • • • •

Un periodista se acercó a Isabel y a su papá.

El periodista: Por favor, Sr. Molina, ¿me permite Ud. sacar una foto de Ud. con su hija?

Sr. Molina: Sí ... con mucho gusto.

El periodista: Sr. Molina, ¡su hija tuvo una suerte increíble!

Sr. Molina: ¿Ud. dijo «una suerte increíble»? ... No es ésa la palabra, señor. ¡Mi hija no tuvo suerte sino presencia de ánimo!

El periodista: ¡Claro! Ud. debe estar muy orgulloso y muy feliz.

Sr. Molina: ¡Por supuesto! ¡Estoy muy orgulloso de mi Isabelita! ... No hay muchos padres con hijas tan inteligentes y tan listas, ¿verdad?

me sorprendí: *I was surprised*
papel: *paper*
adivina: *guess*

llamada: *call*
Nada menos: *No one less*
ladrón: *thief*
huyó: *fled*

El Banco de Bilbao is one of the largest Spanish banks.

felicitó: *he congratulated*
recompensa: *reward*
sino: *but rather*

se acercó: *approached*

orgulloso: *proud*

¿A qué hora volvió a casa el Sr. Molina? ¿Qué vio? ¿A quiénes vio? ¿Le dijo la verdad a su papá Isabel? ¿Qué escribió en el papel? ¿A quién llamó inmediatamente después? ¿A quién arrestó la policía? ¿Qué encontraron en el coche? ¿Quién llamó a Isabel? ¿Cuánto ganó de recompensa Isabel?

NOTA CULTURAL   OPTIONAL

El honor familiar

¿Qué es el honor? ¿Es una cualidad personal o es una cualidad familiar?° En la sociedad hispánica, el honor es una mezcla° de las dos. Se identifica con la persona pero también con la familia. ¡Eso explica por qué el Sr. Molina está tan orgulloso de su hija!

Los jóvenes hispanos son verdaderamente° el orgullo° de sus padres, de sus abuelos y de sus parientes. Ellos tienen que cumplir° no sólo las aspiraciones de sí mismos,° sino° también las de su familia. Deben mantener° las tradiciones de ella y, sobre todo, los valores de honestidad, valentía° y generosidad.

familiar *family*   **mezcla** *mixture*   **verdaderamente** *truly*
orgullo *pride*   **cumplir** *fulfill*   **sí mismos** *themselves*
sino *but*   **mantener** *maintain, keep*   **valentía** *courage*

¿Están orgullosos los hispanos de su familia? ¿Qué tienen que hacer los jóvenes para mantener el honor familiar?

Vocabulario

sustantivos	*el ánimo	spirit, mind	la gente	people
	*la presencia de ánimo	mental alertness	*una llamada	(phone) call
			una palabra	word
	*un estado	state	*una recompensa	reward
	un ladrón	thief		
	*un papel	paper		
adjetivos	*orgulloso	proud		
	tranquilo	calm		
verbos	*acercarse	to approach, to get near	*huir	to flee
			pasar	to happen
	*adivinar	to guess	*¿Qué pasó?	What happened?
	*felicitar	to congratulate		
	gastar	to spend	*permitir	to permit
	*sorprenderse	to be surprised		
expresión	*sino	but		

Note for recognition only: the irregular forms of **huir** in the present (**huyo, huyes, huye, huyen**) and preterite (**huyó, huyeron.**)

NOTA: **Sino** is used instead of **pero** *(but)* in a statement which contradicts a previous negative statement. It means *but* in the sense of *on the contrary* or *but instead.*

No conduzco un Jaguar **sino** un Ferrari.	*I do not drive a Jaguar,* **but** *a Ferrari.*
Isabel no tuvo suerte, **sino** presencia de ánimo.	*Isabel was not lucky,* **but** *alert.*

• ADDITIONAL EXAMPLES: **No somos mexicanos** *sino* **norteamericanos. La capital de los Estados Unidos no es Nueva York** *sino* **Washington.**
• ACTIVITY: Have students complete these statements with *sino* + correct information. **En esta clase no estudiamos francés...** (*sino* **español**). **En la clase no hay 50 alumnos...** (*sino* **20**).

Vamos a hablar de lo que hiciste ayer.

¿Hiciste la tarea? Sí (No, no) hice . . .
¿Hiciste algo especial? ¿Qué?
¿Hiciste algo divertido? ¿Qué?
¿Hiciste algo interesante? ¿Qué?

¿Tuviste tiempo para escribirles a tus abuelos? Sí (No, no) tuve . . .
¿Tuviste tiempo para mirar la televisión?
¿Tuviste que ayudar a tus padres?
¿Tuviste que estudiar mucho?

Estructuras

A. Repaso: el pretérito del verbo *conducir*

Note the preterite forms of **conducir** *(to drive)*.

(yo)	conduje	(nosotros)	condujimos
(tú)	condujiste	(vosotros)	condujisteis
(él, ella, Ud.)	condujo	(ellos, ellas, Uds.)	condujeron

In the preterite, **decir** *(to say)*, **traer** *(to bring),* and verbs ending in **–ucir** are conjugated like **conducir**.

They have a preterite stem ending in **–j.**

They all have the same endings in the preterite:

–e, –iste, –o, –imos, –isteis, -eron.

INFINITIVE	PRETERITE STEM	
decir	**dij-**	Carlos **dijo** la verdad.
traer	**traj-**	Mis amigos **trajeron** sus discos a la fiesta.
traducir	**traduj-**	**Traduje** un artículo de un periódico español.

Use these sentences for practice by varying the subjects. **Tú y yo dijimos la verdad.**

Verbs derived from the above have the same irregularities: **predecir** (to predict), **contradecir** (to contradict), **producir** (to produce), **atraer** (to attract).

ACTIVIDAD 1   El secreto de Isabel

Isabel les dijo un secreto a sus amigos. Di quiénes repitieron el secreto y quiénes no.

Carlos (no)   Carlos no lo dijo.

1. Enrique (sí)
2. Uds. (sí)
3. nosotros (no)
4. yo (no)

5. tú (sí)
6. Marta y yo (no)
7. Elena y Susana (sí)
8. Ud. (no)

WB
A1

B. Repaso: otros pretéritos irregulares

Note the preterite forms of **estar**. Pay special attention to the endings.

(yo)	estuve	(nosotros)	estuvimos
(tú)	estuviste	(vosotros)	estuvisteis
(él, ella, Ud.)	estuvo	(ellos, ellas, Uds.)	estuvieron

▷ Note that the **yo** and **él** forms have no accent marks.

▷ Other irregular verbs have the same preterite endings, but different preterite stems. These verbs can be grouped according to their stem vowels.

Act. 3, 4

INFINITIVE	PRETERITE STEM	
the "i" group		
hacer	**hic-**	¿Qué **hiciste** ayer?
querer	**quis-**	Carmen **quiso** ir al cine conmigo.
venir	**vin-**	¿A qué hora **vinieron** Uds.?
the "u" group		
andar	**anduv-**	Enrique **anduvo** rápidamente.
estar	**estuv-**	Anita y yo **estuvimos** de buen humor.
poder	**pud-**	No **pude** ir a la fiesta.
poner	**pus-**	El papá de Isabel **se puso** furioso.
saber	**sup-**	¿**Supiste** la verdad?
tener	**tuv-**	¡No **tuve** tiempo para escribirte!

Use these sentences for practice by varying the subjects. **¿Qué hizo Ana ayer?**

▷ The **él** form of the preterite of **hacer** is **hizo**. The c → z change is needed to maintain the sound of the stem.

¿Qué **hizo** Isabel después del accidente?

In addition to their regular meanings, a few verbs may have special meanings in the preterite.

	regular meaning (present tense)	special preterite meaning	
conocer	I know	I met (for the first time)	*Ayer, conocí a una chica española.*
querer	I want	I tried	*Quise aprenderlo pero no pude.*
no querer	I don't want	I refused	*Yo no quise invitar a Carlos.*
saber	I know	I found out, learned	*Yo supe quién robó el banco.*
tener	I have	I got, received	*Tuve una carta ayer con malas noticias. ¡Qué lata!*

ACTIVIDAD 2   Las vacaciones de verano

Unos amigos están hablando de las vacaciones pasadas. Di adónde fue cada uno.

▷ Isabel: a Colombia   Isabel hizo un viaje a Colombia.

1. Manuel: a España
2. Uds.: a México
3. tú: a Francia

4. yo: a Puerto Ricc
5. nosotros: a Italia
6. mis primos: a Suecia *(Sweden)*

VARIATION with **estar: Isabel estuvo en Colombia.**

ACTIVIDAD 3   En lugar de eso *(Instead . . .)*

Las siguientes personas quisieron hacer varias cosas el sábado pasado. En lugar de eso, tuvieron que hacer cosas diferentes. Expresa eso.

Isabel: ir a la playa / a la biblioteca   Isabel quiso ir a la playa pero no pudo. Tuvo que ir a la biblioteca.

1. Rafael: invitar a María al cine / a su prima
2. yo: hacer un viaje / la tarea
3. tú: salir con Olga / con Susana
4. nosotros: almorzar en el restaurante / en casa
5. mis amigos: leer historietas *(comics)* / el libro de inglés
6. Concepción: ir a la discoteca / de compras
7. Uds. y yo: comprar dulces / un cuaderno
8. Ud.: ir a un partido de tenis / de compras

Y del Cuerpo de Paz vino un voluntario que nos dio esperanza...

El trabajo no puede ser más duro ni la satisfacción mayor.

ACTIVIDAD 4   Excusas

Ana María organizó una fiesta, pero sus amigos no vinieron. Expresa eso, dando la excusa de cada uno.

Carmen: tiene un accidente   Carmen no vino porque tuvo un accidente.

1. Fernando: tiene que ayudar en casa
2. Marta: no puede recordar la fecha
3. Inés: no sabe llegar
4. Enrique y Luis: están enfermos
5. Héctor: su padre se pone enfermo

ACTIVIDAD 5   Diálogo: ¿Qué pasó?

Pregúntales a tus compañeros si hicieron las siguientes cosas el fin de semana pasado.

ir de compras   Estudiante 1: ¿Fuiste de compras?
                            Estudiante 2: Sí (No, no) fui de compras.

1. andar al centro
2. andar por las calles con tus amigos
3. hacer una fiesta
4. hacer un viaje
5. estar en casa de tus amigos
6. estar contento(a)
7. estar enfermo(a)
8. tener disputa *(quarrel)* con tus hermanos
9. tener dificultades con tus padres
10. tener que ayudar en casa

VARIATION using the plural: **¿Fueron Uds. de compras? Sí (No, no) fuimos...**

ACTIVIDAD 6 ¡Un poco de imaginación! OPTIONAL

May be assigned as a special challenge activity.

En cinco minutos, ¿cuántas frases lógicas puedes crear? Usa los elementos de las columnas A, B, C y . . . tu imaginación.

A	B	C	D
anoche	yo	hacer un viaje	
ayer	tú	conducir	
la semana pasada	mis amigos y yo	traducir	
el año pasado	Isabel	traer	
el mes pasado	mis padres	tener	
el lunes pasado	los alumnos	tener que	
		saber	
		poder	

WB
B1, B2

SCRIPT
Act. 5

MASTERS
p. 20

Ayer, mis amigos y yo le trajimos un regalo a la profesora.
El año pasado, mis padres hicieron un viaje a San Francisco.
La semana pasada, (yo) conduje el coche de mi hermana.

C. El pretérito + *hace*

Note the use of **hace** in the following sentences:

El director habló con Isabel **hace diez minutos.**   *The director spoke to Isabel **ten minutes ago.***

Fui a España **hace dos años.**   *I went to Spain **two years ago.***

To express the time elapsed since a past event took place, Spanish speakers use the construction:

verb in the preterite + **hace** + time

In this construction, **hace** corresponds to the English *ago.*

ACTIVIDAD 7   ¿Dónde está Isabel?

Son las seis de la tarde. Carlos está buscando a Isabel. Sus amigos le dicen cuándo la vieron. Haz el papel de Carlos y de los amigos. Calcula el tiempo según el modelo.

> Pedro (4:00)   Carlos: ¿Viste a Isabel?
>   Pedro: Sí, la vi hace dos horas.

1. Pilar (5:00)
2. Ricardo (4:00)
3. Tomás (2:00)
4. Ramón (3:00)
5. Teresa (5:45)
6. Lupe (5:50)

ACTIVIDAD 8   ¿Tienes buena memoria?

Completa las siguientes frases con **hace** + tiempo.

> Me levanté . . .   Me levanté hace (tres horas).

WB
C1, C2

SCRIPT

Act. 7

1. Me desayuné . . .
2. Salí de casa . . .
3. Llegué a la escuela . . .
4. La clase de español empezó . . .
5. Mi papá compró su coche . . .
6. Mis padres se casaron . . .

D. Los adverbios que terminan en –*mente*

The words in heavy print indicate how the subject acts. They are adverbs of manner. Compare these adverbs with the adjectives from which they are derived.

Carlos es inteligente.	*Carlos is intelligent.*	When two adverbs are used together, only the second has the **-mente** ending. **Trabaja fácil y rápidamente.**
Habla **inteligentemente**.	*He speaks **intelligently**.*	
Carmen es prudente.	*Carmen is cautious.*	
Conduce **prudentemente**.	*She drives **carefully**.*	

Many Spanish adverbs of manner are derived from adjectives, as follows:

feminine form of the adjective   +   **-mente**

(masculine)	(feminine)	(adverb)
rico	rica	rica**mente**
prudente	prudente	prudente**mente**
natural	natural	natural**mente**

> The **-mente** ending often corresponds to the *-ly* in English.

VOCABULARIO PRÁCTICO   Algunos adjetivos

*afortunado	≠	*desafortunado	fortunate, lucky	≠	unfortunate, unlucky
*cuidadoso	≠	descuidado	careful	≠	careless
*limpio	≠	*sucio	clean	≠	dirty
*prudente	≠	*imprudente	cautious, careful	≠	careless
*rápido	≠	*lento	quick, fast	≠	slow
*seguro	≠	peligroso	sure, safe	≠	dangerous

For practice, have students derive corresponding adverbs in **-mente**.

ACTIVIDAD 9   Lo contrario

Carlos hace lo contrario de lo que hace Ramón. Expresa eso usando
adverbios derivados de los adjetivos en paréntesis.

> conducir (prudente, peligroso)   Carlos conduce prudentemente.
>   Ramón conduce peligrosamente.

1. comer (rápido, lento)
2. vestirse (rico, pobre)
3. estudiar (cuidadoso, descuidado)
4. hablar (fácil, difícil)
5. contestar en clase (cuidadoso, descuidado)
6. portarse con sus amigos (cortés, descortés)
7. reaccionar en todas ocasiones (prudente, imprudente)
8. jugar al tenis (rápido, lento)

ACTIVIDAD 10   El accidente

En el accidente, cada uno reacciona según su carácter. Expresa eso.

> Carlos es valiente (brave).   Reacciona valientemente.

1. Isabel es segura.
2. Enrique es tonto.
3. Carmen es prudente.
4. Ramón es rápido.
5. Ángela y Encarnación son lentas.
6. Paco es imprudente.

WB
D1

✏️

WB
Una
página

SCRIPT
🔊
Act. 6, 8,
9

MASTERS
p. 20

📄
TRB

QUIZ
pp. 44—45

WB Test/Repaso

Para la comunicación

Un viaje

Describe un viaje que hiciste con tu familia. Si quieres, puedes usar
las siguientes preguntas como inspiración.

¿Cuándo hiciste este viaje? ¿Con quiénes?

¿Adónde fueron?

¿Tomaron Uds. el coche? ¿Quién condujo?

¿Tuvieron problemas con el coche?

¿Hicieron Uds. algo especial?

¿Tuvieron Uds. un accidente? ¿Otras dificultades?

¿Unas disputas pequeñas?

¿Qué tuvieron que hacer?

¿Qué cosas pudieron hacer? ¿Qué cosas no pudieron hacer?

TEST pp. 46—49

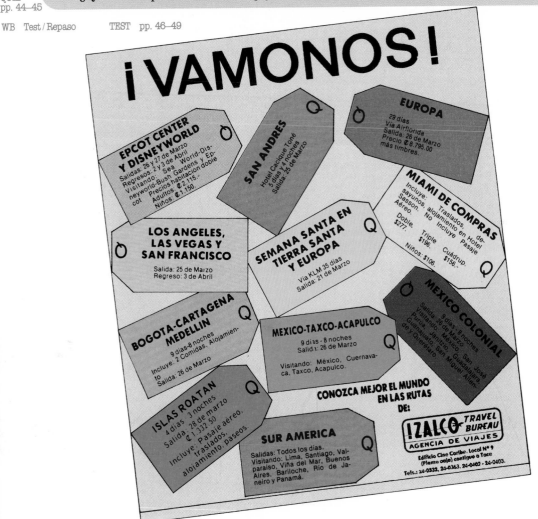

Variedades ¿Tienes sentido de orientación?

¿Tienes sentido de orientación? ¿Sí? Bien. Entonces, puedes ayudar a
Rafael y Marisa.

Rafael y Marisa son dos jóvenes turistas muy confundidos.° Anoche
llegaron muy tarde a Santa Cruz del Mar, un pueblo donde tú pasas
las vacaciones. Esta mañana decidieron dar un paseo pero se
perdieron.

Tú los encontraste y te pidieron direcciones para llegar a su hotel.
Pero no recuerdan el nombre° del hotel. Aquí tienes lo que ellos
recuerdan.

1. Salieron del hotel a las 10 de la mañana.
   Compraron tarjetas postales en una librería°
   que está cerca del hotel.

2. Caminaron un poco, luego pasaron por un
   parque. Allí sacaron una foto de la estatua de
   un hombre a caballo.° Después se sentaron en
   un banco.°

3. Salieron del parque y cruzaron° un puente.°

4. Después de cruzar el puente, se sentaron en
   un café y comieron un sándwich.

5. Dieron un paseo a lo largo del° muelle° y
   sacaron fotos de algunos barcos.

6. Entraron en un banco para cambiar dinero.

7. Cruzaron otro puente.

8. Fueron a otro café y allí se dieron cuenta de
   que estaban° perdidos.°

confundidos: *confused*

nombre: *name*

librería: *bookstore*

a caballo: *on
horseback*
banco: *bench*
cruzaron: *crossed*
puente: *bridge*

a lo largo de: *along*
muelle: *wharf*

estaban: *they were*
perdidos: *lost*

30

Tienes el mapa de Santa Cruz del Mar. ¿Puedes explicarles a Rafael y a Marisa el itinerario° que tomaron? ¿Puedes indicarles el nombre de su hotel?

itinerario: *path*

5

Unidad

¡Cómo transcurre el tiempo!

5.1 Unos «tipos»

5.2 ¿Ángel o diablo?

5.3 ¡Ay, qué día!

5.4 Un accidente en Cartagena

VARIEDADES El robo del museo

OBJECTIVES

Communication

By the end of this unit, students will be able to use Spanish:
- To describe things they used to do in the past
- To describe the circumstances of a specific event (a party, an accident)
- To talk about past events in general

Language

This unit introduces the imperfect: its forms and its uses (as contrasted with the preterite). The unit also reviews negative expressions and presents the construction **lo** + adjective and the expression **lo que.**

Culture

The cultural topics of this unit include Don Quijote, Simón Bolívar, Cartagena, the importance of good manners, and some common superstitions.

Unos «tipos»

Act. 1

En la vida, encontramos a muchas personas simpáticas. De vez en cuando encontramos a un «tipo», es decir a una persona no como las otras . . . Esa persona no es necesariamente antipática. Es solamente diferente . . . ¿Conoces a esos tipos?

«tipo»: *"character"*
es decir: *that is to say*

El holgazán

No estudia nunca.
No trabaja nunca.
No hace nada, excepto divertirse . . .
¡y dormir!

holgazán: *loafer*

El sabelotodo

Naturalmente, cree saberlo todo . . .
pero, en realidad, no sabe nada.

sabelotodo: *know-it-all*

El chismoso

Jamás puede guardar un secreto.
Repite todo lo que le dicen sus amigos.
Por eso, ¡nadie le dice nada!

chismoso: *gossip*
Jamás: *Never*
guardar: *keep*

El sablista

¿Tiene discos, libros, revistas, dinero?
Sí, pero siempre dice que no . . .
Así, pide todo prestado a sus amigos.
Lo terrible es que él no devuelve nada
jamás.

sablista: *sponger*

pide prestado:
borrows

You may test student comprehension with the following activity.
1. **Ricardo duerme siempre. Adivina qué es Ricardo. (un holgazán)**
2. **Felipe le pidió prestado su bicicleta a Carmen, pero no se la devolvió. Adivina qué es Felipe. (un sablista)**
3. **Ana María repitió el secreto que le dijo Paco. Adivina qué es Ana María. (una chismosa)**
4. **Enrique compra la misma ropa y los mismos discos que Rafael. Adivina qué es Enrique. (un imitador)**

El esnob

Para él, lo importante es impresionar
a otros.
Así, prefiere . . .
　　lo caro a lo barato,
　　lo vistoso a lo útil,
　　lo artificial a lo natural.
Por eso, ¡no impresiona a nadie!

vistoso: showy

El imitador

No tiene personalidad.
Siempre hace lo que hacen los otros,
y dice lo que dicen ellos.
¡Imita a todos!

imitador: mimic

El bobo

Cree todo lo que le cuentan sus
amigos.
De vez en cuando, no cree lo
verdadero . . .
¡pero siempre cree lo falso!

bobo: dummy

El payaso

¿Qué toma él en serio?
¡Nada!
Se ríe de todo.
Para él, la vida es una broma.

payaso: clown

*Se ríe: He makes fun
of*

5. **Conchita compra ropa muy cara para impresionar a sus amigas.** Adivina qué es Conchita. (una esnob)
6. **Roberto cree que es Papá Noel quien le trae regalos de Navidad.** Adivina qué es Roberto. (un bobo)
7. **Federico cuenta muchos chistes en la clase de español.** Adivina qué es Federico. (un payaso)
8. **Alonso dice que habla francés, inglés, alemán y japonés. Dice también que es un experto en electrónica, en física, en química...**
　　Adivina qué es Alonso. (un sabelotodo)

NOTA CULTURAL

OPTIONAL

Miguel de Cervantes

Un tipo de la literatura española: don Quijote

No necesitas ser un experto en la literatura española para saber quién es don Quijote. Don Quijote es el personaje° principal de una novela escrita por° Cervantes, uno de los más famosos escritores° españoles.

Acompañado de su fiel° compañero Sancho Panza, don Quijote sobrevive° una serie de aventuras cómicas o fantásticas. Un día, él ataca° molinos de viento,° creyendo que son gigantes.° Otro día toma una posada° por un castillo° que debe defender . . .

Para algunas personas, don Quijote es un idealista, siempre buscando justicia. Para otros, él es un hombre loco y extravagante. Sobre todo, don Quijote es una persona muy independiente y orgullosa;° él es el símbolo del individualismo . . . Don Quijote es realmente más que un «tipo»: ¡Es un hombre extraordinario!

personaje *character*   **escrita por** *written by*
escritores *writers*   **fiel** *faithful*   **sobrevive** *survives*
ataca *attacks*   **molinos de viento** *windmills*
gigantes *giants*   **posada** *inn*   **castillo** *castle*
orgullosa *proud*

¿Quién escribió «Don Quijote»? ¿Cómo se llama el compañero de don Quijote? ¿Por qué ataca molinos de viento? ¿Qué cualidad simboliza don Quijote?

Miguel de Cervantes (1547-1616), the great Spanish novelist and poet, was himself the hero of many adventures. As a soldier, he fought against the Barbary pirates, was captured, and spent five years in captivity before beginning his writing career. **El ingenioso hidalgo don Quijote de la Mancha** was published in 1605.

Vocabulario

sustantivos	**un bobo**	dummy, fool	**una broma**	joke
	un chismoso	tattletale, gossip		
	un holgazán	lazy bum, loafer		
	un payaso	clown		
	un sabelotodo	know-it-all		
	un sablista	sponger		
verbos	**guardar**	to keep		
	impresionar	to impress		
	pedir prestado	to borrow		
expresiones	**excepto**	except		
	jamás	never		

NOTA: The Spanish ending **-idad** corresponds to the English ending *-ity*. Nouns ending in **-idad** are feminine.

en realidad	*in reality*
personalidad	*personality*

Vamos a hablar de lo que hiciste ayer.
¿Hiciste algo especial? Sí, hice algo especial.
                       (No, no hice nada especial.)

¿Hiciste algo extraordinario?   ¿Viste algo extraordinario?
¿Hiciste algo divertido?   ¿Aprendiste algo interesante?
¿Viste algo cómico?   ¿Aprendiste algo raro?

Estructuras

A. La construcción negativa

Compare the affirmative and negative sentences below.

Elena **siempre** sale los sábados.   **No** sale **nunca** los domingos.
                                      Nunca sale los domingos.

Le dice **algo** a Carlos.   **No** le dice **nada** a Carlos.

Most Spanish negative words begin with **n** (**nunca, nada** . . .). When these negative words come after the verb, the construction to use is:

Compare:

    No hablo con **nadie.**   *I do **not** speak to **anyone**.*
    Nadie me habla.   *Nobody speaks to me.*

VOCABULARIO PRÁCTICO   Expresiones afirmativas y negativas

algo	something	—¿Haces **algo** interesante?
nada	nothing, not anything	—No, **no** hago **nada**.
alguien	someone, somebody	—¿Conoces a **alguien** aquí?
nadie	no one, nobody, not anyone	—No, **no** conozco a **nadie**.
alguno	some	—¿Tienes **algunas** ideas interesantes?
ninguno	no, not any, none	—No, **no** tengo **ninguna**.

una vez	once	—Fui a una ópera **una vez**.
a veces	sometimes	—**A veces** voy a un concierto.
siempre	always	—Los sábados, **siempre** voy al cine. ¿Y tú?
nunca	never	—Yo **no** voy **nunca** al cine.
o	or	—¿Quieres té **o** Coca-Cola?
ni . . . ni	neither . . . nor	—**No** quiero **ni** té **ni** Coca-Cola.
también	also, too; so (do I)	—Digo siempre la verdad.
		—¡Yo **también**!
tampoco	neither, nor (do I)	—No digo **mentiras** *(lies)*.
		—¡Yo **tampoco**!

NOTAS: 1. **Alguno** and **ninguno** become **algún** and **ningún** before a masculine singular
noun.

Algún día, voy a hacer un viaje a España.	*Some day I'm going to take a trip to Spain.*
El pobre Guillermo no tiene **ningún** plan de viajes.	*Poor Guillermo hasn't **any** travel plans.*

2. Note also the expressions:

en (a) alguna parte	somewhere	**en (a) ninguna parte**	nowhere
de alguna manera	(in) some way	**de ninguna manera**	(in) no way

3. **Tampoco** is used to express agreement with negative statements.

Carlos no habla inglés.	*Carlos does not speak English.*
Elena **tampoco**.	*Neither does Elena. (Nor does Elena.)*

ACTIVIDAD 1 Las vacaciones

Durante las vacaciones, Isabel no hace lo que hace generalmente. Expresa esto usando la palabra **nunca.**

Trabaja.   Durante las vacaciones no trabaja nunca.

1. Hace la tarea.
2. Ayuda a sus hermanos.
3. Se levanta temprano.
4. Mira la televisión.
5. Toca el piano.
6. Se siente triste.

ACTIVIDAD 2 ¿Estás de mal humor?

Imagina que estás de mal humor. Un amigo quiere saber lo que hiciste el sábado pasado. Contéstale negativamente, usando las expresiones apropiadas (**nada, nunca, nadie** . . .).

¿Hiciste algo especial?   No, no hice nada especial.

1. ¿Leíste algo interesante?
2. ¿Viste algo divertido en la televisión?
3. ¿Compraste algo?
4. ¿Saliste con alguien?
5. ¿Invitaste a alguien al teatro?
6. ¿Jugaste al tenis con alguien?
7. ¿Hablaste con alguno de tus amigos?
8. ¿Viste a alguna de tus amigas?
9. ¿Te llamó alguien por teléfono?
10. ¿Te dijo alguien que eres brillante?

VARIATION in the plural:
¿Hicieron Uds. algo especial?
No, no hicimos...

ACTIVIDAD 3 ¡Yo también!

Elena le dice a Conchita lo que hace y lo que no hace. Conchita le dice que hace (o no hace) las mismas cosas. Haz los papeles según el modelo.

Make sure that students use **yo tampoco** only to express agreement with *negative* statements.

Bailo muy bien.   Elena: Bailo muy bien.
                   Conchita: ¡Yo también!

No nado bien.   Elena: No nado bien.
                 Conchita: ¡Yo tampoco!

1. Hablo inglés.
2. No hablo ruso.
3. Juego al tenis.
4. No juego a los naipes *(cards)*.
5. De vez en cuando, digo una mentira.
6. No digo siempre la verdad.
7. Les pido dinero a mis padres.
8. No les pido dinero a mis amigos.
9. Soy simpática.
10. No soy egoísta.
11. No imito a los otros.
12. Guardo los secretos de mis amigos.
13. Pido prestados discos.
14. No pido prestado dinero.

B. La construcción *lo* + adjetivo OPTIONAL May be taught for recognition.

The Spanish neuter pronoun **lo** is often used with a masculine adjective.
Note the meaning of such constructions in the sentences below.

Elena quiere hacer **lo imposible.**   *Elena wants to do **the impossible.***
   (= las cosas imposibles)

¿Prefieres **lo viejo** o **lo nuevo**?   *Do you prefer **the old** or **the new**?*
   (= las cosas viejas, las cosas   *(Do you prefer **things** that are **old** or **new**?)*
   nuevas)

Lo bueno es que él sabe la verdad.   ***What's good** is that he knows the truth.*
   (= la cosa buena)

The Spanish construction **lo** + masculine adjective corresponds to several
English constructions:

lo nuevo $\begin{cases} \textit{\textbf{the new, the new thing(s)}} \\ \textit{\textbf{the things that are new}} \\ \textit{\textbf{what's new}} \end{cases}$

WB
V2

VOCABULARIO PRÁCTICO   **Algunos adjetivos**

| **común** | common | ≠ | **raro** | strange, rare |
| **fácil** | easy | ≠ | **difícil** | difficult |

hermoso	beautiful	≠	**feo**	ugly
moderno	modern	≠	**antiguo**	antique, old
posible	possible	≠	**imposible**	impossible
sencillo	simple	≠	**complicado**	complicated
útil	useful	≠	**inútil**	useless
verdadero	true	≠	**falso**	false

ACTIVIDAD 4   La filosofía de la vida

Expresa tu filosofía de la vida. Haz frases que empiezan con **debemos hacer** *(we should do)* o con **no debemos hacer** *(we should not do)*.

bueno   (No) Debemos hacer lo bueno.

1. malo
2. útil
3. imposible
4. hermoso
5. feo
6. sencillo
7. fácil
8. ridículo
9. absurdo
10. inútil
11. importante
12. difícil

ACTIVIDAD 5   ¡Por supuesto!

A menudo, nuestras acciones reflejan nuestra personalidad. Expresa esto según el modelo, en frases afirmativas o negativas.

realista / hacer: imposible   Una persona realista no hace lo imposible.

1. buena / hacer: malo
2. mala / hacer: bueno
3. idealista / creer en: absoluto
4. práctica / hacer: útil
5. lógica / creer en: absurdo
6. perezosa / escoger *(to choose)*: difícil
7. moderna / comprar: viejo
8. avara *(miserly)* / comprar: caro
9. prudente / hacer: peligroso
10. supersticiosa / creer en: sobrenatural
11. racional / creer en: lógico
12. realista / creer en: fantástico

ACTIVIDAD 6   ¿Qué hacen?

Lo que hacemos depende de la personalidad de cada uno de nosotros. Puedes expresar esto según el modelo.

VARIATION with negative sentences: **Un artista no hace lo feo.**

un artista hace . . . (¿feo o hermoso?)   Un artista hace lo hermoso.

1. un ángel hace . . . (¿bueno o malo?)
2. un diablo hace . . . (¿bueno o malo?)
3. una persona avara *(miserly)* compra . . . (¿caro o barato?)
4. un estudiante perezoso hace . . . (¿fácil o difícil?)
5. una persona moderna compra . . . (¿antiguo o nuevo?)
6. una persona prudente hace . . . (¿peligroso o fácil?)
7. una persona racional hace . . . (¿posible o imposible?)
8. una persona supersticiosa cree en . . . (¿natural o sobrenatural?)
9. una persona extravagante hace . . . (¿raro o común?)

ACTIVIDAD 7   Unas críticas

Critica a las siguientes personas y cosas expresando lo bueno y lo malo.

▷   la escuela   Lo bueno de la escuela es la clase de español.
Lo malo es la clase de matemáticas.

1. mi ciudad
2. mi casa
3. mi mejor amigo
4. mi mejor amiga
5. mi vida

C. Repaso: *lo que*

Note the meaning of the Spanish expression **lo que.**

Me gusta **lo que** hace Carlos.	*I like **what** Carlos does.*
(= las cosas que)	
Por favor, repite **lo que** dijiste.	*Please repeat **what** you said.*
(= las cosas que)	
Lo que contesta Pedro es ridículo.	***What** Pedro answers is ridiculous.*
(= las cosas que)	

The Spanish expression **lo que** corresponds to the English expression *what,* in the sense of *the thing(s) which.*

▷   The word order is usually:

> **lo que**   +   verb   +   subject (when expressed)

ACTIVIDAD 8   ¡El pobre Ramón!

El pobre Ramón no sabe nada. Haz el papel de Ramón según el modelo.

▷   ¿Qué explicó el profesor?   Ramón: No sé lo que explicó el profesor.

1. ¿Qué dijo Ana?
2. ¿Qué compró Roberto?
3. ¿Qué contestó Carmen?
4. ¿Qué hicieron Paco y Luis?
5. ¿Qué lee Lupe?
6. ¿Qué dice Inés?
7. ¿Qué van a hacer Uds. mañana?
8. ¿Qué van a comprar Uds.?

ACTIVIDAD 9   En la oficina del consejero

Haz el papel del paciente y del consejero según el modelo.

▷   preocupar   el (la) paciente: Hay algo que me preocupa.
el (la) consejero(a): Dígame lo que le preocupa.

Be sure students understand the meanings of these verbs.

1. atormentar
2. molestar
3. alegrar
4. inquietar
5. impresionar
6. enojar
7. aburrir
8. irritar

ACTIVIDAD 10 Expresión personal

¿Hacemos siempre lo que queremos? Claro que no . . . y no nos gusta siempre lo que hacemos. Describe tu experiencia personal en frases afirmativas o negativas usando expresiones como **siempre, a menudo, a veces, nunca.**

WB
C1

SCRIPT

Act. 7

▸ con mis amigos: decir / pensar   Con mis amigos, siempre digo lo que pienso.
(Con mis amigos, a veces no digo lo que pienso.)

1. en clase: decir / pensar
2. en casa: hacer / querer
3. en la cafetería: comer / querer
4. en el examen: contestar / saber
5. en toda ocasión: saber / decir

6. en las tiendas: comprar / necesitar
7. en el periódico: creer / leer
8. en la televisión: creer / ver
9. en la vida: creer / ver
10. en mi cuarto: encontrar / buscar

Para la comunicación

OPTIONAL
May be assigned as
homework.

Expresión personal

Escoge una de las siguientes circunstancias y describe algunos de sus aspectos según el modelo:

• en la escuela
• en casa
• con mis amigos
• en la vida

WB
Tú

SCRIPT

Act. 8

MASTERS
p. 21

TRB

QUIZ
pp. 50–51

▸ esencial   En la escuela lo esencial para mí es aprender algo interesante (sacar buenas notas, divertirme, ser amigo de todos . . .).
En casa, lo esencial es divertirme . . .
En la vida, lo esencial es conocerse . . .

1. importante
2. necesario
3. divertido
4. bueno
5. malo

6. ridículo
7. absurdo
8. aburrido
9. raro
10. magnífico

Lección 2 ¿Ángel o diablo?

STRUCTURES TO OBSERVE: the regular forms of the imperfect and the use of the imperfect to describe repeated events of the past.

Act. 1

No son tan diferentes los niños de los adultos. Tienen las mismas virtudes . . . y los mismos defectos. Hay niños simpáticos y también hay niños antipáticos. Algunos son atentos, otros son mal educados. ¿Recuerdas la época feliz de tu niñez? ¿Cómo eras tú cuando tenías ocho o nueve años? ¿Un ángel o . . . un diablo?

virtudes: *virtues*

atentos: *polite*
mal educados: *ill-mannered*
eras: *were*
tenías: *had / were*

Contesta estas preguntas sinceramente:

	Sí	No
1. ¿Estudiabas mucho en clase?	☐	☐
2. ¿Respetabas a tus maestros?	☐	☐
3. ¿Llegabas a tiempo a las clases?	☐	☐
4. ¿Volvías a casa temprano?	☐	☐
5. ¿Hacías tus tareas todos los días?	☐	☐
6. ¿Escuchabas los consejos de tus padres?	☐	☐
7. ¿Tenías buenos modales?	☐	☐
8. ¿Te acostabas y te levantabas temprano?	☐	☐
9. ¿Te lavabas las manos antes de las comidas?	☐	☐
10. ¿Ayudabas en casa?	☐	☐
11. ¿Les prestabas tus juguetes a tus amigos?	☐	☐
12. ¿Decías siempre la verdad?	☐	☐

Estudiabas: *Did you study*

buenos modales: *good manners*

juguetes: *toys*

O, al contrario . . .

Sí	No	
☐	☐	1. ¿Te gustaba pelear?
☐	☐	2. ¿Te peleabas a menudo con tus amigos?
☐	☐	3. ¿Te peleabas con tus hermanos?
☐	☐	4. ¿Maltratabas a los animales?
☐	☐	5. ¿Insultabas a tus amigos?
☐	☐	6. ¿Rompías los juguetes de tus amigos?
☐	☐	7. ¿Comías muchos dulces?
☐	☐	8. ¿Tenías malos modales?
☐	☐	9. ¿Dormías en clase?
☐	☐	10. ¿Te hacías el payaso en clase?
☐	☐	11. ¿Te enojabas a menudo?
☐	☐	12. ¿Decías mentiras a veces?

Maltratabas: *Did you mistreat*

Te hacías el payaso: *Did you clown around*

You may ask students to give the infinitive form of each verb in the imperfect and to distinguish between the endings of the -ar verbs (-aba) and those of the -er and -ir verbs (-ía).

INTERPRETACIÓN

Las respuestas afirmativas a las preguntas de la izquierda tienen un valor positivo: +1. Las respuestas afirmativas a las preguntas de la derecha tienen un valor negativo: −1. Suma tus puntos. ¿Cuántos tienes?

Eras: *You were*

¿Más de 8?:	Eras un(a) santo(a).
¿De 4 a 8?:	Eras un ángel.
¿De −2 a 4?:	Eras un(a) niño(a) normal.
¿De −3 a −7?:	Eras un diablo.
¿Menos de −7?:	Eras un demonio.

Act. 2

La idea de ser bien educado

¿Qué cualidades consideras más importantes en los jóvenes? ¿Es más importante ser inteligente o ser generoso? ¿Sacar buenas notas o tener buenos modales? ¿Ser independiente o ayudar en casa? Por supuesto, los padres hispanos se sienten orgullosos de tener hijos inteligentes y brillantes . . . pero sobre todo° desean que sus hijos sean° bien educados.

Un joven bien educado respeta a los mayores. Se calla cuando sus padres están hablando, y no los interrumpe con preguntas inútiles. Tiene buenos modales. Obedece a sus profesores y ayuda a sus amigos. No es arrogante sino cortés, no es fatuo° sino servicial.°

¿Eras° tal° joven?

REVIEW: Note that **sino** is used instead of **pero** to contradict a *negative* statement.

sobre todo *above all*   **sean** *be*   **fatuo** *vain*
servicial *helpful*   **Eras** *Were you*   **tal** *such a*

You may stress that **bien educado** means well-mannered or well brought-up, rather than well-educated.

Lección dos
197

Vocabulario

sustantivos	un consejo	(piece of) advice		una época	period, time
	los mayores	adults		la niñez	childhood
	un punto	point			
	un valor	value			
verbo	llegar	to arrive, to get to			
expresiones	a tiempo	on time			
	a la derecha	on the right	≠	a la izquierda	on the left
	temprano	early	≠	tarde	late

Vamos a hablar del sábado pasado. Vamos a ver si hiciste estas actividades.

1. ¿**Jugaste** al fútbol?
   Sí (No, no) **jugué** . . .
2. ¿**Jugaste** al tenis?
3. ¿**Miraste** la televisión?
4. ¿**Nadaste?**
5. ¿**Tomaste** el sol?

Ahora vamos a hablar del verano pasado. Vamos a ver si te ocupabas de estas actividades a menudo durante las vacaciones.

6. ¿**Jugabas** al fútbol a menudo?
   Sí (No, no) **jugaba** . . .
7. ¿**Jugabas** al tenis a menudo?
8. ¿**Mirabas** la televisión a menudo?
9. ¿**Nadabas** a menudo?
10. ¿**Tomabas** el sol a menudo?

OBSERVACIÓN

All of the above questions concern activities which took place in the past.
The verbs are all in the past.
The first five questions concern activities which you did once *on a particular day:*
last Saturday.
- What tense is used?   the preterite
The last five questions do not concern activities that you did once, but rather
activities which you did *regularly* (or *used to do*) during vacation.
- Is the *preterite* used in these questions? The tense used is another past tense, the *imperfect.*
      no

Estructuras

A. El imperfecto de los verbos que terminan en *-ar*

Spanish speakers use two simple past tenses to describe past actions and events: the *preterite,* which you already know, and the *imperfect.* The choice between these two tenses depends on what type of past actions are described.

First you will learn how to form the imperfect. Then you will learn the difference in uses between the imperfect and the preterite.

Note the imperfect forms of **hablar,** paying special attention to the endings.

INFINITIVE	**hablar**	IMPERFECT ENDINGS
IMPERFECT		
(yo)	**Hablaba** español.	**-aba**
(tú)	**Hablabas** inglés.	**-abas**
(él, ella, Ud.)	**Hablaba** portugués.	**-aba**
(nosotros)	**Hablábamos** italiano.	**-ábamos**
(vosotros)	**Hablabais** francés.	**-abais**
(ellos, ellas, Uds.)	**Hablaban** japonés.	**-aban**

Have the students note the accent mark on the **nosotros** form of **hablábamos.** Point out that the **yo** and **él** forms of the imperfect are the same.

> To form the imperfect of **-ar** verbs, the **-ar** ending of the infinitive is replaced by the endings shown above.

> All **-ar** verbs are regular in the imperfect, even those which are irregular in the present.

estar	¿Dónde **estaba** Carlos?	*Where **was** Carlos?*
dar	El Sr. López nunca **daba** buenas notas.	*Sr. López never **gave** good grades.*

ACTIVIDAD 1   La clase de la Srta. Chávez

La Srta. Chávez tenía *(had)* unos alumnos buenos y unos malos. Di quiénes estudiaban y quiénes no.

> Miguel: no   Miguel no estudiaba.

1. Sarita: sí
2. yo: no
3. tú: sí
4. mis primos: no
5. la prima de Danilo: no
6. Uds.: sí
7. Carmen y yo: sí
8. Jacinto y Manuel: no

VARIATIONS with: **trabajar, mirar la televisión, escuchar discos.**

VOCABULARIO PRÁCTICO   Los modales *(Manners)*

sustantivos

un ángel	angel	≠	**un diablo**	devil
una virtud	virtue	≠	**un defecto**	defect
los buenos modales	good manners	≠	**los malos modales**	bad manners

adjetivos

bien educado	well-mannered	≠	**mal educado**	bad-mannered
limpio	clean	≠	**sucio**	dirty
cortés	polite	≠	**descortés**	impolite
atento	attentive, polite	≠	**desagradable**	unpleasant

verbos

compartir	to share	Un niño bien educado **comparte** sus **juguetes** *(toys)* con sus amigos.
cuidar	to care for, to take care of	**Cuida** a sus hermanos menores.
limpiar	to clean	**Limpia** su cuarto.
maltratar	to mistreat	No **maltrata** a los animales.
obedecer	to obey	**Obedece** a sus profesores y a sus padres.
pelear(se)	to fight	No **pelea** con sus hermanos.
saludar	to greet, to say hello	**Saluda** a los mayores.

ACTIVIDAD 2   Diálogo: La niñez de tus compañeros

VARIATION in the plural: ¿Jugaban Uds. al fútbol? Sí, jugábamos al fútbol.

Pregúntales a tus compañeros(as) si hacían *(they did)* estas cosas cuando eran *(they were)* niños(as).

 jugar al fútbol
                Estudiante 1: ¿Jugabas al fútbol?
                Estudiante 2: Sí, jugaba al fútbol.
                           (No, no jugaba al fútbol.)

1. mirar la televisión
2. prestar tu bicicleta
3. jugar con los juguetes de tus compañeros
4. prestar tus juguetes
5. pelearte en la escuela
6. pelearte con tus hermanos
7. portarte bien
8. portarte mal
9. levantarte temprano
10. acostarte temprano
11. limpiar tu cuarto
12. maltratar a los animales

WB
A1

SCRIPT

Act. 4

MASTERS
p. 22

B. El imperfecto de los verbos que terminan en -er y en -ir

In the imperfect, **-er** and **-ir** verbs have the same endings:

You may have the students note that there is an accent on the "i" of all endings.

INFINITIVE	entender	vivir	
IMPERFECT			IMPERFECT ENDINGS
(yo)	**Entendía** español.	**Vivía** en San Juan.	-ía
(tú)	**Entendías** inglés.	**Vivías** en Seattle.	-ías
(él, ella, Ud.)	**Entendía** francés.	**Vivía** en Montreal.	-ía
(nosotros)	**Entendíamos** italiano.	**Vivíamos** en Roma.	-íamos
(vosotros)	**Entendíais** alemán.	**Vivíais** en Berlín.	-íais
(ellos, ellas, Uds.)	**Entendían** portugués.	**Vivían** en Saõ Paulo.	-ían

To form the imperfect of almost all **-er** and **-ir** verbs, the infinitive endings (**-er, -ir**) are replaced by the endings shown above.

tener	¿**Tenías** mucho dinero?	*Did you **use to have** a lot of money?*
decir	¿**Decías** siempre la verdad?	*Did you always **use to tell** the truth?*
hacer	¿**Hacías** tus tareas todas las noches?	*Did you **use to do** your homework every night?*

The imperfect form of **hay** is **había**.

Hay dos cines en mi barrio.
Antes **había** solamente uno.

ACTIVIDAD 3   El Papá Noel

Algunos chicos son más crédulos *(gullible)* que otros. Di cuáles de tus amigos creían en Papá Noel y cuáles no.

VARIATION: They used to write him.
Carmen le escribía.

Carmen: sí   Carmen creía en él.

1. mis primos: no
2. mi hermano mayor: sí
3. yo: no
4. tú: sí
5. nosotros: no
6. Carlos: sí
7. Felipe y Roberto: sí
8. mis otros amigos y yo: no

ACTIVIDAD 4   Aspiraciones profesionales

A menudo cambiamos de idea *(change our mind)*. Di lo que estos amigos quieren ser ahora y lo que querían ser antes.

You may point out that verbs (like **querer**) that have a stem change in the present do not have this stem change in the imperfect.

Carmen: dentista / aeromoza   Ahora Carmen quiere ser dentista.
Antes quería ser aeromoza.

1. nosotros: periodistas / astronautas
2. tú: taxista / piloto de avión
3. Luisa: profesora / doctora
4. Juan: mecánico / actor
5. mis amigos: ingenieros / abogados
6. yo: vendedor(a) viajero(a) / gerente de un banco

ADDITIONAL CUES: **Ud.: presidente/abogado; Uds.: electricistas/plomeros**

Lección dos
201

ACTIVIDAD 5   Elena y su hermano Rafael

Elena le cuenta a su hermano mayor lo que hace en la escuela. Él admite
que era mal estudiante. Dice que hacía lo contrario de lo que hace Elena.
Haz los dos papeles según el modelo.

⟩⟩   tener buenas notas   Elena: Tengo buenas notas.

Make sure that students playing the
role of Elena use the correct **yo** forms
in the present.

Rafael: Yo no tenía buenas notas.

1. leer mucho
2. obedecer al profesor
3. aprender inglés
4. saber las lecciones
5. hacer las tareas
6. no perder el tiempo
7. no leer historietas *(comics)*
8. no dormirme en clase

The purpose of this exercise is to review vocabulary as well
as to practice the forms of the imperfect. Make sure that the
students understand the meanings of the verbs they are using.

ACTIVIDAD 6   Viejas costumbres *(Old habits)*

Describe las viejas costumbres de las siguientes personas, usando los
verbos en frases afirmativas o negativas. Por supuesto, ¡estas costumbres
tienen que corresponder al carácter de cada uno!

⟩⟩   Tú eras *(were)* holgazán: estudiar, hacer la tarea, hacerse el payaso
No estudiabas. No hacías la tarea. Te hacías el payaso.

1. María era generosa: prestar su bicicleta, compartir sus juguetes, ayudar
   a los otros, cuidar a los niños de su vecina

2. Luis era cortés: saludar a los vecinos, respetar a los mayores, obedecer a
   los profesores

3. Mi hermana tenía malos modales: obedecer a sus padres, decir mentiras,
   volver a casa tarde

4. Mis primos eran mal educados: tener buenos modales, dormir en clase,
   pelearse con todo el mundo

5. Felipe era sucio: lavarse, bañarse, cortarse el pelo

6. Carmen y Elena eran pulcras *(neat)*: lavarse el pelo, limpiar su cuarto,
   bañarse

7. Yo era un ángel: decir la verdad, maltratar a los animales, reírse de los
   profesores, criticar a mis amigos

8. Tú y yo éramos hijos modelos: obedecer a nuestros padres, enojarse,
   impacientarse, insultar a nuestros vecinos, compartir todo lo que teníamos

C. El uso del imperfecto para describir sucesos repetidos

Spanish speakers distinguish between habitual or repeated events in the past and past events which are unique in some way. Compare the use of the tenses in the following sentences.

(repeated actions)

Carlos siempre **pasaba** las vacaciones en México . . .

Los sábados, (yo) **jugaba** al tenis con Anita . . .

Generalmente **me levantaba** temprano . . .

(single actions)

pero un año las **pasó** en Puerto Rico.

pero un sábado, **jugué** con Sarita.

pero un día **me levanté** a las diez.

The **imperfect** is used to describe *habitual or repeated events* in the past.
The **preterite** is used to describe a *particular or specific event*.

In English, habitual events are often expressed by the construction *used to* + verb. Such events are expressed in Spanish by the imperfect.

Carlos **pasaba** el verano en México.   *Carlos **used to spend** the summer in Mexico.*
Jugábamos al tenis.   *We **used to play** tennis.*

The *imperfect* is often used with expressions such as **siempre, los sábados, todos los días,** and **a menudo** since these expressions imply repetition.

The *preterite* is often used with expressions such as **una vez, el sábado pasado, un día, esta mañana,** and **anoche** since these expressions do not imply repetition.

ACTIVIDAD 7   ¡Qué vacaciones tan divertidas!

Inés recuerda las cosas que hacía durante las vacaciones y las que no puede hacer ahora. Haz el papel de Inés según el modelo.

Ahora no juego al fútbol.   Durante las vacaciones jugaba al fútbol todos los días.

1. Ahora no nado.
2. Ahora no organizo fiestas.
3. Ahora no invito a mis amigos al cine.
4. Ahora no escucho mis discos.
5. Ahora no miro la televisión.
6. Ahora no salgo.
7. Ahora no juego al tenis.
8. Ahora no me levanto tarde.
9. Ahora no me acuesto tarde.
10. Ahora no me divierto.

Make sure that the students do not make stem changes in the imperfect.

ACTIVIDAD 8   Una vida bien ordenada (*A well-ordered life*)

Cuando era niña, Leonor tenía una existencia bien ordenada. Di qué hacía a las siguientes horas.

⟩⟩   7:00 levantarse   A las siete, Leonor se levantaba.

1. 7:05 bañarse
2. 7:15 vestirse
3. 7:30 hacer la cama
4. 7:45 desayunarse
5. 8:00 salir
6. 8:05 esperar el autobús
7. 8:30 llegar a la escuela
8. 12:00 comer en la cafetería
9. 1:00 jugar
10. 4:30 regresar a casa
11. 5:00 hacer la tarea
12. 10:00 acostarse

ACTIVIDAD 9   ¡Sólo pasó una vez!

Carlos le pregunta a Julia si ella siempre hacía lo mismo durante las vacaciones. Julia le contesta que sólo una vez hizo otras cosas. Haz los dos papeles según el modelo.

⟩⟩   jugar al tenis / al volibol

        Carlos: ¿Jugabas al tenis a menudo?

          Julia: Sí, jugaba al tenis siempre, pero una vez jugué al volibol.

1. levantarte tarde / temprano
2. desayunarte a las ocho / a las diez
3. comer en casa / en un restaurante
4. divertirte con tus amigos / con tus primos
5. comprar el periódico / una revista inglesa
6. salir con Inés / con Raquel
7. montar en bicicleta / en moto
8. acostarte tarde / temprano

ACTIVIDAD 10   Las promesas del primero de enero

Las siguientes personas decidieron cambiar sus malos modales. El primero de enero no actuaron como de costumbre (*habitually*). Expresa esto según el modelo.

⟩⟩   Felipe: comer muchos dulces   Normalmente, Felipe comía muchos dulces.
                                                    El primero de enero, no comió muchos dulces.

WB
C1, C2, C3

SCRIPT
Act. 6

MASTERS
p. 22

1. Carmen: pelearse con sus hermanos
2. Raúl: contar cosas aburridas
3. Luisa y Tomás: pelearse
4. Roberto: decir palabrotas (*dirty words*)
5. yo: maltratar mis libros
6. tú: decir mentiras
7. tú y yo: fumar (*smoke*) en el cuarto de baño
8. los profesores: enojarse con los estudiantes

Para la comunicación

OPTIONAL
May be assigned as homework.

Tu niñez

Describe la época de tu niñez. Si quieres, puedes usar las siguientes ideas.

la residencia
vivir (¿dónde?)

la escuela
estudiar (mucho, poco, ¿qué?)
tener (maestros interesantes,
    compañeros simpáticos)

los amigos
tener (muchos amigos, amigos
    bien educados)
llamarse (¿cómo?)
salir (¿adónde?)
compartir (¿qué?)
prestar (¿qué?)

los hermanos
pelear (¿con quién?)
compartir

los padres
respetar
obedecer (¿cuándo?)

los animales
tener (¿qué?)
llamarse (¿cómo?)
tratar (bien)
cuidar (¿cómo?)

las diversiones
gustar (¿qué?)
jugar (¿a qué? ¿con quién? ¿dónde?)
leer (¿qué?)
escuchar (¿qué?)

los buenos y malos modales
bañarse
lavarse
limpiar
comer
enojarse
ponerse furioso(a)

VARIATION: Have students select a magazine picture and describe the childhood of the person depicted.

Lección 3   ¡Ay, qué día!

Act. 1

31

Ayer me levanté muy contenta. Era martes, y hacía muy buen tiempo.

Pero esto es lo que ocurrió:

Era: *It was*
hacía: *it was*

Me bañé . . .
    pero mientras me bañaba, de repente el agua se puso muy fría. ¡Ay!

Preparé el desayuno . . .
    pero mientras lo preparaba, quemé las tostadas.

mientras: *while*
me bañaba: *I was bathing*
de repente: *suddenly*
tostadas: *pieces of toast*

Me desayuné . . .
    pero mientras me desayunaba, mi gato saltó a la mesa y rompió unos platos.

saltó: *jumped*

Limpié la jaula de Paco, mi papagayo, . . .
    pero mientras la limpiaba, Paco se escapó.

jaula: *cage*

Esperé el autobús . . .
    pero mientras lo esperaba, un taxi me salpicó.

salpicó: *splattered*

Fui a la oficina . . .
    pero mientras iba allá, perdí mi billetera.

iba: *I was going*

Unidad cinco
206

¿Qué día de la semana fue ayer? ¿Qué tiempo hacía? ¿Cómo se sentía la chica al levantarse? ¿Qué hizo con las tostadas? ¿Qué hizo el gato? ¿Qué hizo el papagayo? ¿Qué esperó la chica? ¿Qué perdió? ¿Cómo se llamaba la chica?

Finalmente, a la una me encontré con mi novio, y cuando le conté los eventos del día, él me dijo:

—¡Por supuesto, Gloria! . . . ¿No sabes que hoy es martes trece?

¡Ay, qué día!

NOTA CULTURAL   OPTIONAL

Las supersticiones

¿Piensan los hispanohablantes que el viernes trece es un día de mala suerte? ¡No! Para ellos, el día de mala suerte es el martes trece. Hay otras supersticiones también. Vamos a ver algunas de éstas. ¡Presta° atención!

¡Pobrecito!°

¡Qué mala suerte vas a tener si . . .

es domingo siete!

es martes trece!

atropellas° un gato!

derramas° sal!

rompes un espejo!

¡Estupendo!

¡Qué buena suerte vas a tener si . . .

encuentras un trébol° de cuatro hojas!°

bebes la última copa° de la botella° de vino!

llevas en el dedo un anillo de acero!°

tienes una pata de conejo!°

recibes el ramo de la novia!°

alguien te regala una estatua de un elefante blanco!

Presta Pay   **Pobrecito** Poor thing   **atropellas** you run over
derramas you spill   **trébol** clover   **hojas** leaves   **copa** glass
botella bottle   **acero** steel   **pata de conejo** rabbit's paw
ramo de la novia bride's bouquet

You may ask the students to compare Hispanic and American superstitions.   **¿Cuáles supersticiones son diferentes? ¿Cuáles son las mismas?**

Vocabulario

sustantivos	**un plato**	plate, dish	**el agua**	water
			una oficina	office
verbos	**escaparse**	to escape		
	ocurrir	to occur, to happen		
	quemar	to burn, to scorch		
	saltar	to jump		
	volverse	to become, to turn		
expresiones	**de repente**	suddenly		
	mientras	while		

NOTA: **El** (and **un**) are used in front of a few feminine nouns which begin with a stressed **a** (or **ha**):

> **El** agua está fría.

In the plural, however, the articles **las** and **unas** are used: **las** aguas.

CONVERSACIÓN   OPTIONAL

¿Recuerdas lo que hiciste ayer? Di si hiciste lo siguiente.

1. **¿Escuchaste** discos?
   Sí, **escuché** . . . (No, no **escuché** . . .)
2. **¿Miraste** la televisión?
3. **¿Hablaste** por teléfono con tu mejor amigo?
4. **¿Estudiaste?**
5. **¿Jugaste** con tus amigos?

Ahora, recuerda si hacías las siguientes actividades cuando tu mamá te llamó para la cena.

6. **¿Escuchabas** discos?
7. **¿Mirabas** la televisión?
8. **¿Hablabas** por teléfono con tu mejor amigo?
9. **¿Estudiabas**?
10. **¿Jugabas** con tus amigos?

OBSERVACIÓN

In questions 1–5, you are asked if *you did* certain things yesterday.
• Which tense is used, the *imperfect* or the *preterite?*   the preterite
In questions 6–10, you are asked whether *you were doing* those things *when* your mother called you to dinner.
• Which tense is used, the *imperfect* or the *preterite?*   the imperfect

Estructuras

A. El imperfecto de *ir, ser* y *ver*

In the imperfect, there are only three irregular verbs: **ir, ser,** and **ver.**

INFINITIVE	ir	ser	ver
IMPERFECT			
(yo)	iba	era	veía
(tú)	ibas	eras	veías
(él, ella, Ud.)	iba	era	veía
(nosotros)	íbamos	éramos	veíamos
(vosotros)	ibais	erais	veíais
(ellos, ellas, Uds.)	iban	eran	veían

ACTIVIDAD 1 Preguntas personales

1. ¿Veías muchas películas cuando eras niño(a)? ¿Veías películas del oeste? ¿Veías películas de aventuras?

2. ¿Iban tus padres al cine contigo? ¿Iban Uds. a menudo?

3. ¿Ibas a la escuela cuando tenías cinco años?

4. ¿Eras un(a) niño(a) bien educado(a)? ¿Eras mal educado(a)? ¿Eras bueno(a) con los animales? ¿Eran estrictos tus padres?

5. ¿Veías a menudo a tus abuelos? ¿Ibas a visitarlos con tus padres?

6. ¿Iban Uds. al circo? ¿Al zoológico? ¿Había muchos animales en el zoológico? ¿Te gustaba darles comida?

ACTIVIDAD 2 ¡Cómo cambia la vida!

Unos estudiantes universitarios recuerdan la época de cuando eran alumnos en el colegio. Se dan cuenta de que han cambiado *(they have changed)* mucho desde entonces. Expresa esto según los modelos.

Paco no es tímido con las chicas.   En el colegio, era muy tímido con las chicas.
Teresa está enamorada de Jaime.   En el colegio, no estaba enamorada de Jaime.

1. Elena no es tímida con los chicos.
2. Felipe no es muy generoso con sus amigos.
3. No somos holgazanes.
4. Luisa y tú no están nerviosos durante los exámenes.
5. Carmen no se aburre con sus estudios.
6. Miguel y Felipe no son muy atentos.
7. Voy a menudo a la biblioteca.
8. Soy un estudiante bueno.
9. Tú eres muy paciente con tus profesores.
10. Carlos va al teatro.
11. Susana y Ana María van a la discoteca.

Act. 3
WB
A1
SCRIPT
Act. 4
MASTERS
p. 24

B. El uso del imperfecto para describir acciones continuas

Compare the verbs in the sentences below.

(specific action)	(ongoing action)
Cuando Carlos **llamó** . . .	yo **estudiaba**.
*When Carlos **called** . . .*	*I **was studying**.*
Carmen **llegó** . . .	mientras **nos desayunábamos**.
*Carmen **arrived** . . .*	*when we **were having breakfast**.*
Anita **sacó** una foto . . .	de unos niños que **jugaban** al fútbol.
*Anita **took** a picture . . .*	*of some children who **were playing** soccer.*

The **preterite** is used to describe a *well-defined action or event* which happened at a *specific point in time*.

The **imperfect** is used to describe *ongoing actions or events*. In English such actions are usually expressed by the construction *was (were) + . . .ing*.

Note that the time relationship between the preterite and the imperfect can be shown on a diagram:

specific action
(preterite)   Cuando Carlos **llamó** . . .   Carmen **llegó** . . .   Anita **sacó** una foto . . .

ongoing action
(imperfect)   yo **estudiaba**.   mientras **nos desayunábamos**.   de unos niños que **jugaban** al fútbol.

ACTIVIDAD 3   El robo *(The Burglary)*

Anoche a las diez, ocurrió un robo en el apartamento del Sr. Montero. Un detective les pregunta a los vecinos qué hacían a las diez de la noche. Haz los papeles del detective y de los vecinos.

> Carmen: estudiar   El detective: ¿Qué hacía Ud. anoche a las diez?
> Carmen: ¿Yo? ¡Estudiaba!

1. la Sra. de Chávez: mirar la televisión
2. Miguel: escuchar sus discos
3. la Sra. de Ortiz: hablar por teléfono con una amiga
4. el Sr. García: dar un paseo por la calle
5. Rosario: escribir una carta
6. el Sr. Ruiz: leer el periódico
7. Enrique: comer
8. el Sr. Ávila: visitar a unos amigos
9. la Sra. de Meléndez: dormir
10. el Sr. Herrera: trabajar

ACTIVIDAD 4   Las excusas

Ahora, el detective les pregunta a unos sospechosos *(suspects)* si tomaron parte en el robo. Todos los sospechosos tienen una excusa. Haz los papeles de los sospechosos y del detective.

> estar en el café / volver a casa a las 12:00
> El detective: ¿No tomó Ud. parte en el robo?
> El sospechoso: ¡Claro que no! A la hora del robo estaba en el café. Volví a casa a las 12:00.

1. estar en el cine / volver del cine a las 11:00
2. estar en el estadio / regresar a casa muy tarde
3. cenar con unos amigos / llegar al restaurante a las 8:00
4. visitar a unos amigos / pasar la noche en su casa
5. bailar con mi novia / volver a casa a la 1:00
6. ver una película / salir del cine a las 11:00
7. estar trabajando / salir de la oficina a las 10:00
8. divertirme en una fiesta / después irme a un club

ACTIVIDAD 5   Cuando el director entró . . .

Los alumnos del Sr. Leblanc (el profesor de francés) no son muy atentos.
Di qué hacía cada uno ayer cuando el director entró en la sala de clase.

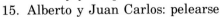 Pedro: pensar en las vacaciones   Pedro pensaba en las vacaciones.

1. Isabel: escribir una carta
2. Paco: comer chocolates
3. Elena: dormir
4. Luisa: leer una novela
5. Carlos: ofrecerles dulces a sus amigos
6. Manuel: peinarse
7. Anita: hacer la tarea de matemáticas
8. Luis y Pablo: leer historietas *(comics)*
9. Marisol: mirarse en el espejo
10. Anita y Gloria: divertirse
11. Pepe y Rolando: mirar a las chicas
12. Benjamín y Mercedes: contar chistes
13. Gloria y Danilo: hablar de modas
14. César y yo: esperar la hora de salir
15. Alberto y Juan Carlos: pelearse
16. Inés: maltratar a Roberto

ACTIVIDAD 6   De visita en la ciudad

En las calles de la ciudad, Dolores observa las siguientes cosas. Más tarde
le cuenta a un amigo lo que vio. Haz el papel de Dolores y dile a tu amigo
lo que viste.

⤳ unos chicos juegan al fútbol   Vi a unos chicos que jugaban al fútbol.

1. unos niños comen dulces
2. dos chicos se pelean
3. una chica espera a su novio
4. unas muchachas cantan
5. un muchacho toca la guitarra
6. unos turistas sacan fotos
7. un hombre vende periódicos
8. unos jóvenes conducen muy rápido
9. una señora llama a su esposo
10. una niña tiene un perro

WB
B1, B2, B3

SCRIPT

Act. 5, 6

MASTERS
p. 24

WB
Al vol-
ver...

SCRIPT

Act. 7

MASTERS
p. 24

TRB

QUIZ
p. 54

Para la comunicación

Unos percances *(Mishaps)*

Describe unos ocho o diez percances (¡reales o inventados!) similares a los que le ocurrieron a Gloria en «¡Ay, qué día!». Puedes encontrar inspiración en los percances de Gloria. Si quieres, puedes usar los siguientes verbos y tu imaginación.

volverse / quemar / escaparse / romper / romperse / chocar / huir / caer / caerse / ponerse / salir / encontrar / perder

Mientras yo estaba en mi cuarto haciendo la tarea, ¡mi perro se escapó a la calle!

Lección 4   Un accidente en Cartagena

Act. 1

32

¿Tienes buen sentido de observación?
¡Vamos a ver!
Imagina que ayer dabas un paseo cerca de la Plaza Bolívar en Cartagena cuando ocurrió un accidente. Como fuiste el único testigo, debes contar los detalles del accidente a la policía.
¿Puedes contestar las preguntas según los dibujos?

único: *only*
testigo: *witness*

dibujos: *drawings*

STRUCTURES TO OBSERVE: the use of the imperfect to describe the circumstances of a main event in the past. As the students answer the questions, have them differentiate between the circumstances (imperfect) and the principal events (preterite) of the accident.

5. ¿Quién conducía el coche?
- ☐ A. Un hombre viejo lo conducía.
- ☐ B. Un muchacho lo conducía.
- ☐ C. Una muchacha lo conducía.

6. ¿Qué llevaba el muchacho?
- ☐ A. Llevaba anteojos de sol.
- ☐ B. Llevaba un sombrero.
- ☐ C. Llevaba una corbata.

7. ¿Qué cruzó la calle enfrente del coche?
- ☐ A. Un gato cruzó la calle.
- ☐ B. Un perro cruzó la calle.
- ☐ C. Un burro cruzó la calle.

cruzó: *crossed*

8. ¿Con qué chocó el coche?
- ☐ A. Chocó con un árbol.
- ☐ B. Chocó con un farol.
- ☐ C. Chocó con una escalera.

farol: *streetlight*

9. ¿Qué hizo el muchacho inmediatamente después del accidente?
- ☐ A. Bajó del coche.
- ☐ B. Se quedó en el coche.
- ☐ C. Corrió tras el gato.

tras: *after*

10. ¿Qué hizo la muchacha?
- ☐ A. Bajó del coche.
- ☐ B. Se quedó en el coche.
- ☐ C. Corrió tras el gato.

11. Entonces, ¿qué hizo el muchacho?
- ☐ A. Llamó a la policía.
- ☐ B. Dio un beso a la chica.
- ☐ C. Se fue de prisa.

beso: *kiss*

12. ¿Qué hizo el gato?
- ☐ A. Trepó a un árbol.
- ☐ B. Subió al coche.
- ☐ C. Se fue de prisa.

Trepó: *It climbed*

alemán: *German*

1. ¿Qué hora era?
- ☐ A. Eran las seis.
- ☐ B. Eran las nueve.
- ☐ C. Eran las siete.

2. ¿Qué tiempo hacía?
- ☐ A. Hacía buen tiempo.
- ☐ B. Hacía mucho sol.
- ☐ C. Llovía.

3. ¿Cuántas personas estaban en el coche?
- ☐ A. dos
- ☐ B. tres
- ☐ C. cuatro

4. ¿Qué tipo de coche era?
- ☐ A. Era un coche norteamericano.
- ☐ B. Era un coche inglés.
- ☐ C. Era un coche alemán.

NOTAS CULTURALES

Cartagena

Cartagena de Indias en Colombia es una de las ciudades más fascinantes del hemisferio occidental.°

Cartagena es una ciudad fortificada fundada° en una isla° en 1533 (mil quinientos treinta y tres). Desde° allí los españoles mandaban las riquezas° del Nuevo Mundo a Europa. Las estrechas calles de la parte antigua de la ciudad dificultan° el tránsito.° Hoy día la nueva Cartagena es una de las ciudades más grandes de Colombia y un centro industrial muy activo.

occidental *western* **fundada** *founded* **isla** *island*
Desde *From* **riquezas** *riches* **dificultan** *make difficult*
tránsito *traffic*

« El Libertador »

Simón Bolívar (1783–1830) fue uno de los líderes del movimiento independentista de la América Latina. Su propósito° era conseguir° la independencia de las colonias de la madre patria,° España.

Bolívar proclamó la independencia y la creación de La Gran Colombia. Fue elegido° su primer presidente.

Hoy día, Simón Bolívar es uno de los héroes más grandes de toda América Latina.

propósito *aim* **conseguir** *to obtain* **patria** *country*
elegido *elected*

- ¿En qué país está Cartagena? ¿Es una ciudad grande o pequeña hoy?
- ¿Quién fue Simón Bolívar? ¿Qué proclamó él? ¿De qué país fue el primer presidente?

Bolívar is a much honored hero. Bolivia is named after him. His own country, Venezuela, calls its currency the **bolívar**. Statues to Bolívar have been erected in most countries of Central and South America.

Vocabulario

sustantivos	**un árbol**	tree	**una escalera**	ladder, stairs
	un beso	kiss		
	un testigo	witness		
verbos	**cruzar**	to cross (a street)		
	llover	to rain		
	trepar	to climb (a tree)		
expresión	**tras**	after, behind		

Act. 2

CONVERSACIÓN

¿Recuerdas los sucesos *(events)* importantes de tu vida? Por ejemplo, ¿puedes recordar el primer día que fuiste a la escuela? Vamos a ver si recuerdas las circunstancias y los hechos *(facts)* memorables de aquel día glorioso.

1. ¿Cuántos años **tenías** entonces?
2. ¿**Estabas** un poco nervioso(a)?
3. ¿**Estabas** un poco tímido(a)?
4. ¿Qué estación del año **era**?
5. ¿**Hacía** buen tiempo aquel día?
6. ¿**Tomaste** el autobús o **fuiste** a pie a la escuela?
7. ¿**Conociste** *(Did you meet)* a nuevos amigos?
8. ¿**Hablaste** con el (la) director(a)?
9. ¿**Te perdiste** en los corredores?
10. ¿**Tomaste** la decisión de ser un(a) estudiante brillante?

OBSERVACIÓN

In the first five questions, you are asked about the *circumstances* of an important event: your first day at school. The circumstances concern *your age, your feelings, the kind of weather.*
- Are the verbs used in the *preterite* or the *imperfect?*   the imperfect

In the last five questions you are asked about *certain specific events*.
- Are the verbs used in the *preterite* or the *imperfect?*   the preterite

Estructuras

A. El imperfecto y el pretérito: circunstancias y acciones

Compare the verbs in these sentences:

(actions)	*(circumstances)*	
	Era el diez de abril.	*time*
	Eran las ocho de la noche.	
Vi un accidente.	**Hacía** mal tiempo.	*weather*
	Llovía.	
	Yo **iba** por la Avenida Libertad.	*location*
	El conductor **tenía** entre veinte y veinte y cinco años.	*age*
Vi al conductor muy bien.	**Era** un hombre alto.	*physical appearance*
	Llevaba un suéter gris.	
	Estaba nervioso.	*emotional state*
El año pasado mi hermano **visitó** México.	**Quería** aprender español.	*attitudes*
	Tenía ganas de conocer México.	

The **preterite** is used to describe *specific actions and events*.
The **imperfect** is used to describe the *circumstances and conditions*
surrounding the action. These circumstances and conditions may refer to:

  time, weather
  location
  age, physical appearance
  mental or emotional state, attitudes, beliefs

⟳ Note the use of the past tense forms of **hay**:

  Hubo un accidente.   ***There was*** *an accident:* a specific event.   (preterite)
  Había tres personas.   ***There were*** *three persons:* circumstances.   (imperfect)

ACTIVIDAD 1   La primera vez

Hay una primera vez para todo. Di cuántos años tenías cuando hiciste
estas cosas por primera vez.

⟳ Fui a la escuela.   La primera vez que fui a la escuela tenía cinco años.

1. Fui al cine.
2. Fui al teatro.
3. Fui a una fiesta.
4. Asistí a un concierto.
5. Asistí a un partido de fútbol
   norteamericano.
6. Bailé.

7. Nadé.
8. Organicé una fiesta.
9. Hice un viaje.
10. Tomé un tren.
11. Tomé un avión.
12. Conduje un coche.

NOTE: The preterite, **fui,** is used
to describe a main event; the imperfect, **tenía,** is used to describe a
condition (age).

ACTIVIDAD 2   Excusas

Ayer estos alumnos no vinieron a la clase de español. Di la excusa de cada
uno.   NOTE: The preterite, **no vino,** is used to describe a main event; the imperfect, **estaba,** is used to describe a circumstance
                                                                                                (physical condition).

⟳ Carlos: está cansado   Carlos no vino porque estaba cansado.

1. Felipe: está enfermo
2. Inés: su mamá está enferma
3. Luisa: no tiene ganas de estudiar

4. Rafael: tiene gripe *(flu)*
5. Carmen: es su cumpleaños
6. Isabel: cree que es domingo

ACTIVIDAD 3   Tus excusas

Ahora explica por qué no hiciste las siguientes cosas. Inventa una excusa,
usando tu imaginación.

⟳ No fui a la escuela . . .   No fui a la escuela porque estaba enfermo(a).

1. No aprendí los verbos.
2. No hice la tarea.
3. No escribí a mis abuelos.
4. No dije la verdad.

5. No me levanté temprano.
6. No ayudé a mis padres.
7. No presté mis discos.
8. No fui a la fiesta.

VARIATION: Ask about
student responses. **¿Por
qué no fue a la escuela
Susan?**

ACTIVIDAD 4   La pelea *(The fight)*

Imagina que el año pasado pasaste el verano en un país hispánico. Un día estabas en un café y viste una pelea entre dos clientes. Ahora cuéntale los detalles de esa pelea a un amigo. ¡Cuidado! Debes usar ciertos verbos en el pretérito y otros en el imperfecto.

You may have the students explain their choice of the imperfect or preterite by indicating whether the sentence concerns a circumstance or a completed action.

▷   Hace calor.   Hacía calor.

1. Es el diez de agosto.
2. Son las cuatro de la tarde.
3. Tengo mucho calor.
4. Estoy en un café con un amigo.
5. Hablamos del próximo partido de fútbol.
6. Un hombre entra en el café.
7. Es un hombre bastante joven.
8. Lleva pantalones grises y una camisa blanca.
9. Lleva anteojos de sol.
10. Habla con otro cliente.
11. Este cliente lo insulta.
12. Los dos hombres se pelean.
13. Hacen mucho ruido.
14. El camarero llama a la policía.
15. La policía llega inmediatamente.
16. Un policía les pide identificación a los dos hombres.
17. Ellos no tienen identificación.
18. La policía se lleva *(take away)* a los dos hombres.

WB
A1, A2, A3

SCRIPT
Act. 3, 5

MASTERS
p. 25

Have each student find a magazine picture to illustrate one of the expressions below. Use the pictures to practice these expressions in the present and imperfect. **¿Tiene sueño este hombre? ¿Y tú, tienes sueño ahora?**

Act. 6

VOCABULARIO PRÁCTICO   Algunos estados físicos y psicológicos

tener calor	to be warm, hot	**tener celos**	to be jealous
tener frío	to be cold	**tener vergüenza**	to be ashamed
tener hambre	to be hungry	**tener miedo (de** *or* **a)**	to be afraid (of)
tener sed	to be thirsty	**tener la culpa**	to be at fault,
tener razón	to be right		to be to blame
no tener razón	to be wrong	**tener prisa**	to be in a hurry
tener cuidado	to be careful	**tener éxito**	to be successful
tener sueño	to be sleepy		

NOTAS: 1. Spanish speakers use **tener** in many expressions indicating a physical or psychological state. English speakers would use *to be*.
2. Note the use of the expression **tener la culpa** in the following examples:
No tengo la culpa.   *It is not my fault.*
¡Teresa tiene la culpa!   *It is Teresa's fault!*

ACTIVIDAD 5   ¡Lógica!

Explica de una manera lógica qué hicieron (o no hicieron) las siguientes personas. Usa una expresión con **tener**.

Several possibilities exist with items 6 and 8.

⟩⟩ Felipe: no entrar en la casa de fantasmas *(haunted house)*
Felipe no entró en la casa de fantasmas porque tenía miedo.

1. Juan Fernando: ir al restaurante
2. Mari-Carmen: beber una Coca-Cola
3. yo: dormirse enfrente del televisor
4. tú: quitarse el suéter
5. nosotros: ponerse el abrigo

6. Ud. y yo: ponerse rojos *(to blush)*
7. Paco: no invitar al nuevo amigo de su novia al café
8. Roberto y Carlos: salir rápidamente

ACTIVIDAD 6   Expresión personal

Completa las siguientes frases usando tu imaginación.

⟩⟩ Tengo éxito con los (las) chicos(as) cuando . . .
Tengo éxito con los chicos cuando les cuento chistes.
⟩⟩ No tengo éxito con ellos (ellas) cuando . . .
No tengo éxito con ellos cuando me enojo con ellos.

1. Tengo cuidado cuando . . .
2. No tengo cuidado cuando . . .
3. Tengo sueño cuando . . .
4. No tengo sueño cuando . . .
5. Tengo celos cuando . . .

6. No tengo celos cuando . . .
7. Tengo prisa cuando . . .
8. No tengo prisa cuando . . .
9. Tengo miedo cuando . . .
10. No tengo miedo cuando . . .

B. Resumen: el uso del pretérito y del imperfecto

Spanish speakers view past actions and events as being either *continuous* or *isolated*.

—They use the **imperfect** to describe *continuous* actions (that is, actions or events that *were in progress during* a certain period of time).
—They use the **preterite** to describe *isolated* actions (that is, actions which *occurred at a specific moment in time*).

Compare the verbs in the following sentences.

(continuous actions or events)	*(isolated actions)*
Cuando yo **era** niño, no **hablaba** español.	Anoche **hablé** español con Ramón.
Julio **tenía** un tocadiscos.	Julio **vendió** su tocadiscos.
Anita **era** mi mejor amiga.	Anita **se fue** a vivir a México.
En el verano **íbamos** a la playa.	Ayer no **fuimos** a la playa.

More specifically, the preterite and the imperfect are used as follows:

TO DESCRIBE:	USE:	
a specific action or event completed in the past	preterite: **Visité** Puerto Rico . . .	*I visited Puerto Rico . . .*
the circumstances of a past action or event	imperfect: Cuando **tenía** diez y seis años . . .	*When I was sixteen (years old) . . .*
an ongoing past action or event	imperfect: Mis primos **vivían** en San Juan entonces.	*My cousins were living in San Juan then.*
a repeated past action or event	imperfect: Ellos me **invitaban** todos los veranos.	*They used to invite me every summer.*

ACTIVIDAD 7   Los vendedores

Di que estas personas ya no *(no longer)* tienen las cosas que tenían porque las vendieron.

You may have the students explain the use of the imperfect: **tenía** = used to have.

🎗️   Roberto: una bicicleta   Roberto tenía una bicicleta pero la vendió.

1. Alfredo: una moto
2. Inés: una cámara
3. Ramón: una calculadora
4. Fernando: una raqueta de tenis
5. Manuela: un reloj
6. Pepe: un tocadiscos
7. Luis: un coche
8. Gustavo: un televisor

ADDITIONAL CUES: **yo:** una grabadora; **tú:** una escalera; **Ud.:** una casa; **nosotros:** un gran espejo; **Uds.:** unas tijeras.

ACTIVIDAD 8   En 1900

Lee cada descripción del mundo moderno y di si es aplicable al mundo de mil novecientos o no.

> La gente tiene coches.   En mil novecientos la gente no tenía coches.

> La gente trabaja mucho.   En mil novecientos la gente también trabajaba mucho.

1. La gente mira la televisión.
2. La gente viaja mucho por avión.
3. Los niños tienen bicicletas.
4. Los niños van a la escuela.
5. Muchos jóvenes van a la universidad.
6. Los jóvenes se divierten.
7. Los jóvenes montan en moto.
8. El tenis es un deporte muy popular.

9. Las casas tienen teléfono.
10. Las casas tienen electricidad.
11. La contaminación (pollution) del aire es un problema.
12. Mucha gente de origen hispano vive en ciudades norteamericanas.
13. La vida no es fácil para todos.

WB
B1, B2

Plaza de las Tres Culturas in Mexico, D.F.

Para la comunicación

OPTIONAL
May be assigned as homework.

Recuerdos *(Memories)*

Cuenta uno de los siguientes sucesos *(events)* usando por lo menos *(at least)* cinco verbos en el imperfecto y cinco verbos en el pretérito.

Éstos son los sucesos:

- tu cumpleaños
- una fiesta
- un picnic
- una reunión familiar *(family reunion)*
- la cena del día de acción de gracias *(Thanksgiving)*
- la Navidad

VARIATION: Find a photo or drawing in this book or a magazine picture that shows an event. Describe it according to the suggested guidelines.

Y éstas son algunas sugerencias:

Las circunstancias

la fecha: ¿el día? ¿la hora?

el tiempo: ¿Hacía calor? ¿Hacía frío? ¿Llovía? ¿Nevaba?

el lugar: ¿tu casa? ¿la casa de tus amigos? ¿otro lugar?

los invitados *(guests)*: ¿Cuántos eran? ¿Quiénes eran? ¿Qué ropa llevaban? ¿Estaban de buen humor?

la comida: ¿Qué había para comer? ¿para beber?

Lo que ocurrió

¿Con quiénes hablaste? ¿De qué hablaste?

¿Qué comiste? ¿Qué bebiste?

¿Hubo una sorpresa? ¿para ti? ¿para otros?

¿Bailaste? ¿Cantaste? ¿A qué jugaste?

¿Pasó algo extraordinario? ¿qué?

WB
Un
evento

SCRIPT
Act. 4, 8

MASTERS
p. 25

TRB

QUIZ
pp. 55–56

WB   Test / Repaso   TEST   pp. 57–61   ACHIEVEMENT TEST   pp. 62–72

Variedades   El robo del museo

33

El domingo pasado, temprano por la mañana, ocurrió un robo° en el Museo de Arte Moderno. Los ladrones° entraron en el museo y se escaparon con algunas obras° de arte muy valiosas.°

robo: *robbery*
ladrones: *robbers*
obras: *works*
   valiosas: *valuable*

Afortunadamente, dos personas observaron el robo. Esto es lo que declararon a la policía. (Atención a los detalles, ¡por favor! ¡Los testigos° no están de acuerdo!°)

testigos: *witnesses*
no están de
acuerdo: *don't agree*

• • • •

La Sra. de Muñoz:

Como todos los domingos, el domingo pasado fui a misa° muy temprano. Iba por la Avenida de la Libertad cuando vi un coche negro que se paró enfrente del Museo de Arte Moderno. Como era de día,° pude observar muy bien lo que pasó.

misa: *Mass*

de día: *daylight*

Como acabo de decir, el coche se paró enfrente del museo. Era un coche grande, de tipo norteamericano, probablemente un Ford o un Chevrolet. En el coche había dos personas: un hombre y una mujer.

La mujer era bastante joven. Creo que tenía menos de veinte y cinco años. Era rubia y llevaba anteojos de sol. (¡Qué raro! ¡A las seis y media de la mañana!) Ella era la conductora del coche y se quedó en el coche todo ese tiempo, esperando a su cómplice.°

chofer

cómplice: *accomplice*

Poco después que se paró el coche, el hombre se bajó. Pude verlo bien. Era bastante alto y moreno, con un bigote° pequeño. Llevaba pantalones de color anaranjado, una chaqueta gris y un sombrero. En la mano tenía un revólver.

bigote: *mustache*

Cruzó la calle y entró en el museo por una ventana que estaba abierta.° Eran exactamente las siete menos veinte y tres. (¡Estoy absolutamente segura de la hora porque miré mi reloj en aquel momento!)

abierta: *open*

Diez minutos después, el hombre salió del museo por la misma° ventana. En los brazos llevaba dos estatuas. Cruzó la calle y se subió al coche donde la mujer lo esperaba. Ella arrancó el coche y los dos se escaparon muy de prisa.

misma: *same*

El Sr. García:

Yo también vi el robo, y ese robo no ocurrió como dice la Sra. de Muñoz. Estoy seguro de lo que digo porque vivo enfrente del museo. Así es que pude observar muy claramente° todo lo que ocurrió.

claramente: *clearly*
ya: *already*

El domingo pasado me levanté a las seis menos cuarto. Como ya° hacía mucho calor, fui a abrir la ventana. La abrí y me quedé mirando la calle. No había nadie, excepto dos o tres personas que iban a misa.

A las seis vi un coche. Como explicó la Sra. de Muñoz, este coche se paró enfrente del museo. ¿Y cómo era? No era negro, sino rojo. No era grande, sino pequeño. No era de tipo norteamericano, sino europeo. Creo que era un Renault o tal vez un Fiat. Es cierto que en el interior había dos personas, un hombre y una mujer, pero era el hombre el que conducía.

A las seis y veinte, los dos ladrones se bajaron del coche, y pude verlos muy bien. La mujer era joven, alta, morena. No llevaba anteojos de sol. El hombre era bajo, moreno y llevaba anteojos. Llevaba pantalones de color anaranjado, pero en vez de° una chaqueta, llevaba un suéter blanco. No llevaba sombrero y no tenía un revólver en la mano. (¡Qué idea más tonta! ¡Es sólo en las películas que los ladrones tienen revólver!)

en vez de: *instead of*

El hombre y la mujer cruzaron la calle. El hombre entró en el museo por la puerta que estaba abierta y no por la ventana. La mujer no entró. Se quedó delante de la puerta. A las seis y media, el hombre salió del museo con dos paquetes muy grandes. La mujer lo ayudó a llevarlos al coche. Después ellos se subieron al coche y desaparecieron° inmediatamente.

desaparecieron: *disappeared*

.   .   .   .   .

¡Es muy difícil ser buen testigo! A menudo, hay una diferencia entre lo que vemos y lo que creemos ver. Por eso, ambos° la Sra. de Muñoz y el Sr. García cometieron ciertos errores en el testimonio.

ambos: *both*

¿Puedes decir cuándo tenían razón y cuándo no?

Mira las ilustraciones y lee la historia otra vez. Después contesta las siguientes preguntas.

Respecto a . . .	¿Quién tenía razón?	
	¿la Sra. de Muñoz?	¿el Sr. García?
1. el tipo de coche	☐	☐
2. el color del coche	☐	☐
3. la hora del crimen	☐	☐
4. el color del pelo de la mujer	☐	☐
5. lo que llevaba la mujer	☐	☐
6. el aspecto físico del hombre	☐	☐
7. lo que llevaba él	☐	☐
8. la manera en que entró en el museo	☐	☐
9. la manera en que salió del museo	☐	☐
10. lo que se llevó	☐	☐

¿Quién fue el mejor testigo? ¿Por qué?

Un poco de historia

¡Qué fácil es imaginar príncipes° que llevan sombreros de plumas° de muchos colores . . . sacerdotes° que leen el futuro en las estrellas° . . . dioses° que demandan sacrificios humanos!

Imaginar esto y mucho más es muy fácil en México y Centroamérica. Aquí la historia comenzó hace miles de años.

Pirámides mayas en Tikal, Guatemala

Tenochtitlán

500 d.C.°

Según los arqueólogos, la gran cultura maya comienza cerca de esta fecha. Más tarde aparecen° las grandes ciudades. En Tikal, Guatemala, los mayas construyen pirámides tan altas como un edificio de veinte pisos.

1325

Con el sacerdote Tenoch, los aztecas llegan a la tierra° prometida,° un lago.° Allí fundan° la ciudad de Tenochtitlán, hoy México. Es una de las ciudades más grandes del mundo.

1519

Hernán Cortés desembarca con 650 hombres y 16 caballos° en el Golfo de México, donde hoy está Veracruz. Comienza entonces la conquista de México por los españoles.

1521

El ejército° de Cortés completa la conquista de México cuando ataca Tenochtitlán y destruye la ciudad casi completamente. Toma a Cuauhtémoc, el último emperador azteca, como prisionero.

Hernán Cortés

príncipes *princes*   **plumas** *feathers*   **sacerdotes** *priests*   **estrellas** *stars*   **dioses** *gods*
d.C. *después de Cristo*   **aparecen** *appear*   **tierra** *land*   **prometida** *promised*   **lago** *lake*
fundan *they found*   **caballos** *horses*   **ejército** *army*

Benito Juárez

1776

Un violento terremoto° destruye la ciudad de Guatemala, sede° del gobierno° colonial en Centroamérica. Así se pierde° una de las ciudades coloniales más importantes del imperio español. Las autoridades deciden fundar la ciudad en otro lugar, donde hoy está la capital.

1810

El sacerdote Miguel Hidalgo y Costilla, padre de la independencia de México, proclama el «Grito° de Dolores», pidiendo el fin del gobierno por los españoles de España («gachupines»).

1821

Una junta política declara la independencia de Centroamérica. Dos años más tarde, se crean° las Provincias Unidas de Centro-américa, una unidad política que, por ambiciones locales, no dura mucho. En menos de veinte años se desintegra en cinco pequeños países.

1846

Una disputa fronteriza da origen a una guerra° entre° México y los Estados Unidos. La guerra termina dos años más tarde y México pierde casi la mitad° de su territorio. La nación victoriosa gana entonces lo que hoy es California, Arizona, Nevada, Utah, Nuevo México, Texas hasta el Río Grande y parte de Colorado.

1862

Los franceses, al mando de° Napoleón III, invaden México y un año después ocupan la capital. En 1864, el archiduque Maximiliano de Austria es coronado emperador de México por orden de Napoleón III. Benito Juárez, al frente de los patriotas, organiza la resistencia y, finalmente, recupera el poder° en 1867. Los mexicanos celebran su victoria sobre los franceses en la batalla de Puebla el cinco de mayo.

La construcción del canal interoceánico en Panamá

1904

Bajo la supervisión del Cuerpo de Ingenieros del Ejército de los Estados Unidos, este país construye un canal interoceánico en Panamá. La construcción del canal toma diez años y los Estados Unidos gastan 375 millones de dólares en ello.

1987

Oscar Arias Sánchez, el presidente de Costa Rica, recibe el Premio Nóbel de la Paz.° Se le concede° este premio por sus esfuerzos° para terminar la guerra entre Nicaragua y sus adversarios y para establecer una paz duradera° en Centroamérica.

terremoto *earthquake* **sede** *seat* **gobierno** *government* **se pierde** *is lost* **Grito** *Cry* **se crean** *are created* **guerra** *war* **entre** *between* **mitad** *half* **al mando de** *under* **el poder** *power* **Premio Nóbel de la Paz** *Nobel Peace Prize* **Se le concede** *He is awarded* **esfuerzos** *efforts* **duradera** *lasting*

229

MÉXICO Y LOS PAÍSES DE CENTROAMÉRICA

México

Población: 81.700.000
Ciudad capital:
México, D.F. (Distrito Federal)
Unidad monetaria: el peso
Productos principales: petróleo,
algodón,° maíz, plata°
Otros datos:°
La ciudad de México es la ciudad más
grande del mundo, después de Tokio y
Shangai.

Guatemala

Población: 8.600.000
Ciudad capital: Guatemala
Unidad monetaria:
el quetzal, en honor del ave° nacional
Animal típico:
el quetzal, un ave pequeña, de cola°
larga y delicada. Es un símbolo de la
libertad.
Producto principal: café
Otros datos:
Además del español, en Guatemala se
hablan más de veinte lenguas°
indígenas.°

algodón *cotton*   **plata** *silver*   **datos** *facts*   **ave** *bird*
cola *tail*   **lenguas** *languages*   **indígenas** *native*

El Salvador

Población: 5.100.000
Ciudad capital: San Salvador
Unidad monetaria:
el colón, en honor de Cristóbal Colón
Productos principales:
café, algodón
Otros datos:
El Salvador es uno de los países
americanos más pequeños. Es más o
menos del mismo tamaño° que el estado
de Massachusetts.

Honduras

Población: 4.600.000
Ciudad capital: Tegucigalpa
Unidad monetaria:
el lempira, en honor de un jefe indígena
que luchó contra° los españoles.
Producto principal: bananas
Otros datos:
El nombre *Honduras (Depths)* viene de
una expresión de Colón. Después de
dominar las malas condiciones de
navegación frente a la costa
centroamericana, Colón dice:—Gracias
a Dios. Salimos de estas honduras.

Nicaragua

Población: 3.300.000
Ciudad capital: Managua
Unidad monetaria:
el córdoba, en honor de Francisco
Fernández de Córdoba, fundador de las
ciudades de León y Granada
Producto principal: algodón
Otros datos:
Nicaragua es el país más grande de
Centroamérica. En 1968, con la ayuda de
los Estados Unidos, construye el camino
Rama que conecta los océanos Atlántico y
Pacífico.

tamaño *size*   **luchó contra** *fought against*

Costa Rica

Población: 2.700.000
Ciudad capital: San José
Unidad monetaria:
   el colón, en honor de Cristóbal Colón
Producto principal: café
Otros datos:
   Los españoles pensaron que ese país
   era rico en minerales.
   Por eso, lo llamaron Costa Rica.

Panamá

Población: 2.200.000
Ciudad capital: Panamá
Unidad monetaria:
   el balboa, en honor de Vasco Núñez de
   Balboa, descubridor° del Océano Pacífico.
   El balboa sólo existe en monedas. Los
   billetes que se usan en Panamá son
   dólares norteamericanos.

Producto principal: bananas
Otros datos:
   Entre 1821 y 1903, Panamá fue parte
   de Colombia. Los panameños se
   independizaron con la ayuda de los
   Estados Unidos, que estaban interesados
   en construir allí un canal interoceánico.
   En 1914 pasó por el canal interoceánico el
   primer barco, el *Ancón*, el cual pesaba
   10.000 toneladas.

descubridor *discoverer*

LOS PRODUCTOS DE LA TIERRA

¿Qué comían los indios antes de la llegada° de los españoles? Bueno, ¡lo mismo que tú! Sí. Tomates, chocolates, maíz, aguacates° . . .

El maíz

¿Dónde se originó el maíz? ¿En Guatemala? ¿En México? ¿En el Perú? Nadie está seguro, pero los indios ya° estaban cultivando maíz en México y Centroamérica hace 4.000 años. El cultivo del maíz hizo posible el desarrollo° de las grandes culturas precolombinas. Comenzó la observación de los fenómenos naturales para saber cuándo plantar. Aparecieron° los primeros dioses° que tenían que dar los recursos° necesarios. Entre° los mayas apareció Chac, el dios de la lluvia.° Entre los aztecas, Tonantzín, la diosa de la tierra.°

El tomate y el aguacate

Estos dos productos, indispensables en una buena ensalada, son de origen mexicano. Los dos nombres se derivan de náhuatl, la lengua de los aztecas. En náhuatl, tomate es tomatl y aguacate es ahuscatl.

El cacao

Éste es el ingrediente principal de algo que los enamorados se dan el 14 de febrero: chocolates. El cacao también es de origen mexicano. Los aztecas usaban granos° de cacao como moneda. Los granos de cacao sirven, también, para hacer chocolate y cacao en polvo.° Mucha gente dice que el chocolate era la bebida favorita del emperador azteca Moctezuma. Pero el chocolate que Moctezuma bebía no tenía azúcar y, seguramente, era muy diferente a la cacao que usas en casa.

---

llegada *arrival*   **aguacates** *avocados*   **ya** *already*   **desarrollo** *development*
Aparecieron *Appeared*   **dioses** *gods*   **recursos** *resources*   **Entre** *Among*   **lluvia** *rain*
tierra *earth*   **granos** *grains*   **en polvo** *powdered*

El mensaje de las piedras

¿Te gusta la arqueología? Un arqueólogo es como un detective. Los dos buscan huellas.° Con las huellas que los arqueólogos encuentran y analizan es posible reconstruir el pasado.

En lugares como México y Guatemala, donde florecieron° grandes civilizaciones precolombinas, el pasado siempre tiene sorpresas. En estos lugares es muy emocionante° ser arqueólogo . . . ¿Quieres ser arqueólogo? ¿Tienes el talento necesario para descifrar° inscripciones antiguas? Vamos a ver:

¿Qué representa esta escultura?° Parece una estrella,° ¿verdad? En realidad, esta escultura se llama la Piedra del Sol. La figura que está en el centro es Tonatiuh o Nahui Ollin, el dios-sol.° Alrededor de él está toda la historia del universo según los aztecas.

En esta piedra, que también se llama la Piedra del Calendario Azteca, todas las figuras significan algo. En el círculo que está más cerca del dios-sol, están los días del mes. Allí están, por ejemplo:

Coatl, la serpiente, el día 5
Mazatl, el venado,° el día 7
Ozomatli, el mono, el día 11
Quiahuitl, el águila,° el día 15

En total, hay 20 símbolos en este círculo, uno por cada día del mes. (Sí, el mes azteca era de sólo veinte días.)

huellas *tracks*   **florecieron** *flourished*   **emocionante** *exciting*   **descifrar** *decipher*
escultura *sculpture*   **estrella** *star*   **dios-sol** *sun god*   **venado** *deer*   **águila** *eagle*

Ahora, mira esta escultura.
¿Ves las rayas y los puntos? . . .
¿Sabes qué representan?

Se encuentran estos símbolos misteriosos en muchas esculturas que tienen más de mil años. Las crearon escultores mayas que vivieron en Guatemala y Honduras durante los primeros siglos° de la era cristiana.

   ¿Y cómo sabemos esto? Por las rayas y los puntos, claro. Estos símbolos representan fechas. Son parte de un sistema numérico inventado por los mayas. Es un sistema que tiene tres símbolos: ▬ , ● y ⬭ . El símbolo ⬭ no tiene valor. Representa el cero.

Mira cómo se escriben los números mayas del uno al diecinueve:

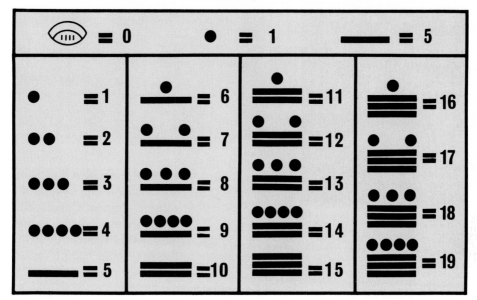

LAS MANOS CREADORAS

Talento, imaginación y manos flexibles. Los artesanos mexicanos necesitan estos tres para crear una gran variedad de objetos de cerámica. La cerámica mexicana no tiene límites. Es un arte popular y folklórico con objetos y estilos diferentes. Mira, por ejemplo:

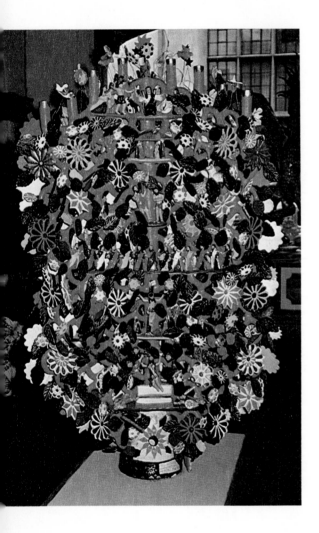

Éste es un candelero, típico de Acatlán, Puebla, cerca de la ciudad de México. Es un árbol con flores,° hojas,° pájaros y ángeles. Está pintado a mano con colores vivos° y fuertes.

Estas figuras son de Coyotepec, Oaxaca. Y como ves, aquí no hay colores alegres. Coyotepec es famoso por su cerámica negra que además de sirenas incluye otras figuras, todas completamente negras.

flores *flowers*   **hojas** *leaves*   **vivos** *lively*

Atzompa es otro pueblo de Oaxaca. Esta figura parece habitante de un cuento de hadas.°

Estos jarrones son de Tonalá, Jalisco, cerca de Guadalajara. ¿Te gustan? Ésta es cerámica pulida,° moderna, de colores suaves.° El estilo de esta cerámica es único. Está pintada a mano y la decoración es típicamente mexicana.

cuento de hadas *fairytale*   **pulida** *polished*   **suaves** *delicate*

LA CREACIÓN DEL HOMBRE

Cuando Dios creó al hombre, ¿lo hizo de barro?° Sí, según la Biblia. No, según los mayas. La literatura de los mayas describe la creación del hombre en un libro antiguo y sagrado:° el *Popol Vuh.* Dice así:

Llegó el momento de la creación. Los dioses creadores,° Ahau Tepeu y Ahau Gucumatz, tenían que buscar la sustancia para hacer la carne° del hombre.

Los dioses creadores comenzaron a planear y a decidir cómo iban a hacer al hombre. Los hombres creados anteriormente habían salido° imperfectos. Era necesario encontrar la sustancia para hacer la carne del hombre.

Cuando los dioses creadores estaban reunidos, cuatro animales les revelaron la existencia de las mazorcas° de maíz blanco y de maíz amarillo.

La abuela Ixmucané tomó el maíz blanco y el maíz amarillo. Los usó para preparar una comida y una bebida de la que salió la carne y la gordura° del hombre. Sus brazos y sus pies también salieron de esta comida.

Los señores Tepeu y Gucumatz formaron así a nuestros primeros padres y madres.

barro *mud*   **sagrado** *sacred*   **creadores** *creators*   **carne** *flesh*   **salido** *come out*
mazorcas *ears*   **gordura** *thickness*

Rubén Darío El poeta niño

Cuando era todavía un niño, Rubén Darío (1867–1916) era famoso en partes de Centroamérica. Se le llamaba «el poeta niño». Nació° en Nicaragua y publicó sus primeros versos cuando tenía 14 años.

Además de escribir poesía durante toda su vida,° era corresponsal° del periódico *La Nación* de Buenos Aires. También viajaba en misiones diplomáticas y consulares por Nicaragua.

En su viaje a España en 1898, fue recibido como un héroe por los poetas jóvenes.

Darío revolucionó el ritmo y la métrica de la poesía española. Llegó a ser el líder de una escuela poética que se llama «el modernismo».

LOS TRES REYES MAGOS

Dice la tradición cristiana que Melchor, Gaspar y Baltasar, los tres reyes magos° de Oriente, vieron en el cielo° una brillante estrella° que los guió° hasta Belén.° Allí ofrecieron sus regalos al niño Jesús: incienso, mirra y oro.° En este poema de Rubén Darío, el poeta embellece° la tradición con sus palabras.

Tesuque Pueblo, NM / Artist: Manuel Vigil

—*Yo soy Gaspar. Aquí traigo el incienso.*
Vengo a decir: La vida es pura y bella.°
Existe Dios. El amor es inmenso.
¡Todo lo sé por la divina Estrella!

—*Yo soy Melchor. Mi mirra aroma todo.*
Existe Dios. Él es la luz del día.
¡La blanca flor tiene sus pies en lodo°
y en el placer° hay la melancolía!

—*Soy Baltasar. Traigo el oro. Aseguro*
que existe Dios. Él es el grande y fuerte.
Todo lo sé por el lucero° puro
que brilla en la diadema° de la Muerte.°

—*Gaspar, Melchor y Baltasar, callaos.°*
Triunfa el amor, y a su fiesta os convida.°
¡Cristo resurge, hace la luz del caos
y tiene la corona de la Vida!   —Rubén Darío

Tonalá, México / Artist Unknown

Nació *He was born*   **vida** *life*   **corresponsal** *correspondent*   **tres reyes magos** *three kings*
cielo *sky*   **estrella** *star*   **guió** *guided*   **Belén** *Bethlehem*   **oro** *gold*   **embellece** *embellishes*
bella *beautiful*   **lodo** *mud*   **placer** *pleasure*   **lucero** *bright star*   **diadema** *crown*
Muerte *Death*   **callaos** *be still*   **os convida** *invites you*

LAS POSADAS

¿Cuándo celebras la Navidad?
¿El 25 de diciembre o antes?

Bueno, en algunas ciudades hispanas la fiesta comienza diez días antes. Sí. Comienza el 16, con la primera posada. Hay nueve posadas en total: una todas las noches del 16 al 24 de diciembre. Las posadas son fiestas. Conmemoran un episodio en la vida de San José y la Virgen María. Todos sabemos que cuando ellos llegaron a Belén,° pasaron muchos apuros° buscando un lugar donde pasar la noche. Por fin,° alguien les ofreció un lugar donde podían quedarse. En otras palabras, alguien les dio posada.

Las posadas siempre se celebran de noche. Comienzan cuando los invitados se separan en dos grupos. Así, los invitados se preparan para actuar en una minicomedia musical. Un grupo sale a la calle, o al jardín, o al patio de la casa. Este grupo hace los papeles de la Virgen y San José. El otro grupo se queda en la casa, con los dueños.°

El grupo que está afuera comienza a cantar pidiendo posada. San José canta:

En nombre del cielo°
pedimos posada.
Ábranle° la puerta,
a mi esposa amada.°

Pero, claro, los que están en la casa no abren la puerta. ¡Cómo le van a abrir la puerta a gente a quien no conocen! El diálogo musical continúa hasta que se descubre la identidad de la Virgen y San José. Entonces, ¡se abren las puertas! Todos se abrazan.° Termina la canción. Sigue la fiesta.

Actividades culturales

1. *Prepara un informe° sobre° el conquistador español Hernán Cortés.*
2. *En un mapa de México y Centroamérica, indica cada país de los que se encuentran en las páginas 230–232. Indica también la capital de cada país, los productos principales y, si es posible, otros datos de interés. Puedes usar dibujos,° estampillas, fotos o tarjetas postales.*
3. *Prepara un informe sobre el canal de Panamá—su historia en los años 1904–1914 y su historia reciente.*
4. *Prepara una exposición° sobre los escultores aztecas, los escultores mayas o los artesanos mexicanos.*

informe *report*   **sobre** *about*   **dibujos** *drawings*   **exposición** *exhibit*

Belén *Bethlehem*   **apuros** *difficulties*   **Por fin** *Finally*   **dueños** *owners*   **cielo** *heaven*
Ábranle *Open*   **amada** *beloved*   **se abrazan** *embrace*

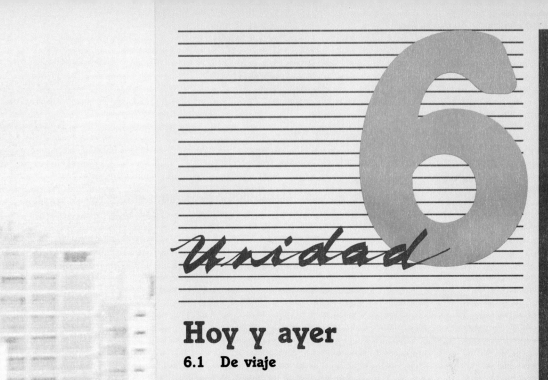

6

Unidad

Hoy y ayer

6.1 De viaje

6.2 La vida está llena de misterios

6.3 Dos chicas

6.4 ¡Demasiado tarde!

VARIEDADES   La vida: una visón humorística

OBJECTIVES
Communication
By the end of this unit, students will be able to use Spanish:
   • To describe what is generally done and not done
   • To describe how they look and feel
   • To talk about their accomplishments
Language
This unit stresses two main topics:
   • The use of the reflexive in impersonal constructions (**se habla español**)
   • The compound past tenses: the present perfect and the pluperfect
Culture
This unit introduces the Dominican Republic and focuses on several aspects of Hispanic culture: the difference between **Ud.** and **tú**, the value of time, and the use of the telephone.

Lección 1   De viaje

Act. 1, 3   Anuncios, letreros, señales de todo tipo . . . Por lo general, éstas son las primeras cosas que se ven cuando se viaja por un país extranjero. Lo importante es comprenderlas, ¿verdad?

¿Comprendes los siguientes anuncios?

Vamos a ver. Examina cada anuncio atentamente y después contesta las preguntas con sí o con no.

anuncios: *announcements*
letreros: *posters*
señales: *signs*
se ven: *one sees*
extranjero: *foreign*
atentamente: *carefully*

sí   no

Un amigo te ofrece un
   cigarrillo.
¿Vas a aceptarlo?   ☐ ☐

cigarrillo: *cigarette*

AQUÍ SE HABLA FRANCÉS
ICI ON PARLE FRANÇAIS

En ese lugar hablan otro
   idioma.
¿Se dan clases de francés
   allí?   ☐ ☐

¡Qué linda playa!
¿Se puede nadar allí?   ☐ ☐

Éste es un lugar muy bonito.
¿Se puede tener un picnic aquí?   ☐ ☐

lugar: *place*

Me gustaría sacar una foto de
   este monumento.
¿Se puede parar aquí por cinco
   minutos?   ☐ ☐

estacionar: *park*

Mi reloj no funciona bien.
¿Puedo dejarlo allí?

☐ ☐

Quiero vender mi guitarra.
¿Puedo venderla en esta tienda?

☐ ☐

Mi moto no anda.
¿Puedo dejarla allí?

☐ ☐

Necesitan una empleada.
¿Es ésta una compañía
internacional?

☐ ☐

Allí se arreglan coches.
¿Es este lugar una estación
de servicio?

☐ ☐

Se solicitan: *Are needed*

¡Qué cantidad de coches!
¿Puedo comprar un coche allí?

☐ ☐

Se alquilan:
Are rented
cantidad: *quantity*

NOTA CULTURAL

El tabaco, un producto de origen indio

¿Sabes que el tabaco es un producto de origen americano? Los indios lo cultivaban antes del descubrimiento° del Nuevo Mundo y lo tomaban como° medicina. Cuando los españoles llegaron a América, los indios les ofrecieron el tabaco como señal de amistad y de paz.° En 1500 (mil quinientos) los españoles llevaron este producto a Europa. En 1560 (mil quinientos sesenta) el embajador francés en Portugal mandó polvo° de tabaco a su reina° para usarlo como medicina contra fuertes dolores de cabeza.°

Durante los siglos el tabaco ha tenido° gran variedad de usos. Se masticaba,° se usaba como polvo aromático y se fumaba en pipas o cigarros. Alrededor de 1830 (mil ochocientos treinta), se empezó a fumar tabaco en cigarrillos.

Hoy día° todos conocen el peligro° que representa para la salud° fumar tabaco. Los que fuman se exponen° a graves enfermedades° y pueden dañar°

la salud de otras personas con el humo° del tabaco.

Para mantenerse en buena salud uno debe informarse sobre los efectos negativos del tabaco.

descubrimiento *discovery* **como** *as* **paz** *peace* **polvo** *powder* **reina** *queen* **dolores de cabeza** *headaches* **ha tenido** *has had* **se masticaba** *was chewed* **Hoy día** *Today* **peligro** *danger* **salud** *health* **se exponen** *expose themselves* **enfermedades** *illnesses* **dañar** *harm* **humo** *smoke*

¿De qué origen es el tabaco? ¿Quiénes cultivaban el tabaco en el Nuevo Mundo? ¿Cuáles son algunos de los unos que el tabaco ha tenido durante los siglos? ¿Por qué hoy día se considera el uso de tabaco un gran peligro para la salud?

Vocabulario

sustantivos	**un anuncio**	advertisement	**una cantidad**	quantity
	un letrero	sign, notice, poster	**una señal**	(traffic) sign
	un lugar	place		
adjetivo	**extranjero**	foreign		
verbos	**estacionar**	to park (a car)		
	fumar	to smoke		
	prohibir	to prohibit		

CONVERSACIÓN

1. ¿**Se habla** español en España?
2. ¿**Se habla** español en México?
3. ¿**Se habla** español en el Brasil?
4. ¿Qué lengua **se habla** en Francia?
5. ¿Qué lengua **se habla** en la clase de español?
6. ¿Qué lengua **se habla** en tu casa?

OBSERVACIÓN

In the above questions, you have been asked where certain languages *are spoken*.

• Which expression is used?   se habla
• Which pronoun is used in this expression?   the reflexive pronoun **se**

Estructuras

A. El uso impersonal del pronombre reflexivo *se*

In the sentences below, the reflexive pronoun **se** refers to specific persons
(Paco, Elena y Pedro) who perform the action.

Paco **se** lava.	*Paco washes **himself**.*
Elena y Pedro **se** hablan.	*Elena and Pedro talk **to each other**.*

Se can also be used in sentences where it does not refer to any specific
person. Note this impersonal use of **se** in the following sentences.

Se habla español en México.	***They (people, one) speak(s)** Spanish in Mexico.*
Se necesita trabajar.	***People (you, we, one) need(s)** to work.*
¿Cómo **se** escribe . . .?	*How does **one** (do **you**) write . . .?*
¿Cómo **se** va al restaurante?	*How does **one** (do **we**) go to the restaurant?*

The Spanish impersonal construction **se** + verb often corresponds to
constructions in English that use impersonal subjects such as *people, they,
you, we, one* . . . The subjects are not expressed in Spanish.
Note also the expression:

Se prohibe fumar. { *Smoking **is prohibited.***
*People **cannot** smoke.*
***No** smoking.* }

ACTIVIDAD 1   Preguntas personales

1. ¿Siempre se habla español en la clase de español?
2. ¿Se estudia mucho en el colegio?
3. ¿Se necesita estudiar mucho para sacar buenas notas?
4. ¿Se trabaja mucho en los Estados Unidos?
5. ¿Se necesita trabajar mucho en la vida?
6. ¿Se necesita tener mucho dinero para ser feliz?
7. ¿Se come bien en la cafetería del colegio?
8. ¿Se come bien en los restaurantes de tu ciudad?
9. ¿Se prohibe fumar en tu escuela?
10. ¿Se prohibe fumar en el autobús?

¡SE BUSCA! MAD EN ESPAÑOL

ACTIVIDAD 2 ¡Prohibiciones!

Algunas personas hacen cosas que no deben hacer. Diles que se prohibe
hacer esas cosas.

⟩⟩ (en el autobús) Un señor fuma.   ¡Lo siento, señor! Se prohibe fumar aquí.

1. (en el tren) Una señora fuma.
2. (en el museo) Una señorita saca fotos.
3. (en el parque) Una señora coge *(picks)* flores.
4. (en el hospital) Un señor habla en voz alta *(in a loud voice).*
5. (en la calle) Un señor estaciona su coche.
6. (durante el concierto) Un señor hace ruido.
7. (en la biblioteca) Un señor habla.

WB
A1

SCRIPT

Act. 4, 5, 6

MASTERS
p. 26

ACTIVIDAD 3 En un país extranjero

Imagina que estás visitando España. Hay ciertas cosas que quieres hacer,
pero no sabes cómo hacerlas. Pídele ayuda a un amigo, según el modelo.

⟩⟩ Quiero ir al museo.   Por favor, ¿cómo se va al museo?

1. Quiero ir al centro.
2. Quiero ir al cine.
3. Quiero telefonear.
4. Quiero estacionar.
5. Quiero invitar a un chico al café.

B. Otro uso impersonal del pronombre reflexivo *se*

Note the use of the impersonal construction with **se** in the following
sentences.

Se necesita un mecánico.	*A mechanic **is needed.***
Se necesitan dos secretarias.	*Two secretaries **are needed.***
Se vende pan en la panadería.	*Bread **is sold** in the bakery.*
Se venden pasteles allí también.	*Cakes **are sold** there also.*

Often the impersonal construction **se** + verb + subject corresponds to the
English passive construction:

> noun + *is (are)* + past participle.

In such cases, the verb agrees with the noun subject, which follows it.

ACTIVIDAD 4 La agencia de empleo *(The employment office)*

Imagina que trabajas para una agencia de empleo. Esa oficina necesita a
las siguientes personas. Prepara los anuncios según el modelo.

VARIATION with **buscar:**
Se buscan dos secretarias...

⟩⟩ dos secretarias bilingües   Se necesitan dos secretarias bilingües.

1. un mecánico
2. dos electricistas
3. una enfermera
4. dos camareros
5. una camarera
6. una mecanógrafa *(typist)*
7. tres cocineros *(cooks)*
8. una farmacéutica *(druggist)*

VOCABULARIO PRÁCTICO   Las tiendas

alquilar	to rent	En esa tienda **se alquilan** bicicletas.
arreglar	to fix	En una relojería **se arreglan** relojes.
reparar	to repair	En una estación de servicio **se reparan** los coches.
solicitar	to solicit,	**Se solicitan** mecánicos.
	to seek (employees)	

NOTA: In Spanish, the names of many shops end in **–ería**.

zapato	→ zapat**ería**	*shoe store*
helado	→ helad**ería**	*ice cream parlor*
perfume	→ perfum**ería**	*perfume shop*
peluca *(wig)*	→ peluqu**ería**	*barber shop, hair dresser*

ACTIVIDAD 5   ¿Sí o no?

Di si las siguientes tiendas se especializan en los productos que están entre
paréntesis. En tus respuestas usa los verbos sugeridos.

⟩⟩   librería (zapatos): vender   En una librería no se venden zapatos.

1. librería (mapas): vender
2. carnicería (pan): vender
3. panadería (pasteles): vender
4. zapatería (sandalias): vender
5. mueblería (discos): vender
6. lavandería (ropa): lavar
7. relojería (televisores): reparar
8. lechería (crema): comprar

ACTIVIDAD 6   Turistas

Unos turistas norteamericanos van de compras en Quito. El guardia les
indica donde se venden las cosas que buscan. Haz los dos papeles según el
modelo.

El guardia is a policeman.

Las tiendas: la carnicería, la florería, la frutería, la lechería, la librería,
              la mueblería, la panadería, la perfumería, la zapatería

⟩⟩   ¿Dónde puedo comprar un litro de leche?
          Turista: ¿Dónde puedo comprar un litro de leche?
          Guardia: Se vende leche en esa lechería.

Only two forms are used in
the responses: **se vende** and
se venden.

WB
B1, B2

SCRIPT
[◉━◉]
Act. 7, 9

MASTERS
p. 26

1. ¿Dónde puedo comprar bistec?
2. Me gustaría comprar zapatos nuevos.
3. Quiero comprar una lámpara para mi cuarto.
4. ¿Dónde se venden libros en inglés?
5. Deseo comprar dos panes y dos pasteles.
6. Necesitamos frutas frescas.
7. ¿Dónde venden perfumes franceses?
8. Deseo comprar flores *(flowers)*.

ACTIVIDAD 7   En casa

Describe las costumbres *(habits)* de tu casa, usando una de las expresiones
sugeridas.

⟩⟩   servir el desayuno: a las siete, a las ocho, a las nueve
          Se sirve el desayuno a las ocho.

1. servir la cena: a las cinco, a las seis, a
   las siete
2. comer: bien, mucho, muchas frutas,
   muchas legumbres
3. tomar: café, té, café con leche, leche,
   gaseosas

4. celebrar: la Navidad, la Pascua
   (Easter/Passover), los cumpleaños, los
   aniversarios
5. hablar: mucho, de los vecinos, de la
   política

ACTIVIDAD 8   En México y en los Estados Unidos

Un estudiante mexicano te habla de su país. Háblale de los Estados
Unidos, según el modelo.

∑⟩   En México hablamos español.
        En los Estados Unidos se hablan inglés y español también.

1. En México comemos tacos.
2. En México bebemos café.
3. En México jugamos al fútbol.
4. En México celebramos el día de la
   Independencia el 16 de septiembre.

5. En México usamos pesos.
6. En México cultivamos maíz *(corn)*.

This is an open-ended activity which may be used for vocabulary
review and expansion. POSSIBLE ANSWERS:
1. **hamburguesas, perritos calientes**
2. **leche, Coca-Cola, gaseosas**
3. **al fútbol americano, al tenis, al básquetbol, al béisbol**
6. **trigo** (wheat), **algodón** (cotton)

ACTIVIDAD 9   Expresión personal

Completa las frases siguientes.

Have students use infinitives in items 3–4 and clauses in items 5–6.

∑⟩   Se come bien en mi casa (en la cafetería, en los restaurantes franceses, en México, etc.).

1. Se come mal . . .
2. Se vive bien . . .
3. Se necesita dinero para . . .
4. Se necesita trabajar para . . .
5. Se necesitan amigos porque . . .
6. Se necesitan consejos cuando . . .

Para la comunicación   OPTIONAL

El mundo hispánico

Escoge un país hispánico (por ejemplo, México, la Argentina, Cuba, el
Perú) y escribe un párrafo describiendo algunos aspectos de la vida de allá.
Si quieres, puedes usar las siguientes preguntas:

¿Qué idiomas se hablan?
¿Qué fiestas se celebran?
¿Qué deportes se juegan?
¿Qué moneda se usa?
¿Qué productos se cultivan?
¿Qué alimentos se comen?
¿Qué religiones se practican?

This may be assigned as a class culture project. The information requested
may be obtained from the **Vista** sections and general sources such as
almanacs and encyclopedias. Groups of students may be asked to prepare
bulletin board exhibits of the country they have selected (with maps, pictures,
stamps, and other realia).

∑⟩   En el Perú se hablan español y quechua . . .

La vida está llena de misterios

Act. 1

35

STRUCTURE TO OBSERVE: the formation of regular past participles. You may point out the examples of the past participles of the lesson and ask the students to give the corresponding infinitive form. Limit this exercise to verbs they have already learned: **ocupar, cerrar, descansar.**

¿Por qué está Luis enamorado de Pilar y por qué está ella enamorada de Rafael?

¿Por qué siempre parece bronceada Elena aun en el invierno . . .?

¿Por qué está Paco siempre pálido, aun en el verano?

bronceada: *tanned*

pálido: *pale*

¿Por qué siempre está ocupada la línea de nuestros amigos cuando queremos llamarlos?

línea: *line*

¿Por qué quiere darle su asiento a la Sra. de Oliva todo el mundo cuando el autobús está casi vacío . . . ?

¿Por qué no quiere darle su asiento nadie cuando el autobús está atestado y ella tiene muchos paquetes?

asiento: *seat*
todo el mundo:
everyone
vacío: *empty*

atestado: *crowded*
paquetes: *packages*

¿De quién está enamorado Luis? ¿De quién está enamorada Pilar? ¿Quién está bronceado, Paco o Elena? ¿Puede sentarse la Sra. de Oliva cuando el autobús está vacío? ¿Puede sentarse cuando el autobús está atestado? ¿Cuándo están abiertas las ventanas de la clase? ¿Cuándo están cerradas? ¿Cómo nos sentimos cuando no hacemos nada?

¿Por qué están abiertas las ventanas de la clase cuando hace frío y están cerradas cuando hace mucho calor?

abiertas: *open*

¿Por qué está encendido el televisor y no hay nadie en la sala?

encendido: *turned on*

¿Por qué nos sentimos cansados cuando no hacemos nada y por qué nos sentimos descansados después de bailar toda la noche?

descansados: *rested*

¿Por qué . . .? ¿Por qué . . .?

¡Ay, la vida está llena de misterios!

llena: *full*

NOTA CULTURAL   OPTIONAL

El teléfono

¿Qué haces cuando quieres invitar a un amigo a un café, charlar° un ratito° con tu mejor amigo, discutir un problema de matemáticas o un problema sentimental? Tal vez, quieres saber qué tiempo va a hacer, cuánto cuesta algo, o a qué hora empieza una película. Pues,° usas el teléfono.

En los países hispánicos, principalmente en las grandes ciudades, muchas familias tienen teléfono y hasta° lo consideran una necesidad de la vida diaria. Pero en las ciudades pequeñas y en los pueblos y aldeas,° pocas personas lo tienen.

A veces, en las aldeas muy pequeñas, sólo hay una oficina de teléfonos. Si quieres llamar a alguien que vive en esa aldea, el jefe de la oficina envía a un empleado para que busque° a la persona que llamas. Esto es posible porque algunas aldeas son muy pequeñas y la mayoría de la gente se conoce.

Así que para la gente de la ciudad, el teléfono es una necesidad. Pero para mucha gente de las aldeas, el teléfono es un lujo.°

charlar *chat* **ratito** *little while* **Pues** *Well* **hasta** *even*
aldeas *villages* **para que busque** *to look for* **lujo** *luxury*

¿Usas mucho el teléfono? ¿Para qué usas el teléfono? En los países hispánicos, ¿dónde se considera el teléfono una necesidad de la vida diaria? En las pequeñas aldeas, ¿es común tener teléfono?

—— Vocabulario ——

sustantivos	**un asiento**	seat		**una línea**	(phone) line
	un paquete	package			
adjetivos	**abierto**	open			
	atestado	crowded			
	lleno	full	≠	**vacío**	empty
	pálido	pale	≠	**bronceado**	tanned

CONVERSACIÓN   OPTIONAL

¿Cómo estás en este momento?

1. ¿Estás **sentado(a)** ahora?
2. ¿Estás **cansado(a)**?
3. ¿Estás **descansado(a)**?
4. ¿Estás muy **ocupado(a)**?

5. ¿Estás **preocupado(a)**?
6. ¿Estás **enojado(a)**?
7. ¿Estás **aburrido(a)**?
8. ¿Estás **dormido(a)**?

OBSERVACIÓN

The words in heavy print in the questions above are used as adjectives. These words, which are derived from verbs, are called *past participles.*

• From which verbs are these past participles derived?

sentar, cansar, descansar, ocupar,
preocupar, enojar, aburrir, dormir

Estructuras

A. Los participios pasados regulares

Compare the past participles and the infinitives of the verbs in the following examples:

preocupar	*(to worry)*	Pedro está muy **preocupado.**	*(worried)*
cerrar	*(to close)*	¿Está el banco **cerrado?**	*(closed)*
aburrir	*(to bore)*	Jorge está **aburrido.**	*(bored)*
vestir	*(to dress)*	Paco está bien **vestido.**	*(dressed)*

Past participles are formed by replacing the infinitive endings –**ar**, –**er**, –**ir** with –**ado**, –**ido**, –**ido**.

–ar verbs	**-ado**	hablar	→	**hablado**
–er verbs	**-ido**	comer	→	**comido**
–ir verbs	**-ido**	vivir	→	**vivido**

These endings often correspond to the English past participle ending -*ed*.

Past participles are often used as adjectives. When this occurs, they take the regular adjective endings.

María está **casada.**   *María is **married.***
Tengo dos hermanos **casados.**   *I have two **married** brothers.*

The verb **estar** is used with the past participle to indicate a state or condition or the result of an action.

Estoy cansado.   *I **am** (I feel) **tired.***
La ventana **está cerrada.**   *The window **is closed.***

ACTIVIDAD 1   Preguntas personales

1. ¿Quién está sentado a tu derecha? ¿a tu izquierda?
2. ¿En qué calle está situada tu casa?
3. ¿Está tu casa situada en el centro? ¿cerca del colegio?
4. ¿Vives en una casa alquilada *(rented)*? ¿un apartamento alquilado?
5. ¿Tienes hermanos casados? ¿hermanas casadas?

ACTIVIDAD 2   En la clase de matemáticas

Describe la actitud de los siguientes alumnos usando participios pasados derivados de los verbos que están entre paréntesis.

Luisa (preocupar)   Luisa está preocupada.

1. Rafael (ocupar)
2. Inés y Sofía (ocupar)
3. Josefina (enojar)
4. Paco y Roberto (enfadar)
5. Raquel y Susana (interesar)
6. Pilar y Mercedes (aburrir)
7. Juan (dormir)
8. Carmen y Luisa (dormir)

ACTIVIDAD 3   ¡Un poco de lógica!

Lo que sentimos depende a veces de lo que acabamos de hacer. Expresa
esto usando los elementos de las columnas A, B y C en diez frases lógicas
por lo menos.

The past participle of **leer** (and verbs ending
in vowel + **er/ir**) has an accent: **leído.**

A	B	C
yo	cansar	dormir 24 horas
tú	descansar	correr 5 kilómetros
Susana	enfadar	sacar una mala nota
Raúl y Pedro	enojar	conocer *(to meet)* a un(a) chico(a) muy simpático(a)
Ana María y Elena	aburrir	oír malas noticias
mis hermanos y yo	preocupar	pasar una hora estudiando
	dormir	perder diez dólares
	enamorar	leer una novela tonta
	irritar	montar a caballo
	emocionar	hablar con un actor muy famoso

 Susana está enojada porque acaba de perder diez dólares.

VOCABULARIO PRÁCTICO   Estados y condiciones

apagar	to turn off	El radio está **apagado.**
atestar	to crowd, to cram	El tren está **atestado.**

Act. 3

cerrar (e → ie)	to close	Los domingos, las tiendas están **cerradas.**
encender (e → ie)	to light, to turn on	Las luces están **encendidas.**
esconder	to hide	¿Dónde está **escondido** el dinero?
quebrar (e → ie)	to break	Tiene el brazo **quebrado.**
quemar	to burn, to scorch	¡Dios mío! Las tostadas *(pieces of toast)* están **quemadas.**

ACTIVIDAD 4   Depende de la hora *(A matter of time)*

Describe las cosas siguientes,
   a)   a las ocho de la mañana,
   b)   a las nueve de la noche.
Usa frases afirmativas o negativas.

   ⊃⊃   el televisor (apagar)   A las ocho de la mañana, el televisor está apagado.
                                     (A las nueve de la noche, no está apagado.)

1. el radio (apagar)   4. la escuela (cerrar)
2. las luces (encender)   5. los restaurantes (cerrar)
3. los autobuses (atestar)   6. el cine (atestar)

ACTIVIDAD 5   La clase de español

Describe la clase de español en frases afirmativas o negativas, según el
modelo.

   ⊃⊃   el (la) profesor(a): sentar   El (la) profesor(a) (no) está sentado(a).
1. los alumnos: sentar   4. la puerta: cerrar
2. la clase: atestar   5. las ventanas: cerrar
3. las luces: encender   6. la calefacción *(heat)*: apagar

ACTIVIDAD 6   ¡Más lógica!

Completa las siguientes frases con una explicación lógica. Usa los
participios pasados de los verbos del vocabulario.

   ⊃⊃   No deposité el dinero en el banco. El banco estaba . . . cerrado.

1. No encontré mis libros. Estaban . . .
2. No compré los pasteles. Estaban . . .
3. No miré la televisión. El televisor
   estaba . . .
4. Hace mucho frío. La calefacción está . . .
5. Hace fresco. El aire acondicionado está . . .
6. El niño se cayó. Ahora tiene la pierna . . .

WB
A1, A2,
A3

SCRIPT
Act. 4, 5,
6

MASTERS
p. 27

B. Preposiciones de lugar

Note the prepositions of place in the sentences below:

El coche está **en** el garaje.	*The car is **in** the garage.*
La antena está **sobre** el televisor.	*The antenna is **on** the TV set.*
Vivo **cerca de** un teatro.	*I live **near** a theater.*
Vivo **lejos de** la escuela.	*I live **far from** the school.*

Prepositions of place may consist of one or several words.

VOCABULARIO PRÁCTICO   **Algunas preposiciones de lugar**

one word

en	in, into, on	El libro está **en** la mesa.
entre	between	El Ecuador está situado **entre** Colombia y el Perú.
hacia	toward	Caminamos **hacia** la escuela.
sobre	on, over, about	¿Está el lápiz **sobre** el cuaderno?
tras	after	El policía corre **tras** el ladrón.

several words

cerca de	near, close to	≠	**lejos de**	far from
debajo de	below, under(neath)	≠	**encima de**	on top of
alrededor de	around	≠	**en medio de**	in the middle of
dentro de	inside	≠	**fuera de**	outside
detrás de	behind, in back of	≠	**delante de**	before, in front of
a la derecha de	to the right of	≠	**a la izquierda de**	to the left of
al lado de	beside		**enfrente de**	facing, in front of
junto a	next to			

NOTA: The above expressions that consist of two or more words may be used alone,
that is, without introducing a noun. In these cases, the **de** is dropped.

¡El gato está **fuera de** la casa!   *The cat is **outside of** the house.*
¡El gato está **fuera**!   *The cat is **outside**.*

ACTIVIDAD 7 ¿Dónde vives?   OPTIONAL

Di dónde vives en relación a las siguientes personas y lugares.

⤳   mi mejor amigo   Vivo al lado de (cerca de, lejos de,
enfrente de) mi mejor amigo.

1. mi mejor amiga
2. mis abuelos
3. mis primos
4. unos vecinos simpáticos
5. la escuela
6. la iglesia
7. un parque
8. una gran ciudad
9. Nueva York
10. Texas

ACTIVIDAD 8   Los animales de Ana María

Ana María tiene tres animales: un gato (Sultán), un pájaro (Paco) y un pez (Gordo). Por razones obvias, los tres animales están separados. Describe la posición de cada uno.

Various answers are possible.

Paco / Sultán

Paco está encima de Sultán (a la derecha de Sultán, lejos de Sultán, etc.).

WB
B1

SCRIPT
Act. 7

MASTERS
p. 27

1. Gordo / Sultán
2. Gordo / el acuario
3. el acuario / la mesa
4. los discos / la mesa
5. Paco / la jaula
6. los discos / el suelo
7. la bombilla / la jaula
8. el agua / el acuario

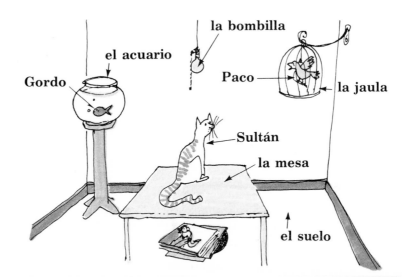

Para la comunicación   OPTIONAL

May be assigned as homework.

Tus emociones

A veces estamos de buen humor. Otras veces estamos de mal humor. Di si sientes (a menudo, raras veces, nunca) las siguientes emociones y cuándo las sientes.

WB
Tú

SCRIPT
Act. 8

MASTERS
p. 27

TRB

QUIZ
pp. 75–76

- cansar
- descansar
- aburrir
- enojar
- agitar
- preocupar
- ocupar
- impresionar

aburrir

Estoy aburrido(a) de vez en cuando. Por ejemplo, estoy aburrido(a) cuando escucho música romántica o cuando no hay nada que hacer.

Lección 3   Dos chicas

Act. 1

Dos chicas están en la playa «La Romana» en la República Dominicana. Bárbara se acerca y saluda a Marta.

You may have the students read the cultural note on **el tuteo** before beginning the reading.

Bárbara: Perdóneme, Srta., ¿conoce Ud. a Conchita Beltrán?

Marta: Por supuesto, somos compañeras de colegio.

Bárbara: ¿La ha visto Ud. recientemente?

Marta: Sí, acabo de verla. Ella estaba aquí en la playa.

Bárbara: Pues . . . algo terrible ha pasado.

Marta: ¡Dios mío! ¿Qué ha ocurrido?

Bárbara: ¡Mire! Ella ha tomado su bolsa, sus llaves, su moped y se ha ido al centro, se ha ido al cine con su novio.

Marta: ¿Con su novio? ¡Qué bien! . . . Esa chica tiene mucha suerte . . . y me alegro mucho por ella.

Bárbara: Un momentito . . . Veo que Ud. no ha comprendido bien la situación. ¿Puedo tutearla?

Marta: Está bien, no me importa.

Bárbara: Es que Conchita ha tomado tu bolsa, tus llaves, tu moped y se ha ido al centro. ¡Se ha ido al cine con tu novio!

Marta: ¿Cómo? ¿Qué has dicho? ¡Qué horror!

ha pasado: has happened

tutearla: use "tú" with you
no me importa: it doesn't matter to me

You may have to explain why the shift from **usted** to **tú** opened Marta's eyes. When Barbara used the form **su novio**, she could have been referring either to Conchita's or to Marta's boyfriend. But when she used the form **tu novio,** she could only mean Marta's boyfriend.

¿Cómo se llaman las dos chicas? ¿Dónde están? ¿Quién es Conchita Beltrán? ¿Qué ha tomado ella? ¿Adónde ha ido? ¿Con quién ha ido al centro?

Act. 2

NOTAS CULTURALES OPTIONAL

La República Dominicana

La República Dominicana está situada en la isla de Santo Domingo, la isla más grande de las Antillas.° Tiene costas° sinuosas° y playas muy largas y bonitas como la de «La Romana».

Santo Domingo, la capital de la República Dominicana, fue fundada° en 1496 (mil cuatrocientos noventa y seis) por Bartolomé Colón, el hermano de Cristóbal Colón. ¡Es la ciudad de origen europeo más antigua de las Américas!

Antillas *West Indies* **costas** *coastline* **sinuosas** *winding*
fundada *founded*

Statue of Bartolomé Colón in Santo Domingo

El tuteo

¿Te preguntas por qué Marta y Bárbara se hablan de "Ud."? Porque estas dos chicas no se conocen muy bien. Una señal de la buena educación es hablarle a la gente de "Ud.", por lo menos° al principio.° Casi siempre se les habla de "Ud." a las personas mayores y a aquéllas° con las que el trato° es más formal.

Poco a poco el uso de "tú" va aumentando.° En algunos países hispanos se tutea más que en otros. En el Perú, Colombia, Venezuela y México, "tú" es de uso muy frecuente en las ciudades pero no en los pueblos. En Nicaragua, El Salvador, Guatemala y Costa Rica se usa más "Ud." que "tú", aun° con la gente que se conoce bien. En la Argentina y el Uruguay no se usa el "tú", se usa el "vos" que equivale° al "tú", y se usa el "Ud." para situaciones más formales.

A pesar de° esto, al visitar un país hispano, siempre es mejor usar "Ud." con todos. No olvides° que "Ud." es una señal de cortesía y de respeto. Usa "tú" solamente cuando alguien te invita a hacerlo: "Por favor, háblame de tú."

por lo menos *at least* **al principio** *at first* **aquéllas** *those people* **trato** *dealings* **va aumentando** *is increasing* **aun** *even* **equivale** *is equivalent to* **A pesar de** *In spite of* **olvides** *forget*

For more information on the Dominican Republic see **Vista** 2, pp. 133–144.
• The oldest university in the Americas is also located in Santo Domingo.
• REALIA: travel brochures.

¿Dónde está la República Dominicana? ¿Cómo se llama su capital? ¿Por quién fue fundada? ¿Se hablan de *tú* o *usted* las personas que no se conocen bien? ¿En la Argentina y el Uruguay se usa el "tú"? ¿Qué se usa?

Vocabulario

verbos	**olvidar**	to forget
	tutear	to say "**tú**" to someone (instead of "**Ud.**")
expresión	**¡No me importa!**	It doesn't matter to me!

Lección tres
259

Estructuras

Act. 3

A. **La formación del pretérito perfecto**   When referring to this tense in English, note that *present perfect* is used.

The *present perfect,* in Spanish as in English, is used to describe certain
past events. Note the forms of this tense.

INFINITIVE		jugar		divertirse	
PRESENT PERFECT					
(yo)	**he**	**jugado**	me **he**		**divertido**
(tú)	**has**	**jugado**	te **has**		**divertido**
(él, ella, Ud.)	**ha**	**jugado**	se **ha**		**divertido**
(nosotros)	**hemos**	**jugado**	nos **hemos**		**divertido**
(vosotros)	**habéis**	**jugado**	os **habéis**		**divertido**
(ellos, ellas, Uds.)	**han**	**jugado**	se **han**		**divertido**

As in English, the present perfect consists of two words:

He hablado.   *I have spoken.*

It is formed as follows:

present of **haber** (*to have*)   +   past participle

▷ In *compound tenses,* such as the present perfect, the past participle does not change with the subject. It always ends in **o.**

María **ha ido** al cine.   *María **has gone** to the movies.*

Tus hermanos **han ido** con ella.   *Your brothers **have gone** with her.*

▷ This construction, present of **haber** + past participle, forms a block that is never broken. Thus, the object pronouns and the negative word **no** always come before the verb.

¿Ha llamado Ud. a Carmen?   ***Have** you **called** Carmen?*

No, no la **he llamado.**   *No, I **have** not **called** her.*

EXPANSION: Ask students to explain their answers. For example, **¿Qué has comprado? ¿A quién has conocido? ¿Con quiénes has ido al cine?**

ACTIVIDAD 1   Preguntas personales

1. ¿Has comprado algo bonito recientemente?

2. ¿Has conocido *(Have you met)* a una persona simpática recientemente?

3. ¿Has ido al cine recientemente?

4. ¿Has estado de buen humor recientemente?

5. ¿Te has divertido recientemente?

6. ¿Te has peleado con tus amigos recientemente?

7. ¿Has estado enfermo(a) recientemente?

8. ¿Has asistido a un concierto recientemente?

ACTIVIDAD 2   Turismo

Las siguientes personas han ido a países extranjeros pero no han visitado la capital. Expresa eso.

▷ Marta (España: Madrid)

     Marta ha ido a España, pero no ha visitado Madrid.

1. Roberto (Italia: Roma)
2. Ud. (la Argentina: Buenos Aires)
3. Uds. (el Brasil: Brasilia)
4. mis padres (Francia: París)
5. yo (Chile: Santiago)
6. tú (Bolivia: La Paz)
7. nosotros (el Perú: Lima)
8. Felipe y Raúl (Colombia: Bogotá)

• ADDITIONAL CUES: **Ud. (el Ecuador: Quito); Clara y yo (Uruguay: Montevideo)**
• ACTIVITY: Have students locate these places on the map.

Colombia
una ruta diferente

corporación nacional de turismo-colombia

ACTIVIDAD 3   Hay días buenos

Explica por qué estos jóvenes están contentos.

> 🖙   Ana María (recibir una carta de su novio)
>   Hoy, Ana María ha recibido una carta de su novio.

1. Paco (recibir 100 pesetas)
2. Ramón (llamar a su novia por teléfono)
3. Beatriz (comprar unos pendientes lindos)
4. Manuel (vender su tocadiscos)
5. Luis (encontrar a un amigo en el centro)
6. Carmen (correr 5 kilómetros)
7. Pilar (tener suerte en el examen)
8. Gloria (salir con un chico simpático)
9. Clara (ser invitada a una fiesta)
10. Rafael (ganar mucho dinero)

You may point out that **tener** and **ser** have regular past participles.

ACTIVIDAD 4   Acusaciones

Paco acusa a Isabel de ciertas cosas. Isabel le dice que no ha hecho (*done*) nada y le indica quiénes lo han hecho. Haz los dos papeles, según el modelo.

The past participles of verbs ending in vowel + er/ir have an accent: **leer → leído**.

> 🖙   leer mi diario: Rafael
>
> Paco: ¡Caramba! ¿Has leído mi diario?
> Isabel: ¡Claro que no! ¡Es Rafael quien lo ha leído!

1. leer mis cartas: Roberto
2. beber mi Coca-Cola: Inés
3. esconder mi libro: Susana
4. perder mis revistas: tu hermano
5. comer mi sándwich: Felipe
6. apagar el televisor: tus padres
7. desarreglar (*to mess up*) mi cuarto: tus hermanas

ACTIVIDAD 5   Diálogo: Recientemente

Pregúntales a tus compañeros si han hecho las siguientes cosas recientemente.

WB
A1, A2

SCRIPT

Act. 4, 5

MASTERS
p. 28

> 🖙   comprar algo especial
>
> Estudiante 1: ¿Has comprado algo especial recientemente?
> Estudiante 2: Sí (No, no) he comprado algo (nada) especial.

1. tomar una decisión importante
2. ganar dinero
3. ganar un premio (*prize*)
4. oír noticias importantes
5. estar enfermo(a)
6. olvidar algo importante
7. ir a un restaurante francés
8. ir de vacaciones
9. crecer (*to grow*)
10. adelgazar (*to get thin*)

VARIATION in the plural:
¿Han comprado Uds. ...? Sí, hemos comprado...

B. El uso del pretérito perfecto

Note the use of the present perfect tense in the following sentences:

¿**Ha llamado** alguien?	***Has*** anyone ***called?***
He recibido tu telegrama.	*I **have received** your telegram.*
El mes pasado, **he perdido** dos libras.	*In the past month, I **have lost** two pounds.*
Pedro no **ha mirado** la televisión.	*Pedro **has** not **watched** television.*
No **ha tenido** tiempo.	*He **has** not **had** time.*

As in English, the present perfect tense is used to describe events that
have (or *have not*) happened. The present perfect may be used in Spanish
whenever it is used in English, with the exception of constructions with **hace.**

Hace dos años **que vive** en Nueva York.   *He **has been living** in
New York for two years.*

VOCABULARIO PRÁCTICO   Algunas expresiones de tiempo

alguna vez	*ever,* *once*	¿Has ido **alguna vez** a México? No, no he ido nunca a México.	*Have you **ever** gone to Mexico?* *No, I have never gone to Mexico.*
ya	*already*	¿Has llamado a Ramón? Sí, **ya** lo he llamado.	*Have you called Ramón?* *Yes, I have **already** called him.*
ya **no ... todavía**	*yet* *not yet*	¿Has comido **ya**? No, **no** he comido **todavía.**	*Have you eaten **yet?*** *No, I have **not** eaten **yet.***

NOTA: Note the use of the present perfect with the above expressions.

ACTIVIDAD 6   El director y su asistente

El director le hace algunas preguntas a su asistente. El asistente contesta
negativamente. Haz los dos papeles.

⟯ llamar / el Sr. Pérez   El director: ¿Ha llamado el Sr. Pérez?

El asistente: No, no ha llamado todavía.

1. venir / la Sra. de Gonzales
2. llegar / la secretaria
3. llegar / el correo (*mail*)
4. comprar el periódico / Ud.

5. recibir el dinero / nosotros
6. llamar / el Sr. Suárez
7. contestar / la Sra. de Muñoz
8. irse / los clientes

ACTIVIDAD 7 Diálogo: Actividades

This may be used as the basis for a class survey.

Pregúntales a tus compañeros si han hecho las siguientes cosas alguna vez.

 conducir un coche   Estudiante 1: ¿Has conducido un coche alguna vez?

                               Estudiante 2: Sí, he conducido un coche.

                                               (No, no he conducido un coche todavía.)

WB
B1

1. conducir un coche deportivo
2. pilotar un avión
3. montar a caballo
4. montar en globo (*hot-air balloon*)
5. esquiar
6. jugar al tenis
7. jugar al ajedrez (*chess*)
8. correr dos kilómetros

SCRIPT

Act. 6, 7

9. correr diez kilómetros
10. nadar cinco kilómetros
11. montar en bicicleta cincuenta kilómetros
12. estar en Nueva York
13. estar en un país extranjero
14. dormirse en la clase de español
15. tener animales domésticos
16. cuidar un perro

C. Los participios pasados irregulares

A few verbs have irregular past participles.

Act. 8

decir	**dicho**	¿Qué **han dicho** por la radio?
hacer	**hecho**	¿Quién **ha hecho** eso?
escribir	**escrito**	¿Le **has escrito** a tu primo?
ver	**visto**	No **hemos visto** a Paco.
abrir	**abierto**	¿Quién **ha abierto** la puerta?
descubrir	**descubierto**	**Hemos descubierto** la verdad.
romper	**roto**	¡Caramba! ¡**He roto** tu cámara!
morir (*to die*)	**muerto**	**Se ha muerto** de risa (*laughter*).
poner	**puesto**	¿Dónde **has puesto** mi raqueta?
volver	**vuelto**	Rafael no **ha vuelto** todavía.

ACTIVIDAD 8 Diálogo: Sucesos pasados (*Past events*)

Pregúntales a tus compañeros si ya han hecho las siguientes cosas.

     hacer un viaje en avión   Estudiante 1: ¿Ya has hecho un viaje en avión?

                                     Estudiante 2: Sí. Ya he hecho un viaje en avión.

                                             (No, no he hecho nunca un viaje en avión.)

1. hacer un viaje en helicóptero
2. hacer un viaje en globo (*hot-air balloon*)
3. decir mentiras a tus padres
4. decir mentiras a tus profesores
5. ver una película española
6. ver un fantasma (*ghost*)
7. escribir un poema

8. escribir una novela
9. escribirle al presidente
10. descubrir un tesoro (*treasure*)
11. romper una ventana
12. romperte un brazo
13. ponerte furioso(a)
14. volver a casa a las dos de la mañana

ACTIVIDAD 9 Los pequeños demonios (*Little devils*)

Hay chicos que no se portan bien. Explica lo que han hecho estos chicos.

∅ Pedrito: romper la lámpara   Pedrito ha roto la lámpara.

1. Isabelita: romper el radio
2. mis hermanitos: romper un vaso
3. Carlitos: decir mentiras
4. mis primos: decir palabrotas (*dirty words*)
5. Raúl: abrir la carta de su hermano
6. nosotros: abrir la jaula (*cage*) del pájaro
7. yo: poner sal en el té de mi abuela
8. tú: poner cola (*glue*) en la silla de tu compañero

WB
C1

SCRIPT
Act. 9

MASTERS
p. 28

Para la comunicación

OPTIONAL
May be assigned as homework.

1. Este mes
Describe cinco cosas importantes que has hecho y cinco cosas que no has hecho durante este mes.

∅ He sacado una buena nota en español.

∅ No he sacado una buena nota en biología.

2. Los hechos más importantes
Haz una entrevista (*interview*) a tres personas que conoces bien. Pueden ser amigos, vecinos, parientes o amigos de la familia. Pídeles información sobre sus actividades importantes. Uds. pueden hablar de:

    los deportes
    un viaje
    los pasatiempos

∅ Antonio ha corrido una milla en menos de seis minutos.

∅ El Sr. Montoya ha pasado dos meses en la selva (*forest*) tropical del Ecuador.

∅ Concepción ha ido al cine cinco veces este mes.

WB
Tú

SCRIPT
Act. 10

MASTERS
p. 28

TRB

QUIZ
pp. 77–78

¿Ha hecho ya
su declaración
de humanidad?

Teléfono (93) 205 14 14

¡Demasiado tarde!

STRUCTURE TO OBSERVE: the pluperfect.

Act. 1

36

Hay un refrán inglés que dice «El tiempo es oro».
¿Es el tiempo tan importante?
Depende.

¿Miras el reloj cuando descansas? ¿Cuando te diviertes en una
fiesta? . . . ¿Cuando estás en la playa con tus amigos? ¡Claro que no!
En esas ocasiones, el tiempo no cuenta.

Pero otras veces, por ejemplo, cuando tomas el autobús, cuando
vas a una entrevista, cuando tienes un examen, el tiempo es
importante. Tú tienes que ser puntual . . . De lo contrario . . .

refrán: *proverb*
oro: *gold*

entrevista: *interview*

De lo contrario:
Otherwise

parada: *stop*
había ido: *had gone*

Carlos quería comprar una entrada para el partido de fútbol . . .

. . . pero cuando llegó a la taquilla, el empleado había vendido la última entrada . . . ¡Ay, qué lástima!

taquilla: *ticket office*

Anita hizo una torta de chocolate . . .

. . . pero cuando quiso decorarlo, alguien se había comido un pedazo.

pedazo: *piece*

Todos los días, la Sra. de Ortiz miraba su magnífica sandía . . .

. . . pero cuando decidió cogerla, ya había desaparecido (. . . en el estómago de Carlos y Paco).

sandía: *watermelon*
había desaparecido: *had disappeared*
estómago: *stomach*

La liebre corrió tan rápido como pudo . . .

. . . pero la tortuga ya había llegado a la meta.

tan rápido como: *as fast as*
meta: *goal*

¿Tomó el autobús el Sr. Fonseca? ¿Por qué no? ¿Invitó a Gabriela al baile Héctor? ¿Por qué no? ¿Compró una entrada Carlos? ¿Por qué no? ¿Decoró el pastel Anita? ¿Por qué no? ¿Comió la sandía la Sra. de Ortiz? ¿Por qué no? ¿Llegó primero a la meta la liebre? ¿Por qué no?

NOTA CULTURAL   OPTIONAL

El valor del tiempo

Imagina que tienes una cita con un amigo a las dos de la tarde. ¿Te enfadas si tu amigo no está allí a las dos en punto?° ¿Te enojas si llega a las dos y cuarto . . . o a las dos y media?

En los países hispanos la noción del tiempo no es tan rígida como en los Estados Unidos, pero en cuestiones de° negocios°, la puntualidad° es muy importante. Esto es evidente especialmente en las ciudades grandes. Sin embargo,° en la vida social la idea del tiempo es muy flexible. No importa si un amigo llega a una cita con diez, veinte o treinta minutos de retraso. Y en muchas ocasiones no hay una hora exacta para la cita.

Lo importante° es disfrutar° de la vida. No es una carrera contra el reloj.

en punto on the dot **en cuestiones de negocios** in business **la puntualidad** punctuality **Sin embargo** However **Lo importante** The important thing **disfrutar** enjoy

En los países hispanos, ¿es la noción del tiempo tan rígida como en los Estados Unidos? ¿Importa si un amigo llega a una cita con un retraso de treinta minutos?

—— Vocabulario ——

sustantivos	**el oro**	gold	**una entrevista**	interview
	un refrán	proverb, saying	**una meta**	goal
			una parada	stop, bus stop
			una taquilla	ticket office
verbo	**desaparecer**	to disappear		
expresiones	**de lo contrario**	otherwise		
	tan . . . como	as . . . as		

CONVERSACIÓN

The following questions concern things that people do while on vacation. Say that you did these things <u>last summer</u> and that you had done them <u>before</u> by answering the questions affirmatively.

1. ¿Viajaste en avión el verano pasado?
2. ¿Habías viajado en avión antes?
3. ¿Visitaste México el verano pasado?
4. ¿Habías visitado México antes?
5. ¿Corriste las olas el verano pasado?
6. ¿Habías corrido las olas antes?
7. ¿Navegaste un bote de vela el verano pasado?
8. ¿Habías navegado un bote de vela antes?

OBSERVACIÓN

The odd-numbered questions refer to events that *happened* last summer.
The even-numbered questions refer to events that *had happened* before, at some unspecified moment in the past.
• Are the verbs in the same tense in each set of sentences?
In the odd-numbered questions, the verbs are in the *preterite*.
In the even-numbered questions, they are in the *pluperfect*.

Unidad seis
268

Estructuras

Act. 6

37

VOCABULARIO PRÁCTICO La naturaleza

sustantivos

un parque

un bosque

unas flores

una rosa

un clavel

un árbol de frutas

una planta

una margarita

un jardín

unas legumbres

ACTIVIDAD 1 Preguntas personales

1. ¿Hay un jardín alrededor de tu casa? ¿Hay plantas allí? ¿flores? ¿árboles?

2. ¿Cultivas flores en tu casa? ¿de qué tipo?

3. ¿Qué frutas se cogen en la región donde vives? ¿naranjas? ¿manzanas? ¿peras? ¿cerezas? ¿melocotones *(peaches)*?

4. ¿Hay un parque cerca de tu casa? ¿un bosque? ¿un lago? ¿un río?

5. ¿Prefieres nadar en una piscina, en un río, en un lago o en el mar?

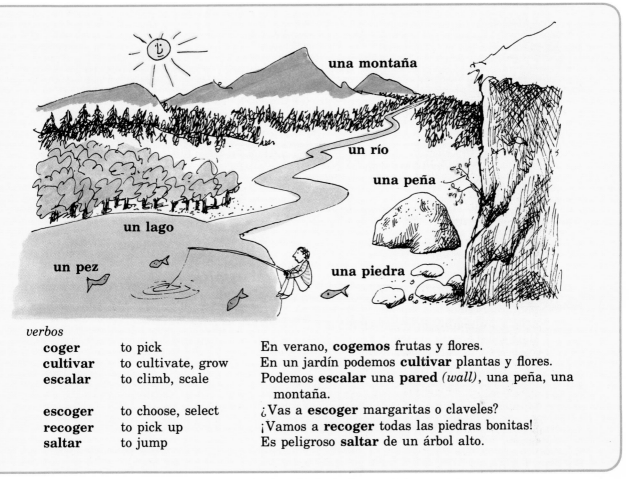

una montaña

un río

una peña

un lago

un pez

una piedra

verbos

coger	to pick	En verano, **cogemos** frutas y flores.
cultivar	to cultivate, grow	En un jardín podemos **cultivar** plantas y flores.
escalar	to climb, scale	Podemos **escalar** una **pared** *(wall)*, una peña, una montaña.
escoger	to choose, select	¿Vas a **escoger** margaritas o claveles?
recoger	to pick up	¡Vamos a **recoger** todas las piedras bonitas!
saltar	to jump	Es peligroso **saltar** de un árbol alto.

The plural of **pez** is **peces.** You may remind the students that a fish that has been caught is **un pescado.**

6. Cuando eras niño(a), ¿te gustaba escalar las paredes? ¿las peñas?

7. ¿Has pescado alguna vez en un río? ¿en el mar? ¿en el océano?

8. ¿Has escalado alguna vez una peña? ¿una montaña? ¿dónde?

9. ¿Has nadado alguna vez en el Océano Atlántico? ¿en el Océano Pacífico? ¿en el Mar Mediterráneo?

10. ¿Has saltado alguna vez de una ventana? ¿de un árbol? ¿de una pared alta?

A. El pluscuamperfecto

Note the *pluperfect* forms of the verb **trabajar.**

Act. 3

INFINITIVE	**trabajar**				
PLUPERFECT					
(yo)	**había**	**trabajado**	(nosotros)	**habíamos**	**trabajado**
(tú)	**habías**	**trabajado**	(vosotros)	**habíais**	**trabajado**
(él, ella, Ud.)	**había**	**trabajado**	(ellos, ellas, Uds.)	**habían**	**trabajado**

Like the present perfect, the pluperfect is a compound tense.
It is formed as follows:

imperfect of **haber**   +   past participle

As in English, the pluperfect is used to describe past events that occurred
before other past events.

Cuando llegué a la estación,
   el tren ya **había salido.**
	*When I arrived at the station, the
	   train **had** already **left**.*

¿**Habías hablado** con esa chica antes? No, no le **había hablado** nunca.	***Had** you **talked** with that girl before?* *No, I **had** never **talked** to her.*
He vendido mi reloj por veinte dólares. Lo **había comprado** por diez. ¡Qué suerte!	*I have sold my watch for twenty dollars.* *I **had bought** it for ten. What luck!*

VARIATION with
**estudiar: Roberto no
había estudiado.**

ACTIVIDAD 2   El examen

Los alumnos de una clase de español sacaron las siguientes notas. ¿Puedes
adivinar quiénes se habían preparado para el examen y quiénes no?

    Roberto (D)   Roberto no se había preparado para el examen.

1. Silvia (A)
2. Mercedes (D)
3. nosotros (A)
4. yo (una buena nota)
5. tú (una mala nota)
6. Felipe (F)
7. Paco y Andrés (F)
8. mis primas (B+)

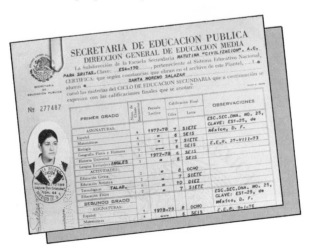

ACTIVIDAD 3   ¡Qué suerte!

Las siguientes personas han vendido ciertas cosas por el doble de lo que
habían pagado. Expresa esto.

> yo (mi reloj: 20 dólares)   He vendido mi reloj por 20 dólares.
>   Lo había comprado por 10 dólares.

1. tú (tu tocadiscos: 40 dólares)
2. yo (mi raqueta: 20 dólares)
3. nosotros (nuestro radio: 30 dólares)
4. Carmen (su bicicleta: 100 dólares)
5. mis primos (su cámara: 40 dólares)
6. tú (tus discos: 20 dólares)
7. Ud. (su ciclomotor *(moped)*: 50 dólares)
8. Uds. (sus libros de español: 16 dólares)
9. Rafael y yo (nuestra grabadora: 120 dólares)
10. Antonio (su moto: 200 dólares)

ACTIVIDAD 4   Siempre se empieza por primera vez

Durante las vacaciones pasadas, las siguientes personas han hecho cosas
que nunca habían hecho antes. Expresa esto según el modelo.

> Paco ha montado a caballo.   Nunca había montado a caballo antes.

1. Carmen ha escalado una peña muy alta.
2. Silvia se ha bañado en el Océano Pacífico.
3. Yo he jugado al ajedrez *(chess)*.
4. Nosotros hemos pescado en un lago.
5. Francisco ha cogido una manzana enorme.
6. Uds. han visto el Mar Mediterráneo.
7. Mi padre ha alquilado un coche.
8. Tú has conducido un coche deportivo.
9. Yo he esquiado en el agua.
10. Nosotros hemos corrido las olas.

75 AÑOS

ICAI   ICADE
UNIVERSIDAD PONTIFICIA COMILLAS

"AYER, HOY, MAÑANA"

"Encuentro
de la Comunidad Universitaria"

VOCABULARIO PRÁCTICO   Otras expresiones de tiempo

esta noche	tonight	**Esta noche** voy a ir al teatro.
anoche	last night	**Anoche** fui al concierto.
anteanoche	the night before (last)	**Anteanoche** fui a la ópera por primera vez. Nunca había ido antes.
ayer	yesterday	**Ayer** esquié.
anteayer	the day before yesterday	**Anteayer** esquié por primera vez. Nunca había esquiado antes.
el (la) . . . pasado(a)	last . . .	**La semana pasada** invité a Marta al cine.
el (la) . . . antepasado(a)	the . . . before (last)	**La semana antepasada** la invité por primera vez. Nunca la había invitado antes.

Since this activity contains several irregular past participles (**vuelto, hecho, visto, roto**), you may want to review these forms.

ACTIVIDAD 5   ¡Demasiado tarde!

Es importante hacer las cosas a tiempo. Describe lo que occurre cuando las siguientes personas no lo hacen.

WB
A1, A2,
A3

SCRIPT
Act. 4, 5

MASTERS
p. 29

☾ Regresas de vacaciones.   Hizo frío.
      Cuando regresaste de vacaciones ya había hecho frío.

1. Llegamos al cine. La película empezó.
2. Mis amigos llegan al teatro. Se vendieron todas las entradas.
3. Tomás llega a la pastelería. Se vendieron todos los pasteles.
4. Felipe llama a Elena para invitarla a un concierto. Ella aceptó la invitación de otro chico.
5. Salgo a dar un paseo. Empezó a llover.
6. Llego a la fiesta de unos amigos. Cenaron.

Para la comunicación

OPTIONAL
May be assigned as homework.

Cosas interesantes

Describe algunas cosas interesantes que hiciste recientemente. Di si antes las habías hecho o no.

WB
Tus vaca-
ciones

SCRIPT
Act. 8

MASTERS
p. 29

TRB

QUIZ
pp. 79–80

WB   Test/Repaso   TEST pp. 81–85

- esquiar en el agua
- jugar al ajedrez
- visitar Disneylandia
- montar a caballo
- asistir al ballet
- conocer al presidente de los Estados Unidos

VARIATION: Describe some interesting things a famous person might do in his or her everyday life.

☾ el viernes pasado, cenar en un restaurante vietnamita
      El viernes pasado cené en un restaurante vietnamita.
      Nunca había cenado en un restaurante vietnamita antes.
      (Había cenado en un restaurante vietnamita antes.)

Variedades La vida: una visión humorística

Miguel Mihura nació° en Madrid en 1905. Escribe obras de teatro que nos dan una visión humorística de la vida. En esta escena de *Mi adorado Juan,* Juan da a Irene, su novia, varias razones, graciosas, para no casarse con ella.

Irene. ¡Juan!

Juan. Hola, Irene.

Irene. ¿Es verdad que se ha ido mi padre?

Juan. Sí. Al café con mi amigo. . . Me esperan allí.

Irene. Entonces. . . ¿le has conquistado?

Juan. Es muy simpático.

Irene. ¿Y has hablado con él de algo?

Juan. Sí, naturalmente. . . De muchas cosas.

Irene. ¿De lo nuestro?

Juan. ¿Qué es lo nuestro?

Irene. De casarnos, Juan.

Juan. Sí, hemos hablado; pero yo no me caso contigo.

Irene. ¿Por qué?

Juan. No puedo casarme, compréndelo. Tú tienes dinero. . . Una casa puesta con lujo. . .° Un coche con chófer. . . Yo no tengo fortuna para sostener este plan de vida.

Irene. Bueno. . . me parece muy bien. . . Viviré como tú vivas. . .°

Juan. No te acostumbrarías,° Irene. Además cuando yo era joven, gané algún dinero y vivo de él, estirándolo° mucho. . . Tal como vivo y según mis cálculos, ese dinero podrá° durarme hasta que cumpla ochenta años. . .° Repartiéndolo° contigo, sólo me alcanzaría° hasta los cincuenta. . . Perdería° por ti casi treinta de vida.

Irene. *(Abrazándole.)* ¡Yo la perdería toda por ti!

Juan. Eso piensas ahora. . . Pero más tarde. . .
Es mejor que rompamos esto nuestro de una manera definitiva.

Irene. ¡No puedes hacer eso, Juan!

Juan. Sí. . . Y debo hacerlo antes que la cosa se complique más. . . Yo lo siento mucho, porque me gustas, porque te quiero, porque me había acostumbrado a pasear contigo por el parque y junto a los barcos del muelle° y a charlar° de mil cosas. . . Pero es preferible dejarlo y ésta será la última vez que nos veamos. . . Adiós, Irene. . . Me voy al café.

Irene. ¡Pero, Juan!

---

nació: *was born*

lujo: *luxury*

viviré como tú vivas: *I will live as you live*
no te acostumbrarías: *You wouldn't get used to it*
estirándolo: *stretching it*
podrá: *will be able*
hasta que cumpla ochenta años: *until I am eighty years old* Repartiéndolo: *Sharing it*
alcanzaría: *would reach* Perdería: *I would lose*

muelle: *dock* charlar: *chat*

Adapted from *Mi adorado Juan*, John Wiley & Sons, New York, 1964. Reprinted by permission of John V. Falconieri and Anthony M. Pasquariello.

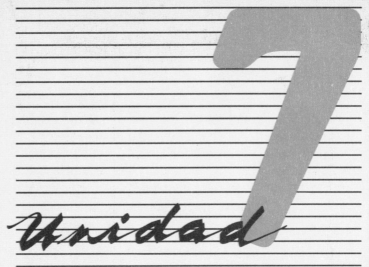

Unidad 7

Mañana será otro día

7.1 **El año 2000**

7.2 **Bobby**

7.3 **Si un día . . .**

7.4 **El perro de Manolito**

VARIEDADES El secreto del jefe indio

OBJECTIVES
Communication
By the end of this unit, students will be able to use Spanish:
- To describe their plans for the future (career, family, contributions to society)
- To make predictions about the future of society
- To describe how they would react in certain situations

Language
This unit concentrates on the forms and uses of the future and the conditional. Other topics include:
- A review of the comparative
- **Para** vs. **por**
- The construction: preposition + infinitive

Culture
The cultural notes of this unit examine a variety of topics, such as Hispanic achievement in the sciences, gypsies and flamenco music, Ecuador.

 Module 15

Lección 1 # El año 2000

Act. 1

El año 2000 es casi mañana . . . o muy pronto. Dentro de veinte años, estaremos en el año dos mil. ¿Cómo será la vida entonces? No podemos saber exactamente qué va a ocurrir en el futuro, pero casi siempre es posible imaginarlo.

Aquí vamos a ver algunas predicciones. ¡Atención: di si estas cosas serán imposibles, posibles o ciertas!

pronto: *soon*
estaremos: *we will be*
    Cómo será: *What will it be like*

ciertas: *certain*

En el año 2000 . . .	imposible	posible	cierto
1. La gente trabajará solamente tres horas al día y tres días a la semana.	☐	☐	☐
2. La gente hablará un idioma universal. (¡Y este idioma no será ni el inglés, ni el francés, sino el español!)	☐	☐	☐

al día: *per day*

3. Los estudiantes no irán al colegio. Estudiarán sus lecciones en casa con su propia computadora.	☐	☐	☐
4. Los cohetes reemplazarán a los aviones como medio de transporte intercontinental. Tomará veinte minutos para ir de Nueva York a Madrid.	☐	☐	☐

irán: *will go*

su propia: *their own*

cohetes: *rockets*
    reemplazarán: *will replace*

This reading may be the basis of a class survey about attitudes towards the future.

	imposible	posible	cierto
5. La gente pasará sus vacaciones en la luna.	☐	☐	☐
6. Los habitantes de otros planetas nos visitarán regularmente.	☐	☐	☐
7. La gente vivirá en edificios de cien pisos y cada casa estará equipada con una computadora.	☐	☐	☐
8. Existirá una cura contra el cáncer.	☐	☐	☐
9. La población de los Estados Unidos será de más de seiscientos millones de habitantes.	☐	☐	☐
10. La gente será más feliz y el mundo será mejor que hoy.	☐	☐	☐

contra: *against*

ANÁLISIS

Ahora anota: 0 punto por cada contestación «imposible».

1 punto por cada contestación «posible».

2 puntos por cada contestación «cierto».

¿Cuántos puntos tienes?

menos de 2: Tú no crees en el progreso.

de 2 a 8: Tú tienes confianza en el futuro de la humanidad.

más de 8: Tú eres un super-optimista.

confianza: *confidence*

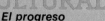

NOTA CULTURAL   OPTIONAL
El progreso

Cuando piensas en el progreso, ¿en qué clase de progreso piensas? Quizá tú piensas en el aterrizaje° de los astronautas norteamericanos en la luna,° en el lanzamiento° de un nuevo satélite por los rusos o en el futuro medio de transporte espacial entre la tierra° y la luna.

Pero el progreso no se limita a los desarrollos° de la tecnología espacial. Hay muchas otras áreas básicas como medicina, física y química° que afectan nuestra vida diaria. En estos dominios° y otros, los científicos hispanos han hecho contribuciones importantes. Algunas de estas contribuciones han merecido el Premio Nóbel.

aterrizaje *landing*   **luna** *moon*   **lanzamiento** *launching*
tierra *earth*   **desarrollos** *developments*   **química** *chemistry*
dominios *domains*

Bernardo Houssay	Argentina	Premio Nobel de Medicina	Por sus estudios de las glándulas
Luis Leloir	Argentina	Premio Nobel de Química	Por sus investigaciones sobre la glucosa
Severo Ochoa	España	Premio Nobel de Medicina	Por sus estudios acerca de las enzimas

— Vocabulario —

adjetivos	**cierto**	sure, certain
	(su) propio	(his, her, its, your, their) own
expresiones	**al día**	per day
	contra	against
	pronto	soon, quickly

CONVERSACIÓN   OPTIONAL

Vamos a hablar de lo que vas a hacer durante el verano próximo.

1. **¿Viajarás?**   Sí (No, no) **viajaré.**
2. **¿Trabajarás?**
3. **¿Visitarás** a tus primos?

4. ¿Te **quedarás** en casa?
5. **¿Irás** a México?
6. **¿Irás** a Puerto Rico?

OBSERVACIÓN

In the above questions you are asked about what you *will do* next summer. The verbs are in a new tense: the *future*.

• In Spanish, does the future tense consist of one or two words?   one word
• In which two letters does the **tú** form end? In which letter does the **yo** form end?
  in **-ás**   in **-é**

Estructuras

A. El futuro

Note the use of the future tense in the sentences below.

Hablaré con el profesor después de la clase.	*I will speak to the teacher after the class.*
Paco **visitará** México el año próximo.	*Paco will visit Mexico next year.*
No **seremos** ricos pero **seremos** felices.	*We will not be rich, but we will be happy.*

The future tense is used to describe actions and events that will happen in the future.

You may have the students observe that all future endings, except **-emos,** have accent marks.

In Spanish, the future is a simple tense: it consists of *one* word.

Note the future forms of **comprar,** paying special attention to the endings.

INFINITIVE	**comprar**	INFINITIVE STEM	FUTURE ENDINGS
FUTURE			
(yo)	**Compraré** un coche deportivo.		**-é**
(tú)	**Comprarás** un reloj.		**-ás**
(él, ella, Ud.)	**Comprará** una guitarra.	**comprar-**	**-á**
(nosotros)	**Compraremos** un bote de vela.		**-emos**
(vosotros)	**Compraréis** una computadora.		**-éis**
(ellos, ellas, Uds.)	**Comprarán** unos pendientes.		**-án**

As in other simple tenses, the forms of the future consist of a stem and an ending.

☞ For most verbs, the future *stem* is the *infinitive*. Since the infinitive always ends in **r,** you always hear the consonant sound /r/ before the future ending.

☞ The future *endings* are the same for all verbs, regular and irregular.

hablar	Tomás nunca **hablará** inglés en España.
leer	Ud. no **leerá** los periódicos norteamericanos.
vivir	Isabel **vivirá** en Madrid un año.
ir	¿Adónde **irá** Ud. para las vacaciones?
ser	¿**Será** Juan millonario algún día?

Aprende en tu propio domicilio esta profesión que tanto te gusta

EMPIEZA A CONSTRUIR TU FUTURO

Nosotros te ayudaremos

ELECTRONICA
FOTOGRAFIA PUERICULTURA
MECANICO DE ELECTRICIDAD
AUTOMOVILES DEL AUTOMOVIL DECORACION
ALBAÑIL

ACTIVIDAD 1   Viajes

Un grupo de estudiantes va a pasar el verano en otros lugares. Di adónde
irá cada uno y qué idioma (¿español, francés o inglés?) hablará.

⟯⟯   Javier (San Juan)   Javier irá a San Juan. Hablará español.

1. Mari-Carmen (Londres)
2. Esteban y Jorge (Santiago)
3. Pilar y Concepción (Quebec)
4. yo (París)
5. tú (Chicago)
6. Uds. (Buenos Aires)
7. nosotros (Montreal)
8. Ud. (Barcelona)

VARIATIONS: with **visitar / vivir en / pasar
un mes en**: Javier visitará (vivirá en, pasará un
mes en) San Juan.

ACTIVIDAD 2   Diálogo: La bola de cristal

Dile el futuro a un compañero, usando los siguientes verbos en frases
afirmativas o negativas. Tu compañero reaccionará a tus predicciones,
según el modelo.

⟯⟯   casarse   Estudiante 1: Un día te casarás. (Nunca te casarás.)
　　　　　　　　Estudiante 2: Tienes razón. (No tienes razón.)
　　　　　　　　　　　　　　Un día me casaré. (Nunca me casaré.)

1. hablar español perfectamente
2. comprar un Rolls Royce
3. conocer a una persona extraordinaria
4. descubrir la cura contra el cáncer
5. conducir un coche deportivo
6. escribir una novela
7. ganar el Premio Nóbel
8. vivir en un palacio
9. escalar los Andes
10. recibir un regalo fabuloso
11. ser millonario(a)
12. ser el (la) presidente(a) de los
    Estados Unidos
13. ser campeón (campeona) de tenis
14. recibir un «Oscar»
15. ir a la China
16. casarse con un(a) millonario(a)
17. visitar el planeta Marte *(Mars)*
18. ser gerente de una carnicería

VOCABULARIO PRÁCTICO
El futuro

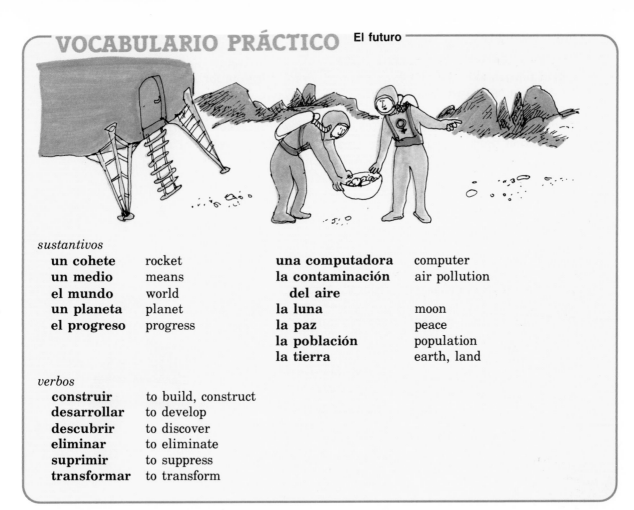

sustantivos

un cohete	rocket	**una computadora**	computer
un medio	means	**la contaminación**	air pollution
el mundo	world	**del aire**	
un planeta	planet	**la luna**	moon
el progreso	progress	**la paz**	peace
		la población	population
		la tierra	earth, land

verbos

construir	to build, construct
desarrollar	to develop
descubrir	to discover
eliminar	to eliminate
suprimir	to suppress
transformar	to transform

ACTIVIDAD 3   El futurismo

The plural of **paz** is **paces.**
You may introduce the
expressions: **hacer las
paces con** (to make peace
with), **¡déjame en paz!**
(leave me in peace, leave
me alone).

Haz predicciones para el año 2000. Haz predicciones para **la gente** en las frases 1–5, para **los hombres** en las frases 6–10 y para **nosotros** en las frases 11–15.

⟩⟩ vivir cien años   En el año dos mil, la gente (no) vivirá cien años.

1. trabajar diez semanas por año
2. ir a la luna los fines de semana
3. viajar en cohete
4. usar «robots»
5. vivir en casas de cristal *(glass)*
6. dormir dos horas al día
7. vivir en paz
8. ser como hoy
9. ser inmortales
10. descubrir otros planetas
11. desarrollar un medio de comunicación con los extraterrestres *(people from space)*
12. construir casas en el fondo *(bottom)* del mar
13. construir edificios de 300 (trescientos) pisos
14. eliminar la contaminación del aire
15. ser muy felices

Lección uno

283

B. Para + sustantivo

Note the use of **para** in the sentences below:

¿Es el telegrama **para** mí?　　　　　　Is the telegram **for** me?

En España, compraré una guitarra　　　In Spain, I will buy a guitar **for** my
　para mi hermana.　　　　　　　　　sister.

Trabajaremos **para** una línea aérea.　We will work **for** an airline company.

The construction **para** + noun is often used to express an objective or goal.
In this case **para** is usually equivalent to the English *for*.
The goal may involve:

- a *person*
  - Trabajo **para el Sr. Díaz.**
- a *thing*
  - ¿Estudiarán tus amigos **para el examen?**
  - Mi mamá comprará una mesa **para el comedor** *(dining room)*.
- a *place*
  - Tomaremos el avión **para Buenos Aires.**
- a *point in time*
  - Tengo que leer el poema **para mañana.**

¡PARA NIÑOS!
Cómodos shorts y frescas camisetas para un verano energético.

ACTIVIDAD 4　¡Un poco de lógica!

En cinco minutos, ¿cuántas frases puedes crear? Usa los elementos de las
columnas A, B, C y D.

A	B	C	D
yo	comprar	un regalo	mí
tú	llevar	un hueso *(bone)*	el examen
mi hermana	necesitar	aspirinas	el profesor
nosotros	estudiar	los verbos	la fiesta
Uds.	tomar	el avión	el perro
Paco y Carmen		unos discos	el cumpleaños de Enrique
		una guitarra	mañana
		el autobús	Madrid
		una caja *(box)*	Nueva York
		de chocolates	la gripe *(flu)*

WB
B1

SCRIPT
Act. 7

MASTERS
p. 30

Compraré un hueso para el perro.

C. Repaso: el comparativo de los adjetivos

To form comparisons with adjectives, Spanish speakers use the following constructions:

(+) **más** + adjective + **que**	En diez años, seremos **más ricos que** hoy.	
(−) **menos** + adjective + **que**	¿Será el mundo **menos loco que** hoy?	
(=) **tan** + adjective + **como**	Soy **tan seria como** mi hermana.	

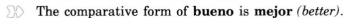 The comparative form of **bueno** is **mejor** *(better)*.

No soy tan **buen** estudiante como Andrés, pero soy **mejor** compañero que él.

*I am not as **good** a student as Andrés, but I am a **better** companion than he.*

ACTIVIDAD 5   Dentro de diez años . . .

Compara la vida dentro de diez años con la vida de hoy, según el modelo, usando el futuro de **ser.**

yo: rico   Yo seré más (menos) rico(a) que hoy.
(Yo seré tan rico[a] como hoy.)

1. yo: serio
2. mis padres: generoso
3. los profesores: tolerante
4. nosotros: racional
5. la vida: fácil
6. los aviones: rápido
7. las medicinas: barato

8. las mujeres: independiente
9. el mundo: peligroso
10. la tierra: fértil
11. la contaminación del aire: fuerte
12. la paz entre las naciones: necesario
13. las computadoras: caro
14. la población mundial: grande

Para la comunicación   OPTIONAL

Tu trabajo futuro

Escribe un pequeño párrafo sobre tu trabajo futuro. Puedes usar las siguientes preguntas como guía.

¿Dónde vivirás?
¿Dónde trabajarás? ¿en un hospital? ¿en una oficina?
    ¿en una fábrica *(factory)*? ¿en una tienda?
    ¿en un laboratorio?
¿Para qué compañía trabajarás?
¿Trabajarás solo(a) o con otras personas?
¿Viajarás mucho?
¿Ganarás mucho dinero?
¿En qué consistirá tu trabajo?

Lección 2 # Bobby

Act. 1

38

La directora del colegio «Eugenio Espejo» de Quito, Ecuador, siempre tiene ideas excelentes.

Este año ella ha tenido la idea de organizar un intercambio con un colegio en San José, California.

intercambio: *exchange*

El colegio norteamericano mandará a Bobby Williams (su mejor estudiante de español) a Quito por tres meses.

Los estudiantes del colegio «Eugenio Espejo» esperan con impaciencia la llegada de Bobby. Por fin . . . ¡el gran día es hoy! Una delegación de cinco alumnos va al aeropuerto a recoger a Bobby Williams.

llegada: *arrival*

Pero, los pobres chicos tienen un problema enorme . . . ¿cómo van a reconocer a Bobby Williams? En efecto, nadie tiene una foto de Bobby.

reconocer: *to recognize*
En efecto: *In fact*

Cada uno tiene una idea de cómo será Bobby. Pero cada idea es diferente.

Marina Ortega: Yo reconoceré a Bobby en seguida. Será un chico alto, moreno y atlético.

en seguida: *right away*

Rocío Villanueva: ¡No! No será moreno, será rubio como todos los norteamericanos.

Roberto García: ¡Ridículo! Reconoceré a Bobby por su ropa. Llevará blue-jeans, botas y una camisa de cuadros.

botas: *boots*
camisa de cuadros: *checked shirt*

Francisco Eugenio de Santa Cruz y Espejo (1747-1795) was an Ecuadorian doctor, thinker, and journalist of Indian ancestry. His writings contributed to the development of the independence movement in South America. He died in prison.

Héctor Montero: Y un sombrero de cowboy, ¿verdad? Eso es absurdo. Yo reconoceré a Bobby por sus maletas. Tendrá una guitarra y una bolsa al hombro.

bolsa al hombro: *backpack*

Consuelo Pérez: Yo digo que Bobby tendrá anteojos de sol y una bufanda.

bufanda: *scarf*

Finalmente llega el avión de San Francisco. Hay muchísimos pasajeros. Los pasajeros salen unos tras otros ... ¿Cuál de ellos es Bobby Williams?

Hay muchos turistas, hombres de negocios, personas de edad ... pero no aparece Bobby Williams. Finalmente una joven llega. Es de estatura mediana, con pelo de color castaño y está vestida como todo el mundo.

hombres de negocios: *businessmen*
personas de edad: *older persons*
aparece: *appears*
estatura mediana: *medium height*
vestida: *dressed*

—¡Hola! Me llamo Bobby Williams ... ¿Son Uds. alumnos del Colegio «Eugenio Espejo»? Yo los reconocí en seguida. Pero, ¡Uds. parecen sorprendidos! ¿Por qué?

sorprendidos: *surprised*

¿Dónde está el colegio Eugenio Espejo? ¿Cómo se llama el primer estudiante de intercambio? Según Marina, ¿cómo será Bobby? ¿Según Rocío, ¿cómo será Bobby? Según Roberto, ¿qué llevará Bobby? Según Héctor, ¿qué tendrá Bobby? Según Consuelo, ¿qué tendrá Bobby? ¿Por qué están sorprendidos los chicos al ver a Bobby?

NOTAS CULTURALES

¿Por qué se llama «Ecuador»?

Situado en la costa occidental de la América del Sur, entre Colombia y el Perú, el Ecuador es uno de los países más pintorescos° de Latinoamérica.

¿Por qué se llama Ecuador? Porque lo cruza la línea equinoccial o el ecuador,° que es una línea imaginaria que divide el mundo en dos hemisferios: el norte y el sur.

Quito, su capital, es una ciudad colonial de las más bellas, llena de iglesias, edificios y monumentos que reflejan° la gloria del pasado.

Otra ciudad de gran importancia es Guayaquil. Esta ciudad, muy comercial y activa, es el puerto° principal del país.

La variedad del Ecuador es asombrosa.° ¡Qué contraste entre la costa, la sierra° y el «oriente» o región amazónica! Si quieres dar un paseo en la época colonial, o la moderna o la prehistórica, ¡visita el Ecuador!

pintorescos *picturesque* **ecuador** *equator* **reflejan** *reflect*
puerto *port* **asombrosa** *amazing* **sierra** *mountain range*

The Galápagos Islands, located in the Pacific Ocean about 600 miles off the coast of Ecuador, constitute a national park known for its particular wildlife: iguanas, giant turtles, flamingos, albatrosses, and many other sea birds.

Vocabulario

sustantivos	**un hombre de negocios**	businessman	**una llegada**	arrival
	un intercambio	exchange	**una persona de edad**	older person
			una salida	departure
verbo	**reconocer**	to recognize		
expresiones	**en efecto**	in fact		
	en seguida	immediately		

Reconocer is conjugated like **conocer: reconozco.**

¿Dónde está situado el Ecuador? ¿Qué es el ecuador? ¿Cómo se llama la capital del Ecuador? ¿Qué tipo de ciudad es Guayaquil? ¿Cómo se llama la región amazónica del Ecuador?

Estructuras

A. Futuros irregulares

A few verbs have irregular futures. Such verbs have:

—an irregular stem (that is, a stem that is different from the infinitive)

—regular future endings: **-é, -ás, -á, -emos, -éis, -án.**

Act. 3

VERBS	FUTURE STEMS	
decir	**dir-**	¿**Dirás** la verdad?
hacer	**har-**	**Haré** un viaje a Francia.
poder	**podr-**	**Podremos** visitar París.
poner	**pondr-**	Me **pondré** una camisa azul.
salir	**saldr-**	Carlos **saldrá** con una chica mexicana.
tener	**tendr-**	**Tendremos** que aprender español.
venir	**vendr-**	Mis primos **vendrán** mañana.
querer	**querr-**	Mis amigos **querrán** ver a sus amigos.
haber (hay)	**habr-**	¿**Habrá** mucha gente en la fiesta?
saber	**sabr-**	¿**Sabrás** tú los futuros irregulares para el examen?

Note that all future stems end in the consonant **r**.   You may use the sentences above for extra practice of future forms by suggesting different subjects. **nosotros: ¿Diremos la verdad?**

ACTIVIDAD 1   En el aeropuerto

¿Cómo podemos reconocer a personas que no conocemos? No es difícil cuando esas personas deciden ponerse ropa distintiva. Di qué ropa se pondrán los siguientes estudiantes para ser reconocidos.

⇨ Juan: una chaqueta azul   Juan se pondrá una chaqueta azul.

1. Felipe: una corbata roja
2. Carmen: un vestido amarillo
3. yo: unos pantalones verdes
4. tú: un sombrero de cowboy
5. nosotros: un impermeable *(raincoat)*
6. mis amigos: un poncho de colores

ADDITIONAL CUES: **Ud.: una camisa negra; Uds.: suéteres violetas; Jaime y yo: sombreros mexicanos.**

ACTIVIDAD 2 Dentro de diez años . . .

¿Cuántos años tendrás dentro de diez años? Unos veinte y cinco, más o menos . . . ¿Puedes imaginar cómo será tu vida entonces? Di cuáles de las siguientes cosas harás.

This activity contains both regular and irregular verbs.

〰️ tener un coche   Dentro de diez años, (no) tendré un coche.

1. estar casado(a)
2. tener hijos
3. tener un trabajo de mucha responsabilidad
4. vivir en un apartamento cómodo (comfortable)
5. ser independiente
6. hacer muchos viajes
7. hacer cosas interesantes
8. ser alguien importante
9. salir mucho
10. saber correr las olas
11. saber hablar español muy bien
12. saber pilotar un avión
13. tener un bote de vela (sailboat)
14. tener un coche deportivo

ACTIVIDAD 3 Preguntas personales

Vamos a hablar del verano próximo.

1. ¿Harás un viaje? ¿adónde? ¿con quién?
2. ¿Qué harás si no haces un viaje?
3. ¿Tendrás trabajo? ¿dónde? ¿de qué tipo?
4. ¿Saldrás mucho? ¿con quién?
5. ¿Podrás usar el coche de tus padres?
6. ¿Tendrás que ayudar en casa?
7. ¿Vendrán tus primos a tu casa?

Ask about student responses.
¿Hará un viaje Jim?

ACTIVIDAD 4 Optimismo

Un optimista piensa que la realidad de hoy cambiará por algo mejor. Haz predicciones optimistas según el modelo.

〰️ No soy rico(a).   No soy rico(a) ahora pero pronto seré rico(a).

1. Mis padres no tienen mucho dinero.
2. Paco no tiene amigos.
3. Dice mentiras.
4. Carmen dice cosas estúpidas.
5. Cometemos muchos errores.
6. No puedo usar la moto de Juan.
7. No podemos salir tarde.
8. Enrique no quiere salir conmigo.
9. Susana no sale con Roberto.
10. Mis amigos no salen los sábados.
11. No tenemos dinero.
12. Mis hermanas no saben conducir.
13. Hay mucha contaminación del aire.
14. Hay muchos problemas en el mundo.

B. El uso del futuro para indicar probabilidad

Note the use of the future in the following sentences.

¿Qué hora es?	*What time is it?*
No sé. **Serán** las dos.	*I don't know.* **It is probably (it may be)** *two o'clock.*
¿Cuántos años tiene el profesor?	*How old is the teacher?*
Tendrá unos cuarenta años.	*He is probably (he may be) about forty.*

In Spanish the future is sometimes used to express a guess about
the present.

ACTIVIDAD 5   En busca del culpable *(Looking for the culprit)*

Cuando Carlos volvió de vacaciones, descubrió que alguien había pintado
(painted) su cuarto de rojo. Sospecha *(He suspects)* de muchas personas. Haz
el papel de Carlos.

> Felipe   ¿Será Felipe el culpable?

1. Paco
2. Carmen
3. tu hermano
4. Uds.
5. tú
6. Conchita y Elena

ACTIVIDAD 6   El nuevo profesor

El director de la escuela anuncia que habrá un nuevo profesor. Cada
alumno trata de adivinar cómo es el profesor y cuántos años tiene. Haz el
papel de los siguientes alumnos.

> Carmen (muy guapo / 25)   Según Carmen, el nuevo profesor será muy guapo.
> Tendrá unos 25 años.

1. Felipe (estricto / 60)
2. Elena (brillante / 40)
3. Manuel (un dictador / 50)
4. Silvia (como todos los profesores / 35)

ACTIVIDAD 7   ¡Un poco de psicología!

Explica cómo se sienten las personas de la columna A, usando los
elementos de las columnas B y C en frases lógicas.

A	B	C
tú	enfermo	tener una cita
Carlos	cansado	tener gripe *(flu)*
Marisol	contento	tener un problema serio
nosotros	agitado	tener que hablar en público
mis amigos	ocupado	tener mucho que hacer
Paco y Enrique	preocupado	acabar de jugar al tenis
Ud. y yo	pálido	acabar de perder el partido de fútbol

> Paco y Enrique están cansados. Acabarán de jugar al tenis.

C. *Por* + sustantivo

The construction **por** + noun has many different uses.
It may express:

- *duration*

  for, during   Estaré en Puerto Rico **por dos semanas.**

  in   Te veré **por la tarde.**

- *manner or means*

  by   Mandaré las maletas **por barco.**

       Te llamaré **por teléfono.**

       Mandarás el paquete **por correo.**

       Reconoceré a Juan **por su sombrero.**

- *movement*

  along   Damos un paseo **por la avenida** José Antonio.

  through   Si no tengo la llave, entraré **por la ventana.**

  by   El tren pasará **por Nueva York** sin parar.

  around   ¿Te gusta caminar **por la ciudad?**

- *exchange*

  for   Te venderé mi bicicleta **por cincuenta dólares.**

  in exchange for   ¿Quieres cambiarme tu tocadiscos **por mi guitarra?**

- *cause, motive*

  for   Me casaré **por amor.**

  because of   Me preocupo mucho **por ti.**

  on behalf of   Hablaré con el profesor **por los otros alumnos.**

  for the sake of   Haré lo imposible **por mis amigos.**

  instead of   José trabaja **por Antonio.**

Por is also used in certain expressions:

ciento **por ciento**	one hundred **percent**
cien kilómetros **por hora**	one hundred kilometers **per hour**

Although both **por** and **para** often correspond to the English preposition *for,* they have distinct uses and cannot be substituted for one another.

ACTIVIDAD 8   En la estación

Di cómo reconocerás a los siguientes pasajeros.

⚭   Alberto llevará una corbata amarilla.   Lo reconoceré por su corbata amarilla.

1. Carmen tendrá una guitarra.
2. Felipe viajará con su perro.
3. Esteban llevará una maleta gris.
4. Isabel y Susana llevarán un bolso negro.
5. Carlos traerá un saco de dormir (sleeping bag).
6. María y Ana llevarán pendientes de oro.

ACTIVIDAD 9   Despachos internacionales (International shipments)   OPTIONAL

Imagina que trabajas para una compañía de despachos internacionales
situada en Nueva York. Debes despachar las siguientes cosas y animales.
¿Cómo (por avión, por barco, por autobús, por tren) los despacharás?

⚭   una guitarra a Filadelfia   La despacharé por tren (autobús).

1. un tocadiscos a Miami
2. un piano a Los Ángeles
3. un televisor a Chicago
4. unos discos a Buenos Aires
5. un elefante a Río de Janeiro
6. un perro a Madagascar
7. un pájaro a Tokio
8. una boa a Vancouver

Since several answers are usually possible, students
may be asked to select the fastest means of transportation, the least expensive, the most expensive,
etc.

ACTIVIDAD 10   Preguntas personales

1. ¿Llamas a tus amigos por teléfono a menudo?
2. Cuando vas de vacaciones, ¿te vas por una semana? ¿quince días? ¿un mes?
3. ¿Te preocupas mucho por tus amigos?
4. ¿Cuál es más barato, mandar cartas a Europa por avión o por barco?
5. ¿Estudias mucho por la tarde? ¿por la mañana?
6. ¿Das muchos paseos por las calles? ¿por el campo?
7. ¿Te gusta dar paseos por los bosques? ¿por los parques?
8. ¿Adónde vas los sábados por la tarde?
9. ¿Te casarás por amor o por dinero?
10. ¿Por cuánto venderás tu bicicleta? ¿y tus discos?
11. ¿Haces muchas cosas por tus hermanos? ¿por tus amigos?
12. ¿Tienes mucho respeto por tus amigos? ¿por tus profesores?

Para la comunicación

Tu futuro

Imagina cómo será tu vida:
- dentro de cinco años
- dentro de veinte años
- dentro de cuarenta años

Para cada época, escribe un párrafo de cinco o seis líneas, usando los siguientes verbos: **ser / estar / tener / hacer / saber / tener que / poder.**

Dentro de cinco años, estaré casado(a) . . .

This text may serve as the basis for a class attitude survey.

STRUCTURE TO OBSERVE: the conditional. You may have the students note the examples of this form in the text. They can identify the stem and the **tú** ending.

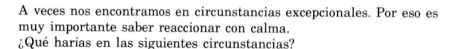

Lección 3   Si un día . . .

A veces nos encontramos en circunstancias excepcionales. Por eso es muy importante saber reaccionar con calma.
¿Qué harías en las siguientes circunstancias?

reaccionar: *to react*
harías: *would you do*

1. Ves una casa que está ardiendo . . .

   A. Entrarías a la casa para salvar a los ocupantes.
   B. Llamarías a los bomberos.
   C. Sacarías fotos del incendio.

ardiendo: *burning*
Entrarías: *You would enter*
salvar: *save*
bomberos: *firemen*
incendio: *fire*

2. Te paseas por un puente alto y ves a alguien que se ahoga . . .

   A. Saltarías del puente para ayudar a la víctima.
   B. Bajarías a la orilla y tomarías un bote para ayudar a la víctima.
   C. Te marcharías sin hacer nada.

puente: *bridge*
se ahoga: *is drowning*

orilla: *bank*

3. Estás solo(a) en una casa aislada. A las dos de la mañana, oyes unos ruidos misteriosos afuera . . .

aislada: *isolated*

   ¡TLONK!

   A. Tomarías una pistola y dispararías en la oscuridad.
   B. Encenderías la luz para identificar el ruido.
   C. Te esconderías debajo de la cama.

dispararías: *would shoot*

4. Ganas diez mil dólares en la lotería . . .

   A. Irías a Las Vegas para probar fortuna.
   B. Depositarías la mitad del dinero en el banco y gastarías el resto.
   C. Gastarías todo el dinero en seguida.

probar fortuna: *to try your luck*
mitad: *half*

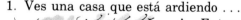

5. Estás en el banco en el momento de un robo . . .

    A. Perseguirías a los bandidos.
    B. Anotarías el número del coche de los bandidos.
    C. Te marcharías del banco muy rápidamente.

robo: robbery
Perseguirías: You would chase
Anotarías: You would note

6. Descubres un tesoro fabuloso en una casa abandonada . . .

tesoro: treasure

    A. Lo compartirías inmediatamente con tus amigos.
    B. Les dirías a tus padres la buena noticia.
    C. Guardarías el tesoro sin decirle nada a nadie.

7. Estás pescando con un amigo, estalla una tormenta y el barco se hunde. Tu amigo está herido y estás a cinco kilómetros de la costa . . .

estalla una tormenta: a storm breaks out
se hunde: sinks
herido: injured

    A. Nadarías hasta la costa con tu amigo.
    B. Buscarías un madero para sostenerse tú y tu amigo.
    C. Nadarías solito hasta la costa.

madero: plank
sostenerse: support
solito: alone

INTERPRETACIÓN

- Si has escogido la letra «A» cuatro veces o más, eres una persona dinámica, valiente y generosa. Pero eres demasiado impulsivo. ¡Piensa antes de actuar!

valiente: brave
actuar: acting

- Si has escogido la letra «B» cuatro veces o más, eres una persona prudente. Actúas con calma. Tus amigos pueden contar contigo.
- Si has escogido la respuesta «C» cuatro veces o más, no tienes los reflejos necesarios para actuar racionalmente en casos de urgencia.
- Si no perteneces a ninguna de estas categorías, eres como todo el mundo: un poco indeciso frente a lo excepcional.

contar contigo: count on you
reflejos: reflexes

NOTA CULTURAL

En busca de tesoros

En los cuentos infantiles, a menudo el héroe o la heroína está buscando un tesoro escondido y lo encuentra.

¿Existen estos tesoros escondidos? ¡Claro que sí! Y uno de los lugares donde hay muchos tesoros escondidos está entre Cuba, la Florida y la mayor de las islas Bahamas. Esta región contiene restos° de naufragios° de muchos barcos españoles que eran parte de una famosa "flota° de plata".° Por más de dos siglos,° estos barcos, llamados "galeones", llevaron no solamente plata, sino también oro y esmeraldas° de México y del Perú a España. A causa de° los huracanes, el viaje era muy peligroso y muchos barcos naufragaron° en los arrecifes° lejos de los cayos° de la Florida. Muchas veces la valiosa° carga° de oro, plata y esmeraldas ha permanecido° allí para los buscadores de tesoros.°

Mel Fisher es buscador de tesoros. Más de mil personas invirtieron° en su proyecto de buscar el galeón español "Nuestra Señora de Atocha", que se hundió° en 1662, en la costa de la Florida.

El 20 de julio de 1985, después de 16 años de búsqueda°, encontraron el tesoro y, en ese año, encontraron 177 barras° de oro, 900 barras de plata y miles de monedas y objetos. En 1986 encontraron más de 2.500 esmeraldas, 35 barras de oro, 85 barras de plata y otros objetos.

A pesar de que estos descubrimientos han sido° valiosos, las personas dedicadas a esta exploración consideran que no han encontrado todo el tesoro

de "Nuestra Señora de Atocha." Y que, además,° hay muchos otros barcos con tesoros insospechados.°

¿Quién sabe? Tal vez un día tú irás en busca de tesoros escondidos.

restos *remains* **naufragios** *shipwrecks* **flota** *fleet* **plata** *silver* **siglos** *centuries* **esmeraldas** *emeralds* **A causa de** *Because of* **naufragaron** *were wrecked* **arrecifes** *reefs* **cayos** *keys* **valiosa** *valuable* **carga** *cargo* **permanecido** *remained* **buscadores de tesoros** *treasure hunters* **invirtieron** *invested* **se hundió** *sunk* **búsqueda** *searching* **barras** *bars* **han sido** *have been* **además** *in addition* **insospechados** *unsuspected*

¿Dónde se puede encontrar tesoros escondidos? ¿Qué es un «galeón»? ¿Qué llevaban los galeones? ¿Por qué era peligroso el viaje de los galeones? ¿Se cree que todos los barcos con tesoros en el fondo del mar ya han sido descubiertos?

Vocabulario

sustantivos	**un puente**	bridge	**una mitad**	half
	un tesoro	treasure		
adjetivo	**valiente**	courageous, brave		
verbos	**actuar**	to act		
	entrar (en, a)	to enter		
	reaccionar	to react		
expresión	**probar fortuna**	to try one's luck		

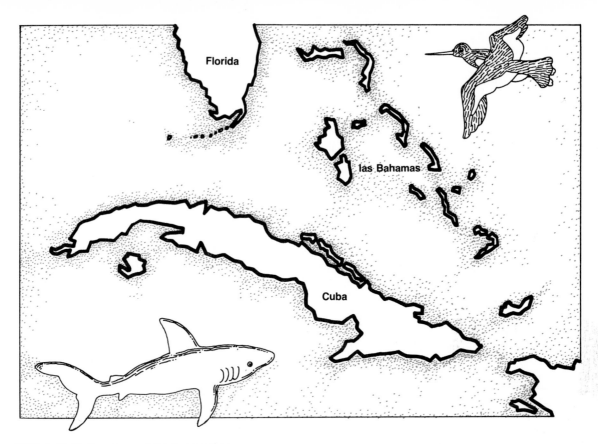

Florida

las Bahamas

Cuba

NOTE: In Florida Keys, the word "key" comes from the Spanish **cayo** (reef).

CONVERSACIÓN   OPTIONAL

Imagina que puedes hacer solamente una de las siguientes cosas. ¿Cuál harías?

1. ¿**Comprarías** una bicicleta o una guitarra?
   Compraría una bicicleta (una guitarra).
2. ¿**Visitarías** México o España?
3. ¿**Vivirías** en una ciudad o en el campo?

OBSERVACIÓN

In the above questions, you are asked what you *would do* if you had certain choices.
The verbs used are in the *conditional*.

- Does the conditional consist of one or two words in Spanish?   one word
- In which three letters does the **tú** form end?   -ías
- In which two letters does the **yo** form end?   -ía

Estructuras

A. El condicional

Note the use of the conditional in the sentences below:

Con cincuenta dólares, me **compraría** una guitarra.	*With fifty dollars, I **would buy** myself a guitar.*
Haríamos un viaje a México, si . . .	*We **would take** a trip to Mexico if . . .*
¿**Te gustaría** vivir en una isla desierta?	***Would** you **like** to live on a deserted island?*

Forms

1. In Spanish the conditional is a *simple verb form:* it consists of *one* word. Note the conditional forms of **comprar**, paying special attention to the endings.

INFINITIVE CONDITIONAL	comprar	FUTURE STEM	CONDITIONAL ENDINGS
(yo)	**Compraría** un avión.		-**ía**
(tú)	**Comprarías** un coche.		-**ías**
(él, ella, Ud.)	**Compraría** un perro.	**comprar-**	-**ía**
(nosotros)	**Compraríamos** una moto.		-**íamos**
(vosotros)	**Compraríais** una grabadora.		-**íais**
(ellos, ellas, Uds.)	**Comprarían** una calculadora.		-**ían**

As with other simple verb forms, the forms of the conditional consist of a stem and endings. The conditional is formed as follows:

> stem of the future + conditional endings

You may remind the students that for most verbs the future stem is the infinitive.

Note that the conditional endings for all verbs are the same as the imperfect endings of **-er** and **-ir** verbs.

2. Verbs with an irregular future stem have the same stem in the conditional.

decir	**diría**	salir	**saldría**
hacer	**haría**	saber	**sabría**
poder	**podría**	tener	**tendría**
poner	**pondría**	venir	**vendría**
querer	**querría**	haber (hay)	**habría**

Uses

1. The conditional is used to express what would happen under certain conditions.
2. It is also used to soften requests.

Compare

(present)	Me gusta viajar.	*I like to travel.*
(conditional)	**Me gustaría** viajar contigo.	***I would like** to travel with you.*
(present)	¿Puedes ayudarme, José?	*José, can you help me?*
(conditional)	**¿Podría Ud.** ayudarme, Sr. Chávez?	***Could you** help me, Sr. Chávez?*

ACTIVIDAD 1 Con un coche

Estos estudiantes norteamericanos dicen adónde irían y lo que visitarían con un coche. Explica el plan de cada uno usando el condicional de **ir** y **visitar.**

Linda (Washington: la Casa Blanca)
> Linda iría a Washington. Visitaría la Casa Blanca.

1. Silvia (San Antonio: el Álamo)
2. Mis amigos (San Francisco: la misión Dolores)
3. Uds. (Boston: el barco «Constitución»)
4. yo (el Canadá: Quebec)
5. tú (México: Acapulco)
6. nosotros (California: Santa Bárbara)
7. Tom y Jack (Nueva York: el Museo del Barrio)
8. María (Florida: San Agustín)

ACTIVIDAD 2 El (la) presidente(a)

¿Serás presidente algún día? ¿Por qué no? De las siguientes cosas, di cuáles harías y cuáles no.

vivir en la Casa Blanca   (No) viviría en la Casa Blanca.

1. pintar (*to paint*) la Casa Blanca de azul
2. comprar un Mercedes para todos los miembros de mi familia
3. viajar mucho
4. hablar en público a menudo
5. desarrollar los armamentos nucleares
6. invitar al presidente de México a la Casa Blanca
7. ir a África
8. transformar la sociedad
9. darles dinero a los pobres
10. mantener la paz por todo el mundo
11. construir palacios y monumentos en mi honor
12. suprimir los impuestos (*taxes*)

¿Le gustaría ir a la piscina sin salir de su casa?

Hemos conjugado lo mejor de la naturaleza y de la ciudad para que usted y su familia disfruten de un piso amplio. Exclusivamente, para usted y los suyos. 12.000 m² de tranquilidad en la mejor zona de Sevilla.

Note that item 10 has an irregular conditional stem: **mantendr-**.

ACTIVIDAD 3   Diálogo: Preferencias

Pregúntales a tus compañeros si les gustaría hacer las siguientes cosas.

> vivir en una isla desierta
>> Estudiante 1: ¿Te gustaría vivir en una isla desierta?
>> Estudiante 2: Sí, me gustaría mucho.
>>> (No, no me gustaría. Nunca viviría en una isla desierta.)

1. ser presidente de los Estados Unidos
2. vivir en otro planeta
3. comer ranas (*frogs*)
4. asistir a una corrida de toros
5. conducir un coche a 100 millas por hora
6. viajar en un cohete
7. estar en un submarino
8. nadar con tiburones (*sharks*)

VARIATION with the plural:
¿Pondrían Uds. el dinero en el banco?
Sí (No, no) pondríamos...

ACTIVIDAD 4   Diálogo: Con 1.000 dólares

Supón que todos los alumnos van a recibir unos mil dólares cada uno(a).
Pregúntales a tus compañeros qué harían y qué no harían.

> poner el dinero en el banco
>> Estudiante 1: ¿Pondrías el dinero en el banco?
>> Estudiante 2: Sí (No, no) lo pondría en el banco.

1. hacer un viaje
2. dar una fiesta fabulosa
3. dejar la escuela
4. ir de vacaciones
5. salir para España
6. salir para Francia

ACTIVIDAD 5   ¡Emergencias!   OPTIONAL

Cada uno reacciona diferentemente en caso de emergencia. Lee la lista de
emergencias. En tu opinión, di qué cosas (B) harían las personas (A) en
estas emergencias.

Lista de emergencias:

	A	**B**
1. Hay un incendio (*fire*).	yo	quedarse quieto(a)
2. Hay un huracán (*hurricane*).	mi papá	escaparse
3. Hay una explosión nuclear.	un loco	saltar por la ventana
4. Los extraterrestres llegan.	las personas valientes	sacar fotos
5. Un platillo volante (*flying saucer*)		llamar a la policía
aterriza (*lands*).		rezar (*to pray*) a Dios
		ponerse nervioso(a)
		gritar (*to scream*)
		buscar refugio (*shelter*)
		llevarse el dinero
		leer el horóscopo
		mirar lo que ocurre

WB
A1, A2, A3

SCRIPT
Act. 4, 5, 6, 7, 9

MASTERS
p. 32

∅⟩ Hay un temblor.   Yo (no) me pondría nervioso(a).
Mi papá. . .

B. Repaso: preposición + infinitivo

Note the use of the infinitives in the following sentences:

Infinitive constructions with **al, antes de, después de** are presented on p. 336.

Ahorro mi dinero **para comprar** un coche.   *I save my money in order to buy a car.*
Carlos se divierte **en vez de estudiar.**   *Carlos is having fun instead of studying.*
¿Es posible ser feliz **sin tener** amigos?   *Is it possible to be happy without having friends?*

In Spanish, the infinitive may be used after prepositions such as **para** (*to,
in order to*), **sin** (*without*), and **en vez de** (*instead of*).

ACTIVIDAD 6   Expresión personal

This may be done as a written activity in small groups.

Di para qué (*for what reason*) te gustaría hacer o tener las siguientes
cosas. Completa las frases con **para** + infinitivo. ¡Usa tu imaginación!

∅⟩ Me gustaría tener dinero . . .
Me gustaría tener dinero para comprar una moto, para ayudar a
los pobres, para dárselo a mis amigos o . . .

1. Me gustaría tener un coche . . .   4. Me gustaría ser presidente . . .
2. Me gustaría asistir a la universidad . . .   5. Me gustaría vivir cien años . . .
3. Me gustaría hablar español muy bien . . .   6. Me gustaría casarme . . .

Olímpica Stereo
¡Para bailar se necesita! ⓐ
Barranquilla · Bogotá · Cartagena · Montería · Santa Marta · Sincelejo

Lección tres
303

ACTIVIDAD 7   Los distraídos (*The absent-minded ones*)

Las siguientes personas son un poco distraídas. Se olvidan de hacer cosas
importantes. Expresa esto usando la construcción **sin** + infinitivo en las
frases de uno a siete y la construcción **en vez de** + infinitivo en las frases
de ocho a doce.

⟯⟩   Carlos se va del restaurante pero no paga.

Carlos se va del restaurante sin pagar.

⟯⟩   Felipe pone agua en el coche pero no pone gasolina.

Felipe pone agua en el coche en vez de poner gasolina.

1. Hablo pero no pienso.
2. Mi papá va a México pero no lleva
   pasaporte.
3. Mis amigos salen pero no dicen adiós.
4. Tú entras en la sala pero no saludas a
   tu familia.
5. Los alumnos quieren contestar pero no
   comprenden la pregunta.
6. El Sr. Vargas sale pero no se pone la
   corbata.
7. Me acuesto pero no me baño.
8. Pones sal en el té pero no pones
   azúcar.
9. Juego pero no estudio.
10. Mi hermano mira la televisión pero no
    aprende los verbos.
11. Mari-Carmen se divierte pero no
    ayuda a su hermanita.
12. Voy al cine pero no voy a la escuela.

Viaje 500 Kms. con coche... sin perder el sueño.

Auto-Expreso: La mejor idea sobre automóviles.

RENFE

ACTIVIDAD 8   Expresión personal

Expresa unas ideas personales completando las siguientes frases con infinitivos. ¡Usa tu imaginación!

⋙   Es imposible ser feliz sin . . .

>Es imposible ser feliz sin tener amigos, tener dinero . . .

1. No es posible sacar buenas notas sin . . .
2. No es posible ganar dinero sin . . .
3. No es posible divertirse sin . . .
4. A veces me divierto en vez de . . .
5. A veces me quedo en casa en vez de . . .
6. A veces me gustaría . . . en vez de . . .

WB
31, B2

Para la comunicación

OPTIONAL   May be assigned as homework.

WB
El con-
curso...

SCRIPT

Act. 10

MASTERS
p. 32

TRB

QUIZ
p. 90

El gordo (*The top prize*)

Imagina que las personas siguientes sacan el gordo (*biggest prize*) de la lotería. Describe qué haría cada uno (o qué no haría) en un párrafo de seis frases.

- yo
- mi mejor amigo(a)
- mis padres

⋙   Yo haría un viaje a Puerto Rico. Tomaría el sol en la playa . . .

Lección 4 El perro de Manolito

Act. 1

Para su cumpleaños, Manolito ha recibido un lindo perrito blanco. Es un perro inteligente, vivo, listo, que solamente tiene un defecto. Cuando Manolito no lo mira, el perro se escapa a la calle.
Hoy, otra vez, Manolito busca a su perro por todos lados y no puede encontrarlo.
¿Qué le habrá pasado a su perro?
Manolito está muy preocupado por él. Manolito está angustiado.

Note the use of the personal **a** with an animal, because of the close relationship between Manolito and his dog.

vivo: *lively*

por todos lados: *everywhere*

habrá pasado: *could have happened*
angustiado: *anguished*

¡Mi pobre perro! ¿Lo habrá atropellado un coche? o se habrá caído en un pozo . . .

atropellado: *run over*
pozo: *well*

o se habrá caído en el río y se habrá ahogado . . .

ahogado: *drowned*

o los gitanos lo habrán encontrado y se lo habrán llevado con ellos . . .

gitanos: *gypsies*

o un guardia civil lo habrá llevado a la estación de policía . . .

¿Qué ha recibido Manolito para su cumpleaños? ¿Qué cualidades tiene el perro de Manolito? ¿Qué defecto tiene? ¿Por qué está muy preocupado Manolito? ¿Dónde está escondido el perro?

o habrá entrado en la carnicería y el carnicero lo habrá encerrado en el sótano por haber robado las salchichas . . .

¡Ay qué lástima! ¡Qué será de mí, sin mi perro! ¡Mi primero y único perro!

Manolito llora. Con tristeza va a su cuarto y se tira en la cama . . . y despierta a su perro que dormía tranquilamente debajo de la cama. ¡Qué alivio!

carnicero: *butcher*
encerrado: *locked*
  sótano: *basement*
  por haber robado: *for stealing*
  salchichas: *sausages*
¡Qué será de mí!: *What will become of me!*

llora: *cries*
  tristeza: *sadness*
  se tira: *throws himself*
¡Qué alivio!: *What a relief!*

NOTAS CULTURALES OPTIONAL

La guardia civil

En España, la guardia civil es una clase especial de la policía. Llevan un sombrero muy distinto, una moda del siglo XVIII.

Los gitanos

Hay algunos gitanos° en España, especialmente en el sur. ¿De dónde vinieron los gitanos? En realidad no se sabe. Muchos historiadores° piensan que vinieron del noroeste de la India. Eran un pueblo nómada° con cultura e idioma propios. La música popular española tiene mucha influencia gitana. Una de sus contribuciones más importantes es la creación del flamenco. El flamenco es un baile, una música y un canto° típico de los gitanos. Se cree que° el flamenco se originó° en el "cante hondo"° de los gitanos de Andalucía. Para mediados° del siglo XIX (diecinueve), el flamenco ya se había convertido en° un arte popular.

gitanos *gypsies* **historiadores** *historians* **pueblo nómada** *nomadic people* **canto** *song* **Se cree que** *It is believed that* **se originó** *originated* **cante hondo** *deep song* **mediados** *middle* **se había convertido en** *had become*

Vocabulario

sustantivo	**la tristeza**	sadness
verbos	**llorar**	to cry
	robar	to rob, to take away
expresiones	**por todos lados**	everywhere, on all sides
	¡qué alivio!	what a relief!
	¡qué será de mí!	what will become of me!

EXTRA VOCAB.: **las razas de perros más populares en los países hispánicos: pastor alemán** (German shepherd); **perro de aguas** (spaniel); **perro sabueso** (beagle); **galgo** (greyhound); **perro de lanas** (poodle); **pachón inglés** (English setter); **perro lobo** (wolfhound).

Vamos a anticipar un poco . . . Vamos a hablar de las cosas interesantes que
habrás hecho al terminar tus estudios secundarios.

1. **¿Habrás aprendido** muchas cosas
   interesantes?
   Sí (No, no) **habré aprendido** . . .
2. **¿Habrás aprendido** cosas útiles?
3. **¿Habrás aprendido** a hablar español?

4. **¿Habrás recibido** muchas «As»?
5. **¿Habrás conocido** a muchos chicos
   simpáticos?
6. **¿Habrás conocido** a muchas chicas
   simpáticas?

OBSERVACIÓN

In the above questions, you are asked about certain things that you *will have done*
by the time you finish high school. The verbs you are using are in the *future perfect*.

• How many words does the future perfect consist of in Spanish?   two
• What verb form is the second word of the future perfect?   the past participle
• Is this the same verb form that is used in the present perfect and in the pluperfect?   yes

WB
V1

40

VOCABULARIO PRÁCTICO   La casa del futuro

el techo

el dormitorio

la cocina

el comedor

la sala

ACTIVIDAD 1 Tu casa futura

1. ¿Tendrá tu casa una piscina? ¿un sistema de aire acondicionado? ¿un sistema de calefacción solar? ¿un garaje para tres coches? ¿un sótano muy grande?

2. ¿Cuántos pisos tendrá? ¿Cuántos cuartos?

3. ¿Será una casa de piedra? ¿de madera?

4. ¿Será el techo de vidrio (glass)? ¿el suelo de madera? ¿las paredes de vidrio?

5. ¿Cómo será la sala? ¿el comedor? ¿la cocina? ¿tu dormitorio?

POR 685.000 ptas. ·Bungalows· EN LA COSTA BLANCA
1, 2 y 3 dormitorios •comedor •cocina •aseo •patio y jardín.

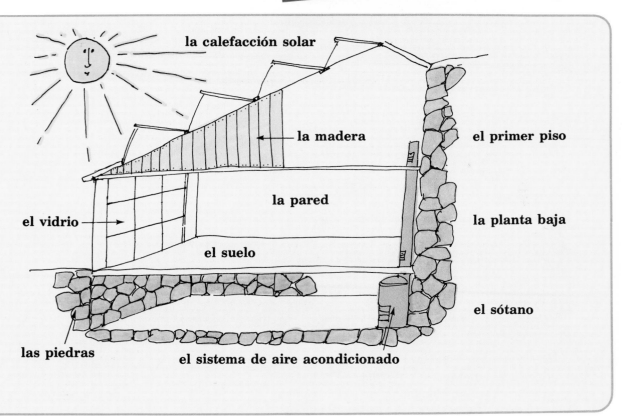

la calefacción solar

la madera

el vidrio

la pared

el suelo

las piedras

el sistema de aire acondicionado

el primer piso

la planta baja

el sótano

Estructuras

A. El futuro perfecto

Note the use of the future perfect in the following sentences.

Dentro de unos dos años, **me habré graduado.** *Within about two years, I will have graduated.*

Dentro de unos cinco años, Elena **se habrá casado con** Carlos. *Within about five years, Elena will have married Carlos.*

Antes del año dos mil, los científicos **habrán descubierto** una cura contra el cáncer. *Before the year 2000, scientists will have discovered a cure for cancer.*

Forms

1. The future perfect, like the present perfect, is a compound tense. In Spanish, it consists of *two* words. Note the forms of the future perfect tense of **comprar.**

Act. 2

INFINITIVE	**comprar**		
FUTURE PERFECT			
(yo)	**habré comprado**	(nosotros)	**habremos comprado**
(tú)	**habrás comprado**	(vosotros)	**habréis comprado**
(él, ella, Ud.)	**habrá comprado**	(ellos, ellas, Uds.)	**habrán comprado**

The future perfect is formed as follows:

> future of **haber** + past participle

2. Reminder: Regular past participles are formed as follows:

replace the infinitive ending:	with the ending:		
-ar →	**-ado**	tomar	→ tom**ado**
-er →	**-ido**	comer	→ com**ido**
-ir →	**-ido**	vivir	→ viv**ido**

Here are a few common irregular past participles:

decir	**dicho**	hacer	**hecho**
descubrir	**descubierto**	poner	**puesto**
escribir	**escrito**	ver	**visto**

Uses

1. As in English, the future perfect is used to express what *will have happened* by a certain point in time.

2. In Spanish, the future perfect, like the future, is used to make a guess or to express OPTIONAL probability, but about a *past* event.

¿Con quién ha salido Carlos?	*With whom has Carlos gone out?*
No sé. **Habrá salido** con Carmen.	*I don't know. He **may have gone out** with Carmen.*
	*(He **has probably gone out** with Carmen.)*

You may review the reflexive pronouns before beginning this activity.

ACTIVIDAD 2   Planes matrimoniales

Unos amigos están hablando de sus planes matrimoniales. Di quién se habrá casado dentro de cinco años, y quién no.

VARIATION: Will they have bought a house? **Felipe no habrá comprado una casa.**

⟩⟩ Felipe (no)   Felipe no se habrá casado.

1. Carmen (sí)
2. Raúl y Marisela (sí)
3. yo (no)
4. tú (sí)
5. nosotros (sí)
6. mis hermanos (sí)
7. el primo de Roberto (no)
8. Ud. y yo (no)

ACTIVIDAD 3   Los planes de Marisela

Marisela tiene muchos planes interesantes. Di qué espera realizar *(accomplish)* dentro de cinco años. Di también si tú habrás realizado planes similares.

⟩⟩ graduarse de la universidad

Dentro de cinco años, Marisela se habrá graduado de la universidad.
Yo (no) me habré graduado de la universidad.

1. pilotar un avión
2. conducir un Ferrari
3. correr el maratón de Boston
4. correr una milla en menos de cinco minutos
5. hablar con el presidente de los Estados Unidos
6. lanzarse en paracaídas *(parachute jump)*
7. aprender cinco idiomas
8. viajar a África
9. correr las olas en el Perú
10. esquiar en los Alpes
11. vivir en París
12. ir a Moscú
13. ver los canguros *(kangaroos)* en Australia
14. escribir una novela
15. hacer un viaje a la China
16. visitar las pirámides de Egipto

$457 mensuales.
2 dormitorios
2 baños

El LAGO

70 apartamentos listos para ocupación inmediata.

Es por eso que El Lago se habrá vendido antes de terminar el verano.

Make sure that the students are using the appropriate forms of the past participle for **escribir** (escrito), **hacer** (hecho), **ver** (visto).

Make sure that the students use the appropriate forms of the past participles for **poner (puesto)**, **descubrir (descubierto)**, **hacer (hecho)**.

ACTIVIDAD 4   El progreso

Di si, en tu opinión, los hombres habrán realizado las siguientes cosas antes
del año 2000.

⟩⟩   los científicos: descubrir una cura contra el cáncer
    Los científicos (no) habrán descubierto una cura contra el cáncer.

1. los astronautas: descubrir otros
   planetas
2. los astronautas: ir a Marte *(Mars)*
3. los medicos: descubrir una cura
   contra el catarro *(common cold)*
4. los ecologistas: suprimir la
   contaminación del aire
5. los arquitectos: construir ciudades en
   la luna
6. los hombres: ponerse en contacto con
   otras civilizaciones
7. los médicos: descubrir el elixir de la
   vida eterna
8. los políticos: transformar la sociedad
9. las mujeres: conseguir la igualdad
   (equality) con los hombres
10. los norteamericanos: hacer las paces
    con los rusos
11. los extraterrestres: establecer buenas
    relaciones con nosotros
12. yo: ganar el premio Nóbel

WB
A1, A2,
A3

SCRIPT
Act. 3, 4,
5

MASTERS
p. 33

B. *Por* + infinitivo   OPTIONAL

May be presented for recognition only.

Note the use of the construction **por** + infinitive in the following sentences.

El profesor me castigó   *The teacher punished me*
    por no saber la lección.   *for not knowing the lesson.*
Tengo un dolor de cabeza   *I have a headache from watching*
    por mirar la televisión demasiado.   *television too much.*

The construction **por** + infinitive usually corresponds to the English
construction *for, because of, for reason of + . . . ing.*

ACTIVIDAD 5   Excusas

Los siguientes alumnos no vinieron al examen. Da la excusa de cada uno.

⟩⟩   Rafael está enfermo.   Rafael no vino por estar enfermo.

1. Yo tengo dolor de estómago
   (stomachache).
2. Nosotros estamos cansados.
3. Teresa ayuda en casa.

4. Mis amigos acompañan a su padre al
   aeropuerto.
5. Tú no te sientes bien.
6. Uds. están en México.

ACTIVIDAD 6   Excesos y consecuencias

May be assigned as a special challenge activity.

Los excesos son peligrosos. Expresa esto en frases lógicas usando los elementos de las columnas A, B y C. ¡Usa tu imaginación!

A	**B**	**C**	
yo	estar enfermo	hablar	mirar la televisión
tú	estar cansado	beber	jugar
Carlos	estar ronco *(hoarse)*	cantar	divertirse
Susana y Elena	tener dolor de cabeza	leer	comer
Uds.	tener dolor de estómago *(stomachache)*	gritar *(to scream)*	reírse

WB
B1, B2,
B3

SCRIPT

Act. 6

Carlos tiene dolor de estómago por reírse demasiado.

Para la comunicación

OPTIONAL   May be assigned as homework.

XXV reunión de la clase

WB
Tus
planes

Imagina que la clase se reúne después de veinte y cinco años. Por supuesto, tus compañeros y tú habrán hecho muchas cosas interesantes durante ese tiempo. Describe lo que tú y otras dos personas de la clase habrán realizado. Escribe un párrafo de seis frases para cada persona. Puedes usar los siguientes verbos:

ser / ir / tener / ganar / trabajar / casarse / ver / hacer / viajar / comprar / construir / descubrir / visitar

SCRIPT

Act. 7

MASTERS
p. 33

TRB

QUIZ
pp. 91–92

WB   Test/Repaso   TEST   pp. 93–96

Variedades   El secreto del jefe indio

Un día, un joven explorador norteamericano llegó a una aldea° de la región amazónica.

En esta aldea vivía una tribu de indios pacíficos.° Muy pronto el jefe de la tribu, un viejo de unos ochenta años, había hecho amistad° con el explorador. Un día el viejo le dijo al explorador:

—Yo sé que has organizado una expedición a la selva° y que quieres salir mañana. Pero, escúchame . . . Tú no irás. Te quedarás en la aldea con nosotros. Esta noche, habrá una tempestad° fuertísima. Hará un tiempo horrible por veinte días. Tendrás que esperar pacientemente el fin de la tempestad. Si después hace buen tiempo, podrás hacer la expedición. Entonces, si quieres, yo iré contigo.

Esa noche, tal como° había dicho el viejo, empezó una desastrosa tempestad que duró veinte días y que arrasó° un gran número de árboles de esta selva tropical. El joven explorador agradeció° al jefe indio que le había salvado° la vida.

De allí en adelante,° antes de cada expedición, él consultaba con su amigo. Éste° le pronosticaba° el tiempo con una exactitud increíble:

—Sí, podrás partir° . . .

—Hará buen tiempo por quince días . . .

—Hará mucho sol esta semana . . .

—Hará mucho calor por tres días . . .

O algo como:

—No, no podrás viajar porque hará mal tiempo por cinco o seis días.

Y cada vez, las predicciones del jefe indio se realizaban.°

El joven explorador estaba tan intrigado por el talento de su amigo pero nunca le preguntó nada de su secreto.

—Será sin duda un viejo secreto indígena, transmitido de generación a generación. Si yo le pregunto, él se enojará y nunca más me dirá nada.

Finalmente después de seis meses, el explorador norteamericano tuvo que partir. El día de su salida° el jefe indio le llamó y le dijo:

—Eres un joven muy simpático y yo estuve muy contento de poder ayudarte. Ahora, me toca° a mí pedirte un favor. Dentro de poco estarás en Nueva York. Allá, ¿podrás comprarme pilas° nuevas para mi radio-transistor? Las mías están bastante gastadas° y muy pronto no podré escuchar más las informaciones meteorológicas° que vienen de la estación cercana.° Pero con las pilas nuevas yo podré ayudar a los otros exploradores norteamericanos que vendrán después de ti . . .

Glosses:
aldea: *village*

pacíficos: *peaceful*
había hecho amistad: *had become friends*

selva: *forest*

tempestad: *storm*

tal como: *just as*
arrasó: *tore down*
agradeció: *was grateful to*
salvado: *saved*

De allí en adelante: *From then on*
Éste = el jefe
pronosticaba: *would predict*
partir: *leave*

se realizaban: *would come true*

salida: *departure*

me toca: *it's my turn*
pilas: *batteries*
gastadas: *used*
meteorológicas: *weather*
cercana: *nearby*

4

Un poco de historia

¿Sabes cuándo comienza la historia del hombre en la América del Sur? Comienza cuando llegan tribus de indios cazadores,° 10.000 años antes de Cristo. Y desde entonces, ¡bueno! ¡Han pasado muchas cosas! Hoy vamos a recordar los grandes hechos.°

Machu Picchu Perú

Francisco Pizarro

1438–1493

Los emperadores incas Pachacútec y Túpac dirigen la expansión imperial que crea en las montañas de los Andes un imperio extraordinario. Ocho millones de indios llegan a ser parte de este imperio.

1532

Francisco Pizarro, un español inquieto y ambicioso, llega al Perú y conquista a los incas.

1535

El imperio de los incas derrotado,° comienzan tres siglos° de dominación española. Francisco Pizarro funda° la «Ciudad de los Reyes»,° ciudad que llega a ser el centro del poder° español en la América del Sur. La «Ciudad de los Reyes» es hoy Lima, la capital del Perú.

1735

Con la autorización de la Corona° española, una expedición francesa° visita el territorio que hoy es el Ecuador. Es una expedición científica que llega a la región para tomar algunas medidas° de la tierra y marcar la posición exacta del ecuador.° Su jefe es el famoso científico Charles Marie de La Condamine.

cazadores *hunters* **hechos** *deeds* **derrotado** *defeated* **siglos** *centuries* **funda** *founds* **Reyes** *Monarchs* **poder** *power* **Corona** *Crown* **francesa** *French* **medidas** *measurements* **ecuador** *Equator*

Bolívar y San Martín

1810

En Caracas y en Buenos Aires, la gente declara su oposición a las autoridades españolas. Así comienza la lucha° por la independencia de la América del Sur. Surgen° dos grandes héroes: Simón Bolívar y José de San Martín.

1824

Bajo el mando de otro gran patriota, Antonio José de Sucre, 6.000 tropas libertadoras derrotan° a 9.000 tropas españolas en Ayacucho, Perú. Es el golpe° decisivo. Es la última gran batalla en las altas cumbres° de los Andes. Después de tres siglos, el poder español por fin° se retira de la América del Sur.

1879–1883

Durante la llamada «Guerra° del Pacífico», Chile, por un lado,° y el Perú y Bolivia, por el otro, pelean por el control de ciertos recursos° naturales. Como resultado de esta guerra, Bolivia pierde su salida° al mar (hoy es un país sin costas) y Chile gana el control del desierto de Atacama donde hay grandes depósitos de cobre° y de nitrato natural, un fertilizante.

1904

Los gobiernos de Chile y Argentina erigen° una estatua de Cristo como símbolo de la paz entre los dos países. Situada en la frontera, la estatua es de bronce y mide° 26 pies.

1912

En Maracaibo, Venezuela, se descubre petróleo. Este gran recurso natural transforma el país.

1948

En una reunión interamericana celebrada en Bogotá, Colombia, se crea oficialmente la Organización de Estados Americanos (OEA). Esta organización tiene su sede° en Washington, D.C. Veinte y seis naciones americanas, incluyendo los Estados Unidos, forman parte de la OEA.

1974

Muere° Juan Perón. Es sucedido por su esposa, Isabel Perón, que gobierna hasta 1976. Ella es la primera mujer que llega a ser presidente de un país del hemisferio occidental.

1983

Raúl Alfonsín es elegido presidente después de años de gobierno militar en la Argentina. Promete el reestablecimiento de la democracia y los derechos humanos.

---

lucha *struggle* **Surgen** *Arise* **derrotan** *defeat* **golpe** *blow* **cumbres** *peaks* **por fin** *finally*
Guerra *War* **por un lado** *on one hand* **recursos** *resources* **salida** *exit* **cobre** *copper*
erigen *erect* **mide** *measures* **sede** *headquarters* **Muere** *Dies*

LOS PAÍSES HISPANOS
DE LA AMÉRICA DEL SUR

Colombia

Población: 30.000.000
Ciudad capital: Bogotá
Unidad monetaria: el peso
Productos principales:
café, esmeraldas,° petróleo
Otros datos:°
Establecida en 1525, Santa Marta, en Colombia, es la población permanente más antigua de la América del Sur.

Venezuela

Población: 17.800.000
Ciudad capital: Caracas
Unidad monetaria:
el bolívar, en honor del héroe de la independencia, Simón Bolívar
Productos principales: petróleo, hierro°
Otros datos:
Venezuela es el noveno productor de petróleo en el mundo. La mayor parte del petróleo venezolano sale del Lago de Maracaibo.

esmeraldas *emeralds*   **datos** *facts*   **hierro** *iron*

Ecuador

Población: 9.600.000
Ciudad capital: Quito
Unidad monetaria:
   el sucre, en honor del héroe de la
   independencia, Antonio José de Sucre
Productos principales:
   bananas, cacao, petróleo
Otros datos:
   El Ecuador toma su nombre de la línea
   imaginaria que divide al mundo en los
   hemisferios norte y sur. Pero aunque°
   el ecuador pasa por el Ecuador, los
   espectaculares volcanes de este páis
   siempre están cubiertos° de nieve.

Perú

Población: 20.200.000
Ciudad capital: Lima
Unidad monetaria: el inti y
   el sol (Los incas adoraban al sol.)
Productos principales:
   cobre, harina de pescado°
Otros datos:
   El Perú es el país con la industria
   pesquera° comercial más grande del
   mundo hispano.

Bolivia

Población: 6.400.000
Ciudad capital: La Paz
Unidad monetaria: el peso
Producto principal: el estaño°
Otros datos:
   La Paz es la capital más alta del
   mundo. Está a 3.900 metros sobre el
   nivel del mar° (más de 12.000 pies).

aunque *although*   **cubiertos** *covered*   **harina de pescado** *fishmeal*   **pesquera** *fishing*
estaño *tin*   **nivel del mar** *sea level*

Chile

Población: 12.300.000
Ciudad capital: Santiago
Unidad monetaria: el peso
Productos principales:
    cobre,° mineral de hierro°
Otros datos:
    En Chile están los picos más altos de la impresionante Cordillera de los Andes. Ésta se extiende desde Colombia y Venezuela hasta Chile, donde muchas expediciones han intentado° conquistar la cumbre° del Aconcagua. Con una elevación de casi 7.000 metros (más de 22.000 pies), es el pico más alto de América.

Argentina

Población: 31.200.000
Ciudad capital: Buenos aires
Unidad monetaria: el austral
Productos principales:
    trigo,° carne, cuero°
Otros datos:
    La Argentina es un país formado casi completamente por emigrantes europeos. Muchas familias italianas, inglesas, irlandesas, alemanas° y, por supuesto, españolas llegaron a la Argentina hace 100 años.

Paraguay

Población: 4.100.000
Ciudad capital: Asunción
Unidad monetaria:
    guaraní, nombre de la cultura precolombina
Productos principales: madera,° carne
Otros datos:
    El Paraguay es un país bilingüe. El español y el guaraní, la lengua precolombina, se hablan en todas partes. También hay libros y periódicos en guaraní.

cobre *copper*   **hierro** *iron*   **intentado** *have tried*   **cumbre** *peak*   **trigo** *wheat*
cuero *leather*   **alemanas** *German*   **madera** *wood*

Uruguay

Población: 3.000.000
Ciudad capital: Montevideo
Unidad monetaria: el peso
Productos principales: carne, lana°
Otros datos:
Uruguay es la república más pequeña de la América del Sur. Tiene un área comparable a la del estado de Washington.

¡SE SALVA LA VIDA CON UNOS POLVOS MILAGROSOS!

En la década de 1630, Luis Fernández, conde° de Chinchón, era el virrey° del Perú. Él era el hombre que gobernaba el Perú en representación del Rey° de España. El conde vivía con su esposa, Ana Ossorio, condesa de Chinchón, en Lima.

Luis quería mucho a Ana; desafortunadamente, un día ella se enfermó.° Tenía una fiebre° muy alta. Los médicos no podían controlársela.

—Imposible,— dijeron los médicos. —Es imposible curar a la condesa.

Pero cuando más triste estaba el conde, ocurrió algo maravilloso: llegó un indio con unos polvos° para la condesa. El indio anunció que traía un secreto inca, una sustancia mágica para la condesa.

Efectivamente, así fue. La condesa se curó milagrosamente.°

Los polvos que trajo el indio fueron de la corteza° de un árbol de las laderas° de los Andes. La corteza de este árbol contiene una sustancia química° que hoy se llama quinina (del quechua, que hablaban los incas). La expresíon quechua *quina-quina* quiere decir corteza de cortezas.

¿Sabes para qué usan la quinina los médicos hoy día?

---

lana *wool*   **conde** *count*   **virrey** *viceroy*   **Rey** *King*   **se enfermó** *fell ill*   **fiebre** *fever*
polvos *powders*   **milagrosamente** *miraculously*   **corteza** *bark*   **laderas** *slopes*   **química** *chemical*

Una ciudad perdida y encontrada

Cuzco. Estación San Pedro. Son las siete de la mañana y el tren va a
partir para Machu Picchu, la ciudad perdida de los incas. Son cuatro horas
de viaje. Cuatro horas subiendo y bajando montañas . . . Por fin,° ¡allí está!

Machu Picchu: nubes° y montañas, misterio y silencio, escaleras° y
murallas° de piedra . . . ¿Fue Machu Picchu el último
refugio de los incas? ¿Fue una fortaleza° militar? ¿Fue un
centro ceremonial? ¿Fue una ciudad sagrada?°

Nadie lo sabe exactamente. Los arqueólogos creen que
la ciudad de Machu Picchu fue construida por los incas
hace 600 años. Pero los españoles nunca llegaron a
Machu Picchu. La ciudad desapareció con la derrota° del
imperio inca sin ser vista por ningún europeo.

Pasaron 400 años. Entonces, un norteamericano, Hiram
Bingham, condujo una expedición arqueológica de «Yale
University» en busca de la ciudad perdida. Y, en 1911,
¡la encontró! Una ciudad completamente de piedra,
construida en la cima° de una montaña. Una ciudad
abandonada, desierta, misteriosa. Escondida bajo una
sábana° de vegetación. Una ciudad llamada Machu
Picchu, hoy visitada por gente de todo el mundo.

Por fin *Finally* **nubes** *clouds* **escaleras** *stairs* **murallas** *walls* **fortaleza** *fortress*
sagrada *sacred* **derrota** *defeat* **cima** *top* **sábana** *sheet*

EL MISTERIOSO MUNDO DEL PASADO

¿Cómo eran los pueblos del pasado? ¿Cómo vivían los incas, por ejemplo? ¿Existían comunicaciones entre pueblos distantes? ¿Cómo comprendían la vida? En la América del Sur los misterios abundan.

El Dorado

Este misterio se refiere a un rey° de origen desconocido. No ha sido posible determinar dónde estaba su reino.° Este rey indio celebraba todos los años una ceremonia religiosa muy misteriosa. Primero se cubría° todo el cuerpo con polvos° de oro y después se bañaba en un lago. Hoy hay gente que todavía busca el lago de El Dorado. ¿Crees tú en la existencia de este lago?

Los egipcios en el Nuevo Mundo

En el lago Titicaca, entre el Perú y Bolivia, los indios que descienden de los incas navegan en balsas de junco° que son muy interesantes. Por su construcción y diseño° estas balsas son similares a las balsas que usaban los antiguos egipcios para navegar en el río Nilo. Este parecido° hace pensar en contactos antiguos entre el norte de África y el sur de América. Claro que hoy es imposible demostrar que los antiguos egipcios les enseñaron a los indios a fabricar balsas. Pero hay personas (como el antropólogo noruego, Thor Heyerdahl) que creen que los antiguos egipcios fueron capaces° de cruzar el Océano Atlántico en sus balsas.

Los gigantes de la Isla de Pascua

Al llegar a la Isla de Pascua,° un remoto territorio chileno en el Pacífico, los visitantes son recibidos por figuras gigantescas, tan altas como un edificio de cuatro o cinco pisos. Estos enormes gigantes de piedra sonríen irónicamente porque el hombre moderno no ha podido descubrir su secreto. Es fácil imaginar que esta isla fue una prisión precolombina, y que las estatuas fueron creadas por criminales. Pero ¿cómo puedes demostrar esta posibilidad?

rey *king*   **reino** *kingdom*   **se cubría** *was covered*   **polvos** *dust (particles)*   **balsas de junco** *boats (rafts) made of bulrushes*   **diseño** *design*   **parecido** *similarity*   **capaces** *capable*   **Isla de Pascua** *Easter Island*

El zoológico natural

Aquí hay cinco animales.
Todos son de origen sudamericano.

1. La llama es el amigo indispensable de los indios que viven en los Andes. Pero es un animal temperamental. Además las llamas no pueden llevar a una persona. Solamente pueden llevar cosas que no pesan° mucho.

4. ¿Conoces este animal? ¡Es una chinchilla! Este animalito es feliz entre la nieve y el frío de los Andes. Su piel° se usa para hacer finísimos abrigos.

2. Éste es un oso hormiguero. Las hormigas° son su plato favorito. Usa su gran hocico° y su lengua° de 30 centímetros (1 pie) para tomar las hormigas de la tierra.

3. Ésta es la anaconda. Vive cerca de los ríos. Come animales pequeños que estruja° entre los anillos° de su cuerpo.

5. El cóndor es un ave° similar al águila.° Los dos son enormes y vuelan° muy alto. Los dos son símbolos nacionales. El cóndor vive en las altas montañas de los Andes y en el escudo° de cuatro repúblicas. Es el ave nacional de Colombia, Ecuador, Bolivia y Chile.

pesan *weigh* **hormigas** *ants* **hocico** *snout* **lengua** *tongue* **estruja** *it squeezes*
anillos *rings* **piel** *fur* **ave** *bird* **águila** *eagle* **vuelan** *fly* **escudo** *shield*

Los campeones de la libertad

Francisco Miranda, 1750-1816

Este general venezolano tomó parte en la Guerra de la Independencia de los Estados Unidos. Fue amigo de Jorge Washington y de Tomás Jefferson. Después, viajó por Europa buscando dinero, armas y hombres para luchar contra° los españoles en la América hispana.

Simón Bolívar, 1783-1830

Rico, aristocrático y muy guapo. Así fue Bolívar, un joven distinguido, nacido° en Caracas. Cuando era estudiante juró° solemnemente dedicar su vida a la libertad del Nuevo Mundo. Como todo gran romántico, fue idealista en sus ideas y dramático en sus acciones. Hizo gloriosamente lo que prometió porque liberó Colombia, Venezuela, Ecuador, el Perú y Bolivia.

Antonio José de Sucre, 1795-1830

Fue el más joven de los héroes. Cuando tenía 15 años se unió° al movimiento libertador. Fue el mejor amigo de Bolívar, y con él comparte la gloria de haber dirigido las grandes batallas. Después, creó la república de Bolivia, y la llamó así en honor a su amigo.

José de San Martín, 1778-1850

Con su ejército° que organizó y entrenó° en la Argentina, San Martín cruzó los Andes, liberó Chile y llegó al Perú. Luchó contra España y la naturaleza:° el frío, la nieve y la falta° de oxígeno en las altas cumbres° de los Andes.

Bernardo O'Higgins, 1778(?)-1842

Héroe nacional de Chile que se unió a las fuerzas de San Martín. Con él cruzó los Andes en 1817. Después, fue autor de la primera constitución de Chile. Su padre, nacido en Irlanda, fue representante de la Corona° española en Chile y en el Perú.

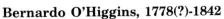

luchar contra *to fight against* **nacido** *born* **juró** *swore* **se unió** *joined* **ejército** *army* **entrenó** *trained* **naturaleza** *nature* **falta** *lack* **cumbres** *peaks* **Corona** *Crown*

Gabriela Mistral

Gabriela Mistral (1889-1957). Nacida° en Chile, Mistral figura entre° los grandes poetas de Latinoamérica. Además de escritora° fue maestra.° También trabajó en el servicio diplomático de Chile y fue Ministro de Cultura. En 1945 ganó el Premio Nóbel y en 1951 su país le concedió° el Premio Nacional de Literatura.

Las obras° de Mistral han sido traducidas a muchos idiomas.° Todo el mundo conoce a esta mujer que en sus viajes por Europa y América siempre defendió los derechos° humanos. Algunos de los temas de sus poemas son el dolor,° la consolación religiosa, la maternidad y la infancia.

BALADA DE LA ESTRELLA

Este poema es un diálogo entre Mistral y una estrella.° La poetisa° quiere saber si hay alguien más triste y más sola que ella misma. La estrella responde de una manera sorprendente.

> Estrella, estoy triste.
> Tú dime° si otra
> como mi alma° viste.
> —Hay otra más triste.
>
> —Estoy sola, estrella.
> Di a mi alma si existe
> otra como ella.
> —Sí, dice la estrella.
>
> —Contempla mi llanto.°
> Dime si otra lleva
> de lágrimas manto.°
> —En otra hay más llanto.
>
> —Di quién es la triste,
> di quién es la sola,
> si la conociste.
>
> —Soy yo, la que encanto,
> soy yo la que tengo
> mi luz° hecha llanto.

DAME° LA MANO

Este poema es una invitación a una danza. ¿Qué simbolizan la flor, la espiga° y la danza? Para contestar esta pregunta, considera que las palabras *y nada más* son muy importantes en este poema.

> Dame la mano y danzaremos;
> dame la mano y me amarás.
> Como una sola flor seremos,
> como una flor, y nada más . . .
>
> El mismo verso cantaremos,
> al mismo paso° bailarás.
> Como una espiga ondularemos,°
> como una espiga, y nada más.
>
> Te llamas Rosa y yo Esperanza;
> pero tu nombre olvidarás,
> porque seremos una danza
> en la colina,° y nada más . . .

From *Poesías Completas*, Aguilar, 1968. Reprinted by permission of Aguilar, S.A. de Ediciones, Madrid, Spain.

Nacida *Born*   **figura entre** *ranks among*   **escritora** *writer*   **maestra** *teacher*
concedió *awarded*   **obras** *works*   **idiomas** *languages*   **derechos** *rights*   **dolor** *pain*
estrella *star*   **poetisa** *poet*   **dime** *tell me*   **alma** *soul*   **llanto** *weeping*
de lágrimas manto *a cloak of tears*   **luz** *light*   **Dame** *Give me*   **espiga** *wheat stalk*
paso *step*   **ondularemos** *we will wave*   **colina** *hill*

La cocina sudamericana

¿Te gustan los postres? Aquí está la receta° del dulce de leche. Es el dulce más fácil de preparar. Aprende a prepararlo y si te piden la receta, di que es un secreto de tus amigos argentinos y brasileños. Necesitas tres cosas:

una olla° pequeña

una lata° de leche condensada con azúcar

un poco de agua

Ahora, vamos a preparar la lata. NOTA: Antes de abrir la lata, tienes que cocinarla. Así es que, ¡NO LA ABRAS!

Preparación
1. Quítale el papel a la lata.
2. Pon la lata en la olla.
3. Ponle agua a la olla. La lata tiene que estar cubierta° de agua.
4. Cocínala a fuego lento° durante dos o tres horas.
5. Cuando la lata esté° fría, ábrela y . . . ¡buen provecho!°

Actividades culturales

1. *Prepara un cartel° que anuncie uno de los países hispanos de la América del Sur.*
2. *Escoge uno de los campeones de la libertad de la página 325 y prepara un informe° sobre su vida.*
3. *Prepara una exposición° de estampillas sudamericanas.*
4. *Escoge uno de los países hispanos de la América del Sur y prepara un informe oral. Puedes hablar de su historia, sus costumbres,° su economía, etc. Prepara también una exposición, usa algunas fotos.*
5. *Prepara un informe sobre la Isla de Pascua.*

cartel *poster*   **informe** *report*   **exposición** *exhibit*   **costumbres** *customs*

---

receta *recipe*   **olla** *pot*   **lata** *tin can*   **cubierta** *covered*   **a fuego lento** *over low heat*   **esté** *is*
¡buen provecho! *Enjoy it!*

Perspectivas de hoy

8.1 Una lección de conducir

8.2 El arte de la persuasión

8.3 El vendedor de la suerte

8.4 Sí, pero . . .

VARIEDADES El ojo de Dios

OBJECTIVES
Communication
By the end of this unit, students will be able to use Spanish:
- To give advice, make suggestions, give orders
- To give instructions to their friends
- To prepare advertising material
- To make indirect requests

Language
This unit introduces the regular formation of the subjunctive and the use of the subjunctive mood in indirect commands. As preparation for the study of the subjunctive, the unit also presents commands and infinitive constructions.

Culture
The cultural notes examine the role of the family in career planning, the lottery, the learning of languages, the significance of the driver's license for an Hispanic teenager.

 Module 20

 **Una lección de conducir**

Act. 1

41

Beatriz está muy contenta.

Acaba de obtener el permiso de conducir.

Un día, ella le pide a su hermano su coche. Le dice que es para ir de compras . . . En realidad, Beatriz tiene otra intención. Ella va a darle una lección de conducir a su amiga Gabriela. Las dos chicas están en el coche . . .

Es obvio que Beatriz todavía no es una experta en el manejo . . . Por eso, todos los consejos que ella le da a Gabriela no siempre son los mejores . . . En efecto, algunos son bastante malos.

manejo: *driving*

¿Puedes determinar cuáles son los buenos consejos y cuáles no lo son?

	buen consejo	mal consejo	
1. Ponte el cinturón de seguridad.	☐	☐	cinturón de seguridad: *seat belt* toca la bocina: *honk the horn*
2. Antes de arrancar, toca la bocina.	☐	☐	
3. Al arrancar, mira a la derecha y a la izquierda.	☐	☐	
4. Después de arrancar, acelera de repente.	☐	☐	de repente: *suddenly*
5. Al ver la luz roja, para.	☐	☐	
6. Al ver la luz amarilla, acelera.	☐	☐	
7. Ten mucho cuidado al pasar por un pueblo.	☐	☐	
8. Pon las luces direccionales antes de doblar la esquina.	☐	☐	doblar la esquina: *turning the corner*
9. Pon las luces direccionales después de parar.	☐	☐	
10. Ve más despacio cuando llueve.	☐	☐	más despacio: *slower*
11. Al doblar la esquina, acelera.	☐	☐	
12. Al ver a un policía, ve más de prisa.	☐	☐	más de prisa: *faster*

You may ask the students to identify the infinitive form of the verb used in the commands.

NOTA CULTURAL   OPTIONAL

El permiso de conducir

¿Cuándo recibirás tu permiso de conducir? ¿Dentro de un año o dos? ¿O tal vez, ya lo tienes?

Para los jóvenes hispanos, el sacar° el permiso de conducir es un hecho emocionante.° Primero porque el examen es muy difícil y muchos salen mal en° el examen. También, el sacar el permiso de conducir es como un símbolo, una señal de que eres cuidadoso y responsable, que eres de confianza,° en otras palabras, que ahora eres un adulto.

el sacar *getting*   **emocionante** *thrilling*   **salen mal en** *fail*
de confianza *worthy of confidence*

¿Tienes el permiso de conducir?   ¿Cuándo vas a obtenerlo?   ¿Es el examen de conducir muy difícil en los Estados Unidos?   En los Estados Unidos, ¿es el sacar el permiso de conducir la señal de que eres un adulto?

sustantivo	**un pueblo**	town
verbo	**obtener**	to obtain, to get
expresiones	**de repente**	suddenly
	tocar la bocina	to honk

Practice the forms of **obtener** by having students vary subjects or sentences like: **Ana obtiene el permiso. Ud. obtuvo el permiso. Uds. obtendrán el permiso.**

NOTA: **Obtener** is conjugated like **tener**.

¿Cuándo **obtendrás** tu permiso de conducir?

CONVERSACIÓN   OPTIONAL

Vamos a hablar de lo que haces todos los días.

1. ¿Te lavas las manos **antes de** comer?
2. ¿Te lavas los dientes **antes de** acostarte?
3. ¿Miras **antes de** cruzar la calle?

4. ¿Estudias mucho **antes de** tomar un examen?
5. ¿Piensas **antes de** hablar?

OBSERVACIÓN

In the above questions, you are asked whether you do certain things before doing others.

• What is the expression that corresponds to *before?*   antes de
• Which form of the verb is used after this expression?   the infinitive

Estructuras

A. Repaso: mandatos afirmativos: la forma familiar (*tú*)

Commands are used to make a suggestion, to give a warning, or to give an order. In the following sentences, orders are given to people addressed as **tú**.

¡María, **escucha**!	*María, listen!*
¡Paquito, **come** el pan!	*Paquito, eat the bread!*
¡**Escribe** la carta, Manuel!	*Write the letter, Manuel!*

For most verbs, the affirmative **tú** form of the command is the same as the **él** form of the present tense.

NOTE: Verbs that have a stem change in the present have the same change in commands: **Paco no cierra la puerta. ¡Cierra la puerta, Paco!**

> endings for the familiar or **tú** form of commands
> for **-ar** verbs: **-a**
> for **-er** verbs: **-e**
> for **-ir** verbs: **-e**

ACTIVIDAD 1 Unos consejos

Imagina que eres profesor(a). Unos alumnos necesitan
cambiar sus actitudes. Aconséjalos.

> Paco no lee libros interesantes.
>> Por favor, Paco, ¡lee libros interesantes!

1. Carmen no estudia para el examen.
2. Rubén no estudia el vocabulario.
3. Felipe no saluda a sus profesores.
4. Isabel no aprende los verbos.
5. Federico no llega a clase a tiempo.
6. Inés no termina la tarea.
7. Alberto no escribe en su cuaderno.
8. Teresa no habla inglés en clase.

ACTIVIDAD 2 En la fiesta

Carlos ha invitado a algunos amigos a una fiesta en su casa. Le pide
ayuda a cada uno. Haz el papel de Carlos. (Cuidado: Los verbos que Carlos
usa tienen un cambio en el radical.)

Make sure that the students make the
appropriate stem changes. You may
want to review these changes by having
students first give sentences in the present
tense: **Ana cierra las ventanas.**

> cerrar las ventanas   ¡Cierra las ventanas, por favor!

1. cerrar la puerta
2. encender las luces
3. pedir prestado unos discos
4. mostrar tus fotos
5. jugar con Alberto

6. contar un chiste
7. servir las gaseosas
8. devolver los discos
9. contar algo divertido
10. servir los sándwiches

B. Repaso: mandatos afirmativos: la forma familiar (*tú*) irregular

A few verbs are irregular in the affirmative **tú** form of the command.

NOTE: All of these verbs are irregular in
the **yo** form of the present. Have students
review: **digo, hago, voy,** etc.

decir	**di**	¡**Di** la verdad!
hacer	**haz**	¡**Haz** la tarea!
ir	**ve**	¡**Ve** a la escuela!
poner	**pon**	¡**Pon** la mesa!
salir	**sal**	¡**Sal** conmigo!
ser	**sé**	¡**Sé** generoso!
tener	**ten**	¡**Ten** paciencia!
venir	**ven**	¡**Ven** aquí!

> With the exception of **decir, hacer, ser,** and **ir,** the affirmative **tú**
> form of the above verbs is the stem of the verb, that is, the infinitive
> minus -**er** or -**ir.**

WB
A1, A2

SCRIPT

Act. 3, 4

MASTERS
p. 34

Act. 5

> Note the idiomatic expressions with **tener.**

tener cuidado (con)	to watch out (for)	**¡Ten cuidado con** el perro!
	to be careful (about)	**¡Ten cuidado con** el coche!
tener paciencia	to be patient	**¡Ten paciencia,** por favor!
tener la bondad (de)	to be good enough (to)	**¡Ten la bondad de** ayudarme!
	(would you please)	

ACTIVIDAD 3   ¡Cuidado!

Un papá les da a sus hijos ciertas órdenes y les recomienda cuidado con
ciertas cosas. Haz el papel del papá.

> Roberto: ir a la playa / el sol   ¡Ve a la playa, Roberto, pero ten cuidado con el sol!

1. Marta: ir al centro / los coches
2. Enrique: poner la mesa / los vasos
3. Silvia: hacer la tarea / los errores
4. Marta: salir con Gloria / su perro
5. Silvia: salir de casa / el tránsito (traffic)
6. Enrique: venir aquí / el perro

Act. 7

42

VOCABULARIO PRÁCTICO   El tránsito

el tranvía

el semáforo

el conductor

los pasajeros

la parada del tranvía

los peatones

la señal de tránsito

la acera

la esquina

el paso de peatones

ACTIVIDAD 4 Una lección de conducir

Supón *(Suppose)* que estás enseñándole a una amiga española el arte de conducir. ¿Qué consejo vas a darle en las circunstancias descritas abajo? Escoge entre **tener cuidado (con)**, **ir más despacio** y **parar**.

▷ Un gato cruza la calle. ¡Ten cuidado con el gato!
(¡Ve más despacio!)
(¡Para!)

1. Los peatones cruzan la calle.
2. El semáforo está verde.
3. El semáforo está amarillo.
4. El semáforo está rojo.
5. Hay un accidente.
6. El conductor del otro coche no tiene cuidado.
7. El coche de enfrente *(ahead)* anda muy despacio.
8. Hay un tremendo lío de tránsito.
9. El coche de atrás *(behind)* está tocando la bocina.
10. Estamos en una carretera.
11. Llegamos a un pueblo.
12. Llegamos a un peaje *(tollbooth)*.
13. El tranvía que está delante del coche para de repente.
14. Los pasajeros están subiendo al tranvía.

WB
B1, B2

SCRIPT
Act. 6

cruzar	to cross, to go to the other side	Los peatones **cruzan** la calle.
doblar	to turn (a corner)	**Dobla** a la izquierda y después **dobla** a la derecha.
parar	to stop	Los coches **paran** cuando el semáforo está rojo.
seguir (e → i)	to follow, to continue	¡**Sigue** el taxi! ¡**Sigue** derecho *(straight ahead)*!
ir de prisa	to go quickly	**Ve** más **de prisa** en la carretera.
ir despacio	to go slowly	**Ve despacio** en el pueblo.

la carretera

el camión

C. Repaso: preposición de tiempo + infinitivo

Note the use of the infinitives in the following sentences.

Cierra la puerta **al salir** de casa.	*Close the door **on leaving** the house.*
Ten cuidado **al cruzar** la calle.	*Be careful **when crossing** the street.*
Enciende las luces direccionales **antes de doblar.**	*Put on your turn signal **before turning.***
Apaga las luces direccionales **después de doblar.**	*Turn off the turn signal **after turning.***

⟴ The infinitive is used after prepositions of time such as **al** (*while, on, when*), **después de** (*after*), and **antes de** (*before*).

⟴ Reminder: The construction **al** + infinitive is used to express the fact that two actions are going on at the same time.

Al entrar, saludo a mis amigos.	*When I come in, I say hello to my friends.*
Al volver a casa, te llamaré.	*When I get back home, I will call you.*

ACTIVIDAD 5   Preguntas personales   OPTIONAL

1. ¿Qué haces al llegar a la escuela?
2. ¿Qué haces al volver a casa?
3. ¿Qué haces al encontrar a tus amigos?
4. ¿Qué harías al ver un accidente?
5. ¿Qué harías al ver un tigre?
6. ¿Qué harías al encontrarte con el presidente? ¿Frankenstein? ¿Paul Newman?
7. ¿Qué harías al ganar mil dólares en la lotería?

Ask about student responses. **¿Qué hace Sam al llegar a la escuela?**

Items 4, 5, 6 and 7 require the conditional. You may have the students review these verb forms on p. 300.

ACTIVIDAD 6   Primero uno, luego otro

Hay un orden cronológico en lo que hacemos. Describe este orden lógico con la construcción **antes de** o **después de** + infinitivo.

⟴ Carmen (estudiar / tomar el examen)   Carmen estudia antes de tomar el examen.

1. tú (lavarte las manos / comer)
2. yo (cepillarme los dientes / comer)
3. nosotros (vestirnos / levantarnos)
4. Felipe (quitarse la ropa / acostarse)
5. los alumnos (pensar / hablar)
6. las personas limpias (bañarse / vestirse)

ACTIVIDAD 7   Expresión personal

WB
C1, C2

SCRIPT

Act. 8

MASTERS
p. 34

Completa las siguientes frases con una idea personal. ¡Usa tu imaginación!

1. Al llegar a casa esta tarde . . .
2. Al salir de clase . . .
3. Después de cenar esta noche . . .
4. Al recibir mi diploma . . .
5. Después de graduarme . . .
6. Antes de buscar trabajo . . .
7. Al recibir mi primer cheque . . .
8. Al decidir que voy a casarme . . .
9. Después de casarme . . .

Since these items concern future events, you may have the students use either **voy a** + infinitive or the future.

Para la comunicación

May be assigned as homework.
OPTIONAL

Direcciones

Supón que un alumno hispano te pide direcciones para ir a los siguientes lugares. Dale las direcciones, usando verbos como **ir, cruzar, doblar en la esquina** y **seguir.**

⊅ para ir de la escuela a la biblioteca
   Ve hasta el semáforo. Cruza la calle ... En la esquina, dobla a la izquierda en la calle de Colón. Sigue derecho hasta la biblioteca municipal.

1. para ir de la biblioteca al cine
2. para ir del cine a la parada del autobús
3. para ir de la parada del autobús a la Plaza Mayor
4. para ir de la Plaza Mayor a la farmacia

VARIATION: Pairs of students may act out skits on these topics.

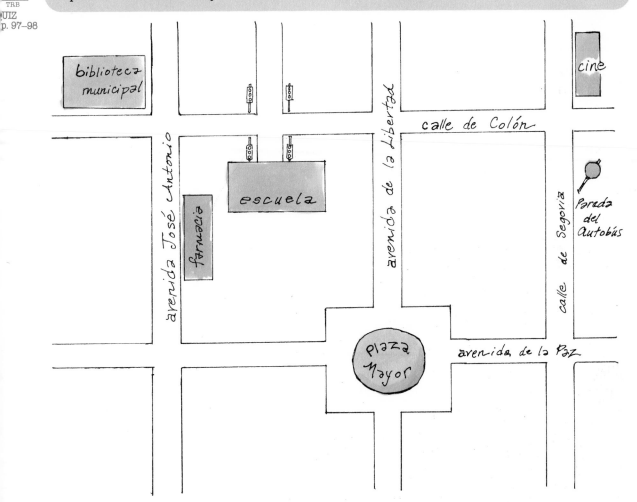

Lección 2 El arte de la persuasión

Act. 1

La gente del siglo veinte ha inventado un arte nuevo: el arte de la persuasión. Hoy día, con la publicidad, vemos este arte constantemente.
Por ejemplo:

¡Beba Ud. QUICK, el agua mineral de los campeones!

campeones: *champions*

¡Sean Uds. modernos!
¡Beban TROPICAL, la bebida de los jóvenes!

bebida: *drink*

¡Piense Ud. en el verano!
¡Piense Ud. en el sol!
¡Piense en su bronceado!
¡Compre hoy la loción bronceadora SOMBRA!

bronceado: *tan*
loción bronceadora: *suntan lotion*

¡Damas!
Para el pelo seco, para el pelo grasoso,
para el pelo fino, para el pelo grueso . . .
un solo champú
Usen el champú BRILLOR, el champú
de las estrellas de cine.

seco: *dry*
grasoso: *greasy*
grueso: *thick*
champú: *shampoo*
estrellas: *stars*

¡Jóvenes!
¡Lleven los blue-jeans YANKIS!
Los blue-jeans de la juventud internacional.

juventud: *youth*

Aprenda Ud. inglés electrónicamente
en menos de dos meses
con el método SINPENA.

«sinpena»: *easily*

¡No sean ridículos en sociedad!
Aprendan Uds. a bailar en 5 lecciones
en el ESTUDIO ESTRELLA.

Desarrolle Ud. su talento artístico.
Aprenda a dibujar con
la Escuela de Correspondencia
de Estudios Gráficos.

¿Sueñan Uds. con pasar unas vacaciones inolvidables?
¡No sueñen más!
Pasen sus vacaciones en las Islas Baleares
con el Club Internacional de Turismo.

inolvidables:
unforgettable

¡Piensen Uds. en la salud!
Dejen de fumar inmediatamente:
Para eso, tomen las pastillas FUMASTOP.

salud: *health*

pastillas: *tablets*

La publicidad está por todas partes: en la televisión, en los
periódicos, en la radio, en las paredes, en las carreteras, en el cine.
¿Cómo podemos resistirla?

por todas partes:
everywhere

NOTA CULTURAL

La enseñanza° del inglés

¿Cuál es la lengua extranjera más popular entre los estudiantes norteamericanos? Naturalmente, es el español. El español viene primero, antes del francés, del alemán y del italiano.

¿Y cuál es la lengua extranjera más popular en los países hispanos? Es el inglés ... hasta en España, que es el vecino de Francia.

¿Por qué es el inglés tan popular?

... Tal vez porque el inglés es la lengua de los negocios y de las ciencias.

... Tal vez porque más gente está viajando al extranjero° y si sabe inglés puede comunicarse.

... Tal vez porque es la lengua de un país muy importante en el mundo: los Estados Unidos.

... Tal vez porque existe cierto grado° de americanización en la vida de los hispanos.

... Tal vez porque la mayoría° de los hispanos se considera amigos de los Estados Unidos.

Al visitar un país hispano, te darás cuenta de que muchas personas pueden hablar inglés — pero que también a ellos les gusta mucho y lo aprecian cuando haces el esfuerzo° de hablar español.

enseñanza *teaching*   **al extranjero** *abroad*   **grado** *level*
mayoría *majority*   **esfuerzo** *effort*

¿Cuál es la lengua más popular en los países hispanos? ¿Cuál es la lengua más popular entre los estudiantes norteamericanos? ¿Hay muchos países en que se habla español? ¿Es el español una lengua internacional?

Vocabulario

sustantivos	**un bronceado**	tan		**una bebida**	drink, beverage
	un campeón	champion		**una estrella**	star
	un método	method		**la juventud**	youth
	un siglo	century		**la mayoría**	majority
				una pastilla	tablet, pill
				la salud	health

adjetivos	**grasoso**	greasy
	grueso	thick
	inolvidable	unforgettable
	seco	dry

expresiones	**en menos de dos meses**	in less than two months
	hoy día	today, nowadays

NOTA: Note the following constructions:

más de	+	number	_more than_	+	number
menos de	+	number	_less than_	+	number

Tengo **más de** dos meses de vacaciones.

¿Hay **menos de** treinta alumnos en la clase?

CONVERSACIÓN   OPTIONAL

Vamos a conversar sobre lo que aprendes.

1. ¿Aprendes **a tocar** el piano?
2. ¿Aprendes **a tocar** la guitarra?
3. ¿Aprendes **a conducir**?
4. ¿Aprendes **a escribir** a máquina?
5. ¿Aprendes **a hablar** francés?

OBSERVACIÓN

In the above questions, you are asked about things you are learning to do.

- What is the form of the verb that follows **aprendes?**   the infinitive
- Does that verb come immediately after **aprendes?** What word comes between **aprendes** and the verb?   a   no

Estructuras

A. Mandatos: las formas negativas regulares de *tú* y de *Ud., Uds.*

Compare the stems of the verbs in the following questions and commands.
Note that in the questions, the verbs are in the **yo** form of the present.

It is very important that the students master the formation of the **Ud.** and **Uds.** commands since the subjunctive formation follows the same pattern.

questions	commands
¿**Hablo** inglés?	¡No, no **hables** inglés!
¿**Salgo** con Manuel?	¡No, no **salgas** con él!
¿Cuántas aspirinas **tomo?**	¡**Tome** Ud. una, Sra. de Móntez!
¿**Salgo** con Felipe?	¡Sí, **salga** Ud. con él!
¿Dónde **estudio** con Marisela?	¡**Estudien** Uds. en la biblioteca!
¿**Hago** la tarea con Roberto?	¡Sí, **hagan** Uds. la tarea juntos!

stem: the **yo** form of the present minus **-o**
ending vowels: **-e** for **-ar** verbs; **-a** for **-er** and **-ir** verbs.

The forms of the commands (except for the affirmative **tú** form) are derived from the **yo** form of the present. The **-o** of the present is replaced by the following endings:

COMMANDS	-ar verbs	-er and -ir verbs			
(negative **tú**)	-es	-as	¡No mires!	¡No comas!	¡No escribas!
(Ud.)	-e	-a	¡Mire Ud.!	¡Coma Ud.!	¡Escriba Ud.!
(Uds.)	-en	-an	¡Miren Uds.!	¡Coman Uds.!	¡Escriban Uds.!

Note that the vowel of the endings is:
-e for **-ar** verbs
-a for **-er** and **-ir** verbs

This pattern for forming commands also applies to stem-changing verbs and to many verbs that are irregular in the **yo** form of the present.

infinitive	present	commands (tú negativo, Ud., Uds.)
cerrar	**cierro**	¡No **cierres** la ventana!
		¡Por favor, Sr. Móntez, **cierre** Ud. la puerta!
decir	**digo**	¡No **digas** mentiras, Carlos!
		¡No **digan** Uds. mentiras, José y Antonio!
		¡**Digan** Uds. la verdad!

In order to preserve the sound of the stem, some verbs have a spelling change in the stem:

ending	change	commands (tú negativo, Ud., Uds.)
-car	c → qu	¡Por favor, no **toques** el piano!
-gar	g → gu	¡Carlos y Felipe, **jueguen** Uds. con sus compañeros!
-zar	z → c	¡**Almuerce** Ud. conmigo, Sr. Chávez!

ACTIVIDAD 1   En el consultorio del médico *(In the doctor's office)*

La doctora Sánchez tiene un paciente, el Sr. Montero, que trabaja en una oficina y no hace ejercicio. Haz los papeles de la médica y del paciente. (Por supuesto, la médica usa *Ud.* con su paciente.)

> fumar   el Sr. Montero: ¿Puedo fumar?
> la Dra. Sánchez: ¡No! ¡No fume Ud.!
>
> comer fruta   el Sr. Montero: ¿Puedo comer fruta?
> la Dra. Sánchez: ¡Por supuesto! ¡Coma Ud. fruta!

VARIATION in the plural: Sr. and Sra. Montero visit the doctor. **¿Podemos fumar? ¡No, no fumen Uds.!**

1. nadar
2. esquiar
3. fumar cigarros
4. comer legumbres
5. comer dulces
6. beber wiski
7. comer helado
8. beber gaseosas
9. beber agua mineral
10. vivir en el campo
11. tomar pastillas para dormir *(sleeping pills)*
12. correr unas millas por día
13. montar en bicicleta al trabajo
14. trabajar 12 horas al día
15. trabajar los sábados y los domingos
16. saltar a la cuerda *(to jump rope)*
17. usar el ascensor *(elevator)*
18. subir la escalera a pie

ACTIVIDAD 2   ¡Nuevo, sí! ¡Viejo, no!

Un compañero te dice qué va a hacer. Ayúdale y dile que debe escoger las cosas nuevas, no las viejas.

> Voy a comprar libros.   Compra los libros nuevos.
> No compres los libros viejos.

1. Voy a escuchar cintas.
2. Voy a leer revistas.
3. Voy a comprar un diccionario.
4. Voy a estudiar verbos.
5. Voy a aprender canciones.

ACTIVIDAD 3   ¡No!

Imagina que tienes hijos. Eres un papá (una mamá) muy estricto(a) y les dices que *no* cuando te dicen lo que van a hacer. Contéstales a tus hijos.

> Salgo con Inés.   ¡No, no salgas con ella!

1. Salgo con Pablo.
2. Vuelvo a las doce.
3. Pongo unos discos de música popular.
4. Conduzco el coche.
5. Cuento un chiste.
6. Enciendo el radio.
7. Duermo en el saco de dormir *(sleeping bag)*.
8. Juego con Isabel.

This activity contains stem-changing verbs and verbs that are irregular in the **yo** form of the present.

VARIATION (for review): Respond in the affirmative. **Sí, sal con ella.**

ACTIVIDAD 4   ¡Son las doce!

This activity includes verbs with a spelling change, stem-changing verbs, and verbs with an irregular **yo** form.

Has invitado a algunos amigos a tu casa. Ahora son las doce de la noche y tus padres están en su cuarto. Tus amigos te preguntan si pueden hacer varias cosas. Contéstales sí o no.

VARIATION in the singular: **¿Puedo tocar el piano? No, no toques el piano.**

 ¿Podemos tocar el piano?   No, no toquen el piano.

 ¿Podemos jugar a los naipes *(cards)*?   Por supuesto, jueguen a los naipes.

1. ¿Podemos tocar la guitarra?
2. ¿Podemos sacar el coche del garaje?
3. ¿Podemos jugar con el perro?
4. ¿Podemos jugar al «Monopolio»?
5. ¿Podemos sacar fotos?
6. ¿Podemos cantar?
7. ¿Podemos bailar?
8. ¿Podemos poner discos de jazz?
9. ¿Podemos hacer ruido?
10. ¿Podemos usar el teléfono?
11. ¿Podemos apagar el radio?
12. ¿Podemos poner el tocadiscos?
13. ¿Podemos abrir las ventanas?
14. ¿Podemos cerrar la puerta?
15. ¿Podemos mostrar nuestras fotos?
16. ¿Podemos contar chistes?

WB
A1, A2,
A3, A4

SCRIPT
Act. 3, 4

MASTERS
p. 35

B. Mandatos: las formas negativas irregulares de *tú* y de *Ud., Uds.*

A few verbs have irregular commands in the **Ud., Uds.** and negative **tú** forms.

Act. 5

INFINITIVES	IRREGULAR COMMANDS: STEMS AND FORMS		
dar	**d-**	**(no des, dé, den)**	No **des** un paseo por el parque.
estar	**est-**	**(no estés, esté, estén)**	¡**Estén** Uds. aquí a las dos!
ser	**se-**	**(no seas, sea, sean)**	¡**Sean** Uds. buenos!
ir	**vay-**	**(no vayas, vaya, vayan)**	¡**Vayan** Uds. a la playa con ellos!
saber	**sep-**	**(no sepas, sepa, sepan)**	¡**Sepan** Uds. los verbos para el examen!

⟩⟩ Note that the verbs with irregular command stems are those that do not end in **-o** in the **yo** form of the present (**doy, estoy, soy, voy,** and **sé).**

⟩⟩ The imperative endings of these verbs are regular. Exception: there are accent marks on the following forms: **dé, esté, estés, estén.**

ACTIVIDAD 5   La clase

Imagina que eres el (la) profesor(a). Diles a los alumnos que deben hacer las siguientes cosas.

⋙   estar atentos   ¡Estén Uds. atentos!

1. estar a tiempo
2. estar tranquilos
3. ser bien educados
4. ser buenos alumnos
5. saber los verbos
6. saber el vocabulario
7. ir al laboratorio
8. ir a España
9. darle regalos a su profesor(a)
10. darles buenos consejos a sus amigos

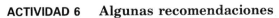

ACTIVIDAD 6   Algunas recomendaciones

Las siguientes personas quieren hacer muchas cosas. Diles que deben tener cuidado con ciertas cosas.

⋙   Paco y Elena quieren ir a la playa: el sol
        ¡Vayan a la playa! ¡Pero tengan cuidado con el sol!

1. Marisa y Roberto quieren ir a mi casa: el perro
2. El Sr. Gutiérrez quiere ir al centro: el tránsito *(traffic)*
3. Isabel y Marisol quieren dar un paseo por el campo: la hiedra venenosa *(poison ivy)*
4. Caperucita Roja *(Little Red Riding Hood)* quiere dar un paseo por el bosque: el lobo *(wolf)*
5. La Srta. de Clemente quiere ir al lago: los mosquitos
6. Mis hermanos quieren ir de compras: los coches

WB
B1

C. Repaso: verbo + preposición + infinitivo

Note the use of the infinitive after the verb in heavy print.

Quiero hablar francés.   *I want to speak French.*
Paco **aprende a** bailar.   *Paco is learning how to dance.*
¡**Dejen de** fumar!   *Stop smoking!*
Pienso ir a México.   *I am planning to go to Mexico.*

REMINDER: When a verb immediately follows another verb, the second verb is usually in the infinitive form.

Some verbs are followed directly by the infinitive. Others follow the pattern:

verb   +   preposition (**a, de, con, en**)   +   infinitive

VOCABULARIO PRÁCTICO
Algunos verbos y preposiciones con infinitivos

a	acostumbrarse a	to get used to	**Me acostumbro a** no tener mucho dinero.
	aprender a	to learn	**Aprendemos a** tocar la guitarra.
	comenzar a (e → ie)	to begin	¿**Comienzas a** tocar bien?
	empezar a (e → ie)	to begin	Paco **empieza a** conducir.
	enseñar a	to teach	Voy a **enseñarte a** hablar inglés.
de	**alegrarse de**	to be happy about	**Me alegro de** aprender cosas interesantes
	cansarse de	to get tired of	. . . pero **me canso de** ir al colegio todos los días.
	dejar de	to quit, to stop	¡**Dejen de** decir cosas estúpidas!
	tratar de	to try	¡**Trata de** estar tranquilo!

ACTIVIDAD 7 Buenos consejos

Imagina que escribes una columna en un periódico español. En esa columna, tratas de ayudar a las personas que te escriben. Dale un consejo a cada una de las siguientes personas. Empieza cada consejo con uno de los siguientes verbos: **dejar / aprender / comenzar / tratar**. También usa el infinitivo del verbo que las personas usan.

⚡ Fumo.   Deje de fumar.
⚡ No tengo paciencia.   Trate de tener paciencia.

1. Compro cosas inútiles.
2. Como muchos dulces.
3. Tomo muchas gaseosas.
4. Como mucho helado.
5. Duermo diez horas cada noche.
6. No hago ejercicios.
7. No juego al tenis.
8. No bailo bien.
9. No soy tolerante.
10. No nado.

ACTIVIDAD 8 Otros consejos OPTIONAL

Ahora, da consejos similares a las siguientes personas. ¡Usa tu imaginación!

⚡ a una persona gorda   Aprenda Ud. a comer menos.
(Deje de comer demasiado.)

1. a una persona muy flaca
2. a un chico tímido
3. a un estudiante que saca malas notas
4. a un alumno que se duerme en la clase
5. a una persona que no tiene amigos
6. a una persona que no sale nunca
7. a un chico que no practica ningún deporte

en	complacerse en	to take pleasure in	¿**Te complaces** mucho **en** decir tonterías?
	consistir en	to consist of, in	El trabajo **consiste en** vender discos.
	convenir en (e → ie)	to agree on	Hemos **convenido en** ir a las dos.
	insistir en	to insist on	**Insisto en** hablar con Ud.
	tardar en	to be late in	Paco **tarda en** venir.
	vacilar en	to hesitate	No **vacilo** nunca **en** decir la verdad.
con	soñar con (o → ue)	to dream about	Los alumnos **sueñan con** ir a Europa.

NOTAS: 1. **Convenir** is conjugated like **venir: convengo, convienes** . . .
2. The present tense forms of **complacerse** are like those of **conocer:**
Me **complazco** en escuchar música clásica.

ACTIVIDAD 9 Expresión personal

Expresa algo sobre las siguientes situaciones. Empieza cada frase con la forma **yo** de uno de los verbos del vocabulario.

⊙⊃ Hablo español en clase.

Empiezo a (aprendo a, me complazco en, vacilo en, sueño con . . .) hablar español en clase.

1. Tengo muchas amigas.
2. Soy norteamericano(a).
3. Tengo mucho dinero.
4. Voy a España.

5. Salgo con amigos simpáticos.
6. Conduzco.
7. Veo programas idiotas en la televisión.
8. Escucho discos de música popular.

Para la comunicación

OPTIONAL
May be assigned as homework.

Un poco de publicidad

Imagina que trabajas para una estación de televisión. Tienes que anunciar los siguientes productos:

la crema dental (*toothpaste*) LUX
la crema RUBY
el champú (*shampoo*) BELCOLOR
los discos MATADOR
el banco PACÍFICO
las aspirinas BADER

el hotel MIRAMAR
la gaseosa DÍNAMO
la revista MAÑANA
el método PERFECT para aprender inglés
el bolígrafo MARCA
BLANCO para lavar la ropa

Escoge tres productos y escribe un anuncio de tres o cuatro frases para cada producto. ¡Usa tu imaginación y tu sentido de la publicidad! Como modelo puedes usar los anuncios de «El arte de la persuasión».

El vendedor de la suerte

STRUCTURE TO OBSERVE: the position of pronouns with commands.

Act. 1

La suerte por unos pesos . . . o por unas pesetas . . . o por unos quetzales . . . En los países hispánicos hay una persona que puede traer a todo el mundo la felicidad eterna . . . Es el vendedor de lotería.

Desde la esquina de la calle, les ofrece la suerte a los transeúntes.
— . . . Lotería . . . Billetes de lotería . . . ¿Quién quiere transformar unos pesos en unos millones de pesos?
¿Quién quiere comprarse unos billetes de lotería?

transeúntes:
passers-by
Billetes: *Tickets*

Un chico se acerca.
—Tú, chico. Cómprate este billete . . .
—No tengo dinero.

Una señorita pasa.
—Cómpreselo, señorita . . . ¡Es el último!
—¿El último? ¡Bueno! ¡Démelo, por favor!
—Gracias, señorita. Cuesta solamente diez pesos . . . Diez pesos que pueden transformar su vida . . .

La señorita se va. Y mientras se va, el vendedor les ofrece de nuevo sus «últimos» billetes a los transeúntes.
—La suerte por diez pesos . . . ¿Quién quiere comprarse billetes de lotería . . .? ¡Me quedan sólo dos! ¡Ud., señor, cómpreselos! . . . ¡Mire! Mañana podrá ser millonario. ¡Ud., señora, cómpreselos! . . . ¿Ud. quiere uno? Bueno, diez pesos, ¡por favor!

¡Me quedan sólo dos!:
I have only two left!

¿Quién es el hombre que puede traer la felicidad eterna? ¿Qué les ofrece a los transeúntes? ¿Quién se acerca primero? ¿Por qué no compra billetes el chico? ¿Cuánto cuestan los billetes? ¿Compra un billete la señorita? ¿Compra un billete la señora?

La señora se aleja . . . y el vendedor sigue:
—Lotería . . . Lotería . . . ¡Me queda sólo uno! ¡Lléveselo hoy! ¿Quién quiere comprárselo? ¡Tú, chica, cómpratelo! ¿Sí? ¡Gracias! ¡Y que Dios te ayude!

se aleja: *moves on*

que Dios te ayude: *may God help you*

Act. 2

NOTA CULTURAL OPTIONAL

Los millonarios instantáneos

¿Cómo puedes ganar un millón de dólares de la noche a la mañana sin trabajar? Pues, puedes encontrar un tesoro, o heredar° una fortuna de un

tío rico o descubrir que hay un pozo° de petróleo en tu propio patio. En los países hispanos hay otra manera de hacerse millonario: sacar el gordo° de la lotería.

¿Quieres probar tu suerte? Es muy fácil: compra un billete de lotería. ¿Dónde? ¿De quién? Del vendedor ambulante,° el lotero, la persona que se gana la vida vendiendo billetes de lotería.

En algunos sitios,° la lotería se juega cada semana y los números que salen determinan la cantidad de tu premio. Para los días de fiesta como Semana Santa, la Navidad o el Año Nuevo, el premio es mayor.° Si todos los números que tienes salen, quiere decir que sacaste el gordo. Sí, hijo mío, ¡eres millonario . . . y de la noche a la mañana!

heredar *inherit* **pozo** *well* **gordo** *top prize*
ambulante *walking* **sitios** *places* **mayor** *greater*

¿Cómo es posible ganar mucho dinero sin trabajar? ¿Cómo se llama el hombre que vende billetes de lotería? ¿Para qué ocasiones hay un premio más grande? ¿Qué quiere decir la expresión «sacar el gordo»?

Vocabulario

sustantivos	**un billete**	ticket	**la felicidad**	happiness
	un premio	prize	**la lotería**	lottery
	un transeúnte	passer-by	**una transeúnte**	passer-by
	un vendedor	salesman, vendor	**una vendedora**	saleswoman, vendor
verbo	**alejarse**	to move away		
expresiones	**me queda(n)**	I have . . . left	**Que Dios te ayude.**	May God help you.

Note: **Alejarse** is derived from **lejos** (far).
Similarly, **acercarse** is derived from **cerca**.

Lección tres
349

For most verbs (except those that have an irregular **yo**
form in the present), the **nosotros** form of the imperative
is simply the **nosotros** form of the present in which:

a is replaced by **e**	¿Bail<u>a</u>mos?	¡Sí, bail<u>e</u>mos!
e, i are replaced by **a**	¿Com<u>e</u>mos?	¡Sí, com<u>a</u>mos!
	¿Escrib<u>i</u>mos?	¡Sí, escrib<u>a</u>mos!

Estructuras

Act. 3

A. Mandatos: la primera persona del plural *(nosotros)*

Note the forms and use of commands in the following sentences.

¡**Compremos** un billete de lotería!	*Let's buy a lottery ticket.*
¡**No vendamos** el coche!	*Let's not sell the car.*
¡**No decidamos** nada ahora!	*Let's not decide anything now.*
¡**Salgamos** con nuestros amigos!	*Let's go out with our friends.*
¡**Pongamos** música de baile!	*Let's put on dance music.*
¡**Demos** una fiesta!	*Let's give a party.*

To express *let's* or *let's not,* Spanish speakers use the **nosotros** command form.
For most verbs this form is derived from the **yo** form of the present as follows:

STEM	ENDINGS
yo form of the present minus **-o**	**-emos** for **-ar** verbs **-amos** for **-er** and **-ir** verbs

For stem-changing verbs in **-ar** and **-er**:

The forms for stem-changing verbs in
-ir will be presented on p. 388.

STEM		ENDINGS	
infinitive minus	**-ar**	**-emos**	¡Cerr**emos** la puerta!
	-er	**-amos**	¡No volv**amos** tarde!

The spelling changes that occur in the
Ud. or **Uds.** forms also occur in the
nosotros form: **organizar → organicemos
jugar → juguemos tocar → toquemos**

♪) The **nosotros** form of the command for **ir** is **vamos.**

  Vamos a la playa.   *Let's go to the beach.*

♪) The *let's* construction may also be rendered by **vamos a** + infinitive.

  Vamos a bailar.   *Let's dance.*
  Vamos a salir.   *Let's go out.*

  This construction, however, cannot be used in the negative.

ACTIVIDAD 1   La revolución

Imagina que los alumnos se niegan *(refuse)* a estudiar. En vez de estudiar,
deciden hacer cosas más divertidas. Eres el (la) líder de esta revolución
estudiantil. ¿Qué vas a proponerles a tus compañeros?

♪) estudiar (no)   ¡No estudiemos más!
♪) jugar a la pelota (sí)   ¡Juguemos a la pelota!

1. aprender los verbos (no)
2. escuchar la radio (sí)
3. escuchar las cintas (no)
4. regresar a casa (sí)
5. leer historietas *(comics)* (sí)
6. perder el tiempo (sí)
7. dibujar en los cuadernos (sí)
8. pintar el autobús de negro (sí)
9. hacer ruido (sí)
10. hacer la tarea (no)
11. saludar a los profesores (no)
12. hablar español (sí)

ACTIVIDAD 2   Diálogo: Planes para el fin de semana

Hablemos del fin de semana. Estás pensando en las siguientes actividades
para ti y tus compañeros. Usa la forma **nosotros** en el presente. Tus
compañeros aceptan tus ideas o no las aceptan, usando la forma **nosotros**
en el imperativo.

♪) estudiar   Estudiante 1: ¿Estudiamos?
                Estudiante 2: ¡Sí (no, no) estudiemos!
                            ¡Qué buena idea! (¡Qué idea más tonta!)

WB
A1, A2

SCRIPT
[●═●]
Act. 4

MASTERS
p. 36

1. organizar una fiesta
2. invitar a unos chicos (unas chicas) al cine
3. visitar un museo
4. tener un picnic
5. discutir la política
6. jugar al béisbol
7. correr el maratón
8. correr las olas
9. hacer un viaje al campo
10. salir con unos chicos (unas chicas)
11. ir al centro
12. ir a nadar

B. La posición de los pronombres con los mandatos

Note the position of the object pronouns in the following commands.

PRESENT	COMMAND (AFFIRMATIVE)	COMMAND (NEGATIVE)
¿Te invito?	¡Sí, invítame!	¡No, no me invites!
¿Me levanto?	¡Sí, levántate!	¡No, no te levantes!
¿Invitamos a Carlos?	¡Sí, invitémoslo!	¡No, no lo invitemos!
¿Nos lavamos?	¡Sí, lávense!	¡No, no se laven!

Object pronouns come before the verb in negative commands. In affirmative commands, they come after the verb and are attached to it.

☞ When one pronoun is attached to the command verb, there is an accent mark on the next-to-last syllable of the verb. If the verb has only one syllable, it does not have an accent: **Ponlo.**

☞ When the pronoun **nos** is attached to a **nosotros** command form, the final **s** of the verb is dropped.

OPTIONAL

¿Nos levantamos?   ¡Sí, **levantémonos**!
¿Nos vamos?   ¡Sí, **vámonos**!

ACTIVIDAD 3   La mudanza *(Moving)*

Make sure that students use the **Ud.** form of commands when talking to the agent of the moving company.

VARIATION: Marisela's older brother is helping her. Use the **tú** form: **No, no la pongas allá. Ponla en la cocina.**

Marisela va a pasar un año en Buenos Aires. Ha alquilado un apartamento pequeño que tiene tres cuartos: una cocina, un dormitorio y una sala. El agente de mudanzas *(mover)* quiere saber en qué cuarto tiene que poner los varios objetos. Haz los papeles del agente y de Marisela según el modelo.

☞   la refrigeradora / el dormitorio

> El agente: ¿Pongo la refrigeradora en el dormitorio?
> Marisela: No, no la ponga allá. Póngala en la cocina.

1. la cama / la cocina
2. el televisor / la cocina
3. los discos / la cocina
4. los libros / la cocina
5. los cuchillos / el dormitorio
6. los vasos / el dormitorio
7. el sofá / el dormitorio
8. la máquina de escribir / la cocina

ACTIVIDAD 4   **Para mantenerse en buena salud** *(To stay healthy)*

Un médico les dice a sus clientes lo que tienen que hacer para mantenerse sanos. Haz el papel del (de la) médico(a) usando mandatos afirmativos o negativos según la lógica del caso.

⤳   divertirse   ¡Diviértanse!
             (¡No se diviertan!)

1. levantarse temprano
2. levantarse tarde
3. acostarse temprano
4. acostarse tarde
5. lavarse a menudo
6. enfadarse

7. irritarse
8. quedarse siempre enfrente del televisor
9. ponerse furiosos
10. preocuparse inútilmente
11. calmarse siempre
12. pelearse con otros

VOCABULARIO PRÁCTICO   Para el camping

ir de camping   to go camping

unos gemelos

una mochila

una tienda de campaña

un saco de dormir

una linterna eléctrica

un cacharro

una sartén

una manta

ACTIVIDAD 5 **Regalos de cumpleaños** OPTIONAL

Isabel es una chica muy generosa pero no sabe nunca qué regalarles a sus amigos para su cumpleaños. Dile cuál de los siguientes regalos puede comprarles a estas personas.

For some items various
answers are possible.

unos discos	un saco de dormir	unos cacharros
una raqueta	una sartén eléctrica	una manta
unos libros	una mochila	una tienda de campaña
un perro	unos gemelos	una linterna eléctrica

A Jaime le gusta observar los pájaros.   Cómprale unos gemelos.

1. A Paco y Roberto les gusta la música.
2. A mí me gusta el tenis.
3. A mis primos les gusta leer.
4. A Isabel le gusta ir de camping.
5. A nosotros nos gusta cocinar.
6. A Manuel le gustan los animales.
7. A Gloria y Adela no les gusta viajar con muchas maletas.
8. A Andrés no le gusta tener frío cuando duerme.

WB
B1, B2

SCRIPT

Act. 5, 7, 8

MASTERS
p. 36

C. Los mandatos con dos pronombres OPTIONAL

May be taught for recognition
only.

Note the pronouns in the sentences on the right.

¿Te muestro mis fotos?	No **me las muestres** hoy.
	Muéstramelas mañana.
¿Me pongo la corbata?	No **te la pongas** para ir a clase.
	Póntela para ir a la fiesta.

When two object pronouns are used, the order is:

> indirect object pronoun + direct object pronoun

When the two pronouns are attached to the verb, there is an accent mark on the next to the last syllable of the verb. If the verb has only one syllable, the accent is on that syllable.

Compare: **Compre** la mochila.   *Buy the backpack.*
Cómpreme la mochila.   *Buy me the backpack.*
Cómpremela.   *Buy it for me.*

ACTIVIDAD 6   El amigo norteamericano

Supón que un amigo norteamericano va a pasar el mes de agosto contigo en México. Te pregunta si tiene que comprarse *(buy himself)* las siguientes cosas. Dile si tiene que comprárselas o no. Usa el mandato de **comprarse** en frases negativas o afirmativas.

¿Debo comprarme anteojos de sol?   ¡Sí, cómpratelos!
(¡No, no te los compres!)

1. ¿Debo comprarme un traje de baño?
2. ¿Debo comprarme un saco de dormir?
3. ¿Debo comprarme una tienda de campaña?
4. ¿Debo comprarme una manta?

5. ¿Debo comprarme esquís?
6. ¿Debo comprarme unos suéteres?
7. ¿Debo comprarme una mochila?
8. ¿Debo comprarme discos de música latina?

ACTIVIDAD 7   Mañana

Hay muchas cosas que Carlos quiere hacer para Marina. Desafortunadamente, Marina está muy ocupada hoy. Carlos tiene que hacer estas cosas mañana. Haz el papel de Carlos y de Marina.

mostrar mis fotos   Carlos: ¿Te muestro mis fotos?
Marina: No me las muestres hoy.
Muéstramelas mañana.

WB
C1

SCRIPT
Act. 6

1. comprar el periódico
2. prestar la sartén
3. llevar los libros
4. mandar las cartas

5. devolver el saco de dormir
6. devolver la tienda de campaña
7. contar chistes
8. contar cuentos

Para la comunicación

OPTIONAL
May be assigned as homework.

¿Tienes talento para vender?

Imagina que quieres vender las siguientes cosas:

VARIATION: Pairs of students can prepare skits.

- unas entradas para la comedia musical organizada por tu escuela
- unas entradas para un partido de béisbol en que el equipo de tu escuela va a jugar (es un equipo muy bueno)
- unas entradas para un partido de fútbol en que el equipo de tu escuela va a jugar (es un equipo terrible)
- unas entradas para la fiesta del club de español

WB
¿Quién va...

TRB
QUIZ
pp. 101–102

Haz unas frases en que tratas de vender estas cosas a una persona que no conoces bien. Si quieres, puedes inspirarte en el texto «El vendedor de la suerte».

¡No pierda la oportunidad! ¡Cómprese una entrada para la comedia musical!

Lección 4 Sí, pero . . .

Act. 1

Avisos, sugerencias, consejos, mandatos o prohibiciones . . . son parte de nuestra existencia.

Por eso, todos los días tenemos que escuchar mil recomendaciones diferentes, en el colegio y en casa también.

Por ejemplo . . .

Avisos: *Warnings*
sugerencias: *suggestions*

Yo: Mamá, ¿puedo usar el teléfono?
Mamá: Claro, úsalo . . .
    pero no permito que lo uses
    más de cinco minutos.

Yo: Hay un programa de deportes
    esta noche . . . ¿Puedo verlo?
Papá: Sí, por supuesto . . .
    pero . . . antes de verlo, insisto
    en que termines la tarea . . . y
    que limpies tu cuarto . . . y que
    ayudes a tu mamá . . .
    y que . . .

Yo: ¿Puedo ir al cine?
Papá: Sí . . . pero quiero que vuelvas
    a casa a las diez en punto . . .
    e insisto en que no vayas allá
    con la moto de tu amigo
    Fernando . . . y que la película
    sea sin violencia . . .

en punto: *on the dot*

sea: *be*

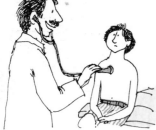

Yo: ¿Qué profesión me aconsejan
    Uds.?
Papá: Por supuesto, la decisión es
    tuya . . . pero espero que sea
    una profesión respetable . . .
    como la de médico . . . o la de
    arquitecto.
Mamá: ¡Yo prefiero que seas abogado!
Tío Andrés: Y yo, espero que seas oficial
    . . . ¡como yo!
La abuela: ¡Y yo prefiero que seas
    sacerdote!

aconsejan: *advise*

seas: *you be*
oficial: *officer*

sacerdote: *priest*

Students may observe that the subjunctive forms (after **permito que, insisto en que,** etc.) are similar to those of direct commands.

A veces me pregunto: ¿Es posible sobrevivir cuando hay tantas limitaciones en la vida?

sobrevivir: *to survive*

NOTA CULTURAL OPTIONAL

La familia y la selección de una carrera

¿Sabes qué profesión escogerás o en qué campo° profesional entrarás? ¿Lo consultarás con tus amigos? ¿Con tu consejero escolar?° ¿O con tus padres? ¿O vas a tomar la decisión tú mismo?

En los países hispanos, la familia desempeña° un papel muy importante en la selección de las profesiones. En efecto, muchísimas veces los hijos escogen la profesión de sus padres. Ésta es la costumbre especialmente en los pueblos donde el comercio y la artesanía° son transmitidos de generación a generación.

Por eso, si el padre es carpintero, joyero,° albañil° o hacendado,° a menudo los hijos seguirán la misma profesión que el padre. En las ciudades grandes, las profesiones serán diferentes. Pero si el padre es médico, dentista, abogado, hombre de negocios o político, es probable que alguno de los hijos seguirán la misma profesión.

campo *field*   **consejero escolar** *guidance counselor*
desempeña *plays*   **artesanía** *crafts*   **joyero** *jeweler*
albañil *mason*   **hacendado** *rancher*

Aunque° la familia sigue desempeñando° un papel muy importante en la selección de las profesiones, los jóvenes hispanos gozan de° más libertad en esta selección. Sin embargo, por la abundancia de nuevas carreras, los jóvenes siguen pidiendo consejo° a sus padres sobre qué les convendría mejor° estudiar.

Aunque *Although*   **sigue desempeñando** *continues to play*   **gozan de** *enjoy*   **consejo** *advice*   **les convendría mejor** *would be best for them*

CONVERSACIÓN   OPTIONAL

Vamos a hablar de tus relaciones con tus amigos.

1. ¿Quieres que tus amigos te **admiren**?
   Sí (No, no) quiero que mis amigos me
   admiren.

2. ¿Quieres que tus amigos te **imiten**?

3. ¿Quieres que tus amigos te **comprendan**?

4. ¿Quieres que tus amigos te **digan** siempre
   la verdad?

5. ¿Quieres que tus amigos **tengan** paciencia
   contigo?

OBSERVACIÓN

In the above questions, you were asked if you want your friends to do certain
things. To express your request, you used the expression **quiero que** *(I want)*.
Your command was *indirect* rather than direct. The verb form that follows **quiero
que** and expresses the indirect command is called the *subjunctive*.

• Are the subjunctive forms the same as the **Uds.** command form?   yes

Estructuras

A. El subjuntivo: la formación regular

A command, order, recommendation or suggestion may be given either:

—directly   **Study!**
—or indirectly   **I want you to study!**

Compare the verb forms used in the following direct and indirect
commands.

direct commands
¡No **hables** inglés, María!
¡**Aprenda** inglés, Sr. Chávez!
¡**Salgamos** esta noche!
¡**Pongan** los discos aquí, Ana y Luis!

Quiero que

indirect commands
no **hables** inglés.
aprenda inglés.
salgamos esta noche.
pongan los discos aquí.

Except for the **tú** commands in the affirmative, Spanish speakers use the same verb forms for both direct and indirect commands. These are called *subjunctive* verb forms.

Note the subjunctive forms of the verbs in the chart below:

ct. 3, 5

INFINITIVE	cantar	leer	escribir	salir
yo form of present	canto	leo	escribo	salgo
SUBJUNCTIVE				
(yo)	cante	lea	escriba	salga
(tú)	cantes	leas	escribas	salgas
(él, ella, Ud.)	cante	lea	escriba	salga
(nosotros)	cantemos	leamos	escribamos	salgamos
(vosotros)	cantéis	leáis	escribáis	salgáis
(ellos, ellas, Uds.)	canten	lean	escriban	salgan

As we have seen, the subjunctive is derived from the **yo** form of the present, as follows:

STEM	ENDINGS	
yo form of the present minus **-o**	**-e, -es, -e, -emos, -éis, -en**	(for **-ar** verbs)
	-a, -as, -a, -amos, -áis, -an	(for **-er** and **-ir** verbs)

As in the imperative, certain spelling changes are necessary to preserve the sound of the stem.

-car (c → qu)   Quiero que no **toques** la guitarra.
-gar (g → gu)   Quiero que **paguen.**
-zar (z → c)   Quiero que **empiecen** el trabajo.

ACTIVIDAD 1   En el campamento de veraneo *(At summer camp)*

Imagina que trabajas como asistente del director de un campamento de veraneo. Insistes en que todos los chicos se laven antes de acostarse. Expresa esto, usando **quiero que** + el subjuntivo de **lavarse.**

Raúl   Quiero que Raúl se lave.

1. tú
2. Isabel
3. Carlos
4. Uds.

5. tus amigos
6. Rafael y Esteban
7. Mari-Carmen
8. nosotros

VARIATIONS: with bañarse, comer más, escribir cartas, hacer la cama, tener cuidado.

ACTIVIDAD 2　En la clase

El (la) profesor(a) es muy exigente. Para él (ella), hay tres cosas muy importantes: hablar español, aprender los verbos y no hacer ruido. Expresa que el (la) profesor(a) espera esto de cada uno de los alumnos.

> María　　El profesor quiere que María hable español.
> 　　　　　Quiere también que aprenda los verbos.
> 　　　　　Finalmente quiere que no haga ruido.

1. Felipe
2. Manuel y Roberto
3. Ud.
4. Uds.
5. Teresa y yo

6. toda la clase
7. yo
8. tú
9. nosotros
10. todos los alumnos

ACTIVIDAD 3　¿Sí o no?

Carlos le pregunta a su papá si tiene que hacer las siguientes cosas. Su papá le dice que sí o que no. Haz los dos papeles.

*This exercise practices the subjunctive of verbs with irregular **yo** forms in the present.*

> poner la mesa (sí)　　　Carlos: ¿Pongo la mesa, papá?
> 　　　　　　　　　　　　Papá: ¡Por supuesto! . . . ¡Quiero que pongas la mesa!

> decir un chiste (no)　　Carlos: ¿Te digo un chiste, papá?
> 　　　　　　　　　　　　Papá: No, no quiero que me digas ningún chiste.

1. hacer la tarea (sí)
2. hacer un viaje con mis amigos (no)
3. poner el coche en el garaje (sí)
4. salir con Pedro (sí)
5. salir con Manuel (no)
6. conducir tu coche (no)
7. conducir el coche de mi abuelo (sí)
8. poner aceite en la ensalada (sí)
9. poner vinagre en el yogur (no)
10. poner una rana *(frog)* en la cama de la tía Isabel (no)
11. tener cuidado con el perro (no)
12. tener cuidado con el tránsito (sí)
13. decir la verdad (sí)
14. decir mentiras (no)

ACTIVIDAD 4 **¡Un poco de lógica!** OPTIONAL

En cinco minutos haz tantas frases lógicas como puedas, usando los elementos de las columnas A, B, C y D. Las frases pueden ser afirmativas o negativas.

May be assigned as a special challenge activity.

A	B	C	D
tú		yo	organizar una fiesta
Carlos		nosotros	ayudar en casa
mi mejor amigo(a)	querer que	Manuela	estudiar
el profesor		los alumnos	hablar inglés
mis padres		tú y yo	usar el teléfono
			comprar cosas inútiles
			tocar la guitarra
			llevar el tocadiscos
			conducir el coche
			hacer ruido
			tener cuidado
			venir a la fiesta

SCRIPT
Act. 4, 6

⟩⟩ Mis padres no quieren que (yo) use el teléfono.

B. El uso del subjuntivo: mandatos indirectos

In each of the sentences below, the subject expresses a wish (or an indirect command) that concerns someone else. Note the use of the subjunctive.

El profesor **quiere que los alumnos estudien**.	*The teacher **wants the students to study**.*
Mi papá **me pide que le ayude**.	*My father **is asking me to help him**.*
Inés **no quiere que su novio vea a Elena**.	*Inés **does not want her boyfriend to see Elena**.*

Spanish speakers use the subjunctive after verbs and expressions in which a wish (weak or strong) is made. Note that the wish must concern someone (or something) other than the subject. When the wish concerns the subject, the infinitive is used.

Contrast:

the wish concerns the subject (infinitive)	the wish concerns someone else (subjunctive)
Espero visitar México.	(Yo) **espero que Paco visite** México.
Mi padre **quiere aprender** español.	Mi padre **quiere que yo aprenda** español.

⟩⟩ Some of the verbs and expressions that are used to express a wish or indirect command appear in the **Vocabulario práctico**.

El papá de Felipe quiere que su hijo haga ciertas cosas . . . pero Felipe no
quiere hacerlas. Haz los dos papeles según el modelo.

☞   estudiar   el papá: Quiero que estudies.
                    Felipe: Y yo, no quiero estudiar.

1. aprender francés
2. estudiar para hacerte médico
3. aprender a tocar el violín
4. escuchar música clásica
5. leer poesía
6. conocer a personas importantes

7. salir con compañeros serios
8. levantarte temprano
9. cortarte el pelo
10. limpiar tu cuarto
11. hacer la cama
12. cuidar a tus hermanitos

The following verbs and expressions are used to express indirect commands and strong wishes.

VOCABULARIO PRÁCTICO   Mandatos indirectos

preference

| **(me) gusta que** | (I) like | No **me gusta que** salgas con mi novia. |
| **preferir (e → ie) que** | to prefer | **Prefiero que** no vengas a la fiesta. |

suggestion, advice

tolerar que	to tolerate	¿**Toleras que** tus amigos se burlen de ti?
sugerir (e → ie) que	to suggest	¿Qué **sugieres que** hagamos?
recomendar (e → ie) que	to advise	¿Qué **recomiendas que** yo le diga al profesor?

ACTIVIDAD 6   Sí, pero . . .

Carlos quiere hacer ciertas cosas para Mari-Carmen, pero Mari-Carmen
tiene ideas diferentes. Haz los dos papeles según el modelo.

⟩⟩⟩   invitarte al teatro / al cine   Carlos: ¿Quieres que te invite al teatro?
                                    Mari-Carmen: Sí, pero . . . prefiero que me invites al cine.

1. comprarte un helado / dulces
2. prestarte mis libros / discos
3. llamarte hoy / mañana
4. invitar a tus hermanos al teatro / primas
5. salir con Elena / conmigo
6. prestarte 5 dólares / 10 dólares

hope, wish

desear que	to wish	¿**Deseas que** hable español contigo?
esperar que	to hope	¿**Esperas que** tus amigos te inviten al cine?
ojalá (que)	let's hope that	**Ojalá (que)** haga buen tiempo mañana.

prohibition

| **oponerse a que** | to be against | **Me opongo a que** leas mi diario. |
| **prohibir que** | to forbid | Mi papá **prohibe que** conduzca el coche. |

request, command

pedir (e → i) que	to ask	Mis padres me **piden que** estudie más.
insistir en que	to insist	Mis amigos **insisten en que** me divierta con ellos.
mandar que	to order	La policía **manda que** los conductores sean prudentes.
rogar (o → ue) que	to beg	Los abogados **ruegan que** sus clientes digan la verdad.
exigir que	to demand	Los profesores **exigen que** los alumnos los respeten.

NOTA: The expression **ojalá** (or **ojalá que**), which must be followed by the subjunctive, is
      derived from an Arabic expression meaning "May Allah grant that." It has several
      English equivalents:

  Let's hope that . . .   ¡**Ojalá** haga buen tiempo el próximo sábado!
  I wish (hope) that . . .   ¡**Ojalá que** Carmen acepte mi invitación!

The Arabs occupied Spain for about eight centuries (711–1492). As a result, there are many words of Arabic origin in
Spanish, e.g., **naranja, álgebra, algodón** (cotton).

ACTIVIDAD 7   Expresión personal

¿Cómo reaccionas en las siguientes circunstancias? Para expresar tu
actitud, usa una de las siguientes expresiones: **(no) acepto que** / **(no)
tolero que** / **insisto en que** / **me opongo a que** / **prohibo que** / **ruego que.**

☞   Mi hermano toma mi guitarra.   (No) Tolero que mi hermano tome mi guitarra.

1. Mis profesores respetan mis ideas.
2. Mis padres me comprenden.
3. Mis amigos me ayudan.
4. Mis amigos olvidan mi cumpleaños.
5. Mi mejor amigo(a) sale con mi novio(a).
6. Mi mejor amigo(a) no me dice la verdad.
7. Mis hermanos me molestan.
8. Mis profesores reconocen mi talento.

ACTIVIDAD 8   Recomendaciones   OPTIONAL

Hazle una sugerencia a cada una de las siguientes personas. Empieza tus
sugerencias con **Sugiero o recomiendo que . . .** . Puedes usar uno de los
siguientes verbos. ¡Usa tu imaginación!

  comprar / **llevarse** / **aprender** / **tener** / **tener cuidado con**

☞   Paco va a pasar un año en los Estados Unidos.
          Sugiero (Recomiendo) que Paco aprenda inglés (que se lleve sus discos . . .).

1. Mari-Carmen va a pasar un año en Francia.
2. Gil y Roberto van a pasar unos dos meses en Italia.
3. Isabel va a la playa.
4. Manuel y Clara van a la montaña.
5. Vamos a las Islas Galápagos.
6. Vamos a pescar.

ACTIVIDAD 9   Expresión personal: ¡Ojalá!   OPTIONAL

Haz tres frases para cada una de las siguientes personas. Empieza cada
frase con **Ojalá que.** Si quieres, usa los siguientes verbos: **comprar** /
recibir / **sacar** / **tener** / **vender** / **salir** / **conocer** / **hacer** / **invitar** /
descubrir. Usa también tu imaginación.

☞   Mi mejor amigo   Ojalá que compre una moto.
                    Ojalá que conozca chicas simpáticas.
                    Ojalá que haga algo interesante el próximo fin de semana.

1. mi mejor amiga   4. los vecinos   7. Ud.
2. el (la) profesor(a)   5. mis compañeros   8. Uds.
3. mis padres   6. yo   9. tú

WB
B1, B2,
B3

SCRIPT
Act. 7, 8

MASTERS
p. 37

C. El concepto del subjuntivo

Tenses and moods

In a sentence, the verbs tell what the action is. Each verb form is characterized by its tense and its mood.

- The *tense* indicates the time of the action.
  The present, the future, the imperfect and the preterite are different tenses.
- The *mood* reflects the attitude of the speaker toward the action.
  The indicative and the subjunctive are different moods.

Indicative vs. subjunctive

In English, the subjunctive, although rare, is still occasionally used.
Compare the verbs in the following sentences.

indicative	*subjunctive*
He *is* not a good student.	I wish he *were* an excellent student.
Carlos *is* in Mexico.	It is important that he *be* home for Christmas.
Elena *studies* English.	Her parents insist that she *study* French also.

Spanish speakers, on the other hand, use the subjunctive mood frequently.
Therefore, it is very important to know when to use it and why.
Compare the uses of the indicative and the subjunctive in the following sentences.

PRESENT INDICATIVE (what is)	PRESENT SUBJUNCTIVE (what may be)
Sé Veo } que Uds. **estudian** poco. Observo	Quiero Prefiero } que Uds. **estudien** más. Insisto en

Indicative

When you say **Uds. estudian poco** or **Sé que Uds. estudian poco,** you express a fact or your knowledge of this fact. In Spanish the indicative is used to *state facts*. It is the mood of *what is*.

Subjunctive

When you say **Quiero que Uds. estudien más** or **Insisto en que Uds. estudien más,** you express a wish. In Spanish, the subjunctive is used to express *wishes* and other *feelings* and *attitudes* about an idea or fact. It is the mood of *what may be*.

In this lesson, you have learned that the subjunctive is used to express indirect commands. In Units 9 and 10, you will learn more about other uses of the subjunctive.

If appropriate, you may want to refine the above concept further by contrasting the uses of the indicative and the subjunctive after **decir** and **escribir**.
INDICATIVE: **Digo (escribo) que Carlos conduce bien.** I say (I write) that Carlos drives well. Here **decir** (and **escribir**) are used to express a *fact.*
SUBJUNCTIVE: **Le digo (Le escribo) a Carlos que conduzca bien.** I am telling (I am writing) Carlos that he should drive well. Here **decir** and **escribir** are used to express a *wish* or *indirect command.*

ACTIVIDAD 10   La perfección

Imagina que eres una persona muy exigente *(demanding)*. Sabes que las siguientes personas hacen ciertas cosas bien pero quieres que las hagan mejor. Expresa esto según el modelo.

 Carlos toca la guitarra.

Sé que Carlos toca la guitarra bien . . . pero quiero que toque mejor.

1. Inés canta.
2. Tú tocas el piano.
3. Pedro nada.
4. Mis primos bailan.
5. Tú hablas francés.
6. Hablan italiano.
7. Corren las olas.
8. Juegas al béisbol.
9. Marina monta a caballo.
10. Felipe esquía.
11. Carmen escala montañas.
12. Mis amigos se lanzan en paracaídas *(parachutes)*.

ACTIVIDAD 11   Lo que sabemos y lo que esperamos

¿Son reales las siguientes cosas o son solamente cosas deseables *(desirable)*? Expresa tu punto de vista personal usando **ojalá que** + subjuntivo o **sé que** + indicativo.

WB
C1, C2,
C3

SCRIPT
Act. 9, 10

MASTERS
p. 37

 los norteamericanos: hablar inglés   Sé que los norteamericanos hablan inglés.

 los norteamericanos: hablar español   Ojalá que los norteamericanos hablen español.

1. yo: tener un coche / ganar dinero / tener amigos simpáticos
2. los vecinos: tener un bote / ganar la lotería / invitar a mis padres a su casa
3. el (la) profesor(a): tener paciencia / ayudar a los alumnos / hablar español / hablar inglés
4. mis amigos: tener un coche deportivo / salir conmigo / invitarme a la fiesta
5. los norteamericanos: ayudar a los otros países / hacer las paces con todos

Para la comunicación

OPTIONAL
May be assigned as homework.

Expresión personal

Tú también quieres que los otros hagan ciertas cosas. Di lo que esperas *(expect)* de las siguientes personas. ¡Usa tu imaginación!

WB
Recomen-
daciones

TRB

QUIZ
pp. 103–104

WB   Test/Repaso   TEST pp. 105–108

 mi papá   Espero que mi papá me compre una moto.
(Espero que mi papá no me hable de mis estudios.)

1. mi mamá
2. mi mejor amigo
3. mi mejor amiga
4. mis profesores
5. mis hermanos
6. el presidente
7. el (la) alcalde *(mayor)*
8. todo el mundo

VARIATION: Have students cut out pictures of several people and indicate what they would like them to do.

Variedades   El ojo de Dios

Para los indios en el oeste de México, el ojo de Dios° es algo mágico. Estos objetos sirven para asegurar° el bienestar:° comida para todos, larga vida y salud para los niños. El ojo de Dios es un talismán° que protege° la casa y a las personas que viven en ella.

   ¿Y tú? ¿No quieres proteger tu casa? Pues,° mira. Hacer un ojo de Dios es muy fácil.

Materiales:

  2 varillas° delgadas (más o menos del grueso°
    de un lápiz) de 25 centímetros de largo cada una
  2 madejas° de lana,° una de cada color: rojo y
    negro, amarillo y verde, azul y rosado, o
    cualquier° otra combinación
  goma° blanca
  tijeras

Instrucciones:

1. Haz una cruz° con las
   varillas, cruzándolas
   en el centro.

2. Escoge el color que
   deseas para el centro
   del ojo y usa una
   punta° de lana para
   atar° las varillas con
   un nudo.°

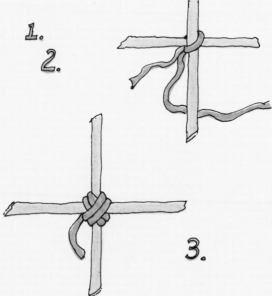

3. Enrolla° la lana
   alrededor de las
   varillas, haciendo
   una ✕ . Haz esto
   dos o tres veces.

Dios: *God*
asegurar: *to insure*
  bienestar: *well-being*
talismán: *good-luck
  piece*
protege: *protects*
Pues: *Then*

varillas: *sticks*
  grueso: *thickness*

madejas: *skeins*
  lana: *yarn*

cualquier: *any*

goma: *glue*

cruz: *cross*

punta: *end*
atar: *to tie*
nudo: *knot*

Enrolla: *Wrap*

4. Ahora, toma la lana
   y comienza a
   enrollarla en cada
   varilla. Primero,
   pásala delante de la varilla,
   luego por detrás y
   luego delante
   otra vez.

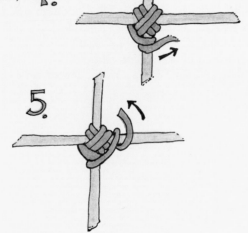

5. Trae la lana a la
   varilla más cerca a
   tu derecha, tirándola°
   para que quede
   tensa° y junto al
   centro.

tirándola: *pulling it*

tensa: *tight*

6. Haz la misma
   operación que hiciste
   en la primera varilla
   (Punto 4).

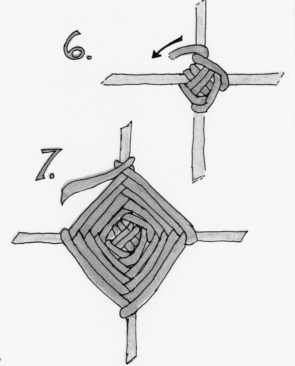

7. Sigue haciendo esta
   operación pasando la
   lana siempre a la
   próxima varilla.
   Cuando tienes una
   banda de color de
   unos tres o cuatro
   centímetros de ancho,
   cambia de color.

8. Corta la lana y pega° la punta a la parte de atrás° de la varilla. Toma la punta del nuevo color y pégala a la parte de atrás de esta varilla. Luego enrolla, como hiciste con la primera banda de color.

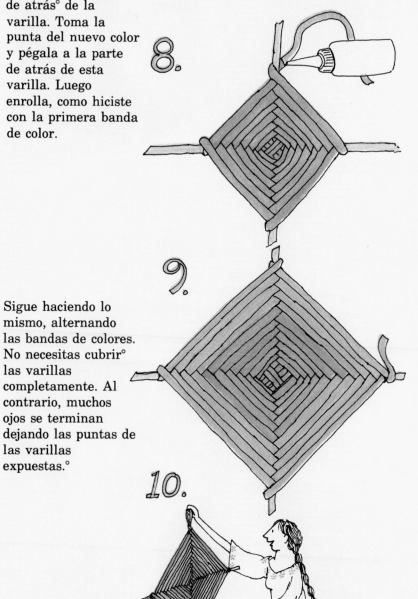

9. Sigue haciendo lo mismo, alternando las bandas de colores. No necesitas cubrir° las varillas completamente. Al contrario, muchos ojos se terminan dejando las puntas de las varillas expuestas.°

10. Para colgar° el ojo, amarra° una argolla° de lana a la punta de una de las varillas.

pega: *glue*

de atrás: *in back*

cubrir: *to cover*

expuestas: *uncovered*

colgar: *to hang*
amarra: *fasten*
argolla: *loop*

9

Unidad

¡Así es la vida!

OBJECTIVES

Communication

By the end of this unit, students will be able to use Spanish:

- To talk about *what is* and *what may be*
- To express an opinion, an emotion, a personal attitude about an event
- To express doubts about people and things

Language

This unit expands on the forms of the subjunctive (irregular, stem-changing verbs) and on its uses:

- After expressions of emotion
- After impersonal expressions
- After verbs and expressions of opinion
- After verbs and expressions of doubt
- After relative pronouns

Culture

The cultural notes of this unit introduce the role of the teacher and of the school in Hispanic society, problems related to life in large cities and life in the country, and hypotheses about the mysterious Nazca drawings.

Lección 1   Un distraído

Act. 1

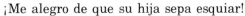
STRUCTURE TO OBSERVE: the use of the subjunctive after expressions of emotion.
Have students note the various instances of this use in the reading.

El profesor Ramos es un señor muy amable . . . pero un poco distraído.
Y de vez en cuando, él mete la pata.

distraído:
   absent-minded
mete la pata:
   blunders

¡Me alegro de que su hija sepa esquiar!

¡Siento que haya un apagón!

apagón: *blackout*

¿Le molesta que abra la ventana un poco?

You may have the students describe what happens in each cartoon.

¡Estoy contento de que lleguemos muy temprano para la película!

¡Me alegro de que Uds. se vayan de vacaciones!

Act. 2

NOTA CULTURAL OPTIONAL

El profesor en la sociedad hispana

¿Qué te parece° el profesor Ramos? ¿Lo encuentras un poco distraído o demasiado distraído? ¿ . . . Y casi un poco tonto?

Pues, en realidad, en los países de habla hispana, los profesores y maestros son muy estimados° y respetados dentro y fuera de la clase. De hecho la gente hispánica considera la profesión de maestro o profesor una de las carreras° que tienen más prestigio.

Si pensamos que los profesores de los colegios urbanos son apreciados y queridos, los maestros rurales son aun° más estimados. Son como parte de la familia. Los padres y los maestros, juntos, cooperan° para darle la mejor educación e instrucción al estudiante.

¡Qué cooperación más fantástica!

Qué te parece What do you think of **estimados** held in esteem **carreras** careers **aun** even **cooperan** work together

¿Tienen mucho prestigio los maestros y profesores en los países hispánicos? ¿Tienen mucho prestigio en los Estados Unidos? ¿Son los profesores como parte de la familia en los Estados Unidos?

Vocabulario

sustantivo	**un apagón**	blackout
adjetivo	**distraído**	absent-minded
verbo	**meter**	to put (in)
expresión	**meter la pata**	to make a blunder

Estructuras

You may want to first review the irregular command forms from Unit 8, pp. 333, 344.

A. Los subjuntivos irregulares

We have seen that the stem of the subjunctive is the same as the stem of the command form. This is also true of irregular verbs. Verbs that have an irregular stem in the command form have an irregular subjunctive stem.

Act. 3

INFINITIVE STEM OF THE COMMAND SUBJUNCTIVE	ser se-	ir vay-	saber sep-
Mis profesores quieren que . . .			
(yo)	sea	vaya	sepa
(tú)	seas	vayas	sepas
(él, ella, Ud.)	sea	vaya	sepa
(nosotros)	seamos	vayamos	sepamos
(vosotros)	seáis	vayáis	sepáis
(ellos, ellas, Uds.)	sean	vayan	sepan

NOTE: These verbs have irregular subjunctive stems but regular subjunctive endings.

⟩⟩ The subjunctive of **hay** is **haya**.

¡Me alegro de que no **haya** examen!

⟩⟩ Note also the accent marks on some of the subjunctive forms of **dar** and **estar**.

| dar | dé | des | dé | demos | (deis) | den |
| estar | esté | estés | esté | estemos | (estéis) | estén |

ACTIVIDAD 1 Buenos consejos

Las siguientes personas aprenden idiomas. ¿A cuál de estos países quieres que vaya cada uno?

Francia / Italia / el Japón / Portugal / Alemania / España / Inglaterra

⋙ Carlos aprende inglés.   Quiero que vaya a Inglaterra.

1. Paco y Ramón aprenden francés.
2. Maribel aprende italiano.
3. Uds. aprenden japonés.
4. Aprendemos portugués.
5. Aprendes español.
6. Ud. aprende alemán.

VARIATIONS: You want them to know how to speak these languages.
Quiero que Carlos sepa hablar inglés.
You want them to be bilingual.
Quiero que Carlos sea bilingüe.

ACTIVIDAD 2 ¡Un poco de lógica!

May be assigned as a special challenge activity.

En cinco minutos, ¿cuántas frases lógicas puedes crear? Usa los elementos de las columnas A, B, C, D y E, según el modelo. Las frases pueden ser afirmativas o negativas.

A	B	C	D	E
yo	querer	tú	ser	al (en el) laboratorio
Carlos	preferir	el profesor	estar	aquí a las dos
el profesor	desear	Mari-Carmen	dar	de buen humor
los alumnos	esperar	los alumnos	saber	los verbos
mis padres		nosotros	ir	buenas notas
		mis / sus amigos		dinero
		yo		hablar español
				bailar
				a tiempo
				a (en) la fiesta
				más generoso

⋙ Los alumnos esperan que el profesor dé buenas notas.

B. El uso del subjuntivo después de las expresiones que muestran emociones

The subjunctive is used to describe feelings and emotions, which are subjective. Note the use of the subjunctive in the sentences below.

Me alegro de que mi hermana **tenga** amigas simpáticas.
I am happy (that) my sister has nice friends.

Siento que mis amigos no **tengan** mucho dinero.
I am sorry (that) my friends do not have much money.

¿Te molesta que yo **me lleve** tu guitarra?
Do you mind if I take your guitar?

To express the subject's feelings about the actions of someone else, Spanish speakers use the construction:

expression of emotion + **que** + subjunctive

▷ While the word *that* may be omitted in English, **que** must be used in Spanish.

▷ When the feelings concern the actions of the subject, the infinitive is used instead of the subjunctive.
Contrast:

Me alegro de hacer un viaje.
I am happy to go on a trip.

Me alegro de que hagas un viaje.
I am happy that you are going on a trip.

Siento marcharme.
I am sorry to leave.

Siento que te marches.
I am sorry that you are leaving.

Me encanta aprender español.
I am delighted to learn Spanish.

Me encanta que mis hermanos aprendan español.
I am delighted that my brothers are learning Spanish.

ACTIVIDAD 3   La fiesta

VARIATIONS: with **bailar bien, divertirse.**

Las fiestas son buenas ocasiones para ver a los amigos. Di que las siguientes personas se alegran de que sus amigos vengan a la fiesta.

▷ Felipe (Carmen)   Felipe se alegra de que Carmen venga a la fiesta.

1. Susana (Rafael)
2. Roberto y Luis (Ana y Elena)
3. mis amigos (sus novias)
4. yo (tú)
5. Teresa y yo (Uds.)
6. tú (mi hermana)
7. nosotros (los chicos mexicanos)
8. mi prima (Jaime)

ACTIVIDAD 4   Decepciones *(Disappointments)*

Luis se alegra de que Elena haga las siguientes cosas, pero siente que ella
no las haga con él. Haz los dos papeles según los modelos.

⟯⟯   invitar a Paco al cine   Elena: Invito a Paco al cine.
                                            Luis: Me alegro de que invites a Paco al cine, pero siento
                                                     que no me invites.

⟯⟯   salir con Felipe   Elena: Salgo con Felipe.
                                            Luis: Me alegro de que salgas con Felipe, pero siento que no
                                                     salgas conmigo.

1. invitar a Rafael al café
2. escribirle a Jaime
3. llamar a Roberto
4. salir con Tomás

5. trabajar con Manuel
6. hacer un viaje con Juan Carlos
7. bailar con Antonio
8. ir al teatro con Pablo

ACTIVIDAD 5   Expresión personal

Describe tus reacciones en las siguientes circunstancias. Empieza cada
frase con **Me alegro de que** . . . o **Siento que** . . .

⟯⟯   Tu mejor amigo va a España.
           Me alegro de que (Siento que) mi mejor amigo vaya a España.

1. El profesor está enfermo.
2. El profesor no viene a clase.
3. El profesor va de vacaciones.
4. El profesor da malas notas.
5. Tus padres compran un coche nuevo.
6. Tus padres no te comprenden siempre.
7. Tus amigos organizan una fiesta.
8. Tus amigos no te invitan a salir.
9. Tu mejor amigo está enojado contigo.
10. Tu mejor amigo va a vivir en otra ciudad.
11. Tu mejor amigo se burla de ti.
12. Tu mejor amigo(a) sale con tu novio(a).

ACTIVIDAD 6   Un egoísta

Raúl es muy egoísta. Se alegra de hacer las siguientes cosas, pero no se
alegra de que sus amigos las hagan también. Expresa esto, según el
modelo.

⟯⟯   ir de vacaciones   Raúl se alegra de ir de vacaciones.
                                   No se alegra de que sus amigos vayan de vacaciones.

Have a student explain the difference between the construction **me alegro de** + *infinitive and* **me alegro de que** + *subjunctive.*

1. salir
2. sacar buenas notas
3. hacer un viaje

4. tener un trabajo interesante
5. saber tocar la guitarra
6. ir a España

estar
{
alegre
contento
desilusionado (*disappointed*)
enojado
furioso
orgulloso
sorprendido (*surprised*)
triste
}
de que . . .

alegrarse de que . . .	to be happy that	**Me alegro de que** mis amigos me comprendan.
sentir (e → ie) **que** . . .	to be sorry that	**Siento que** mis hermanos no me comprendan.
temer que . . .	to fear that	**Temo que** mi primo esté enojado conmigo.
tener miedo de que . . .	to be afraid that	**Tengo miedo de que** mi novio no venga.
(me) molesta que . . .	it bothers (me) that, (I) mind	**Me molesta que** Uds. fumen.

NOTAS: 1. Note the use of **de** in the constructions with **estar** + adjective.
   Estoy sorprendido de que mis amigos no me llamen.
   El profesor **está orgulloso de que** los alumnos hablen bien el español.
2. The **me molesta** construction is similar to the **me gusta** construction.
   ¿**Te molesta** que yo fume?   *Do you mind (does it bother you) that I smoke?*
   Amigos, ¿**les molesta**   *Friends, do you mind (does it bother you) that*
   que yo abra la ventana?   *I open the window?*

ACTIVIDAD 7   Un chico bien educado

Ramón es un chico bien educado (pero un poco indiscreto). Siempre les pregunta a sus amigos si les molesta que haga ciertas cosas. Unos dicen que sí, otros que no. Haz los papeles de Ramón y de sus amigos.

⟩⟩ abrir la puerta (no)   Ramón: ¿Te molesta que abra la puerta?
                El amigo: No, no me molesta que abras la puerta.

1. abrir la ventana (sí)
2. apagar el radio (no)
3. apagar el tocadiscos (sí)
4. invitar a tus amigos al cine (no)
5. invitar a tu novia al cine (sí)
6. leer tus revistas (no)

7. leer tu diario (sí)
8. llevarme tus discos (no)
9. llevarme tu dinero (sí)
10. ir a la playa (no)
11. ir a tu cuarto (sí)
12. usar tu bicicleta (no)

ACTIVIDAD 8   Expresión personal: temores *(fears)*

Di si temes que las siguientes cosas ocurran. Empieza cada frase con **(no)
temo que** o **(no) tengo miedo de que.**.

    El profesor me da una mala nota.   (No) temo que el profesor me dé una mala nota.

1. El examen es difícil.
2. Mis amigos se burlan de mí.
3. Mi mejor amigo me olvida.
4. Mis amigos no me escriben.
5. No hay vacaciones este año.

6. Hay un terremoto *(earthquake)*.
7. Los extraterrestres invaden la tierra.
8. La tierra deja de girar *(turn)*.
9. El fin del mundo ocurre mañana.
10. Drácula existe.

ACTIVIDAD 9   ¡Un poco de lógica!

May be assigned as a special challenge activity.

En cinco minutos, ¿cuántas frases lógicas puedes crear? Usa los elementos
de las columnas A, B, C y D. Tus frases pueden ser afirmativas o
negativas.

A	B	C	D
yo	contento	novio(a)	ser egoísta
tú	alegre	amigos	estar enfermo
Carlos	orgulloso	profesor(a)	ir de vacaciones
Marina	sorprendido	padres	salir con otros chicos (otras chicas)
mis amigos	furioso	vecinos	tener dinero
mis padres	enojado		tener buen trabajo
Ud. y yo	triste		saber hablar francés
	desilusionado		organizar una fiesta
			comprar un coche nuevo

    Carlos está sorprendido de que su novia esté enferma.

Para la comunicación

OPTIONAL
May be assigned as homework.

Expresión personal

¿Qué piensas del mundo que te rodea *(surrounds)*? Expresa tus sentimientos
con ideas personales.

Estoy enojado(a) de que . . .
Estoy alegre de que . . .
Estoy triste de que . . .
Estoy furioso(a) de que . . .
Estoy desilusionado(a) de que . . .
Temo que . . .
No tengo miedo de que. . .
Me molesta que . . .
No me molesta que . . .

    Estoy triste de que haya mucha discriminación en el mundo.

WB
B1, B2,
B3

SCRIPT
Act. 4, 5,
6

MASTERS
p. 38

WB
sin
noticias

SCRIPT
Act. 7, 8

MASTERS
p. 38

TRB

QUIZ
pp. 109–
110

Lección 2

Una cuestión de interpretación

Hay cien maneras de poner en práctica los consejos que recibimos.
Escucha lo que la maestra les dice a sus alumnos . . .
Luego, ve cómo los alumnos interpretan los consejos.

¡Chicos! . . .

¡Es importante que Uds. demuestren su talento!

¡Es bueno que Uds. encuentren soluciones a sus
problemas personales!

¡Es normal que Uds. muestren cariño a los
compañeros menos afortunados que Uds.!

¡Es bueno que Uds. puedan expresarse!

¡Es útil que piensen en el futuro!

¡Es esencial que Uds. se sientan cómodos en
presencia de los mayores!

¡Es importante que Uds. sigan el ejemplo de los
mayores!

¡Es justo que Uds. les devuelvan a sus amigos lo
que reciben de ellos!

demuestren:
demonstrate

cariño: *affection*

cómodos: *comfortable*

¡Es importante que demostremos nuestro
talento!

¡Es bueno que encontremos soluciones
a nuestros problemas personales!

¡Es normal que mostremos cariño a los compañeros menos afortunados que nosotros!

¡Es bueno que podamos expresarnos!

Papá, necesito 300 pesetas para ir al cine mañana.

¡Es útil que pensemos en el futuro!

¡Es esencial que nos sintamos cómodos en presencia de los mayores!

¡Es importante que sigamos el ejemplo de los mayores!

¡Es justo que les devolvamos a nuestros amigos lo que recibimos de ellos!

Have the students describe the various cartoons.

Act. 2

NOTA CULTURAL   OPTIONAL

El papel de las escuelas y los colegios en el mundo hispano

¿Piensas que el colegio tiene un papel muy importante en la formación moral de los alumnos norteamericanos? Las escuelas y los colegios hispanos les enseñan responsabilidad y patriotismo a sus estudiantes. Todos tienen que tomar el curso de Instrucción Cívica. Allí aprenden a sentir orgullo por su patria° y a ser ciudadanos° responsables.

Las escuelas y colegios urbanos ponen menos énfasis° en esto porque muchos de sus estudiantes asistirán a la universidad. Pero las escuelas y los colegios rurales ponen más énfasis en la educación cívica porque saben que para muchos de sus alumnos esto es el fin de la vida estudiantil.°

¿Sabes mucho de la historia de tu país? ¿Crees que serás un(a) ciudadano(a) responsable?

patria *country*   **ciudadanos** *citizens*   **énfasis** *emphasis*
estudiantil *student*

— Vocabulario —

sustantivos	**una cuestión (de)**	a matter (of)
	una manera	manner
adjetivos	**cómodo**	comfortable, at ease
	justo	fair
verbos	**demostrar (o → ue)**	to demonstrate, show
	expresarse	to express oneself

CONVERSACIÓN

Vamos a hablar de lo que piensas del papel que tus profesores tienen en tu vida.

1. Según tú, ¿es necesario que tus profesores te **den** consejos?
2. ¿Es necesario que **hablen** de tu progreso escolar con tus padres?
3. ¿Es necesario que **se preocupen** por tu vida personal?
4. ¿Es necesario que **se preocupen** por tu futuro?
5. ¿Es necesario que **discutan** tu futuro con tus padres?

OBSERVACIÓN

Each of the above questions begins with the impersonal expression **¿Es necesario que ...?**
• Is the verb that follows that expression in the indicative or the subjunctive?

the subjunctive

Estructuras

A. El uso del subjuntivo después de expresiones impersonales

Each of the following sentences begins with the impersonal construction **es** + adjective + **que.** Such constructions are used to express a particular opinion. Note the use of the subjunctive in the following examples.

Es necesario que los alumnos **estudien.**	*It is necessary that the students study.*
Es importante que digas la verdad.	*It is important that you tell the truth.*
Es bueno que Marisela **aprenda** inglés.	*It is good that Marisela is learning English.*
Es justo que ayudemos a los otros.	*It is fair that we help others.*

Spanish speakers use the subjunctive after many impersonal expressions.

⋙ The above impersonal expressions are used to express an indirect command (**es necesario que ...**) or an opinion (**es bueno que ...**).

You may want to review indirect commands on p. 361.

⋙ Note that these impersonal expressions may be followed by:
—**que** + subjunctive when the expressions concern someone in particular
—the infinitive when the expression does not specifically refer to anyone.

Es importante **que trabajes.**	*It is important that you work.*
Es importante **trabajar.**	*It is important to work.*

ACTIVIDAD 1 Expresión personal: lo más importante

De las dos cualidades, di cuál es la más importante para las siguientes personas, según el modelo.

▷ mis profesores: justos o interesantes
     Es más importante que sean justos (interesantes).

1. mi papá: generoso o enérgico
2. mi mamá: cariñosa *(loving)* o paciente
3. mi mejor amigo: sincero o divertido
4. mi mejor amiga: entusiasta o inteligente
5. mi futuro(a) esposo(a): rico(a) o responsable
6. mi futuro(a) jefe(a): brillante o tolerante
7. mis amigos: simpáticos o inteligentes

ACTIVIDAD 2 Unos alumnos perezosos

This activity contains only regular verbs.

Imagina que eres el (la) profesor(a) de unos alumnos perezosos. Di que es necesario que cambien sus actitudes.

VARIATION: with **Es importante que.**

▷ Felipe no estudia. Es necesario que Felipe estudie.

1. Silvia y Carlos no estudian.
2. Ramón no escucha las cintas.
3. Mari-Carmen no lee.
4. Ana María y Luisa no me escuchan.
5. Roberto no llega a tiempo.
6. Raúl y Elena no hablan inglés.
7. Los alumnos no preparan la tarea.
8. Juan Manuel no usa el diccionario.
9. Inés y Jaime no aprenden los verbos.
10. Consuelo no asiste a la clase.

This activity contains a mix of regular verbs, verbs with irregular **yo** forms in the present, and verbs with irregular subjunctive forms.

ACTIVIDAD 3 Una lección de conducir *(A driving lesson)*

Imagina que le enseñas a una amiga española a conducir. Dile si las siguientes cosas son necesarias o no. Empieza cada frase con **(No) es importante** o **(No) es necesario** o **(No) es útil.**

VARIATION with **Ud.** form: **...que tenga cuidado.**

▷ tener cuidado (No) es necesario que tengas cuidado.

1. usar las luces direccionales
2. mirar en el espejo
3. llenar el tanque a menudo
4. parar ante *(in front of)* los peatones
5. quedarte tranquila en toda ocasión
6. ir de prisa
7. ser amable con los otros conductores
8. ser paciente
9. estar de buen humor
10. tener un coche rápido
11. tener un coche nuevo
12. conocer bien el código de tránsito *(traffic rules)*
13. conocer bien las señales de tránsito
14. ponerte un casco *(helmet)*

ACTIVIDAD 4   Requisitos profesionales

Para ciertos empleos se necesitan habilidades *(skills)* especiales. Di cuáles
de las siguientes habilidades son importantes o útiles para las siguientes
personas y cuáles no.

las habilidades: hablar inglés   ser cortés
                  hablar español   asistir a la universidad
                  escribir a máquina   tener paciencia
                  saber conducir

Felipe quiere ser abogado en Panamá.
> Es útil que hable inglés y que asista a la universidad.
> No es importante que escriba a máquina.

1. Carlos quiere ser taxista.
2. Susana quiere ser intérprete.
3. Paco y Silvia quieren ser secretarios bilingües.
4. Rafael quiere ser policía.
5. Isabel y Raúl quieren trabajar en una agencia de viajes.

VOCABULARIO PRÁCTICO   Expresiones impersonales

es sorprendente *(surprising)* **(que)**

es bueno (que)
es malo (que)
es mejor (que)
es peligroso (que)

es agradable (que)
es natural (que)
es justo (que)
es lógico (que)

es importante (que)
es necesario (que)
es útil (que)
es indispensable (que)
es esencial (que)

es absurdo (que)
es ridículo (que)
es raro *(strange)* **(que)**
es triste (que)

importa (que)	it matters	**Importa que** todos los hombres sean iguales.
es lástima (que)	it's a pity	**Es lástima que** no lo sean.
vale la pena (que)	it is worthwhile	**¿Vale la pena que** estudiemos **tanto** *(so much)*?

ACTIVIDAD 5   Lo que importa

Éstas son ciertas cualidades: **generoso** / **justo** / **inteligente** / **divertido** / **paciente** / **tranquilo** / **cortés** / **honrado** (*honest*) / **hábil** (*skillful*) / **prudente**. En tu opinión, ¿qué cualidad importa que las siguientes personas tengan y qué no importa?

🗲   un(a) profesor(a)   Importa que sea justo. No importa que sea generoso.

1. un taxista
2. un(a) arquitecto(a)
3. un(a) abogado(a)
4. un político
5. un(a) fotógrafo(a)

6. un(a) médico(a)
7. el presidente
8. yo
9. tus amigos
10. tus hermanos

ACTIVIDAD 6   Expresión personal

Expresa tu opinión personal sobre las siguientes cosas, usando las expresiones del vocabulario.

*This activity contains a mix of regular verbs, verbs with irregular **yo** forms and verbs with irregular subjunctive forms.*

🗲   No tengo mucho dinero.

(No) es importante (justo, necesario . . .) que no tenga mucho dinero.

1. Tenemos mucho trabajo.
2. Hay exámenes.
3. Los profesores son estrictos.
4. Mis amigos me prestan sus discos.
5. La vida es complicada.
6. Ayudamos a los pobres.
7. Hay mucha contaminación del aire.
8. Hay discriminación.
9. Los Estados Unidos ayudan a otros países.
10. Los Estados Unidos hacen las paces con Rusia.

11. Los jóvenes ayudan a los viejos.
12. Los padres castigan (*punish*) a sus hijos.
13. Los niños respetan a los mayores.
14. Los hombres exploran el espacio.
15. Los científicos inventan productos nuevos.
16. Los científicos desarrollan armas atómicas.
17. Los hombres son civilizados.
18. Las mujeres son iguales a los hombres.

Mujer, lee
Mujeres
es tu revista

ACTIVIDAD 7   Expresión personal: yo   OPTIONAL

¿Qué es importante en tu vida y qué no es importante? Completa las
siguientes frases con una idea personal.

> Es importante que yo . . .
>> Es importante que yo sea feliz (tenga mucho dinero, tenga
>> muchas amigas, asista a la universidad . . .).

WB
A1, A2,
A3, A4

SCRIPT
Act. 3, 4

1. Es necesario que yo . . .
2. Es natural que yo . . .
3. Es absurdo que yo . . .

4. Es lástima que yo . . .
5. Importa que yo . . .
6. Vale la pena que yo . . .

VARIATIONS with other subjects: **Es importante que el profesor..., que nosotros..., que los
norteamericanos...**

B. El subjuntivo de los verbos en -*ar* y en -*er* con cambios en el radical

The **-ar** and **-er** verbs with a stem change in the present indicative have
the same stem change in the subjunctive.

Act. 5

INFINITIVE STEM CHANGE SUBJUNCTIVE: Es importante que . . .	pensar e → ie	volver o → ue	jugar u → ue
(yo)	piense	vuelva	juegue
(tú)	pienses	vuelvas	juegues
(él, ella, Ud.)	piense	vuelva	juegue
(nosotros)	pensemos	volvamos	juguemos
(vosotros)	penséis	volváis	juguéis
(ellos, ellas, Uds.)	piensen	vuelvan	jueguen

> Stem-changing verbs in **-ar** and **-er** have regular subjunctive endings.

> Note that there is no stem change in the **nosotros** and **vosotros**
> forms.

ACTIVIDAD 8   ¿Es bueno?

VARIATION in the singular:
¿**Es bueno que piense...? Sí,
es necesario que pienses...**

Los alumnos le preguntan a la maestra si es bueno que hagan (o no
hagan) ciertas cosas. La maestra les contesta afirmativamente o
negativamente. Haz los papeles de los alumnos y de la maestra según el
modelo.

Make sure that the
students use the re-
flexive pronoun **nos** in
items 4, 5, 6.

> pensar en el futuro (sí)   Alumnos: ¿Es bueno que pensemos en el futuro?
>> Maestra: Sí, es necesario que Uds. piensen en el futuro.

WB
B1, B2

SCRIPT
Act. 6

1. pensar en otros (sí)
2. cerrar la puerta de la clase (sí)
3. cerrar los libros (sí)
4. despertarse temprano (sí)

5. despertarse temprano los domingos (no)
6. acostarse temprano (no)
7. volver a casa a tiempo (sí)
8. querer a otros (sí)

C. El subjuntivo de los verbos en *-ir* con cambios en el radical

The **-ir** stem-changing verbs have the same stem changes in the present subjunctive as in the present indicative. In addition, in the **nosotros** and **vosotros** forms, these verbs have the following stem changes: **e → i** and **o → u.**

INFINITIVE STEM CHANGES SUBJUNCTIVE: Es importante que . . .	sentir e → ie, i	pedir e → i, i	dormir o → ue, u
(yo)	sienta	pida	duerma
(tú)	sientas	pidas	duermas
(él, ella, Ud.)	sienta	pida	duerma
(nosotros)	sintamos	pidamos	durmamos
(vosotros)	sintáis	pidáis	durmáis
(ellos, ellas, Uds.)	sientan	pidan	duerman

ACTIVIDAD 9   ¿Es importante?

Ahora los alumnos de la Actividad 8 le preguntan a la maestra si es importante o no que hagan ciertas cosas. Haz los dos papeles según el modelo.

VARIATION in the singular:
¿Es importante que me sienta...? Sí, es importante que te sientas...

sentirse contento (sí)   Alumnos: ¿Es importante que nos sintamos contentos?
                        Maestra: Sí, es importante que Uds. se sientan contentos.

1. pedir consejos a sus padres (sí)
2. pedir dinero a sus abuelos (no)
3. seguir los buenos ejemplos (sí)
4. seguir los malos ejemplos (no)
5. dormir bien (sí)
6. dormir diez horas (no)
7. vestirse bien (no)
8. divertirse en casa (sí)
9. divertirse durante los exámenes (no)

May be assigned as a special
challenge activity.

ACTIVIDAD 10   ¡Un poco de humor!

En diez minutos, ¿cuántas frases divertidas puedes crear? Usa los
elementos de A, B, C y tu imaginación para completar la columna D.

A	B	C	D
Es agradable	yo	poder	
Es raro	nosotros	querer	
Es absurdo	mis amigos	pensar	
Es ridículo	el (la) profesor(a)	volver	
Es bueno	los alumnos	despertarse	
Es malo	mi amigo y yo	sentirse	
Es normal		dormirse	
Es lástima		dormir	
Es triste		cerrar	
		pedir	
		preferir	

 Es normal que los alumnos se duerman cuando el profesor habla.

Para la comunicación

OPTIONAL
May be assigned as homework.

Para un mundo mejor

En tu opinión, ¿cómo es posible crear un mundo mejor? Expresa tus ideas
personales. Si quieres, puedes usar una de las siguientes palabras con cada
expresión impersonal.

el presidente / los hombres / los jóvenes / los mayores / los
norteamericanos / los rusos / los ricos / los pobres / los científicos / los
médicos / los políticos

> Es esencial . . .
> Es indispensable . . .
> Es necesario . . .
> Es útil . . .
> Es importante . . .
> Vale la pena . . .
> No vale la pena . . .

 Es importante . . .   Es importante que los políticos transformen la sociedad.

WB
Tu eres...

SCRIPT

Act. 8

MASTERS
p. 39

TRB

QUIZ
pp. 111–
112

Lección 3   El mundo misterioso

Act. 1

Todos tenemos una mente racional. Y con esta mente, podemos explicar muchas cosas . . . pero no todas. Hay todavía muchas cosas que no pueden ser explicadas lógicamente. Éstas constituyen los misterios del universo . . .

mente: *mind*

¿Qué piensas de los siguientes misterios? Y ¿crees que estos misterios existan?

	Sí, es posible.	No, no es posible.
1. Muchas personas creen que los fantasmas existen. ¿Y tú? ¿Crees que haya fantasmas?	☐	☐
2. De vez en cuando, unas personas declaran que han observado objetos misteriosos en el cielo. ¿Y tú? ¿Crees que los OVNIS (objetos volantes no identificados) existan?	☐	☐
3. Ciertas personas dicen que tienen poderes extraordinarios como lo de trasladar o romper objetos sin tocarlos. En tu opinión, ¿es posible que ellas tengan tales poderes?	☐	☐

fantasmas: *ghosts*

cielo: *sky*
   OVNIS: *UFOs*
volantes: *flying*
poderes: *powers*
trasladar: *moving*
tocarlos: *touching them*
tales: *such*

Unidad nueve
390

4. De vez en cuando, un vidente predice una catástrofe como un accidente de aviación o un terremoto. ¿Crees que sea posible predecir el futuro? ☐ ☐

vidente: fortune teller
predice: predicts
terremoto: earthquake

5. Ciertas personas parecen tener el talento de adivinar lo que pensamos. ¿Crees que esas personas tengan poderes extrasensoriales? ☐ ☐

adivinar: guessing

6. De vez en cuando, alguien dice que ha visto el famoso monstruo del Loch Ness. ¿Crees que tal monstruo exista? ☐ ☐

7. En África y Asia, hay curanderos que mantienen hacer operaciones quirúrgicas sin usar ningún instrumento. ¿Crees que esas operaciones sean reales? ☐ ☐

curanderos: healers
mantienen: claim
quirúrgicas: surgical

8. Muchas personas creen en la vida eterna. ¿Crees que haya vida después de la muerte? ☐ ☐

muerte: death

9. Muchas personas consultan el horóscopo antes de tomar decisiones importantes. ¿Crees que las estrellas determinen nuestro destino? ☐ ☐

estrellas: stars

10. Para los científicos es muy difícil explicar el origen de ciertas líneas misteriosas de la región de Nazca en el Perú. ¿Crees que astronautas extraterrestres hayan dibujado esas líneas hace muchos años? ☐ ☐

extraterrestres: from outer space
hace muchos años: many years ago

INTERPRETACIÓN

- Si has contestado sí a ocho preguntas o más: la gente pensará que eres crédulo(a).

crédulo: gullible

- Si has contestado sí a de cinco a siete preguntas: crees en el poder de la razón . . . aunque para ti las razones no lo explican todo.

razón: reason

- Si has contestado sí a de dos a cuatro preguntas: eres muy racional. Crees lo que ves. Para ti no hay nada como la experiencia.

- Si has contestado afirmativamente menos de dos preguntas: piensas que puedes explicarlo todo racionalmente. ¿No crees que haya un lugar en tu vida para un poquito de imaginación y misterio?

poquito: little bit

You may use this text as the basis for a class poll.

NOTA CULTURAL OPTIONAL

Las líneas misteriosas de Nazca

Estas líneas fueron descubiertas en los años de 1920 (mil novecientos veinte) por un piloto que estaba volando° sobre Nazca, una región desértica° del Perú. Él observó un diseño° muy curioso que solamente se podía distinguir desde arriba.° Estas líneas representaban figuras geométricas de triángulos y cuadrados.° También había° flores y animales gigantescos como pájaros, culebras,° un mono y una araña.°

Los científicos han tratado de descubrir el origen de estas líneas y su propósito.° Naturalmente hay muchas teorías. Por ejemplo:

¿Representan estas líneas un calendario solar gigantesco?

¿Eran caminos° usados por civilizaciones antiguas?

¿Son estas líneas vestigios° de canales de irrigación antiguos?

¿Es un mapa que apunta° a un tesoro escondido?°

¿Fueron usadas por los antiguos astronautas como aeropuerto?

¿Tienen significado religioso? ¿Son vestigios de un culto antiguo?

¿Cuál es la verdadera explicación? ¡Nadie lo

sabe! Hoy día, las líneas de Nazca son todavía uno de los numerosos misterios de la América del Sur.

volando *flying* **desértica** *deserted* **diseño** *pattern*
arriba *above* **cuadrados** *squares* **había** *there were*
culebras *snakes* **araña** *spider* **propósito** *meaning*
caminos *roads* **vestigios** *remains* **apunta** *points*
tesoro escondido *hidden treasure*

¿En qué país está Nazca? ¿Quién descubrió las líneas misteriosas? ¿Cómo? ¿Qué representan esas líneas? ¿Hay una explicación que todos los científicos aceptan?

—— Vocabulario ——

sustantivos	**un científico**	scientist	**una estrella**	star
	un fantasma	ghost	**una línea**	line
	un poder	power	**la mente**	mind
			la muerte	death
			la razón	reason
adjetivos	**crédulo**	gullible, credulous		
	eterno	eternal		
verbos	**predecir**	to predict		
	tocar	to touch		
	trasladar	to move, to transfer		
	volar (o → ue)	to fly		

Have students practice the forms of **predecir** by changing the subjects in sentences like: **No predigo el futuro. ¿Qué predirá Ud.? ¿Has predicho una catástrofe? ¿Quién predijo la muerte?**

NOTA: **Predecir** is conjugated like **decir.**

Estructuras

A. El uso del subjuntivo después de expresiones de duda

In the sentences below, Carmen considers some things as certain, whereas Manuel considers them doubtful, untrue, or at best only possible. Compare the verbs in each pair of sentences.

The doubt may be strong (**no creo que**) or weak (**es posible que**).

(certainty)

Carmen:
Sé que Raúl **es** generoso.

Creo que Felipe **habla** inglés.
Es cierto que mis amigos **van** a la fiesta.

(doubt or uncertainty)

Manuel:
Dudo *(I doubt)* **que** Raúl **sea** generoso.

No creo que Felipe **hable** inglés.
Es posible que mis amigos **vayan** a la fiesta.

The *indicative* is used after expressions of *certainty*.
The *subjunctive* is used after expressions of *doubt* or *uncertainty*.

NOTE: **Saber** conveys information and is always followed by the indicative, even when used negatively or in questions.

⇥ Some expressions of certainty may become expressions of doubt when used in the negative or interrogative form. In such cases, the subjunctive can be used.

certainty: **Creo que** Paco **es** simpático.
   doubt: **No creo que** Paco **sea** simpático.
       ¿Crees que Paco **sea** buen compañero?

Some expressions of doubt may become expressions of certainty in the negative. For instance, *Dudo que* Carlos *sea* rico. *No dudo que* Carlos *es* buen compañero.

¿Crees que may be followed by the indicative if there is no doubt in the mind of the person asking the question: **¿Crees que Carlos es buen compañero?**

⇥ While the word *that* may be omitted in English after an expression of certainty or doubt, the word **que** must always be used in Spanish.

ACTIVIDAD 1 Opiniones

María y Alberto están hablando de sus amigos. Es obvio que no tienen las mismas opiniones. Haz los papeles de María y Alberto según el modelo.

⟨⟩ Enrique es simpático.   María: Creo que Enrique es simpático.
                            Alberto: ¡Bah! No creo que Enrique sea simpático.

1. Inés es bonita.
2. Tomás y Felipe son interesantes.
3. Gloria y Susana son aburridas.
4. Paco habla francés muy bien.
5. Isabel estudia mucho.
6. Elena y Manuel juegan bien al tenis.
7. Ana dice la verdad.
8. Esteban sale siempre con Consuelo.

ACTIVIDAD 2 Expresión personal: sí o no

Expresa tu opinión de lo siguiente. Empieza cada frase con **Creo que** + indicativo o **No creo que** + subjuntivo.

⟨⟩ El español es difícil.   Creo que el español es difícil.
                            (No creo que el español sea difícil.)

1. El español es útil.
2. El (la) profesor(a) es estricto(a).
3. Los alumnos de la clase hablan español bien.
4. Los chicos son más inteligentes que las chicas.
5. Los hombres son mejores conductores que las mujeres.
6. Los jóvenes son más idealistas que los mayores.
7. Los alumnos tienen más paciencia que los profesores.
8. La China es más pequeña que los Estados Unidos.

VOCABULARIO PRÁCTICO   Expresiones de duda

Es posible que	No es verdad que
Es imposible que	No es cierto que
Es probable que	No es seguro que
Es improbable que	Es dudoso (doubtful) que

dudar que	to doubt that	**Dudo que** los marcianos existan.
no creer que	not to believe that	**No creo que** haya hombres en la luna.
no estar seguro(a) de que	not to be sure that	**No estoy seguro de que** digas la verdad.
negar (e → ie) que	to deny that	**Niego que** haya vida después de la muerte.

Unidad nueve
394

ACTIVIDAD 3   Expresión personal

Di lo que piensas de lo siguiente. Empieza cada frase con **creo que** + el indicativo o una expresión de duda + el subjuntivo.

> Los fantasmas existen.   Creo que los fantasmas existen.
> (Es posible [dudoso . . .] que los fantasmas existan.)

1. La percepción extrasensorial existe.
2. Dios existe.
3. Los OVNIS existen.
4. Las brujas *(witches)* existen.
5. El número 13 trae mala suerte.
6. El número 7 trae buena suerte.
7. Los gatos negros traen mala suerte.
8. Hay vida después de la muerte.
9. Los muertos *(dead)* pueden comunicarse con los vivos *(living)*.
10. Es necesario consultar el horóscopo antes de tomar una decisión importante.
11. Ciertas personas pueden predecir el futuro.
12. El universo es un misterio.
13. Hay vida en la luna.
14. Hay vida extraterrestre.
15. Las estrellas determinan nuestro destino.
16. El fin del mundo es mañana.

ACTIVIDAD 4   Una disputa

Juan Carlos contradice todo lo que le dice Elena. Haz los dos papeles.

> El profesor habla inglés bien (es cierto).
> Elena: Es cierto que el profesor habla inglés bien.
> Juan Carlos: No es cierto que el profesor hable inglés bien.

In Juan Carlos' replies, students should use **tu** and **tus** in sentences 3 and 4 and **yo** in sentence 6.

1. Los chicos norteamericanos son simpáticos (es cierto).
2. Las chicas norteamericanas son deportistas (es verdad).
3. Mi novio es muy inteligente (estoy segura).
4. Mis amigas son generosas (creo).
5. Los chicos son impacientes (es cierto).
6. Tú eres tonto (es verdad).

WB
A1, A2, A3

SCRIPT

Act. 3, 4, 5

MASTERS
p. 40

B. El pretérito perfecto del subjuntivo

Note the use and the forms of the present perfect of the subjunctive in the sentences below.

Me alegro de que Carlos **haya llamado.**	*I am happy that Carlos (has) called.*
Es bueno que haya hablado contigo.	*It's good that he (has) talked with you.*
No creo que Felipe **haya asistido** a una corrida.	*I do not believe that Felipe has been to a bullfight.*
¿Es posible que haya ido a España?	*Is it possible that he went (has gone) to Spain?*

The present perfect subjunctive is sometimes used instead of the present subjunctive to refer to past actions and events.

The present perfect subjunctive is a compound tense. It is formed as follows:

> present subjunctive of **haber** + past participle

Act. 6

PRESENT PERFECT SUBJUNCTIVE	Es importante que . . .	
(yo)	**haya estudiado**	(nosotros)	**hayamos estudiado**
(tú)	**hayas estudiado**	(vosotros)	**hayáis estudiado**
(él, ella, Ud.)	**haya estudiado**	(ellos, ellas, Uds.)	**hayan estudiado**

Remind the students of the formation of the past participle:
-ar verbs: -ar → -ado   hablado, estudiado
-er, -ir verbs: -er, -ir → -ido   comido, vivido
Review the irregular past participles:

decir	*dicho*	poner	*puesto*	abrir	*abierto*
hacer	*hecho*	escribir	*escrito*	descubrir	*descubierto*
ver	*visto*	romper	*roto*		

ACTIVIDAD 5   El profesor se alegra

El profesor se alegra de que los alumnos hayan visitado países interesantes durante las vacaciones, pero siente que no hayan asistido a ciertos espectáculos. Haz el papel del profesor.

Carmen: España / un concierto de música flamenca
   Me alegro de que Carmen haya visitado España,
      pero siento que no haya asistido a un concierto de música flamenca.

1. Antonio: Colombia / una corrida
2. Roberto y Marta: la Argentina / un partido de fútbol
3. tú: los Estados Unidos / un partido de béisbol
4. Uds.: el Canadá / un partido de hockey
5. María y Consuelo: Inglaterra / un concierto de rock
6. Ud.: México / el Ballet Folklórico

ACTIVIDAD 6 Expresión personal: los misterios del universo

¿Qué piensas de lo siguiente? Expresa tu opinión personal, empezando tus frases con: **Es posible que** . . . o **No es cierto que** . . . o **Dudo que** . . . + el pretérito perfecto del subjuntivo.

> los egipcios (¿descubrir la electricidad?)
>> Es posible (Dudo) que los egipcios hayan descubierto la electricidad.

1. los vikingos (¿descubrir América?)
2. los marcianos (¿explorar la tierra?)
3. Cristóbal Colón (¿vivir más de cien años?)
4. Drácula (¿existir?)
5. los indios (¿venir de Asia?)
6. los rusos (¿inventar el avión?)

ACTIVIDAD 7 Un jactancioso (A boaster)

Raúl dice que ha hecho muchas cosas extraordinarias. Carmen no lo cree.
Haz los dos papeles según el modelo.

> visitar la China
>> Raúl: He visitado la China.
>> Carmen: ¡Bah! No creo que hayas visitado la China.

WB
B1, B2

SCRIPT

Act. 7

MASTERS
p. 40

1. visitar el Japón
2. hablar con el presidente
3. vivir en Tahití
4. actuar en una película del oeste
5. salir con una actriz famosa
6. correr el maratón de Boston
7. conducir en las quinientas millas de Indianapolis
8. viajar en cohete
9. ganar una medalla de oro en los juegos olímpicos

Para la comunicación

OPTIONAL
May be assigned as homework.

Tus creencias (Your beliefs)

Expresa lo que crees y lo que no crees sobre tres de las siguientes cosas:

los fantasmas
los OVNIS
la vida después de la muerte
Nessie (el monstruo del Loch Ness)
el triángulo de las Bermudas
los poderes extrasensoriales

WB
El mundo...

TRB

QUIZ
pp. 113–
114

> Muchísimas personas dudan que Nessie sea un verdadero monstruo.

> Mi amigo Juan sabe mucho de lo que piensan otros. Creo que tiene poderes extrasensoriales.

Lección 4   **Nunca satisfechos**

Have students note the differences in uses (*what is* vs. *what is* |*wished for*) in the text.

Act. 1

45–46

Hay personas que son felices con poco y . . .
hay otras . . .

La Srta. García tiene un coche
que es muy cómodo, pero que no anda rápido.

anda: *goes*

Quiere cambiarlo por otro coche
que sea pequeño y que ande a doscientos
kilómetros por hora.

El Sr. Meléndez tiene una casa muy grande y muy moderna
que está situada en un barrio muy elegante
y que tiene muchas habitaciones, un garaje para tres coches
y una piscina.

barrio: *district*
habitaciones: *rooms*

Pero quiere vivir en una casita
que esté situada en el campo
y que tenga pocas habitaciones, con
un jardín grande con árboles y flores.

Unidad nueve
398

**¿Qué tipo de coche tiene la Srta. García? ¿Qué tipo de coche quiere comprar?
¿En qué tipo de casa vive el Sr. Meléndez? ¿En qué tipo de casa quiere vivir?**

Ramón conoce a una chica muy inteligente y muy seria
que habla francés, inglés e italiano, que va a la universidad
y que tiene padres muy ricos.

Pero prefiere salir con chicas
que no hablen idiomas extranjeros, ni
que vayan a la universidad,
pero que tengan buen sentido del humor.

Carmen conoce a un chico muy simpático
que es alto, rubio y buen mozo,
que tiene trabajo interesante,
que sabe jugar al tenis muy bien
y a quien le gustan todos los deportes.

buen mozo:
good-looking

¿Y con quién sueña Carmen?
Ella sueña con tener otro novio
que sea moreno y romántico,
que tenga poco,
pero que sepa tocar la guitarra,
a quien le guste la poesía
y que no le hable nunca de deportes.

¿Qué tipo de chica es la amiga de Ramón? ¿Con qué tipo de chica quiere salir Ramón?
¿Qué tipo de chico es el amigo de Carmen? ¿Qué tipo de chico quiere conocer Carmen?

NOTA CULTURAL   OPTIONAL

La vida de la ciudad y la del campo

¿Dónde te gustaría vivir? ¿En la ciudad o en el campo? En la caricatura,° el Sr. Meléndez vive en una casa muy cómoda en la ciudad, pero él sueña con vivir en el campo. ¿Crees que este sueño es típico?

En muchos países hispanos, lo opuesto° es lo verdadero.° Mucha gente que vive en el campo sueña con mudarse° a las ciudades grandes. ¿Por qué? En el campo, las condiciones de la vida son muy difíciles. Muchas veces la gente no puede encontrar trabajo, y cuando lo encuentra, es trabajo duro° y no recibe mucho dinero. La vida en la ciudad significa mejores condiciones de trabajo, mejor paga,° mejor educación y las posibilidades de divertirse.

Pero esto es un sueño . . .

Para muchísima gente, la vida en la ciudad es dura y a veces más dura que la del campo. Sin embargo, las ciudades hispanas crecen° cada día más por la afluencia° de las personas del campo que llegan en busca° de una vida mejor.

caricatura *cartoon*   **opuesto** *opposite*   **verdadero** *truth*
mudarse *moving*   **duro** *hard*   **paga** *pay*   **crecen** *grow*
afluencia *influx*   **busca** *search*

¿Por qué mucha gente quiere mudarse a las ciudades grandes? ¿Cómo es el trabajo en el campo? ¿Gana mucho dinero la gente que trabaja en el campo? ¿Qué significa la vida en la ciudad para la gente que vive en el campo? ¿Cómo es la vida en la ciudad para mucha gente?

—— Vocabulario ——

sustantivos	**un barrio**	district, neighborhood	**una habitación**	room
adjetivo	**satisfecho**	satisfied, happy		
expresiones	**andar a doscientos kilómetros por hora**		to go 200 km. per hour (≅ 120 mph)	
	buen mozo	good-looking		

CONVERSACIÓN   OPTIONAL

Vamos a hablar de tu mejor amigo(a). Después vamos a hablar de ciertas personas que te gustaría conocer.

1. ¿Es tu mejor amigo(a) un(a) chico(a) que **habla** español?
2. ¿Es un(a) chico(a) que **vive** en la misma ciudad que tú?
3. ¿Es un(a) chico(a) que **tiene** buen sentido del humor?
4. ¿Es un(a) chico(a) que te **comprende** bien?

5. ¿Quieres encontrar un chico que **hable** español?
6. ¿Quieres tener correspondencia con una chica que **viva** en otro país?
7. ¿Quieres conocer un chico que **tenga** buen sentido del humor?
8. ¿Quieres casarte con una persona que te **comprenda**?

OBSERVACIÓN

In the first four sentences, you are asked questions about a specific person, namely your best friend.

• Is the verb that follows **que** *(who)* in the indicative or the subjunctive?   the indicative

In the last four sentences, you are asked questions about people who may exist but who have not yet been identified.

• Is the verb that follows **que** in the indicative or the subjunctive?   the subjunctive

Estructuras

Act. 3

A. Los pronombres relativos

The words in heavy print are used to connect two sentences. They are
called *relative pronouns*. Note the forms and uses of these pronouns in the
sentences below:

Tengo un amigo **que** vive en México.
Los amigos **que** tengo son generosos.

*I have a friend **who** lives in Mexico.*
*The friends (**whom**) I have are generous.*

Tengo una guitarra **que** es de España.
Los libros, **que** están aquí,
   son interesantes.

*I have a guitar **that** comes from Spain.*
*The books, **which** are here,*
   are interesting.

The relative pronoun **que** may refer to people or things. It
corresponds to the English pronouns *who, whom, that, which.*

> While *whom, that,* and *which* may be omitted in English, **que** must
> always be used in Spanish.

Have the students observe that **que** and **quien** do not have accent marks
when used as relative pronouns.

> After a preposition (**a, de, con, para . . .**), **quien** (**quienes**) is used
> instead of **que** to refer to people.

Compare:

NOTE: In Spanish, the preposition always comes immediately
before the relative pronoun (and not at the end of the sentence).

¿Dónde están los instrumentos
   con que trabajas?

*Where are the instruments **with which** you work?*

¿Dónde están los chicos
   con quienes trabajas?

*Where are the boys **with whom** you work?*

Ésa es la revista **de que** te hablé.
Ése es el chico **de quien** te hablé.

*That is the magazine **about which** I spoke to you.*
*That is the boy **about whom** I spoke to you.*

ACTIVIDAD 1   ¿Cómo se llaman?

María quiere saber cómo se llaman ciertas personas y objetos. Haz el papel de María según los modelos. Empieza cada pregunta con **¿Cómo se llama(n) . . .?**

⊗   Un chico entra.   ¿Cómo se llama el chico que entra?

⊗   Carlos lee unas revistas.   ¿Cómo se llaman las revistas que Carlos lee?

1. Una chica toca la guitarra.
2. Unos chicos hablan.
3. Enrique invita a una chica al baile.
4. Silvia llama a unos chicos.
5. Juan Miguel compra una revista.
6. Elena compra unos libros.
7. Alberto escucha unas cintas.
8. Clara escucha a unos amigos.

ACTIVIDAD 2   ¿Quién es?

Roberto quiere saber los nombres de las personas de quienes habla Susana. Haz el papel de Roberto, empezando cada pregunta con **¿Quién es . . .?** o **¿Quiénes son . . .?**

⊗   Le escribo a un chico.   ¿Quién es el chico a quien le escribes?

1. Les escribo a unas chicas.
2. Hablo con una profesora.
3. Hablo de unos vecinos.
4. Trabajo para una persona.
5. Salgo con unas chicas.
6. Estoy enamorada de un chico.
7. Estoy enojada con unos chicos.

ACTIVIDAD 3   Expresión personal: las personas que figuran en tu vida   OPTIONAL

Describe las siguientes personas, usando el pronombre relativo apropiado.
¡Usa tu imaginación!

⊗   Tengo un amigo . . .
       Tengo un amigo que se llama Roberto (tiene un coche, es mi compañero de tenis, corre las olas . . .).

⊗   Tengo una amiga con . . .
       Tengo una amiga con quien voy al cine (salgo mucho, juego al volibol . . .).

1. Tengo una amiga . . .
2. Tengo un amigo con . . .
3. Tengo vecinos . . .
4. Tengo vecinos con . . .
5. Tengo un(a) profesor(a) de español . . .
6. Tengo compañeros con . . .
7. Tengo padres . . .
8. Tengo hermanos con . . .
9. Tengo amigos . . .
10. Tengo amigos a . . .

B. El uso del subjuntivo después de los pronombres relativos

Note that the personal **a** is not used with a direct object noun when this noun does not refer to a specific person. This is the case in the examples below and in certain exercise items.

In the sentences on the left, Carlos is speaking about friends or possessions *he has*. In the sentences on the right, he is speaking about friends or possessions *he would like to have*. Compare the verbs in each pair of sentences.

(what is)	*(what may be)*
Conozco a un amigo **que habla** inglés.	Busco un amigo **que hable** francés.
Tengo amigas **que juegan** al volibol.	Prefiero tener amigas **que jueguen** al tenis.
Tengo un coche **que es** muy viejo y **que gasta** mucha gasolina.	Quiero comprar un coche **que sea** nuevo y **que no gaste** mucha gasolina.
Vivo en un apartamento **que es** pequeño y **que cuesta** mucho.	Quiero vivir en un apartamento **que sea** grande y **que no cueste** mucho.

In Spanish, the indicative or the subjunctive may be used after a relative pronoun. The choice between the two depends on what the speaker wants to describe:

The *indicative* is used to describe *what is*.

Carlos conoce a un amigo **que habla** inglés.	Carlos knows a friend **who speaks** English (that is, **who does** indeed **speak** English).

In the above sentence, Carlos has a very specific person in mind. The indicative describes *facts* and *realities*.

The *subjunctive* is used to describe *what may* or *could be*.

Carlos busca un amigo **que hable** francés.	Carlos is looking for a friend **who speaks** French (that is, **who could speak** French).

In the above sentence, Carlos does not have a particular person in mind. The subjunctive describes *possibilities*.

ACTIVIDAD 4   En búsqueda de . . .

Las siguientes personas buscan a otras personas u objetos con ciertas cualidades. Expresa esto según el modelo.

> Carlos: coche (ir despacio/ir rápido)
> Carlos tiene un coche que va despacio. Busca un coche que vaya rápido.

1. Alicia: amiga (hablar italiano/hablar ruso)
2. Yo: máquina de escribir (funcionar mal/funcionar bien)
3. Yo: reloj de pulsera (andar mal/andar bien)
4. Carmen: amigos (jugar a los naipes/jugar al ajedrez)
5. Felipe: moto (hacer mucho ruido/no hacer mucho ruido)

ACTIVIDAD 5   La envidia (Envy)

VARIATION in the plural:
Tenemos amigos que nos ayudan. Queremos tener amigos que nos ayuden.

Rafael tiene una amiga que tiene mucha suerte. Es un poco envidioso *(envious)* de ella. Haz los dos papeles según el modelo.

> Tengo amigos que me ayudan.

Alicia: Tengo amigos que me ayudan.
Rafael: Quiero tener amigos que me ayuden.

1. Tengo amigas que me invitan a salir.
2. Tengo una amiga que me presta su coche.
3. Tengo profesores que me dan buenas notas.
4. Tengo padres que me comprenden.
5. Tengo hermanos que no se enfadan conmigo.
6. Tengo abuelos que son generosos.

ACTIVIDAD 6   Anuncios de empleo (Want ads)

Imagina que trabajas para una agencia de empleo. Estás encargado(a) de *(in charge of)* escribir anuncios de empleo. Prepara los anuncios según el modelo.

> Buscamos una secretaria: debe hablar español y escribir a máquina.
> Buscamos una secretaria que hable español y que escriba a máquina.

1. Buscamos un dependiente: debe tener una buena presentación y hablar inglés.
2. Necesitamos dos agentes de viajes: deben tener coche y ser ambiciosos.
3. Se busca un ingeniero: debe tener título *(degree)* de ingeniero y estar especializado en electrónica.
4. Se necesitan dos dibujantes: deben tener experiencia y ser de nacionalidad española.
5. Buscamos una intérprete: debe hablar francés e italiano y tener título universitario.

ACTIVIDAD 7   ¡Sueños imposibles!   OPTIONAL

Todo el mundo tiene sueños. Describe los sueños imposibles de las siguientes personas.

> Roberto quiere comprar un coche: ser cómodo / andar a 200 kilómetros por hora / no gastar mucha gasolina.
> Roberto quiere comprar un coche que sea cómodo, que ande a 200 kilómetros por hora y que no gaste mucha gasolina.

1. Teresa quiere vivir en un apartamento: ser grande / estar situado en el centro / costar poco.
2. El Sr. Navarro busca una casa: tener una piscina / ser muy espaciosa / ser barata.
3. Carmen quiere encontrar un chico: hablar tres idiomas / tocar la guitarra muy bien / ser un campeón de tenis / no ser presumido *(stuck-up)*.
4. Los alumnos quieren tener un profesor: ser muy divertido / enseñar cosas interesantes / no dar exámenes.

ACTIVIDAD 8   Un chico bien informado

Es muy útil conocer a Paco porque es un chico que conoce a todos y que lo sabe todo. Haz los papeles de Paco y sus amigos según el modelo.

⊃⊂   Quiero encontrar un chico: hablar inglés

Un amigo: Quiero encontrar un chico que hable inglés.

Paco: Pues, yo conozco a un chico que habla inglés.

1. Quiero conocer una chica: vivir en México
2. Quiero hablar con una persona: poder ayudarme
3. Quiero conocer chicos: tener un coche deportivo
4. Quiero ir a un restaurante: servir comida francesa
5. Quiero ir a una tienda: vender anteojos de sol
6. Quiero ir a una agencia: alquilar apartamentos baratos

ACTIVIDAD 9   Los novios ideales   OPTIONAL

Cada persona tiene una idea diferente de la persona con quien espera casarse. Di si quieres casarte con un hombre o con una mujer que tenga las siguientes características.

⊃⊂   ser más inteligente que yo

(No) quiero casarme con un hombre (una mujer) que sea más inteligente que yo.

1. ser mucho mayor que yo
2. ser más rico(a) que yo
3. ser menos instruido(a) *(educated)* que yo
4. tener buenas cualidades morales
5. tener un futuro estable pero limitado
6. tener un trabajo que requiere viajes frecuentes
7. ser muy conservador(a)
8. respetarme
9. tratar de dominarme
10. desear tener una familia grande
11. no desear tener hijos
12. tener una religión diferente de la mía

ACTIVIDAD 10   La agencia matrimonial OPTIONAL

May be done in groups,
with each group preparing
one item.

Imagina que trabajas en una agencia matrimonial. Di con qué clase de esposo(a) deben casarse las siguientes personas.

WB
B1, B2,
B3, B4

SCRIPT

Act. 4, 5,
6, 7

MASTERS
p. 41

⌒ Paco es muy tímido.
   Debe casarse con una chica que sea cariñosa (con quien se sienta cómodo . . .).

1. Teresa es muy inteligente.
2. Esteban es muy rico.
3. A Elena le gustan los deportes.
4. A Enrique le gusta la música.
5. Federico quiere tener una familia grande.
6. Mari-Carmen quiere continuar con su profesión.

Para la comunicación

OPTIONAL
May be assigned as homework.

Tus preferencias

¿Qué esperas? Describe tus preferencias, completando las siguientes frases. Usa tu imaginación (¡y tu sentido del humor!).

WB
Tus
sueños

SCRIPT

Act. 8

MASTERS
p. 41

TRB

QUIZ
p. 115

   Deseo conocer personas que . . .
   Quiero hacer un viaje con una persona con quien . . .
   Espero tener un(a) jefe(a) que . . .
   No me gusta trabajar para una persona que . . .
   Quiero comprar un coche que . . .
   Prefiero vivir en una casa que . . .
   Quiero vivir en una ciudad en que . . .
   Deseo vivir en un mundo en que . . .
   Quiero casarme con una persona con quien . . .
   No quiero casarme con una persona que . . .

⌒ No quiero casarme con una persona que lo sepa todo (que no sepa reír . . .).

WB   Test / Repaso   TEST pp. 116–120

Variedades   Pablo Neruda

Pablo Neruda (1904-1973), nacido° en Chile, es uno de los poetas
sudamericanos más conocidos° de este siglo.° Empezó a publicar sus
poemas cuando era muy joven. Después de escribir varios libros, viajó
como diplomático a muchos países. Tuvo que salir de Chile por razones
políticas en 1948, pero volvió en 1952.

    La poesía de Neruda es fuerte, lírica y profunda. Su obra° es una de
las cumbres° de la poesía española. Ganó el premio° Nobel de
literatura en 1971.

    En este poema, ¿cuáles son las cinco cosas que quiere el poeta?

nacido: *born*
conocidos: *famous*
  siglo: *century*

obra: *work*
cumbres: *peaks*
  premio: *prize*

Pido silencio

Ahora me dejen tranquilo.
Ahora se acostumbren sin mí.

Yo voy a cerrar los ojos.°

Y sólo quiero cinco cosas,
cinco raíces° preferidas.

Una es el amor sin fin.°

Lo segundo es ver el otoño.
No puedo ser sin que las hojas°
Vuelen° y vuelvan a la tierra.°

Lo tercero es el grave° invierno,
la lluvia que amé,° la caricia°
del fuego° en el frío silvestre.°.

En cuarto lugar el verano
redondo° como una sandía.°

La quinta cosa son tus ojos.
Matilde[1] mía, bienamada,°
no quiero dormir sin tus ojos,
no quiero ser sin que me mires:
yo cambio la primavera
porque tú me sigas mirando.

Amigos, eso es cuanto quiero.
Es casi nada y casi todo.

ojos: *eyes*

raíces *roots*

fin: *end*

hojas: *leaves*
Vuelen: *They fly*
  tierra: *ground*
grave: *serious*
amé: *I loved*
  caricia: *caress*
fuego: *fire*
  silvestre: *wild*

redondo: *round*
  sandía: *watermelon*

bienamada: *beloved*

[1]Matilde: Neruda's wife.

VISTA

España

5

Un poco de historia

¿Qué es España? . . . Bueno, podemos hablar de muchas Españas. Por ejemplo, hay una España romana, una España árabe, una España cristiana . . . Hay una España increíblemente poderosa,° y una España profundamente dividida. En todas las Españas hay cosas memorables. Éstas son algunas.

133 a.C.°

Cae Numancia, ciudad que ha resistido la invasión romana durante mucho tiempo. Pero sus habitantes no se rinden.° Antes de ser prisioneros, prefieren quitarse la vida. Cuando el general romano Escipión Emiliano y sus 60.000 hombres entran a la ciudad, ni siquiera° los caballos están vivos.

711

Bajo el mando del general Tarik, los moros° cruzan el Estrecho de Gibraltar.° En poco tiempo ocupan la región. Los cristianos que huyen° del poder° árabe se refugian en las montañas de Asturias. Allí comienza la reconquista cristiana de España. Dura° más de ocho siglos.

El Cid

1094

El Cid conquista Valencia durante una de sus más famosas campañas militares contra los moros. El Cid es uno de los grandes héroes de España.

La Alhambra

1492

Cae el último reino° moro cuando las fuerzas de los Reyes° Católicos, Fernando e Isabel, vencen° a Boabdil, rey° moro de Granada. Boabdil, su familia y su corte° son obligados a abandonar el maravilloso palacio de La Alhambra.

poderosa *powerful*   **a.C.** *antes de Cristo*   **se rinden** *surrender*   **ni siquiera** *not even*
moros *Moors*   **Estrecho de Gibraltar** *Strait of Gibraltar*   **huyen** *flee*   **poder** *power*
Dura *It lasts*   **reino** *kingdom*   **Reyes** *Sovereigns*   **vencen** *conquer*   **rey** *king*   **corte** *court*

Los Reyes Católicos reciben a Colón.

1493

Los Reyes Católicos reciben a Colón en Barcelona. Es su gran triunfo. A los reyes les presenta los indios, los papagayos° y las otras cosas que ha traído. Y dice Colón:—A los pies de Vuestras° Majestades, pongo las Indias españolas.

1588

España sufre una gran derrota.° El poder del viento y el poder de los ingleses destruyen la Armada Invencible, un ejército° naval creado por el rey Felipe II de España para derrotar a la reina Isabel I de Inglaterra.

1808

El emperador francés Napoleón se apodera de° España. En Madrid el pueblo se subleva.° Así comienza la llamada Guerra° de Independencia contra la ocupación francesa. Inspirado por la brutalidad y la crueldad de esta guerra, el pintor Francisco de Goya crea algunas de sus obras maestras.°

1936

Estalla° otra guerra. Esta vez es una guerra civil. Durante tres años España se destruye a sí misma.° La guerra deja un millón de muertos. Termina cuando Madrid se rinde.° Las fuerzas victoriosas son las del general Francisco Franco. Franco pasa a ser jefe del nuevo gobierno° y gobierna a España durante casi 40 años, hasta su muerte en 1975.

1975

Juan Carlos I, nieto° del último rey de España. Alfonso XIII, llega a ser rey. Establece un gobierno nuevo basado en principios democráticos.

1986

En enero España se hizo° miembro de la Comunidad Económica Europea.° Este ingreso° en la Comunidad contribuye a su mejor desarrollo° económico y amplía° sus relaciones con los países de Europa.

1992

Se celebran los Juegos Olímpicos de Verano en Barcelona.

---

papagayos *parrots* **Vuestras** *Your* **derrota** *defeat* **ejército** *army* **se apodera de** *seizes*
se subleva *rebels* **Guerra** *War* **obras maestras** *masterpieces* **Estalla** *Breaks out*
sí misma *herself* **se rinde** *surrenders* **gobierno** *government* **nieto** *grandson* **se hizo** *became*
Comunidad Económica Europea *European Economic Community* **comercio** *trade* **ingreso** *entry*
desarrollo *development* **amplía** *broadens*

España

Población: 38.800.000
Ciudad capital: Madrid
Unidad monetaria: la peseta
Productos principales:
  hierro,° coches, barcos, aceitunas,°
  naranjas, sardinas
Otros datos:
  España está formada de varias regiones.
  Por todo el país hay una gran variedad
  de clima. Es también un país muy
  montañoso. Después de Suiza, su
  elevacíon media° es la más alta de Europa.

hierro *iron*   **aceitunas** *olives*   **datos** *facts*   **media** *average*

Algunas regiones de España

Galicia

Población: 2.754.000
Ciudades principales: La Coruña,
Santiago de Compostela
Lengua:° el gallego, una lengua que se
parece° al portugués

Vascongadas

Población: 2.135.000
Ciudades principales: Bilbao, San
Sebastián
Lengua: el vasco, una lengua de origen
desconocido

Cataluña

Población: 5.958.000
Ciudad principal: Barcelona
Lengua: el catalán

Castilla la Vieja

Población: 2.577.000
Ciudades principales: Ávila, Burgos,
Segovia
Lengua: el castellano (el español)

Andalucía

Población: 6.442.000
Ciudades principales: Sevilla, Córdoba,
Granada
Lengua: el andaluz, una variedad del
español

Castilla la Nueva

Población: 6.355.000
Ciudad principal: Madrid
Lengua: el castellano

This map represents some of Spain's traditional regions. A
regrouping has occurred in recent years and some new
regions now exist.

Lengua *Language*   **se parece** *is similar*

413

¿Sabes quién es quién?

Hombres y mujeres de todos los tiempos.
Gente que hay que° conocer porque es extraordinaria.
¿No has oído hablar de . . .

Teodosio I, el Grande?

Fue uno de los emperadores romanos nacidos° en España. Durante su gobierno el paganismo desapareció para siempre. Cristo reemplazó° a Júpiter, Venus, Neptuno y todos los demás dioses.° Al morir,° Teodosio dividió el imperio entre sus hijos Arcadio y Honorio.

Isabel la Católica?

Fue reina de Castilla y gobernó junto° con su esposo, Fernando el Católico, rey de Aragón. Fue protectora de Colón y promotora de sus planes. Durante su gobierno terminó la dominación árabe de España. Las acciones de Isabel y su esposo cambiaron profundamente el destino de España.

Miguel Servet?

Famoso médico del siglo XVI que descubrió la circulación de la sangre.° (Sobre esto hay una controversia. Los ingleses dicen que fue William Harvey.) Servet también fue un teólogo y esto le costó la vida. Juan Calvino lo condenó a morir en la hoguera.°

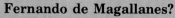

Fernando de Magallanes?

Este navegante, nacido en Portugal, sirvió a la Corona° española como comandante de una expedición fantástica. Su increíble viaje de 1519 a 1522 alrededor del mundo demostró que el mundo era redondo.° De los 240 hombres que comenzaron el viaje en cinco barcos, sólo regresaron 18. Magallanes no fue uno de ellos. Y de los cinco barcos, solamente regresó el *Victoria*. ¡Qué apropiado para los 18 hombres que sobrevivieron!

Don Quijote?

No fue un ser° humano de verdad, pero tiene más vida que todos nosotros. Este héroe idealista, creado por Miguel de Cervantes hace cuatrocientos años, no ha perdido su popularidad. ¿Has oído hablar de la obra teatral *Man of la Mancha*?

Felipe de Borbón y Grecia?

Es el hijo mayor de los Reyes de España. Este chico es hoy el Príncipe° de Asturias. Será el futuro rey de España. Nacido el 30 de enero de 1968, es rubio, de ojos azules. Le gusta nadar y jugar al fútbol.

---

hay que *one ought to*   **nacidos** *born*   **reemplazó** *replaced*   **dioses** *gods*   **Al morir** *When he was dying*   **junto** *together*   **sangre** *blood*   **hoguera** *stake*   **Corona** *Crown*   **redondo** *round*   **ser** *being*   **Príncipe** *Prince*

LA FIESTA BRAVA

Hay varias clases de fiesta. Hay una fiesta que es para bailar, y hay una fiesta que es para morir.° Ésta es la fiesta brava. Siempre (o casi siempre) muere el toro. A veces, también muere el torero. Los aficionados° nunca olvidarán que Bailaor mató° a Joselito . . . que Islero mató a Manolete. Bailaor e Islero eran toros. Joselito y Manolete eran toreros con un talento muy especial. Eran dos personalidades magnéticas.

La fiesta brava es un espectáculo que se puede interpretar de muchas maneras. Veamos lo que dicen estos jóvenes:

José María Arrazola es vasco. Vive en Pamplona y dice: —La fiesta brava es una danza de vida o muerte. Es una obra de arte en movimiento. El torero juega con la muerte que es el toro.

María de los Ángeles Ibarra es de Galicia. Vive en Vigo y dice: —Es el drama del hombre que pone su vida en peligro° y sabe dominar su miedo.° Los toros de lidia° no son como otros toros. Son animales creados para atacar, y son más rápidos y más poderosos° que el hombre.

Antonio Vargas es valenciano. Vive en Valencia y dice: —La fiesta brava es un espectáculo que hay que° prohibir. Hay maneras menos sangrientas° y menos bárbaras de hacer arte. No lo digo por el toro, sino por el torero que puede perder la vida para satisfacer al público.

Luz Marina Mendizábal es andaluza. Vive en Córdoba y dice: —En España, para ser millonario, hay que ser torero. Además, las corridas de toros son una atracción turística muy popular. Así es que es imposible prohibir un espectáculo que es una mina de oro.°

---

morir *dying* **aficionados** *fans* **mató** *killed* **peligro** *danger* **miedo** *fear* **toros de lidia** *fighting bulls*
poderosos *powerful* **hay que** *they ought to* **sangrientas** *bloody* **oro** *gold*

PEQUEÑO RETRATO
DE UN GRAN PINTOR

Fue un niño precoz. Después, un muchacho rebelde. A los 25 años hizo una revolución.
Y desde entonces el arte de pintar cambió para siempre.

¿Quién no conoce por lo menos un cuadro° de Picasso? . . . Picasso, el gran rebelde, es posiblemente el pintor más popular de nuestro siglo. Cuando la gente ve uno de sus cuadros siempre reacciona. A veces, bien. A veces, mal. Pero reacciona. Los seres humanos fueron el tema favorito del pintor, especialmente la mujer.

A veces, la pintó así:

PICASSO, Pablo. *Woman with blue veil.* 1923. Oil on canvas, 39¾″ × 32″. Collection, Los Angeles County Museum of Art. Museum purchase with DeSylva funds.

PICASSO, Pablo. *Seated Woman*. 1927. Oil on wood, 51⅛″ × 38¾″. Collection, The Museum of Modern Art, New York. Fractional gift of James Thrall Soby.

Otras veces, así:

Picasso nació° para pintar. Y afortunadamente, la familia reconoció inmediatamente el gran talento de un niño prodigio. Su padre también era pintor. Así es que padre e hijo comenzaron a pintar juntos. Claro que la familia esperaba un pintor tradicional. Pero no fue así.

A los 16 años Picasso aprobó° el examen de admisión para entrar a estudiar en la Real Academia de San Fernando en Madrid. Trabajó con intensidad. En un solo día creó todos los trabajos que tenía que presentar para ser admitido. Después, las clases comenzaron, y Picasso nunca asistió a ellas. Prefería pasar las horas en el Museo del Prado. Pablo Ruiz Picasso pintaba según sus propias ideas. Más tarde fue a Francia donde pintó sus obras más famosas.

nació *was born* **aprobó** *passed* **417**

EL CID

SUS SUFRIMIENTOS Y SU TRIUNFO

En la Edad Media° el norte de España estaba bajo el control de los cristianos y el sur estaba bajo el control de los moros.° En general los cristianos y los moros convivían en paz. Pero en el siglo XI los cristianos decidieron reconquistar las tierras del sur y unificar el país. Al mismo tiempo un nuevo grupo de moros vino del norte del África para conquistar toda España. Así comenzó una lucha° larga por el dominio del país.

Por ese entonces° vivió el hombre más famoso de toda la historia de España: Rodrigo Díaz de Vivar, llamado «el Cid». Este valiente y noble guerrero° llegó a ser° un gran héroe, pero primero debía sufrir muchas adversidades. Aquí está su historia.

El Cid fue inicialmente el vasallo° de Sancho, rey° de Castilla, quien lo hizo capitán de su ejército° y su cortesano° favorito. Pero cuando Sancho fue asesinado, sus tierras pasaron a su hermano Alfonso, rey de León. Como Sancho y Alfonso habían sido rivales, el nuevo rey no confiaba° mucho en el Cid. Además, los cortesanos le envidiaban° al Cid el prestigio que había obtenido bajo el rey Sancho. Veían al Cid como a un rival.

A pesar de° la hostilidad de los cortesanos y de la desconfianza° del rey, el Cid continuó sirviendo a Alfonso. Un día el rey mandó al Cid a Sevilla, una ciudad mora, para cobrar° un tributo. El conde don García Ordóñez, el rival

principal del Cid, incitó a los moros de otra ciudad para atacarlo. En la batalla el Cid salió victorioso, y como castigo° encarceló° al conde y le cortó la barba . . . ¡la mayor humillación para un caballero!°

Los cortesanos aprovecharon° esta oportunidad para deshonrar al Cid. Organizaron una protesta ante el rey.

—El Cid ha humillado a una persona importante de esta corte— declararon los cortesanos.

—El Cid ha robado parte del tributo— acusó falsamente Ordóñez a su rival.

Vocabulario

Edad Media	los años desde el siglo V hasta la mitad del siglo XV
moros	el nombre dado a los árabes que viven en el norte del África
vasallo	persona subordinada a un señor feudal que recibe protección por su lealtad
cortesano	persona que pertenece a la corte del rey
tributo	lo que se paga a un rey por su protección
conde	título de nobleza

Edad Media *Middle Ages* **moros** *Moors* **lucha** *struggle* **Por ese entonces** *At that time* **guerrero** *warrior* **llegó a ser** *became* **vasallo** *vassal* **rey** *king* **ejército** *army* **cortesano** *courtier* **confiaba** *trusted* **envidiaban** *envied* **A pesar de** *Despite* **desconfianza** *distrust* **cobrar** *to collect* **castigo** *punishment* **encarceló** *he imprisoned* **caballero** *knight* **aprovecharon** *took advantage*

Alfonso no dijo nada, pero escuchó atentamente. «Cuando mi hermano estaba vivo,° el Cid era mi enemigo principal. Ahora ha insultado a un cortesano mío. Tal vez haya robado mi tesoro. Ha faltado a la fidelidad que todo vasallo debe al rey.» Estos pensamientos terminaron por enojar mucho al rey. Éste mandó al Cid un mensaje en el cual lo exiliaba. ¡El Cid tenía nueve días para dejar su casa y salir de las tierras del rey!

Ofendido pero fiel° al rey, el Cid obedeció. Con mucho dolor se despidió de su esposa y de sus dos hijas.

—Me da pena abandonarlas.

—Pero, ¿cuándo volverás?

—Sólo Dios sabe. Pero les seré fiel a ustedes y al rey hasta que él se dé cuenta que no soy su enemigo.

Acompañado de unos pocos hombres y servidores, el Cid partió. Pero antes de salir de las tierras del rey sufrió otra ofensa. En la ciudad de Burgos, por donde pasó primero, todos se apartaron° de él y no querían ni hablarle. El Cid se quedó confuso y triste. Pero todo se explicó cuando una niña se le acercó y le dijo:

—Por favor, márchese usted de este lugar, gran señor, pues° el rey ha ordenado que nadie le dé alojamiento° ni le dirija la palabra.°

«¿Ha sufrido jamás un caballero una desgracia tan grande?» se preguntó el Cid. «Soy fiel, honrado° y valiente, pero he perdido el respeto de todos. ¿Qué debo hacer ahora?»

El Cid decidió partir para otro reino.° Después de poco tiempo encontró un lugar donde lo acogieron.° Allí reunió a sus hombres. ¿Para qué? Para luchar contra los moros. A pesar de la injusticia que Alfonso le había hecho, el Cid luchaba contra los enemigos del rey. «Así demostraré al rey . . . y a todos . . . que soy un caballero honorable.»

En los años siguientes toda España oyó hablar de las valientes conquistas del Cid «Campeador».° Sus hazañas° le dieron fama, dinero y tierras. De ser una persona pobre y humillada pasó a ser una persona rica, famosa y admirada por muchos. Pero todavía le faltaba lo que más deseaba: estar con su familia y tener el favor del rey.

«¿Qué debo hacer para obtener el perdón del rey? Si le presentara° una ofrenda° rica . . .» El Cid decidió ofrecerle al rey un regalo. Mandó a un mensajero° para llevárselo.

—El Cid, mi señor, besa° sus manos y sus pies y le ruega que acepte estos 30 caballos como ofrenda para obtener su perdón.

—Es demasiado pronto para que lo perdone. Él no ha pagado suficientemente por sus ofensas. Pero acepto este regalo porque viene de las tierras de los moros.

Así el Cid debía continuar en su exilio. Siguió peleando contra los moros, y no sólo ganó más batallas sino que también ganó el nombre que lo hizo famoso. Este héroe era tan justo con sus enemigos que fue respetado aún por los moros, quienes en señal de admiración le dieron el nombre de «Cid», una palabra que viene del árabe. Quiere decir «Gran Señor» en español.

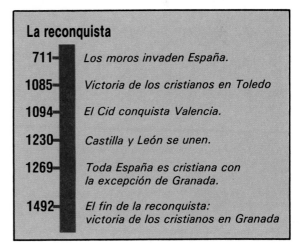

La reconquista

711	Los moros invaden España.
1085	Victoria de los cristianos en Toledo
1094	El Cid conquista Valencia.
1230	Castilla y León se unen.
1269	Toda España es cristiana con la excepción de Granada.
1492	El fin de la reconquista: victoria de los cristianos en Granada

vivo *alive*   **fiel** *loyal*   **se apartaron** *kept away*   **pues** *for*   **alojamiento** *lodging*
dirija la palabra *speak*   **honrado** *honest*   **reino** *kingdom*   **acogieron** *welcomed*   **Campeador** *Warrior*
hazañas *deeds*   **presentara** *I presented*   **ofrenda** *gift*   **mensajero** *messenger*   **besa** *kisses*

Finalmente el Cid conquistó Valencia, una importante ciudad mora. Allí se apoderó de° un gran botín.° Por segunda vez decidió mandar un rico regalo al rey, pidiéndole ser perdonado para poder reunirse con su familia. Esta vez el rey no pudo rehusar.°

—El Cid, mi señor, manda saludos a su majestad, besa sus manos y sus pies y pide que en el nombre del Creador acepte estos 200 caballos que le manda como ofrenda de paz.

—El Cid, su señor, ha dado prueba° de su valor y fidelidad. Mi corazón se alegra de sus conquistas. Recibo este regalo en buena fe.°

—El Cid, mi señor, pide que le conceda° el favor de su perdón para poder reunirse con su esposa y sus hijas.

—Al Cid, su señor, le concedo mi perdón. Desde este momento lo considero como un vasallo fiel. Pongo en libertad a su esposa y a sus hijas y les doy una escolta° hasta los límites de mi reino.

Así fue que el Cid pudo reunirse con su familia en sus nuevas tierras de Valencia.

se apoderó de *he seized* **botín** *booty* **rehusar** *refuse*
ha dado prueba *has proved* **fe** *faith*
conceda *you grant* **escolta** *escort* **a través de** *through*

La historia del Cid fue muy popular en la Edad Media y es popular aún hoy. El Cid es admirado porque conservó su honor a través de° todos sus infortunios y nunca abandonó sus principios de fidelidad y justicia.

ESPAÑA EN LA ÉPOCA DEL CID

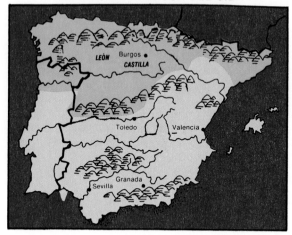

■ *El territorio de los cristianos*
■ *El territorio de los moros*

EL CID EL CID EL CID EL C

La historia del Cid fue conservada en el «Poema del Cid», el primer monumento de la literatura española. Escrito hacia 1140, este poema épico combina elementos históricos y elementos ficticios al contar la leyenda del héroe nacional de España.

Abajo° hay un pasaje del poema antiguo. Relata la parte donde el mensajero del Cid le presenta al rey Alfonso el primer regalo. Puede compararse con la versión moderna del mismo pasaje para establecer cuánto la lengua° española ha cambiado desde los tiempos del Cid.

Un pasaje del poema antiguo	*Versión moderna*
Mio Çid Roy Díaz de Dios aya su graçia!	¡El Cid Ruy Díaz, por todos, que Dios lo tenga en su gracia!
Ido es a Castiella Albar Fáñez Minaya,	Ya se fue para Castilla Alvar Fáñez el Minaya.
treynta cavallos al rey los enpresentava;	El don° de treinta caballos° ante el Rey lo presentaba;
vídolos el rey, fermoso sonrrisava:	Violos el Rey, que sonríe con hermosa y gentil cara:°
"¿quin los dio estos, si vos vala Dios, Minaya?"	—¿Quién os dio estos caballos, que Dios os valga° Minaya?
—"Mio Çid Roy Díaz, que en buen ora cinxo espada.	—Nuestro Cid Rodrigo Díaz, que en buena hora ciño espada.°
. . . .	. . . .
A vos, rey ondrado, enbía esta presentaja;	y a vos, Rey honrado, envía° este don para que os plazca.°
bésavos los piedes e las manos amas	Los pies os besa, señor, y también las manos ambas,°
quel ayades merçed, si el Criador vos vala."	y os pide le hagáis favor, ¡así el Creador os valga!

Abajo *Below* **lengua** *language* **don** *present* **caballos** *horses* **cara** *face* **valga** *may protect*
ciñó espada *wore a sword* **envía** *he sends* **plazca** *it please* **ambas** *both*

Sorprende a tus amigos con una sopa fría

El gazpacho es una sopa° española muy popular. Es una sopa fría, deliciosa y muy fácil de preparar. ¿Deseas preparar el gazpacho español?

Los ingredientes:

 3 tomates medianos°

 1 cebolla° pequeña

 1 pimiento° rojo o verde, no muy grande

 1 pepino° mediano

 1 diente de ajo°

 1 taza de jugo de tomate

2 cucharadas° de vinagre

2 cucharadas de aceite (de oliva, si es posible)

 1 cucharadita de sal

pan

La preparación:
1. Pela° los tomates.
2. Corta en cubitos los tomates, la cebolla, el pimiento, el pepino y el ajo.
3. Pon los ingredientes, excepto el pepino, en una licuadora.°
4. Mézclalos° durante uno o dos minutos con un poco de pan para espesarlo.°
5. Pon la sopa a enfriar° en la refrigeradora durante dos horas o más, si es necesario. ¡Tiene que estar bastante fría!
6. Revuelve° el gazpacho frío con una cuchara.
7. Sírvelo con los pepinos. ¡Buen provecho!

Actividades culturales

1. *Prepara un informe° sobre Juan Carlos, el rey de España.*
2. *Escoge una de las regiones de España y prepara una exposición.° Puedes usar mapas, carteles,° fotos o folletos° turísticos.*
3. *Aprende algo de un aspecto de la cultura árabe en España y descríbelo a la clase.*
4. *Prepara un informe sobre Pablo Ruiz Picasso. Si es posible, ve al museo para ver sus obras o míralas en varios libros.*

informe *report*   **exposición** *exhibit*   **carteles** *posters*   **folletos** *brochures*

sopa *soup*   **medianos** *medium-sized*   **cebolla** *onion*   **pimiento** *pepper*   **pepino** *cucumber*
diente de ajo *garlic clove*   **cucharadas** *spoonfuls*   **Pela** *Peel*   **licuadora** *mixer*   **Mézclalos** *Mix them*
espesarlo *thicken it*   **enfriar** *to cool*   **Revuelve** *Stir*

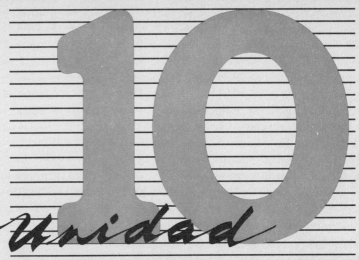

10 Unidad

Cambios

OBJECTIVES

Communication

By the end of this unit, the students will be able to use Spanish:
- to formulate certain objectives
- to describe future events that depend on specific conditions
- to describe what would happen if certain other things were to occur

Language

In this final unit, which may be considered optional, the basic uses of the present subjunctive are reviewed, and the imperfect subjunctive is presented. The principal topics covered are:
- the use of the subjunctive after **para que**
- Subjunctive vs. indicative after **cuando**
- Summary of the uses of the present subjunctive
- Review of the future and the conditional
- Forms and uses of the imperfect subjunctive
- Imperfect subjunctive after **si**

Culture

The cultural topics of this unit include the importance of music for Hispanic teenagers, the role of the marketplace, parents' treatement of male and female teenagers, and the attitude toward change in Spanish-speaking societies.

Lección 1 La generosidad tiene límites

Act. 1

47–48

Hay personas muy generosas.
Otros ponen condiciones a su generosidad.
Por ejemplo:

Aquí tienes diez pesos . . .

. . . para que vayas a la heladería y me compres un helado.

Aquí tienes: *Here are*
para que: *in order that*

Voy a invitarte a mi casa . . .

. . . para que me ayudes a pintar mi cuarto.

Te invito a mi fiesta . . .

. . . con la condición de que me prestes tu tocadiscos y que lleves tus discos de Elio Roca.

Unidad diez
424

Voy a presentarte a mi mejor amigo . . .

. . . con la condición de que me presentes a tus hermanas y primas.

presentarte: *to introduce you*

Por supuesto, puedes usar mi bicicleta . . .

. . . con tal que repares los frenos, infles las llantas y arregles el asiento.

con tal que: *provided that*

Claro, voy a prestarte mi diccionario de inglés . . .

. . . con tal que me prestes tu guitarra y tu moto y que me invites al picnic.

Have the students describe the various cartoons. If needed, ask lead questions.

Act. 2

NOTA CULTURAL OPTIONAL

Los jóvenes hispanos y la música

¿Te gusta la música? Para los jóvenes hispano-hablantes, la música es sin duda el pasatiempo favorito. Muchos tocan la guitarra o el piano. Otros escuchan los últimos «hits» del momento. Hay muchos cantantes populares: Julio Iglesias de España, José José de México, Elio Roca de la Argentina. Y a casi todos los jóvenes les encanta bailar.

¿Qué clase de música es popular? Naturalmente la música hispana: el merengue, la cumbia,

el bolero, la salsa y también la música norte-americana: el jazz, el rock and roll y la música disco. El hecho es que «Miami Sound Machine», «Santana» y muchos conjuntos° famosos son tan populares en el mundo hispanohablante como en los Estados Unidos. Para la juventud hispánica, la música y el baile son más que diversiones. Son parte de la cultura y de la vida.

conjuntos *groups*

¿Te gusta la música? ¿Les gusta la música a los jóvenes norteamericanos? ¿Tocas la guitarra? ¿Tocas el piano? ¿Quiénes son los cantantes populares en los Estados Unidos? ¿Les gusta el jazz a los jóvenes norteamericanos? ¿Les gusta la música disco? ¿Cuál es el conjunto más popular en los Estado Unidos?

Vocabulario

sustantivo	**un hecho**	fact, deed
verbo	**presentar**	to introduce
expresión	**aquí tiene(s)**	here is, here are

Unidad diez
426

De vez en cuando invitas a tus amigos a tu casa. ¿Los invitas por las siguientes razones?

1. ¿Los invitas **para que pasen** unas horas contigo?
2. ¿Los invitas **para que jueguen** al ping pong contigo?
3. ¿Los invitas **para que conozcan** a tus padres?
4. ¿Los invitas **para que** te **ayuden** con tus tareas?
5. ¿Los invitas **para que** te **hablen** de sus problemas?
6. ¿Los invitas **para que** te **cuenten** su vida?

OBSERVACIÓN

In the above sentences, you are asked about certain objectives you may have in mind for inviting your friends to your house.

- Are these objectives or conditions realized or not at the time you make the invitation?
  they are not yet realized

- Are the verbs describing these objectives or conditions in the indicative or the subjunctive?
  the subjunctive

Estructuras

Act. 3

A. El subjuntivo después de *para que*

Note the use of the subjunctive after **para que** in the following sentences.

Voy a invitar a Carlos **para que** me **preste** sus discos.	*I am going to invite Carlos **so that** he **will lend** me his records.*
Te llamo **para que vengas** a mi fiesta.	*I am calling you **so that** you **will come** to my party.*
Aquí tienes un dólar **para que** te **compres** la revista.	*Here is a dollar **so that** you **can buy** yourself the magazine.*

The subjunctive is always used after the conjunction **para que** to express objectives or conditions not yet realized.

Note the constructions in the following chart.

When the objective concerns	the construction to use is
the subject	**para** + infinitive
another person	**para que** + subjunctive

Compare the following sentences.

Compro el periódico **para leer** el horóscopo.	*I buy the newspaper **(in order) to read** the horoscope.*
Compro el periódico **para que tú leas** la página de deportes.	*I buy the newspaper **so that you may read** the sports page.*

ACTIVIDAD 1   Un tío generoso

El tío Alberto es muy generoso. Manda dinero para que sus sobrinos
(nephews) se compren algo. Haz el papel del tío Alberto.

⟯⟩   Ricardo (5 dólares: anteojos de sol)
        Manda 5 dólares para que Ricardo se compre anteojos de sol.

1. Luisa (15 dólares: un traje de baño)
2. tú (1 dólar: dulces)
3. Felipe (50 dólares: una bicicleta)
4. Uds. (20 dólares: un radio)
5. Elena y Carmen (40 dólares: un tocadiscos)
6. tú y Pepe (2 dólares: helado)

ACTIVIDAD 2   La compañía internacional

Una compañía internacional manda a sus empleados a países extranjeros.
Explica los objetivos de la compañía.

⟯⟩   Silvia (México / hablar español)
        La compañía manda a Silvia a México para que hable español.

1. Rafael (Francia / hablar francés)
2. Elena (Roma / aprender italiano)
3. Carlos y Pedro (Tokio / aprender japonés)
4. Felipe (Nueva York / estudiar electrónica)
5. Luisa (Londres / establecer relaciones comerciales) establezca
6. Raúl y Guillermo (Los Ángeles / hacer investigaciones [*research*] técnicas) hagan

ACTIVIDAD 3   ¡Un poco de lógica!   OPTIONAL

May be assigned as a special challenge activity.

Explica los objetivos de las personas de la columna A. ¿Cuántas frases
lógicas puedes crear usando los elementos de A, B y C?

A	B	C
yo	darle dinero a Enrique	venir a la fiesta
tú	escribirles a (mis) padres	comprender la situación
Elena	invitar a Carlos a la fiesta	traer sus discos
nosotros	llamar a Raúl y Felipe	prestar su coche
Luis y Ana	explicarle el problema a Antonio	saber la verdad
	decirle la verdad al profesor	comprar billetes de lotería
	mandarle un regalo a Felicia	comprar un coche
	mandarle un telegrama a Teresa	estar de buen humor
	mandarle un cheque de mil dólares	quedarse en casa
	a Carmen	(no) enojarse
		(no) irritarse
		(no) ponerse furioso

WB
A1, A2,
A3

SCRIPT
Act. 4, 5

MASTERS
p. 42

⟯⟩   Elena le da dinero a Enrique para que compre billetes de lotería.

B. El subjuntivo después de ciertas conjunciones

The following sentences describe certain actions that are subject to certain conditions that have not yet been fulfilled.
Note the use of the subjunctive after the conjunctions in heavy print that introduce these conditions.

Voy a terminar la tarea **antes de que** Carlos venga.	*I am going to finish the assignment **before** Carlos comes.*
Te presto mis discos **con la condición de que** me prestes tu guitarra.	*I am lending you my records **with the condition that** you lend me your guitar.*
Te presto mi bicicleta **con tal que** no la rompas.	*I am lending you my bicycle **provided that** you do not break it.*
Vamos a hacer un picnic **a menos que** llueva.	*We will have a picnic **unless** it rains.*
En caso de que llueva, vamos a ir al cine.	***In case** it rains, we will go to the movies.*

The subjunctive is always used after the following conjunctions that introduce conditions not yet fulfilled.

a menos que	unless
antes de que	before
con la condición de que	on the condition that
con tal que	provided that
en caso de que	in case (that)

The construction **antes de que** + subjunctive is replaced by **antes de** + infinitive when the conditions concern the subject.
Compare:

Pablo me llama **antes de venir**.	*Pablo calls me **before coming (he comes)**.*
Pablo me llama **antes de que yo venga**.	*Pablo calls me **before I come**.*

ANTES DE VIAJAR
¡CONSULTENOS!
Rio
CHARTERS CORP.
285-0400
CHILE $658 IDA Y VUELTA
BRAZIL RIO – SAO $610 IDA Y VUELTA

ACTIVIDAD 4   Invitaciones recíprocas

Las siguientes personas invitan a sus amigos a bailar con la condición de
que sus amigos las inviten también. Expresa esto según el modelo.

🐸 yo: tú   Te invito a bailar con la condición de que tú me invites también.

1. yo: Paco
2. Paco: Elena
3. nosotros: tus primos

4. tú: Jaime
5. Héctor: Rafaela
6. Ana y Susana: Felipe y Carlos

ACTIVIDAD 5   El picnic de Teresa

Teresa ha organizado un picnic. Sus amigos van al picnic a menos que algo
ocurra. Expresa esto según el modelo.

🐸 Elena: sentirse cansada   Elena va al picnic a menos que se sienta cansada.

1. Raúl: sentirse enfermo
2. Felipe: tener mucho trabajo
3. Bárbara: no tener tiempo
4. mis primos: no tener su moto
5. tú: tener que estudiar
6. yo: salir con mi novio(a)
7. nosotros: estar de viaje
8. Roberto y Consuelo: estar cansados

ACTIVIDAD 6   ¡Una cuestión de tiempo!   OPTIONAL   May be assigned as homework.

Hay cosas que tenemos que hacer antes de que otras cosas ocurran.
Expresa esto según el modelo.

🐸 yo: limpiar mi cuarto / mis amigos llegan
       Tengo que limpiar mi cuarto antes de que mis amigos lleguen.

1. tú: estudiar más / el profesor da el examen
2. Carlos: invitar a Elena al cine / Raúl la invita
3. el cocinero (cook): preparar la comida / los clientes llegan
4. los bandidos: salir del banco / la policía llega
5. la policía: llegar / los bandidos se escapan
6. el Sr. Montero: llegar a la estación / el tren sale

WB
B1, B2,
B3

Para la comunicación

May be assigned as homework.

SCRIPT

Act. 6

MASTERS
p. 42

TRB

QUIZ
pp. 121–
122

Planes

Completa las siguientes frases con una idea personal.

Voy a salir el fin de semana con tal que . . .

Voy a sacar una «A» en español con la condición de que . . .

Voy a pasar unas vacaciones muy buenas a menos que . . .

Voy a asistir a la universidad con la condición de que . . .

Voy a casarme a menos que . . .

Siempre estoy de buen humor con la condición de que . . .

No me pongo furioso a menos que . . .

Voy a salir el fin de semana con tal que mis amigos me inviten (mis padres me den dinero).

Lección 2 · La próxima vez

Act. 1

49

¿Eres una persona cuidadosa?

A veces somos un poco negligentes. Como resultado algo estúpido o vergonzoso nos pasa. La experiencia nos enseña a ser más cuidadosos . . . la próxima vez.

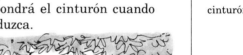

La Sra. de Ramos no lleva nunca paraguas cuando sale.

La próxima vez, llevará su paraguas cuando salga.

El Sr. Cárdenas no se pone el cinturón de seguridad cuando conduce.

La próxima vez, el Sr. Cárdenas se pondrá el cinturón cuando conduzca.

La Sra. de Martínez no cierra la puerta cuando va al mercado.

La próxima vez, cerrará la puerta cuando vaya al mercado.

Como resultado: *As a result*
vergonzoso: *embarrassing*

paraguas: *umbrella*

cinturón: *belt*

Unidad diez
432

This lesson presents the uses of the indicative and subjunctive after **cuando.** Have the students observe the verb forms used with ongoing events and events which have not yet happened.

Micifus no mira cuando cruza la calle.

La próxima vez, él mirará cuando cruce la calle.

Felipe no tiene cuidado cuando pasa debajo de una escalera.

La próxima vez, él tendrá cuidado cuando pase debajo de una escalera.

Cuando pasean, Jaime y Carmen no llevan su cámara.

La próxima vez, Jaime y Carmen llevarán su cámara cuando paseen.

pasean: *they take a walk*

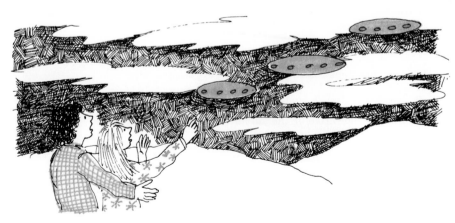

You may have the students describe each cartoon.

¿Adónde vas para comprar carne, pan, leche, etc.? ¿Dónde se encuentran los supermercados en el mundo hispánico? ¿Qué institución reemplaza los supermercados en los pequeños pueblos?

¿Qué productos se venden en el mercado? ¿Qué se lleva al mercado el fotógrafo? el barbero? el curandero?

Act. 2

NOTA CULTURAL   OPTIONAL

El mercado

En los Estados Unidos, hay un lugar muy práctico donde se puede comprar todo. Éste es el supermercado. Los supermercados existen también en el mundo hispano, pero se encuentran principalmente en las ciudades grandes. No hay supermercados en los pueblecitos, pero hay otra institución muy pintoresca:° el mercado.

El día del mercado, los comerciantes° de la región se reúnen en la plaza mayor e instalan sus tiendas°... Venden frutas y legumbres, ropa y utensilios de cocina, productos de belleza° y medicinas... Viene también el fotógrafo con su cámara, el barbero° con sus tijeras, el dentista con sus instrumentos... el curandero ambulante° con sus drogas milagrosas° y la adivinadora°...

El día del mercado es el día en que la gente del campo va de compras, vende sus productos y se reúne con sus amigos... En verdad, ¡es un día de gran actividad!

pintoresca *picturesque* **comerciantes** *merchants* **instalan sus tiendas** *set up their booths* **belleza** *beauty* **barbero** *barber* **curandero ambulante** *traveling healer* **milagrosas** *miraculous* **adivinadora** *fortune teller*

—— Vocabulario ——

sustantivos	**un cinturón**	belt
	un mercado	market, open-air market
	un paraguas	umbrella
verbo	**pasear**	to take a walk
expresión	**como resultado**	as a result

CONVERSACIÓN   OPTIONAL

1. ¿Estás contento(a) **cuando sacas** una buena nota?
2. ¿Estás contento(a) **cuando sacas** una mala nota?
3. ¿Estás contento(a) **cuando sales** con amigos simpáticos?
4. ¿Estás contento(a) **cuando** tus padres te **dan** dinero?

5. ¿Estarás contento(a) **cuando recibas** tu diploma?
6. ¿Estarás contento(a) **cuando te ganes** la vida?
7. ¿Estarás contento(a) **cuando compres** tu primer coche?
8. ¿Estarás contento(a) **cuando te cases?**

OBSERVACIÓN

Reread questions 1 to 4. These questions concern events that are happening to you now.
- Is the first verb in the present or in the future?   in the present
- Is the verb after **cuando** in the indicative or the subjunctive?   in the indicative

Now reread questions 5 to 8.
- Do these questions concern events that are happening now or events that may happen to you in the future?   future events
- Is the first verb in the present or in the future?   in the future
- Is the verb after **cuando** in the indicative or the subjunctive?   in the subjunctive

Estructuras

You may remind the students that the future tense is formed by adding future endings to the future stem (usually the infinitive). Review the irregular stems: **dir-, har-, podr-, pondr-, querr-, saldr-, sabr-, tendr-, vendr-, habr-.**

A. Repaso: el futuro

Review the forms of the future in the chart below:

yo	hablaré	nosotros	hablaremos
tú	hablarás	vosotros	hablaréis
él, ella, Ud.	hablará	ellos, ellas, Uds.	hablarán

VARIATION in the plural: **¿Visitarán Uds. España? Sí, un día visitaremos España.**

ACTIVIDAD 1   Diálogo: Un día

Pregúntales a tus compañeros si algún día harán las siguientes cosas.

> visitar España   Estudiante 1: ¿Visitarás España?
> Estudiante 2: Sí, un día visitaré España.
> (No, no visitaré nunca España.)

1. hablar español perfectamente
2. asistir a la universidad
3. comprar un coche
4. ganarse la vida
5. casarse
6. comprar una casa
7. vivir en un país extranjero
8. ir a México
9. ser profesor(a)
10. ser médico(a)
11. ser famoso(a)
12. ir a la luna
13. conocer al presidente de los Estados Unidos
14. viajar en cohete

ACTIVIDAD 2   Varias profesiones   OPTIONAL

Describe lo que harán las siguientes personas en sus profesiones. Usa por lo menos 3 de los siguientes verbos en frases afirmativas o negativas: **trabajar / vivir / cuidar / asistir a / ser / estar / viajar / ganar / recibir / comprar / ver.**

> Teresa será ingeniera.
> Trabajará para una compañía de petróleo. Vivirá en Texas.
> De vez en cuando viajará a Alaska. Se ganará la vida muy bien.
> Con su dinero comprará un Jaguar.

1. Carlos será político.
2. Nosotros seremos trabajadores sociales.
3. Tú serás médico.
4. Felipe y Manuel serán fotógrafos.
5. Ana María será periodista.
6. Adela será jugadora profesional de tenis.
7. Uds. serán instructores de esquí acuático.
8. Yo seré el rey (king) / la reina (queen) de los holgazanes.

WB
A1, A2

SCRIPT
Act. 3

MASTERS
p. 43

B. El subjuntivo o el indicativo después de algunas conjunciones de tiempo

In the sentences below, Carlos (age nineteen) describes what he does.
He speaks about events that actually do happen to him.
His little sister Luisa (age eight) speaks about what she will do.
She speaks about events that may happen, but that have not yet
happened. Compare the verbs used after **cuando** in each set of sentences.

Act. 4

Carlos: **Cuando tengo** tiempo, llamo a mis amigos.	*When I have time, I call my friends.* (actual event)
Luisa: Y yo, **cuando tenga** tiempo, llamaré a mi novio.	*When I have time, I will call my boyfriend.* (future event)
Carlos: **Cuando estoy** con mi novia, vamos al cine.	*When I am with my girlfriend, we go to the movies.* (actual event)
Luisa: Y yo, **cuando esté** con mi novio, iremos a bailar.	*When I am with my boyfriend, we will go dancing.* (future event)

After **cuando,** the verb may be in the indicative or the subjunctive.

It is in the *indicative* if the action or event is actually taking place, takes place regularly, or has taken place.   indicative = certainty

It is in the *subjunctive* if the action or event is yet to take place.   subjunctive = uncertainty

ACTIVIDAD 3   Enrique

Enrique habla de lo que hace regularmente y de lo que va a hacer en el
futuro. Completa las frases de Enrique con **estoy** o **esté,** según el caso.

1. Cuando ___ en la clase de francés, me duermo.   1. estoy
2. Cuando ___ en la universidad, no estudiaré francés.   2. esté
3. Cuando ___ con mi novia, vamos al cine.   3. estoy
4. Cuando ___ en la biblioteca, leo los periódicos.   4. estoy
5. Cuando ___ en Nueva York, hablaré inglés.   5. esté
6. Cuando ___ con mis amigos, hablamos de la política.   6. estoy
7. Cuando ___ casado, me compraré un coche deportivo.   7. esté
8. Cuando ___ enfermo, tomo aspirinas.   8. estoy
9. Cuando ___ en mi palacio, invitaré a todos mis amigos.   9. esté
10. Cuando ___ en mi yate *(yacht)*, organizaré fiestas.   10. esté

ACTIVIDAD 4   Planes universitarios

Unos alumnos están hablando de lo que van a estudiar en la universidad.
Expresa lo que dicen según el modelo, usando el subjuntivo de **estar.**

∑ᐳ   Juan Carlos (biología)

Cuando esté en la universidad, Juan Carlos estudiará biología.

1. Felipe (arquitectura)
2. Alberta (medicina)
3. yo (electrónica)
4. tú (física)
5. nosotros (matemáticas)
6. Ignacio y Roberto (astronomía)

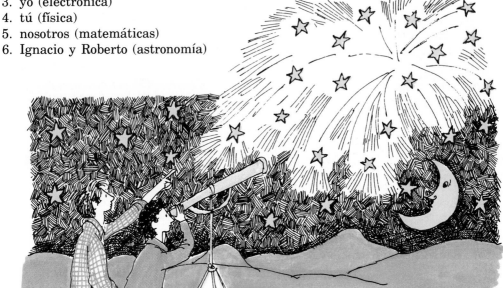

ACTIVIDAD 5   ¡La felicidad!

Nadie es completamente feliz. Por ejemplo, las siguientes personas están
bastante contentas ahora . . . pero estarán más contentas en el futuro
cuando . . . Expresa esto según el modelo.

Have a student explain the use of the indicative and the subjunctive after **cuando** in the model sentences.

∑ᐳ   Carmen sale con Ricardo (con Felipe).

Carmen está contenta cuando sale con Ricardo.
Estará más contenta cuando salga con Felipe.

1. Susana sale con Eduardo (con Roberto).
2. Alberto tiene una cita con Inés (con Ana María).
3. Rafaela nada bien (como una campeona).
4. Nosotros cantamos en el coro *(choir)* de la escuela (en la Ópera
   Metropolitana de Nueva York).
5. Emilio y Esteban juegan para el equipo de la escuela (para los Yankis).
6. Yo saco una «B» («A»).

ACTIVIDAD 6   Esperanzas *(Hopes)*

La felicidad es diferente para cada uno de nosotros. Di qué significa la felicidad para las siguientes personas, según el modelo.

〰️ María espera tener trabajo.   María estará feliz cuando tenga trabajo.

1. Felipe espera vivir en México.
2. Isabel espera trabajar como abogada.
3. Raúl espera casarse con Isabel.
4. Ramón espera graduarse.
5. Manuela espera descubrir el novio ideal.
6. Luisa espera ser arquitecta.
7. Raquel espera recibir una carta de Roberto.
8. Carlos espera encontrar la novia ideal.
9. Elena espera asistir a la universidad.
10. José espera tocar bien la guitarra.

ACTIVIDAD 7   Paco y Carlitos

Carlitos (8 años) no quiere hacer lo que hace su hermano Paco (20 años). Haz el papel de Paco y de Carlitos.

〰️ estar en la universidad / estudiar mucho
    Paco: Cuando estoy en la universidad, estudio mucho.
    Carlitos: Y yo, cuando esté en la universidad, no estudiaré mucho.

1. estar con amigos / discutir de política
2. estar en casa / mirar la televisión
3. estar de buen humor / invitar a mis amigos a un café
4. salir con una chica / pagar por ella
5. tener dinero / prestarles mi dinero a mis amigos
6. tener tiempo / leer poemas

ACTIVIDAD 8   ¡Un poco de lógica!   OPTIONAL

May be assigned as a special challenge activity.

En cinco minutos, ¿cuántas frases lógicas (afirmativas o negativas) puedes crear, usando los elementos de las columnas A, B y C y tu imaginación? Para la columna D, usa tu imaginación.

WB
B1, B2,
B3, B4

SCRIPT
Act. 5, 6

MASTERS
p. 43

A	B	C	D
yo	estar en España	hablar	
tú	ir a Francia	visitar	
Roberto	encontrar a los chicos (las chicas)	estar	
nosotros	tener un coche	comprar	
Manuela y Ana	tener dinero	invitar	
		ir	

〰️ Cuando esté en España, compraré una guitarra (visitaré Madrid, etc.).

C. Resumen: el uso del subjuntivo

The main uses of the subjunctive are summarized in the following chart.

LESSON	The subjunctive is used after . . .	
8.4	1. verbs and expressions of indirect command	**Quiero que toques** la guitarra.
9.1	2. verbs and expressions of emotion	**Me alegro de que toques** la guitarra.
9.3	3. verbs and expressions of doubt	**No creo que toques** el piano.
9.2	4. many impersonal expressions (indirect command, emotion, or doubt)	**¡Es estupendo que toques** bien!
9.4	5. **que** + possible facts or events that have not yet happened	Quiero encontrar a **alguien que toque** el clarinete.
10.1	6. conjunctions + objectives or conditions that have not yet been fulfilled	Voy a invitarte **con la condición de que toques** la guitarra.
10.2	7. **cuando** + events that have not yet happened	Te escucharé **cuando toques** la guitarra.

ACTIVIDAD 9   Reacciones personales

Expresa tus reacciones a lo siguiente. Para eso empieza cada frase con una expresión que requiera el subjuntivo.

Mis padres me compran un Ferrari.

> Quiero que (No creo que, Dudo que, Ojalá que, Es imposible que) mis padres me compren un Ferrari.

1. Mis amigos me respetan.
2. Mis padres me comprenden.
3. Mis profesores son tolerantes.
4. Todos los hombres son iguales *(equal)*.
5. Los políticos son sinceros.
6. Somos inmortales.
7. La vida extraterrestre existe.

Giant head at the Museum of Anthropology in Mexico, D.F.

WB
Las es-
peranzas

TRB

QUIZ
pp. 123–
124

Para la comunicación

Expresión personal

Completa las siguientes frases usando tu imaginación y un verbo en el subjuntivo.

Me casaré cuando . . .
Espero conocer personas que . . .
Quiero tener un trabajo que . . .
Quiero casarme con una persona que . . .
Seré independiente cuando . . .

Estaré muy contento(a) con la condición de que . . .
Compraré un coche deportivo cuando . . .
Iré a España cuando . . .
Iré a la luna cuando . . .

Me casaré cuando tenga trabajo (esté en la universidad, etc.).

Lección 3   ¿Víctimas o no?

Act. 1

¿Eran tus padres estrictos . . . o muy tolerantes contigo?
Por lo general, la disciplina familiar es más fuerte en los países
hispánicos que en los Estados Unidos.
Cuatro jóvenes hablan de cómo era la disciplina familiar cuando
eran niños. En tu opinión, ¿eran víctimas de esa disciplina o no?

familiar: *of the family*

Emilio Fiestas

¡Ay, la disciplina familiar!
En el colegio importaba que yo sacara
buenas notas y en casa importaba que
estudiara antes y después de comer. ¡Pero
eso no era todo! Mis padres exigían también
que me bañara todos los días, que me lavara
las manos antes de comer, que me cepillara
los dientes, que limpiara mi cuarto, que . . .

Ana María Clemente

En mi casa, mis padres no insistían en
que sacara buenas notas ni que estudiara
siempre. Otras cosas eran más importantes.
Era importante que yo respetara a los
mayores y que escuchara sus consejos. Mis
padres exigían que compartiera lo que tenía
y que me llevara bien con todos. Y
naturalmente, no querían que me peleara
con mis hermanos ni que me burlara de mis
compañeros.

Carlos Ramos

Mis padres no eran muy estrictos
conmigo . . . Pero sí lo eran con mi
hermana. Durante la semana, mi mamá
insistía en que ella regresara
inmediatamente después de las clases y
que ayudara en casa después de estudiar
y los fines de semana. Mi papá no le
permitía que saliera con sus compañeras (y
mucho menos con chicos). ¡Ay, la pobrecita!

You may use these texts as models for the students to describe
family discipline when they were younger.

Marisa Fuentes

No, no eran mis padres muy estrictos. No insistían en que estudiara y me permitían salir con mis compañeras ... (¡y de vez en cuando con chicos también!).

Sin embargo, había muchas cosas que querían que yo hiciera. Querían que tocara el piano (¡quizás esperaban que llegara a ser una gran artista!). Querían que tomara clases particulares de francés. Querían que aprendiera a montar a caballo y a patinar. Querían que aprendiera a cantar. Querían que ...

NOTA CULTURAL OPTIONAL

¿Más igualdad?

En los Estados Unidos, las chicas reciben mensualidades,° tienen empleos,° participan en todos los deportes y seleccionan° cursos ... ¡como los chicos!

En los países hispanos, tradicionalmente los padres eran más estrictos con las hijas que con los hijos. Ellas recibían menos dinero y generalmente no podían salir solas con chicos. Empezaban a salir solas cuando se hacían novias y solamente salían con sus novios.

Ahora la situación es muy diferente. Muchas chicas empiezan a salir solas o con sus amigas y amigos. Comienzan a participar más en todos los deportes y a estudiar carreras donde tradicionalmente había solamente chicos. Cada vez más,° se encuentran chicas que estudian, trabajan o son deportistas.

mensualidades *allowances* **empleos** *jobs* **seleccionan** *choose* **Cada vez más** *More and more*

¿Recibes una mensualidad? ¿Tienes un empleo? ¿En los países hispanos, tradicionalmente tratan los padres a los chicos y a las chicas de la misma manera?

── Vocabulario ──

adjetivos	**exigente**	demanding
	familiar	(of the) family
expresiones	**peor**	worse
	por lo general	in general

CONVERSACIÓN

Vamos a hablar de la disciplina familiar de ahora y de cuando estabas en la escuela primaria.

Ahora . . .

1. **¿Insisten** tus padres **en que estudies** mucho?
2. **¿Insisten en que saques** buenas notas?
3. **¿Insisten en que trabajes** durante las vacaciones?
4. **¿Insisten en que ayudes** en casa?

Cuando estabas en la escuela primaria . . .

5. **¿Insistían** tus padres **en que estudiaras** mucho?
6. **¿Insistían en que sacaras** buenas notas?
7. **¿Insistían en que trabajaras** durante las vacaciones?
8. **¿Insistían en que ayudaras** en casa?

OBSERVACIÓN

Carefully reread questions 1 to 4.
- Do these questions concern the present or the past?   the present
- Is the verb of indirect command (**insistir**) in the present or the past?   the present
- Are the verbs that follow **que** in the present subjunctive?   yes

Carefully reread questions 5 to 8.
- Do these questions concern the present or the past?   the past
- Is the verb **insistir** in the present or in the past?   the past
  In what tense is it?   the imperfect
- Are the verbs that follow **que** in the present subjunctive?   no

The verbs here are in a new tense: the *imperfect subjunctive*.

Estructuras

A. El imperfecto del subjuntivo: formas regulares

So far we have been using the subjunctive mainly in the present tense. The most frequently used past tense in the subjunctive is the *imperfect*. The forms of the *imperfect subjunctive* are easy to remember because they are derived from a form you already know: the **ellos** form of the preterite.

Have students note the accent mark on the **nosotros** form.

Note these forms in the chart below, paying attention to the endings.

Act. 3

INFINITIVE	hablar	comer	vivir
ellos form of the preterite	hablaron	comieron	vivieron

IMPERFECT SUBJUNCTIVE			
Era importante que . . .			
yo	hablara	comiera	viviera
tú	hablaras	comieras	vivieras
él, ella, Ud.	hablara	comiera	viviera
nosotros	habláramos	comiéramos	viviéramos
vosotros	hablarais	comierais	vivierais
ellos, ellas, Uds.	hablaran	comieran	vivieran

The **-se** form of the imperfect subjunctive is not presented in this book. These endings are: **-se, -ses, -se, -semos, -seis, -sen.**

The imperfect subjunctive is formed as follows:

ellos form of the preterite	-ra	´-ramos
minus **-ron** +	-ras	-rais
	-ra	-ran

This pattern applies to both regular and irregular verbs. We will review the irregular preterites in the next lesson.

ACTIVIDAD 1 ¡Ay, qué catástrofe!

Felipe estuvo fuera de su casa por unas dos horas. Durante ese tiempo sus amigos hicieron cosas que no le gustaban mucho a Felipe. Expresa esto, empezando cada frase con **Felipe no quería . . .**

⚭ Miraron sus fotos. Felipe no quería que miraran sus fotos.

1. Sacaron fotos con su cámara.
2. Llamaron a su novia por teléfono.
3. Usaron su moto.
4. Hablaron mal de los vecinos.
5. Usaron su tocadiscos.
6. Jugaron a la pelota en su cuarto.
7. Tocaron su guitarra.
8. Bebieron su Coca-Cola.
9. Comieron sus dulces.
10. Leyeron su diario.
11. Rompieron su radio.
12. Le pidieron dinero a su hermana.
13. Durmieron en su cama.
14. Cogieron las flores de su jardín.

ACTIVIDAD 2 La familia Hernández

La familia Hernández tiene diez hijos. Para cada uno, la Sra. de Hernández tenía un plan especial. Describe esos planes según el modelo.

⚭ Paco: estudiar francés La Sra. de Hernández esperaba que Paco estudiara francés.

1. Ana María: estudiar medicina
2. Felipe: aprender inglés
3. Raúl: estudiar música
4. Isabel: asistir a la universidad
5. Raquel: asistir al Conservatorio de Música
6. Andrea: casarse con un médico
7. Pedro: casarse con la hija de una amiga
8. Clara: ganar mucho dinero
9. Roberto: trabajar en los Estados Unidos

ACTIVIDAD 3 ¡Qué vida!

WB
A1, A2,
A3

SCRIPT
Act. 4

MASTERS
p. 44

A cada uno de los alumnos, el profesor le decía que estudiara más y que se divirtiera menos. Expresa esto según el modelo.

⚭ a Carmen
   A Carmen, el profesor le decía que estudiara más y que se divirtiera menos.

1. a Roberto
2. a mí
3. a ti
4. a Isabel y Consuelo
5. a Paco y Manuel
6. a nosotros
7. a Uds.
8. a Bárbara

50

B. El imperfecto del subjuntivo: usos

The imperfect subjunctive is used after the same verbs and expressions as the present subjunctive, when these expressions and verbs are in the past. In the sentences below, Carmen and her father compare their lives as students. Carmen speaks about the present. Her father speaks about the past.

For simplicity, the present perfect and the pluperfect of the subjunctive are omitted here. You may remind students that the present perfect subjunctive is used after expressions in the present when this expression concerns a past event. Compare:
Es importante **que estudies**.
*It is important **that you study**.*
Es importante **que hayas estudiado**.
*It is important **that you studied**.*
Era importante **que estudiaras**.
*It was important **that you studied**.*

Act. 3

Compare the forms of the subjunctive in each pair of sentences.

Carmen	el papá de Carmen
Ahora . . .	Hace unos veinte años . . .
El profesor sugiere que **trabaje** más.	El profesor sugería que **trabajara** más.
Es importante que **estudiemos**.	Era importante que **estudiáramos**.
Espero que mis amigos me **inviten** a sus fiestas.	Esperaba que mis amigos me **invitaran** a sus fiestas.

When an expression that requires the subjunctive (that is, an expression of indirect command, doubt, emotion . . .) is in a past tense, the subjunctive is usually in the imperfect.

EXPRESSIONS REQUIRING THE SUBJUNCTIVE	SUBJUNCTIVE TENSE
present tense	present subjunctive
past tense	imperfect subjunctive

ACTIVIDAD 4   Expresión personal: en tu casa

¿Eran las siguientes cosas importantes cuando eras niño(a)? Para contestar estas preguntas, comienza tus frases con una de las siguientes expresiones afirmativas o negativas:

(no) era importante / esencial / necesario / bueno / malo

∑⊃ comer mucho   (No) Era importante que yo comiera mucho.

1. estudiar mucho
2. respetar a los mayores
3. pelearme con mis hermanos
4. hablar bien de todos
5. limpiar mi cuarto
6. lavar los platos (*dishes*)
7. ayudar en casa
8. aprender a tocar el piano
9. compartir mis juguetes con mis amigos
10. volver temprano a casa
11. salir sin permiso
12. escribirles a mis abuelos
13. vivir en paz con mis hermanos
14. cortarme el pelo
15. bañarme todos los días

ACTIVIDAD 5 ¡Pobre Antonio!

Antonio sólo hizo las siguientes cosas después de que alguien le pidió que las hiciera. Expresa esto en un diálogo según el modelo.

∑⊃ estudiar mucho / el profesor   Estudiante 1: ¿Por qué estudió mucho Antonio?
Estudiante 2: El profesor le pidió que estudiara mucho.

1. estudiar más / su papá
2. comer más / su mamá
3. comer menos / su hermana
4. cerrar la ventana / Anita
5. pagar las entradas / su novia
6. comprar helados para todos / sus amigos

ACTIVIDAD 6 ¿Alegre o triste?

Explica las reacciones de Carmen en las siguientes situaciones. Empieza cada frase con: **Se alegró de que ...** o **Sintió que ...**

 Su mejor amiga le escribió una carta.

Carmen se alegró de que su mejor amiga le escribiera una carta.

1. Su papá le mandó dinero.
2. Héctor la invitó al cine.
3. Silvia y Elena la invitaron a un restaurante.
4. Carlos no la invitó a la fiesta.
5. Felipe no habló bien de ella.
6. Raúl le vendió su bicicleta.
7. Sus padres le compraron un radio.
8. Su novio le compró un anillo.

ACTIVIDAD 7 ¡Nada cambia!

Carmen es una estudiante de la universidad de Madrid. Un día visita a su tía que vive cerca de la universidad. Le habla de su vida. Su tía le dice que la vida era igual cuando ella era estudiante. Haz el papel de la tía.

WB
B1, B2

SCRIPT

Act. 6

MASTERS
p. 44

Carmen: Mi papá quiere que estudie para ser profesora.

su tía: Mi papá también quería que estudiara para ser profesora.

1. Mi mamá espera que estudie para ser médica.
2. Mis profesores insisten en que estudiemos siempre.
3. Mi novio quiere que coma más.
4. Mi novio se alegra de que salga con él.
5. Mis amigos se alegran de que los invite a un restaurante.

Para la comunicación

WB
Tú y
los otros

TRB

QUIZ
pp. 125–
126

OPTIONAL
May be assigned
as homework.

Cuando eras más joven ...

Describe como era tu vida cuando eras más joven. Puedes completar las siguientes frases con una idea personal.

Importaba que yo ...

Importaba que mis amigos / mis hermanos / mis primos ...

Me alegraba de que mis amigos / mis padres / mis abuelos ...

Sentía que mis amigos / mis padres / mis profesores ...

Mis padres esperaban que yo / mis hermanos ...

Los maestros insistían en que yo / mis compañeros ...

 Importaba que yo limpiara mi cuarto y lavara los platos cada día.

Lección 4   Todo cambia

Act. 1

Cada día nos levantamos a una hora más o menos fija. Nos lavamos, nos desayunamos y vamos a la escuela. Tenemos nuestras costumbres . . .
Tenemos discos favoritos, revistas favoritas y tiendas favoritas . . .
Y cuando salimos, salimos con los mismos amigos . . .

¿Es decir que somos esclavos de la rutina? No, porque nuestras costumbres cambian. A veces pueden cambiar rápidamente, especialmente cuando ocurre un suceso importante o excepcional en nuestra existencia.

¿Cambiarías completamente tu estilo de vida en las siguientes circunstancias?

fija: *fixed*
costumbres: *habits*

¿Es decir que: *Is that
   to say?*
 esclavos: *slaves*
suceso: *event*

A sí	B no	
☐	☐	1. Si me mudara a otra ciudad
☐	☐	2. Si fuera a España por un año
☐	☐	3. Si asistiera a la universidad
☐	☐	4. Si ganara un millón de dólares
☐	☐	5. Si me casara con alguien muy rico
☐	☐	6. Si me quedara solamente un año de vida
☐	☐	7. Si fuera un atleta famoso
☐	☐	8. Si me dieran un papel importante en una película
☐	☐	9. Si tuviera un coche deportivo
☐	☐	10. Si pudiera participar en una expedición espacial

me mudara: *I moved*

papel: *role*

espacial: *in space*

You may use this text as the basis for a class poll. You may also have some students describe how their lives would change in one or two of the circumstances mentioned.

Unidad diez

INTERPRETACIÓN

Cuenta tus respuestas «A».

Si tienes menos de cuatro respuestas:
> Tus amigos siempre pueden contar contigo porque tú eres una persona muy estable.

Si tienes de cuatro a ocho respuestas:
> Te adaptas fácilmente a los cambios de situación . . . pero sabes también mantener tus principios y conservar tus amistades.

Si tienes más de ocho respuestas:
> Cambias de opinión muy rápidamente y también de sentimientos. ¡Tienes que ser un poco más estable si quieres conservar tus amistades!

estable: *stable, solid*

mantener: *to keep*
amistades:
  friendships

Act. 2

NOTA CULTURAL OPTIONAL

Cambio y estabilidad

¿Has vivido siempre en la ciudad donde vives ahora? ¿Has asistido siempre al mismo colegio? ¿Y tus amigos? ¿Han vivido en esta ciudad toda su vida? Probablemente conoces a mucha gente que son de otros lugares. Esto pasa porque los norteamericanos se mudan con frecuencia. Se mudan de una ciudad a otra, de un estado a otro; y por lo tanto° de un colegio a otro y de una compañía a otra.

Esto no ocurre tanto en la sociedad hispánica. A menudo la gente vive en el mismo pueblo o ciudad donde su familia ha vivido por generaciones. Es allí donde nace, va a la escuela, trabaja, se casa y establece una familia.

No hay muchos cambios. No hay tantos cambios como en la sociedad norteamericana. Esta estabilidad permite que se conserven mejor las tradiciones.

¿Qué prefieres? ¿El cambio o la estabilidad?

por lo tanto *even*

—— Vocabulario ——

sustantivos	**un esclavo**	slave
	una costumbre	habit
	un papel	role
verbos	**conservar**	to keep, to preserve
	mudarse	to move
expresión	**es decir (que)**	that is to say (that), this means (that)

¿Conoces a mucha gente de otros lugares? Generalmente, ¿se mudan con frecuencia los norteamericanos? Y los hispanos, ¿se mudan con frecuencia también? En los países hispanos, ¿hay tantos cambios como en la sociedad norteamericana? ¿Qué con-secuencias tiene esta estabilidad para la sociedad?

Estructuras

A. El imperfecto del subjuntivo: formas irregulares

We have seen that the stem of the imperfect subjunctive is always derived from the **ellos** form of the preterite. Note the **yo** forms of the imperfect subjunctive of the following irregular verbs.

Act. 3

INFINITIVE	PRETERITE (ellos form)	IMPERFECT SUBJUNCTIVE (yo form)
ser	fueron	**fuera**
ir	fueron	**fuera**
tener	tuvieron	**tuviera**
estar	estuvieron	**estuviera**
hacer	hicieron	**hiciera**
venir	vinieron	**viniera**
dar	dieron	**diera**
decir	dijeron	**dijera**

You may want to make a general review of all the irregular preterites that the students have learned. In addition to those listed they have had:

andar	anduvieron	producir	produjero
poder	pudieron	traducir	tradujero
poner	pusieron	querer	quisieron
saber	supieron	caer	cayeron
conducir	condujeron	traer	trajeron

The endings of the imperfect subjunctive of the above verbs are the same as those of the regular verbs:

-ra   -ras   -ra   ´ramos   -rais   -ran

ACTIVIDAD 1   Lo que importa

Lo que importa es diferente para cada persona.
¿Qué les importaba más a las siguientes personas?
Haz dos frases usando el verbo **ser** en la primera y el verbo **tener** en la
segunda.

Teresa (buena alumna / buenas notas)   Importaba que Teresa fuera buena alumna.
                                          Importaba que tuviera buenas notas.

1. Rafael (cortés / buenos modales)
2. mis primos (buenos compañeros / amigos simpáticos)
3. tú (elegante / ropa bonita)
4. nosotros (los mejores alumnos / notas excelentes)
5. yo (el [la] mejor atleta de la escuela / muchos trofeos)
6. Sara y Manuela (populares / muchos admiradores)

ACTIVIDAD 2   La fiesta de Ana María

Los amigos y parientes de Ana María hicieron las siguientes cosas.
Di cuáles fueron las reacciones de Ana María (entre paréntesis) según el modelo.

Rafael y Carlos no vinieron a la fiesta. (Era lástima)
        Era lástima que Rafael y Carlos no vinieran a la fiesta.

1. Silvia y Elena le regalaron unos discos. (Era fabuloso)
2. Roberto y Alfredo fueron muy amables con sus padres. (Era importante)
3. Julia y Teresa estuvieron muy coquetas *(flirtatious)* con su novio. (No era bueno)
4. Emilio y Manuel le contaron chistes. (Era interesante)
5. Luisa y Carmen le hicieron un pastel delicioso. (Era impresionante)
6. Sus primas vinieron tarde. (Era lástima)
7. Sus padres le regalaron una bicicleta. (Era impresionante)
8. Sus primas no tuvieron regalos para ella. (Era lástima)

ACTIVIDAD 3   El profesor dijo . . .

El profesor les dijo a sus alumnos que hicieran ciertas cosas. Expresa esto
en un diálogo según el modelo.

a Pedro: tener cuidado   Estudiante 1: ¿Qué le dijo el profesor a Pedro?
                          Estudiante 2: Le dijo que tuviera cuidado.

WB
A1, A2

SCRIPT
Act. 4

MASTERS
p. 45

1. a Rafaela: tener mejores notas
2. a Silvia: ir al laboratorio
3. a Mari-Carmen: ir a la biblioteca
4. a Roberto: irse a casa
5. a Alberto: decir la verdad

6. a José: no decir mentiras
7. a Susana: hacer la tarea
8. a Antonio: no hacerse el payaso
9. a Elena: estar más atenta
10. a Julio: venir en seguida

B. Repaso: el condicional

The conditional is equivalent to the English *would* + verb.

Me gustaría tener un coche deportivo.　　*I would like to have a sports car.*
¿Conducirías rápidamente?　　　　　　　　*Would you drive fast?*
Sí, pero **conduciría** prudentemente.　　　　*Yes, but I would drive carefully.*

Review the forms of the conditional in the chart below.

yo	hablaría	nosotros	hablaríamos
tú	hablarías	vosotros	hablaríais
él, ella, Ud.	hablaría	ellos, ellas, Uds.	hablarían

⚏ The stem of the conditional is the same as the future stem: for most verbs this stem is the infinitive.

⚏ The endings are: **-ía, -ías, -ía, -íamos, -íais, -ían**

ACTIVIDAD 4　Con cien dólares

Imagina que alguien va a darles 100 dólares a las siguientes personas. Di lo que cada uno se compraría.

⚏　Alfredo: un tocadiscos　　　Alfredo se compraría un tocadiscos.

1. nosotros: una bicicleta
2. tú: una grabadora
3. Felipe: un traje nuevo
4. Elena: un par de esquís (*a pair of skis*)
5. Roberto y Andrés: una tienda de campaña
6. yo: una calculadora

ACTIVIDAD 5　Con un millón de dólares

Estas personas sueñan con recibir un millón de dólares. Di que con este dinero no harían lo que hacen ahora.

⚏　Felipe: trabajar de mecánico
　　　　Felipe trabaja de mecánico.
　　　　Con un millón de dólares, no trabajaría de mecánico.

1. Susana: trabajar de secretaria
2. Alberto: aprender a escribir a máquina
3. nosotros: comer hamburguesas todos los días
4. tú: vivir en un apartamento muy pequeño
5. el Sr. Morales: conducir un coche muy viejo
6. yo: ir a la escuela

WB
B1, B2

C. El uso del imperfecto del subjuntivo: después de *si*

In each group of sentences, people are talking about what they would do under certain conditions. Both conditions are introduced by **si** (*if*). Note that in the first sentence in each group the condition expresses something that is possible. In the second sentence, the condition expresses something that is contrary to reality. Compare the use of the verb forms in Spanish and English.

Si tengo cuatro dólares este fin de semana, **iré** al cine.	*If I have* four dollars this weekend, *I will go* to the movies.
Si tuviera un millón de dólares, **iría** a Tahiti.	*If I had* a million dollars, *I would go* to Tahiti.
Si estoy aquí mañana, te **llamaré.**	*If I am* here tomorrow, *I will call* you.
Si estuviera en San Juan, **llamaría** a tus primos.	*If I were* in San Juan, *I would call* your cousins.

The following verb forms are used with **si**:

	condition (**si**)	result
when the condition expresses something possible	present indicative	future
when the condition expresses something contrary to reality	imperfect subjunctive	conditional

ACTIVIDAD 6 ¡Es obvio!

Las siguientes personas dicen qué idioma hablarían si vivieran en el extranjero. Expresa esto según el modelo.

⟩⟩ Paco: París / francés   Si Paco viviera en París, hablaría francés.

1. Amalia: Nueva York / inglés
2. Carlos: Moscú / ruso
3. Uds.: Hong Kong / chino
4. yo: Río / portugués
5. nosotros: Amsterdam / holandés
6. tú: Berlín / alemán
7. Raúl y Juan: México / español

FONART
GENUINO ARTE
POPULAR MEXICANO

May be assigned
as a special challenge
activity.

ACTIVIDAD 7   Un poco de lógica   OPTIONAL

Di lo que harían las siguientes personas si tuvieran ciertos empleos.
¿Cuántas frases lógicas puedes crear, usando los elementos de las columnas
A, B y C?

A	B	C
yo	médico(a)	trabajar mucho
tú	enfermero(a)	ganar mucho dinero
mi hermana	abogado(a)	viajar mucho
Carlos y Rafael	policía	conocer a muchas personas
Elena y Amalia	periodista	trabajar en una oficina
nosotros	fotógrafo(a)	ayudar a otras personas
	instructor(a) de esquí	trabajar al aire libre (*outdoors*)
	actor (actriz)	
	cantante	

Si tú fueras instructor de esquí, trabajarías al aire libre.

ACTIVIDAD 8   Sueños

Los siguientes estudiantes hablan de lo que harían si no fueran estudiantes.
Expresa esto.

Raúl quiere viajar.   Si no fuera estudiante, Raúl viajaría.

1. Dolores quiere ser actriz.
2. Mis primos quieren vivir en España.
3. Nosotros queremos aprender judo.
4. Tú quieres correr las olas.
5. Yo quiero ser pintor (*painter*).
6. Elena quiere esquiar todo el año.

ACTIVIDAD 9   Expresión personal

Di lo que harías si no hicieras las siguientes cosas.

estudiar español
        Si no estudiara español, estudiaría italiano (francés, música, etc.).

WB
C1, C2

SCRIPT

Act. 6, 7

MASTERS
p. 45

1. vivir en los Estados Unidos
2. ser alumno(a)
3. estar en esta clase
4. asistir a esta escuela
5. vivir en esta ciudad
6. comer en la cafetería

Para la comunicación

Soñar no cuesta nada

Escoge una de las siguientes situaciones y sueña un poco en un párrafo de seis líneas.

ser millonario(a)
ser campeón (campeona) de tenis
pasar un año en México
tener un avión
tener un yate (*yacht*)
conocer al presidente
ser presidente
ser un(a) cantante famoso(a)

WB
En la
vida

TRB

QUIZ
pp. 127–
128

⤳ Si fuera millonario(a), compraría un yate enorme, iría a Europa, viajaría por todo el mundo y no trabajaría.

⤳ Si tuviera un yate, iría a Hawai, visitaría todas las islas del Pacífico y me divertiría muchísimo.

WB   Test / Repaso   TEST pp. 129–132   ACHIEVEMENT TEST pp. 133–143

Variedades   Dos temas

Hay cosas que conocemos y que no podemos explicar. Estos dos poetas nos hablan de dos temas:° la vida y la juventud.°

temas: *themes*
juventud: *youth*

la vida

¿Qué es la vida? un frenesí;°
¿Qué es la vida? una ilusión,
una sombra,° una ficción,
y el mayor° bien es pequeño;
que toda la vida es sueño,°
y los sueños, sueños son.

frenesí: *frenzy, madness*

sombra: *shadow*
mayor: *greatest*
sueño: *a dream*

De *La vida es sueño* por Calderón de la Barca (1600-1681), de España, autor de muchos dramas simbólicos y religiosos.

la juventud

Juventud, divino tesoro,
¡ya te vas para no volver!
Cuando quiero llorar, no lloro,
¡y a veces lloro sin querer!

De «Canción de otoño en primavera»,* por
Rubén Darío (1867-1916), poeta de Nicaragua.

*In Rubén Darío, *Cantos de vida y esperanza,* Colección Austral No. 118, 12th edition, 1971, Madrid (Espasa-Calpe), p. 90.

APPENDIX 1 LOS NÚMEROS

A. Cardinal numbers

0	cero	16	diez y seis (dieciséis)	90	noventa
1	uno	17	diez y siete (diecisiete)	100	cien (ciento)
2	dos	18	diez y ocho (dieciocho)	101	ciento uno
3	tres	19	diez y nueve (diecinueve)	102	ciento dos
4	cuatro	20	veinte	200	doscientos
5	cinco	21	veinte y uno (veintiuno)	201	doscientos uno
6	seis	22	veinte y dos (veintidós)	300	trescientos
7	siete	23	veinte y tres (veintitrés)	400	cuatrocientos
8	ocho	30	treinta	500	quinientos
9	nueve	31	treinta y uno	600	seiscientos
10	diez	40	cuarenta	700	setecientos
11	once	41	cuarenta y uno	800	ochocientos
12	doce	50	cincuenta	900	novecientos
13	trece	60	sesenta	1.000	mil
14	catorce	70	setenta	2.000	dos mil
15	quince	80	ochenta	1.000.000	un millón (de)

NOTAS:
1. **Uno** becomes **un** before a masculine noun: **treinta y un** chicos
   una before a feminine noun: **treinta y una** chicas
2. **Ciento** is used before numbers under 100: **ciento** veinte
3. The hundreds from two to nine hundred agree
   with the nouns they introduce: **doscientas** pesetas

B. Ordinal numbers

1°	primero(a)	6°	sexto(a)
2°	segundo(a)	7°	séptimo(a)
3°	tercero(a)	8°	octavo(a)
4°	cuarto(a)	9°	noveno(a)
5°	quinto(a)	10°	décimo(a)

NOTAS:
1. **Primero** becomes **primer** before a masculine singular noun: **el primer** libro
2. **Tercero** becomes **tercer** before a masculine singular noun: **el tercer** papel

APPENDIX 2 VOCABULARIO PRÁCTICO

This Appendix reviews selected vocabulary by topics from Book One of *Spanish for Mastery*.

La hora (Time)

¿Qué hora es?	*What time is it?*
Es la una.	*It is 1:00.*
Son las dos.	*It is 2:00.*
Son las dos y cinco.	*It is 2:05.*
Son las dos y diez.	*It is 2:10.*

Son las dos y cuarto.	*It is 2:15.*
Son las dos y veinte.	*It is 2:20.*
Son las dos y veinte y cinco.	*It is 2:25.*
Son las dos y media.	*It is 2:30.*
Son las tres menos veinte y cinco.	*It is 2:35. (It is 25 of 3.)*
Son las tres menos veinte.	*It is 2:40. (It is 20 of 3.)*
Son las tres menos cuarto.	*It is 2:45. (It is quarter of 3.)*
Son las tres menos diez.	*It is 2:50. (It is 10 of 3.)*
Son las tres menos cinco.	*It is 2:55. (It is 5 of 3.)*
Son las tres.	*It is 3:00.*

NOTAS:
y cuarto	*quarter past*
y media	*half past*
menos cuarto	*quarter of*

To express the English concept of *past* or *after*, Spanish uses the word **y**.
To express the English concept of *of* or *to*, Spanish uses the word **menos**.

¿A qué hora?	*At what time?*
A la una y cinco **de la mañana**.	*At 1:05 in the morning (A.M.)*
A las tres y cuarto **de la tarde**.	*At 3:15 in the afternoon (P.M.)*
A las ocho y media **de la noche**.	*At 8:30 at night (P.M.)*

Los días de la semana *(The days of the week)*

(el) lunes	*Monday*	hoy	*today*
(el) martes	*Tuesday*	mañana	*tomorrow*
(el) miércoles	*Wednesday*	ayer	*yesterday*
(el) jueves	*Thursday*	el jueves pasado	*last Thursday*
(el) viernes	*Friday*	el sábado próximo	*next Saturday*
(el) sábado	*Saturday*		
(el) domingo	*Sunday*		

NOTA: In Spanish, the definite article is used before days of the week except after *ser*:

el lunes (martes, etc.)	*(on) Monday (Tuesday, etc.)*
los lunes (martes, etc.)	*(on) Mondays (Tuesdays, etc.)*

but:	¿Qué día es hoy (mañana)?	*What day is it today (tomorrow)?*
	Hoy (Mañana) es lunes (martes).	*Today (Tomorrow) is Monday (Tuesday).*

Los meses del año *(The months of the year)*

enero	*January*	julio	*July*
febrero	*February*	agosto	*August*
marzo	*March*	septiembre	*September*
abril	*April*	octubre	*October*
mayo	*May*	noviembre	*November*
junio	*June*	diciembre	*December*

Las estaciones *(The seasons)*

la primavera	*spring*	el otoño	*fall*
el verano	*summer*	el invierno	*winter*

La fecha *(The date)*

To express the date, Spanish uses the construction **el** + number + **de** + month.
However, the first day of the month is always expressed as **el primero**.

¿Cuál es la fecha de hoy (mañana)?	*What is today's (tomorrow's) date?*
Hoy (Mañana) es el trece de enero.	*Today (Tomorrow) is January 13th.*
Es el primero de mayo.	*It is May first.*

El tiempo *(The weather)*

¿Qué tiempo hace (hoy, en mayo, en el otoño)?	*How's the weather (today, in May, in the fall)?*
Hace buen tiempo.	*It's nice.*
Hace mal tiempo.	*It's bad.*
Hace (mucho) calor.	*It's (very) hot.*
Hace frío.	*It's cold.*
Hace viento.	*It's windy.*
Hace sol.	*It's sunny.*
Está nublado.	*It's cloudy.*
Llueve.	*It's raining.*
Nieva.	*It's snowing.*
¿Cuál es la temperatura?	*What's the temperature?*
—doce grados	*—twelve degrees*
—tres grados bajo cero	*—three degrees below zero*

Los países y los adjetivos de nacionalidad

las Américas

la América del Norte

el Canadá	canadiense
los Estados Unidos	norteamericano

la América Central

México	mexicano
Panamá	panameño

la América del Sur

la Argentina	argentino
el Brasil	brasileño
Chile	chileno

Asia

China	chino
el Japón	japonés (japonesa)
Rusia	ruso

el Caribe

Cuba	cubano
Puerto Rico	puertorriqueño

Europa

Alemania	alemán (alemana)
España	español
Francia	francés (francesa)
Inglaterra	inglés (inglesa)
Italia	italiano
Portugal	portugués (portuguesa)

El cuerpo *(The body)*

la boca	*mouth*	la cara	*face*	el pelo	*hair*
el brazo	*arm*	la frente	*forehead*	el pie	*foot*
la cabeza	*head*	la mano	*hand*	la pierna	*leg*
los dedos	*fingers*	la nariz	*nose*	la rodilla	*knee*
los dientes	*teeth*	el ojo	*eye*		
la espalda	*back*	la oreja	*ear*		

La ropa *(Clothing)*

un abrigo	*(over)coat*	un impermeable	*raincoat*
unos anteojos	*eyeglasses*	unos pantalones	*pants*
unos anteojos de sol	*sunglasses*	unos pantalones cortos	*shorts*
una blusa	*blouse*	unas sandalias	*sandals*
unos calcetines	*socks*	un suéter	*sweater*
una camisa	*shirt*	un sombrero	*hat*
una camiseta	*tee shirt*	un traje	*suit*
una corbata	*necktie*	un traje de baño	*bathing suit*
una chaqueta	*jacket*	un vestido	*dress*
una falda	*skirt*	unos zapatos	*shoes*

Ocupaciones

un abogado, una abogada	*lawyer*
un aeromozo, una aeromoza	*flight attendant*
un agente de viajes, una agente de viajes	*travel agent*
un carpintero	*carpenter*
un científico, una científica	*scientist*
un dentista, una dentista	*dentist*
un dibujante, una dibujante	*designer*
un electricista, una electricista	*electrician*
un empleado, una empleada	*employee*
un enfermero, una enfermera	*nurse*
un fotógrafo, una fotógrafa	*photographer*
un gerente, una gerente	*manager*
un guía, una guía	*guide*
un ingeniero, una ingeniera	*engineer*
un locutor, una locutora	*announcer*
un mecánico	*mechanic*
un médico, una médica	*doctor*
un modista, una modista	*dressmaker*
un periodista, una periodista	*journalist*
un pescador, una pescadora	*fisherman*
un policía	*police officer*
un programador, una programadora	*programmer*
un secretario, una secretaria	*secretary*
un trabajador social, una trabajadora social	*social worker*
un vendedor (viajero), una vendedora (viajera)	*(traveling) salesperson*
un veterinario, una veterinaria	*veterinarian*

Los colores

¿De qué color . . . ?	*What color . . . ?*	gris	*gray*
		negro	*black*
amarillo	*yellow*	rojo	*red*
blanco	*white*	verde	*green*
castaño	*brown*		

NOTA: Colors are adjectives and agree with the nouns they describe. Tengo **un abrigo negro** y **una blusa roja. Las corbatas** son **azules** y **los pantalones** son **verdes**.

La comida *(Food)*

Los alimentos *(Foods)*

la carne	*meat*	un pastel	*pastry*
el bistec	*steak*	una torta, una tarta,	
el jamón	*ham*	un bizcocho	*cake*
el pollo	*chicken*	otros alimentos	*other foods*
		el aceite	*oil*
las frutas y los vegetales	*fruits and vegetables*	el azúcar	*sugar*
el arroz	*rice*	una ensalada	*salad*
una banana	*banana*	una hamburguesa	*hamburger*
los frijoles	*beans*	un huevo	*egg*
el maíz	*corn*	la mantequilla	*butter*
una manzana	*apple*	el pan	*bread*
una naranja	*orange*	la pimienta	*pepper*
una papa	*potato*	el queso	*cheese*
una pera	*pear*	la sal	*salt*
un plátano	*banana, plantain*	un sándwich	*sandwich*
un tomate	*tomato*	el vinagre	*vinegar*
los postres	*desserts*		
un helado	*ice cream*		

Las bebidas *(Drinks)*

el agua	*water*	un jugo de frutas	*fruit juice*
el café	*coffee*	la leche	*milk*
la cerveza	*beer*	el té	*tea*
una gaseosa	*soda, carbonated drink*	el vino	*wine*

Las comidas *(Meals)*

el desayuno	*breakfast*	la merienda	*late afternoon snack*
desayunarse	*to have breakfast*	merendar (e → ie)	*to have a late afternoon snack*
el almuerzo	*lunch*		
almorzar (o → ue)	*to have lunch*	la cena	*dinner*
		cenar	*to have dinner*

Los muebles *(Furniture)*

una cama	*bed*	un radio	*radio*
un estante	*bookcase*	una silla	*chair*
una lámpara	*lamp*	un televisor	*television set*
una mesa	*table*	un tocadiscos	*record player*

APPENDIX 3 VERBOS

A. REGULAR VERBS

Simple Tenses

INFINITIVE:	**hablar** *(to speak)*		**comer** *(to eat)*		**vivir** *(to live)*	
	INDICATIVE					
PRESENT	hablo	hablamos	como	comemos	vivo	vivimos
	hablas	habláis	comes	coméis	vives	vivís
	habla	hablan	come	comen	vive	viven
IMPERFECT	hablaba	hablábamos	comía	comíamos	vivía	vivíamos
	hablabas	hablabais	comías	comíais	vivías	vivíais
	hablaba	hablaban	comía	comían	vivía	vivían
PRETERITE	hablé	hablamos	comí	comimos	viví	vivimos
	hablaste	hablasteis	comiste	comisteis	viviste	vivisteis
	habló	hablaron	comió	comieron	vivió	vivieron
FUTURE	hablaré	hablaremos	comeré	comeremos	viviré	viviremos
	hablarás	hablaréis	comerás	comeréis	vivirás	viviréis
	hablará	hablarán	comerá	comerán	vivirá	vivirán
CONDITIONAL	hablaría	hablaríamos	comería	comeríamos	viviría	viviríamos
	hablarías	hablarías	comerías	comeríais	vivirías	viviríais
	hablaría	hablarían	comería	comerían	viviría	vivirían

	COMMANDS			
tú	habla		come	vive
negative tú	no hables		no comas	no vivas
Ud.	hable		coma	viva
Uds.	hablen		coman	vivan

	SUBJUNCTIVE					
PRESENT	hable	hablemos	coma	comamos	viva	vivamos
	hables	habléis	comas	comáis	vivas	viváis
	hable	hablen	coma	coman	viva	vivan
IMPERFECT	hablara	habláramos	comiera	comiéramos	viviera	viviéramos
	hablaras	hablarais	comieras	comierais	vivieras	vivierais
	hablara	hablaran	comiera	comieran	viviera	vivieran

	PARTICIPLE		
PRESENT	hablando	comiendo	viviendo
PAST	hablado	comido	vivido

Compound Tenses

			INDICATIVE		

PRESENT PERFECT

he	hemos				
has	habéis	}	hablado	comido	vivido
ha	han				

PLUPERFECT

había	habíamos				
habías	habíais	}	hablado	comido	vivido
había	habían				

FUTURE PERFECT

habré	habremos				
habrás	habréis	}	hablado	comido	vivido
habrá	habrán				

			SUBJUNCTIVE		

PRESENT PERFECT

haya	hayamos				
hayas	hayáis		hablado	comido	vivido
haya	hayan				

IRREGULAR PAST PARTICIPLES OF REGULAR VERBS

abrir	**abierto**	descubrir	**descubierto**
cubrir	**cubierto**	escribir	**escrito**
describir	**descrito**	romper	**roto**

B. STEM-CHANGING VERBS

INFINITIVE IN -ar:	cerrar (e → ie) *(to close)*		probar (o → ue) *(to try)*		jugar (u → ue) *(to play)*	
			INDICATIVE			
PRESENT	**cierro**	cerramos	**pruebo**	probamos	**juego**	jugamos
	cierras	cerráis	**pruebas**	probáis	**juegas**	jugáis
	cierra	**cierran**	**prueba**	**prueban**	**juega**	**juegan**
			SUBJUNCTIVE			
PRESENT	**cierre**	cerremos	**pruebe**	probemos	**juegue**	juguemos
	cierres	cerréis	**pruebes**	probéis	**juegues**	juguéis
	cierre	**cierren**	**pruebe**	**prueben**	**juegue**	**jueguen**

like **cerrar**: comenzar, despertarse, empezar, encerrar, gobernar, negar(se), pensar, recomendar, regar, sentarse, tropezar

like **probar**: acostarse, almorzar, aprobar, contar, costar, demostrar, encontrar(se), mostrar, recordar, revolver, sonar, soñar, tostar, volar

INFINITIVE IN -er:	perder (e → ie) *(to lose)*		volver (o → ue) *(to return)*	
INDICATIVE				
PRESENT	**pierdo**	perdemos	**vuelvo**	volvemos
	pierdes	perdéis	**vuelves**	volvéis
	pierde	**pierden**	**vuelve**	**vuelven**
SUBJUNCTIVE				
PRESENT	**pierda**	perdamos	**vuelva**	volvamos
	pierdas	perdáis	**vuelvas**	volváis
	pierda	**pierdan**	**vuelva**	**vuelvan**

like **perder:** defender, descender, encender, entender, extenderse
like **volver:** devolver, doler, llover *(used only in third-person singular)*, revolver

INFINITIVE IN -ir:	pedir (e → i, i) *(to ask)*		dormir (o → ue, u) *(to sleep)*		sentir (e → ie, i) *(to feel)*	
INDICATIVE						
PRESENT	**pido**	pedimos	**duermo**	dormimos	**siento**	sentimos
	pides	pedís	**duermes**	dormís	**sientes**	sentís
	pide	**piden**	**duerme**	**duermen**	**siente**	**sienten**
PRETERITE	pedí	pedimos	dormí	dormimos	sentí	sentimos
	pediste	pedisteis	dormiste	dormisteis	sentiste	sentisteis
	pidió	**pidieron**	**durmió**	**durmieron**	**sintió**	**sintieron**
SUBJUNCTIVE						
PRESENT	**pida**	**pidamos**	**duerma**	**durmamos**	**sienta**	**sintamos**
	pidas	**pidáis**	**duermas**	**durmáis**	**sientas**	**sintáis**
	pida	**pidan**	**duerma**	**duerman**	**sienta**	**sientan**
IMPERFECT	**pidiera**	**pidiéramos**	**durmiera**	**durmiéramos**	**sintiera**	**sintiéramos**
	pidieras	**pidierais**	**durmieras**	**durmierais**	**sintieras**	**sintierais**
	pidiera	**pidieran**	**durmiera**	**durmieran**	**sintiera**	**sintieran**
PRESENT PARTICIPLE	**pidiendo**		**durmiendo**		**sintiendo**	

like **pedir:** conseguir, despedirse, perseguir, reír, rendirse, repetir, seguir, servir, sonreír, vestirse
like **dormir:** morir (past participle: **muerto)**
like **sentir:** divertir(se), hervir, mentir, preferir, referir, requerir, sugerir

C. SPELLING-CHANGING VERBS

actuar *(to act)*

present indicative: **actúo, actúas, actúa,** actuamos, actuáis, **actúan**
present subjunctive: **actúe, actúes, actúe,** actuemos, actuéis, **actúen**

like **actuar:** continuar, graduarse

464

buscar *(to look for)*

preterite: **busqué,** buscaste, buscó, buscamos, buscasteis, buscaron
present subjunctive: **busque, busques, busque, busquemos, busquéis, busquen**
    like **buscar:** acercarse, arrancar, atacar, comunicar, criticar, chocar, dedicar(se), desembarcar,
        equivocarse, explicar, fabricar, identificar, indicar, marcar, mascar, pescar,
        pronosticar, publicar, sacar, salpicar, secarse, significar, tocar

coger *(to seize, grasp, gather)*

present indicative: **cojo,** coges, coge, cogemos, cogéis, cogen
present subjunctive: **coja, cojas, coja, cojamos, cojáis, cojan**
    like **coger:** dirigir(se), elegir, erigir, escoger, exigir, proteger, recoger, surgir

conducir *(to drive)*

present indicative: **conduzco,** conduces, conduce, conducimos, conducís, conducen
preterite: **conduje, condujiste, condujo, condujimos, condujisteis, condujeron**
present subjunctive: **conduzca, conduzcas, conduzca, conduzcamos, conduzcáis, conduzcan**
imperfect subjunctive: **condujera, condujeras, condujera, condujéramos, condujerais, condujeran**
    like **conducir:** producir, traducir

conocer *(to know, be acquainted with)*

present indicative: **conozco,** conoces, conoce, conocemos, conocéis, conocen
present subjunctive: **conozca, conozcas, conozca, conozcamos, conozcáis, conozcan**
    like **conocer:** aparecer, crecer, complacer(se), desaparecer, establecer, florecer, merecer, nacer,
        obedecer, ofrecer, parecer(se), permanecer, pertenecer, reconocer

construir *(to construct, build)*

present indicative: **construyo, construyes, construye,** construimos, construís, **construyen**
preterite: construí, construiste, **construyó,** construimos, construisteis, **construyeron**
present subjunctive: **construya, construyas, construya, construyamos, construyáis, construyan**
imperfect subjunctive: **construyera, construyeras, construyera, construyéramos, construyerais,**
               construyeran
present participle: **construyendo**
    like **construir:** constituir, destruir, huir, influir, reconstruir

creer *(to believe)*

preterite: creí, **creíste, creyó, creímos, creísteis, creyeron**
present participle: **creyendo**
imperfect subjunctive: **creyera, creyeras, creyera, creyéramos, creyerais, creyeran**
past participle: **creído**   like **creer:** leer

cruzar *(to cross)*

preterite: **crucé,** cruzaste, cruzó, cruzamos, cruzasteis, cruzaron
present subjunctive: **cruce, cruces, cruce, crucemos, crucéis, crucen**
    like **cruzar:** abrazar, adelgazar, almorzar (o → ue), analizar, aterrizar, cazar, colonizar,
        comenzar (e → ie), cristianizar, empezar (e → ie), especializarse, gozar, lanzarse,
        organizar, popularizar; realizar(se), reemplazar, rezar, tropezar (e → ie)

distinguir *(to distinguish)*

present indicative: **distingo,** distingues, distingue, distinguimos, distinguís, distinguen
present subjunctive: **distinga, distingas, distinga, distingamos, distingáis, distingan**
    like **distinguir:** conseguir (e → i, i), perseguir (e → i, i), seguir (e → i, i)

esquiar *(to ski)*

present indicative: **esquío, esquías, esquía,** esquiamos, esquiáis, **esquían**
present subjunctive: **esquíe, esquíes, esquíe,** esquiemos, esquiéis, **esquíen**
     like **esquiar:** enfriar

llegar *(to arrive)*

preterite: **llegué,** llegaste, llegó, llegamos, llegasteis, llegaron
present subjunctive: **llegue, llegues, llegue, lleguemos, lleguéis, lleguen**
     like **llegar:** ahogarse, apagar, castigar, colgar (o → ue), entregar, jugar (u → ue), navegar,
          negar(se) (e → ie), pagar, pegar, regar (e → ie), rogar (o → ue)

vencer *(to conquer)*

present indicative: **venzo,** vences, vence, vencemos, vencéis, vencen
present subjunctive: **venza, venzas, venza, venzamos, venzáis, venzan**   like **vencer:** convencer

D. IRREGULAR VERBS

andar *(to walk, go)*

preterite: **anduve, anduviste, anduvo, anduvimos, anduvisteis, anduvieron**
imperfect subjunctive: **anduviera, anduvieras, anduviera, anduviéramos, anduvierais, anduvieran**

caer *(to fall)*

present indicative: **caigo,** caes, cae, caemos, caéis, caen
preterite: caí, **caíste, cayó, caímos, caísteis, cayeron**
present subjunctive: **caiga, caigas, caiga, caigamos, caigáis, caigan**
imperfect subjunctive: **cayera, cayeras, cayera, cayéramos, cayerais, cayeran**
present participle: **cayendo**
past participle: **caído**

dar *(to give)*

present indicative: **doy,** das, da, damos, dais, dan
preterite: **di, diste, dio, dimos, disteis, dieron**
present subjunctive: **dé,** des, **dé,** demos, deis, den
imperfect subjunctive: **diera, dieras, diera, diéramos, dierais, dieran**

decir *(to say, tell)*

present indicative: **digo, dices, dice,** decimos, decís, **dicen**
preterite: **dije, dijiste, dijo, dijimos, dijisteis, dijeron**
future: **diré, dirás,** etc.   conditional: **diría, dirías,** etc.
command: **di** (tú), no **digas** (neg. tú), **diga** (Ud.), **digan** (Uds.)
present subjunctive: **diga, digas, diga, digamos, digáis, digan**
imperfect subjunctive: **dijera, dijeras, dijera, dijéramos, dijerais, dijeran**
present participle: **diciendo**
past participle: **dicho**   like **decir:** contradecir, predecir

estar *(to be)*

present indicative: **estoy, estás, está,** estamos, estáis, **están**
preterite: **estuve, estuviste, estuvo, estuvimos, estuvisteis, estuvieron**
present subjunctive: **esté, estés, esté,** estemos, estéis, **estén**
imperfect subjunctive: **estuviera, estuvieras, estuviera, estuviéramos, estuvierais, estuvieran**

haber *(to have–auxiliary)*

present indicative: **he, has, ha, hemos,** habéis, **han**
preterite: **hube, hubiste, hubo, hubimos, hubisteis, hubieron**
future: **habré, habrás,** etc.   conditional: **habría, habrías,** etc.
present subjunctive: **haya, hayas, haya, hayamos, hayáis, hayan**
imperfect subjunctive: **hubiera, hubieras, hubiera, hubiéramos, hubierais, hubieran**

hacer *(to make, do)*

present indicative: **hago,** haces, hace, hacemos, hacéis, hacen
preterite: **hice, hiciste, hizo, hicimos, hicisteis, hicieron**
future: **haré, harás,** etc.   conditional: **haría, harías,** etc.
command: **haz** (tú), no **hagas** (neg. tú), **haga** (Ud.), **hagan** (Uds.)
present subjunctive: **haga, hagas, haga, hagamos, hagáis, hagan**
imperfect subjunctive: **hiciera, hicieras, hiciera, hiciéramos, hicierais, hicieran**
past participle: **hecho**   like **hacer:** satisfacer

ir *(to go)*

present indicative: **voy, vas, va, vamos, vais, van**
imperfect indicative: **iba, ibas, iba, íbamos, ibais, iban**
preterite: **fui, fuiste, fue, fuimos, fuisteis, fueron**
command: **ve** (tú), no **vayas** (neg. tú), **vaya** (Ud.), **vayan** (Uds.)
present subjunctive: **vaya, vayas, vaya, vayamos, vayáis, vayan**
imperfect subjunctive: **fuera, fueras, fuera, fuéramos, fuerais, fueran**
present participle: **yendo**   past participle: **ido**

oír *(to hear)*

present indicative: **oigo, oyes, oye,** oímos, oís, **oyen**
preterite: oí, oíste, **oyó,** oímos, oísteis, **oyeron**
present subjunctive: **oiga, oigas, oiga, oigamos, oigáis, oigan**
imperfect subjunctive: **oyera, oyeras, oyera, oyéramos, oyerais, oyeran**   present participle: **oyendo**

poder *(to be able, can)*

present indicative: **puedo, puedes, puede,** podemos, podéis, **pueden**
preterite: **pude, pudiste, pudo, pudimos, pudisteis, pudieron**
future: **podré, podrás,** etc.   conditional: **podría, podrías,** etc.
present subjunctive: **pueda, puedas, pueda,** podamos, podáis, **puedan**
imperfect subjunctive: **pudiera, pudieras, pudiera, pudiéramos, pudierais, pudieran**
present participle: **pudiendo**

poner *(to put, place)*

present indicative: **pongo,** pones, pone, ponemos, ponéis, ponen
preterite: **puse, pusiste, puso, pusimos, pusisteis, pusieron**
future: **pondré, pondrás,** etc.   conditional: **pondría, pondrías,** etc.
command: **pon** (tú), no **pongas** (neg. tú), **ponga** (Ud.), **pongan** (Uds.)
present subjunctive: **ponga, pongas, ponga, pongamos, pongáis, pongan**
imperfect subjunctive: **pusiera, pusieras, pusiera, pusiéramos, pusierais, pusieran**
past participle: **puesto**   like **poner:** componer, oponerse, proponer, suponer

querer *(to want)*

present indicative: **quiero, quieres, quiere,** queremos, queréis, **quieren**
preterite: **quise, quisiste, quiso, quisimos, quisisteis, quisieron**
future: **querré, querrás,** etc.   conditional: **querría, querrías,** etc.
present subjunctive: **quiera, quieras, quiera,** queramos, queráis, **quieran**
imperfect subjunctive: **quisiera, quisieras, quisiera, quisiéramos, quisierais, quisieran**

467

saber *(to know)*

present indicative: **sé,** sabes, sabe, sabemos, sabéis, saben
preterite: **supe, supiste, supo, supimos, supisteis, supieron**
future: **sabré, sabrás,** etc.   conditional: **sabría, sabrías,** etc.
present subjunctive: **sepa, sepas, sepa, sepamos, sepáis, sepan**
imperfect subjunctive: **supiera, supieras, supiera, supiéramos, supierais, supieran**

salir *(to go out, leave)*

present indicative: **salgo,** sales, sale, salimos, salís, salen
future: **saldré, saldrás,** etc.   conditional: **saldría, saldrías,** etc.
command: **sal** (tú), no **salgas** (neg. tú), **salga** (Ud.), **salgan** (Uds.)
present subjunctive: **salga, salgas, salga, salgamos, salgáis, salgan**

ser *(to be)*

present indicative: **soy, eres, es, somos, sois, son**
imperfect indicative: **era, eras, era, éramos, erais, eran**
preterite: **fui, fuiste, fue, fuimos, fuisteis, fueron**
command: **sé** (tú), no **seas** (neg. tú), **sea** (Ud.), **sean** (Uds.)
present subjunctive: **sea, seas, sea, seamos, seáis, sean**
imperfect subjunctive: **fuera, fueras, fuera, fuéramos, fuerais, fueran**

tener *(to have)*

present indicative: **tengo, tienes, tiene,** tenemos, tenéis, **tienen**
preterite: **tuve, tuviste, tuvo, tuvimos, tuvisteis, tuvieron**
future: **tendré, tendrás,** etc.   conditional: **tendría, tendrías,** etc.
command: **ten** (tú), no **tengas** (neg. tú), **tenga** (Ud.), **tengan** (Uds.)
present subjunctive: **tenga, tengas, tenga, tengamos, tengáis, tengan**
imperfect subjunctive: **tuviera, tuvieras, tuviera, tuviéramos, tuvierais, tuvieran**

like **tener:** contener, detener, mantener(se), obtener, sostenerse

traer *(to bring)*

present indicative: **traigo,** traes, trae, traemos, traéis, traen
preterite: **traje, trajiste, trajo, trajimos, trajisteis, trajeron**
present subjunctive: **traiga, traigas, traiga, traigamos, traigáis, traigan**
imperfect subjunctive: **trajera, trajeras, trajera, trajéramos, trajerais, trajeran**
present participle: **trayendo**   past participle: **traído**

venir *(to come)*

present indicative: **vengo, vienes, viene,** venimos, venís, **vienen**
preterite: **vine, viniste, vino, vinimos, vinisteis, vinieron**
future: **vendré, vendrás,** etc.   conditional: **vendría, vendrías,** etc.
command: **ven** (tú), no **vengas** (neg. tú), **venga** (Ud.), **vengan** (Uds.)
present subjunctive: **venga, vengas, venga, vengamos, vengáis, vengan**
imperfect subjunctive: **viniera, vinieras, viniera, viniéramos, vinierais, vinieran**
present participle: **viniendo**   like **venir:** convenir, intervenir

ver *(to see)*

present indicative: **veo,** ves, ve, vemos, veis, ven
imperfect indicative: **veía, veías, veía, veíamos, veíais, veían**
preterite: **vi,** viste, **vio,** vimos, visteis, vieron
present subjunctive: **vea, veas, vea, veamos, veáis, vean**
past participle: **visto**

SPANISH-ENGLISH VOCABULARY

The Spanish-English Vocabulary lists the words and expressions in the student text except for specialized vocabulary glosses in the *vistas* and *Notas culturales*. Active words and expressions, that is, vocabulary items that students are expected to know, are followed by a number. The number (2.1), for example, indicates that the item is active in Unit 2, Lesson 1. An asterisk (*) in front of a verb means that the verb is irregular or that it has a spelling change. See the verb charts in Appendix 3.

a

a to, at
a la casa de __ to __'s house **(1.3)**
a la derecha on the right **(5.2)**
a la izquierda on the left **(5.2)**
a lo largo de along
a menos que unless **(10.1)**
a menudo often **(1.3)**
a tiempo on time **(5.2)**
a veces at times, sometimes **(1.3)**
a ver let's see
abajo down (with) . . .
abandonado abandoned
abandonar to abandon
abierto open: *see* **abrir (6.2)**
un **abogado, una abogada** lawyer
la **abolición** abolition
* **abrazar** to embrace
un **abrigo** overcoat
abrir to open **(1.4)**
absoluto absolute
absurdo absurd **(9.2)**
una **abuela** grandmother **(1.2)**
un **abuelo** grandfather **(1.2)**
los **abuelos** grandparents **(1.2)**
una **abundancia** abundance
aburrido bored **(1.4)**, boring **(1.2)**
aburrir to bore
aburrirse to get bored **(3.3)**
acabar de + inf. to have just + *p.p.* **(4.1)**
una **academia** academy
un **accesorio, una accesoria** accessory
accidentalmente accidentally
un **accidente** accident
una **acción** *(pl.* **acciones)** action
el **aceite** oil **(4.2)**
una **aceituna** olive
un **acelerador** accelerator
acelerar to accelerate
aceptar to accept
una **acera** sidewalk **(8.1)**
acerca de on, about
* **acercarse a** to approach, to get near **(4.4)**

el **acero** steel
acomodado wealthy
la **clase acomodada** upper middle class
acompañar to accompany
acondicionado conditioned
el **sistema de aire acondicionado** air conditioning system **(7.4)**
aconsejar to advise, counsel **(8.4)**
acostarse (o → ue) to go to bed **(3.2)**
acostumbrarse a to get used to **(8.2)**
una **actitud** attitude
una **actividad** activity
activo active **(1.2)**
un **acto** act
un **actor** actor
una **actriz** *(pl.* **actrices)** actress
la **actuación** acting out, performance
actual present, current
actuar (u → ú) to act **(7.3)**
un **acuario** aquarium, fishbowl
acuático aquatic
unos **esquís acuáticos** water skis
un **acuerdo** agreement
estar de acuerdo to agree **(4.2)**
una **acusación** *(pl.* **acusaciones)** accusation
la **acústica** acoustics
una **adaptación** *(pl.* **adaptaciones)** adaptation
adaptar to adapt
adelante ahead, forward
de allí en adelante from then on
* **adelgazar** to get thin, lose weight
además besides **(1.2)**
un **adivinador, una adivinadora** fortuneteller
adivinar to guess **(4.4)**
un **adjetivo** adjective
la **admiración** admiration
un **admirador, una admiradora** admirer

admirar to admire **(1.3)**
la **admisión** admission
admitido admitted
admitir to admit
¿adónde? (to) where?
adorar to adore
un **adulto** adult
un **adverbio** adverb
aérea concerning air
una **línea aérea** airline
un **aeromozo, una aeromoza** flight attendant
afectar to affect
una **afeitadora** razor **(3.2)**
afeitarse to shave *(oneself)* **(3.2)**
un **aficionado, una aficionada** fan
afirmativamente affirmatively
afirmativo affirmative
la **afluencia** influx
afortunadamente fortunately
afortunado fortunate, lucky **(4.4)**
africano African
afrocubano Afro-Cuban
afuera outside
una **agencia** agency
una **agencia de coches** car dealer
una **agencia de empleo** employment agency
una **agencia de viajes** travel agency
una **agencia matrimonial** marriage counselor
un **agente, una agente** agent
un **agente de mudanzas** mover
un **agente de viajes** travel agent
la **agilidad** agility
agitado agitated, irritated, excited
agitar to agitate, irritate, excite
agosto August
agradable pleasant, agreeable **(9.2)**
agradar to be pleasing
me **agrada(n)** I enjoy **(2.4)**
agradecido grateful

agresivo aggressive

el agua (f.) water (5.3)

    el agua dulce fresh water

    esquiar en el agua to water-ski

un aguacate avocado

un águila (f.) eagle

ahí there (2.2)

* **ahogarse** to drown

ahora now (1.4)

ahorrar to save

el aire air

    al aire libre outdoors

    el sistema de aire acondicionado air conditioning system (7.4)

    la contaminación del aire air pollution (7.1)

aislado isolated

el ajedrez chess

    jugar al ajedrez to play chess

el ajo garlic

    un diente de ajo clove of garlic

al (a + el) to the, at the (1.3)

    al + inf. when, on (doing something), while, upon (doing something), at the (moment of) + verb (4.3)

    al contrario on the contrary (4.3)

    al día per day (7.1)

una alameda mall, public walk

un albañil mason

un alcalde mayor

una aldea village

alegrarse (de) to get/be happy (because of) (3.3)

alegre happy (1.4)

alejarse (de) to move away (from) (8.3)

alemán (f. alemana) German

el alemán German (language)

un alemán, una alemana German (person)

Alemania Germany

una alfombra rug

algo something, anything (5.1)

el algodón cotton

alguien someone, somebody (5.1)

algún, alguno some (4.1)

    alguna vez ever, once (6.3)

    algunos some, several (4.1)

el aliento breath

    sin aliento out of breath

alimentarse to eat

el alimento nourishment, food

el alivio relief

    ¡qué alivio! what a relief! (7.4)

el alma (f.) soul

un almacén (pl. almacenes) (department) store (1.3)

* **almorzar (o → ue)** to have lunch (3.1)

el alpinismo mountain climbing (2.4)

alquilado rented

alquilar to rent (6.1)

alrededor de around (6.2)

alternar to alternate

alto tall (1.2), high

    en voz alta aloud

un alumno, una alumna student (1.2)

allá over there (2.2)

allí there (2.2)

    de allí en adelante from then on

    desde allí from there (4.3)

amable kind (2.1), friendly

amado beloved

amarillo yellow

amarrar to fasten

amazónico Amazon

una ambición (pl. ambiciones) ambition

ambicioso ambitious

el ambiente atmosphere

ambos both

ambulante walking, traveling

la América America

    la América del Sur South America

la americanización Americanization

un amigo, una amiga friend (1.2)

la amistad friendship (3.4)

un amo master

el amor love (3.4)

una anaconda anaconda

un análisis analysis

* **analizar** to analyze

la anarquía anarchy

ancho wide

el andaluz language of Andalusia

un andaluz, una andaluza person from Andalusia

* **andar** to walk, work, run (function) (4.3), go (9.4)

los Andes Andes mountains

un ángel angel (5.2)

la angustia anguish

un anglohablante, una anglohablante English-speaking person

angustiado anguished

un anillo ring (2.3)

un animal animal

un animalito little animal

el ánimo spirit, mind (4.4)

    la presencia de ánimo mental alertness (4.4)

anoche last night (6.4)

anotar to note

anteanoche the night before last (6.4)

anteayer the day before yesterday (6.4)

una antena antenna

unos anteojos eyeglasses

    unos anteojos de sol sunglasses (2.2)

antepasado ___ before last (6.4)

los antepasados ancestors

anterior before

anteriormente previously

antes (de) before (1.4)

anticipar to anticipate

antiguo old, antique (5.1)

antillano Caribbean

un antillano, una antillana person from the West Indies (Caribbean)

las Antillas West Indies (Caribbean)

antipático unpleasant, disagreeable (1.2)

un antropólogo anthropologist

anunciar to announce

un anuncio announcement, advertisement (6.1)

    un anuncio de empleo want ad

un año year

    el Año Nuevo New Year

apagado extinguished, shut off

* **apagar** to turn off (6.2)

un apagón (pl. apagones) blackout (9.1)

* **aparecer** to appear, seem

un apartamento apartment

un edificio de apartamentos
apartment building **(4.3)**
un **apellido** last name
apenas hardly, scarcely
un **aperitivo** apéritif
aplicable applicable
apoderarse de to seize
apreciado appreciated
apreciar to appreciate
aprender (a) to learn **(1.4)**
aprobar (o → ue) to
approve, pass
apropiado appropriate
apuntar to point
el **apuro** difficulty
aquel *(f.* **aquella)** that *(over there)* **(2.2)**
aquél *(f.* **aquélla)** that one *(over there)* **(2.2)**
aquellos those *(over there)* **(2.2)**
aquéllos those *(over there)* **(2.2)**
aquí here **(2.2)**
aquí tiene(s) here is, here are **(10.1)**
árabe Arabic
un **aragonés, una aragonesa**
person from Aragon
una **araña** spider
arawako Arawak
un **árbol** tree **(5.4)**
un árbol de frutas fruit tree **(6.4)**
ardiendo burning
un **área** *(f.)* area
la **arena** sand **(2.2)**
la **Argentina** Argentina
argentino Argentinean
una **argolla** loop
aristocrático aristocratic
un **arma** *(f.)* weapon, arm
una **armada** armada, navy, fleet
un **armamento** armament
los armamentos nucleares
nuclear armaments
aromático aromatic
la **arqueología** archeology
arqueológico archeological
un **arqueólogo** archeologist
un **arquitecto** architect
* **arrancar** to pull out, start *(a car)* **(4.2)**
arrasar to tear down
un **arrecife** reef
arreglar to fix **(2.1)**

el **arreglo** care
arrestado arrested
arrestar to arrest
arriba above
arrogante arrogant
un **arroyo** stream
el **arte** art
la **artesanía** crafts
un **artesano, una artesana**
artisan, craftsman
un **artículo** article
artificial artificial
un **artista, una artista** artist
artístico artistic
un **ascensor** elevator
asegurar to insure
asesinado assassinated
así so, like that
así (es que) therefore, so (it is that) **(3.1)**
Asia Asia
asiático Asian
un **asiento** seat **(6.2)**
un **asistente, una asistenta** assistant
asistir a to attend
asociado associated
asomar to appear
asomarse to look out
asombroso amazing
un **aspecto** aspect
la **aspiración** aspiration, ambition
una **aspirina** aspirin
un **astronauta, una astronauta**
astronaut
la **astronomía** astronomy
asumir to assume
un **asunto** matter, topic
* **atacar** to attack
atar to tie
la **atención** attention
prestar atención to pay attention
atentamente attentively
atento attentive, polite **(5.2)**
un **aterrizaje** landing
* **aterrizar** to land
atestado crowded **(6.2)**
atestar to crowd, cram **(6.2)**
Atlántico Atlantic
un **atleta, una atleta** athlete
atlético athletic
el **atletismo** athletics
atómico atomic
atormentar to torment, torture

una **atracción** *(pl.* **atracciones)**
attraction
atractivo attractive
atrás behind
atropellar to run over
aumentar to augment, increase
aun even **(3.4)**
aunque though, although **(1.2)**
el **auspicio** auspice, protection
Australia Australia
auténtico authentic
una **autobiografía** autobiography
autobiográfico
autobiographical
un **autobús** *(pl.* **autobuses)** bus **(1.3)**
un **automóvil** automobile
un **automovilista, una automovilista** motorist, driver
la **autoridad** authority
la **autorización** authorization
avanzado advanced
avaro miserly
un **ave** *(f.)* bird
una **avenida** avenue
una **aventura** adventure
una película de aventuras
adventure film
un **avión** *(pl.* **aviones)** airplane
un **aviso** warning **(8.4)**, information
¡ay! oh!
ayer yesterday **(6.4)**
la **ayuda** aid, help
ayudar to aid, help **(1.3)**
un **azteca, una azteca** Aztec
azteca Aztec
el **azúcar** sugar
la caña de azúcar sugarcane
azul blue

b

¡bah! bah!
bailar to dance **(1.1)**
un **bailarín, una bailarina** dancer
un **baile** dance **(2.4)**
bajar (de) to descend, get off **(4.3)**
bajo short **(1.2)**, low
la planta baja ground floor, street floor **(7.4)**
los Países Bajos The Low Countries *(Netherlands, Belgium, Luxembourg)*

bajo   below, under

el balboa   *money of Panama*

un balcón *(pl.* balcones)   balcony

una balsa de junco   bulrush raft

el ballet   ballet

una banana   banana (6.1)

un banco   bank (3.4), bench

una banda   band

una bandera   flag

un bandido, una bandida   bandit

bañarse   to bathe, take a
   bath (3.2)

un baño   bathroom, bath
   un traje de baño   bathing
      suit (2.2)

barato   cheap, inexpensive

una barba   beard

una barbacoa   barbecue

la barbaridad   outrage
   ¡qué barbaridad!   what
      nonsense! (1.4)

bárbaro   barbaric

un barbero   barber

un barco   boat

un barrio   district, neighborhood (9.4)

el barro   mud

básico   basic

el básquetbol   basketball (2.4)

bastante   rather, enough (1.1)

una batalla   battle

batallar   to fight a battle

la bauxita   bauxite

beber   to drink (1.4)

una bebida   drink, beverage (8.2)

el béisbol   baseball

Belén   Bethlehem

la belleza   beauty

bello   beautiful

las Bermudas   Bermuda

un beso   kiss (5.4)

la Biblia   Bible

una biblioteca   library (1.3)

una bicicleta   bicycle (1.3)

bien   well (1.1)
   bien educado   well-
      mannered (5.2)
   portarse bien   to behave (3.3)

el bienestar   well-being

un bigote   mustache (3.2)

bilingüe   bilingual

un billete   bill, paper money
   (2.3), ticket (8.3)

una billetera   wallet (2.3)

una biografía   biography

la biología   biology

el bistec   steak (6.1)

blanco   white

los blancos   white people

unos blue-jeans   blue jeans

una blusa   blouse

una boa   boa

un bobo, una boba   dummy, fool (5.1)

una boca   mouth

una bocina   horn
   tocar la bocina   to honk
      (the horn) (8.1)

una boda   wedding (3.4)

una bola de cristal   crystal ball

el bolero   bolero *(dance)*

un bolígrafo   pen (2.3)

el bolívar   *money of Venezuela*

Bolivia   Bolivia

una bolsa   bag
   una bolsa al hombro
      backpack

un bolsillo   pocket (2.3)

un bolso   purse (2.3)

un bombero   fireman

una bombilla   light bulb

la bonanza   prosperity, success

la bondad   kindness
   tener la bondad (de)   to be
      good enough (to) *(would you
      please)* (8.1)

bonito   pretty (1.2)

un borlote   dance, party

un bosque   forest (6.4)

un bote   boat (2.2)
   un bote de vela   sailboat (2.2)

una botella   bottle

Brasil   Brazil

brasileño   Brazilian

bravo   brave, valiant

un brazo   arm (3.4)

brillante   brilliant

una broma   joke (5.1)

bronceado   tanned (6.2)

un bronceado   tan (8.2)
   la loción bronceadora
      suntan lotion

una bruja   witch

la brutalidad   brutality

bucear   to go scuba diving

buen, bueno   good (1.2)
   buen mozo   good-looking (9.4)
   ¡buen provecho!   enjoy it!
   de buen humor   in a good
      mood (1.4)

los buenos modales   good
   manners (5.2)
   ¡qué bueno!   how great (3.1)

una bufanda   scarf

burlarse de   to make fun of (3.3)

un burro   donkey

la busca   search
   en busca de   looking for,
      in search of

un buscador de tesoro   treasure-
   hunter

* buscar   to look for (1.3)

un buzo   diver

C

un caballero   gentleman, knight

un caballo   horse
   a caballo   on horseback
   montar a caballo   to ride
      a horse

caber   to fit

una cabeza   head
   me duele la cabeza   my
      head hurts
   un dolor de cabeza
      headache

el cacao   cocoa

un cacharro   pot, saucepan
   (8.3)

cada   each (3.2)
   cada uno   each one (3.2)

una cadena   chain

* caer   to fall (3.4)

* caerse   to fall (3.4)

el café   coffee, café (2.1)

una cafetería   cafeteria

una caja   box

un cajón *(pl.* cajones)   drawer

un calcetín *(pl.* calcetines)   sock

una calculadora   calculator (1.3)

la calefacción   heat
   la calefacción solar   solar
      heating (7.4)

un calendario   calendar

calentar   to heat

la calma   calmness, tranquility

calor   hot
   hace calor   it's hot
      (weather) (2.2)
   tener calor   to be warm,
      hot (5.4)

caluroso   hot (2.2)

callarse   to keep quiet, silent (3.2)

una **calle** street **(2.1)**
    estar en la calle to be out
una **cama** bed **(6.1)**
    hacer la cama to make the bed
una **cámara** camera **(1.3)**
una **camarera** waitress
un **camarero** waiter **(2.1)**
    cambiar to change, to
      exchange **(2.3)**
    cambiar de idea to
      change one's mind
el **cambio** change *(money)*
un **cambio** change
    caminar to walk **(2.2)**
un **camino** road, way
    El Camino Real The
      Royal Way
un **camión** *(pl.* **camiones)** truck **(8.1)**
una **camisa** shirt
    una camisa de cuadros
      checked shirt
un **campamento de veraneo**
    summer camp
una **campana** bell
la **campaña** country(side)
    una tienda de campaña
      tent **(8.3)**
una **campaña** campaign
un **campeón, una campeona**
    champion **(8.2)**
el **camping** camping
    ir de camping to go
      camping **(8.3)**
el **campo** country(side) **(1.3)**
un **campo** field
    un trabajador del campo
      field worker
    canadiense Canadian **(1.2)**
un **canal de irrigación**
    irrigation canal
el **cáncer** cancer
una **canción** *(pl.* **canciones)** song
un **candado** padlock
un **candelero** candlestick
un **candidato, una candidata**
    candidate
un **canguro** kangaroo
una **canica** marble
una **canoa** canoe
    cansado tired **(1.4)**
    cansarse (de) to get tired
      (of) **(3.3)**
un **cantante, una cantante** singer
    cantar to sing **(1.1)**

una **cantidad** quantity **(6.1)**
una **caña** cane, pole
    la caña de azúcar
      sugarcane
    una caña de pescar
      fishing pole
    capaz *(pl.* **capaces)** capable
la **Caperucita Roja** Little Red
    Riding Hood
una **capital** capital
    capturado captured
una **cara** face
el **carácter** character
una **característica** characteristic
    ¡caramba! wow! **(1.3)**
una **carga** cargo, load, burden
el **Caribe** Caribbean
una **caricatura** cartoon
el **cariño** affection **(3.4)**
    cariñoso loving, affectionate
la **carne** flesh, meat
    el chile con carne chile
      with meat
    la carne de res beef **(6.1)**
una **carnicería** butcher shop **(6.1)**
un **carnicero, una carnicera**
    butcher
un **carpintero, una carpintera**
    carpenter
una **carrera** career, race **(8.4)**
una **carretera** highway
una **carta** card, letter
un **cartel** poster
un **cartero, una cartera** mail
    carrier **(2.1)**
una **casa** house **(1.3)**
    a casa home **(1.3)**
    a la casa de __ at __'s
      house **(1.3)**
    en casa at home
    una casa de fantasmas
      haunted house
el **casamiento** marriage
    casarse to get married **(3.4)**
    casarse con to marry **(3.4)**
una **cáscara** peel
un **casco** helmet
    casero domestic
    casi almost **(2.4)**
una **casita** little house
un **caso** case
    en caso de que in case
      (that) **(10.1)**
el **castellano** *Spanish language*

un **castellano, una castellana**
    person from Castile
  * **castigar** to punish
un **castillo** castle
el **catalán** *language of*
    Catalonia
un **catalán, una catalana**
    person from Catalonia
una **catástrofe** catastrophe
una **catedral** cathedral
una **categoría** category
    católico Catholic
    catorce fourteen
una **causa** cause
un **cayo** key *(island)*
la **caza** hunting **(2.4)**
un **cazador, una cazadora**
    hunter
  * **cazar** to hunt **(2.4)**
una **cebolla** onion
    ceder to cede, yield
    celebrado celebrated
    celebrar to celebrate
una **celebridad** celebrity
los **celos** jealousy
    tener celos to be jealous **(5.4)**
la **cena** dinner
un **centavo** cent
un **centímetro** centimeter
    central central
el **centro** downtown **(1.3)**
    Centroamérica Central
      America
    cepillarse to brush one's hair **(3.2)**
un **cepillo** brush **(3.2)**
la **cerámica** pottery **(2.4)**
    cerca de near **(6.2)**
    cercano nearby
una **ceremonia** ceremony
    ceremonial ceremonial
una **cereza** cherry **(6.1)**
    cero zero
    cerrado closed **(6.2)**
    cerrar (e → ie) to close, to
      shut **(3.1)**
    cerrar con llave to lock **(3.1)**
un **cerro** hill
un **ciclomotor** moped
    ciego blind
el **cielo** sky, heaven
    cien one hundred
la **ciencia** science
    la ciencia ficción science
      fiction

**una película de ciencia
ficción** science-fiction movie
científico scientific
un **científico, una científica**
scientist **(9.3)**
ciento one hundred
por ciento percent **(1.2)**
cierto certain, sure **(7.1)**
un **cigarrillo** cigarette
un **cigarro** cigar
la **cima** top
cinco five
cincuenta fifty
un **cine** movie theater **(1.3)**
la **cinemanía** movie madness
una **cinta** tape, cassette **(1.3)**
un **cinturón** belt **(10.2)**
un **cinturón de seguridad** seat belt
un **circo** circus
la **circulación** circulation
un **círculo** circle
una **circunstancia** circumstance
una **cita** date, meeting, appointment
una **ciudad** city **(1.3)**
un **ciudadano, una ciudadana**
citizen
cívico civic
civil civil
una **civilización** (pl.
civilizaciones) civilization
civilizado civilized
claramente clearly
un **clarinete** clarinet
claro light (colored)
¡claro! of course!
¡claro que no! of course not!
una **clase** kind, type **(2.4)**; class
la **clase acomodada**
upper middle class
una **sala de clase** classroom
clásico classical
clavar to fix
un **clavel** carnation **(6.4)**; key
(in music)
un **cliente, una cliente**
customer, client
el **clima** climate
un **club** club
el **cobre** copper
una **Coca-Cola** Coca-Cola
la **cocina** cooking **(2.4)**
una **cocina** kitchen **(7.4)**
cocinar to cook **(1.1)**
un **cocinero, una cocinera** cook

un **coche** car **(1.3)**
una **agencia de coches**
car dealer
un **código** set of rules, code
coeducacional coeducational
* **coger** to pick **(6.4)**
un **cohete** rocket **(7.1)**
la **cola** glue, tail, line
hacer cola to stand in line
una **colección** (pl. **colecciones**)
collection **(2.4)**
coleccionar to collect **(2.4)**
un **colegio** high school
colgar (o → ue) to hang
Colombia Colombia
el **colón** money of Costa Rica
and El Salvador
una **colonia** colony
colonial colonial
la **colonización** colonization
* **colonizar** to colonize
un **color** color
color de rosa rose-
colored, "fun"
una **columna** column
un **collar** necklace **(2.3)**
un **comandante, una
comandante** commander
una **combinación** (pl. **combinaciones**)
combination
una **comedia** comedy **(2.4)**
una **comedia musical**
musical comedy
un **comedor** dining room **(7.4)**
* **comenzar** (e → ie) to begin,
start **(3.1)**
comer to eat **(1.4)**
comercial commercial
un **comerciante, una
comerciante** merchant
el **comercio** commerce, trade
cometer to commit
cómico comical, funny
la **comida** food, meal
el **comino** cumin
como since **(3.2)**, like, as, because
como resultado as a
result **(10.2)**
tal como just as
tan __ como as __ as
tanto __ como as much __ as
¿cómo? how? **(1.1)** what?
¿cómo es __? what is __
like?

¿Cómo te llamas? What's
your name?
cómodo comfortable **(9.2)**
un **compañero, una compañera**
classmate **(1.2)**
una **compañía** company
una **compañía aérea**
airline company
una **compañía de seguros**
insurance company
comparable comparable
comparar to compare
comparativo comparative
compartir to share **(5.2)**
una **competencia** competition
* **complacer** to please
* **complacerse en** to take
pleasure in **(8.2)**
complemento complement
completamente completely
completar to complete
complicado complicated **(5.1)**
un **cómplice, una cómplice**
accomplice
* **componer** to compose
un **comprador, una compradora**
buyer
comprar to buy **(1.3)**
las **compras** shopping **(4.1)**
ir de compras to go
shopping **(4.1)**
comprender to understand **(1.4)**
comprometerse to get engaged
un **compromiso** engagement
una **computadora** computer **(7.1)**
común common **(5.1)**
la **comunicación** communication
* **comunicar** to communicate
el **comunismo** communism
comunista communist
con with **(2.3)**
con la condición de que
on the condition that **(10.1)**
con tal que provided that **(10.1)**
un **concepto** concept
un **concierto** concert **(1.3)**
un concierto de rock
rock concert
una **conclusión** (pl. **conclusiones**)
conclusion
un **conde** count
condenar to condemn
condensado condensed
una **condesa** countess

una **condición** *(pl.* **condiciones)**
condition
con la condición de que
on the condition that **(10.1)**
el **condicional** conditional
un **condimento** condiment, spice
un **condor** condor
* **conducir** to drive **(4.4)**
un permiso de conducir
driver's license **(4.2)**
un **conductor, una conductora**
driver **(8.1)**
conectar to connect
una **conexión** *(pl.* **conexiones)**
connection
un **conejo** rabbit
una **conferencia** conference
confiable worthy of confidence
la **confianza** confidence
un **conflicto** conflict
confundido confused
el **Congreso** Congress
una **conjunción** *(pl.* **conjunciones)**
conjunction
un **conjunto** group
conmemorar to commemorate
conmigo with me
* **conocer** to know, be
acquainted with, to be
familiar with **(2.1)**; to
meet for the first time
* **conocerse** to meet
conocido famous
un **conocido, una conocida**
acquaintance
una **conquista** conquest
conquistado conquered
un **conquistador, una**
conquistadora conqueror
conquistar to conquer
una **consecuencia** consequence
* **conseguir (e → i, i)** to obtain
un **consejero, una consejera**
adviser, counselor
un consejero escolar
guidance counselor
un **consejo** *(piece of)* advice **(5.2)**
los consejos advice
conservador conservative
conservar to preserve, keep **(10.4)**
un **conservatorio** conservatory
considerado considered
considerar to consider
consistir en to consist of **(8.2)**

constantemente constantly
constipado congested with a cold
una **constitución** *(pl.* **constituciones)**
constitution
* **constituir** to constitute
la **construcción** construction
construido constructed
* **construir** to construct **(4.3)**
consultar to consult
un **consultorio** office
un consultorio del médico
doctor's office
un **contacto** contact
la **contaminación** pollution
la contaminación del aire
air pollution **(7.1)**
contar (o → ue) to count,
tell **(3.1)**
contar con to count on
contemplar to contemplate
* **contener (e → ie)** to contain
contento content, happy **(1.4)**
una **contestación** *(pl.*
contestaciones) answer
contestar to answer
contigo with you *(fam.)*
la **continuación** continuation
continuar (u → ú) to continue
continuo continuous
contra against **(7.1)**
en contra against
* **contradecir** to contradict
el **contrario** contrary, opposite
al contrario on the
contrary **(4.3)**
de lo contrario on the
other hand, on the
contrary **(6.4)**
lo contrario the opposite
un **contraste** contrast
un **contrato** contract
una **contribución** *(pl.* **contribuciones)**
contribution
un **control** control
controlar to control
una **controversia** controversy
* **convencer** to convince
convencido convinced
* **convenir (e → ie, i) en** to
agree on **(8.2)**
una **conversación** *(pl.* **conversaciones)**
conversation
conversar to converse
cooperar to cooperate

una **copa** cup
coqueta flirtatious
coquetear to flirt
un **coquí** coqui *(small frog from
Puerto Rico)*
un **corazón** *(pl.* **corazones)** heart
una **corbata** tie
una **cordillera** mountain chain
el **córdoba** *money of Nicaragua*
un **coro** choir
una **corona** crown
un **corral** corral
un **corredor** corridor
el **correo** mail
un **correo** post office **(2.1)**
correr to run **(1.4)**
correr las olas to surf **(2.2)**
la **correspondencia** correspondence
corresponder to correspond
una **corrida** run, bullfight
una corrida de toros
bullfight
cortar to cut
cortarse to cut *(oneself)* **(3.2)**
la **corte** king's court
cortés polite **(5.2)**
la **cortesía** courtesy
la **corteza** bark of a tree
corto short
unos pantalones cortos
shorts
una **cosa** thing **(1.3)**
¿qué cosa? what thing?,
what is it? **(2.3)**
cosmopolita cosmopolitan
una **costa** coastline
Costa Rica Costa Rica
costar (o → ue) to cost **(3.1)**
el **costo** cost
una **costumbre** custom, habit
de costumbre habitually
un **cowboy** cowboy
la **creación** creation
creado created
creador creator
crear to create **(3.3)**
* **crecer** to grow
crédulo gullible, credulous **(9.3)**
una **creencia** belief
* **creer** to believe **(1.4)**
una **crema** cream **(6.1)**
la crema dental toothpaste
criar (i → i) to bring up
una **criatura** creature

un **crimen** (*pl.* **crímenes**) crime
un **criminal, una criminal**
    criminal
    cristal crystal
        una bola de cristal
            crystal ball
    * **cristianizar** to Christianize
    cristiano Christian
un **cristiano, una cristiana**
    Christian
    Cristo Christ
la **crítica** criticism
    * **criticar** to criticize (1.3)
el **crol** crawl (*swimming*)
un **cruce** crossing
    crudo raw
la **crueldad** cruelty
una **cruz** (*pl.* **cruces**) cross
    * **cruzar** to cross (5.4)
un **cuadrado** square
    cuadrangular square
un **cuadro** painting, square
        una camisa de cuadros
            checked shirt
    ¿cuál(es)? which? (2.4)
una **cualidad** quality
    cualquier any
    cuando when (10.2)
        de vez en cuando once in
            a while, from time to
            time (3.1)
    ¿cuándo? when? (1.1)
    ¿cuánto? how much? (1.1)
        ¿cuántas veces? how
            often?, how many times?
        ¿cuánto tiempo? how
            long?
        ¿cuántos? how many? (1.3)
    cuarenta forty
    cuarto fourth
un **cuarto** room
    cuatro four
    cuatrocientos four hundred
    cubano Cuban
    cubierto covered
un **cubito** small pail
    cubrir to cover
una **cuchara** spoon
una **cucharada** spoonful
un **cuchillo** knife
    cuenta: darse cuenta (de)
        to realize (3.3)
un **cuento** story
        un cuento de hadas
            fairytale

una **cuerda** cord, rope
        saltar a la cuerda to
            jump rope
el **cuero** leather
un **cuerpo** body, corps
    cuesta it costs; *see* **costar**
una **cuestión** (*pl.* **cuestiones**)
    matter (9.2)
el **cuidado** care (5.4)
        tener cuidado to be
            careful (5.4)
    cuidadoso careful (4.4)
    cuidar to take care of (2.1)
una **culebra** snake
la **culpa** guilt, blame
        tener la culpa to be to
            blame, be at fault (5.4)
    culpable guilty (4.3)
un **culpable, una culpable**
    guilty person
    cultivar to cultivate, grow (6.4)
el **cultivo** cultivation
un **culto** cult
una **cultura** culture
    cultural cultural
la **cumbia** *dance from Colombia*
la **cumbre** top
un **cumpleaños** birthday
un **cumplido** complement
    cumplir to fulfill
la **cuna** birthplace, cradle
una **cuñada** sister-in-law
un **cuñado** brother-in-law
una **cura** cure
un **curandero, una curandera**
    healer
        un curandero ambulante
            traveling healer
    curarse to be cured
la **curiosidad** curiosity
    curioso curious
un **curso** course

ch

el **champú** shampoo (3.2)
el **chantaje** blackmail (2.3)
una **chaqueta** jacket
el **chaquete** backgammon
        jugar al chaquete to play
            backgammon
    charlar to chat
un **cheque** check
el **chicle** gum (2.3)

una **chica** girl (1.2)
un **chico** boy (1.2)
    Chile Chile
el **chile con carne** chile with meat
    chileno Chilean
    China China
una **chinchilla** chinchilla
un **chinchoso, una chinchosa** a
    "pain" (3.3)
    chino Chinese
    chismoso gossipy, tattling
un **chismoso, una chismosa**
    gossip, tattle-tale (5.1)
un **chiste** joke (3.1)
    * **chocar con** to run into,
        bump into (4.3)
el **chocolate** chocolate
una **chuleta** cutlet (6.1)

d

una **dama** lady
las **damas** checkers
        jugar a las damas to
            play checkers
una **danza** dance
el **daño** damage
    * **dar** to give (2.2)
        dar un paseo to go for a
            walk, ride (4.3)
        dar una ojeada to glance
        dar una vuelta to go for
            a ride (4.2)
        darse cuenta (de) to
            realize (3.3)
        darse prisa to hurry (3.2)
un **dato** fact
    de of (2.1) from
        de alguna manera (in)
            some way (5.1)
        de buen humor in a good
            mood (1.4)
        de costumbre habitually
        de hecho in fact (1.1)
        de lo contrario otherwise (6.4)
        de mal humor in a bad
            mood (1.4)
        de ninguna manera (in)
            no way (5.1)
        de nuevo again (3.4)
        de prisa quickly (4.2)
        ¿de quién(es)? whose? (2.1)
        de repente suddenly (5.3)

de vez en cuando once in a while, from time to time **(3.1)**

de visita on a visit

debajo de below, under(neath) **(6.2)**

deber to owe **(1.4)**

deber + inf. should, ought to **(1.4)**

una **década** decade

una **decepción** *(pl. decepciones)* disappointment

decidir to decide

décimo tenth

* **decir** to say, tell **(2.2)**

es decir this means, that is to say **(10.4)**

una **decisión** *(pl. decisiones)* decision

tomar una decisión to make a decision

decisivo decisive

declarado declared

declarar to declare

la **decoración** decoration

decorar to decorate

* **dedicar** to dedicate

* **dedicarse** to devote *(oneself)*

un **dedo** finger

un **defecto** fault **(5.2)**

defender (e → ie) to defend

definido definite

dejar to leave, let

dejar de + inf. to quit, stop + verb **(8.2)**

del (de + el) of the, from the, about the **(1.3)**

delante de before, in front of **(6.2)**

una **delegación** *(pl. delegaciones)* delegation

un **delfín** *(pl. delfines)* dolphin

delgado thin **(1.2)**

delicado delicate

delicioso delicious

demandar to demand

los **demás** the rest, the others **(3.3)**

demasiado too, too much **(1.1)**

la **democracia** democracy

un **demonio** demon, devil

demostrar (o → ue) to demonstrate **(9.2)**

demostrativo demonstrative

dental dental

la **crema dental** toothpaste

un **dentista, una dentista** dentist **(2.1)**

dentro de inside **(6.2);** within

depender to depend

un **dependiente, una dependienta** clerk **(2.1)**

deportado deported

un **deporte** sport **(2.4)**

deportista athletic, sports-loving **(1.2)**

deportivo concerning sports

depositar to deposit

un **depósito** deposit

la **derecha** right (side)

a la derecha on the right **(5.2)**

derecho straight ahead

un **derecho** right

derivado derived

derivar to derive

derrotado defeated

derrotar to defeat

desafortunadamente unfortunately

desafortunado unfortunate **(4.4)**

desagradable unpleasant **(5.2)**

* **desaparecer** to disappear **(6.4)**

desarreglar to mess up

desarrollar to develop **(7.1)**

el **desarrollo** development

desastroso disastrous

desayunarse to have breakfast

el **desayuno** breakfast

descansado relaxed, rested

descansar to rest **(1.1)**

descender (e → ie) to descend

un **descendiente, una descendiente** descendant

descifrar to decipher

desconocido unknown

descontento discontent, unhappy

descortés impolite **(5.2)**

describir to describe

una **descripción** *(pl. descripciones)* description

descrito described

descubierto discovered **(6.3)**

un **descubridor, una descubridora** discoverer

un **descubrimiento** discovery

descubrir to discover **(7.1)**

desde from **(4.3),** since

desde allí from there **(4.3)**

desde entonces from then on

deseable desirable

desear wish **(1.1),** to desire

* **desembarcar** to disembark

desempeñar to play a role *(in an organization)*

desértico deserted

desgraciadamente unfortunately

desierto deserted

desigualdad inequality

desilusionado disappointed **(9.1)**

desintegrar to disintegrate

despacio slowly **(8.1)**

despachar to ship, dispatch

un **despacho** shipment

despedirse (e → i, i) to say goodbye, take leave **(3.2)**

me despido I say goodbye

despertarse (e → ie) to wake *(oneself)* up **(3.2)**

despierto awake

soñar despierto to daydream

después (de) after **(1.4)**

el **destino** destiny

destructivo destructive

* **destruir** to destroy

detalladamente in detail

un **detalle** detail **(3.3)**

un **detective, una detective** detective

* **detener (e → ie)** to stop

determinar to determine

detrás de behind **(6.2)**

un **devastador, una devastadora** devastator, harasser

devolver (o → ue) to return *(an object)*, give back **(3.1)**

di say: *see* decir

un **día** day

al día per day **(7.1)**

de día in the daytime

el día de acción de gracias Thanksgiving

hoy día nowadays **(8.2)**

por el día during the day **(3.2)**

todos los días every day

un día someday, one day **(1.1)**

un **diablo** devil **(5.2)**

diagonalmente diagonally

un **diálogo** dialog

diario daily **(3.2)**

un **diario** diary

dibujar to design, draw

un **dibujo** design, drawing

un **diccionario** dictionary

un **dictador** dictator

dicho said: *see* decir

diecinueve nineteen

un **diente** tooth **(3.4)**

un diente de ajo clove of
garlic

diez ten

diez y nueve nineteen

una **diferencia** difference

diferente different

diferentemente differently

difícil difficult **(5.1)**

dificilísimo very difficult

una **dificultad** difficulty

dificultar to make difficult

digital digital

digo I say: *see* **decir**

dijo he (she) (you) *(formal)*
said: *see* **decir**

dime tell me: *see* **decir** **(2.3)**

dinámico dynamic

el **dinero** money

dio he (she) (you) *(formal)*
gave: *see* **dar**

un **dios** god

Dios God **(4.3)**

¡Dios mío! my goodness! **(4.3)**

el **dios-sol** sun-god

que Dios te ayude may
God help you **(2.3)**

¡Válgame Dios! God help
me! **(4.3)**

una **diosa** goddess

un **diploma** diploma

dirás you will say: *see* **decir**

una **dirección** *(pl.* **direcciones)**
address, direction

las luces direccionales
directional lights **(4.2)**

directo direct

un **director, una directora** director

diría I would say: *see* **decir**

* **dirigir** to direct **(2.1)**

* **dirigirse (a)** go toward
(4.2); to head

la **disciplina** discipline

disciplinado disciplined

disco disco

un **disco** record **(1.3)**

descompuesto not working

una **discoteca** discotheque

la **discriminación** discrimination

discutir to discuss

un **diseño** design

disgustar to disgust, not to
like, hate **(2.4)**

disparar to shoot

un **disparo** shot

una **disputa** dispute

distante distant

* **distinguir** to distinguish

distintivo distinctive

distinto distinct

distraído absent-minded
(9.1); scatterbrained

un **distraído, una distraída**
scatterbrained person

la **distribución** distribution

un **distrito** district

una **diversión** *(pl.* **diversiones)**
entertainment

divertido entertaining,
amusing **(1.2)**

divertir (e → ie, i) to amuse **(3.3)**

divertirse (e → ie, i) to have
fun **(3.3);** to enjoy oneself

dividido divided

dividir to divide

divino divine

el **divorcio** divorce

doblar to turn **(8.1)**

doblar la esquina to turn
the corner

un **doctor, una doctora** doctor

un **dólar** dollar

doler (o → ue) to be in pain,
to feel pain

me duele la cabeza my
head hurts **(3.1)**

un **dolor** pain, ache

un dolor de cabeza headache

un dolor de estómago
stomachache

doméstico domestic

la **dominación** domination

dominar to dominate

domingo Sunday

el domingo (on) Sunday **(1.3)**

los domingos (on)
Sundays **(1.3)**

dominicano Dominican

la República Dominicana
Dominican Republic

un **dominicano, una dominicana**
*person from the Dominican
Republic*

el **dominio** domain, mastery

el dominio de ti mismo
self-control

¿dónde? where? **(1.1)**

dorado browned

dorar to brown

dormido asleep

dormir (o → ue, u) to sleep **(3.1)**

un saco de dormir
sleeping bag **(8.3)**

una pastilla para dormir
sleeping pill

dormirse (o → ue, u) to fall
asleep **(3.2)**

un **dormitorio** bedroom **(7.4)**

dos two

dos veces seguidas twice
in a row

doscientos two hundred

doy I give: *see* **dar**

un **drama** drama

dramático dramatic

una **droga** drug

una **duda** doubt

sin duda without a doubt,
doubtless

dudar to doubt **(9.3)**

dudoso doubtful **(9.3)**

un **dueño, una dueña** owner

duermo I sleep: *see* **dormir**

dulce sweet, fresh

el agua dulce fresh water

los **dulces** candy **(2.3)**

la **duración** duration

durante during **(1.4)**

durar to last **(3.4)**

durmió he (she) (you, *formal)*
slept: *see* **dormir**

duro hard

e

e and *(before words beginning
with* **i** *or* **hi)** **(1.3)**

un **ecologista, una ecologista**
ecologist

económico economical

el **ecuador** equator

el **Ecuador** Ecuador

echar to throw, cast, pour
out, add

la **edad** age

una persona de edad
older person **(7.2)**

un **edificio** building

**un edificio de
apartamentos**
apartment building **(4.3)**

una **editorial** publishing house

la **educación** education

educado educated

bien educado polite **(5.2)**
mal educado impolite **(5.2)**
efectivamente effectively
efecto: en efecto in fact
(7.2), in effect
un **egipcio, una egipcia** Egyptian
Egipto Egypt
el **egoísmo** selfishness
egoísta selfish
un **ejemplo** example
por ejemplo for example
un **ejercicio** exercise
un **ejército** army
el *(pl. los)* the **(1.2)**
El Salvador El Salvador
él he **(1.1);** him, it *(m.) (after prep.)*
la **electricidad** electricity
un **electricista, una electricista** electrician
eléctrico electric, electrical
una linterna eléctrica flashlight **(8.3)**
la **electrónica** electronics
electrónicamente electronically
un **elefante** elephant
la **elegancia** elegance
elegante elegant
elegido elected
* **elegir** to elect, choose
elemental elementary
un **elemento** element
la **elevación** elevation
elevado elevated
eliminar to eliminate **(7.1)**
un **elixir** elixir
ella she **(1.1);** her *(after prep.)*
ellas they *(f.);* them *(f.) (after prep.)*
ello it *(neuter)*
ellos they *(m.);* them *(m.) (after prep.)*
un **embajador, una embajadora** ambassador
la **emigración** emigration
un **emigrante, una emigrante** emigrant
emigrar to emigrate
una **emoción** *(pl. emociones)* emotion
emocionante exciting, thrilling
un **emperador** emperor
* **empezar (e → ie)** to start, begin **(3.1)**

un **empleado, una empleada** employee **(2.1)**
un **empleo** job, employment
una agencia de empleo employment agency
un anuncio de empleo want ad
empujar push **(4.2);** to step on
en in, on, at **(6.2)**
en alguna parte somewhere **(5.1)**
en busca de in search of, looking for
en casa at home
en contra against
en efecto in fact **(7.2)**
en ninguna parte nowhere **(5.1)**
en particular in particular
en pro for
en punto on the dot **(8.4)**
en seguida immediately **(7.2)**
en vano in vain
enamorado in love **(1.4)**
estar enamorado de to be in love with **(1.4)**
un **enamorado, una enamorada** loved one
enamorarse (de) to fall in love (with) **(3.4)**
encadenado in chains
encantado enchanted, haunted
encantador delightful
encantar to enchant, delight
me encanta I very much like **(1.1)**
encender (e → ie) to light, turn on **(6.2)**
encendido turned on
encerar to wax
encerrar (e → ie) to lock
encima de on top of **(6.2)**
encontrado found
encontrar (o → ue) to find (like) **(3.1),** meet
encontrarse (o → ue) con to meet
enérgico energetic
enero January
enfadarse (con) to get angry (with, at) **(3.3)**
un **énfasis** emphasis

enfermarse to fall ill
un **enfermero, una enfermera** nurse **(2.1)**
enfermo sick **(1.4)**
un **enfermo, una enferma** sick person **(2.1)**
enfrentarse to face, meet face to face
enfrente de facing, in front of **(6.2)**
enfriar (i → í) to cool
engordar to get fat
un **enigma** enigma
enojado angry **(9.1)**
enojarse (con) to get angry (with, at) **(3.3)**
enorme enormous
enrollar to wrap
una **ensalada** salad
la **enseñanza** teaching
enseñar (a) to teach, show **(2.2)**
entender (e → ie) to understand **(3.1),** hear
enterrado buried
entonces then **(2.4)**
desde entonces from then on
una **entrada** ticket **(2.4)**
entrar (en) to enter **(7.3)**
entre among, between **(6.2)**
* **entregar** to deliver **(2.1)**
el **entrenamiento** training
entrenar to train
una **entrevista** interview **(6.4)**
entusiasta enthusiastic
envidioso envious, jealous
una **enzima** enzyme
un **episodio** episode
una **época** time, period **(5.2)**
equinoccial: la línea equinoccial line of the equator
equipado equipped
un **equipo** team **(2.4)**
la **equitación** horseback riding **(2.4)**
* **equivocarse** to make a mistake, be mistaken **(3.3)**
era was: *see* **ser**
una **era** era
eres you *(fam.)* are: *see* **ser**
* **erigir** to erect
un **error** error
es he (she) is, you *(formal)* are: *see* **ser**
es decir that is to say **(10.4)**
esa that *(f.)* **(2.2)**

ésa that one *(f.)* **(2.2)**
esas those *(f.)* **(2.2)**
ésas those *(f.)* **(2.2)**
escalar to climb, scale **(2.4)**
    escalar la montaña to
      climb the mountain.
una **escalera** stairway, ladder **(5.4)**
    escaparse to escape **(5.3)**
la **esclavitud** slavery
un **esclavo, una esclava** slave **(10.4)**
* **escoger** to choose, select **(6.4)**
    escolar scholastic
    un consejero escolar
      guidance counselor
    esconder to hide **(6.2)**
    escondido hidden **(6.2)**
    escribir to write **(1.4)**
    escribir a máquina to
      typewrite
    una máquina de escribir
      typewriter
    escrito written **(6.3)**
un **escritor, una escritora**
    writer
un **escritorio** desk
    escuchar to listen to **(1.1)**
un **escudo** coat of arms, shield
una **escuela** school **(1.3)**
un **escultor, una escultora**
    sculptor
una **escultura** sculpture
    ese that *(m.)* **(2.2)**
    ése that one *(m.)* **(2.2)**
    esencial essential **(9.2)**
un **esfuerzo** effort
una **esmeralda** emerald
un **esnob, una esnob** snob
    eso that *(neuter)* **(2.3)**
    por eso because of that
      (3.1)
    esos those *(m.)* **(2.2)**
    ésos those *(m.)* **(2.2)**
    espacial spacial, in space
el **espacio** space
    espacioso spacious
una **espalda** back
    nadar de espalda to
      swim on one's back
    España Spain
    español *(f.* **española)**
      Spanish **(1.2)**
    especial special
    especializado specialized
* **especializarse** to specialize
    especialmente especially

    espectacular spectacular
un **espectáculo** sight, spectacle
    (4.3); show
un **espectador, una espectadora**
    spectator
un **espejo** mirror **(2.3)**
la **esperanza** hope
    esperar hope **(1.1)**, wait for,
      to expect
un **espíritu** spirit
una **esposa** wife **(3.4)**
un **esposo** husband **(3.4)**
    los esposos spouses,
      husband and wife
la **espuma** foam
un **esquí** ski
    unos esquís acuáticos
      water skis
    esquiar (i → í) to ski **(1.1)**
    esquiar en el agua to
      waterski **(2.2)**
una **esquina** corner **(8.1)**
    doblar la esquina to turn
      the corner
    esta this *(f.)* **(2.2)**
    esta noche tonight **(6.4)**
    ésta this one *(f.)* **(2.2)**
la **estabilidad** stability
    estable stable, solid
* **establecer** to establish
    establecido established
una **estación** *(pl.* **estaciones)**
    season, station
    una estación de servicio
      service station **(2.1)**
    estacionar to park **(6.1)**
un **estadio** stadium
un **estado** state **(4.4)**
los **Estados Unidos** United States
    estallar to break out
el **estaño** tin
* **estar** to be **(1.4)**
    estar de acuerdo to agree **(4.2)**
    estar de vacaciones to
      be on vacation **(4.1)**
    estar de viaje to be on a
      trip
    estar en la calle to be
      out **(4.1)**
    estas these *(f.)* **(2.2)**
    éstas these *(f.)* **(2.2)**
una **estatua** statue
la **estatura** stature, height
    la estatura mediana
      medium height

    este this *(m.)* **(2.2)**
    éste this one *(m.)* **(2.2)**
un **estereotipo** stereotype
un **estilo** style
    el estilo de vida lifestyle
    estimado held in esteem
    esto this *(neuter)* **(2.3)**
un **estómago** stomach
    un dolor de estómago
      stomachache
    estornudar to sneeze
    estos these *(m.)* **(2.2)**
    éstos these *(m.)* **(2.2)**
una **estrategia** strategy
    estrecho narrow
un **estrecho** strait
una **estrella** star **(8.3)**
un **estreno** premiere
    estricto strict
una **estructura** structure
    estrujar to squeeze
un **estudiante, una estudiante**
    student **(1.2)**
    estudiantil student
    estudiar to study **(1.1)**
    estupendo stupendous
    estúpido stupid **(1.2)**
    estuve I was: *see* **estar**
    eterno eternal **(9.3)**
    étnico ethnic
    Europa Europe
    europeo European
un **europeo, una europea**
    person from Europe
un **evento** event
    exactamente exactly
    exacto exact
una **exageración** *(pl.* **exageraciones)**
    exaggeration
un **examen** *(pl.* **exámenes)** exam
    excelente excellent
una **excepción** *(pl.* **excepciones)**
    exception
    excepcional exceptional
    excepto except **(5.1)**
un **exceso** excess
    excitante exciting
    exclamar to exclaim **(4.3)**
una **excusa** excuse
    excusarse to excuse oneself
    exigente demanding **(10.3)**
* **exigir** to demand **(8.4)**
la **existencia** existence
    existir to exist
el **éxito** success **(5.4)**

tener éxito to be
successful **(5.4)**
exótico exotic
la **expansión** expansion
una **expectación** *(pl.* **expectaciones)**
expectation
una **expedición** *(pl.* **expediciones)**
expedition
una **experiencia** experience
un **experto, una experta** expert
una **explicación** *(pl.* **explicaciones)**
explanation
explicado explained
* **explicar** to explain **(4.2)**
una **exploración** *(pl.* **exploraciones)**
exploration
un **explorador, una exploradora**
explorer
explorar to explore
una **explosión** *(pl.* **explosiones)**
explosion
expresar to express
expresarse to express oneself **(9.2)**
una **expresión** *(pl.* **expresiones)**
expression
expuesto uncovered
expulsado expelled, driven out
exquisito exquisite
extenderse (e → ie) to extend
la **extensión** extension
extranjero foreign **(6.1)**
un **extranjero, una extranjera**
foreigner, stranger
al extranjero abroad
en el extranjero abroad
extraordinario extraordinary
extrasensorial extrasensory
la **percepción**
extrasensorial
extrasensory perception
extraterrestre from outer space
un **extraterrestre** being from
outer space
extravagante extravagant
el **extremo** end, extreme
al extremo to the extreme

f

una **fábrica** factory
* **fabricar** to manufacture,
create
fabuloso fabulous

fácil easy **(5.1)**
fácilmente easily
una **falda** skirt
falso false **(5.1)**
una **falta** lack
faltar to lack, be lacking **(2.4)**
la **fama** fame
el **Salón de Fama** Hall of
Fame
una **familia** family
familiar *(of the)* family
(10.3), familiar
los **familiares** family members
famoso famous
un **fantasma** ghost **(9.3)**
una **casa de fantasmas**
haunted house
fantástico fantastic
un **farmacéutico, una**
farmacéutica pharmacist,
druggist
una **farmacia** pharmacy, drugstore
un **faro** headlight **(4.2)**
un **farol** streetlight
fascinante fascinating
fascinar to fascinate
fatal fatal
fatuo vain
favor: por favor please
favorito favorite
la **fe** faith
febrero February
la **fecha** date
federal federal
la **felicidad** happiness **(8.3)**
las **felicitaciones** congratulations
felicitar to congratulate **(4.4)**
feliz *(pl.* **felices)** happy
un **fenómeno** phenomenon
feo ugly **(1.2)**
una **feria** fair
feroz *(pl.* **feroces)** ferocious
fértil fertile
el **fertilizante** fertilizer
la **ficción** fiction
la **ciencia ficción** science
fiction
una **fiebre** fever
fiel faithful
una **fiesta** party **(1.3)**
una **figura** figure
figurar (en) to be part (of),
figure (in)
fijar to fix
fijo fixed, firm, secure

una **fila** row
la **filosofía** philosophy
el **fin** end
el **fin de semana** weekend
(1.4)
por fin finally
final final
finalmente finally
una **finca** farm
finísimo very fine
fino thin, fine
la **física** physics
físico physical
flaco skinny **(1.2)**
flamenco flamenco
flexible flexible
una **flor** flower **(6.4)**
* **florecer** to flourish
una **florería** flower shop
un **florero, una florera** florist
una **flota** fleet
folklórico folk
el **fondo** bottom
una **forma** form
una **formación** *(pl.* **formaciones)**
formation
formar to form
una **fortaleza** fortress
fortificado fortified
la **fortuna** fortune
probar (o → ue) fortuna
to try one's luck **(7.3)**
una **foto** photo **(2.4)**
la **fotografía** photography **(2.4)**
un **fotógrafo, una fotógrafa**
photographer
un **fragmento** fragment
francés *(f.* **francesa)** French **(1.2)**
Francia France
franciscano Franciscan
una **frase** phrase, sentence
frecuente frequent
frecuentemente frequently
freír (e → i, i) to fry
el **frenesí** frenzy, madness
los **frenos** brakes **(4.2)**
frente a opposite, facing **(4.3)**
enfrente de in front of,
facing **(6.2)**
el **frente** front
fresco cool **(2.2),** fresh
hace fresco it's cool
(weather) **(2.2)**
un **frijol** bean
frío cold **(2.2)**

481

hace frío it's cold *(weather)* **(2.2)**

tengo frío I'm cold **(5.4)**

frito fried

fronterizo border, bordering

la **fruta** fruit **(6.4)**

una **frutería** fruit market **(6.1)**

fue he (she) was, you *(formal)* were: *see* **ser**

un **fuego** fire

una **fuente** fountain

fuera (de) outside (of) **(2.1)**

fuerte strong

la **fuerza** force, strength

fuiste you *(fam.)* were: *see* **ser**

fumar to smoke **(6.1)**

una **función** *(pl.* **funciones)** function

funcionar to function

fundado founded

un **fundador, una fundadora** founder

fundar to found

furioso furious **(1.4)**

el **fútbol** soccer **(2.4)**

jugar al fútbol to play soccer

el **futurismo** futurism

futurista futuristic

el **futuro** future

g

un **gachupín, una gachupina** *Spanish settler in Latin America*

un **galeón** *(pl.* **galeones)** galleon

una **galería** gallery

el **galope** gallop

el **gallego** *language of Galicia*

un **gallego, una gallega** *person from Galicia*

el **ganado** cattle

ganar to earn, win **(1.1)**

ganarse la vida to earn a living

un **garaje** garage

una **gaseosa** soda, carbonated drink

la **gasolina** gasoline **(4.2)**

gastado used

gastar to spend **(4.4)**

un **gasto** expense

un **gato, una gata** cat

el **gazpacho** gazpacho *(soup with tomato, oil, spices; served cold)*

unos **gemelos** binoculars **(8.3)**

una **generación** *(pl.* **generaciones)** generation

general general **(10.3)**

un **general** general

una **generalización** *(pl.* **generalizaciones)** generalization

generalmente generally

el **género** gender

la **generosidad** generosity

generoso generous

un **genio** genius **(3.3)**

la **gente** people **(4.4)**

la **geografía** geography

geométrico geometric

un **gerente, una gerente** manager **(2.1)**

gigante giant

un **gigante** giant

gigantesco gigantic

girar to turn

un **gitano, una gitana** gypsy

una **glándula** gland

un **globo** (hot air) balloon

la **gloria** glory

gloriosamente gloriously

glorioso glorious

la **glucosa** glucose

gobernar (e → ie) to govern

un **gobierno** government

un **golpe** blow

golpear to hit

gordo fat **(1.2)**

el **gordo** top prize

la **gordura** thickness

* **gozar de** to enjoy **(4.1)**

una **grabadora** tape recorder **(1.3)**

grabar to record

gracias thank you

el día de acción de gracias Thanksgiving

gracioso gracious, funny

un **grado** level

graduarse (u → ú) to graduate

gráfico graphic

gran great **(1.3)**

grande big, large; great **(1.3)**

un **grano** grain

grasoso greasy **(8.2)**

Grecia Greece

la **gripe** flu

gris gray

gritar to scream

un **grito** cry

grueso thick **(8.2)**

el **grueso** thickness

un **grupo** group

un **guante** glove

guapísimo very handsome

guapo handsome, beautiful **(1.2)**

el **guaraní** *money of Paraguay, pre-Columbian language*

guardar to keep **(5.1),** put away

la **guardia** guard

un **guardián nocturno** night guard

Guatemala Guatemala

una **guerra** war

una película de guerra war movie

guerrero warlike

un **guía, una guía** guide

una **guía** guidebook **(6.1)**

una **guitarra** guitar

gustar to like, to please, be pleasing **(2.4)**

me gusta(n) I like **(1.1)**

me gusta(n) más I prefer **(1.1)**

me gustaría(n) I would like **(1.1)**

el **gusto** taste

a cada uno su gusto each to his or her own taste

al gusto to your taste

h

* **haber** to have *(auxiliary)* **(6.3)**

había there was, there were: *see* **haber**

hábil skillful

una **habilidad** skill

una **habitación** *(pl.* **habitaciones)** room **(9.4)**

un **habitante, una habitante** inhabitant

un **hábito** habit **(10.4)**

el **habla** *(f.)* speech

de habla hispana Spanish-speaking

hablado spoken

hablar to talk, speak **(1.1)**

habrá there will be: *see* **haber**

un **hacendado, una hacendada**
   rancher
* **hacer** to do, make (3.4)
   hace + *time* (*time*) ago (4.4)
   hace + *time* + **que** +
      (*verb*) to have been ___
      ing for + *time*
   **hace calor (frío, fresco,
      sol, viento)** it's hot
      (cold, cool, sunny,
      windy) (2.2)
   hacer cerámica to make
      pottery (2.4)
   hacer cola to stand in line
   hacer el papel to play
      the role (3.4)
   hacer el payaso to clown
      around
   hacer la cama to make
      the bed
   hacer la maleta to pack a
      suitcase (3.4)
   hacer un viaje to take a
      trip (3.4)
   ¿qué tiempo hace?
      what's the weather?
   se hace is made
* **hacerse** to become (3.4)
   se hizo became
   hacia toward, in the direction
      of (4.2)
una **hacienda** farm
un **hada** (*f.*) fairy
   un cuento de hadas fairytale
una **hamaca** hammock
el **hambre** (*f.*) hunger
   tener hambre to be
      hungry (5.4)
   haré I will make, do; *see* **hacer**
la **harina** flour
   la harina de pescado
      fishmeal
   hasta even, until, down to
   hawaiano Hawaiian
   una tabla hawaiana
      surfboard
   hay there is, there are
   hay que one must, it is
      necessary to (2.4)
   ¿qué hay? what's up?,
      what is it? (2.3)
   haya (*subjunctive of* **haber**)
      there is, there are
   haz do: *see* **hacer**
   he I have (*auxiliary*): *see* **haber**

   hecho done: *see* **hacer**
un **hecho** fact, deed (10.1)
   de hecho in fact (1.1)
una **heladería** ice cream parlor (2.1)

el **helado** ice cream
un **helicóptero** helicopter
un **hemisferio** hemisphere
   hemos we have (*auxiliary*);
      see **haber**
   heredar to inherit
   herido wounded
una **hermana** sister (1.2)
una **hermanita** little sister
un **hermano** brother (1.2)
   los hermanos brothers
      and sisters (1.2)
   hermosísimo very beautiful
   hermoso beautiful (5.1)
un **héroe** hero
una **heroína** heroine
   hervir (e → ie, i) to boil
   hice I did: *see* **hacer**
la **hiedra venenosa** poison ivy
el **hierro** iron
   hierve it boils: *see* **hervir**
una **hija** daughter (1.2)
un **hijo** son (1.2)
   los hijos children (1.2)
un **himno** hymn
   hispano, hispánico Hispanic
un **hispano, una hispana**
      Hispanic person
un **hispanohablante, una
   hispanohablante**
      Spanish-speaking person
la **historia** history
una **historia** story
un **historiador, una historiadora**
      historian
   histórico historical
unas **historietas** comics
un **hocico** snout
el **hockey** hockey
una **hoguera** bonfire, stake
una **hoja** leaf
   hola hi, hello
   holandés (*f.* **holandesa**) Dutch
un **holgazán, una holgazana**
      loafer (5.1)
un **hombre** man (1.2)
   un hombre de negocios
      businessman (7.2)
un **hombrecito** little man
un **hombro** shoulder

   una bolsa al hombro
      backpack
   homogéneo homogeneous
   Honduras Honduras
las **honduras** depths
la **honestidad** honesty
el **honor** honor
   honrado honest
una **hora** hour
un **horario** schedule
una **hormiga** ant
   un oso hormiguero anteater
el **horóscopo** horoscope
el **horror** horror
   ¡qué horror! how
      terrible!, how horrible!
   una película de horror
      horror movie
un **hospital** hospital (2.1)
la **hospitalidad** hospitality
un **hotel** hotel
   hoy today (1.4)
   hoy día today, nowadays (8.2)
   hubo there was: *see* **haber**
   huele it smells
una **huella** track
un **hueso** bone
* **huir** to flee (4.4)
la **humanidad** humanity
   humano human
   un ser humano human being
   húmedo humid
el **humor** mood, humor
   de buen humor in a good
      mood (1.4)
   de mal humor in a bad
      mood (1.4)
   hundirse to sink
un **huracán** (*pl.* **huracanes**)
      hurricane
   huyen they flee

   iba I was going: *see* **ir**
una **idea** idea
   cambiar de idea to
      change one's mind
   ideal ideal
el **idealismo** idealism
   idealista idealistic
un **idealista, una idealista** idealist
la **identidad** identity
la **identificación** identification

* **identificar** to identify
un **idioma** language
  idiota idiotic
un **idiota, una idiota** idiot
  ido gone: *see* **ir**
una **iglesia** church
  igual equal, same
la **igualdad** equality
una **ilusión** *(pl.* **ilusiones)** illusion
una **ilustración** *(pl.* **ilustraciones)**
  illustration
una **imagen** image
la **imaginación** imagination
  imaginar(se) to imagine
  imaginario imaginary
  imaginativo imaginative
un **imitador, una imitadora** mimic
  imitar to imitate
la **impaciencia** impatience
  impacientarse (con) to get
    impatient (because of) **(3.3)**
  impaciente impatient
  imperativo imperative
  imperfecto imperfect
  imperial imperial
un **imperio** empire
un **impermeable** raincoat
  impersonal impersonal
  impertinente impertinent
la **importancia** importance
  importante important **(9.2)**
  importantísimo very
    important
  importar to matter
    me importa(n) it matters
      to me **(2.4)**
    no me importa it doesn't
      matter to me **(6.3)**
  imposible impossible **(5.1)**
  impresionante impressive
  impresionar to impress **(5.1)**
  improbable improbable **(9.3)**
  imprudente careless **(4.4),**
    imprudent, indiscreet
un **impuesto** tax
  impulsivo impulsive
  inaugurar to inaugurate
un **inca, una inca** Inca
  incendiar to burn
un **incendio** fire
  incluyendo including
  increíble unbelievable **(4.3),**
    incredible
  increíblemente incredibly
  indeciso indecisive

  indefinido indefinite
la **independencia** independence
  independentista
    Independent *(political party)*
  independiente independent
  independizarse to become
    independent
  India India
las **Indias** the Indies
* **indicar** to indicate
  indicativo indicative
  indiferente indifferent
  indígena native
  indio Indian
un **indio, una india** Indian
  indirecto indirect
  indisciplinado undisciplined
  indiscreto indiscreet
  indispensable indispensable **(9.2)**
el **individualismo** individualism
  individualista individualist
una **industria** industry
  industrial industrial
  infantil for children, children's
un **infinitivo** infinitive
  inflar to inflate
una **influencia** influence
  influenciar to influence
* **influir** to influence
las **informaciones**
    meteorológicas weather report
  informado informed
  informarse to inform oneself,
    find out
un **ingeniero, una ingeniera**
    engineer
  Inglaterra England
  inglés *(f.* **inglesa)** English **(1.2)**
el **inglés** English *(language)*
un **inglés, una inglesa** *person*
    from England
la **ingratitud** ingratitude
un **ingrediente** ingredient
la **injusticia** injustice
  inmediatamente immediately
un **inmigrante, una inmigrante**
    immigrant
  inmortal immortal
  inolvidable unforgettable **(8.2)**
  inquietar to worry
  inquieto worried
  inquisitivo inquisitive,
    curious **(2.3)**
una **inscripción** *(pl.* **inscripciones)**
    inscription

  insistente insistent
  insistir (en) to insist (on) **(8.2)**
el **insomnio** insomnia
una **inspiración** *(pl.* **inspiraciones)**
    inspiration
  inspirado inspired
  inspirarse to be inspired
  instalar to install, set up
  instantáneo instantaneous
una **institución** *(pl.* **instituciones)**
    institution
una **instrucción** *(pl.* **instrucciones)**
    instruction
un **instructor, una instructora**
    instructor
  instruido educated
un **instrumento** instrument
  un instrumento musical
    musical instrument
  insultar to insult
un **insulto** insult
  intelectual intellectual **(1.2)**
  inteligente intelligent **(1.2)**
  inteligentemente intelligently
una **intención** *(pl.* **intenciones)**
    intention
la **intensidad** intensity
  intentar to try
un **intento** attempt
  interamericano inter- American
un **intercambio** exchange **(7.2)**
  intercontinental
    intercontinental
el **interés** interest
  interesado interested
  interesante interesting **(1.2)**
  interesantísimo very
    interesting
  interesar to interest
    me interesa(n) I am
      interested in **(2.4)**
  interesarse to be interested **(2.4)**
  interior interior
un **intermedio** intermission
  internacional international
  interoceánico interoceanic
  interplanetario interplanetary
una **interpretación** *(pl.*
    interpretaciones)
    interpretation
  interpretar to interpret
un **intérprete, una intérprete**
    interpretor
  interrogativo interrogative
  interrumpir to interrupt

* **intervenir (e → ie, i)** to
    intervene
íntimo intimate
intrigado intrigued
inútil useless **(2.4)**
inútilmente uselessly
invadir to invade
una **invasión** (pl. **invasiones**)
    invasion
invencible invincible,
    unconquerable
inventado invented
inventar to invent
la **investigación** investigation,
    research
un **investigador, una
    investigadora**
    investigator
el **invierno** winter
una **invitación** (pl. **invitaciones**)
    invitation
un **invitado, una invitada** guest
invitar to invite **(1.3)**
* **ir** to go **(1.3)**
    ir de camping to go
        camping **(8.3)**
    ir de compras to go
        shopping **(4.1)**
    ir de vacaciones to go on
        a vacation **(4.1)**
irlandés (f. **irlandesa**) Irish
irónicamente ironically
irregular irregular
la **irrigación** irrigation
irritable irritable **(1.4)**
irritarse (con) to be irritated
    (at, with) **(3.3)**
* **irse (a)** to go (away), to leave
    (for) **(3.2)**
una **isla** island
Italia Italy
italiano Italian
el **italiano** Italian (language)
un **italiano, una italiana** Italian
    (person)
un **itinerario** path
la **izquierda** left (side) **(5.2)**
    a la izquierda on the left **(5.2)**

j

el **jabón** soap **(3.2)**
jactancioso boastful
el **jai alai** jai alai

jamás never **(5.1)**
el **jamón** ham **(6.1)**
el **Japón** Japan
japonés (f. **japonesa**) Japanese
el **japonés** Japanese (language)
un **japonés, una japonesa**
    Japanese (person)
un **jardín** (pl. **jardines**) garden **(6.4)**
una **jaula** cage
el **jazz** jazz
un **jefe, una jefa** chief, boss **(2.1)**
la **jota** national dance of
    Aragon
joven (pl. **jóvenes**) young **(1.2)**
    más joven younger
un **joven, una joven** young
    person **(1.2)**
    jóvenes young people **(1.2)**
un **joyero, una joyera** jeweler
el **judo** judo
un **juego** game
    jueves Thursday
un **jugador, una jugadora** player
* **jugar** (u → ue) to play **(2.4)**
el **jugo** juice
un **juguete** toy **(5.2)**
    julio July
    junco bulrush
        una balsa de junco bulrush raft
una **junta** junta
    junto together **(3.1)**; joined
    junto a next to **(6.2)**
    jurar to swear
la **justicia** justice
    justo fair **(1.4)**
        no es justo it's not fair **(2.4)**
la **juventud** youth **(8.2)**

k

un **kilómetro** kilometer

l

la the (f.) **(1.2)**; her, you (f.
    formal), it **(2.1)**
un **labio** lip
    un lápiz de labios
        lipstick **(3.2)**
un **laboratorio** laboratory
una **ladera** slope
un **lado** side
    al lado de beside **(6.2)**

    por todos lados
        everywhere **(7.4)**
    por un lado on one hand
un **ladrón, una ladrona** thief
un **lago** lake **(6.4)**
una **lámpara** lamp **(6.1)**
la **lana** wool
el **lanzamiento** launching, launch
* **lanzar** to launch, throw
    lanzarse en paracaídas
        to parachute jump
un **lápiz** (pl. **lápices**) pencil
    un lápiz de labios lipstick
    largo long
    a lo largo de along
    las the (f. pl.) **(1.2)**; them
        (f.), you (f. pl.) **(2.1)**
la **lástima** pity
    es lástima (que) it's a
        pity **(9.2)**
    ¡qué lástima! what a
        pity!, too bad! **(3.1)**
la **lata** boredom
    ¡qué lata! what a bore! **(3.1)**
una **lata** tin can
    latín Latin
    Latinoamérica Latin America
    latinoamericano Latin American
una **lavandería** laundry
    lavar to wash **(3.2)**
    lavarse to get washed **(3.2)**
un **lazo** lasso
    le to him, to her, to you
        (formal) **(2.2)**
una **lección** (pl. **lecciones**) lesson
la **lectura** reading **(2.4)**
la **leche** milk **(6.1)**
una **lechería** dairy **(6.1)**
* **leer** to read **(1.4)**
una **legumbre** vegetable **(6.4)**
    lejano far
    lejos (de) far away (from) **(6.2)**
el **lempira** money of Honduras
una **lengua** language, tongue
    lento slow **(4.4)**
    les to them, to you (pl.) **(2.2)**
una **letra** letter
un **letrero** sign, poster, notice **(6.1)**
    levantarse to get up **(3.2)**
una **leyenda** legend
    leyó he (she) (you) (formal)
        read: see **leer**
    liberar to liberate
la **libertad** liberty

un libertador, una libertadora
   liberator
Libra Libra *(zodiac sign)*
una libra pound
libre free
   al aire libre outdoors
una librería bookstore **(6.1)**
una libreta memo book **(2.3)**
un libro book **(1.3)**
una licuadora blender
un líder, una líder leader
una lidia fight, bullfight
   unos toros de lidia
     fighting bulls
una liebre hare
una limitación *(pl.* **limitaciones)**
   limitation
limitado limited
limitar to limit
un límite limit
limpiar to clean **(4.2)**
la limpieza cleanliness
limpio clean **(4.4)**
lindo pretty
una línea line **(6.2)**
   la línea equinoccial line
     of the equator
   una línea aérea airline
una linterna lantern
   una linterna eléctrica
     flashlight **(8.3)**
un lío entanglement, mess
   ¡qué lío! what a mess!,
     what a mix-up! **(3.1)**
   un lío de tránsito traffic jam
una lista list
listo clever *(with* **ser)** **(1.2)**;
   ready, prepared *(with*
   estar) **(1.4)**
la literatura literature
un litro liter
lo it, that; him, you *(m.*
   formal) **(2.1)**
   lo que that which, what **(5.1)**
   lo siguiente the following,
     what follows
   por lo tanto therefore
un lobo, una loba wolf
local local
localizar to localize
una loción *(pl.* **lociones)** lotion
   la loción bronceadora
     suntan lotion
loco crazy **(1.2)**
lógicamente logically

lógico logical **(9.2)**
lograr to manage to
los the *(m. pl.)* **(1.2)**; them
   (m.), you *(m. pl.)* **(2.1)**
una lotería lottery **(8.3)**
un lotero, una lotera lottery
   ticket seller
las luces direccionales
   directional lights
la lucha fighting
luchar to fight
luego then **(3.2)**
un lugar place **(6.1)**
   en lugar de instead of
   tener lugar to take place
un lujo luxury
la luna moon **(7.1)**
lunes Monday
una luz *(pl.* **luces)** light **(4.2)**
   una luz de semáforo
     traffic light **(8.1)**

11

una llama llama
una llamada call **(4.4)**
   llamar to call **(1.3)**
   llamar por teléfono to
     call on the telephone **(1.3)**
   llamarse to be called
una llanta tire **(4.2)**
una llave key **(2.3)**
la llegada arrival **(7.2)**
 * **llegar** to arrive, get to **(5.2)**
   llegar a oídos to reach
     the ears
llenar to fill **(4.2)**
lleno full **(6.2)**; crowded
llevar take (along) **(1.1)**
llevarse to take away, carry away
   llevarse (con) to get
     along (with) **(3.4)**
llorar to cry **(7.4)**
llover (o → ue) to rain **(3.1)**
la lluvia rain

m

una madeja skein
la madera wood **(7.4)**
un madero beam
una madre mother **(1.2)**
   maduro ripe

maestro master
   una obra maestra work
     of art, masterpiece
mágico magic, magical
magnético magnetic
magnífico magnificent
el maíz corn, maize
la majestad majesty
   vuestras majestades
     your majesties
mal badly **(1.1)**
   de mal humor in a bad
     mood **(1.4)**
   mal educado impolite **(5.2)**
   portarse mal to
     misbehave **(3.3)**
una maleta suitcase **(3.4)**
   hacer la maleta to pack a
     suitcase **(3.4)**
malo bad **(1.2)**, sick **(1.4)**
   malos modales bad
     manners **(5.2)**
   ¡qué malo! how awful! **(3.1)**
maltratar to mistreat **(5.2)**
mamá mom, mother **(1.2)**
mandar to send **(2.2)**, to
   order **(8.4)**
un mandato order, command **(8.4)**
el mando command
el manejo driving, management **(9.2)**
una manera manner **(9.2)**, way
   de alguna manera (in)
     some way **(5.1)**
   de ninguna manera (in)
     no way **(5.1)**
   de una manera in a way **(3.2)**
una mano hand **(3.4)**
una manta blanket **(8.3)**
 * **mantener (e → ie)** to claim,
   maintain, keep
 * **mantenerse (e → ie)** to
   remain, keep *(oneself)*
la mantequilla butter **(6.1)**
una manzana apple **(6.1)**
mañana tomorrow **(1.4)**
una mañana morning **(1.4)**
   por la mañana in the
     morning **(1.4)**
un mapa map **(6.1)**
una máquina machine
   escribir a máquina to
     typewrite
   una máquina de escribir
     typewriter
el mar sea

el nivel del mar sea level
un maratón (*pl.* **maratones**) marathon
una maravilla wonder
maravilloso marvelous **(1.1)**, wonderful
una marca brand
marcado marked, branded
* **marcar** to mark
un marciano Martian
marcharse to leave **(3.2)**
una margarita daisy **(6.4)**
un marido husband
Marte Mars
martes Tuesday
marzo March
más more **(1.1)**
  más de more than **(8.2)**
  más joven younger
  más o menos more or less **(3.4)**
  me gusta(n) más I prefer **(1.1)**
* **mascar** to chew
una máscara mask
matar to kill
el mate herb tea
las matemáticas mathematics
el material material
una matrícula license
  un número de matrícula license plate **(4.2)**
matrimonial matrimonial
  una agencia matrimonial marriage counselor
el matrimonio marriage **(3.4)**
un maya, una maya Maya
mayor greater, greatest, older, main
  la plaza mayor main square
los mayores adults **(5.1)**
la mayoría majority **(8.2)**
una mazorca ear *(of corn)*
me me, to me **(2.3)**; myself **(3.2)**
un mecánico, una mecánica mechanic **(2.1)**
un mecanógrafo, una mecanógrafa typist
una medalla medal **(2.3)**
la media mean, half
  (las dos) y media half past (two)
mediano medium
  la estatura mediana medium height
la medicina medicine
un médico, una médica doctor **(2.1)**

una medida measurement
medio half
el medio middle
  en medio de in the middle of **(6.2)**
un medio means **(7.1)**
Mediterráneo Mediterranean
mejor better **(3.1)**, best **(1.2)**
un melocotón (*pl.* **melocotones**) peach
memorable memorable
una memoria memory
menor younger, youngest **(4.1)**
menos less **(1.1)**; minus
  a menos que unless **(10.1)**
  (en) menos de (in) less than **(8.2)**
  más o menos more or less **(3.4)**
  por lo menos at least
un mensaje message
una mensualidad monthly allowance
la mente mind **(9.3)**
mentir (e → ie, i) to lie **(3.1)**
una mentira lie **(5.1)**
una menudencia small thing
menudo: a menudo often **(1.3)**
un mercado market **(1.3)**
* **merecer** to deserve **(2.1)**; to merit
el merengue merengue *(dance)*
un mes month
una mesa table **(6.1)**
un mestizo, una mestiza *person of Indian and European ancestry*
una meta goal **(6.4)**
meter to put (in) **(9.1)**
  meter la pata to blunder **(9.1)**
meteorológico weather
un método method **(8.2)**
un metro meter
mexicano Mexican **(1.2)**
México Mexico
una mezcla mix
mezclar to blend, mix
mi, mis my **(2.1)**
mí me *(after prep.)*
el miedo fear
  tener miedo to be afraid **(5.4)**
un miembro member
mientras while **(5.3)**
miércoles Wednesday
mil thousand, a thousand
milagrosamente miraculously

milagroso miraculous
un militar military man
una milla mile
un millón (*pl.* **millones**) million
un millonario, una millonaria millionaire
una mina mine
mineral mineral
una minicomedia mini-comedy
un mini-drama mini-drama
mínimo minimum
un minuto minute
mío my, of mine **(4.2)**
  ¡Dios mío! my goodness! **(4.3)**
el mío mine
mirar to watch, look at **(1.1)**
una misa Mass
una misión (*pl.* **misiones**) mission
mismo same **(2.1)**
  sí mismo oneself
un misterio mystery
  una película de misterio mystery movie
misterioso mysterious **(2.3)**
una mitad half **(7.3)**
mitológico mythological
una mochila knapsack, backpack **(8.3)**
la moda fashion **(1.4)**
los modales manners
  buenos modales good manners **(5.2)**
  malos modales bad manners **(5.2)**
modelo model
un modelo model
moderno modern **(5.1)**
molestar to bother, annoy **(3.3)**
  (me) molesta (que) it bothers (me) (that), I mind **(9.1)**
molido ground
un molino de viento windmill
un momento moment
  ¡un momento! wait a minute! **(2.4)**
una monarquía monarchy
un monasterio monastery
una moneda coin **(2.3)**
monetario monetary
un mono, una mona monkey
un monstruo monster
una montaña mountain **(6.4)**
montar to get on
  montar a caballo to ride a horse **(2.4)**
un monumento monument

un **moped** moped
moral moral
moreno dark (1.2), brown
morir (o → ue, u) to die
mortal mortal
un **mosquito** mosquito
mostrar (o → ue) to show (3.1)
un **motivo** motive, reason
una **moto** motorcycle (1.3)
una **motocicleta** motorcycle
un **motor** motor (4.2)
móvil mobile
un **movimiento** movement
mozo: buen mozo good-looking (9.4)
una **muchacha** girl (1.2)
un **muchacho** boy (1.2)
los **muchachos** boys and girls
muchísimo very much, a great deal
mucho much (1.1)
muchos many (1.3)
la **mudanza** moving
un **agente de mudanzas** moving agency
mudarse to move (10.4)
una **mueblería** furniture store (6.1)
un **muelle** wharf
la **muerte** death (9.3)
muere he (she) dies, you (formal) die: see **morir**
muerto dead: see **morir**
un **muerto, una muerta** dead person
una **mujer** woman (1.2)
una **mula** mule
un **mulero** mule-boy
una **multitud** multitude
mundial world, worldly
el **mundo** world (1.3)
el **Nuevo Mundo** New World
todo el mundo everyone
municipal municipal
un **mural** mural
una **muralla** wall
un **museo** museum
la **música** music (2.4)
musical musical
un **instrumento musical** musical instrument
una **comedia musical** musical comedy
un **músico, una música** musician
muy very (1.1)

n

* **nacer** to be born
nacido born
una **nación** (pl. **naciones**) nation
nacional national
la **nacionalidad** nationality
nada nothing, not anything (5.1)
nadar to swim (1.1)
nadar de espalda to swim on one's back
nadie nobody, no one, not anyone (5.1)
el **náhuatl** language of the Aztecs
los **naipes** playing cards
jugar a los naipes to play cards
una **naranja** orange (fruit) (6.1)
una **nariz** (pl. **narices**) nose
la **natación** swimming (2.4)
nativo native
natural natural (9.2)
la **naturaleza** nature
naturalmente naturally
un **naufragio** shipwreck
una **navaja** folding knife, penknife (2.3)
naval naval
una **nave** ship
la **navegación** navigation
un **navegante, una navegante** navigator
* **navegar** to sail (2.2), to navigate
la **Navidad** Christmas
necesariamente necessarily
necesario necessary (2.4)
necesitar to need (1.3)
la **negación** negation
* **negar (e → ie)** to deny (9.3)
* **negarse (e → ie)** to refuse
negativamente negatively
negativo negative
la **negligencia** negligence
negligente negligent
negociar to negotiate
los **negocios** business
un **hombre de negocios** businessman (7.2)
negro black
nervioso nervous (1.4)
ni nor (5.1)
ni ... ni neither ... nor (5.1)
ni siquiera not even
Nicaragua Nicaragua
nicaragüense Nicaraguan

la **nieve** snow
ninguno none, no (5.1)
la **niñez** childhood (5.2)
un **niño, una niña** child (1.2)
el **níquel** nickel
el **nitrato** nitrate
un **nivel** level
el **nivel del mar** sea level
no no, not (1.1)
¡claro que no! of course not!
no ... todavía not yet (6.3)
no me importa it doesn't matter to me (6.3)
ya no no longer
nocturno nighttime
un **guardián nocturno** night guard
una **noche** night (1.4)
de noche at night
esta noche tonight (6.4)
por la noche at night (1.4)
Noel Christmas
el **Papá Noel** Father Christmas, Santa Claus
nombrar to name
un **nombre** name
normal normal
el **norte** north
norteamericano North American (1.2)
noruego Norwegian
nos us, to us (2.3); ourselves (3.2), each other (3.4)
nosotros(as) we (1.1), us (after prep.)
una **nota** note, mark, grade
las **noticias** news (2.1)
novecientos nine hundred
una **novela** novel
noveno ninth
un **novio, una novia** boyfriend, girlfriend (1.2); sweetheart, fiancé(e)
un **ramo de novia** bridal bouquet
una **nube** cloud
nublado cloudy (2.2)
nuclear nuclear
los **armamentos nucleares** nuclear arms
un **nudo** knot
nuestro our (2.1); of ours (4.2)
nueve nine
nuevo another, different, new (1.3)
de nuevo again (3.4)

el **Año Nuevo** New Year
el **Nuevo Mundo** New
World
numeral numeral
numérico numerical
un **número** number
un **número de matrícula**
license plate (4.2)
un **número de teléfono**
telephone number
numeroso numerous
nunca never (1.1)

o

o or (1.3)
* **obedecer** to obey (2.1)
un **obelisco** obelisk
un **objetivo** objective
un **objeto** object (1.3)
una **obligación** (*pl.* **obligaciones**)
obligation
obligado obliged, obligated
una **obra** work
una **obra de teatro**
(*theatrical*) play (2.4)
una **obra maestra** work
of art, masterpiece
una **obra teatral**
(*theatrical*) play
la **observación** observation
observar to observe
* **obtener** (e → ie) to obtain,
get (8.1)
obvio obvious
una **ocasión** (*pl.* **ocasiones**)
occasion
occidental western
un **océano** ocean
octavo eighth
una **ocupación** (*pl.* **ocupaciones**)
occupation
ocupado occupied, busy
un **ocupante, una ocupante**
occupant
ocupar to occupy
ocuparse (de) to occupy
oneself (in) (3.3); be busy (in)
ocurrir to occur, happen (5.3)
ochenta eighty
ocho eight
ochocientos eight hundred
una **oda** ode

odiar to hate (1.1)
el **oeste** West
una **película del oeste**
western
una **oferta** offer
oficial official
oficialmente officially
una **oficina** office (5.3)
* **ofrecer** to offer (2.1)
el **oído** hearing, ear
llegar a oídos to reach
the ears
* **oír** to hear (3.4)
ojalá (que) I wish, let's hope
that, if only (8.4)
una **ojeada** glance
dar una ojeada to glance
un **ojo** eye
una **ola** wave
correr las olas to surf
olímpico Olympic
una **oliva** olive tree
olvidar to forget (6.3)
una **olla** pot
una **ópera** opera (2.4)
una **operación** (*pl.* **operaciones**)
operation
una **opinión** (*pl.* **opiniones**) opinion
* **oponerse** to be against (8.4)
una **oportunidad** opportunity
la **oposición** opposition
el **optimismo** optimism
optimista optimistic
un **optimista, una optimista** optimist
el **opuesto** opposite
un **orden** order
ordenado ordered
ordinal ordinal
ordinario ordinary
una **organización** (*pl.*
organizaciones)
organization
la **Organización de**
Estados Americanos
Organization of
American States (OAS)
organizado organized
* **organizar** to organize
el **orgullo** pride
orgulloso proud (4.4)
la **orientación** orientation
oriental oriental, eastern
el **oriente** Orient
un **origen** (*pl.* **orígenes**) origin
la **originalidad** originality

originarse to originate
una **orilla** bank (*of a river*), shore
el **oro** gold (6.4)
un **Oscar** Oscar (*award*)
la **oscuridad** obscurity,
darkness
un **oso hormiguero** anteater
otro other, another (1.3)
un **OVNI** UFO
el **oxígeno** oxygen
¡**oye!** listen! (2.3)
oyen they hear: *see* **oír**

p

la **paciencia** patience (8.1)
tener paciencia to be patient
(8.1)
paciente patient
un **paciente, una paciente**
patient
pacífico peaceful
el **Pacífico** Pacific
un **padre** father (1.2)
los **padres** parents
la **paella** paella (*rice dish with*
fish and chicken)
la **paga** pay, payment
el **paganismo** paganism
* **pagar** to pay
un **país** country (3.4)
un **paisaje** landscape
los **Países Bajos** the Low
Countries (*Netherlands,*
Belgium, Luxembourg)
un **pájaro** bird
una **palabra** word (4.4)
una **palabrota** dirty word
un **palacio** palace
pálido pale (6.2)
una **palma** palm tree
el **pan** bread (6.1)
una **panadería** bakery (6.1)
Panamá Panama
un **panameño, una panameña**
Panamanian
unos **pantalones** pants
unos **pantalones cortos**
shorts
un **pañuelo** handkerchief (2.3)
papá dad (1.2)
el **Papá Noel** Father
Christmas, Santa Claus
un **papagayo** parrot

una **papaya** papaya
el **papel** paper, piece of paper (4.4)
    una **toalla de papel**
      paper towel
un **papel** role, part (3.4)
    hacer el papel to play
      the part (3.4)
un **paquete** package (6.2)
un **par** pair
    para for (1.3); in order to
un **parabrisas** windshield (4.2)
un **paracaídas** parachute
    lanzarse en paracaídas
      to parachute jump
una **parada** stop (6.4)
un **paraguas** umbrella (10.2)
el **Paraguay** Paraguay
    parar(se) to stop (4.3)
un **parasol** parasol
 * **parecer** to seem, look (2.1)
 * **parecerse** to resemble
un **parecido** similarity
una **pared** wall (6.4)
un **paréntesis** parenthesis
un **pariente** relative (1.2)
un **parque** park (6.4)
un **párrafo** paragraph
una **parte** part
    en (a) alguna parte
      somewhere (5.1)
    en (a) ninguna parte
      nowhere (5.1)
un **participante, una**
    participante participant
un **participio** participle
particular particular
    en particular in particular
particularmente particularly
un **partido** game (2.4)
    un partido de básquetbol
      basketball game
    partir to leave (6.4)
    pasado last (1.4) (6.4); passed by
el **pasado** past
un **pasajero, una pasajera**
    passenger (8.1)
    pasar to happen (4.4) (4.1)
un **pasatiempo** pastime
la **Pascua** Easter, Passover
    la Isla de Pascua Easter
      Island
    pasear to walk (10.2)
un **paseo** walk, ride
    dar un paseo to go for a
      walk, ride (4.3)

la **pasión** passion
un **paso** crossing
    un paso de peatones
      pedestrian crossing,
      crosswalk (8.1)
un **pastel** pastry, pie (6.1)
una **pastilla** pill, tablet (8.2)
    una pastilla para dormir
      sleeping pill
una **pata** paw
    meter la pata to blunder
paternal paternal
paterno paternal
el **patinaje** skating (2.4)
    patinar to skate (2.4)
los **patines de ruedas** roller
    skates
un **patio** patio
la **patria** mother country,
    homeland
un **patriota, una patriota**
    patriot
el **patriotismo** patriotism
un **payaso** clown (5.1)
    hacer el payaso to clown
      around
la **paz** peace (7.1)
un **peaje** toll booth
un **peatón, una peatona**
    pedestrian (8.1)
    un paso de peatones
      pedestrian crossing,
      crosswalk (8.1)
una **peculiaridad** peculiarity
un **pedazo** piece
un **pedigüeño** leech
    pedir (e → i, i) to ask (for)
      (3.1)
    pedir prestado to borrow
      (5.1)
el **pegamento** glue
 * **pegar** to stick, glue
    peinarse to comb *(one's hair)*
      (3.2)
un **peine** comb (2.3)
    pelar to peel
una **pelea** fight
    pelear(se) to quarrel, fight (3.4)
una **película** film, movie (2.4)
    una película de vaqueros
      cowboy movie
el **peligro** danger
    peligroso dangerous (2.4)
el **pelo** hair
una **pelota** ball (1.3)

una **pelota de tenis** tennis ball
una **peluca** wig
una **peluquería** barber shop, hair-
    dresser
la **pena** grief
un **pendiente** earring (2.3)
    pensar (e → ie) to think (3.1)
      pensar + *inf*. to intend (3.1)
      pensar de to think of,
        have an opinion about (3.1)
      pensar en to think about (3.1)
una **peña** rock, large stone, cliff (6.4)
    peor worse (10.3) worst
un **pepino** cucumber
    pequeño small, little (1.3)
una **pera** pear (6.1)
un **percance** mishap
la **percepción** perception
    la percepción
      extrasensorial
      extrasensory perception
    perder (e → ie) to lose,
      waste, miss (3.1)
    perder el tiempo to
      waste time
    perdido lost
    perdonar to pardon, excuse
      perdóneme excuse me
    perezoso lazy (1.2)
la **perfección** perfection
    perfectamente perfectly
    perfecto perfect
un **perfume** perfume
una **perfumería** perfume shop
un **periódico** newspaper (1.3)
un **periodista, una periodista**
    journalist
un **periquito** parakeet
una **perla** pearl
 * **permanecer** to stay
    permanente permanent
el **permiso** permission, permit (4.2)
    un permiso de conducir
      driver's license (4.2)
    permitir to permit (4.4)
    pero but (1.3)
un **perrito** little dog
un **perro** dog
 * **perseguir (e → i, i)** to chase
una **persona** person
    una persona de edad
      older person (7.2)
un **personaje** character
    personal personal
una **personalidad** personality (5.1)

personalmente personally

una **perspectiva** perspective

la **persuasión** persuasion

* **pertenecer** to belong to, be a
member of **(2.1)**

el **Perú** Peru

pesar to weigh

a pesar de in spite of

un **pescado** fish *(caught)*

un **pescador** fisherman

la harina de pescado
fishmeal

* **pescar** to fish **(2.2)**

una caña de pescar
fishing pole

la **peseta** *money of Spain*

pesimista pessimistic

el **peso** *Hispanic money*

pesquero fishing

el **petróleo** oil

una **petición** *(pl.* **peticiones)**
petition

un **pez** *(pl.* **peces)** fish *(live)* **(6.4)**

un **piano** piano

picado minced

un **picnic** picnic

un **pico** peak

pide he (she) asks, you
(formal) ask; *see* **pedir**

un **pie** foot **(3.4)**

a pie by foot

una **piedra** stone **(2.2)**

la **piel** fur

pienso I think: *see* pensar

pierdo I lose: *see* **perder**

una **pierna** leg

unos **pijamas** pajamas

una **pila** battery

pilotar to pilot

un **piloto** pilot

el **pimiento** pepper

el **ping pong** ping-pong **(2.4)**

jugar al ping pong to
play ping-pong **(2.4)**

pintado painted

pintar to paint **(2.4)**

pintarse to put on makeup **(3.2)**

un **pintor, una pintora** painter

pintoresco picturesque

la **pintura** painting **(2.4)**

una **pipa** pipe

una **pirámide** pyramid

un **pirata** pirate

pisar to step on

una **piscina** swimming pool **(1.3)**

un **piso** floor *(of a building)* **(4.3)**

una **pistola** pistol

una **pizza** pizza

un **plan** plan

planear to plan

un **planeta** planet **(7.1)**

una **planta** plant **(6.4)**

la **planta baja** street floor

una **plantación** *(pl.* **plantaciones)**
plantation

plantar to plant

el **plástico** plastic

la **plata** silver

un **plátano** plantain, banana

un **platillo volador** flying saucer

un **plato** dish, plate **(5.3)**

una **playa** beach **(1.3)**

una **plaza** plaza, square

la plaza mayor main square

una plaza de toros bullring

una **pluma** feather

el **pluscuamperfecto** pluperfect

la **población** population **(7.1)**

poblar to populate

pobre poor **(1.2)**

pobre de ti poor you

un **pobre, una pobre** poor person

pobrecito poor you, poor him

poco little **(1.1)**

pocos few

un **poco** a little **(2.1)**

* **poder** (o → ue) to be able
(to), can **(3.1)**

el **poder** power **(9.3)**

poderoso powerful

podremos we will be able to:
see **poder**

un **poema** poem

la **poesía** poetry

un **poeta, una poeta** poet

el **póker** poker

jugar al póker to play poker

la **policía** police

un **policía** police officer **(2.1)**

policíaco detective

una película policíaca
detective movie

la **política** politics

un **político, una política** politician

un **polvo** powder

los polvos particles, dust

un **pollo** chicken **(6.1)**

un **poncho** poncho

pondrá he (she) (you)
(formal) will put: *see* **poner**

* **poner** to put, put on **(3.4)**

* **ponerse** to become, to put on
(clothing) **(3.4)**

ponerse + adj. to get,
become + *adj.* **(3.4)**

ponerse rojo to blush

popular popular

la **popularidad** popularity

* **popularizar** to popularize

poquito little bit

por for **(2.3)**, during, in, by,
along, through, in exchange
for **(2.3) (7.2)**

ciento por ciento one
hundred percent **(1.2)**

por ciento percent **(1.2)**

por ejemplo for example

por el día during the day
(3.2)

por eso because of that **(3.1)**

por favor please

por fin finally

por la mañana in the
morning **(1.4)**

por la noche at night **(1.4)**

por la tarde in the
afternoon **(1.4)**

por lo general in general
(10.3)

por lo menos at least

por lo tanto even, therefore

¿por qué? why? **(1.1)**

por supuesto of course

por todos lados
everywhere **(7.4)**

por un lado on one hand

¡va por … ! it's a deal
for … !

porque because

portarse to behave

portarse bien to behave
(3.3)

portarse mal to
misbehave **(3.3)**

porteño *from Buenos Aires*

un **portero, una portera** doorkeeper

portugués *(f.* **portuguesa)**
Portuguese

un **portugués, una portuguesa**
Portuguese

una **posada** inn

las posadas *pre-
Christmas celebration*

una **posesión** *(pl.* **posesiones)**
possession

una **posibilidad** possibility
posible possible **(5.1)**
posiblemente possibly
una **posición** *(pl.* **posiciones)**
position
positivamente positively
positivo positive
postal postal
una **postal** postcard
el **postre** dessert
un **pozo** well
una **práctica** practice, custom
práctico practical
un **precio** price
precioso precious
precolombino pre-Columbian
precoz precocious
* **predecir** to predict **(9.3)**
una **predicción** *(pl.* **predicciones)**
prediction
una **preferencia** preference, right
of way
preferir (e → ie, i) to prefer
(3.1)
una **pregunta** question
preguntar to ask, ask a
question
prehistórico prehistoric
un **premio** prize **(8.3)**
el **premio Nóbel** Nobel prize
preocupado preoccupied,
worried **(1.4)**
preocupar to worry **(2.4)**, to
preoccupy
me preocupa(n) I am
worried (by) **(2.4)**
preocuparse (por) to be
worried (because of) **(3.3)**
una **preparación** *(pl.*
preparaciones)
preparation
preparar to prepare
prepararse to get ready **(3.2)**
una **preposición** *(pl.*
preposiciones)
preposition
la **presencia** presence
la **presencia de ánimo**
presence of mind **(4.4)**
presentar to introduce **(10.1)**
presente present
el **presente** present
un **presidente, una presidente**
president
prestado borrowed

pedir prestado to borrow
(5.1)
prestar to lend **(2.2)**
prestar atención to pay
attention
el **prestigio** prestige
presumido stuck up, snobbish
el **pretérito** preterite, past tense
primero first **(3.4)**
un **primo, una prima** cousin **(1.2)**
principal principal, main
lo principal the main
thing
principalmente principally,
mainly
un **príncipe** prince
un **principio** principle, beginning
una **prisa** hurry
darse prisa to hurry **(3.2)**
de prisa quickly **(4.2)**
tener prisa to be in a
hurry **(5.4)**
una **prisión** *(pl.* **prisiones)** prison
un **prisionero, una prisionera**
prisoner
privado private
pro favor, advantage
en pro for, in favor of
la **probabilidad** probability
probable probable **(9.3)**
probablemente probably
probar (o → ue) to try out
(4.2), test, taste **(3.1)**
probar fortuna to try
one's luck **(7.3)**
un **problema** problem
proclamar to proclaim
un **prodigio** prodigy, marvel
* **producir** to produce
un **producto** product
un **productor, una productora**
producer
profesional professional
un **profesor, una profesora**
professor, teacher **(2.1)**
profundamente profoundly
un **programa** program **(2.4)**
**un programa de
variedades** variety show
progresivo progressive
el **progreso** progress **(7.1)**
la **prohibición** prohibition **(8.4)**
prohibir to prohibit **(6.1)**
se prohibe it is forbidden
una **promesa** promise

prometer to promise **(3.4)**
prometido promised
un **promotor, una promotora**
promoter
un **pronombre** pronoun
* **pronosticar** to predict
pronto soon, quickly **(7.1)**
una **pronunciación** *(pl.*
pronunciaciones)
pronunciation
una **propina** tip
propio own **(4.3)**
* **proponer** to propose
una **propiedad** property
el **propósito** aim, meaning
próspero prosperous
la **protección** protection
un **protector, una protectora**
protector
* **proteger** to protect
provecho: ¡buen provecho!
enjoy it!, good appetite!
una **provincia** province
próximo next **(1.4)**
prudente cautious, careful **(4.4)**
prudentemente carefully
la **psicología** psychology
psicológico psychological
un **psicotest** psychotest
* **publicar** to publish
la **publicidad** publicity
público public
el **público** public
pude I could: *see* **poder**
un **pueblecito** small town
un **pueblo** town **(8.1)**
puedo I can: *see* **poder**
un **puente** bridge **(7.3)**
una **puerta** door
un **puerto** port
Puerto Rico Puerto Rico
un **puertorriqueño, una
puertorriqueña** Puerto Rican
pues then, therefore, well
puesto put: *see* **poner** **(6.3)**
un **puesto** stand
pulcro neat
pulido polished
una **pulsera** bracelet **(2.3)**
un reloj de pulsera wrist
watch **(2.3)**
una **punta** end
un **punto** point **(5.2)**, dot
en punto on the dot **(8.4)**
puntual punctual

la **puntualidad** punctuality
una **pupila** pupil *(eye)*
un **purista, una purista** purist
puro pure
puse I put: *see* **poner**

q

que who, whom, which, that
(9.4), than
hay que one has to, one
ought to, it is necessary
que Dios te ayude may
God help you (8.3)
¡qué! what!, how!
¡qué ...! what a ...!
(2.4)
¡qué alivio! what a relief!
(7.4)
¡qué barbaridad! what
nonsense! (1.4)
¡qué bueno! how great!
(3.1)
¡qué horror! how
horrible!
¡qué lástima! what a
pity! (3.1)
¡qué lata! what a bore! (3.1)
¡qué lío! what a mess! (3.1)
¡qué malo! how awful! (3.1)
¡qué será de mí! what
will become of me! (7.4)
¡qué va! nonsense! (3.1)
¿qué? what? (1.1)
¿por qué? why? (1.1)
¿qué cosa? what thing?,
what is it? (2.3)
¿qué hay? what's up?,
what is it? (2.3)
¿qué más? what else?
¿qué pasó? what
happened? (4.4)
quebrado broken (6.2)
quebrar (e → ie) to break
(6.2)
el **quechua** *Inca language
spoken in Peru*
quedarse to stay (3.2);
remain
me queda(n) __ I have __
left (8.3)
quejarse de to complain
about (3.3)

quemado burned, scorched
(6.2)
una **quemadura** burn
una quemadura de sol
sunburn
quemar to scorch, burn (5.3)
* **querer (e → ie)** to want,
wish (3.1)
querer a to like, love
(someone) (3.1)
querido dear, loved
querrá he (she) (you)
(formal) will want: *see*
querer
el **queso** cheese (6.1)
el **quetzal** quetzal, *money of
Guatemala*
quien who, whom (9.4)
¿quién(es)? who?, whom? (1.1)
¿de quién(es)? whose?
quiero I want: *see* **querer**
quieto quiet, peaceful
la **química** chemistry
químico chemical
quince fifteen
quinientos five hundred
la **quinina** quinine
quinto fifth
quirúrgico surgical
quise I wanted, tried: *see*
querer
quitarse to take *(something)*
off (3.2)
quizá perhaps, maybe (2.1)

r

racial racial
racional rational
racionalmente rationally
un **radiador** radiator (4.2)
el **radical** root, stem *(of a word)*
la **radio** radio *(emission)*
un **radio** radio *(set)* (1.3)
una **raíz** *(pl.* **raíces)** root
un **ramo** bouquet
un ramo de novia bridal
bouquet
una **rana** frog
un **rancho** ranch
rápidamente rapidly, quickly
rápido rapid, fast (4.4)
una **raqueta** racket (1.3)
raro rare, strange (5.1)

raras veces rarely
un **rascacielos** skyscraper
un **rasgo** characteristic
un **rastro** flea market
un **ratito** little while
un **rato** short time
un **ratón** *(pl.* **ratones)** mouse
una **raya** line, line between two
countries, frontier
una **raza** race, generation
la **razón** reason (9.3)
no tener razón to be
wrong (5.4)
tener razón to be right (5.4)
una **reacción** *(pl.* **reacciones)** reaction
reaccionar to react (7.3)
real real, royal
la **realidad** reality
realista realistic
* **realizar** to accomplish
* **realizarse** to come true
realmente really
una **reata** lariat
una **rebelión** *(pl.* **rebeliones)**
rebellion
una **receta** recipe
recibido received
recibir to receive, get (1.4)
reciente recent
recientemente recently
la **reciprocidad** reciprocity
recíproco reciprocal
* **recoger** to pick up (6.4)
una **recomendación** *(pl.*
recomendaciones)
recommendation
recomendar (e → ie) to
recommend (8.4), to advise
una **recompensa** reward (4.4)
* **reconocer** to recognize (7.2)
una **reconquista** reconquest
* **reconstruir** to reconstruct
recordar (o → ue) to
remember (3.1)
rectangular rectangular
un **recuerdo** memory
un **recurso** resource
redondo round
* **reemplazar** to replace
referir (e → ie, i) to refer
reflejar to reflect
un **reflejo** reflex, reflection
reflexivo reflexive
un **refrán** *(pl.* **refranes)** proverb,
saying (6.4)

un **refresco** refreshment
una **refrigeradora** refrigerator
un **refugiado, una refugiada** refugee
   refugiarse to take refuge
un **refugio** shelter
   regalar to give *(as a gift)* **(2.2)**
un **regalo** gift **(1.3)**
* **regar (e → ie)** to spill
un **régimen** *(pl.* **regímenes)**
   regimen, diet
una **región** *(pl.* **regiones)** region
una **regla** rule
   regresar to return **(4.1)**
   regular regular
   regularmente regularly
una **reina** queen
un **reino** kingdom
   reír (e → i, i) to laugh **(3.1)**
   reírse (e → i, i) de to laugh,
      make fun of
una **relación** *(pl.* **relaciones)** relation
   relativo relative
una **religión** *(pl.* **religiones)** religion
   religioso religious
un **reloj** watch, clock **(1.3)**
      un **reloj pulsera** wrist
         watch **(2.3)**
una **relojería** watch shop
un **remedio** remedy
   remoto remote
   rendirse (e → i, i) to surrender
   reparar to repair **(6.1)**
un **repaso** review
   repente: de repente
      suddenly **(5.3)**
   repetido repetitive, repeated
   repetir (e → i, i) to repeat **(3.1)**
la **representación**
   representation
un **representante, una**
   representante
   representative
   representar to represent
una **república** republic
la **República Dominicana**
   Dominican Republic
   requerir (e → ie, i) to
      require
un **requisito** requirement
una **res** head of cattle
      la **carne de res** beef
   reservado reserved
una **residencia** residence
   resistir to resist
   respectivamente respectively

respecto a with respect to
respetable respectable
respetado respected
respetar to respect **(1.3)**
el **respeto** respect
responder to respond,
   answer **(1.4)**
una **responsabilidad**
   responsibility
responsable responsible
una **respuesta** response, answer **(2.1)**
un **restaurante** restaurant **(1.3)**
el **resto** rest, remainder
   los **restos** remains
un **resultado** result
   como resultado as a
      result **(10.2)**
un **resumen** summary
retirarse to retire, retreat
un **retraso** delay
retratar to paint a portrait
un **retrato** portrait
reunido united
reunirse (u → ú) con to
   meet **(3.2)**
revelar to reveal
revisar to check **(4.2)**
una **revista** magazine **(1.3)**
una **revolución** *(pl.* **revoluciones)**
   revolution
revolucionario revolutionary
revolver (o → ue) to stir
un **revólver** revolver
revuelto rough
revuelve he (she) stirs, you
   (formal) stir: *see* **revolver**
un **rey** king
* **rezar** to pray
ricamente richly
rico rich **(1.2)**
ridículo ridiculous **(9.2)**
riego I spill: *see* **regar**
río I laugh: *see* **reír**
un **río** river **(6.4)**
las **riquezas** riches
la **risa** laughter
robar to rob **(7.4)**
un **robo** robbery, burglary
un **robot** robot
el **rock** rock music
   el **rock and roll** rock and roll
una **rodaja** slice
rodeado surrounded
rodear to surround
un **rodeo** rodeo

* **rogar (o → ue)** to beg **(8.4)**
   rojo red
      la **Caperucita Roja** Little
         Red Riding Hood
      ponerse rojo to blush
   romano Roman
   romántico romantic
      una **película romántica**
         romantic movie
un **rompecabezas** puzzle
   romper to break, **(4.3)**, to
      tear
   romperse to break *(part of
      oneself)* **(4.3)**
   ronco hoarse
la **ropa** clothing
una **rosa** rose **(6.4)**
      color de rosa rose-
         colored, "fun"
   rosado pink
el **rosbif** roast beef
las **rositas de maíz** popcorn
   roto broken: *see* **romper** **(6.3)**
   rubio blond **(1.2)**
una **rueda** wheel **(4.2)**
un **ruedo** ring
un **ruido** noise **(3.4)**
una **ruina** ruin
   rural rural
   ruso Russian
el **ruso** Russian *(language)*
un **ruso, una rusa** Russian
   (person)
una **ruta** route
una **rutina** routine

S

   sábado Saturday **(1.3)**
      el **sábado** (on) Saturday
         (1.3)
      los **sábados** (on)
         Saturdays **(1.3)**
la **sabana** savanna
una **sábana** sheet
un **sabelotodo, una sabelotodo**
   know-it-all **(5.1)**
* **saber** to know **(2.2)**
un **sablista, una sablista**
   sponger **(5.1)**
   sabrá he (she) (you) *(formal)*
      will know: *see* **saber** **(4.2)**
* **sacar** to take out **(4.2)**, get
   (1.1)

sacar fotos to take pictures (1.1)
el sacar getting
un sacerdote priest (8.4)
un saco sack, bag
    un saco de dormir sleeping bag (8.3)
un sacrificio sacrifice
sacudir to shake
sagrado sacred
la sal salt
una sala living room (7.4)
    una sala de clase classroom
un salario salary
una salchicha sausage
saldrá he (she) (you) (formal) will leave: see salir
una salida departure (7.2), exit
* salir to leave, go out (3.4), to come out
el Salón de Fama Hall of Fame
* salpicar to splatter
la salsa salsa (dance)
saltar to jump (5.3)
    saltar a la cuerda to jump rope
la salud health (8.2)
saludar to greet (5.2)
salvar to save
una sandalia sandal
una sandía watermelon
un sándwich sandwich
la sangre blood
sangriento bloody
sano healthy (2.4)
un santo, una santa saint
    la Semana Santa Holy Week
saqué I took: see sacar
una sardina sardine
una sartén (pl. sartenes) frying pan (8.3)
un satélite satellite
* satisfacer to satisfy
satisfecho satisfied (9.4)
se (to) himself, herself, yourself (formal), themselves, yourselves, onself (3.2), each other (3.4)
sé I know: see saber
sé be: see ser
una secadora dryer (3.2)
* secarse to dry (oneself) (3.2)
seco dry (8.2)
un secretario, una secretaria secretary

un secreto secret
secundario secondary
la sed thirst
    tener sed to be thirsty (5.4)
la sede seat, headquarters
una seguida series
    dos veces seguidas twice in a row
    en seguida immediately (7.2)
* seguir (e → i, i) to follow, continue to be (3.1)
    seguir + pres. part. to keep on, still be (3.1)
según according to (1.2)
segundo second
seguramente surely
la seguridad safety
    un cinturón de seguridad safety belt
seguro sure, safe (4.4)
el seguro insurance
    una compañía de seguros insurance company
seiscientos six hundred
una selección (pl. selecciones) selection
seleccionar to select
una selva forest, jungle
un sello stamp (2.1)
un semáforo traffic light (8.1)
una semana week
    el fin de semana weekend (1.4)
    la Semana Santa Holy Week
sencillo simple (5.1)
sentado seated
sentarse (e → ie) to sit down (3.2)
un sentido sense
    un sentido del humor sense of humor
sentimental sentimental
un sentimiento sentiment, feeling
sentir (e → ie, i) to feel, regret, be sorry about (3.1)
sentirse (e → ie, i) to feel
    me siento I feel (3.3)
una señal sign, signal (6.1)
    una señal de tránsito traffic sign (8.1)
sepa he, she, you (formal) know (subjunctive of saber)
separado separated

separar to separate
un separatista, una separatista separatist
septiembre September
séptimo seventh
* ser to be (1.2)
    ser de to belong to (2.1)
    volver a ser to become
un ser being
    un ser humano human being
una serenata serenade
una serie series
serio serious (1.2)
una serpiente serpent, snake
servicial helpful
un servicio service
    una estación de servicio service station
servir (e → i, i) to serve (3.1)
sesenta sixty
setenta seventy
sexto sixth
si whether, if
sí mismo oneself
sido been: see ser
siempre always (1.1)
una sierra mountain range
un siglo century (8.2)
un significado meaning, significance
* significar to signify, mean
sigo I follow: see seguir
siguiente following
    lo siguiente the following
el silencio silence
una silla chair (6.1)
un sillón (pl. sillones) armchair (6.1)
un símbolo symbol
similar similar
la simpatía liking, friendliness
simpático nice, pleasant (1.2)
simplemente simply
sin without
    sin aliento out of breath
    sin duda doubtless
    sin embargo however, nevertheless
sinceramente sincerely
sincero sincere
sino but (4.4)
sinuoso winding
siquiera: ni siquiera not even
una sirena siren, mermaid

un **sistema** system
    el sistema de aire acondicionado air conditioning system **(7.4)**
un **sitio** place
una **situación** (*pl.* **situaciones**) situation
    situado situated
    sobre on, over, about **(6.2)**
    sobre todo above all
    sobrenatural supernatural
    sobrevivir to survive
una **sobrina** niece
un **sobrino** nephew
    sociable sociable
    social social
una **sociedad** society
un **sofá** sofa
    sois you (*fam. pl.*) are: *see* **ser**
el **sol** sun **(2.2)** *money of Peru*
    el dios-sol sun god
    hace sol it's sunny **(2.2)**
    tomar el sol to sunbathe **(1.1)**
    una quemadura de sol sunburn
    unos anteojos de sol sunglasses **(2.2)**
    solamente only **(2.1)**
    solar solar
    la calefacción solar solar heating **(7.4)**
    soleado sunny **(2.2)**
    solicitar solicit, seek, to need **(6.1)**
    se solicita we need, we're looking for **(6.1)**
    solito alone
    solo alone **(4.1)**
    sólo only
    soltero single
una **solución** (*pl.* **soluciones**) solution
una **sombra** shadow
un **sombrero** hat **(2.2)**
    somos we are: *see* **ser**
    son they (you) (*pl.*) are: *see* **ser**
    sonar (o → ue) to ring, sing out
    sonreír (e → i, i) to smile **(3.1)**
    soñar (o → ue) (con) to dream (about) **(3.1)**
    soñar despierto to daydream
la **sopa** soup

sorprenderse to be surprised **(4.4)**
sorprendente surprising **(9.2)**
una **sorpresa** surprise **(2.1)**
sospechar to suspect
sospechoso suspicious **(2.3)**
un **sospechoso, una sospechosa** suspect
* **sostenerse** (e → ie) to support
un **sótano** basement **(7.4)**
    soy I am: *see* **ser**
    su, sus his, her, your (*formal, fam. pl.*), their **(2.1)**
    suave delicate
    subir (a) to go up, get (in, on), climb **(4.3)**
el **subjuntivo** subjunctive
sublevarse to rebel
un **submarino** submarine
una **sucesión** (*pl.* **sucesiones**) succession
un **suceso** event
un **sucesor, una sucesora** successor
    sucio dirty **(4.4)**
el **sucre** *money of Ecuador*
    sudamericano South American
    Suecia Sweden
el **suelo** floor **(4.3)**; ground
el **sueño** sleep
    tener sueño to be sleepy **(5.4)**
un **sueño** dream
la **suerte** luck **(1.3)**
un **suéter** sweater
una **sugerencia** suggestion **(8.4)**
    sugerir (e → ie, i) to suggest **(8.4)**
    Suiza Switzerland
un **sujeto** subject
    sumar to add
    supe I knew, I found out: *see* **saber**
    superficialmente superficially
    superior superior
un **supermercado** supermarket
un **super-optimista, una super-optimista** superoptimist
una **superstición** (*pl.* **supersticiones**) superstition
    supersticioso superstitious
la **supervisión** supervision
* **suponer** to suppose

suprimir to suppress **(7.1)**; omit
    supuesto: por supuesto of course
el **sur** south
    la América del Sur South America
    suramericano South American
* **surgir** to arise
el **suroeste** southwest
una **suscripción** (*pl.* **suscripciones**) subscription
una **sustancia** substance
un **sustantivo** noun
    suyo his, her, your (*formal*), their **(4.2)**

t

el **tabaco** tobacco
una **tabla hawaiana** surfboard
un **taco** *meat in folded tortilla*
    Tahiti Tahiti
los **taínos** *Arawak tribe*
    tal such
    con tal que so that, provided that
    ¿qué tal? how are you?
    tal + *noun* such a + *noun* **(3.3)**
    tal como just as
    tal vez perhaps **(1.2)**
un **talento** talent
un **talismán** (*pl.* **talismanes**) good-luck piece
el **tamaño** size
    también also, too **(1.1)**
    tampoco neither, not either **(5.1)**
    tan so **(2.1)**; that
    tan (*adj.*) **como** as (*adj.*) as **(6.4)**
el **tango** tango (*dance*)
un **tanque** tank **(4.2)**
    tanto so
    por lo tanto therefore
    tanto __ como as much __ as
una **taquilla** ticket office **(6.4)**
    tardar (en) to be late (in) **(8.2)**, to delay
    tarde late **(5.2)**
una **tarde** afternoon, evening **(1.4)**

por la tarde in the afternoon, evening **(1.4)**

una tarea task, work

las tareas homework

una tarjeta card **(6.1)**

un taxi taxi

un taxista, una taxista taxi driver

una taza cup

te you, to you **(2.3)**; yourself *(fam.)* **(3.2)**

el té tea

teatral theatrical

una obra teatral *(theatrical)* play

un teatro theater **(1.3)**

una obra de teatro *(theatrical)* play **(2.4)**

técnico technical

la tecnología technology

un techo roof **(7.4)**

telefonear to telephone

un teléfono telephone

llamar por teléfono to call on the telephone

un número de teléfono telephone number

un telegrama telegram

un telescopio telescope

la televisión television *(transmission)*

un televisor television *(set)* **(1.3)**

un televisor de color color television

un tema theme

un temblor trembling

temer to fear **(9.1)**

el temor fear

temperamental temperamental

una tempestad storm

una temporada season

temprano early **(5.2)**

tendrá he (she) (you) *(formal)* will have: *see* **tener**

* **tener (e → ie)** to have **(1.3)**

no tener razón to be wrong **(5.4)**

tener __ años to be __ years old **(1.3)**

tener calor to be *(feel)* hot **(5.4)**

tener celos to be jealous **(5.4)**

tener cuidado to be careful **(5.4)**

tener éxito to be successful **(5.4)**

tener frío to be *(feel)* cold **(5.4)**

tener ganas de to want to, to feel like **(1.3)**

tener hambre to be hungry **(5.4)**

tener la bondad (de) to be good enough (to) *(would you please)* **(8.1)**

tener la culpa to be guilty, to be at fault **(5.4)**

tener lugar to take place

tener miedo to be afraid **(5.4)**

tener paciencia to be patient **(8.1)**

tener prisa to be in a hurry **(5.4)**

tener que + inf. to have to **(1.3)**

tener razón to be right **(5.4)**

tener sed to be thirsty **(5.4)**

tener sueño to be sleepy **(5.4)**

tener suerte to be lucky **(1.3)**

tener vergüenza to be ashamed **(5.4)**

tengo I have: *see* **tener**

el tenis tennis **(2.4)**

jugar al tenis to play tennis **(2.4)**

unos zapatos de tenis sneakers, tennis shoes

la tensión tension

tenso tight

la tentación temptation

un teólogo clergyman

una teoría theory

tercer, tercero third

terminar to end **(3.4)**

un terremoto earthquake

terrible terrible

un territorio territory

un tesoro treasure **(7.3)**

un buscador de tesoro treasure-hunter

un testigo, una testigo witness **(5.4)**

un testimonio testimony

un texano, una texana Texan

un texto text

ti you *(fam.) (after prep.)*

pobre de ti poor you

una tía aunt **(1.2)**

un tiburón *(pl. tiburones)* shark

el tiempo time, weather

a tiempo on time **(5.2)**

¿cuánto tiempo? how long?

¿qué tiempo hace? what is the weather like? **(2.2)**

una tienda store **(1.3)**

una tienda de campaña tent **(8.3)**

la tierra earth, land **(7.1)**

un tigre tiger

unas tijeras scissors **(3.2)**

tímido timid, shy

un tío uncle **(1.2)**

los tíos uncles and aunts **(1.2)**

típicamente typically

típico typical

un tipo type

un «tipo» "character"

tirar to pull

tirarse to throw oneself

un título degree

una toalla towel **(2.2)**

una toalla de papel paper towel

un tocadiscos record player **(1.3)**

* **tocar** to touch **(9.3)**; play *(a musical instrument)* **(1.1)** be one's turn

me toca it's my turn

tocar la bocina to honk *(horn)* **(8.1)**

todavía still, yet **(4.2)**

no ... todavía not yet **(6.3)**

todo every, all, the whole, **(4.1)** everything **(3.3)**

después de todo after all

por todos lados everywhere

sobre todo above all

todo el mundo everyone **(3.3)**

todo el tiempo all the time **(1.3)**

todos every **(2.4)**; all, everyone **(2.1)**

todos los días every day **(2.4)**

tolerante tolerant

tolerar to tolerate **(8.4)**

tomar to take **(1.1)**

tomar el sol to sunbathe **(1.1)**

tomar una decisión to make a decision

tomarse por to take oneself for, think one is **(3.3)**

un **tomate** tomato

la **tontería** foolishness

tonto foolish **(1.2)**

tordo dapple-gray

un **torero, una torera** bullfighter

una **tormenta** storm

estalla una tormenta a storm breaks out

un **tornado** tornado

un **torneo** tournament

un **toro** bull

una corrida de toros bullfight

una plaza de toros bullring

unos toros de lidia fighting bulls

una **torre** tower

una **torta** cake **(6.1)**

una **tortuga** tortoise

toser to cough

la **tostada** toast

tostado toasted **(6.2)**

tostar (o → ue) to toast **(6.2)**

total total

totalmente totally

un **trabajador, una trabajadora** worker

un trabajador del campo field worker

un trabajador social social worker

trabajar to work **(1.1)**

un **trabajo** job

una **tradición (pl. tradiciones)** tradition

tradicional traditional

tradicionalmente traditionally

* **traducir** to translate **(2.1)**

* **traer** to bring **(3.4)**

una **tragedia** tragedy **(2.4)**

traje I brought: see **traer**

un **traje** suit **(2.2)**

un traje de baño bathing suit **(2.2)**

un traje de luces "suit of lights"

tranquilamente tranquilly

tranquilo tranquil, calm **(1.4)**

transcurrir to pass (away), elapse

un **transeúnte, una transeúnte** passer-by **(8.3)**

transformar to transform **(7.1)**

el **tránsito** traffic **(8.1)**

un lío de tránsito traffic jam

una señal de tránsito traffic sign **(8.1)**

transmitido transmitted

el **transporte** transportation

un **tranvía** tramway, streetcar **(8.1)**

tras after, behind **(5.4)**

trasladar to move, transfer **(9.3)**

tratar de to try **(8.2)**

un **trébol** clover

trece thirteen

treinta thirty

tremendo tremendous

un **tren** train

trepar to climb **(5.4)**

trescientos three hundred

un **triángulo** triangle

una **tribu** tribe

el **trigo** wheat

triste sad **(1.4)**

la **tristeza** sadness **(7.4)**

un **triunfo** triumph

un **trofeo** trophy

un **trombón (pl. trombones)** trombone

una **tropa** troop

* **tropezar (con) (e → ie)** to stumble (against) **(4.3)**, to bump into

tropical tropical

tu, tus your (fam.) **(2.1)**

tú you (fam.) **(1.1)**

un **turista, una turista** tourist

turístico tourist

tutear to use "tú" with someone **(6.3)**

tuve I had: see **tener**

tuyo yours (fam.) **(4.2)**

u

u or (before words beginning with o or ho) **(1.3)**

Ud. you (formal sing.) **(1.1)**

Uds. you (pl.) **(1.1)**

último last

un, una one, an, a **(1.2)**

único unique, only **(1.4)**

una **unidad** unit

unido united

los Estados Unidos United States

unirse to join

universal universal

una **universidad** university

universitario university

el **universo** universe

uno one

cada uno each one

unos some **(1.2)**

unos + number about + number

una **uña** fingernail **(3.2)**

urbano urban

la **urgencia** urgency, emergency

el **Uruguay** Uruguay

usar to use

el **uso** use

usted (Ud.) you (formal sing.)

ustedes (Uds.) you (pl.)

un **utensilio** utensil

útil useful **(2.4)**

v

va he (she) goes, you (formal) go: see **ir**

¡qué va! nonsense! **(3.1)**

¡va por ...! it's a deal for ...! **(2.3)**

va y viene coming and going

una **vaca** cow

las **vacaciones** vacation **(4.1)**

estar de vacaciones to be on vacation **(4.1)**

ir de vacaciones to go on vacation **(4.1)**

vaciar (i → i) to empty

vacilar en to hesitate **(8.2)**, to vacilate, to waver

vacío empty **(6.2)**

el **valenciano** language of Valencia

un **valenciano, una valenciana** person from Valencia

la **valentía** courage

valer to be worth, protect

valer la pena to be worthwhile **(9.2)**

¡válgame Dios! God help me! (4.3)

valiente courageous, brave (7.3)

valioso valuable

el **valor** value (5.1) courage

vamos let's go, we go: *see* **ir**

vamos a ver let's see (1.4)

vanidoso vain

vano vain

en vano in vain

un **vaquero** cowboy

una película de vaqueros cowboy movie

una **variación** (*pl.* **variaciones**) variation

una **variedad** variety

un programa de variedades variety show

una **varilla** stick

varios several

el **vasco** *language of the Basque region*

un **vasco, una vasca** Basque

un **vaso** *(drinking)* glass

vaya he, she, it goes, you *(formal)* go *(subjunctive of* **ir**)

ve go: *see* **ir**

un **vecino, una vecina** neighbor (2.1)

la **vegetación** vegetation

veía I (he) (she) was seeing, you *(formal)* were seeing: *see* **ver**

veinte twenty

veinte y uno twenty-one

una **vela** sail

un bote de vela sailboat

una **vena** vein

un **venado** deer

* **vencer** to beat, conquer

un **vendedor, una vendedora** salesperson (8.3)

un vendedor viajero traveling salesperson

vender to sell (1.4)

vendrá he (she) (you) *(formal)* will come: *see* **venir**

venenoso poisonous

la hiedra venenosa poison ivy

venezolano Venezuelan

Venezuela Venezuela

* **venir** (e → ie, i) to come (4.4)

una **ventana** window (4.3)

* **ver** to see (1.4)

a ver let's see (1.2)

veranear to spend the summer

veraneo: un campamento de veraneo summer camp

el **verano** summer

un **verbo** verb

verdad true

la **verdad** truth (1.1)

es verdad that's right, true (1.1)

no es verdad that's not right, true (1.1)

verdaderamente truly, really

verdadero true (5.1), real

verde green

vergonzoso embarrassing

la **vergüenza** shame

tener vergüenza to be ashamed (5.4)

un **verso** verse

vestido dressed

un **vestido** dress

un **vestigio** vestige

vestirse (e → i, i) to get dressed (3.2)

me visto I get dressed

una **vez** (*pl.* **veces**) time

a veces at times (1.3)

alguna vez ever, sometime

¿cuántas veces? how many times?

de vez en cuando from time to time, once in a while (3.1)

dos veces seguidas twice in a row

en vez de instead of

raras veces rarely

tal vez perhaps

una vez once (5.1)

vi I saw: *see* **ver**

viajar to travel (1.1)

un **viaje** trip (3.4), voyage

estar de viajes to be on a trip

hacer un viaje to take a trip (3.4)

una agencia de viajes travel agency

viajero traveling

un vendedor viajero traveling salesperson

una **víctima** victim

victorioso victorious

la **vida** life

el estilo de vida lifestyle

ganarse la vida to earn a living

un **vidente, una vidente** fortune teller

un **vidrio** glass (7.4)

viejo old (1.2)

viene he (she) (it) comes, you *(formal)* come: *see* **venir**

va y viene coming and going

el **viento** wind (2.2)

hace viento it's windy (2.2)

un molino de viento windmill

viernes Friday (1.3)

el viernes (on) Friday (1.3)

los viernes (on) Fridays (1.3)

un **vikingo** Viking

el **vinagre** vinegar

vine I came: *see* **venir**

vinieron they (you) *(pl.)* came: *see* **venir**

el **vino** wine

la **violencia** violence

violento violent (2.4)

un **violín** (*pl.* **violines**) violin

la **Virgen** Virgin Mother

un **virrey** viceroy

una **virtud** virtue (5.2); quality

una **visión** (*pl.* **visiones**) vision

una **visita** visit

de visita (en) on a visit (to, in)

un **visitante, una visitante** visitor

visitar to visit (1.1)

visto seen: *see* **ver**

vistoso showy

¡viva __ long live __!

vivir to live (1.4)

vivo lively, alive

un **vivo** living person

un **vocabulario** vocabulary

volador flying

un platillo volador flying saucer

volante flying

volar (o → ue) to fly (9.3)

un **volcán** (*pl.* **volcanes**) volcano

el **volibol** volleyball

jugar al volibol to play volleyball

volver (o → ue) to return
    (3.1)
    volver a ser to become
volverse (o → ue) to
    become, turn (5.3)
vosotros(as) you *(fam. pl.)*
voy I go: *see* ir
una voz *(pl.* voces) voice (4.2)
    en voz alta aloud
vuela he (she) flies, you
    (formal) fly: *see* volar
un vuelo flight
una vuelta turn, stroll
    dar una vuelta to take a
    walk, ride (4.2)
vuelto returned: *see* volver

vuelvo I return: *see* volver
vuestro yours, of yours *(fam.
    pl.)*

el wiski whisky

Y

y and (1.3)
ya already, yet (6.3)
    ya no no longer
los Yankis Yankees

un yate yacht
yo I (1.1)
el yogur yogurt
yoruba yoruba

Z

una zapatería shoe store
un zapato shoe
    unos zapatos de tenis
    tennis shoes, sneakers
zoológico zoological
    un jardín zoológico zoo
un zoológico zoo

ENGLISH-SPANISH VOCABULARY

The English-Spanish Vocabulary lists only the active words and expressions in the student text.

a

a un, una **(1.2)**
able: to be able *poder (o → ue) **(3.1)**
about sobre **(6.2)**
absent-minded distraído **(9.1)**
absurd absurdo **(9.2)**
accident un accidente
according to según **(1.2)**
to act actuar (u → ú) **(7.3)**
active activo **(1.2)**
activity una actividad
to be acquainted with *conocer **(2.1)**
adjective un adjetivo
to admire admirar **(1.3)**
adults los mayores **(5.1)**
adventure una aventura
   adventure film una película de aventuras
adverb un adverbio
advertisement un anuncio **(6.1)**
advice unos consejos **(5.2)**
   piece of advice un consejo **(5.2)**
to advise aconsejar **(8.4)** recomendar **(8.4)** (e → ie)
affection el cariño **(3.4)**
affirmative afirmativo
afraid: to be afraid tener miedo **(5.4)**
after después (de) **(1.4)** tras **(5.4)**
afternoon una tarde **(1.4)**
   in the afternoon por la tarde **(1.4)**
again de nuevo **(3.4)**
against contra **(7.1)**
   to be against *oponerse a **(8.4)**
ago hace + *period of time* **(4.4)**
to agree on estar de acuerdo **(4.2)** *convenir (e → ie, i) en **(8.2)**
agreeable agradable **(9.2)**
air conditioning system el sistema de aire acondicionado **(7.4)**
air pollution la contaminación del aire **(7.1)**
alertness: mental alertness la presencia de ánimo **(4.4)**
all todo **(4.1)** todos **(2.4)**

all the time todo el tiempo **(1.3)**
almost casi **(2.4)**
alone solo **(4.1)**
along: to get along (with) llevarse (con) **(3.4)**
already ya **(6.3)**
also también **(1.1)**
although aunque **(1.2)**
always siempre **(1.1)**
American americano, *(from the U.S.)* norteamericano **(1.2)**
to amuse divertir (e → ie, i) **(3.3)**
amusing divertido **(1.2)**
an un, una **(1.2)**
and y (e *before words starting with* i *or* hi) **(1.3)**
angel un ángel **(5.2)**
angry enojado **(9.1)**
   to get angry (with, at) enfadarse (con) **(3.3)** enojarse (con) **(3.3)**
to annoy molestar **(3.3)**
another otro **(1.3)**
answer una respuesta **(2.1)**
to answer responder **(1.4)** contestar
antique antiguo **(5.1)**
anything algo **(5.1)**
apartment building un edificio de apartamentos **(4.3)**
apple una manzana **(6.1)**
to approach *acercarse (a) **(4.4)**
arm un brazo **(3.4)**
armchair un sillón (*pl.* sillones) **(6.1)**
around alrededor (de) **(6.2)**
arrival una llegada **(7.2)**
to arrive *llegar **(5.2)**
article un artículo
artistic artístico
as como
   as *(adj.)* **as** tan *(adj.)* como **(6.4)**
   as a result como resultado **(10.2)**
ashamed: to be ashamed tener vergüenza **(5.4)**
to ask pedir (e → i, i) **(3.1)** preguntar
to ask for pedir (e → i, i) **(3.1)**

asleep: to fall asleep dormirse (o → ue, u) **(3.2)**
aspect un aspecto
at a
   at times a veces **(1.3)**
athletic deportista **(1.2)**
attentive atento **(5.2)**
aunt una tía **(1.2)**
automobile un automóvil
awful: how awful! ¡qué malo! **(3.1)**

b

back: in back of detrás de **(6.2)**
backpack una mochila **(8.3)**
bad malo **(1.2)**
   in a bad mood de mal humor **(1.4)**
   too bad! ¡qué lástima! **(3.1)**
bad-mannered mal educado **(5.2)**
badly mal **(1.1)**
bakery una panadería **(6.1)**
ball una pelota **(1.3)**
ban una prohibición (*pl.* prohibiciones) **(8.4)**
banana una banana **(6.1)**
bank un banco **(3.4)**
basement un sótano **(7.4)**
basketball el básquetbol **(2.4)**
bath un baño
   to take a bath bañarse **(3.2)**
bathing suit un traje de baño **(2.2)**
to be *ser **(1.2)** *estar **(1.4)**
   to be __(years old) tener __ años **(1.3)**
   to be a member (of) *pertenecer (a)
   to be able *poder (o → ue) **(3.1)**
   to be afraid tener miedo **(5.4)**
   to be against *oponerse a **(8.4)**
   to be ashamed tener vergüenza **(5.4)**
   to be at fault tener la culpa **(5.4)**
   to be careful tener cuidado **(5.4)**

501

to be cold tener frío **(5.4)**

to be good enough (to) tener la bondad (de) **(8.1)**

to be happy (about) alegrarse (de) **(3.3)**

to be hot tener calor **(5.4)**

to be hungry tener hambre **(5.4)**

to be in a hurry tener prisa **(5.4)**

to be jealous tener celos **(5.4)**

to be late in tardar en **(8.2)**

to be lucky tener suerte **(1.3)**

to be on vacation estar de vacaciones **(4.1)**

to be out estar en la calle **(4.1)**

to be patient tener paciencia **(8.1)**

to be right tener razón **(5.4)**

to be sleepy tener sueño **(5.4)**

to be successful tener éxito **(5.4)**

to be thirsty tener sed **(5.4)**

to be to blame tener la culpa **(5.4)**

to be warm tener calor **(2.2)**

to be wrong no tener razón **(5.4)**

beach una playa **(1.3)**

beard una barba

beautiful guapo **(1.2)** hermoso **(5.1)**

because porque, como

  because of that por eso **(3.1)**

to become volverse (o → ue) **(5.3)** *hacerse (+ *noun*) **(3.4)** *ponerse (+ *adj.*) **(3.4)**

  what will become of me! ¡qué será de mí! **(7.4)**

bed una cama **(6.1)**

  to go to bed acostarse (o → ue) **(3.2)**

bedroom un dormitorio **(7.4)**

beef la carne de res **(6.1)**

before antes (de) **(1.4)**, delante (de) (*position*) **(6.2)**

  the __ before (last) el __ antepasado **(6.4)**

  the day before yesterday anteayer **(6.4)**

  the night before last anteanoche **(6.4)**

to beg *rogar (o → ue) **(8.4)**

to begin *comenzar (e → ie) **(3.1)**, *empezar (e → ie) **(3.1)**

to behave portarse bien **(3.3)**

behind detrás (de) **(6.2)**, tras **(5.4)**

to believe *creer **(1.4)**

to belong *pertenecer **(2.1)**

  to belong to *ser de **(2.1)**

below debajo (de) **(6.2)**

belt un cinturón (*pl.* cinturones) **(10.2)**

beside al lado (de) **(6.2)**

besides además **(1.2)**

best mejor **(1.2)**

  best one el mejor

better mejor **(3.1)**

between entre **(6.2)**

beverage una bebida **(8.2)**

bicycle una bicicleta **(1.3)**

big grande **(1.3)**

bill un billete *(money)* **(2.3)**

binoculars unos gemelos **(8.3)**

birthday un cumpleaños

blackmail el chantaje **(2.3)**

blackout un apagón (*pl.* apagones) **(9.1)**

blame: to be to blame tener la culpa **(5.4)**

blanket una manta **(8.3)**

blond rubio **(1.2)**

blunder: to make a blunder meter la pata **(9.1)**

boat un bote **(2.2)**

book un libro **(1.3)**

bookstore una librería **(6.1)**

bore: what a bore! ¡qué lata! **(3.1)**

bored aburrido **(1.4)**

  to be bored estar aburrido **(1.4)**

  to get bored aburrirse **(3.3)**

boring aburrido **(1.2)**

  to be boring ser aburrido **(1.2)**

to borrow pedir prestado **(5.1)**

boss un jefe, una jefa **(2.1)**

to bother molestar **(3.3)**

  it bothers (me) (that) (me) molesta (que) **(9.1)**

boy un chico **(1.2)**, un muchacho **(1.2)**, un niño **(1.2)**

boyfriend un novio **(1.2)**

bracelet una pulsera **(2.3)**

brakes los frenos **(4.2)**

brave valiente **(7.3)**

bread el pan **(6.1)**

to break quebrar **(6.2)**, romperse **(4.3)**

  to break (one's leg) romperse (la pierna) **(4.3)**

bridge un puente **(7.3)**

to bring llevar **(1.1)**, *traer **(3.4)**

broken quebrado **(6.2)**, roto **(6.3)**

brother un hermano **(1.2)**

  brothers and sisters los hermanos **(1.2)**

brush un cepillo **(3.2)**

to brush cepillar(se) **(3.2)**

to build *construir **(4.3)**

building un edificio **(4.3)**

  apartment building un edificio de apartamentos **(4.3)**

to bump into *chocar con **(4.3)**

to burn quemar **(5.3)**

burned quemado **(6.2)**

bus un autobús (*pl.* autobuses) **(1.3)**

  bus stop la parada (del autobús) **(6.4)**

businessman un hombre de negocios **(7.2)**

but pero **(1.3)**, sino **(4.4)**

butcher shop una carnicería **(6.1)**

butter la mantequilla **(6.1)**

to buy comprar **(1.3)**

C

café un café **(2.1)**

cafeteria una cafetería

cake una torta **(6.1)**

calculator una calculadora **(1.3)**

call: phone call una llamada **(4.4)**

to call (up) llamar (por teléfono) **(1.3)**

calm tranquilo **(1.4)**

camera una cámara **(1.3)**

camping el camping **(8.3)**

  to go camping ir de camping **(8.3)**

can: to be able *poder (o → ue) **(3.1)**

Canadian canadiense **(1.2)**

candy los dulces **(2.3)**

car un coche **(1.3)**, un automóvil

card una tarjeta **(6.1)**

care el arreglo, el cuidado **(5.4)**

to take care of cuidar **(2.1)**

career una carrera **(8.4)**

careful cuidadoso **(4.4)**, prudente **(4.4)**

  to be careful tener cuidado **(5.4)**

careless imprudente **(4.4)**

carnation un clavel (6.4)

case: in case (that) en caso de (10.1)

cassette una cinta (1.3)

cautious prudente (4.4)

century un siglo (8.2)

certain cierto (7.1)

chair una silla (6.1)

champion un campeón, una campeona (8.2)

to change cambiar (2.3)

to check revisar (4.2)

cheese el queso (6.1)

cherry una cereza (6.1)

chicken un pollo (6.1)

child un niño, una niña (1.2)

childhood la niñez (5.2)

children los niños (1.2)

to choose *escoger (6.4)

city una ciudad (1.3)

class una clase

classical clásico

classmate un compañero, una compañera (1.2)

clean limpio (4.4)

to clean limpiar (4.2)

clerk un dependiente, una dependienta (2.1)

clever listo (1.2)

to climb escalar (2.4), subir (a) (4.3), (a tree) trepar (5.4)

mountain climbing el alpinismo (2.4)

clock un reloj (1.3)

close (to) cerca (de) (6.2)

to close cerrar (e → ie) (3.1)

closed cerrado (6.2)

cloudy nublado (2.2)

it's cloudy está nublado (2.2)

clown un payaso (5.1)

coffee el café

coin una moneda (2.3)

cold frío (2.2)

it's cold (weather) hace frío (2.2)

to be (feel) cold tener frío (5.4)

to collect coleccionar (2.4)

collection una colección (pl. colecciones) (2.4)

coin collection una colección de monedas (2.4)

stamp collection una colección de sellos (2.4)

comb un peine (2.3)

to comb (one's hair) peinarse (3.2)

to come venir (e → ie, i) (4.4)

to come back regresar (4.1), volver (o → ue) (3.1)

comedy una comedia (2.4)

comfortable cómodo (9.2)

command un mandato (8.4)

common común (5.1)

comparative el comparativo

to complain (about) quejarse (de) (3.3)

complement un complemento

complicated complicado (5.1)

computer una computadora (7.1)

concert un concierto (1.3)

condition una condición (pl. condiciones)

on the condition con la condición de (10.1)

conductor un conductor (8.1)

to congratulate felicitar (4.4)

conjunction una conjunción (pl. conjunciones)

to consist (of, in) consistir (en) (8.2)

to construct *construir (4.3)

construction la construcción

content contento (1.4)

to continue *seguir (e → i, i) (3.1)

continuous continuo

contrary: on the contrary al contrario (4.3)

conversation una conversación (pl. conversaciones)

to cook cocinar (1.1)

cooking la cocina (2.4)

cool fresco (2.2)

it's cool (weather) hace fresco (2.2)

corner una esquina (8.1)

to cost costar (o → ue) (3.1)

to count contar (o → ue) (3.1)

to counsel aconsejar (8.4)

country un país (3.4)

country(side) el campo (1.3)

courageous valiente (7.3)

cousin un primo, una prima (1.2)

cousins los primos (1.2)

to cram atestar (6.2)

crazy loco (1.2)

cream una crema (6.1)

to create crear (3.3)

credulous crédulo (9.3)

to criticize *criticar (1.3)

to cross *cruzar (5.4)

crosswalk un paso de peatones (8.1)

to crowd atestar (6.2)

crowded atestado (6.2)

to cry llorar (7.4)

to cultivate cultivar (6.4)

curious inquisitivo (2.3)

customer un (una) cliente

to cut cortar(se) (3.2)

cutlets las chuletas (6.1)

d

daily diario (3.2)

dairy una lechería (6.1)

daisy una margarita (6.4)

dance un baile (2.4)

to dance bailar (1.1)

dangerous peligroso (2.4)

dark moreno (1.2)

daughter una hija (1.2)

day un día (1.1)

during the day por el día (3.2)

every day todos los días (2.1)

one day un día (1.1)

per day al día (7.1)

someday un día (1.1)

deal: it's a deal for ___! ¡va por ___! (2.3)

death la muerte (9.3)

defect un defecto (5.2)

definite definido

to deliver *entregar (2.1)

to demand *exigir (8.4)

demanding exigente (10.3)

to demonstrate demostrar (o → ue) (9.2)

demonstrative demostrativo

dentist un (una) dentista (2.1)

to deny *negar (e → ie) (9.3)

department store un almacén (pl. almacenes) (1.3)

departure una salida (7.2)

departure salida

to descend bajar (de) (4.3)

to deserve *merecer (2.1)

to desire desear (1.1)

detail un detalle (3.3)

to develop desarrollar (7.1)

devil un diablo (5.2)

difficult difícil (5.1)

diminutive el diminutivo

dining room un comedor (7.4)

direct directo

to direct *dirigir (2.1)

direction: in the direction of hacia (4.2)

directional lights (on a car) las (luces) direccionales (4.2)

dirty sucio (4.4)

disagreeable antipático (1.2)

to disappear *desaparecer (6.4)

disappointed desilusionado (9.1)

to discover descubrir (7.1)

discovered descubierto (6.3)

dish un plato (5.3)

district un barrio (9.4)

to do *hacer (3.4)

doctor un médico, una médica (2.1)

dollar un dólar

door una puerta

dot: on the dot en punto (8.4)

to doubt dudar (9.3)

doubtful dudoso (9.3)

downtown el centro (1.3)

to dream (about) soñar (o → ue) (con) (3.1)

to dress, get dressed vestirse (e → i, i) (3.2)

drink una bebida (8.2)

to drink beber (1.4), tomar (1.1)

to drive *conducir (4.4)

    driver un conductor, una conductora (8.1)

    driver's license un permiso de conducir (4.2)

dry seco (8.2)

to dry *secar(se) (3.2)

dryer una secadora (3.2)

dummy un bobo, una boba (5.1)

duration la duración

during durante (1.4)

    during the day por el día (3.2)

e

each cada (3.2)

    each one cada uno (3.2)

each other se, nos (3.4)

early temprano (5.2)

to earn ganar (1.1)

earring un pendiente (2.3)

earth la tierra (7.1)

ease: at ease cómodo (9.2)

easy fácil (5.1)

to eat comer (1.4)

effect: in effect en efecto (7.2)

elegance la elegancia

to eliminate eliminar (7.1)

emotion una emoción (pl. emociones)

employee un empleado, una empleada (2.1)

empty vacío (6.2)

to end terminar (3.4)

English (el) inglés (1.2)

to enjoy *gozar (de) (4.1)

    I enjoy me agrada(n) (2.4)

enough bastante (1.1)

to enter entrar (en) (7.3)

entertainment las diversiones

to escape escaparse (5.3)

essential esencial (9.2)

eternal eterno (9.3)

even aun (3.4)

evening una tarde (1.4)

    in the evening por la tarde (1.4)

ever alguna vez (6.3)

every todo (4.1), todos los (2.4)

    every day todos los días (2.4)

    everybody todo el mundo (3.3)

    everyone todo el mundo (3.3); todos (2.1)

    everything todo (3.3)

    everywhere por todos lados (7.4)

exact en punto (8.4)

except excepto (5.1)

exchange un intercambio (7.2)

    in exchange for por (2.3)

to exchange cambiar (2.3)

to exclaim exclamar (4.3)

experience una experiencia

to explain *explicar (4.2)

to express (oneself) expresarse (9.2)

expression una expresión (pl. expresiones)

eye un ojo

f

face una cara

facing enfrente (de) (6.2), frente a (4.3)

fact un hecho (10.1)

    in fact de hecho (1.1) en efecto (7.2)

fair justo (1.4)

    it's not fair no es justo (2.4)

to fall *caer (3.4)

    to fall asleep dormirse (o → ue, u) (3.2)

    to fall down *caerse (3.4)

    to fall in love (with) enamorarse (de) (3.4)

false falso (5.1)

to be familiar with *conocer (2.1)

family una familia

    (of the) family familiar (10.3)

far (from) lejos (de) (6.2)

fashion la moda (1.4)

fast (adj.) rápido (4.4)

fast (adv.) de prisa (4.2), rápidamente

fat gordo (1.2)

father un padre (1.2), (el) papá (1.2)

fault un defecto (5.2)

    to be at fault tener la culpa (5.4)

to fear temer (9.1)

to feel sentir (e → ie, i) (3.1), sentirse (e → ie, i) (3.3)

    to feel very much like tener ganas de (1.3)

feeling un sentimiento

fiesta una fiesta (1.3)

to fight pelear(se) (3.4)

to fill llenar (4.2)

film una película (2.4)

    adventure film una película de aventuras

    horror film una película de horror

to find encontrar (o → ue) (3.1)

fingernail una uña (3.2)

to finish terminar (3.4)

first primero (3.4)

fish (caught) un pescado, (live) un pez (pl. peces) (6.4)

to fish *pescar (2.2)

five cinco

to fix arreglar (2.1)

flashlight una linterna eléctrica (8.3)

to flee *huir (4.4)

floor (of a building), un piso (4.3), (of a room) el suelo (4.3)

    street floor la planta baja (7.4)

flower una flor (6.4)

to fly volar (o → ue) (9.3)

to follow *seguir (e → i, i) (3.1)

fool un bobo, una boba (5.1)

foolish tonto (1.2)

foot un pie (3.4)

for para (1.3), por (2.3)

to forbid prohibir (6.1)

foreign extranjero (6.1)

forest un bosque (6.4)

to forget olvidar (6.3)

form una forma

formation una formación (*pl.* formaciones)

fortunate afortunado (4.4)

French (el) francés (*f.* francesa) (1.2)

Friday viernes (1.3)

friend un amigo, una amiga (1.2)

 best friend el mejor amigo (1.2)

friendship la amistad (3.4)

from de (2.1), desde (4.3)

 from there desde allí (4.3)

 from time to time de vez en cuando (3.1)

front: in front of delante (de) (6.2), enfrente (de) (6.2)

fruit una fruta (6.4)

 fruit market una frutería (6.1)

 fruit tree un árbol de frutas (6.4)

frying pan una sartén (*pl.* sartenes) (8.3)

full lleno (6.2)

fun divertido (1.2)

 to have fun divertirse (e → ie, i) (3.3)

 to make fun of burlarse de (3.3)

funny divertido (1.2)

furious furioso (1.4)

furniture shop una mueblería (6.1)

future el futuro

g

game un partido (2.4)

 soccer game un partido de fútbol (2.4)

garden un jardín (*pl.* jardines) (6.4)

gasoline la gasolina (4.2)

gender el género

general: in general por lo general (10.3)

genius un genio (3.3)

to get recibir (1.4), *obtener (e → ie) (8.1)

 to get + *adj.* *ponerse + *adj.* (3.4)

 to get a grade sacar una nota (1.1)

to get angry (at) enfadarse (con) (3.3), enojarse (con) (3.3)

to get bored aburrirse (3.3)

to get happy alegrarse (3.3)

to get in, on subir (a) (4.3)

to get interested interesarse

to get irritated irritarse (3.3)

to get married casarse (3.4)

to get near *acercarse (4.4)

to get off bajar (de) (4.3)

to get ready prepararse (3.2)

to get tired (of) cansarse (de) (3.3)

to get to *llegar (5.2)

to get up levantarse (3.2)

to get used to acostumbrarse a (8.2)

to get worried preocuparse (3.3)

ghost un fantasma (9.3)

gift un regalo (1.3)

girl una chica (1.2), una muchacha (1.2), una niña (1.2)

girlfriend una novia (1.2)

to give *dar (2.2), *ofrecer (2.1)

 to give (*as a present*) regalar (2.2)

 to give back devolver (o → ue) (3.1)

glass el vidrio (7.4)

to go *ir (1.3), *andar (9.4)

 to go away *irse (3.2)

 to go camping ir de camping (8.3)

 to go for a ride dar una vuelta (4.2)

 to go for a walk, ride dar un paseo (4.3)

 to go on a vacation ir de vacaciones (4.1)

 to go out *salir (3.4)

 to go quickly ir de prisa (4.2)

 to go shopping ir de compras (4.1)

 to go slowly ir despacio (8.1)

 to go to bed acostarse (o → ue) (3.2)

 to go to the other side *cruzar (5.4)

 to go towards *dirigirse (a) (4.2)

 to go up subir (a) (4.3)

goal una meta (6.4)

God el Dios (4.3)

 God help me! ¡Válgame Dios! (4.3)

 may God help you que Dios le ayude (8.3)

gold el oro (6.4)

gone ido

good buen, bueno (1.2)

 in a good mood de buen humor (1.4)

 my goodness! ¡Dios mío! (4.3)

good-looking buen mozo (9.4)

goodbye adiós

gossip un chismoso, una chismosa (5.1)

grade una nota

grandfather un abuelo (1.2)

grandmother una abuela (1.2)

grandparents los abuelos (1.2)

greasy grasoso (8.2)

great gran (1.3), grande (1.3)

 how great! ¡qué bueno! (3.1)

to greet saludar (5.2)

to grow cultivar (6.4)

to guess adivinar (4.4)

guide un (una) guía

 guidebook una guía (6.1)

guilty culpable (4.3)

guitar una guitarra

gullible crédulo (9.3)

gum el chicle (2.3)

h

habit una costumbre, un hábito (10.4)

hair el pelo

half una mitad (7.3)

ham el jamón (6.1)

hand una mano (3.4)

handkerchief un pañuelo (2.3)

handsome guapo (1.2)

to happen ocurrir (5.3), pasar (4.4)

 what happened? ¿qué pasó? (4.4)

happiness la felicidad (8.3)

happy alegre (1.4), contento (1.4), satisfecho (9.4)

 to get (be) happy alegrarse (de) (3.3)

hat un sombrero (2.2)

to hate odiar (1.1)

 I hate me disgusta(n) (2.4)

to have *tener (e → ie) (1.3), tomar (*used with something to drink*) (1.1), *haber (*auxiliary*) (6.3)

I do not have no tengo **(1.3)**, me falta(n) **(2.4)**

to have fun divertirse (e → ie, i) **(3.3)**

to have lunch *almorzar (o → ue) **(3.1)**

to have to tener que + *inf.* **(1.3)**

he él **(1.1)**

headlight un faro **(4.2)**

health la salud **(8.2)**

healthy sano **(2.4)**

to hear *oír **(3.4)**

hello: to say hello saludar **(5.2)**

to help ayudar **(1.3)**

God help me! ¡Válgame Dios! **(4.3)**

may God help you que Dios le ayude **(8.3)**

her ella *(after prep.);* la *(dir. obj.)* **(2.1)**; su, sus *(poss. adj.)* **(2.1)**

to her le **(2.2)**

hers suyo **(4.2)**

herself se **(3.2)**

here aquí **(2.2)**

here is, here are aquí tiene(s) **(10.1)**

to hesitate vacilar en **(8.2)**

hidden escondido **(6.2)**

to hide esconder **(6.2)**

highway una carretera

him él *(after prep.);* lo *(dir. obj.)* **(2.1)**

to him le **(2.2)**

himself se **(3.2)**

his su, sus **(2.1)**; suyo **(4.2)**

home una casa **(1.3)**, a casa **(1.3)**

homework la(s) tarea(s)

to honk tocar la bocina **(8.1)**

to hope desear **(1.1)**, esperar **(1.1)**

let's hope that ojalá que **(8.4)**

horror el horror

horror film una película de horror

horse un caballo

horseback riding la equitación **(2.4)**

hospital un hospital **(2.1)**

hot caluroso **(2.2)**

it's hot *(weather)* hace calor **(2.2)**

to be (feel) hot tener calor **(5.4)**

house una casa **(1.3)**

at __'s house a la casa de __ **(1.3)**

how? ¿cómo? **(1.1)**

how is the weather? ¿qué tiempo hace? **(2.2)**

how many? ¿cuántos? **(1.3)**

how much? ¿cuánto? **(1.1)**

hundred cien *(before nouns)*, ciento

one hundred percent ciento por ciento **(1.2)**

hungry: to be hungry tener hambre **(5.4)**

to hunt *cazar **(2.4)**

hunting la caza **(2.4)**

hurry: to be in a hurry tener prisa **(5.4)**

to hurry darse prisa **(3.2)**

hurt: my __ hurt(s) me duele(n) __ **(3.1)**

husband un esposo **(3.4)**

i

I yo **(1.1)**

ice cream el helado

ice cream parlor una heladería **(2.1)**

idea una idea

ill enfermo **(1.4)**

ill-mannered mal educado **(5.2)**

immediately inmediatamente, en seguida **(7.2)**

impatient: to get impatient impacientarse **(3.3)**

imperfect imperfecto

impolite descortés **(5.2)**, mal educado **(5.2)**

important importante **(9.2)**

impossible imposible **(5.1)**

to impress impresionar **(5.1)**

improbable improbable **(9.3)**

in en **(6.2)**

in a way de una manera **(3.2)**

in fact de hecho **(1.1)**, en efecto **(7.2)**

in general en general

in love enamorado **(1.4)**

in the afternoon por la tarde **(1.4)**

in the evening por la tarde **(1.4)**, por la noche **(1.4)**

in the morning por la mañana **(1.4)**

indicate *indicar

indicative indicativo

indirect indirecto

indispensable indispensable **(9.2)**

infinitive un infinitivo

information un aviso **(8.4)**

inquisitive inquisitivo **(2.3)**

inside dentro (de) **(6.2)**

to insist (on) insistir (en) **(8.2)**

intellectual intelectual **(1.2)**

intelligent inteligente **(1.2)**

to intend pensar (e → ie) + *inf.* **(3.1)**

interesting interesante **(1.2)**

I am interested in me interesa(n) **(2.4)**

interrogative interrogativo

interview una entrevista **(6.4)**

into en **(6.2)**

to introduce presentar **(10.1)**

to invite invitar **(1.3)**

irregular irregular

irritable irritable **(1.4)**

irritated: to get irritated irritarse **(3.3)**

is es, está **(1.4)**

it lo, la **(2.1)**

its su, sus **(2.1)**

j

jealous: to be jealous tener celos **(5.4)**

joke un chiste **(3.1)**, una broma **(5.1)**

July julio

to jump saltar **(5.3)**

just: to have just acabar de + *inf.* **(4.1)**

k

to keep guardar **(5.1)**, conservar **(10.4)**

to keep on *seguir (e → i, i) + *pres. part.* **(3.1)**

to keep quiet callarse **(3.2)**

key una llave **(2.3)**

kind amable **(2.1)**

kind una clase **(2.4)**

kiss un beso **(5.4)**

kitchen una cocina **(7.4)**

knife *(small, folding knife)* una navaja **(2.3)**

to know *(facts)* *saber **(2.2)**, *(people)* *conocer **(2.1)**
   to know how saber + *inf.* **(2.2)**
know-it-all un (una) sabelotodo **(5.1)**

l

to lack faltar **(2.4)**
   I lack me falta(n) **(2.4)**
ladder una escalera **(5.4)**
lake un lago **(6.4)**
lamp una lámpara **(6.1)**
land la tierra **(7.1)**
large grande **(1.3)**
last pasado **(6.4)**
   last Friday el viernes pasado **(6.4)**
   last night anoche **(6.4)**
to last durar **(3.4)**
late tarde **(5.2)**
   to be late in tardar en **(8.2)**
to laugh reír (e → i, i) **(3.1)**
lazy perezoso **(1.2)**
   lazy bum un holgazán, una holgazana **(5.1)**
to learn aprender (a) **(1.4)**
to leave marcharse **(3.2)**, *salir **(3.4)**, *irse **(3.2)**
   to take leave despedirse (e → i, i) **(3.2)**
left izquierda **(5.2)**
   on the left a la izquierda **(5.2)**
left: (I) have left (me) queda(n) **(2.3)**
to lend prestar **(2.2)**
less menos **(1.1)**
   in less than (two months) en menos de (dos meses) **(10.1)**
   more or less más o menos **(3.4)**
let's see a ver **(1.2)**
letter una carta
library una biblioteca **(1.3)**
license: driver's license un permiso de conducir **(4.2)**
   license plate un número de matrícula **(4.2)**
lie una mentira **(5.1)**
to lie mentir (e → ie, i) **(3.1)**
life la vida
light una luz *(pl.* luces) **(4.2)**
   directional lights *(on a car)* las (luces) direccionales **(4.2)**

to light encender (e → ie) **(6.2)**
like como
to like *querer (e → ie) a **(3.1)**, gustar **(2.4)**
   I like me gusta(n) **(1.1)**
   I like very much me encanta(n) **(1.1)**
   I would like me gustaría(n) **(1.1)**
line una línea **(6.2)**
lipstick un lápiz de labios **(3.2)**
listen! ¡oye! **(2.3)**
to listen (to) escuchar **(1.1)**
little pequeño **(1.3)**
   a little poco **(1.1)**, un poco **(2.1)**
to live vivir **(1.4)**
living room una sala **(7.4)**
loafer un holgazán, una holgazana **(5.1)**
to lock cerrar (e → ie) con llave **(3.1)**
logical lógico **(9.2)**
to look mirar **(1.1)**
   to look for *buscar **(1.3)**
   to look like *parecer **(2.1)**
to lose perder (e → ie) **(3.1)**
lot: a lot of mucho **(1.1)**
lottery la lotería **(8.3)**
love el amor **(3.4)**
   in love enamorado **(1.4)**
to love *(someone)* *querer (e → ie) a **(5.1)**
   to fall in love (with) enamorarse (de) **(3.4)**
luck: to try one's luck probar fortuna **(7.3)**
lucky afortunado **(4.4)**
   to be lucky tener suerte **(1.3)**
lunch: to have lunch *almorzar (o → ue) **(3.1)**

m

magazine una revista **(1.3)**
mailman un cartero **(2.1)**
majority la mayoría **(8.2)**
make *(of a car)* una marca
to make *hacer **(3.4)**
   to make a blunder meter la pata **(9.1)**
   to make a mistake *equivocarse **(3.3)**
   to make fun of burlarse de **(3.3)**
makeup: to put on makeup pintarse **(3.2)**
man un hombre **(1.2)**

manager un (una) gerente **(2.1)**
manner una manera **(9.2)**
mannered: ill-mannered mal educado **(5.2)**
   well-mannered bien educado **(5.2)**
manners los modales **(5.2)**
   bad manners los malos modales **(5.2)**
   good manners los buenos modales **(5.2)**
many muchos **(1.3)**
   how many? ¿cuántos? **(1.3)**
map un mapa **(6.1)**
market un mercado **(1.3)**
   fruit market una frutería **(6.1)**
marriage el matrimonio **(3.4)**
to marry, get married casarse (con) **(3.4)**
marvelous maravilloso **(1.1)**
match un partido **(2.4)**
   soccer match un partido de fútbol **(2.4)**
math las matemáticas
matter una cuestión **(9.2)**
   it doesn't matter to me no me importa(n) **(6.3)**
   it matters to me me importa(n) **(2.4)**
maybe quizá **(2.1)**, tal vez **(1.2)**
me me **(2.3)**
   to me me **(2.3)**
means un medio **(7.1)**
means: this means es decir **(10.4)**
mechanic un mecánico, una mecánica **(2.1)**
medal una medalla **(2.3)**
to meet encontrarse (o → ue) (con), reunirse (u → ú) **(3.2)**
member: to be a member (of) *pertenecer (a) **(2.1)**
memo book una libreta **(2.3)**
mental alertness la presencia de ánimo **(4.4)**
mess: what a mess! ¡qué lío! **(3.1)**
method un método **(8.2)**
Mexican mexicano **(1.2)**
middle: in the middle of en medio de **(6.2)**
milk la leche **(6.1)**
mind el ánimo **(4.4)** la mente **(9.3)**
mine mío **(4.2)**
minute un minuto
   wait a minute! ¡un momento! **(2.4)**

mirror un espejo (2.3)
to misbehave portarse mal (3.3)
to miss perder (e → ie) (3.1)
mistaken: to be mistaken
   *equivocarse (3.3)
to mistreat maltratar (5.2)
modern moderno (5.1)
money el dinero
mood el humor (1.4)
   in a bad mood de mal humor
      (1.4)
   in a good mood de buen humor
      (1.4)
moon la luna (7.1)
moral moral
more más (1.1)
   more or less más o menos (3.4)
more than más de (8.2)
moreover además (3.4)
morning una mañana (1.4)
   in the morning por la mañana
      (1.4)
mother una madre (1.2) (la) mamá
      (1.2)
motor un motor (4.2)
motorcycle una moto (1.3)
mountain una montaña (6.4)
   mountain climbing el alpinismo
      (2.4)
mouth una boca
to move *(emotionally)* emocionar,
   trasladar (9.3) mudarse (10.4)
to move away alejarse (8.3)
moved *(emotionally)* emocionado
movement el movimiento
movie theater un cine (1.3)
much mucho (1.1)
   how much? ¿cuánto? (1.1)
   too much demasiado (1.1)
museum un museo
music la música (2.4)
must: one must hay que (2.4)
mustache un bigote (3.2)
my mi, mis (2.1)
my goodness! ¡Dios mío! (4.3)
myself me (3.2)
mysterious misterioso (2.3)

n

nail una uña (3.2)
nationality la nacionalidad
natural natural (9.2)

nature la naturaleza
near cerca (de) (6.2)
   to get near *acercarse (a) (4.4)
necessary necesario (2.4)
   it is necessary to hay que (2.4)
necklace un collar (2.3)
to need necesitar (1.3)
negation la negación
negative negativo
neighbor un vecino, una vecina (2.1)
neighborhood un barrio (9.4)
neither ni, tampoco (5.1)
   neither ___ nor ni ___ ni (5.1)
nervous nervioso (1.4)
neuter neutro
never nunca (1.1) jamás (5.1)
new nuevo (1.3)
news las noticias (2.1)
newspaper un periódico (1.3)
next próximo (1.4)
   next Saturday el sábado
      próximo (1.4)
   next to junto (6.2)
nice simpático (1.2)
night una noche (1.4)
   at night por la noche (1.4)
   last night anoche (6.4)
   the night before (last)
      anteanoche (6.4)
no no (1.1) ningún, ninguno (5.1)
   no one nadie (5.1)
nobody nadie (5.1)
noise un ruido (3.4)
none ningún, ninguno (5.1)
nonsense! ¡qué va! (3.1)
   what nonsense! ¡qué
      barbaridad! (1.4)
nor ni (5.1)
   nor do I yo tampoco (5.1)
not no (1.1)
   not any ningún, ninguno (5.1)
   not anyone nadie (5.1)
   not anything nada (5.1)
   not yet no ... todavía (6.3)
notebook un cuaderno
nothing nada (5.1)
notice un letrero (6.1)
noun un sustantivo
novel una novela
now ahora (1.4)
nowadays hoy día (8.2)
nowhere en (a) ninguna parte (5.1)
numeral numeral
nurse un enfermero, una enfermera
      (2.1)

o

to obey *obedecer (2.1)
object un objeto (1.3)
to obtain *obtener (e → ie) (8.1)
to occupy (oneself) ocuparse (3.3)
to occur ocurrir (5.3)
of de (2.1)
offer *ofrecer (2.1)
office una oficina (5.3)
   post office un correo (2.1)
   ticket office una taquilla (6.4)
often a menudo (1.3)
oil el aceite (4.2)
old antiguo (5.1) viejo (1.2)
   older person una persona de
      edad (7.2)
on en (6.2) sobre (6.2)
   on (Monday) el (lunes) (1.3)
   on the weekend el fin de
      semana (1.4)
on the other hand de lo contrario
      (6.4)
   on time a tiempo (5.2)
once una vez (5.1); alguna vez
      (6.3)
   once in a while de vez en
      cuando (3.1)
one un, uno, una (1.2)
   one hundred cien *(before
      nouns)*, ciento
   one hundred percent ciento
      por ciento (1.2)
oneself se (3.2)
only *(adj.)* único (1.4)
only *(adv.)* solamente (2.1)
open abierto (6.2)
to open abrir (1.4)
open-air market un mercado (1.3)
opera una ópera (2.4)
opposite en frente de, frente a (6.2)
or o (u *before words beginning with
   o or* ho) (1.3)
orange *(fruit)* una naranja (6.1)
order un mandato (8.4)
in order to para
to order mandar (8.4)
ordinal ordinal
other otro (1.3)
others otros (1.3)
   the others, the other people
      los demás (3.3)
otherwise de lo contrario (6.4)
our nuestro (2.1)

ours nuestro **(4.2)**
ourselves nos **(3.2)**
out: to be out estar en la calle **(4.1)**
outside (of) fuera (de) **(2.1)**
over sobre **(6.2)**
to owe deber **(1.4)**
own propio **(4.3)**

p

to pack a suitcase hacer la maleta **(3.4)**
package un paquete **(6.2)**
"pain" un chinchoso, una chinchosa **(3.3)**
to paint pintar **(2.4)**
painting la pintura **(2.4)**
pale pálido **(6.2)**
paper el papel **(4.4)**
pan: frying pan una sartén (pl. sartenes) **(8.3)**
parents los padres **(1.2)**
park un parque **(6.4)**
to park estacionar **(6.1)**
parlor: ice cream parlor una heladería **(2.1)**
participle un participio
party una fiesta **(1.3)**
passenger un pasajero, una pasajera **(8.1)**
passer-by un transeúnte, una transeúnte **(8.3)**
past pasado
pastime un pasatiempo
pastry un pastel **(6.1)**
patience la paciencia **(8.1)**
to be patient tener paciencia **(8.1)**
patient un (una) paciente
peace la paz **(7.1)**
pear una pera **(6.1)**
pedestrian un peatón (pl. peatones) **(8.1)**
pen un bolígrafo **(2.3)**
pencil un lápiz (pl. lápices)
people la gente **(4.4)**
per por **(1.2)**
percent por ciento **(1.2)**
per day al día **(7.1)**
perfect perfecto
perhaps quizá **(2.1)** tal vez **(1.2)**
period una época **(5.2)**
permission el permiso **(4.2)**
permit un permiso **(4.2)**
to permit permitir **(4.4)**
person una persona

older person una persona de edad **(7.2)**
young person un (una) joven **(1.2)**
personal personal
personality una personalidad **(5.1)**
phone call una llamada **(4.4)**
to phone llamar por teléfono **(1.3)**
photo una foto **(2.4)**
photography la fotografía **(2.4)**
physical físico
piano un piano
to pick *coger **(6.4)**
to pick up *recoger **(6.4)**
picture una foto **(2.4)**
pill una pastilla **(8.2)**
ping-pong el ping pong **(2.4)**
pity: it's a pity es lástima **(9.2)**
what a pity ¡qué lástima! **(3.1)**
place un lugar **(6.1)**
to plan pensar (e → ie) + inf. **(3.1)**
planet una planeta **(7.1)**
plant una planta **(6.4)**
plate un plato **(5.3)**
license plate un número de matrícula **(4.2)**
play una obra de teatro **(2.4)**
to play (sports) *jugar (u → ue) **(2.4)**
(a musical instrument) *tocar **(1.1)**
to play a part hacer un papel **(3.4)**
to play ping-pong jugar al ping pong **(2.4)**
to play soccer jugar al fútbol **(2.4)**
player: record player un tocadiscos **(1.3)**
pleasant agradable **(9.2)**
pleasure: to take pleasure (in) *complacerse (en) **(8.2)**
pluperfect el pluscuamperfecto
plural el plural
pocket un bolsillo **(2.3)**
poem un poema
point un punto **(5.1)**
police officer un (una) policía **(2.1)**
polite atento **(5.2)** cortés **(5.2)**, bien educado **(5.2)**
pollution: air pollution la contaminación del aire **(7.1)**
pool: swimming pool una piscina **(1.3)**
poor pobre **(1.2)**
population la población **(7.1)**
position una posición (pl. posiciones)

possession una posesión (pl. posesiones)
possessive posesivo
possible posible **(5.1)**
post office un correo **(2.1)**
poster un letrero **(6.1)**
pot un cacharro **(8.3)**
pottery la cerámica **(2.4)**
to make pottery hacer cerámica **(2.4)**
power un poder **(9.3)**
practical práctico
to predict *predecir **(9.3)**
to prefer preferir (e → ie, i) **(3.1)**
I prefer prefiero **(3.1)** me gusta(n) más **(1.1)**
preoccupied preocupado **(1.4)**
prepared listo **(1.4)**
preposition una preposición (pl. preposiciones)
present (tense) el presente, (gift) un regalo **(1.3)**
to preserve conservar
preterite el pretérito
pretty bonito **(1.2)**
priest un sacerdote **(8.4)**
prize un premio **(8.3)**
probability la probabilidad
probable probable **(9.3)**
program un programa **(2.4)**
progress el progreso **(7.1)**
progressive progresivo
to prohibit prohibir **(6.1)**
prohibition una prohibición (pl. prohibiciones) **(8.4)**
to promise prometer **(3.4)**
pronoun un pronombre
proud orgulloso **(4.4)**
proverb un refrán (pl. refranes) **(6.4)**
provided that con tal que **(10.1)**
to pull out *arrancar **(4.2)**
purse un bolso **(2.3)**
to push empujar **(4.2)**
put puesto **(6.3)**
to put *poner **(3.4)** meter **(9.1)**
to put on (clothing) *ponerse **(3.4)**
to put on makeup pintarse **(3.2)**

q

quantity una cantidad **(6.1)**
to quarrel pelearse **(3.4)**

question   una pregunta
quick   rápido   (4.4)
quickly   de prisa   (4.2) pronto   (7.1)
quiet: to keep quiet   callarse   (3.2)
to quit   dejar (de)   (8.2)

r

race   una carrera   (8.4)
racket   una raqueta   (1.3)
radiator   un radiador   (4.2)
radio *(set)*   un radio   (1.3)
to rain   llover (o → ue)   (3.1)
rapid   rápido   (4.4)
rare   raro   (5.1)
rather   bastante   (1.1)
razor   una afeitadora   (3.2)
to react   reaccionar   (7.3)
to read   *leer   (1.4)
reading   la lectura   (2.4)
ready   listo   (1.4)
   to get ready   prepararse   (3.2)
to realize   darse cuenta (de)   (3.3)
reason   la razón   (9.3)
to receive   recibir   (1.4)
reciprocity   la reciprocidad
to recognize   *reconocer   (7.2)
record   un disco   (1.3)
   record player   un tocadiscos   (1.3)
recorder: tape recorder   una
   grabadora   (1.3)
reflexive   reflexivo
to regret   sentir (e → ie, i)   (3.1)
regular   regular
relative   relativo
relatives   los parientes   (1.2)
relief: what a relief!   ¡qué alivio!
   (7.4)
to remember   recordar (o → ue)   (3.1)
to rent   alquilar   (6.1)
to repair   reparar   (6.1)
to repeat   repetir (e → i, i)   (3.1)
repeated   repetido
to respect   respetar   (1.3)
response   una respuesta   (2.1)
rest: the rest   los demás   (3.3)
to rest   descansar   (1.1)
restaurant   un restaurante   (1.3)
result: as a result   como resultado
   (10.2)
to return   regresar   (4.1) volver
   (o → ue)   (3.1) *(objects)* devolver
   (o → ue)   (3.1)

review   un repaso
reward   una recompensa   (4.4)
rich   rico   (1.2)
ride: to go for a ride   dar una
   vuelta   (4.2) dar un paseo   (4.3)
   to ride a horse   montar a
      caballo   (2.4)
ridiculous   ridículo   (9.2)
riding: horseback riding   la
   equitación   (2.4)
right: that's right   es verdad   (1.1)
   to be right   tener razón   (5.4)
right   la derecha   (5.2)
   on the right   a la derecha   (5.2)
ring   un anillo   (2.3)
river   un río   (6.4)
to rob   robar   (7.4)
rock: large rock   una peña   (6.4)
rocket   un cohete   (7.1)
role   un papel   (3.4)
romantic   romántico
roof   un techo   (7.4)
room   un cuarto, una habitación   (9.4)
rose   una rosa   (6.4)
to run   correr   (1.4) *(function)*
   *andar   (9.4)

s

sad   triste   (1.4)
sadness   la tristeza   (7.4)
safe   seguro   (4.4)
to sail   *navegar (en un bote de
   vela)   (2.2)
sailboat   un bote de vela   (2.2)
salesman   un vendedor   (8.3)
saleswoman   una vendedora   (8.3)
same   mismo   (2.1)
sand   la arena   (2.2)
satisfied   satisfecho   (9.4)
Saturday   sábado   (1.3)
to say   *decir   (2.2) exclamar   (4.3)
   say!   ¡dime!   (2.3)
   that is to say   es decir   (10.4)
   to say goodbye   despedirse
      (e → i, i)   (3.2)
   to say hello   saludar   (5.2)
   to use "tú" with someone
      tutear   (6.3)
saying   un refrán *(pl.* refranes)   (6.4)
to scale   escalar   (2.4)
school   una escuela   (1.3)
scientist   un científico, una científica
   (9.3)

scissors   unas tijeras   (3.2)
to scorch   quemar   (5.3)
scorched   quemado   (6.2)
sea   el mar
seat   un asiento   (6.2) una silla
   (6.1)
to see   *ver   (1.4)
   let's see   a ver   (1.4)
to seek *(employees)*   solicitar   (6.1)
to seem   *parecer   (2.1)
to select   *escoger   (6.4)
to sell   vender   (1.4)
to send   mandar   (2.2)
serious   serio   (1.2)
to serve   servir (e → i, i)   (3.1)
service   un servicio   (2.1)
   service station   una estación de
      servicio   (2.1)
several   algunos   (4.1) varios
shampoo   el champú   (3.2)
to share   compartir   (5.2)
to shave   afeitar(se)   (3.2)
she   ella   (1.1)
shoe   un zapato
   shoe store   una zapatería
shop: butcher shop   una carnicería
   (6.1)
   furniture shop   una mueblería
      (6.1)
shopping   las compras   (4.1)
   to go shopping   ir de compras
      (4.1)
short   bajo   (1.2)
should   deber + *inf.*   (1.4)
to show   enseñar   (2.2) mostrar
   (o → ue)   (3.1) demostrar (o → ue)
   (9.2)
to shut   cerrar (e → ie)   (3.1)
sick   enfermo   (1.4), malo   (1.4)
   sick person   un enfermo, una
      enferma   (2.1)
sidewalk   una acera   (8.1)
sight   un espectáculo   (4.3)
sign   un letrero   (6.1) una señal
   (6.1)
silly   tonto   (1.2)
simple   sencillo   (5.1)
since   como   (3.2)
to sing   cantar   (1.1)
sister   una hermana   (1.2)
to sit (down)   sentarse (e → ie)   (3.2)
situated   situado
to skate   patinar   (2.4)
skating   el patinaje   (2.4)
to ski   esquiar (i → i)   (1.1)

skinny flaco (1.2)

skis unos esquís

    waterskis unos esquís acuáticos

slave un esclavo (10.4)

to sleep dormir (o → ue, u) (3.1)

    to be sleepy tener sueño (5.4)

    to fall asleep dormirse

        (o → ue, u) (3.2)

sleeping bag un saco de dormir (8.3)

slow lento (4.4)

slowly despacio (8.1)

small pequeño (1.3)

smart listo (1.2)

to smile sonreír (e → i, i) (3.1)

to smoke fumar (6.1)

so tan (2.1)

    so do I yo también (1.1)

    so (it is that) así (es que) (3.1)

    so much tanto

soap el jabón (3.2)

soccer el fútbol (2.4)

social social

sock un calcetín (pl. calcetines)

solar heating la calefacción solar

    (7.4)

to solicit solicitar (6.1)

some algún, alguno (4.1) unos (1.2)

    some day un día (1.1) algún

        día (4.1)

somebody alguien (5.1)

someone alguien (5.1)

something algo (5.1)

sometimes a veces (1.3)

somewhere en (a) alguna parte

    (5.1)

son un hijo (1.2)

    sons and daughters los hijos

    (1.2)

song una canción (pl. canciones)

soon pronto (7.1)

Spanish (el) español (1.2)

to speak hablar (1.1)

specialized especializado

spectacle un espectáculo (4.3)

spectator un espectador, una

    espectadora

to spend (money) gastar (4.4)

    (time) pasar (4.1)

spirit el ánimo (4.4)

sponger un sablista, una sablista

    (5.1)

sport un deporte (2.4)

    sports-loving deportista (1.2)

    team sports unos deportes de

        equipo (2.4)

stairs una escalera (5.4)

stamp un sello (2.1)

stand un puesto

star una estrella (8.3)

to start *comenzar (e → ie) (3.1)

    *empezar (e → ie) (3.1)

to start a car *arrancar (4.2)

state un estado (4.4)

station una estación (pl. estaciones)

    (2.1)

    service station una estación de

        servicio (2.1)

to stay quedarse (3.2)

steak el bistec (6.1)

still todavía (4.2)

stone una piedra (2.2)

stop una parada (6.4)

    bus stop la parada del autobús

        (6.4)

    streetcar stop la parada del

        tranvía (6.4)

to stop parar (4.3) dejar (de) (8.2)

    to stop (oneself) pararse (4.3)

store una tienda (1.3)

    department store un almacén

        (1.3)

    watch store una relojería

story un cuento

strange raro (5.1)

street una calle (2.1)

    street floor la planta baja (7.4)

streetcar un tranvía (8.1)

student un (una) estudiante (1.2);

    un alumno, una alumna (1.2)

to study estudiar (1.1)

to stumble (against) *tropezar

    (e → ie) (con) (4.3)

stupid estúpido (1.2)

subjunctive el subjuntivo

successful: to be successful tener

    éxito (5.4)

such a ... tal ... (3.3)

suddenly de repente (5.3)

to suggest sugerir (e → ie) (8.4)

suggestion una sugerencia (8.4)

suit un traje (2.2)

    bathing suit un traje de baño

        (2.2)

suitcase una maleta (3.4)

    to pack a suitcase hacer la

        maleta (3.4)

summary un resumen

summer el verano

sun el sol (2.2)

to sunbathe tomar el sol (1.1)

sunglasses unos anteojos de sol

    (2.2)

sunny soleado (2.2)

    it's sunny hace sol (2.2) está

        soleado (2.2)

to suppress suprimir (7.1)

sure seguro (4.4) cierto (7.1)

to surf correr las olas (2.2)

surprise una sorpresa (2.1)

to be surprised sorprenderse (4.4)

surprising sorprendente (9.2)

suspicious sospechoso (2.3)

sweater un suéter

to swim nadar (1.1)

swimming la natación (2.4)

    swimming pool una piscina

        (1.3)

t

table una mesa (6.1)

tablet una pastilla (8.2)

to take tomar (1.1) (photos) *sacar

    (4.2)

    to take a bath bañarse (3.2)

    to take a ride dar una vuelta

        (4.2)

    to take a trip hacer un viaje (3.4)

    to take a walk pasear (10.2)

    to take along llevar (1.1)

    to take away robar (7.4)

    to take care of cuidar (2.1)

    to take off (clothing) quitarse

        (3.2)

    to take oneself for tomarse por

        (3.3)

    to take out *sacar (4.2)

    to take pleasure (in)

        *complacerse (en) (8.2)

to talk hablar (1.1)

tall alto (1.2)

tan un bronceado (8.2)

to tan tostar (o → ue) (6.2)

tank un tanque (4.2)

tanned bronceado (6.2)

tape una cinta (1.3)

    tape recorder una grabadora

        (1.3)

to taste probar (o → ue) (3.1)

tattletale un chismoso, una

    chismosa (5.1)

tea el té

to teach enseñar (a) (2.2)

teacher un profesor, una profesora; (2.1) un maestro, una maestra

team un equipo (2.4)

telephone un teléfono (1.3)

television la televisión

    television set un televisor (1.3)

to tell contar (o → ue) (3.1) *decir (2.2)

    tell me! ¡dime! (2.3)

ten diez

tennis el tenis (2.4)

tent una tienda de campaña (8.3)

to test probar (o → ue) (3.1)

that ese *(f. esa) (adj.)* (2.2) que

    relative pron. (9.4) tan *(adj.)*; eso

    neuter pron.) (2.3)

    that *(over there)* aquel *(f.* aquella) (2.2)

    that is to say es decir (10.4)

    that one ése, aquél (2.2)

    that's true es verdad (1.1)

the el, la, los, las (1.2)

theater un teatro (1.3)

    movie theater un cine (1.3)

their su, sus (2.1)

theirs suyo (4.2)

them ellos, ellas *(after prep.)*; los, las *(dir. obj.)* (2.1)

    to them les (2.2)

themselves se (3.2)

then entonces (2.4) luego (3.2)

there allí, ahí (2.2)

    over there allá (2.2)

there is, there are hay

therefore así (es que) (2.1)

they ellos, ellas (1.1)

thick grueso (8.2)

thin delgado (1.2)

thing una cosa (1.3) un objeto (1.3)

    what thing? ¿qué cosa? (2.3)

to think pensar (e → ie) (3.1)

    to think about pensar en (3.1)

    to think of pensar de (3.1)

    to think one is tomarse por (3.3)

thirsty: to be thirsty tener sed (5.4)

this este *(f. esta)* (2.2); esto *(neuter pron.)* (2.3)

    this one éste (2.2)

though aunque (1.2)

to thrill emocionar

ticket una entrada (2.4) un billete (8.3)

    ticket office una taquilla (6.4)

time el tiempo, una época (5.2) una vez (5.1)

    all the time todo el tiempo (1.3)

    at times a veces (1.3)

    at what time? ¿a qué hora?

    from time to time de vez en cuando (3.1)

    on time a tiempo (5.2)

tire una llanta (4.2)

tired cansado (1.4)

    to get tired of cansarse de (3.3)

to a

toast la tostada

to toast tostar (6.2)

toasted tostado (6.2)

today hoy (1.1) hoy día (8.2)

together juntos (3.1)

to tolerate tolerar (8.4)

tomorrow mañana (1.4)

tonight esta noche (6.4)

too también (1.1)

    too, too much demasiado (1.1)

tooth un diente (3.4)

top: on top of encima de (6.2)

to touch *tocar (9.3)

toward hacia (4.2)

towel una toalla (2.2)

town un pueblo (8.1)

toy un juguete (5.2)

traffic el tránsito (8.1)

    traffic light un semáforo (8.1)

    traffic sign una señal (de tránsito) (8.1)

tragedy una tragedia (2.4)

train un tren

to transfer trasladar (9.3)

to transform transformar (7.1)

to translate *traducir (2.1)

to travel viajar (1.1)

treasure un tesoro (7.3)

tree un árbol (5.4)

    fruit tree un árbol de frutas (6.4)

trip un viaje (3.4)

    to take a trip hacer un viaje (3.4)

trolley car un tranvía (8.1)

truck un camión *(pl.* camiones) (8.1)

true verdadero (5.1)

    that's not true no es verdad (1.1)

    that's true es verdad (1.1)

truth la verdad (1.1)

to try probar (o → ue) (4.2) tratar (de) (8.2)

    to try one's luck probar fortuna (7.3)

tú: to use "tú" with someone tutear (6.3)

to turn volverse (o → ue) (5.3)

    to turn *(a corner)* doblar (8.1)

    to turn off *apagar (6.2)

    to turn on encender (e → ie) (6.2)

TV set un televisor (1.3)

type una clase (2.4)

typewriter una máquina de escribir

u

ugly feo (1.2)

umbrella un paraguas (10.2)

unbelievable increíble (4.3)

uncle un tío (1.2)

    uncles and aunts los tíos (1.2)

under(neath) debajo (6.2)

to understand comprender (1.4) entender (e → ie) (3.1)

unforgettable inolvidable (8.2)

unfortunate desafortunado (4.4)

unhappy triste (1.4)

unique único (1.4)

United States los Estados Unidos

unless a menos que (10.1)

unlucky desafortunado

unpleasant antipático (1.2) desagradable (5.2)

until hasta

us nosotros(as) *(after prep.)*; nos *(obj. pron.)* (2.3)

    to us nos (2.3)

use el uso

to use usar

useful útil (2.4)

useless inútil (2.4)

v

vacation(s) las vacaciones (4.1)

    to be on (a) vacation estar de vacaciones (4.1)

    to go on (a) vacation ir de vacaciones (4.1)

value valor (5.1)

variety una variedad (2.4)

variety show un programa de variedades **(2.4)**

vegetable una legumbre **(6.4)** un vegetal

vendor un vendedor, una vendedora **(8.3)**

verb un verbo

very muy **(1.1)**

violent violento **(2.4)**

virtue una virtud **(5.2)**

to visit visitar **(1.1)**

vocabulary el vocabulario

voice una voz *(pl. voces)* **(4.2)**

to wait (for) esperar **(1.3)**
   wait a minute! ¡un momento! **(2.4)**

waiter un camarero **(2.1)**

waitress una camarera **(2.1)**

to wake up despertarse (e → ie) **(3.2)**

to walk *andar **(4.3)** caminar **(2.2)**
   to go for a walk dar un paseo **(4.3)** dar una vuelta **(4.2)** pasear **(10.2)**

wall una pared **(6.4)**

wallet una billetera **(2.3)**

to want *querer (e → ie) **(3.1)**

warm: to be warm *(sensation)* tener calor **(2.2)**

warning un aviso **(8.4)**

to wash lavar **(3.2)**
   to wash (oneself) lavarse **(3.2)**

to waste perder (e → ie) **(3.1)**

watch un reloj **(1.3)**
   watch store una relojería

to watch mirar **(1.1)**

water el agua *(f.)* **(5.3)**

to waterski esquiar en el agua **(2.2)**

water skis unos esquís acuáticos

way: in a way de una manera **(3.2)**
   (in) no way de ninguna manera **(5.1)**
   (in) some way de alguna manera **(5.1)**

we nosotros(as) **(1.1)**

to wear llevar

weather el tiempo **(2.2)**
   how's the weather? ¿qué tiempo hace? **(2.2)**

wedding una boda **(3.4)**

Wednesday miércoles **(1.3)**

week una semana **(1.4)**

weekend el fin de semana **(1.4)**
   on the weekend el fin de semana **(1.4)**

well bien **(1.1)**
   well-mannered bien educado **(5.2)**

western (movie) una película del oeste

what lo que **(5.1)**

what? ¿qué? **(1.1)**
   at what time? ¿a qué hora?
   what happened? ¿qué pasó? **(4.4)**
   what is it? ¿qué cosa? **(2.3)**
   what is it? what's up? ¿qué hay? **(2.3)**

what! ¡qué!
   what a . . .! ¡qué . . .! **(2.4)**
   what a bore! ¡qué lata! **(3.1)**
   what a mess! ¡qué lío! **(3.1)**
   what a pity! ¡qué lástima! **(3.1)**
   what a relief! ¡qué alivio! **(7.4)**
   what nonsense! ¡qué barbaridad! **(1.4)**
   what will become of me! ¡qué será de mí! **(7.4)**

wheel una rueda **(4.2)**

when cuando **(10.2)**
   when? ¿cuándo? **(1.1)**

where donde
   where? ¿dónde? **(1.1)**

which? ¿cuál(es)? **(2.4)**

while mientras **(5.3)**, al + *inf.*
   once in a while de vez en cuando **(3.1)**

who? whom? ¿quién(es)? **(9.4)**

the whole todo **(4.1)**

whose? ¿de quién(es)? **(2.1)**

why? ¿por qué? **(1.1)**

wife una esposa **(3.4)**

to win ganar **(1.1)**

wind el viento **(2.2)**
   it's windy hace viento **(2.2)**

window una ventana **(4.3)**

windshield un parabrisas **(4.2)**

to wish desear **(1.1)**

to wish to tener ganas de **(1.3)**

with con **(2.3)**

witness un (una) testigo **(5.4)**

woman una mujer **(1.2)**

wood la madera **(7.4)**

woods un bosque **(6.4)**

word una palabra **(4.4)**

to work trabajar **(1.1)** *(function)* *andar **(4.3)**

world el mundo **(1.3)**

worried preocupado **(1.4)**
   I am worried (by) me preocupa(n) **(2.4)**
   to get worried (because) preocuparse (por) **(3.3)**

worse peor **(10.3)**

worthwhile: it is worthwhile vale la pena **(9.2)**

would: I would like me gustaría **(1.1)**

wow! ¡caramba! **(1.3)**

wrist watch un reloj de pulsera **(2.3)**

to write escribir **(1.4)**

written escrito **(6.3)**

wrong: to be wrong no tener razón **(5.4)**

Y

yesterday ayer **(6.4)**
   the day before yesterday anteayer **(6.4)**

yet todavía **(4.2)** ya **(6.3)**
   not yet no . . . todavía **(6.3)**

you tú *(fam.)*, Ud. *(formal)*, Uds. *(pl.)* **(1.1)** te **(2.3)** lo, la, los, las *(obj. pronouns)* **(2.1)** ti, Ud., Uds. *(after prep.)*
   to you te *(fam.)* **(2.3)** le *(formal)*, les *(pl.)* **(2.2)**

young joven *(pl. jóvenes)* **(1.2)**

young person un (una) joven **(1.2)**

younger menor **(4.1)**

your tu, tus *(fam.)*; su, sus *(formal sing., pl.)* **(2.1)**

yours tuyo *(fam.)* suyo *(formal)* **(4.2)**

yourself te *(fam.)*, se *(formal)* **(3.2)**

youth la juventud **(8.2)**

INDEX